APPLIED DATA COMMUNICATIONS

A BUSINESS-ORIENTED APPROACH

Second Edition

James E. Goldman

Purdue University

John Wiley & Sons, Inc.

New York • Chichester • Weinheim • Brisbane • Singapore • Toronto

Acquisitions Editor	Beth Lang Golub
Marketing Manager	Carlise Paulson
Production Editor	Tony VenGraitis
Designer	Ann Marie Renzi
Illustrator	Curtis A. Snyder
Illustration Coordinator	Anna Melhorn
Cover Design	David Levy
Cover Art	© Jean-François Allaux/SIS

This book was set in Times Roman by Digitype and printed and bound by Quebecor Printing/Kingsport. The cover was printed by Phoenix Color Corp.

This book is printed on acid-free paper. ∞

The paper in this book was manufactured by a mill whose forest management programs include sustained yield harvesting of its timberlands. Sustained yield harvesting principles ensure that the number of trees cut each year does not exceed the amount of new growth.

Library of Congress Cataloging-in-Publication Data
Goldman, James E.
    Applied data communications : a business-oriented approach / James
E. Goldman. — 2nd ed.
        p.   cm.

    Includes bibliographical references and index.
    ISBN 0-471-17067-4 (cloth : alk. paper)
    1. Electronic data interchange.   2. Business Enterprises—
Communication Systems.   3. Data transmission systems.   4. Computer
networks.   I. Title
HF5548.33.G65   1998
658'.0546—DC21   97-35096
                                                                       CIP

Printed in the United States of America

10 9 8 7 6

To Susan, Eric, and Grant

PREFACE

■ WHAT'S NEW IN THE SECOND EDITION

The field of data communications continues to evolve at a rapid pace. To provide the reader with the most timely and important information possible, several changes have been made to the second edition while preserving those unique aspects of the first edition that contributed to its wide acceptance and popularity. Among the most significant changes to the second edition are the following:

- New chapters have been added covering (1) Network security, (2) Network management, (3) Enterprise networking and the Internet, (4) Remote access and wireless networking.
- Local area network coverage has been expanded to three chapters in a dedicated section.
- The overall text has been organized into four major parts to allow easier adaptation to a variety of course outlines.
- Technology and services information has been updated in all chapters.
- Increased emphasis has been placed on the use of the OSI model and top-down model as analytical tools.
- All business cases have been updated.

■ THE NEED FOR THIS BOOK

The field of information systems has been in a transitionary state from the mainframe-oriented, hierarchical networks of yesterday to the distributed, client/server architectures of today. The motivation for this transition was not merely economic in nature but was also largely fueled by increased recognition of information as a corporate asset to be leveraged to competitive advantage. Businesses realized that true financial gains could be achieved by delivering the right information to the right decision-maker at the right place and time for the right cost.

The distributed nature of today's information systems, enabling users to gain quick and easy access to key data regardless of location, has put increased emphasis on the importance of the networking aspects of information systems analysis and design. The often repeated phrase "The network *is* the computer" is a reflection of the central role of networking as the foundation of today's distributed information systems.

This transition from processor-centric, mainframe-oriented computing to network-centric, client/server information systems has not been without difficulty and occasional failures. Designing distributed information systems requires business-oriented analysis, design, and problem-solving skills. Furthermore, networking can no longer be considered a technology-oriented, engineering field of study that can be dealt with in a vacuum. To effectively design the networks that form the backbone of today's distributed information systems, network analysts must thoroughly understand the business implications of their designs as well as the characteristics of the information systems that must travel over their networks.

As the business climate of the 1990s continues to evolve, many of the outcomes of this evolution point to an increasingly strategic role for data communications and networking. Increased emphasis on productivity, the dawn of the mobile professional, the flattening of managerial hierarchies, and the downsizing of corporate information systems all depend on well-designed corporate networks to varying degrees. As a result, there has been a corresponding increase in the demand for data communications professionals fluent in both the language of business and the language of data communications technology.

Designing effective networks to support client/server information systems requires a structured, systems engineering type of approach. Such a structured, top-down approach to network analysis and design requires thinking models or frameworks into which network analysts can organize their thoughts and questions. Just such a process-oriented, top-down model was introduced in the first edition of *Applied Data Communications: A Business-Oriented Approach* by James E. Goldman, associate professor in Purdue University's Department of Computer Technology.

The top-down model equips students with a practical, business-first, technology-last, problem-solving approach with which to attack data communications and networking opportunities. Students are taught to use analytical models to organize networking requirements as well as the functionality of the technology currently available to meet those requirements. Using this methodology, this text teaches students how to *do* data communications and network analysis and design in a client/server information systems environment, rather than merely telling students about data communications and networking concepts and technology.

■ UNIQUE FEATURES OF THE BOOK

Business Orientation/Problem-Solving Approach

Although several business data communications books have been written, none have placed an ongoing emphasis on business orientation as concepts and technology change. None have equipped the student with thinking models through which data communications can be viewed objectively as technology inevitably changes in the future. That is where this book succeeds.

This book starts by familiarizing the student with the forces at work shaping the data communications industry, allowing the student to become an informed player, rather than a victim, of this technology-dominated industry. Realizing that the data communications industry itself is a product of interacting business forces is but a first step toward an awareness of the business orientation of data communications and networking analysis and design.

Rather than addressing business issues and decisions in isolated chapters or sections, this text adheres to a business-oriented, problem-solving approach throughout the entire text. In most cases, design challenges and requirements related to a particular chapter's topics are presented first, followed by alternative technology implementations that meet the outlined technical requirements. Alternative implementations are then analyzed as to advantages and disadvantages from both technical and business perspectives. The top-down model is employed as a means to relate technology implementations to business objectives.

Process-Oriented Thinking Models

Applied Data Communications: A Business-Oriented Approach, Second Edition provides process-oriented thinking models with which students can organize their problem-solving approach. These models are reinforced and used throughout the text rather than merely being introduced in a single chapter on network design. Examples of such models include

1. Top-down model.
2. Input-processing-output model.
3. OSI model.
4. Client-server architecture model.

Most of these models are introduced in Part 1 of the text.

Business Cases

A real-world, practical approach to the industry is supported by the inclusion of business cases from professional periodicals in the text. Students are required to take real-world examples of implemented networking solutions and apply the facts of the case to the top-down model. In doing so, students are able to evaluate delivered networking functionality in terms of the implemented system's ability to deliver on stated business objectives. Additional questions are asked of the students as a means of gaining insight into the objective evaluation of real-world networking solutions. Questions also guide students toward development of analytical skills and business-oriented network design capabilities. Students can become familiar with the current real-world trends in network analysis and design while being provided with the assurance of explanations and supporting conceptual material supplied by the text.

These are not the full-blown business cases typical of MBA programs. Rather, they serve as a basis for students to organize real-world network information in a top-down model for discussion and analysis. Often, significant facts are missing from such news stories, forcing students to develop critical thinking and questioning skills.

Specialized Sections/Notations

In Sharper Focus   *In Sharper Focus* sections highlight more detailed, more advanced, or background information for concepts introduced within a chapter. These sections can be included or excluded at the instructor's discretion.

Managerial Perspective   *Managerial Perspective* sections take a "bottom-line" approach to network analysis and design. The potential business impact of management decisions in a variety of situations is highlighted in these sections which may be of particular interest to MBA audiences.

Applied Problem Solving   Those sections of chapters that focus on the use of analytical models for *Applied Problem Solving* activities are highlighted for the benefit of both instructors and students. By stressing problem-solving activities, students can be assured of learning how to *do* network analysis and design.

Practical Advice and Information   Emphasizing the practical nature of the text, instances of practical advice or warnings are highlighted to call the reader's attention to important but often overlooked information.

■ ORGANIZATION

Overall Organization

The text is organized into four major parts:
1. Introductory Data and Voice Communications.
2. Local Area Networking.
3. Enterprise Networking.
4. Network Administration.

More detailed information regarding chapter headings and topics covered within these major parts can be found in the detailed Table of Contents.

Each of the four major parts of the text begins with an introduction detailing how that part relates to the other parts of the book as well as how the chapters within that part relate to each other. The introduction provides the proverbial "big picture" so that the reader can understand how specific topics fit in the larger scheme of things. A key objective of the text is to keep the reader aware of how the information currently being read relates to previously covered material and to material yet to be covered.

Chapter Organization

Each chapter begins with an outline of new concepts introduced, previous concepts reinforced, and the learning objectives for that chapter. Section and paragraph headings help students to organize and identify key concepts introduced in each chapter. End of chapter material includes a chapter summary, key terms, abundant review questions, and activities and problems for active student learning.

As previously mentioned, business cases from professional periodicals are reprinted at the close of each chapter with associated analysis questions to be answered by students or used as the basis for classroom discussion. A liberal use of diagrams adds to both the usability of the text and the level of understanding of the students.

■ SUPPLEMENTS

Instructor's Resource Guide

The *Instructor's Resource Guide* recognizes the wide variance of backgrounds of instructors of data communications and networking courses. As a result, it is far more comprehensive than a typical instructor's guide. In addition, annotations highlight the significance of individual diagrams and provide instructors with key points to be shared with students. In addition to providing solutions to the text's review questions and business cases, the *Instructor's Resource Guide* also provides additional test questions in a wide variety of formats.

Transparencies in Windows Metafile Format and PowerPoint Format

Included with the *Instructor's Resource Guide* is a CD-ROM containing all of the diagrams and illustrations included in the text. This gives individual instructors the flexibility to use these slides in their existing Windows metafile (.WMF) format, to print them out as transparencies, or to produce student notes versions of the illustrations with their own annotations.*

■ INTENDED AUDIENCE

Due to the modular nature of this text, a variety of audiences/courses could be well served. Among the possible courses are the following:
- A one-semester course in data communications as part of an undergraduate computer information systems curriculum. Such a course may be included in either 2- or 4-year programs.
- A business-oriented course in data communications as part of an MBA program, especially those with concentrations in management information systems or computer information systems.
- Continuing education or industrial seminars offered in data communications fundamentals for professional development.

■ ACKNOWLEDGMENTS

I am indebted to a number of people whose efforts were crucial in the development of this book.

For the outstanding quality illustrations that appear in the book as well as for his unwavering support, I'd like to thank Curt Snyder of Purdue University.

For his efforts in the creation of a meaningful and high-quality *Instructor's Resource Guide*, I'd like to thank my colleague Dr. Mark Smith of the Computer Information Systems and Technology Department at Purdue University.

For their collaborative efforts in turning a manuscript into a professionally published book, I'd like to thank the following professionals at John Wiley & Sons: Beth Lang Golub, Editor; Tony VenGraitis, Senior Production Editor; Ann Marie Renzi, Designer; Anna Melhorn, Illustration Coordinator. Also, thanks to Donna King at Progressive Publishing Alternatives for her supervision of the production of the book.

Reviewers

A special debt of gratitude is owed to the professionals who were kind enough to review the manuscript of this book prior to publication. It is through your effort that an accurate text of high quality can be produced.
- Curtis P. Armstrong   *Tennessee Technological University*
- Lance Besser   *The University of Central Texas*
- Someswar Kesh   *Central Missouri State University*
- Ahmed A. Shabana   *Texas A & M University*
- H. P. Stevenson   *Raritan Valley Community College*
- Graham Thorpe   *McGill University*

---

*All diagrams are also included in PowerPoint presentations. Large diagrams are included in existing form as well as in close-up views of individual portions of the original diagram.

CONTENTS

APPLIED
DATA
COMMUNICATIONS

A BUSINESS-ORIENTED APPROACH

INTRODUCTORY DATA AND VOICE COMMUNICATIONS

INTRODUCTION

The purpose of Part 1 of the text is to familiarize the reader with the fundamental concepts of data and voice communications from both business and technical perspectives. Much of the information provided in Part 1 serves as a foundation for material presented in later chapters.

Chapter 1, "The Data Communications Industry," provides insight into the business side of the data communications industry to allow readers to be active participants rather than victims of this fast-changing field. In addition, Chapter 1 introduces the reader to many of the key analytical models that will be used throughout the text to perform business-first, technology-last, network analysis.

Chapter 2, "Data Communications Concepts," introduces the reader to the basics of data communication by concentrating on asynchronous communications. By examining all that is involved with using a modem, this chapter uses a technology familiar to most readers as a means of introducing most of the fundamental concepts of data communication.

Chapter 3, "Basic Data Communications Technology," follows up on the concepts introduced in Chapter 2 with a structured analysis of currently available hardware and software technology used to achieve the types of communications described therein. As technology will continue to change rapidly, it is essential to develop technology analysis skills that can objectively evaluate technology in terms of its ability to meet stated business objectives.

1

Chapter 4, "Voice Communications Concepts and Technology," introduces the reader to the basics of voice communication from residential dial-up service to voice/data integration on a wide-area corporate network. Services available from the phone companies, more properly known as carriers, are also introduced.

CHAPTER 1

THE DATA COMMUNICATIONS INDUSTRY

Concepts Introduced

Interacting Components of the Data
   Communications Industry
Regulary Process
Deregulation and Divestiture
Standards-Making Process
Top-Down Model
Data Communications as a Profession
Data Communications and
   Information Systems

OSI Model
Internet Suite of Protocols Model
I-P-O Model
Protocols and Compatibility
Job Skills
Career Opportunities

OBJECTIVES

Upon successful completion of this chapter, you should be able to

1. Understand today's data communications industry as a system of interacting components.

2. Understand the current state of the data communications industry as well as the major issues facing each of the industry's constituent components.

3. Understand the challenges and solutions to business-oriented data communications analysis.

4. Understand the importance of structured models such as the top-down model, the OSI model, and the I-P-O model to successful business-oriented data communications analysis.

5. Understand the relationship of network analysis and design to information systems analysis and design.

6. Understand career opportunities in data communications and the job skills required to succeed in this field.

■ INTRODUCTION

Data communication is a field of study and an industry in a most rapid state of change. After familiarizing the reader with the current state of the data communications industry, this chapter introduces a series of models or thinking frameworks into which one can organize thoughts, facts, requirements, solutions, and technology to overcome the challenges faced by today's data communications professionals. By mastering these thinking models, the reader will be developing a business-oriented, technology-independent process for the analysis and design of data communications systems. These models will be used throughout the remainder of the text.

To better appreciate the wonderful opportunities available in data communications as a profession, it is important to understand how network analysis relates to information systems analysis in general, as well as the types of skills required for success in this most exciting field.

■ THE BEST WAY TO APPROACH DATA COMMUNICATIONS

Since the field of data communications is in such a state of constant change—some would refer to it as chaos—how can one study data communications and still keep one's sanity? The primary points to remember are the first two of Goldman's laws of data communications. (For a full listing, see Appendix A.)

Law 1:   You will never know all there is to know about data communications.

Law 2:   Be honest with yourself concerning what you don't know.

If you can accept these facts, you will be well on your way to survival in this most exciting and rewarding field.

What, then, can you expect to master in a one-semester course in data communications based around this textbook? After successful mastery of the material contained in this text, you should be able to:

1. Hold an intelligent conversation on a variety of data communications topics.

2. Analyze networking requirements, evaluate networking options, ask appropriate networking questions, and know where to seek answers to those questions.

Understand, however, that you will not necessarily possess all of the answers. You will not necessarily be qualified to design networks. You will possess enough information to ask essential questions and keep yourself from getting in over your networking head.

What Is Data Communications?

Data communications can be viewed as a foreign language. Just as the mastery of any foreign language requires practice in speaking and writing that language, so it is with data communications as well. I would encourage you to speak the language as often as possible. Don't be afraid of making mistakes. Form informal study groups if possible and review key concepts by forcing yourself to speak data communications. You will be pleasantly surprised at the speed with which you become comfortable with this new language.

Traditionally, data communications is viewed as a subset of **telecommunications.** Whereas telecommunications involves the transmission of voice, data, and video, data communications is typically limited to data transmission only. Telecommunications also often includes radio and television broadcasting.

A classic definition of **data communications** might be:

- The encoded transmission of data via electrical, optical, or wireless means between computers or network processors.

In truth, such a definition is really just a goal or outcome of a much larger process of interacting system components collectively known as data communications. By breaking down a system-oriented representation of the data communications industry into constituent components, interaction between components and the resultant state of the data communications industry can be more easily understood.

■ THE DATA COMMUNICATIONS INDUSTRY: A SERIES OF INTERACTING COMPONENTS

To be an effective participant in the data communications industry, it is important to understand the forces at work behind the scenes in that industry. In this manner, enlightened professionals can be proactive in their decision-making rather than being victimized by an industry that seems at times to be beyond reason and out of control.

Another way in which the classic definition of data communications is misleading is that the field of data communications is no longer concerned only with the transmission of data. Voice, video, image, and fax transmission all fall within the domain of the data communications analyst.

Figure 1-1 shows one way of breaking the complex world of data communications into a group of interacting components. As can be seen from the diagram, data communications is the sum total of the interacting components outlined. There is no distinct beginning or end. No one component is more important than another.

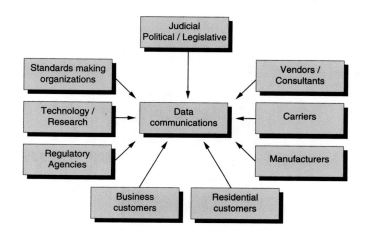

Figure 1-1   The Data Communications Industry: A Series of Interacting Components

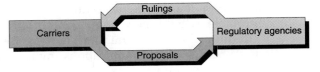

Figure 1-2   Relationship of Regulatory Agencies and Carriers

The Regulatory Process

Two tightly dependent components in a constant and ongoing state of change are the regulatory and carrier components. The **regulatory** component represents local, state, and federal agencies charged with regulating telecommunications, and the **carrier** component represents companies such as telephone and cable TV companies that sell transmission services.

To fully understand these two important components of today's data communications environment, we must focus on their interaction, those forces that join them and influence their present status. This interaction is a rather formal process of a series of proposals, also known as tariffs, from the carriers to the state and federal regulatory agencies and the issuance of rulings and approvals in return. This relationship is illustrated in Figure 1-2.

Basic Telecommunications Infrastructure   To understand the changing regulatory relationship between different phone companies and their associated regulatory agencies, it is important to understand the physical layout of a basic telecommunications infrastructure, and the names of the interacting components and service boundaries contained therein. Figure 1-3 illustrates such a basic telecommunications infrastructure.

Figure 1-3 illustrates the major components of the **public switched network (PSN)** necessary to support long-distance dial-up service for data communications. The acronym **LATA** stands for **local access transport areas**, which were established as a result of divestiture. A LATA is sometimes, but not always, equivalent to the area covered by a given area code. There can be several LATAs per area code. LATAs can cross state boundaries, but area codes cannot. As an example, Figure 1-4 illustrates both the area codes and LATAs for the state of Indiana. All local phone

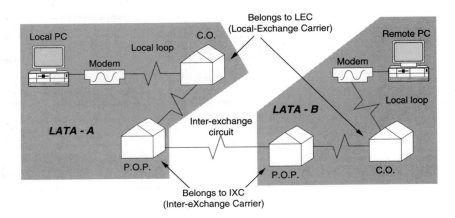

Figure 1-3   Basic Telecommunications Infrastructure

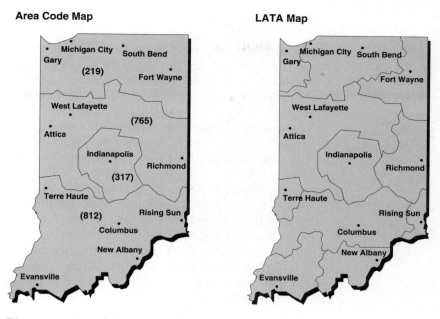

Figure 1-4   Area Codes vs. LATAs

traffic within a LATA is handled by the local phone company, more formally known as a **local exchange carrier** or **LEC,** most often one of the regional Bell operating companies.

The circuits between a residence or business and the local **central office** or **CO** are known as **local loops.** A central office is a facility belonging to the local phone company in which calls are switched to their proper destination. Any phone traffic destined for locations outside of a LATA must be handed off to the long-distance or **inter-exchange carrier (IXC)** of the customer's choice. Competing long-distance carriers wishing to do business in a given LATA maintain a switching office in that LATA known as a **POP** or **point of presence.** This POP handles billing information and routes the call over the long-distance carrier's switched network to its POP in the destination's LATA. The circuit between the POPs may be via satellite, microwave, fiber optical cable, traditional wiring, or some combination of these media. Depending on traffic levels on the long-distance carrier's network, calls may be routed through any combination of switches before reaching their final destination.

Deregulation and Divestiture: 1980s   Having become familiar with the overall interaction of carriers and regulatory agencies and with the basic infrastructure of today's telecommunications industry, the historical aspects of this regulatory relationship must be explored to better understand how today's regulatory environment evolved. Today's competitive telecommunications industry in the United States is largely the result of rulings by the Justice Department in the early 1980s. These rulings are generally referred to as **deregulation** and **divestiture.** These two terms are related but not synonymous.

Prior to deregulation and divestiture. America's telecommunications needs (data and voice), (hardware and services) were all supplied, with few exceptions, by one vendor: AT&T (American Telephone and Telegraph). At that time, homeowners were not allowed to purchase and install their own phones, something we take for granted today.

Local Bell operating companies provided local service but were still a part of AT&T. All telephone service, local as well as long distance, was coordinated through one telecommunications organization. Most indoor wiring was also the responsibility of AT&T, not the owner of the building in which the wiring existed. This top-to-bottom control of the telecommunications industry was seen as a monopoly, especially by other telecommunications vendors wishing to compete in the industry.

As a result, deregulation and divestiture were enacted in the late 1970s and early 1980s. It is important to note that the initial divestiture and deregulation of the telecommunications industry was not the result of a purely regulatory process. This enormously important event was primarily a judicial process, fought out in the courtrooms, largely fostered by one man, Bill McGowan, former president of MCI.

Although the Federal Communications Commission (FCC), a federal regulatory agency, initially ruled in 1971 that MCI could compete with AT&T for long-distance service, it was McGowan's 1974 lawsuit that got the Justice Department involved and led to the actual breakup of the telecommunications monopoly in America. Rulings concerning deregulation and divestiture continue to be handed down until 1996 through interpretation of a ruling known as the **Modified Final Judgment,** or **MFJ,** as issued by Federal Judge Harold Greene in 1982.

Divestiture broke up the network services of AT&T into separate long-distance and local service companies. AT&T would retain the right to offer long-distance services, while the former local Bell operating companies were grouped into new **regional Bell operating companies (RBOCs)** to offer local telecommunications service. Figure 1-5 illustrates the RBOCs and their constituent former Bell operating companies (BOCs) after divestiture.

Deregulation, on the other hand, addressed an entirely different aspect of the telecommunications industry in the United States: the ability of "phone companies" in America to compete in an unrestricted manner in other industries such as the computer and information systems fields.

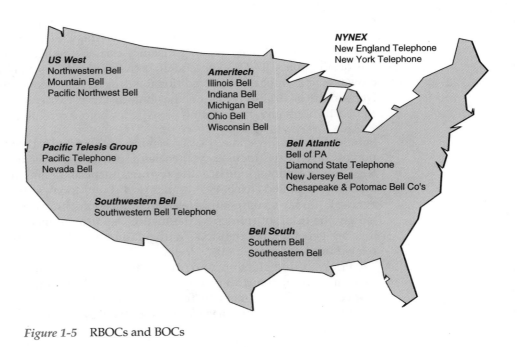

Figure 1-5   RBOCs and BOCs

Prior to deregulation, phone companies either were banned from doing business in other industries or were subject to having their profits and/or rates monitored or "regulated" in a similar fashion to the way in which their rates for phone service were regulated. As a result of deregulation, both AT&T and the RBOCs were allowed to enter into other industries by forming additional subsidiaries. For the first time, phone companies were competing in a market-driven, customer-dictated economy. A common misconception about deregulation is that phone companies became totally deregulated and can basically charge whatever the market will bear for phone services. This is not the case. Phone companies have both regulated and deregulated portions of their business, often segregated into separate companies.

Network services offered by phone companies are still regulated. New rate proposals from phone companies are filed as tariffs with state or federal regulatory authorities. Local service rate changes are filed on the state level with a particular state's Public Utilities Commission and on a federal level with the FCC for interstate service proposals and rate change requests. These commissions must balance objectives that are sometimes contradictory:

- Basic phone service must remain affordable enough that all residents of a state can afford it. This guarantee is sometimes known as universal service or universal access.

- Phone companies must remain profitable to be able to afford to constantly reinvest in upgrading their physical resources (hardware, cables, buildings) as well as educating and training their human resources.

The divestiture and deregulation activities of the 1980s allowed competing long-distance carriers such as MCI and U.S. Sprint to sell long-distance services on a level playing field with AT&T thanks to a ruling known as **equal access.** This means that any other long-distance carrier must be treated equally by the local BOCs in terms of access to the local carrier switching equipment, and ultimately to their customers.

From the end-user's perspective, the divestiture and deregulation activities of the 1980s enabled freedom of choice of long-distance carriers for both voice and data traffic. The competition for business and residential customers' long-distance business has forced down prices for long-distance service. On the other hand, from a telecommunications user's standpoint, one nice thing about having only one phone company in the predivestiture days was that it was easy to know who to call for new service or a repair problem. Installation and maintenance of hardware as well as long-distance and local service for voice or data were all coordinated through one company.

It is this loss of coordinated installation and troubleshooting that is perhaps the biggest loss to telecommunications users as a result of deregulation and divestiture. Service problems can often result in finger-pointing between hardware vendors, local service carriers, and long-distance carriers, while the telecommunications users are left rather helplessly in the middle.

Deregulation, Divestiture, and & Realignment: 1990s   In September 1992, the FCC enacted additional rulings that enabled limited competition in the local loop. The competition was limited to leased or private lines that bypass the phone company's switching equipment. Prior to these rulings, only the RBOCs were allowed to transport calls from a residence to business to the local central office and ultimately to the point of presence of any of the long-distance carriers.

A company would use a leased line to transport voice and/or data between corporate locations on a 24 hr/day, 7 day/week basis. Leased lines have no dial tone. They are private, point-to-point, "pipes" into which customers can transport voice and data to only the predetermined ends of those pipes. The differences among all of the various switched and leased voice and data services will be explored further in Chapters 2, 3, and 4.

Through a mandated process known as **co-location,** RBOCs had to allow alternate local loop carriers to install their equipment in the RBOC's central office. In return, RBOCs were allowed to charge **access charges** for co-location of the alternate carrier's equipment in their COs. End-users could also co-locate networking equipment in the RBOC's CO. Businesses could now build their own virtual private networks by co-locating their own networking equipment in local phone company central offices. Remembering that this ruling only affected leased line traffic, only those businesses that had a need for point-to-point or multipoint leased lines, usually for data transmission, were likely to benefit from this ruling. However, this local loop leased line deregulation was but a shadow of things to come.

The **Telecommunications Act of 1996** seeks to encourage competition in all aspects and markets of telecommunications services including switched and dedicated local and inter-LATA traffic as well as cable TV companies and wireless services such as paging, cellular, and satellite services. The legislation directs the FCC to produce the rules that will allow LECs and IXCs to compete in each other's markets. Companies that seek to offer local access service in competition with RBOCs are known as **competitive access providers** or **CAPs.** Perhaps most importantly, the law expressly preempts the authority of Judge Greene to dictate the operation of the telecommunications industry in the United States, while increasing the burden of the FCC to establish a fair and equitable market environment in which a variety of companies can compete in a deregulated manner. Figure 1-6 summarizes the major implications of the Telecommunications Act of 1996 from a variety of perspectives.

Whereas the divestiture of AT&T in the 1980s was government-imposed, the trivestiture of AT&T in 1995 was self-imposed. To free its various divisions to seek business opportunities without regard for the interests of other AT&T divisions, AT&T split into the following three separate companies:

1. **AT&T**—All of the carrier services, wireless services, and half of Bell Labs.

2. **Lucent Technologies**—All of the data and voice communications and networking equipment manufacturing and half of Bell Labs.

3. **NCR**—Known as AT&T Global Information Solutions after the 1991 takeover, NCR is once again an independent computer manufacturer.

In addition to divestiture and deregulation, the 1990s also saw realignment as various RBOCs proposed mergers to increase territory size, capitalize major new ventures, and create a more formidable competitor for IXCs that may wish to enter these regions. The two major RBOC realignments are as follows:

1. NYNEX and Bell Atlantic combined as Bell Atlantic to control the northeast corridor region from Washington, D.C., to Boston.

2. PacTel (Pacific Telesis) and Southwestern Bell combined as SBC Communications to control telecommunications in the Texas to California high-tech region.

Perspective	Implication/Importance
Strategic Intent	• To provide for a procompetitive deregulatory national policy framework by opening all telecommunications markets to competition • To direct FCC to create rulemakings to produce this deregulated environment
FCC	• Charged with producing new rules as to how the deregulated market is to operate in a manner that is fair to all competitors • Directed to also examine all regulations imposed on carriers and eliminate any that no longer serve a productive purpose
IXCs	• Eliminated need for long-distance carriers to file tariffs; rates determined by competitive pricing and the free market • Allowed to enter into local access markets, gaining access to local loops on a national basis • Will likely resell access to RBOCs' local networks rather than building their own
CAPs	• Gain access to RBOCs' local loop markets • Will likely resell access to RBOCs' local networks rather than building their own
LECs	• Can compete for IXC business within their own region as long as they can prove there is at least potential for competition in the local loop • Can enter into equipment manufacturing businesses
Cable TV companies	• Can enter telephone business but must wait until cable rates are deregulated
Users	• Will be offered more opportunities for bundled services from a single vendor • May regain single source for voice and data services lost in original divestiture/deregulation • May realize lower costs due to increased competition in a variety of markets

Figure 1-6   Telecommunications Act of 1996

The Standards Process

While the regulatory process is most important to carriers and their customers, the standards process is important to all constituencies of the data communications industry. Without standards, data communications would be nearly impossible as single-vendor, customized transmission solutions would probably be the only way to achieve end-to-end transmissions. **Standards** allow multiple vendors to manufacture competing products that can be purchased by data communications professionals. End-users can be confident that devices will operate as specified and will interoperate successfully. Standards can have a tremendous potential economic impact on vendors of data communications equipment and the standards-making process is wrought with political and financial influences.

Although the charter of each standards-making organization dictates the exact procedure for standards development, the process can be generalized as follows:

1. Recognition of the need for a standard.

2. Formation of some type of committee or task force.

3. Information/recommendation gathering phase.

4. Tentative/alternative standards issued.

5. Feedback on tentative/alternative standards.

6. Final standards issued.

7. Compliance with final standards.

Standards-Making Organizations   Standards-making organizations for the data communications industry fall into two major categories:

- Officially sanctioned.

- Ad hoc.

Some of the most significant officially sanctioned standards-making organizations whose standards will be referred to throughout the book are listed in Figure 1-7.

Perhaps because of the lag time often required to produce standards in an officially sanctioned standards-making organization, or perhaps in response to the ever-broadening scope of data communications-related technology, many ad hoc

Organization Name	Abbreviation	Authority/Charter	Mission/Contribution
International Standards Organization	ISO	International; voluntary	OSI 7-layer model
Comite Consultif International Telegraphique et Telephonique	CCITT	International; U.N. chartered	Telecommunications standards
International Telecommunications Union	ITU-T	International; U.N. chartered	Parent organization and successor to CCITT
American National Standards Institute	ANSI	U.S. government representative to ISO	Information systems standards
Institute of Electrical and Electronics Engineers	IEEE	Industrial professional society	Local area network standards
Electronics Industries Association	EIA	Trade organization	Electrical signaling standards, wiring standards

Figure 1-7   Officially Sanctioned Standards-Making Organizations

standards-making organizations continue to be formed. Known by a variety of terms including task forces, user groups, interest groups, consortium, forum, alliances or institutes, these groups have taken it on themselves to develop standards for specific areas of the data communications industry.

Although able to produce standards faster, in most cases, than official standards-making organizations, the existence and operation of these ad hoc standards-making organizations pose a few potential problems. Vendor-initiated ad hoc standards-making organizations are occasionally organized into opposing camps, with users left as victims between multiple standards for a single operation. These vendor-driven consortia do not necessarily have the best interests of end-users as their highest priority. Some ad hoc standards group such as the ATM (asynchronous transfer mode) Forum do not produce final standards, but rather seek to expedite the standards-making process by hammering out technical debates and issuing unified recommendations to official standards-making organizations for official sanction and ratification.

Business Impacts of Standards   The standards-making process is very important to manufacturers and one that they monitor closely and participate in actively. It is important to understand that the development of new technology most often precedes the standardization of that new technology. The development process is often carried out at a significant expense by either individual or groups of manufacturers as part of research and development work. Competing manufacturers may propose differing technological solutions to a given opportunity. It is often only after these competing technologies are about to come to market that the need for standardization prompts the formation of a standards committee. It should be obvious that competing manufacturers have a strong desire to get their own technology declared as "the standard." To capture early market share and thereby influence the standards-making process, manufacturers often produce and sell equipment prior to standards issuance. Make no mistake about it: standards-making can be a very political process. Furthermore, by the time standards are actually adopted for a given technology, the next generation of that technology is sometimes ready to be introduced to the market. Figure 1-8 attempts to illustrate this time lag between technological development and standards creation.

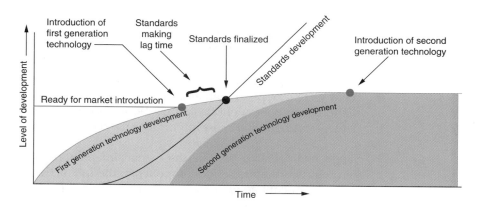

Figure 1-8   Technology Development and Standards Creation

Purchasers of data communications equipment should be wary of buying equipment that complies with proprietary prestandards. Have accommodations been made to upgrade the equipment to comply with official standards once they are issued? Will there be a charge for this upgrade? Will the upgrade require a return to the factory or is it a software upgrade that can be downloaded?

In general, standards work to the advantage of the data communications consumer as they provide assurance as to the interoperability of equipment manufactured by a variety of vendors. However, users should be aware of at least two standards-related issues that can cause confusion and potentially lead to bad purchase decisions and operational nightmares.

Standards Extensions   Recalling the potentially competitive nature of the standards-making process, it should come as no surprise that final standards are sometimes "least common denominator" implementations of competing proposals. To differentiate their own product offerings, vendors are likely to offer "extensions" to a given "standard." Naturally, one vendor's "extensions" do not necessarily match all the other vendors' "extensions." Users must be careful to ensure not only that a particular vendor's equipment meets the industry standard, but that the equipment meets the standard in an *acceptable* and *useful* way and that the vendor has not implemented extensions to the standard.

The Jargon Jungle   Unfortunately, standards do not apply to the vocabulary used by salespeople and marketing agencies to describe data communications hardware and software technology. As a result, the data communications user is trapped in a situation sometimes referred to as the "jargon jungle." Competing manufacturers often call similar features or operational characteristics by different names, leaving it to the data communications consumer to sort out the differences. There is no standards-making body that regulates data communications vocabulary and its use.
      Put another way:

Law 3:   There are no data communications police.

The best way to prevent being lost in the jargon jungle is to ask lots of questions. Be prepared to determine functionality of equipment based on operational characteristics rather than on package labels.

Manufacturing, Research, and Technology

Just as the regulatory and carrier components of the data communications environment were grouped together based on their respective interactions, many of the remaining component entities portrayed in Figure 1-1 can be legitimately grouped together based on their most important interactive force: business.

Supply and Demand   Unlike the formal interactions of proposals and rulings that join regulatory and carrier components, the interacting forces that join the remaining components as well as carriers are supply and demand, basic economic concepts. That's right, *data communications is business*. Figure 1-9 attempts to graphically illustrate the complex relationship between these many data communications environment components. The present status and near-term trends of any particular

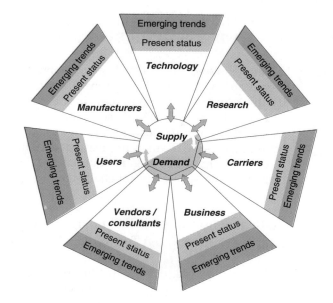

Figure 1-9   Supply and Demand as Driving Forces of
the Data Communications Industry

component are directly related to the net effect of the supply and demand forces of all other components combined.

This same phenomenon is sometimes referred to as **technology push/demand pull.** In technology-push scenario, new technologies may be introduced to the market to spawn innovative uses for this technology and thereby generate demand. Conversely, business needs may create a demand for services or technological innovation that are not currently available. However, the demand pull causes research and development efforts to accelerate, thereby introducing the new technology sooner than it would have otherwise been brought to market.

As an example, business and users may demand faster transfer of data. However, if research has not supplied the technology to accomplish these faster transfers, then manufacturers cannot produce and supply (sell) these products to businesses and users, while vendors and consultants cannot distribute and recommend their use.

Available technology also plays a key role in the relationship between business and carriers. Understanding that

- The phone companies are in business to make a profit.

- The phone companies need to sell the network services that business is willing to buy at a price business is willing to pay.

It therefore should follow that these enabling technologies tie the business demand for network services to the carrier's supply of network services. Stated another way, a carrier cannot provide the network services that businesses demand without the proper technology in place. Carriers can only afford to invest in new technology through profitable operations. Expressing this dynamic relationship in the form of an equation:

Business Demands + Available Technology = Emerging Network Services

■ CHALLENGES AND SOLUTIONS TO BUSINESS-ORIENTED DATA COMMUNICATIONS ANALYSIS

Having explored the interacting components of the data communications industry to gain an appreciation of its dynamic nature, the network analyst must next identify the key challenges to success in the data communications field and the associated potential solutions to those challenges. One of the most important things to realize is that corporations are not interested in investing in technology merely for technology's sake. Rather, implemented technology must produce measurable impact on business goals and requirements. Assuring this technological impact on business goals is a significant challenge.

Challenge: Information Technology Investment vs. Productivity Gains, Assuring Implemented Technology Meets Business Needs

In the past decade, over $1 trillion has been invested by business in information technology. Despite this massive investment, carefully conducted research indicates that there has been little if any increase in productivity as a direct result of this investment. This dilemma is known as the **productivity paradox.** How did so much money get invested in technology that failed to deliver increases in productivity? What was the nature of the analysis and design process that recommended the purchase of this technology? Clearly, something is wrong with an analysis and design process that recommends technology implementations that fail to meet strategic business objectives of increased productivity.

What are the characteristics required of an analysis and design process with the potential to overcome the productivity paradox? How can a network analyst remain properly focused on business requirements while performing technology analysis? Bringing this investment in technology, in general, down to investment in data communications and networking, in particular, it may be safe to say that

> **Law 4:**   If the network doesn't make good business sense, it probably makes no sense.

To overcome the productivity paradox, a structured methodology must be followed to assure that the implemented network technology meets the communications and business needs of the intended business, organization, or individual. The top-down approach and benchmarking are two potential solutions to the productivity paradox.

Solution: The Top-Down Approach

Applied Problem Solving

One such structured methodology is known as the top-down approach. Such an approach can be graphically illustrated in a **top-down model** as shown in Figure 1-10. Using a top-down approach as illustrated in the top-down model is relatively straightforward. Insisting that a top-down approach to network analysis and design is undertaken should ensure that the network design implemented will meet the business needs and objectives that motivated the design in the first place.

This top-down approach requires network analysts to understand business constraints and objectives as well as information systems applications and the data on

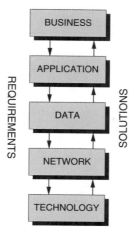

Figure 1-10   The Top-Down Model

which those applications run, before considering data communications and networking options.

Notice where the network layer occurs in the top-down model. It is no accident that data communications and networking form the foundation of today's sophisticated information systems. A properly designed network supports flexible delivery of data to distributed application programs, allowing businesses to respond quickly to customer needs and rapidly changing market conditions.

The Top-Down Model   How does the proper use of the top-down model ensure effective, business-oriented network analysis and design? Figure 1-11 lists the analysis processes associated with each layer of the top-down model.

One must start with the *business-level* objectives. What is the company (organization, individual) trying to accomplish by installing this network? Without a clear understanding of business-level objectives, it is nearly impossible to configure and implement a successful network. In many cases, businesses take this opportunity to critically reexamine their business processes in an analysis methodology known as **business process reengineering (BPR).**

Once business-level objectives are understood, one must understand the *applications* that will be running on the computer systems attached to these networks. After all, it is the applications that will be generating the traffic that will travel over the implemented network.

Once applications are understood and have been documented, the *data* that those applications generate must be examined. In this case, the term *data* is used in a general sense, as today's networks are likely to transport a variety of payloads including voice, video, image, and fax in addition to true data. Data traffic analysis not only must determine the amount of data to be transported but also must determine important characteristics about the nature of that data.

Once data traffic analysis has been completed, the following should be known:

1. Physical locations of data   (Where?)

2. Data characteristics and compatibility issues   (What?)

3. Amount of data generated and transported   (How much?)

Top-Down Model Layer	Associated Analysis Processes
Business layer	• Strategic business planning • Business process reengineering • Identify major business functions • Identify business processes • Identify business opportunities
Applications layer	• Applications development • Systems analysis and design • Identify information needs • Relate information needs to business processes and opportunities
Data layer	• Database analysis and design • Data modeling • Data distribution analysis • Client/server Architecture design • Distributed database design • Relate data collection and distribution to information and business needs
Network layer	• Network analysis and design • Logical network design (what) • Network implementation planning • Network management and performance monitoring • Relate logical network design to data collection and distribution design
Technology layer	• Technology analysis grids • Hardware–software–media technology analysis • Physical network design (how) • Physical network implementation • Relate physical network design to logical network design

Figure 1-11   Analysis Processes of the Top-Down Model

Given these requirements as determined by the upper layers of the top-down model, the next job is to determine the requirements of the *network* that will possess the capability to deliver this data in a timely, cost-effective manner. These network performance criteria could be referred to as *what* the implemented network must do to meet the business objectives outlined at the outset of this top-down analysis. These requirements are also sometimes referred to as the **logical network design.**

The *technology* layer analysis, in contrast, will determine *how* various hardware and software components will be combined to build a functional network that will meet predetermined business objectives. The delineation of required technology is often referred to as the **physical network design.**

Overall, the relationship between the layers of the top-down model could be described as follows: Analysis at upper layers produces requirements that are passed down to lower layers, whereas solutions meeting these requirements are passed back to upper layers. If this relationship among layers holds true throughout the business-oriented network analysis, then the implemented technology (bottom layer) should meet the initially outlined business objectives (top layer). Hence, the name, the top-down model.

Solution: Benchmarking

If using the top-down approach ensures that implemented technology meets business objectives, how can the impact of implemented technology on business objectives be measured? Without measurement, the top-down approach can't be proven to be any more effective at overcoming the productivity paradox than any other analysis and design methodology. In the age of downsized professional staffs and operating budgets, it is essential that network managers be able to prove the strategic importance of networking resources to the achievement of overall business objectives. Without such proof, network managers may soon find themselves and their staff replaced by outside contractors.

One way to demonstrate the impact of implemented technology by tying networking costs to business value is through a process known as **benchmarking.** Benchmarking can be summarized into the following three major steps:

1. Examine and document quantifiable improvements to business processes.

2. Perform surveys to measure customer satisfaction with deployed network services.

3. Compare actual implementation costs with the cost to purchase similar services from outside vendors in a process known as **outsourcing** (alternatively, comparative costs could be determined by examining other companies in the same vertical market).

Benchmarking the impact of networking technology is not an exact science. Although costs are relatively easy to quantify, the same cannot be said for benefits. Controlling all variables affecting business improvement is difficult at best. For example, how can improved business performance be directly attributed to network improvements, while eliminating such variables as an improved economy or a reduction in competition?

Challenge: Analysis of Complex Data Communications Connectivity and Compatibility Issues

Assuming that the proper use of the top-down model will ensure that implemented technical solutions will meet stated business requirements, the more technical challenges of network analysis and design must be addressed.

Introduction to Protocols and Compatibility   Solving incompatibility problems is at the very heart of successful network implementation. Compatibility can be thought of as successfully bridging the gap or communicating between two or more technology components, whether hardware or software. This logical gap between components is commonly referred to as an **interface.**

Interfaces may be physical (hardware to hardware) in nature. For example:

- Cable physically connecting to serial ports on a computer.
- A network interface and card physically plugging into the expansion bus inside a computer.

Interfaces may also be logical or software-oriented (software to software) as well. For example:

- A network operating system client software (Windows for Workgroups) communicating with the clients PC's operating system (DOS).
- A client-based data query tool (Microsoft Excel) gathering data from a large database management system (Oracle).

Finally, interfaces may cross the hardware-to-software boundary. For example:

- A network operating system specific piece of software known as a driver that interfaces to an installed network interface card (NIC).
- A piece of operating system software known as a kernel that interfaces to a computer's CPU chip.

The reason that these various interfaces are able to be bridged successfully, thereby supporting compatibility between components, is due to **protocols.** Protocols are nothing more than rules for how communicating hardware and software components bridge interface or talk to one another. Protocols may be proprietary (used exclusively by one or more vendors) or open (used freely by all interested parties). Protocols may be officially sanctioned by international standards-making bodies such as the International Standards Organization (ISO), or may be purely market-driven (de facto protocols). Figure 1-12 illustrates the relationship between interfaces, protocols, and compatibility.

For every potential hardware-to-hardware, software-to-software, and hardware-to-software interface imaginable, there is likely to be one or more possible protocols supported. The sum of all of the protocols employed in a particular computer is sometimes referred to as that computer's **protocol stack.** Successfully determining which protocols must be supported in which instances for the multitude of interfaces possible in a complicated network design is likely to be the difference between success or failure in a network implementation.

How can a network analyst possibly keep track of all potential interfaces and their associated protocols between all network-attached devices? What is needed is a framework in which to organize the various potential interfaces and protocols in such complicated network designs. More than one such framework, otherwise known as communications architectures, exists. Two of the most popular communications architectures are the seven-layer OSI model and the four-layer internet suite of protocols model.

Solution: The OSI Model

Determining which technology and protocols to employ to meet the requirements determined in the logical network design, yielded from the network layer of the top-down model, requires a structured methodology of its own. Fortunately, a framework for organizing networking technology and protocol solutions has been developed by the ISO and is known as the open systems interconnection (OSI) model. The following

Hardware to Hardware Interface

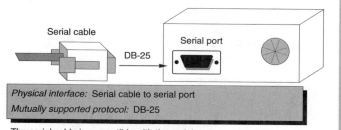

Physical interface: Serial cable to serial port
Mutually supported protocol: DB-25

The serial cable is compatible with the serial port.

Software to Software Interface

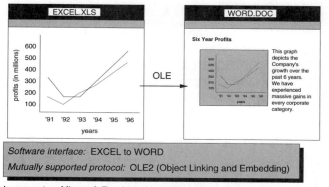

Software interface: EXCEL to WORD
Mutually supported protocol: OLE2 (Object Linking and Embedding)

Incorporate a Microsoft Excel graphic within a Microsoft Word document.

Software to Hardware Interface

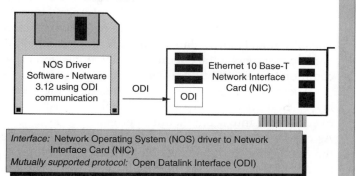

Interface: Network Operating System (NOS) driver to Network
            Interface Card (NIC)
Mutually supported protocol: Open Datalink Interface (ODI)

Implementing mutually supported protocols allows interfacing hardware and/or software technology to communicate, thereby insuring compatibility.

Figure 1-12   Interfaces, Protocols, and Compatibility

section is only intended to offer the reader a brief introduction to the overall functionality of the OSI model as a network analysis tool, with greater detail on the OSI model being provided throughout the remainder of the text. The OSI model should be looked on as a powerful, but somewhat complex, tool. Rather than explaining the tool in great detail now, even though we won't be using it until later, the author has chosen to wait until the tool is actually employed. In Chapter 5, the OSI model is explored in much greater detail in terms of both architecture and functionality as it is employed to simplify the discussion of local area network (LAN) architectures and internetwork connectivity. The **OSI model** is illustrated in Figure 1-13.

OSI Model Layer	Functionality	Automobile Assembly Line
7 Application	Layer where application programs interact and receive services	Dealer Installed Options: Options desired by users are added at the dealership
6 Presentation	Assures reliable session transmission between applications; takes care of differences in data representation	Painting and Finish Work: The vehicle is painted and trim is applied
5 Session	Enables two applications to communicate across the network	Interior: Seats and dashboard are added to passenger compartment
4 Transport	Assures reliable transmission from end-to-end, usually across multiple nodes	Electrical: Electrical system and components are added
3 Network	This layer sets up the pathways or end-to-end connections, usually across a long distance or multiple nodes	Body: Passenger compartment and fenders are attached to the chassis
2 Data Link	Puts messages together, attaches proper headers to be sent out or received, assures messages are delivered between two points	Engine/Drive Train: Engine and transmission components provide the vehicle with propulsion
1 Physical	Layer that is concerned with transmitting bits of data over a physical medium	Chassis/Frame: Steel is fabricated to form the chassis on which all other components will travel

Figure 1-13   The OSI Model

The OSI model divides the communication between any two networked computed devices into seven layers or categories. Network analysts literally talk in terms of the OSI model. When troubleshooting network problems, inevitably the savvy network analyst starts with the physical layer (layer 1) and assures that protocols and interfaces at each layer are operational before moving up the OSI model. The OSI model allows data communications technology developers as well as standards developers to talk about the interconnection of two networks or computers in common terms without dealing in proprietary vendor jargon.

These "common terms" are the result of the layered architecture of the seven-layer OSI model. The architecture breaks the task of two computers communicating to each other into separate but interrelated tasks, each represented by its own layer. As can be seen in Figure 1-13, the top-layer (layer 7) represents services offered to the application programs running on each computer and is therefore aptly named the application layer. The bottom layer (layer 1) is concerned with the actual physical connection of the two computers or networks and is therefore named the physical layer. The remaining layers (layers 2–6) may not be as obvious but, nonetheless, represent a sufficiently distinct logical group of functions required to connect two computers, as to justify a separate layer. As will be seen later in the text, some of the layers are divided into sublayers.

To use the OSI model, a network analyst lists the known protocols for each computing device or network node in the proper layer of its own seven-layer OSI model. The collection of these known protocols in their proper layers is known as the protocol stack of the network node. For example, the physical media employed such as unshielded twisted pair, coaxial cable, or fiber optic cable would be entered as a layer 1 protocol, while ethernet or token ring network architectures might be entered as a layer 2 protocol. As will be seen later in the text as part of the study of network operating systems, a given computer may employ more than one protocol on one or more layers of the OSI model. In these cases, such computers are described as supporting multiple protocol stacks or simply as multiprotocol.

The OSI model allows network analysts to produce an accurate inventory of the protocols present on any given network node. This protocol profile represents a unique personality of each network node and gives the network analyst some insight into what **protocol conversion,** if any, may be necessary to get any two network nodes to communicate successfully. Ultimately, the OSI model provides a structured methodology for determining what hardware and software technology will be required in the physical network design to meet the requirements of the logical network design.

Perhaps the best analogy for the OSI reference model, which illustrates its architectural or framework purpose, is that of an assembly line producing an automobile. Although each process or step is independently managed and performed, each step also depends on previous steps to be performed according to standardized specifications or protocols for the overall process, the production of a functional vehicle, to be successful.

Similarly, each layer of the OSI model operates independently of all other layers, while depending on neighboring layers to perform according to specification while cooperating in the attainment of the overall task of communication between two computers or networks.

The OSI model is neither a protocol nor a group of protocols. It is a standardized, empty framework into which protocols can be listed to perform effective network analysis and design. As will be seen later in the text, however, the OSI has also produced a set of OSI protocols that correspond to some of the layers of the OSI model. It is important to differentiate between the OSI model and OSI protocols.

The OSI model will be used throughout the remainder of the text as the protocol stacks of various network operating systems are analyzed and in the analysis and design of advanced network connectivity alternatives.

Solution: The Internet Suite of Protocols Model

Although the OSI model is perhaps more famous than any OSI protocol, just the opposite could be said for a model and associated protocols known as the **internet suite of protocols model.** Also known as the TCP/IP protocol suite, or TCP/IP architecture, this communications architecture takes its name from **TCP/IP (transmission control protocol/internet protocol),** the de facto standard protocols for open-systems internetworking. As can be seen in Figure 1-14, TCP and IP are just two of the protocols associated with this model.

Like the OSI model, the TCP/IP model is a layered communications architecture in which upper layers use the functionality offered by the protocols of the lower layers. Each layer's protocols are able to operate independently from the protocols of other layers. For example, protocols on a given layer can be updated or modified without having to change all other protocols in all other layers. A recent example is the new version of IP known as IPng (IP next generation), which was developed in response to a pending shortage of IP addresses. This proposed change is possible without the need to change all other protocols in the TCP/IP communication architecture. The exact mechanics of how TCP/IP and related protocols work will be explored in greater depth later in the text.

Layer	OSI	INTERNET	Data Format	Protocols
7	Application	Application	Messages or Streams	TELNET FTP TFTP SMTP SNMP CMOT MIB
6	Presentation			
5	Session	Transport or Host-Host	Transport Protocol Packets	TCP UDP
4	Transport			
3	Network	Internet	IP Datagrams	IP
2	Data Link	Network Access	Frames	
1	Physical			

Figure 1-14   Internet Suite of Protocols vs. OSI

Figure 1-14 compares the four-layer internet suite of protocols model with the seven-layer OSI model. Either communications architecture could be used to analyze and design communications between networks. In the case of the internet suite of protocols model, the full functionality of internetwork communications is divided into four layers rather than seven. Some network analysts consider the internet suite of protocols model simpler and more practical than the OSI model.

Solution: The I-P-O Model

Once the protocols are determined for two or more computers or networks that wish to communicate, the next step is to determine the type of technology required to deliver the identified internetworking functionality and protocols.

To understand the basic function of any piece of networking equipment, one really need only understand the differences between the characteristics of the data that came in and the data that went out. Those differences identified were processed by the data communications equipment being analyzed.

This input-processing-output or **I-P-O model** is another key model that will be used throughout the textbook to analyze a variety of networking equipment and opportunities. The I-P-O model provides a framework in which to focus on the difference between the data that came into a particular networked device (I) and the data that came out of that same device (O). By defining this difference, the processing (P) performed by the device is documented.

As a simple example of the use of the I-P-O model, let's assume that we wish to hook a particular PC to a particular printer. After some investigation, we discover that the PC can only provide input (I) to the printer (O) through the PC's serial port. However, the printer (O) only has a parallel interface. As a result, we have a serial interface (perhaps DB-25, RS-232) as an input and have a parallel interface (Centronics connector) as an output. What is required is a device to provide the necessary (P)rocessing to convert our serial input to the required parallel output. Such devices are readily available. However, before purchasing such a device, it is essential to have organized and documented the required electrical and mechanical protocols that must be interfaced and converted between. By organizing such interfaces in a simple I-P-O model, one can immediately see the exact conversions that must take place.

Although at first glance the I-P-O model may seem overly simplistic, it is another valuable model that can assist network analysts in organizing thoughts, documenting requirements, and articulating needs.

■ THE DATA COMMUNICATIONS PROFESSION

Where Does Data Communications Fit in an Overall Information Systems Architecture?

How is a top-down approach to data communications analysis and design actually implemented in today's corporations? What is the overall information systems structure into which this top-down approach fits? Figure 1-15 illustrates one way in which a top-down approach could be implemented within the overall framework of an information systems architecture.

Several key points illustrated in the diagram are worth noting. Predictably, the entire information systems development process begins with the business analysis process. What is important to note, however, is that all major sections of the top-down approach model business, applications, data, technology, and network—take part in the business analysis process.

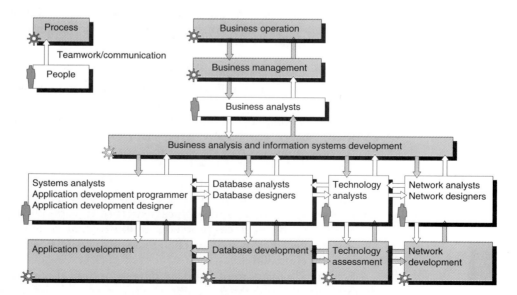

Figure 1-15   The Top-Down Approach to Information Systems Development

In some cases, a separate technology assessment group would exist within a corporation and would partake in the business analysis phase of the information systems development process as well. In so doing, each layer of the top-down model is represented by trained individuals and complementary processes in the top-down approach to information systems development. This initial participation of all segments of the information systems development team in the business analysis portion of the process provides assurance that the system as implemented will adequately support the business functions for which it was intended.

After this initial participation of all segments of the team in the business analysis phase, each segment develops their portion of the information system. However, merely knowing the business needs that an information system is trying to meet is an insufficient guarantee of a successful implementation. It is essential that during the development process, the applications, database, network, and technology development teams communicate continually to assure that their finished subsystems will communicate effectively to support those business needs initially identified. This critical communication between subsystems as well as between the individuals who developed these subsystems is illustrated in Figure 1-15.

Professional Development

The accomplishment of this communication between business, application, database, network, and technology analysts should not be taken for granted. These analysts must be able to speak each other's languages and jargon to communicate effectively. This need to understand all aspects of the information systems architecture has major implications for the proper training of data communications and networking professionals.

Unless one understands "the big picture" of the entire top-down model, one cannot effectively design and implement the data communications and networking foundation that must support this same big picture. Data communications cannot be studied in a vacuum. The study of data communications and networking must be approached from "the big picture" perspective, ever-mindful of the tremendous potential effect that data communications and networking decisions have on this same big picture.

Critical Skills for Data Communications Professionals   To understand the critical skills required of data communications professionals, one first has to thoroughly understand the business environment in which these professionals must operate. Today's economic environment has been alternatively described as the Information Age or a knowledge-based economy. Characteristic of such an economy are the recognition of information as a corporate asset to be leveraged for competitive advantage and the need for highly reliable networks to support the mission-critical applications that deliver that valuable information to key decision-makers.

Such an economic environment requires data communications professionals who can move beyond their technical expertise and specialization by demonstrating the ability to solve business problems. In this role, data communications professionals will be seen increasingly as change agents and partners and less as technology experts and consultants.

So what do the current trends in data communications indicate for employment opportunities? Given the recognition by business of the importance of networks and given the complicated nature of both the data communications technology and the integration of that technology to carrier-provided network services, it would seem that job opportunities should be ideal for a data communications professional who possesses the following qualities:

- Understands and can speak "business"

- Demonstrates an ability to own and solve business problems in a partnership rather than assuming a consultative role

- Demonstrates an ability to look outside his or her own expertise for solutions

- Exhibits an understanding of the need for lifelong learning

- Demonstrates an ability to evaluate technology with a critical eye as to cost/benefit and potential for significant business impact of that technology

- Understands comparative value and proper application of available network services and can work effectively with carriers to see that implementations are completed properly and cost-effectively

- Communicates effectively, both on paper and orally, with technically oriented people as well as with business management personnel

The multitalented nature of these data communications professionals is illustrated in Figure 1-16.

The Certification Question   Certification as an indication of mastery of a particular vendor's technology may be important in some employment situations. Figure 1-17 lists some of the vendor-specific certifications available to data communications professionals.

Some concerns with certification programs are

- The amount of practical, hands-on experience required to earn a given certification.

- The amount of continuing education and experience required to retain a certification.

- Vendor-specific certifications do not provide the broad background required for today's multivendor internetworks.

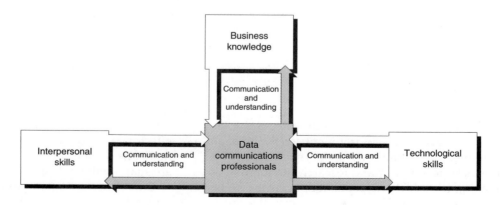

Figure 1-16   Critical Skills for Data Communications Professionals

Vendor	Certification
Banyan	Certified Banyan engineer
Compaq	Accredited system engineer
IBM	Certified LAN server engineer, professional systems engineer
Lotus	Certified Lotus professional
Microsoft	Certified systems engineer
Novell	Certified Novell engineer, master CNE

Figure 1-17   Vendor-Specific Certifications

In an effort to address these concerns, the Network Professional Association has developed a certification known as the certified network professional (CNP). To earn the CNP certification, applicants must

- Already have earned at least two of the vendor-specific certifications listed in Figure 1-17

- Have at least 2 years of employment as a network professional

- Pass the CNP exam, which includes sections on client operating systems, network operating systems, hardware, protocols, and topologies

To remain certified as a CNP, an individual must participate in between 60 and 120 hours of continuing education per year and must remain employed in the networking profession. As the networking profession matures, the importance of certification to the profession will be evident.

The Opportunity   To say that these are exciting times in the field of data communications is an understatement of untold proportions. The opportunities are indeed significant for those individuals properly prepared. I invite you to enter the exciting world of data communications with me. I am confident that it is a journey you will not soon forget. For a more humorous view of pursuing a career in data communications, see Ten Top Reasons to be in Data Communications in Appendix B.

SUMMARY

Today's data communications industry is characterized by an environment consisting of a group of interacting components such as business, technology and research, standards-making organizations, regulatory agencies, and common carriers. The state of the overall industry at any point in time is the product of the interaction of these components. To be an effective participant in the data communications field, one must be aware of the forces at work that are shaping the industry.

Data communications and networking are integral parts of an overall information systems architecture. The ultimate success of an implemented information system depends largely on the design of the network that forms the foundation of that system. This high degree of integration between networking and other information system architecture components is graphically illustrated in a model known as the top-down model.

The top-down model implies that any information system design must begin with a thorough understanding of business requirements before subsequent issues such as applications, data, networking, and technology are addressed.

The integrated nature of the network layer of an information systems architecture is mirrored in the skills required of today's data communications professionals. The demand is high for individuals well versed in business analysis, information systems, and networking design combined with outstanding written and verbal communications skills.

Remember—if the network does not make good business sense, it probably makes no sense at all.

KEY TERMS

access charges, 10
benchmarking, 19
BPR, 17
business process reengineering, 17
CAP, 10
carrier, 6
central office, 7
CO, 7
co-location, 10
competitive access providers, 10
data communications, 5
demand pull, 15
deregulation, 7
divestiture, 7
equal access, 9
inter-exchange carriers, 7
interface, 19

internet suite of protocols model, 23
I-P-O model, 24
IXC, 7
LATA, 6
LEC, 7
local access transport area, 6
local exchange carrier, 7
local loops, 7
logical network design, 18
MFJ, 8
modified final judgment, 8
OSI seven-layer model, 21
outsourcing, 19
physical network design, 18
point of presence, 7
POP, 7
productivity paradox, 16

protocol conversion, 23
protocols, 20
protocol stack, 20
PSN, 6
public switched network, 6
RBOC, 8
regional Bell operating company, 8
regulatory agencies, 6
standards, 11
TCP/IP, 23
technology push, 15
telecommunications, 5
Telecommunications Act of 1996, 10
top-down model, 16
transmission control
    protocol/internal protocol, 23

REVIEW QUESTIONS

1. What are the major interacting components that comprise today's data communications industry?
2. What are the specific interaction scenarios between the following components: Manufacturers and standards-making organizations, Business and manufacturers, Carriers and regulatory agencies, Carriers and political/judicial legislative?
3. Where do data communications and networking fit in an overall information systems architecture?
4. What is the role of business requirements analysis in network analysis and design?
5. What is the top-down model and how is it employed in network analysis and design?

6. Define the relationship between the following terms: inter-LATA and intra-LATA, CO and POP, local loop and RBOC.
7. What is the overall intent of the Telecommunications Act of 1996?
8. What skills are required of today's data communications professional?
9. What is divestiture and how does it differ from deregulation?
10. What is an RBOC?
11. Why is the data communications industry in such a state of change?
12. What is the Modified Final Judgment and why is it important?

13. What are the key events that led up to divestiture and deregulation?
14. Who were the big winners and losers as a result of divestiture?
15. From a data communications user's perspective, what have been the most important impacts of divestiture and deregulation?
16. Explain how carriers can engage in both regulated and unregulated business ventures.
17. Which agencies are responsible for regulation of carriers on both a state and federal level?
18. What is the OSI model and why is it important?
19. Why is the standards-making process so politically charged at times?
20. Why do standards often lag behind technological development?
21. What are the possible business impacts of standards on a manufacturer of data communications equipment?
22. How do the laws of supply and demand apply to the data communications industry? Give examples.
23. What is benchmarking and how is it related to the top-down model?
24. What is the I-O-P model and of what value is it?
25. What are the major processes performed by most data communications equipment?
26. Distinguish between and give an example of each of the three types of interfaces discussed in the chapter.

27. What is the relationship between interfaces, protocols, and standards?
28. What is meant by the statement, "Data communications solutions are business solutions"?
29. What is the internet suite of protocols model?
30. Describe the similarities and differences between the OSI model and the internet suite of protocols model.
31. What are the benefits and shortcomings of vendor-specific certifications?
32. What are the major differences between logical network design and physical network design?
33. Explain how the processes associated with each layer of the top-down model contribute to effective information systems development.
34. How can one avoid wasting money on technology that does not improve productivity?
35. What kinds of opportunities are available in the data communications industry for properly trained graduates?
36. How can equations such as "Business Demands + Available Technology = Emerging Network Services" remain useful to you in the future?
37. What is the productivity paradox and why should a network analyst be concerned with it?

ACTIVITIES

1. Contact the local provider of telecommunications services to your home or business. Inquire as to how long-distance calls are passed along to user-specified long-distance carriers.
2. If your local telecommunications provider is not one of the seven RBOCs, inquire as to the history of this company's providing telecommunications service in this area; why doesn't one of the RBOCs supply local telecommunications service in this area?
3. Contact your state Public Utilities Commission. Inquire as to the current state of intra-LATA (local carrier) competition in your state. Is it currently allowed? Are proposals pending?
4. Inquire of your Public Utilities Commission regarding the regulations in your state for shutting off one's phone service due to nonpayment. Is phone service seen more as a right or privilege in your state?
5. Inquire of your local telecommunications carrier or RBOC as to which aspects of its business are regulated vs. unregulated. Draw a diagram.
6. Are any of your local carrier's unregulated activities being considered for regulation?

7. Invite a telecommunications professional who was in the business at the time of divestiture to speak to your class regarding life before and after divestiture. Try to get speakers representing both the user's and carrier's perspective.
8. Gather job postings for networking-related careers. Put together a scrapbook or bulletin board display. What types of technical and nontechnical skills are required? What are the salary ranges? Do all jobs require experience?
9. What types of professional certifications, if any, are currently available to people in the field of data communications and networking? How are such certifications viewed by companies hiring networking professionals?
10. Who is the current chairman of the FCC and what are his/her qualifications?
11. Find out who are the Public Utility Commissioners in your home state. What are their qualifications for the position.
12. Which committees in the House of Representatives and Senate consider legislation related to telecommunications?

13. Which representatives/senators currently serve on those committees? How much financial support do these elected officials receive from telecommunications companies or lobbyists?
14. What telecommunications-related legislation is currently being considered by Congress?
15. Find out which operations of AT&T are unregulated and which are regulated?
16. Do standards always lag behind technological development? If not, give an example.
17. How much of the Telecommunications Act of 1996 has been implemented to date? Prepare a presentation on the impact of that legislation.

CASE STUDY

Telecom Competition—Rochester, N.Y.: Land of the Free Market

Michael Schauseil must worry sometimes that he'll wake up and find out that the past 15 months have been some crazy, wonderful dream in which phone companies keep forcing lower and lower prices on him.

All Schauseil has to do is wave someone else's lower offer under this provider's nose and the provider whips out an even lower counteroffer.

It all started in January of last year when the state of New York agreed to let the former Rochester Telephone Co. sell long-haul, cable and cellular services in exchange for opening the local loop to competitors. That move made Rochester the nation's first open market for phone service.

So when Schauseil, the manager of telecommunications for Blue Cross/Blue Shield of Rochester (BC/BS), went shopping for one carrier to handle all his telecommunications needs, he had a choice.

Ultimately, Schauseil negotiated an agreement with Frontier Corp., the unregulated entity that has a subsidiary Rochester Telephone, the regulated local exchange carrier.

When Schauseil cut the deal last spring, the Rochester open market was mere months old and real competition hadn't yet materialized. In an effort to seal up BC/BS's business, Frontier put together an attractive bundle of local, long-distance, cellular and private-line services anyway.

Schauseil thought the offer was good enough to dump two of his former service providers—AT&T long-distance and Cellular 1 cellular—and to sign on for two years with Frontier. Then Time Warner Communications of Rochester, the local cable TV provider, stepped in as a local exchange carrier offering even lower rates.

Frontier reacted by ripping open Schauseil's two-year contract and slashing prices: Long-distance came down an extra 27%; cellular, 11%; and local service, 9%. Frontier is also working on a proposal to beat Time Warner's offer of a flat rate or local metered service that is typically billed by the minute.

"They haven't closed the door yet on anything," Schauseil said.

Telecome Test Tube

Since the open market experiment began, the main competitors have been Frontier, AT&T, Time Warner and Citizens Telecom.

AT&T, the long-distance giant that came into the local market as a reseller of local telephone access, has all but dropped out of the residential market, grousing that it cannot make a profit because of the paltry 5% wholesale discount Rochester Telephone offers on local access. AT&T has an appeal in with the PSC. And recently, it decided to resell some local access from Time Warner.

Citizens Telecom also resells local service as well as paging and cellular services, bundled with its own long-distance service.

But Time Warner has come on strong, undercutting Rochester Telephone prices in areas where it competes between 10% and 30%, depending on the service. With its own fiber/coaxial cable network in place locally, Time Warner is not hemmed in by profit margins set by Rochester Telephone's wholesale price.

Time Warner has 13 Synchronous Optical Network (SONET) rings in place as its local backbone, so it offers direct fiber links to large corporate users at discounted rates. Rochester Telephone's SONET deployment, in contrast, lags far behind with only two completed rings.

The University of Rochester has bought some T-1s and fax and Centrex service from Time Warner over its SONET fiber at significant savings. Beyond the price, John Tompkinson, a senior network engineer for the university, said he likes the superior performance of fiber over that of copper and the inherent redundancy of SONET rings.

No Answer on Local Dial Tone

Time Warner's impact on local residential phone service has been less dramatic. The company will not say how many customers it has signed up, but they are restricted to a limited number of apartment buildings where Time Warner is trialing equipment and working out the problems of providing residential telephony.

In fact, Rochester Telephone says the competitors' inroads into local dial-tone service is between 3% and 4%, most of that snapped up by AT&T during its short-lived push into the market.

Time Warner's progress in the local dial-tone area is slowed by difficulties upgrading a cable TV network to telephony standards and by the immaturity of the hardware.

"The in-home technology is being developed as we speak," said Ann Burr, Time Warner's president in Rochester. "It's difficult to move as fast as we would like."

Still, Burr said the company is promising to start deploying cable modem Internet access service offering up to 10M bit/sec by the end of this year or early next.

Time Warner's rapid move into the market for large corporate users has been a wake-up call for Rochester Telephone, according to company President Denise Gutstein.

Rochester Telephone is installing more fiber in SONET rings; looking for a partner, perhaps a wireless provider, to compete against cable TV offerings; and researching a way to deliver high bandwidth to the home over its existing wires.

The company is also consolidating its central offices from 20 to five, meaning decreased costs and faster rollout of new services.

Gutstein said pressure from Time Warner has not only accelerated Rochester Telephone's efforts in those areas, but also has made Frontier more flexible in negotiating deals with users.

Bundling services, such as the Frontier package worked out for BC/BS, is now more common because of competition. "This forces a different consideration when the customer has more options compared to a year ago," Gutstein said.

And that's something Schauseil can enjoy. "They appear open and willing to discuss anything to keep you as a customer," he said.

Source: Tim Greene, "Rochester, N.Y.: Land of the Free Market," *Network World,* vol. 13, no. 20 (May 13, 1996) p. 1. Copyright © May 13, 1996 by Network World, Inc. Framingham, MA 01701. Reprinted by permission of Network World.

BUSINESS CASE STUDY QUESTIONS

Activities

1. Complete a top-down model for this case by gleaning facts from the case and placing them in the proper layer of the top-down model. After having completed the top-down model, analyze and detail those instances where requirements were clearly passed down from upper layers to lower layers of the model and where solutions to those requirements were passed up from lower layers to upper layers of the model. Although the facts in this case pertain primarily to the business layer, cases in future chapters will contain more facts pertaining to all layers of top-down model.

2. Detail any questions about the case that may occur to you for which answers are not clearly stated in the article.

3. After answering the following questions from the article, research and speculate what impact the Telecommunications Act of 1996 might play on any of the issues described in the article.

Business

1. What did Rochester Telephone gain the right to sell?
2. What did Rochester Telephone have to offer in return for the right to sell services not typically sold by local carriers?
3. What is the relationship between Frontier Corp. and Rochester Telephone Co.?
4. How is Frontier Corp. appealing to business users in an effort to get them to switch carriers?
5. What other companies, if any, are competing with Rochester Telephone in the local service offerings?

6. How can alternative local service providers provide local service without running their own networks and local loops?
7. Which alternative local service provider already had its own network?
8. Which types of network services were more advanced from alternative carriers than from Rochester Telephone?
9. What are some of the problems facing alternative service providers?
10. What had been the impact to date of the

alternative service providers in terms of lost market share for Rochester Telephone Co.?

11. What are some of the strategic business changes that Rochester Telephone Co. has undertaken in reaction to local competition?

12. How do residential or industrial customers benefit from competition among local service providers?

13. Can you think of any potential negatives that customers might encounter due to increased local competition?

Application

1. What is Centrex?

2. What types of businesses might be interested in Centrex or a similar service?

Data

1. What is the data rate promised by cable modem access?

2. What is the data rate of a V.34 modem over a dial-up local loop from a local phone service provider?

Network

1. What is SONET?
2. Explain the comment in the article regarding the redundancy of SONET.

3. What is a T-1?

Technology

1. What impact does the availability of technology (or lack thereof) have on an alternative service provider's ability to gain market share?

CHAPTER 2

DATA COMMUNICATIONS CONCEPTS

Concepts Reinforced
....

I-P-O Model   Basic Telecommunications
Protocols and Compatibility   Infrastructure

Concepts Introduced
....

Character Encoding   Modulation/Demodulation
Serial vs. Parallel   Analog vs. Digital
Physical Interfaces vs. Transmission   Modulation Techniques
  Protocols   Carrier Waves
Serial Transmission Standards   Half-Duplex vs. Full-Duplex
Two-Wire vs. Four-Wire Circuits   Synchronous vs. Asynchronous
Dial-up vs. Leased Line   Transmission
Baud Rate vs. Transmission Rate   Echo Cancellation
Transmission Services

OBJECTIVES

Upon successful completion of this chapter, you should be able to

1. Distinguish between the following related concepts and understand the proper application of each:

analog	digital
synchronous	asynchronous
full-duplex	half-duplex
two wire	four wire
serial	parallel
bps	baud rate
leased line	dial-up/switched line

2. Understanding the concepts, processes, and protocols involved with completing a modem-based, point-to-point data communications session, including the following:

character encoding	serial transmission
serial/parallel conversion	modulation/demodulation

3. Understand the impact and limitations of various modulation techniques.

4. Understand the differences and proper application of a variety of carrier transmission services.

■ INTRODUCTION

As new vocabulary and concepts are introduced in this chapter, it's important to understand that these words and concepts will be used throughout your study of data communications. Future concepts will be built upon the foundation of a thorough understanding of the vocabulary in this chapter.

This is the time to begin to speak this foreign language that we call data communications. Don't be timid. Try to get together with other data communications students or professionals outside of class and practice your new vocabulary.

Discussions of specific technology will be kept to a minimum in this chapter, concentrating instead on the conceptual aspects of the "how" of data transmission. Although modems will be mentioned in this chapter, the in-depth study of technology, including its business impact, will begin in Chapter 3.

End-to-End Data Communications

Figure 2-1 serves as a road map for all of the concepts to be studied in this chapter. An end-to-end data communications session between two PCs and their associated modems via a dial-up phone line offers an overall scenario into which most data communications concepts can be introduced. In this manner, each concept can be understood individually as well as in terms of its contribution to the overall end-to-end data communications session.

Another reason for choosing a modem-based data communications session as a means of introducing basic data communications concepts is the likelihood of encountering modems and dial-up connections in real life. This contributes to familiarity with the process as we begin this study and a greater understanding of this common data communications opportunity at the conclusion of the chapter.

However, it is important to understand that the concepts outlined in Figure 2-1 and explained throughout the chapter are not specific to only PCs or modems. These are basic data communications concepts that form the basis of the vast majority of data communications technology. Likewise, although PC modems are discussed in this chapter, modems also have many other applications such as communicating with mainframe computers as described in Chapter 9.

The end-to-end data communications session between two PCs and its constituent concepts and processes as illustrated in Figure 2-1 can be logically subdivided into three major sections:

- From the computer to the modem.

- Within the modem.

- From the modem to the phone service.

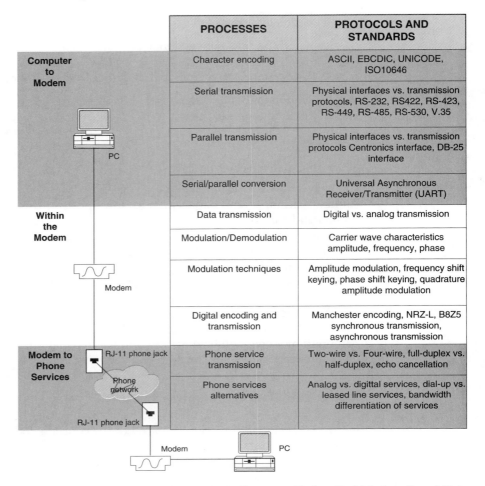

	PROCESSES	PROTOCOLS AND STANDARDS
Computer to Modem	Character encoding	ASCII, EBCDIC, UNICODE, ISO10646
	Serial transmission	Physical interfaces vs. transmission protocols, RS-232, RS422, RS-423, RS-449, RS-485, RS-530, V.35
	Parallel transmission	Physical interfaces vs. transmission protocols Centronics interface, DB-25 interface
	Serial/parallel conversion	Universal Asynchronous Receiver/Transmitter (UART)
Within the Modem	Data transmission	Digital vs. analog transmission
	Modulation/Demodulation	Carrier wave characteristics amplitude, frequency, phase
	Modulation techniques	Amplitude modulation, frequency shift keying, phase shift keying, quadrature amplitude modulation
	Digital encoding and transmission	Manchester encoding, NRZ-L, B8Z5 synchronous transmission, asynchronous transmission
Modem to Phone Services	Phone service transmission	Two-wire vs. Four-wire, full-duplex vs. half-duplex, echo cancellation
	Phone services alternatives	Analog vs. digittal services, dial-up vs. leased line services, bandwidth differentiation of services

Figure 2-1   Basic Data Communications Concepts: End-to-End Modem-Based Data Communications Session

In turn, each of these major subsections is divided into several constituent processes. Each of these processes will be described conceptually. In addition, any significant protocols or standards currently governing these processes, as listed in Figure 2-1, will be explored.

More detailed information on the operation of the carrier network and services will be provided in

- Chapter 4—"Voice Communications Concepts and Technology."

- Chapter 8—"Wide-Area Networking Concepts, Architectures, and Services."

■ COMPUTER TO MODEM

Character Encoding

To get data from its source PC to its destination PC, it must be transformed from its humanly understandable form (letters, numbers, voices, images) to an electronically based machine-understandable form. The process of transforming humanly readable characters into machine-readable code is known as **character encoding.**

In a particular encoding scheme, characters are turned into a series of 1s and 0s. Why 1s and 0s? The 1s and 0s are used as symbols to represent two discrete states, much like a light switch being on or off. These discrete states can be easily represented electrically by discrete voltages of electricity. In turn, these discrete voltages of electricity representing coded characters can then be easily transmitted, received, and examined by data communications equipment.

The individual 1s and 0s that constitute a given character are known as **bits.** The series (usually 8) of bits representing the entire encoded letter is known as a **byte.** These 1s and 0s, or digits, represented by discrete voltages of electricity are in **digital** format and are known as digital data. Now that the humanly readable character is in machine-readable form, it (these bits) can now be transmitted in a process generally known as data communications.

Characters can be encoded according to a variety of protocols or standards. A few of the currently popular encoding standards are described in the following paragraphs.

ASCII **American standard code for information interchange (ASCII)** is one standardized method for encoding humanly readable characters. ASCII uses a series of 7 bits to represent 128 ($2^7 = 128$) different characters including uppercase and lowercase letters, numerals, punctuation, symbols, and specialized control characters. One use of control characters will be explained further in Chapter 3. An eighth-bit known as a parity bit, is added to 7-bit ASCII for error detection. Error detection and parity checking will also be described in Chapter 3. Figure 2-2 is an ASCII table.

EBCDIC **Extended binary coded decimal interchange code (EBCDIC)** is an 8-bit code capable of representing 256 different characters, numerals, and control characters ($2^8 = 256$). EBCDIC is the primary coding method used in IBM mainframe applications. Figure 2-3 is an EBCDIC table.

USING ASCII AND EBCDIC TABLES

Practical Advice and Information

Using ASCII or EBCDIC tables to interpret character encoding is relatively straightforward. The tables are arranged according to groups of bits otherwise known as bit patterns. The bit patterns are divided into groups. In the case of ASCII, bits 6 through 4 are known as the most significant bits (MSB) whereas bits 3 through 0 are known as the least significant (LSB). In the case of EBCDIC, bits 0 through 3 are known as the MSB and bits 4 through 7 are known as the LSB.

To find the bit pattern of a particular character, one needs to just combine the bit patterns that intersect in the table at the character in question, remembering that most significant bits always come before least significant bits. In the case of ASCII, this means that bits are arranged from bit 6 to bit 0, whereas EBCDIC is arranged from bit 0 to bit 7. As an example, representative characters, numerals, and control characters and their bit patterns are highlighted with shading in the ASCII and EBCDIC tables and are displayed in Figure 2-4 in humanly readable, ASCII, and EBCDIC formats.

Unicode and ISO 10646 ASCII and EBCDIC coding schemes have sufficient capacity to represent letters and characters familiar to people whose alphabets use the letters *A, B, C,* etc. However, what happens if the computer needs to support communica-

				MSB	Bit 6	0	0	0	0	1	1	1	1
					Bit 5	0	0	1	1	0	0	1	1
LSB					Bit 4	0	1	0	1	0	1	0	1
Bit 0	Bit 1	Bit 2	Bit 3										
0	0	0	0			NUL	DLE	SP	0	@	P		p
1	0	0	0			SOH	DC1	!	1	A	Q	a	q
0	1	0	0			STX	DC2		2	B	R	b	r
1	1	0	0			ETX	DC3	#	3	C	S	c	s
0	0	1	0			EOT	DC4	$	4	D	T	d	t
1	0	1	0			ENQ	NAK	%	5	E	U	e	u
0	1	1	0			ACK	SYN	&	6	F	V	f	v
1	1	1	0			BEL	ETB		7	G	W	g	w
0	0	0	1			BS	CAN	(	8	H	X	h	x
1	0	0	1			HT	EM	)	9	I	Y	i	y
0	1	0	1			LF	SUB	*	:	J	Z	j	z
1	1	0	1			VT	ESC	+	;	K	[	k	{
0	0	1	1			FF	FS	,	<	L	\	l	|
1	0	1	1			CR	GS		=	M	]	m	}
0	1	1	1			SO	RS	.	>	N	^	n	~
1	1	1	1			SI	US		?	O	-	o	DEL

Figure 2-2   ASCII Table

tion in Chinese or Arabic? It should be obvious that 128 or 256 possible characters will not suffice when other languages and alphabets are considered.

In view of this fact, an international effort was undertaken to establish a new coding standard that could support many more alphabets and symbols than ASCII or EBCDIC. Although **Unicode** and **ISO 10646** were initiated separately, Unicode Version 1.1 and ISO 10646 are identical and were released in 1993.

Unicode is a 16-bit code supporting up to 65,536 possible characters ($2^{16} = 65,536$). It is backward compatible with ASCII as the first 128 Unicode characters are identical to the ASCII table. In addition, Unicode includes over 2000 Han characters for languages such as Chinese, Japanese, and Korean. It also includes Hebrew, Greek, Russian, and Sanskrit alphabets as well as mathematical and technical symbols, publishing symbols, geometric shapes, and punctuation marks.

Application programs that display text on a monitor must encode characters according to an encoding scheme understood by the computer's operating system. It is up to the operating system's vendors to include support for particular encoding schemes such as Unicode/ISO 10646. Microsoft's Windows NT is one example of an operating system that supports Unicode.

		MSB	Bit 0	0	0	0	0	0	0	0	0	1	1	1	1	1	1	1	1
			Bit 1	0	0	0	0	1	1	1	1	0	0	0	0	1	1	1	1
			Bit 2	0	0	1	1	0	0	1	1	0	0	1	1	0	0	1	1
LSB			Bit 3	0	1	0	1	0	1	0	1	0	1	0	1	0	1	0	1
Bit 7	Bit 6	Bit 5	Bit 4																
0	0	0	0	NUL	DLE	DS		SP	&	-									0
1	0	0	0	SOH	DC1	SOS						a	j			A	J		1
0	1	0	0	STX	DC2	FS	SYN					b	k	s		B	K	S	2
1	1	0	0	ETX	DC3							c	l	t		C	L	T	3
0	0	1	0	PF	RES	BYP	PN					d	m	u		D	M	U	4
1	0	1	0	HT	NL	LF	RS					e	n	v		E	N	V	5
0	1	1	0	LC	BS	EOB	UC					f	o	w		F	O	W	6
1	1	1	0	DEL	IL	PRE	EOT					g	p	x		G	P	X	7
0	0	0	1		CAN							h	q	y		H	Q	Y	8
1	0	0	1		EM						\	i	r	z		I	R	Z	9
0	1	0	1	SMM	CC	SM		>>	!		:								
1	1	0	1	VT				.	$	,	#								
0	0	1	1	FF	IFS		DC4	<	*	%	@								
1	0	1	1	CR	IGS	ENQ	NAK	(	)										
0	1	1	1	SO	IRS	ACK		+	;	>	=								
1	1	1	1	SI	IUS	BEL	SUB		_	?									

Figure 2-3   EBCDIC Table

Humanly Readable	ASCII	EBCDIC
A	1000001	11000001
x	1111000	10100111
5	0110101	11110101
LF (line feed)	0001010	00100101

Figure 2-4   Humanly Readable, ASCII, and EBCDIC Coding

	Transmission Characteristic	
	Serial	**Parallel**
Transmission description	Bits transmitted in a linear fashion, one bit after another, one at a time	All bits in a single character transmitted simultaneously
Comparative speed	Slower	Faster
Distance limitation	Farther	Shorter
Application	Between two computers, from a computer to an external modem, from a computer to a relatively slow printer	Within a computer along the computer's bus, from a computer to parallel high-speed printers
Cable description	All bits travel down a single wire, one bit at a time	Each bit travels down its own wire simultaneously with other bits

Figure 2-5   Serial Transmission vs. Parallel Transmission

Serial vs. Parallel Transmission

These bits that represent humanly readable characters can be transmitted in either of two basic transmission methodologies. They can be either transmitted simultaneously **(parallel transmission)** or transmitted in a linear fashion, one after the other **(serial transmission).** The advantages, limitations, and typical applications of each transmission methodology are summarized in Figure 2-5 and illustrated in Figure 2-6.

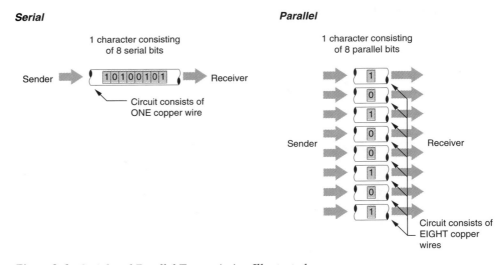

Figure 2-6   Serial and Parallel Transmission Illustrated

PHYSICAL INTERFACES VS. TRANSMISSION PROTOCOLS

With either parallel or serial transmission, it is important to distinguish between those standards that describe the connectors or physical interfaces that are used to connect appropriate cables to a computer's parallel or serial ports and the standards that describe the electrical characteristics or transmission protocol of either serial or parallel transmission. These differences in standards are highlighted in the sections on serial and parallel transmission that follow.

Serial Interface Standards   Figure 2-7 illustrates three of the most common physical interfaces for serial transmission:

- A typical 25-pin serial port, known as a **DB-25** connector.

- A 9-pin serial port most often found on personal computers, known as a **DB-9** connector.

- An **M-block connector** used in high-speed serial transmissions.

It is important to note that the designators DB-25, DB-9, and M-Block only describe the physical connectors and do not imply anything regarding the transmission protocol that defines the electrical specifications for transmission using one of these physical interfaces. As will be seen, these physical interfaces can be employed using a variety of different transmission protocols.

Serial Transmission Standards   Serial transmission is the basis of most data communications between computers and therefore deserves further investigation. The transmission of data between two PCs via modems as illustrated in Figure 2-1 is an example of serial transmission.

RS-232:   In the case of the DB-25 connector illustrated in Figure 2-7, the presence or absence of an electrical charge on each of its 25 pins has been designated as having a specific meaning in data communications. These standard definitions are officially known as **RS-232-C,** were issued by the Electronics Industries Association (EIA), and are listed in Figure 2-8.

Although all 25 pins are defined, in most cases, 10 or fewer of the pins are actually used in the majority of serial transmission applications. On some personal computers as well as many notebook and laptop computers, the serial port has only 9 pins (DB-9 connector) and the RS-232 serial transmission protocol is supported as listed in Figure 2-8.

Recalling that character encoding ensures that all characters can be represented as a series of 1s and 0s, it is the job of the transmission protocol to represent these 1s and 0s as discrete electrical signals. RS-232 defines voltages of between +5 and +15 V dc on a given pin to represent a logical 0, otherwise known as a space, and voltages of between −5 and −15 V dc to represent a logical 1, otherwise known as a mark.

Modem Cables: So how are these meaningful electrical signals transported from the serial port on the local PC to a similar-looking port, or interface, on the local modem? The answer is

- Either buy or make a data cable in a configuration known as a **modem cable.**

DB-25 connector (female)

DB-9 connector (female)

M-Block connector

Figure 2-7   Serial Transmission Physical Interfaces

The cable has several small insulated wires within an outer jacket. These cables come with different numbers of "inner" wires depending on how many signals need to be transferred from one serial port to another. Each signal to be carried, or RS-232 pin to be supported, requires its own individual inner wire.

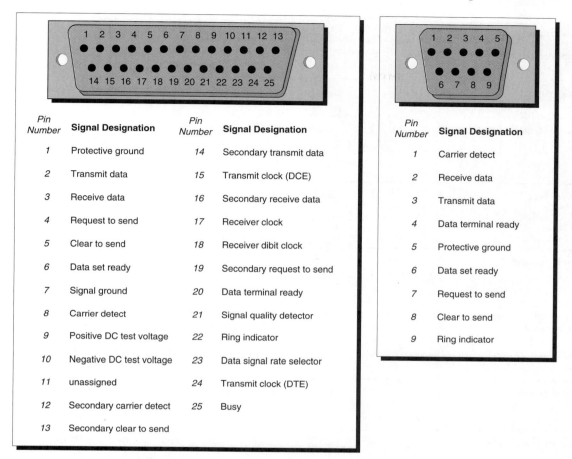

Pin Number	Signal Designation	Pin Number	Signal Designation
1	Protective ground	14	Secondary transmit data
2	Transmit data	15	Transmit clock (DCE)
3	Receive data	16	Secondary receive data
4	Request to send	17	Receiver clock
5	Clear to send	18	Receiver dibit clock
6	Data set ready	19	Secondary request to send
7	Signal ground	20	Data terminal ready
8	Carrier detect	21	Signal quality detector
9	Positive DC test voltage	22	Ring indicator
10	Negative DC test voltage	23	Data signal rate selector
11	unassigned	24	Transmit clock (DTE)
12	Secondary carrier detect	25	Busy
13	Secondary clear to send		

Pin Number	Signal Designation
1	Carrier detect
2	Receive data
3	Transmit data
4	Data terminal ready
5	Protective ground
6	Data set ready
7	Request to send
8	Clear to send
9	Ring indicator

Figure 2-8   RS-232 Serial Transmission Protocol As Defined for DB-25 and DB-9 Connectors

The next question is: Which of the possible 25 signals are most meaningful and therefore worth transferring over the modem cable in this example? Figure 2-9 summarizes the 12 signals that are most commonly included in modem cables and designates which signals are assigned to which pins on both DB-9 and DB-25 connectors. The RS-232 signals described in Figure 2-9 are arranged in logical pairs to increase understanding rather than in order of DB-25 pin number.

The modem cables will have 12 data leads or inner wires, one for each of the commonly used RS-232 pins outlined in Figure 2-9. The wires will be pinned "straight through;" in other words, the wire from pin 2 on the DTE (PC) end will go straight through to pin 2 on the DCE (modem) end, and so on with the remaining pins.

Constructing modem cables or connecting any two devices for data communications involves choosing between a variety of media types. Coaxial cable, unshielded twisted pair, shielded twisted pair, and fiber optic cable are but a few of the possible options. Although media alternatives will be explored in detail in Chapter 6, it is important to understand that media choices are present in every data communications opportunity.

RS-232 Signal	DB-25 Pin	DB-9 Pin	Abbrev.	From	To	Explanation
Protective ground	1	5	PG			Used as a reference voltage to protect circuit boards inside the PC
Signal ground	7	5	SG			Used as a reference voltage to determine proper signal voltage for 1s and 0s
Transmit data	2	3	TXD	DTE	DCE	Used to transmit discrete voltages representing characters encoded as 1s and 0s to deliver the actual data message
Receive data	3	2	RXD	DCE	DTE	Used to receive discrete voltages representing characters encoded as 1s and 0s to receive the actual data message
Request to send	4	7	RTS	DTE	DCE	Used in conjunction with CTS to perform modem-to-modem flow control allowing modems to take turns transmitting to each other
Clear to send	5	8	CTS	DCE	DTE	Used in conjunction with RTS to perform modem-to-modem flow control allowing modems to take turns transmitting to each other
Data set ready	6	6	DSR	DCE	DTE	Used for initial handshaking between local modem and local PC to indicate local modem is functional
Data terminal ready	20	4	DTR	DTE	DCE	Used for initial handshaking between local modem and local PC to indicate local PC is functional
Transmit clock	15		TC	DCE	DTE	Used to transmit clocking signal (required for synchronous modems only)
Receive clock	17		RC	DCE	DTE	Used to receive clocking signal (required for synchronous modems only)
Carrier detect	8	1	CD	DCE	DTE	Used to indicate that the local modem has successfully contacted the remote modem and is ready to transmit data
Ring indicator	22	9	RI	DCE	DTE	Used to indicate to the local modem that a call is incoming and that the modem should auto-answer the call

Figure 2-9   Most Commonly Used RS-232 Signals

DCE vs. DTE: In addition to being able to identify certain signals according to their pin numbers, it is necessary to also be able to identify which end of the cable goes to the PC and which goes to the modem. The PC and the modem in our example are given generic designations of **DTE (data terminal equipment)** and **DCE (data communications equipment),** respectively. DCE is also expanded as **data circuit terminating equipment.**

Many of the RS-232 and signals have a directionality to them. In other words, either the terminal is informing the modem of something by raising or lowering electrical voltages to a certain pin or the modem is informing the terminal of something by the same means. Figure 2-9 outlines the directionality of the signals of commonly used RS-232 pins in the columns labeled "from" and "to."

OTHER SERIAL TRANSMISSION STANDARDS

RS-232 is officially limited to 20 Kbps (kilobits/second) for a maximum distance of 50 ft. The fact of the matter is that dependent on the type of media used and the amount of external interference present, RS-232 can be transmitted at higher speeds and/or over greater distances. Other serial transmission standards overcome both the speed and distance limitations of RS-232 and are listed in Figure 2-10.

Parallel Transmission   As can be seen from Figure 2-6, parallel transmission is primarily limited to transmission of data within a computer and between a computer's parallel port and a parallel printer. Common physical interfaces associated with parallel transmission are the DB-25 connector and the Centronics connector. The Centronics connector is a 36-pin parallel interface. In addition to the physical plug and socket, the Centronics parallel standard also defines electrical signaling for parallel transmission and is a de facto standard. DB-25 and Centronics parallel physical interfaces are illustrated in Figure 2-11.

Serial/Parallel Conversion: UARTs   Remember that data travels via parallel transmission within a PC over the PC's main data highway, known as a bus. The data emerging from the serial port and out into a modem must be in serial format however. Therefore, somewhere inside the PC a parallel to serial conversion must be taking place. A specialized computer chip known as **UART (universal asynchronous receiver transmitter)** acts as the interface between the parallel transmission of the computer bus and the serial transmission of the serial port. UARTs differ in performance capabilities based on the amount of on-chip buffer memory. The 16550 UART chip contains a 16-byte on-chip buffer memory for improved serial/parallel conversion performance. In the case of internal modem, the UART is included on the internal modem card, thereby bypassing the system UART.

Given the transmission speed of today's modems, it is especially important that PCs are equipped with the 16550 UART with its 16-byte buffer rather than previous UARTs, which only contained a 1-byte buffer.

Transmission Monitoring and Manipulation: Breakout Boxes   To effectively troubleshoot serial or parallel transmissions, it is necessary to able to monitor and manipulate the electrical signaling on individual signaling pins. Devices known as **breakout boxes** are used to monitor and manipulate electrical signaling. Breakout boxes are built to monitor a particular electrical transmission specification. As a result, separate

Standard Name	Standards Body	Physical Interface Connector	Description
RS-422	EIA	DB-9, DB-25, DB-37	An electrical specification usually associated with RS-449 (DB-37 connector). Each signal pin has its own ground line (balanced) rather than sharing a common ground. Speeds up to 10 Mbps over 1200 m can be achieved. Use of DB-25 or DB-9 is also possible.
RS-423	EIA	DB-9, DB-25, DB-37	An electrical specification usually associated with RS-449 (DB-37 connector). Signal pins share a common ground wire (unbalanced signaling). Speeds up to 10 Mbps over 1200 m can be achieved. Use of DB-25 or DB-9 is also possible.
RS-449	EIA	DB-37 plus DB-9	A physical/mechanical specification for a DB-37 (37-pin connector) plus an additional DB-9 if required. This specification is usually associated with either the RS-422 or RS-423 electrical specification.
RS-485	EIA	DB-9, DB-25, DB-37	A standard that can be used in multipoint applications in which one computer controls multiple (up to 64) devices. This standard is often used in computer integrated manufacturing operations or in telecommunications management networks.
RS-530	EIA	DB-25	A physical/mechanical specification that works with RS-422 or RS-423 over a DB-25 connector rather than a DB-37 connector. This standard allows speeds of up to 2 Mbps.
V.35	ITU	M-Block	An international standard for serial transmission up to 48 Kbps defined for an M-block connector. This standard is often used on data communications equipment that must interface to high-speed carrier services.

Figure 2-10   Other Serial Transmission Standards

breakout boxes are required to monitor RS-232, V.35, RS-449, or parallel transmission. Figure 2-12 illustrates a typical breakout box.

■ WITHIN THE MODEM

So exactly what does a modem do? To analyze what any piece of data communications equipment does, the input-processing-output (I-P-O) analysis model, introduced in Chapter 1, is employed.

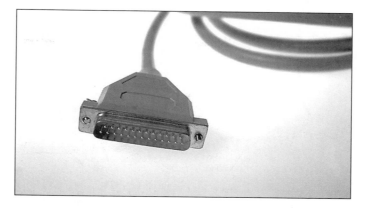

DB-25 (male) parallel interface

Centronics parallel interface

Figure 2-11   Parallel Transmission Physical Interfaces

Applied Problem Solving

THE I-P-O MODEL

The I-P-O model provides a framework in which to focus on the difference between the data that came into the modem (I) and the data that came out of the modem (O). By defining this difference, we have defined how the modem processed the data (P).

In general terms, based on what we have learned thus far, we could say:

- Input data (I)—From the PC: A series of 1s and 0s representing characters and transmitted as discrete voltages of electricity in digital format.

- Output data (O)—To the public phone network on a normal phone line.

It should be obvious that to better understand the processing (P) that goes on in a modem, it is first necessary to have a better understanding of (O), data transmission over a "normal" or dial-up phone line.

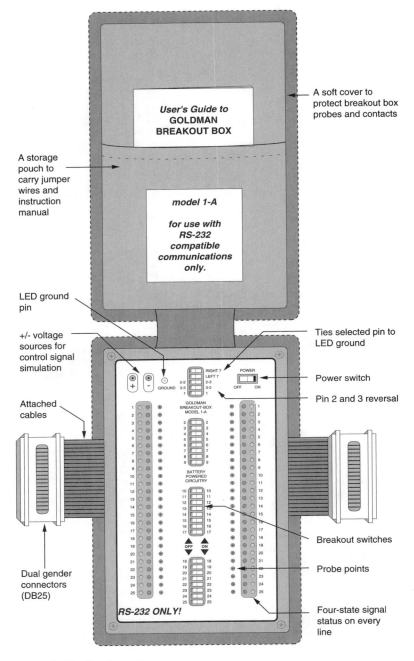

A soft cover to protect breakout box probes and contacts

User's Guide to GOLDMAN BREAKOUT BOX

A storage pouch to carry jumper wires and instruction manual

model 1-A

for use with RS-232 compatible communications only.

LED ground pin

Ties selected pin to LED ground

+/- voltage sources for control signal simulation

Power switch

Pin 2 and 3 reversal

Attached cables

Breakout switches

Dual gender connectors (DB25)

Probe points

RS-232 ONLY!

Four-state signal status on every line

Figure 2-12   Breakout Box

Digital vs. Analog Transmission

A **switched** or **dial-up line** is the type of phone line that you would typically have installed in your home or place of business. To place a call, you pick up the receiver or handset, wait for a dial tone, and dial the number of the location you wish to call. This ordinary type of phone service is sometimes called **POTS** or **plain old tele-**

phone service. More formally, the phone network is referred to as the **public switched telephone network (PSTN).**

As introduced in Chapter 1, a large switch in a telephone company building called a central office (CO) connects your phone equipment to the phone equipment of the party you wish to call by finding an available circuit or path to your desired destination. It is important to understand at this point that the CO switch tries to find a path as quickly as possible to your destination. The actual **circuits** it chooses represent the best path available at that time. The particular circuits or path chosen may vary from one occasion to another, even for calls to the same location. Calls placed over dial-up lines through CO switches that have connections built from available circuits are called circuit-switched connections. To interface transparently to the PSTN, modems must be able to dial and answer phone calls to and from other modems.

The next important characteristic related to transmitting data over a dial-up phone line has to do with how the data is represented on that phone line. First, it is important to realize that today's dial-up phone network was originally designed to carry voice conversations efficiently and with reasonable sound quality. This "efficiency of design with reasonable sound quality" meant reproducing a range of frequencies of human speech and hearing just wide enough to produce reasonable sound quality. That range of frequencies, or **bandwidth,** is 3100 Hz (from 300 to 3400 Hz) and is the standard bandwidth of today's voice-grade dial-up circuits (phone lines). Hz is the abbreviation for hertz. One hertz is 1 cycle/sec. The higher the number of hertz or cycles/second, the higher the frequency. Frequency, wavelength, hertz, and cycles/second will be explained further later in this chapter.

This 3100 Hz is all the bandwidth with which the modem operating over a dial-up circuit has to work. Remember also that because today's dial-up phone network was designed to be able to mimic the constantly varying tones or frequencies that characterize human speech, only these continuous, wavelike tones or frequencies can travel over the dial-up phone network in this limited bandwidth.

The challenge for the modem, then, is to represent the discrete, digitized 1s and 0s from the input (PC) side of the modem in a continuous or **analog** form within a limited bandwidth so that the data may be transmitted over the dial-up network. Figure 2-13 summarizes the results of I-P-O analysis involving modems and the PSTN.

Modulation/Demodulation

It should be clear that a modem's job must be to convert digital data into analog data for transmission over the dial-up phone network and to convert analog data received from the dial-up network into digital data for the terminal or PC. The

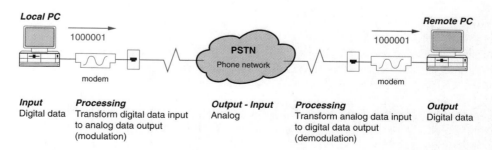

Figure 2-13   I-P-O Analysis: Modems and the PSTN

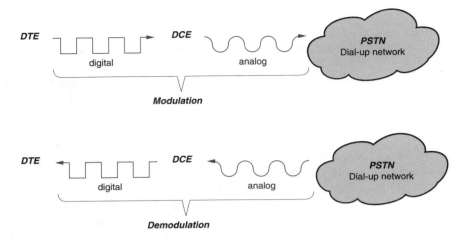

Figure 2-14   Modulation vs. Demodulation

proper names for these processes are **modulation** and **demodulation** as illustrated in Figure 2-14. In fact, the word **modem** is actually a contraction for **mo**dulator/**de**modulator.

Carrier Waves   To represent the discrete-state 1s and 0s or bits of digitized data on a dial-up phone line, an analog or voicelike wave must be able to be changed between at least two different states. This implies that a "normal" or "neutral" wave must exist to start with, which can be changed to represent these 1s and 0s.

This "normal" or "neutral" wave is called a **carrier wave** as illustrated in Figure 2-15. The RS-232 pin 8 (carrier detect) refers to this carrier or reference wave. Modems generate carrier waves that are then altered (modulated) to represent bits of data as 1s and 0s. When a local modem and remote modem are trying to establish communications, they emit a series of high-pitched screeches. These screeches are the two modems trying to detect a common carrier wave in order to establish communication. Once the carrier wave has been detected by both modems, the actual data transmission can begin as the modems manipulate this common carrier wave to represent 1s and 0s.

How can the carrier wave be manipulated to represent 1s and 0s? There are only three physical characteristics of this wave that can be altered or modulated:

1.   **Amplitude.**

2.   **Frequency.**

3.   **Phase.**

Carrier wave

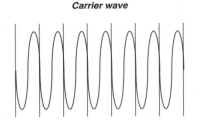

Figure 2-15   Carrier Wave

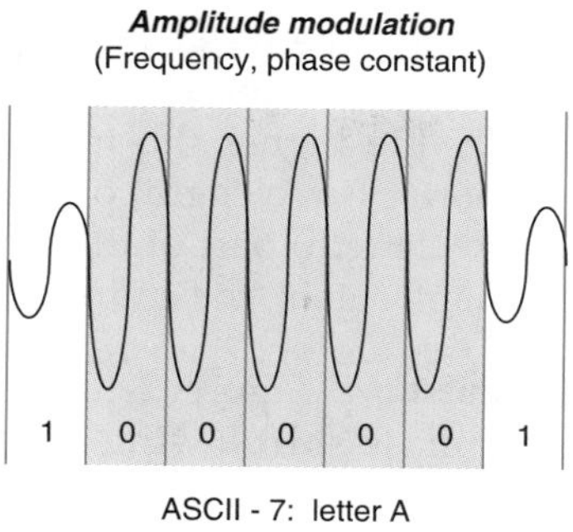

Amplitude modulation
(Frequency, phase constant)

1 0 0 0 0 0 1

ASCII - 7: letter A

Figure 2-16   Amplitude Modulation

As will be seen later in this section, in some modulation schemes more than one of these characteristics are altered simultaneously.

Amplitude Modulation   Figure 2-16 illustrates the **amplitude modulation** of a carrier wave. Notice how only the amplitude changes, while frequency and phase remain constant. In this example, the portions of the wave with increased height (altered amplitude) represent 0s and the lower wave amplitudes represent 1s. Together, this portion of the wave would represent the letter *A* using the ASCII-7 character encoding scheme.

The vertical lines in Figure 2-16 separate the opportunities to identify 1s and 0s. These timed opportunities to identify 1s and 0s by sampling the carrier wave are known as signaling events. The proper name for one signaling event is a **baud.**

Frequency Modulation   Figure 2-17 represents the **frequency modulation** of a carrier wave. Frequency modulation is often referred to as **frequency shift keying** or **FSK.** The frequency can be thought of as how frequently the same spots on two subsequent waves pass a given point. Waves with a higher frequency will take less time to pass whereas waves with a lower frequency will take a greater time to pass.

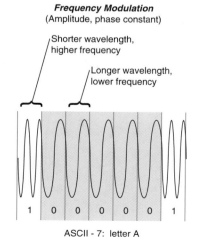

Frequency Modulation
(Amplitude, phase constant)

Shorter wavelength, higher frequency

Longer wavelength, lower frequency

1 0 0 0 0 0 1

ASCII - 7: letter A

Figure 2-17   Frequency Modulation

The distance between the same spots on two subsequent waves is called the **wavelength.** The longer the wavelength, the lower the frequency and the shorter the wavelength, the higher the frequency. Notice in Figure 2-17 how the higher frequency (shorter wavelength) part of the wave represents a 1 and the lower frequency (longer wavelength) part of the wave represents a 0, while amplitude and phase remain constant. Again, the entire bit stream represents the letter *A* in ASCII-7.

Phase Modulation   Figure 2-18 illustrates an example of **phase modulation,** also known as **phase shift keying** or **PSK.** Notice how the frequency and amplitude remain constant in the diagram. Phase modulation can be thought of as a shift of departure from the "normal" continuous pattern of the wave. Notice in Figure 2-18 how we would expect the pattern of the wave to continue normally, but suddenly the phase shifts and heads off in another direction. This phase shift of 180° is a detectable event, with each change in phase representing a change in state from 0 to 1 or 1 to 0 in this example.

Measuring Phase Shift: In Figure 2-18, the detected analog wave was either the carrier wave with no phase shift or the carrier wave phase-shifted 180°. Given that phase shifts are measured in degrees, it should stand to reason that we could shift the phase or carrier waves by varying degrees other than just 180°. By increasing the number of possible phase shifts, we increase the number of potential detectable events. As illustrated in Figure 2-19, when we had just two potential detectable events (no phase shift or 180° phase shift), those two events represented a 0 or a 1, respectively. However, by introducing four potential phase shifts (0, 90, 180, and 270°), we are able to associate two bits with each potential detectable event.

A simpler and perhaps clearer way to represent phase shifts as illustrated in Figure 2-19 is through the use of **constellation points.** Using a four-quadrant representation of the 360° of possible phase shift, we can represent each different shifted wave by individual points. Note that a phase shift of 270° is represented as −90° in a constellation diagram. Phase shift modulation with four different phases is more properly referred to as **quadrature phase shift keying** or **QPSK.**

Baud Rate vs. Transmission Rate   The number of signaling events per second is more properly known as the **baud rate.** Although baud rate and **bps** (bits/second) or **transmission rate** are often used interchangeably, the two terms are in fact related, but not identical. In the first illustration in Figure 2-19, only two detectable events were possible, meaning that only one bit was interpreted at each signaling event (1 bit/baud). Therefore, in this case the baud rate was equal to the transmission rate as expressed in bps.

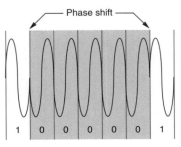

ASCII - 7: letter A

Figure 2-18   Phase Modulation

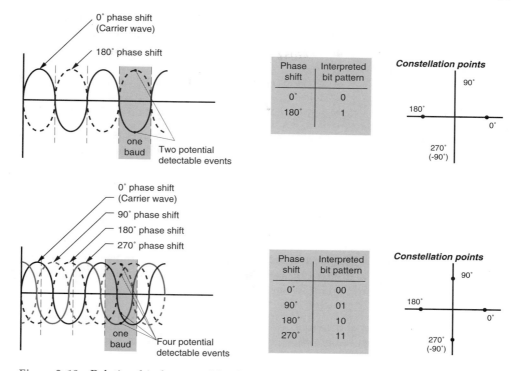

Figure 2-19 Relationship between Number of Phase Shifts and Number of Potential Detectable Events

However, in the second illustration in Figure 2-19, four detectable events are possible for each signaling event, making it possible to interpret 2 bits/baud. In this case, the bit rate or transmission rate as measured in bps would be twice the baud rate.

More sophisticated modulation techniques are able to interpret more than 1 bit/baud. In these cases, the bps is greater than the baud rate. For example, if the baud rate of a modem is 2400 signaling events per second and the modem is able to interpret two bits per signaling event, then the transmission speed is 4800 bps. Mathematically, the relationship between baud rate and transmission rate can be expressed as

$$\text{Transmission rate (bps)} = \text{Baud rate} \times \text{bits/baud}$$

MORE THAN 1 BIT/BAUD

In Sharper Focus

There are really only two ways in which one can modify a given modem to transmit data faster:

1. Increase the signaling events per second, or baud rate, as mentioned previously.

2. Find a way for the modem to interpret more than 1 bit/baud.

Modification of a phase modulation technique such as that illustrated in Figure 2-19 can allow a modem to detect, interpret, and transmit more than 1 bit/baud.

The mathematical equation that describes the relationship between the number of potential detectable events and the numbers of bits per baud that can be interpreted is as follows:

$$\text{Number of potential detectable events} = \text{Number of states}^{\text{bits/baud}}$$

- Number of states = always 2 (data is either a 1 or 0).
- Number of potential detectable events = 4 different phase angles (0, 90, 180, 270°) as shown in the second illustration in Figure 2-19.

To solve:

- 2 (the number of states) raised to what power equals 4 (the number of different detectable events)?

The answer is 2, meaning that 2 bits/baud can be interpreted at a time. Two bits at a time are known as a **dibit.** By extension of the preceding mathematical equation, the following should be obvious:

No. of Potential Detectable Events	No. of bits/baud	Also Known As
8	3	tribit
16	4	quadbit
32	5	
64	6	
128	7	
256	8	
512	9	

Quadrature Amplitude Modulation   How far can we go with increasing the number of phase shift angles or potential detectable events? One limiting factor to increasing the bits/baud in phase shift modulation is, given that the modem is being used on a dial-up line of unpredictable quality, how small (least number of degrees) a phase shift can be reliably detected? Sixteen different phase shifts would require reliable detection of phase shifts of as little as 22.5°. Remembering that phase is not the only wave characteristic that can be varied, 16 different detectable events can also be produced by varying both phase and amplitude. Many of today's high-speed modems use a modulation technique that varies both phase and amplitude known as **quadrature amplitude modulation** or **QAM.**

16QAM, with its 16 different potential detectable events, would allow 4 bits/baud, or quadbits, to be produced or detected per signaling event. In this case the transmission rate in bps would be 4 times the baud rate. Figure 2-20 illustrates a representative set of constellation points and associated quadbits for a QAM scheme. Differences in phase are represented in degrees around the center of the diagram whereas differences in amplitude are represented by linear distance from the center of the diagram. Each point is uniquely identified by combining one of three potential amplitudes (0.311, 0.850, and 1.161 V) with one of twelve potential phase shifts (15, 45, 75, 105, 135, 175, −165, −135, −105, −75, −45, and

$-15°$). Obviously, all potential combinations of these two sets of variables are not used in 16QAM.

NYQUIST'S THEOREM AND SHANNON'S LAW

What are the underlying factors that limit the carrying capacity of a given circuit? The work of Harry Nyquist and Claude Shannon help to answer that question.

Nyquist's Theorem

The constellation points illustrated in Figure 2-20 are sometimes referred to as symbols. It should stand to reason that as the number of constellation points (symbols) increases and symbols are in closer proximity to each other on the constellation diagram, the chance for a modem to misinterpret constellation points increases. Interference between symbols that can cause misinterpretation is known as **intersymbol interference.** Nyquist investigated the maximum data rate (measured in bps) that can be supported by a given bandwidth (measured in Hz) due to the effect of intersymbol interference. He found the relationship between bandwidth (W) and maximum data rate (C) to be

$$C = 2W$$

Consider a voice-grade circuit: $W = 3100$ Hz; therefore the maximum theoretical data rate $C = 6200$ bps. However, this fails to account for the ability of modern modems to interpret more than 1 bit/baud by being able to distinguish between more than just two symbols or potential detectable events. Taking this ability into account, if we call the number of potential detectable events M, Nyquist's Theorem becomes

$$C = 2W \log_2 M$$

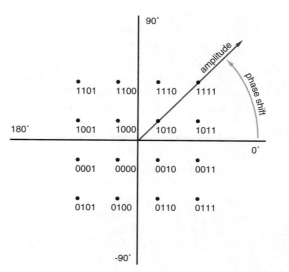

Figure 2-20 QAM Constellation Points and Quadbits

Again, consider a voice-grade circuit: if $M = 16$ potential detectable events, then $\log_2 M = 4$ and $C = 24,800$ bps.

Shannon's Law

The data rates theorized by Nyquist's Theorem are not achieved in reality due to the presence of noise on phone lines. Noise is measured as a ratio of the strength of the data signal to the strength of the background noise. This ratio is known as the **signal to noise ratio (S/N)** and is computed as follows:

$$(S/N)_{dB} = 10 \log(\text{signal power}/\text{noise power})$$

S/N is expressed in decibels (dB). Decibels are a logarithmic measurement using a reference of 0_{dB} for comparison. As a result, a noise level of 10_{dB} is 10 times more intense than a noise level of 0_{dB}, a noise level of 20_{dB} is 100 times more intense than a noise level of 0_{dB}, and a noise level of 30_{dB} is 1000 times more intense than a noise level of 0_{dB}.

Shannon found that the higher the data rate, the more interference is caused by a given amount of noise, thus causing a higher error rate. This should make sense since at higher data rates, more bits are traveling over a circuit in a fixed length of time, and a burst of noise for the same length of time will affect more bits at higher data rates. By taking into account the signal to noise ratio, Shannon expresses the maximum data rate of a circuit (C) as

$$C = W \log_2(1 + S/N)$$

Consider a voice-grade circuit: if $W = 3100$ Hz and $S/N = 30_{dB}$, and remembering that a S/N of 30_{dB} yields a ratio of 1000, then $C = 30,894$ bps. Depending on the value inserted into Shannon's Law for S/N or for W, C will vary accordingly. The value 24,000 bps is also a common value for C using Shannon's Law. By substituting different values for W and for S/N, it should become obvious that data channel capacity (C) can be more drastically affected by changes in bandwidth (W) than by changes in the signal to noise ratio (S/N).

Finally, it should be noted that there are numerous other line impairments such as attenuation, delay distortion, and impulse noise that Shannon's Law does not take into account. As a result, the data channel capacity (C) derived from Shannon's Law is theoretical and is sometimes referred to as error-free capacity.

Synchronous vs. Asynchronous Transmission   Potential detectable events must be produced on one modem, transmitted over the public phone network, and detected reliably on a remote modem. In a modem with a baud rate of 2400 baud (signaling events) per second, the remote modem has exactly 0.416 msec (1 divided by 2400) to accurately detect and interpret the incoming data.

Obviously, the modems must have a reliable way to know exactly when to sample the line for data. Somehow, the local and remote modems must establish and maintain some type of timing between them so that these detectable events are produced, transmitted, and detected accurately. There are two main alternatives to establishing and maintaining the timing for the sampling of detectable events. These two timing alternatives are known as

- **Asynchronous transmission.**

- **Synchronous transmission.**

Figure 2-21 summarizes some important characteristics about asynchronous and synchronous transmission methods. The most noticeable difference is that the synchronization, or detectable event timing, itself is re-established with the transmission of each character in asynchronous transmission via the use of start and stop bits and with each block of characters in synchronous transmission. In asynchronous transmission, there may be 1, 1.5, or 2 stop bits. The timing in the case of synchronous transmission is provided by a clock that may be supplied by either the remote or local modem or by the carrier.

Secondly, when comparing idle time activity, synchronization is maintained, thanks to the ever-present clocking signal, in synchronous transmission and dropped in asynchronous transmission while no characters are being transmitted. The effect of these characteristics on transmission efficiency is illustrated in Figure 2-21.

In terms of application, PC modems use asynchronous transmission as do asynchronous terminals such as a VT-100 to an asynchronous minicomputer such as a VAX. Synchronous transmission is used between mainframe terminals such as IBM 3270 and IBM mainframe computers. Synchronous transmission is also used for most high-speed WAN services such as 64 Kbps or T-1.

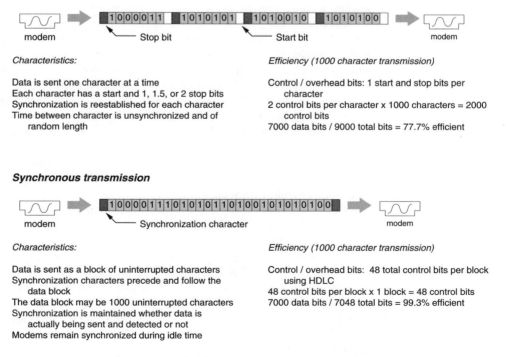

Figure 2-21 Asynchronous vs. Synchronous Transmission

■ MODEM TO PHONE SERVICE

Transmission Concepts

To understand the capabilities and limitations of a variety of phone services available to the consumer, it is first necessary to gain a better understanding of some of the concepts of the phone network infrastructure responsible for delivering those services.

Two-Wire vs. Four-Wire Circuits   Most local loops that are used for connection to the PSTN to supply switched, dial-up phone service are physically described as **two-wire circuits.** Since one of these two wires serves as a ground wire for the circuit, that leaves only one wire between the two ends of the circuit for data signaling. Dial-up or switched circuits generate a dial tone and are connected at a central office-based switch that completes connections to the circuit corresponding to the dialed phone number.

A **four-wire circuit** consists of two wires capable of simultaneously carrying a data signal, each with its own dedicated ground wire. Typically, four-wire circuits are reserved for **leased lines,** otherwise known as dedicated lines or private lines. These circuits bypass telephone company switching equipment. They have no dial tone and are always operational between the locations specified by the customers ordering the leased lines.

Half-Duplex vs. Full-Duplex   Given that two-wire dial-up circuits only have one wire for data signaling, only one modem could be transmitting at a time while the other modem could only be receiving data. This one direction at a time transmission is known as **half-duplex.**

Modems that interfaced to a dial-up circuit had to support this half-duplex transmission method. What this meant was that once the two modems completed initial **handshaking,** one modem would agree to transmit while the other received. In order for the modems to reverse roles, the initially transmitting DTE (terminal or computer) drops its RTS (request to send) (RS-232 pin 4) and the transmitting DCE (modem) drops its CTS (clear to send) (RS-232 pin 5) and perhaps its carrier wave. Next, the initially receiving DTE must raise RTS, the initially receiving DCE (modem) must generate a carrier wave and raise CTS, and the role reversal is complete.

This role reversal is known as **turnaround time** and can take 0.2 sec or longer. This may not seem like a very long time, but if this role reversal needs to be done several thousand times over a long-distance circuit, charged by usage time, it may have a large dollar impact.

Full-duplex transmission supports simultaneous data signaling in both directions. Full-duplex transmission might seem to be impossible on two-wire circuits. Until the advent of the V.32 9600 bps full-duplex modem, the only way to get full-duplex transmission was to lease a four-wire circuit. Two wires (signal and ground) were for transmitting data and two wires (signal and ground) were for receiving data. There was no "role reversal" necessary and therefore no modem turnaround time delays.

Modems manufactured to the CCITT's V.32 standard (and the later V.34 standard) can transmit in full-duplex mode, thereby receiving and transmitting simultaneously over dial-up two-wire circuits. These modems use sophisticated **echo cancellation** techniques and, at least when they were first introduced, were significantly more expensive than slower, half-duplex modems. Figure 2-22 highlights the differences between half-duplex and full-duplex transmission.

Half-duplex: Modems transmit in both directions, only one direction at a time.

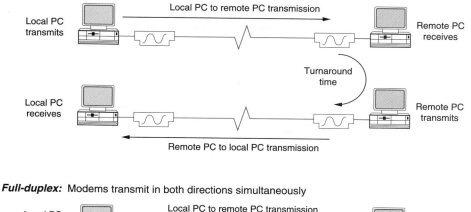

Full-duplex: Modems transmit in both directions simultaneously

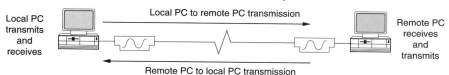

Figure 2-22   Half-Duplex vs. Full-Duplex Transmission

Echo Cancellation   Echo cancellation takes advantage of sophisticated technology known as **digital signal processors (DSP),** which are included in modems that offer echo cancellation. By first testing the echo characteristics of a given phone line at modem initialization time, these DSPs are able to actually distinguish the echoed transmission of the local modem from the intended transmission of the remote modem. The DSP then subtracts or cancels the echoed local transmission from the total data signal received, leaving only the intended transmission from the remote modem to be processed by the modem and passed on to the local PC.

Transmission Services

Having reviewed the processes involved to move a data signal from a computer through a modem, the final step in the overall process is to interface that modem to a transmission service purchased from the local carrier or phone company. Figure 2-23 summarizes some of the potential transmission services that can be purchased from local carriers. Most of these services will be explored further in later chapters.

Analog Services   Modems modulate digital input from computers into analog output compatible with the phone company's analog voice network. As will be seen in our study of data communications technology in Chapter 3, modems may be able to interface to analog dial-up services, analog leased lines, or both.

An analog or **voice-grade leased line** is a normal voice-grade line that bypasses the carrier's switching equipment. When the service is ordered, the two or more locations that are to be connected must be named. A new circuit is installed into these locations with a new RJ-11 jack interface added at each circuit location. There is no dial tone on this new line because it does not go through any switching equipment. With only two locations connected, the circuit is called point-to-point; with more than two locations, the circuit is called multipoint.

Service Name	Dial-up/ Leased	Analog/ Digital	2-wire/ 4-wire	Rates: Flat or Usage	Transmission Rate
Analog					
• **POTS**	D	A	2	U	28.8 Kbps w/V.34 modem
• **Voice-grade leased**	L	A	4	F	28.8 Kbps w/V.34 modem
Narrow-band digital					
• **DDS**	L	D	4	F	9.6, 19.2, 56 Kbps
• **DS-0**	L	D	4	F	64 Kbps
Broad-band digital					
• **T-1**	L	D	4	F	1.544 Mbps
• **T-3**	L	D	Fiber	F	44.736 Mbps
Digital dial-up					
• **ISDN**	D	D	2 or 4	U	144 Kbps
• **Switched 56K**	D	D	4	U	56 Kbps

Figure 2-23   Transmission Services

For leased lines, charges include both an installation charge and a flat monthly charge. The installation charge may be significant, especially if the circuit crosses LATAs. The flat monthly fee does not vary by usage, unlike the dial-up voice-grade circuits. The circuit is exclusively the user's, 24 hr/day.

Digital Services   As can be seen in Figure 2-23, digital transmission services available from carriers can be either dial-up or leased. One very important point to remember about interfacing to digital services is that a modem is not used since there is no need to modulate the computer's digital signaling into an analog signal. Rather than terminating the circuit with a modem, a **CSU/DSU (channel service unit/data service unit)** is employed. CSU/DSU will be explored further in Chapter 3.

Narrowband Digital Services: In addition to being differentiated as either dial-up or leased, digital services can also be differentiated as to amount of bandwidth delivered. Digital services that deliver less than 1.544 Mbps of bandwidth are generally considered as **narrowband digital services.**

When a narrowband digital circuit is ordered, the speed of that circuit must be specified to the phone company at the time the order is placed. Typical choices are

- **Digital Data Services (DDS)** at speeds of 2400, 4800, 9600, 19,200 or 56,000 Kbps
- **DS-0** (digital service level 0) at 64 Kbps.

This "declaring your speed" brings up a key difference in operation of analog and digital circuits. When an analog circuit, dial-up or leased, degrades or has some kind of transmission impairment, many modems use **fallback** or lower speeds automatically and continue with data transmissions. With a digital circuit, the speed of the circuit is set at the CO, the CSU/DSUs are set to the speed of the circuit, and if there is a problem with the line, the data transmission ceases. It should be pointed out that digital circuits tend to be more error free than analog circuits. Simply stated, the key determining factor in the transmission speed of an analog circuit is the modem, whereas the key determining factor in the case of a digital circuit is the configured speed of the circuit itself.

Broadband Digital Services: Higher capacity digital services are also available. **T-1** (1.544 Mbps) and **T-3** (45 Mbps) leased lines are among the most popular services available. Although these services offer flat monthly rates, these rates usually vary with distance. T-1 lines can easily cost thousands of dollars per month while T-3 lines can easily cost tens of thousands of dollar per month.

Dial-Up Digital Services: Digital dial-up services have become increasingly popular and more available with the tremendous increase in interest in Internet access. **Integrated services digital network (ISDN)** is a dial-up digital service that can offer up to 144 Kbps (most often 128 Kbps). Accessing as ISDN service from your home computer requires a device that performs the same basic functions as a CSU/DSU but is called a **terminal adapter, network termination unit (NTU),** or **digital modem.** The term "digital modem" is really a contradiction in terms. Another digital dial-up service is known as **switched 56K.** Interfacing to a switched 56K service requires a switched 56K CSU/DSU.

Practical Advice and Information

ISDN service, switched 56K service, or any of the digital services listed in Figure 2-23 are not necessarily available at any given home or business location. One should never assume that any particular transmission service is available at any network location when performing network planning and design.

SUMMARY

In this chapter, the transmission of data from one PC to another via a dial-up phone line has been used as an example of a simple data communications opportunity to introduce many key concepts.

Because the dial-up phone network was initially designed for voice or analog traffic only, the modem's major task is to transform digital data to analog data and vice versa (modulation/demodulation). Modems can accomplish this modulation by any combination of amplitude, frequency, or phase modulation. The greater the number of bits that can be interpreted per baud, or signaling event, the greater the overall transmission rate of bits as measured in bits/second (bps).

The timing of signaling events between distant modems is crucial to successful data transmission. Asynchronous transmission uses start and stop bits surrounding each character to achieve this intermodem timing, whereas synchronous transmission uses a constant clocking signal to keep modems constantly synchronized.

Once the parallel data of the PC have been modulated into serial format onto the phone network, it may reach its remote destination using a variety of available network services. Circuits may be switched, more commonly known as dial-up, or may be leased, in which case a customer would have access to these lines 24 hr/day, 7 days/week. Charges would be based on the length of this permanent circuit rather than on circuit usage time, as is the case with dial-up lines.

Digital network services are also available, in which case a CSU/DSU rather than a modem is employed, since there is no need for analog to digital conversion on an all-digital link.

Data communications devices such as modems and CSU/DSUs combine with available network services to provide end-to-end transmission between computers. The complicated interaction between hardware, software, and network services is transparent to the end-user. In analyzing and designing such a network, data communications professionals concentrate on how changes in one aspect of a design affect other aspects of a design. For example, changing from analog to digital leased lines would have a major impact on the type of data communications devices employed.

Using network analysis models such as I-P-O (input-processing-output) model provides a framework in which to plan network connections from a simple modem-to-modem transmission to a complex transcontinental wide-area network.

KEY TERMS

16QAM, 54
American standard code for information interchange, 37
amplitude, 50
amplitude modulation, 51
analog, 49
ASCII, 37
asynchronous transmission, 59
bandwidth, 49
baud, 51
baud rate, 52
bit, 37
bps, 52
breakout boxes, 45
broadband digital services, 61
byte, 37
carrier wave, 50
channel service unit/data service unit, 60
character encoding, 37
circuits, 49
constellation points, 52
CSU/DSU, 60
data circuit terminating equipment, 45
data communications equipment, 45
data terminal equipment, 45
DB-25, 41
DB-9, 41
DCE, 45
DDS, 60
demodulation, 50
dial-up line, 48

dibit, 54
digital, 37
digital data services, 60
digital modem, 61
digital signal processors, 59
DS-0, 60
DSP, 59
DTE, 45
EBCDIC, 37
echo cancellation, 58
extended binary coded decimal interchange code, 37
fallback, 60
four-wire circuit, 58
frequency, 50
frequency modulation, 51
frequency shift keying, 51
FSK, 51
full-duplex, 58
half-duplex, 58
handshaking, 58
integrated services digital network, 61
intersymbol interference, 55
ISDN, 61
ISO 10646, 38
leased line, 58
M-block connector, 41
modem, 50
modem cable, 41
modulation, 50
narrowband digital services, 60
network termination unit, 61
parallel transmission, 40

phase, 50
phase modulation, 52
phase shift keying, 52
plain old telephone service, 48
POTS, 48
PSK, 52
PSTN, 49
public switched telephone network, 49
QAM, 54
QPSK, 52
quadrature amplitude modulation, 54
quadrature phase shift keying, 52
RS-232-C, 41
S/N, 56
serial transmission, 40
signal to noise ratio, 56
switched 56K, 61
switched line, 48
synchronous transmission, 57
T-1, 61
T-3, 61
terminal adapter, 61
transmission rate, 52
turnaround time, 58
two-wire circuits, 58
UART, 45
Unicode, 38
universal asynchronous receiver transmitter, 45
voice-grade leased line, 59
wavelength, 52

REVIEW QUESTIONS

1. What is the difference between analog transmission and digital transmission?
2. What is the difference between asynchronous transmission and synchronous transmission? Which is more efficient?
3. What is a carrier wave?
4. What three characteristics of a carrier wave can be varied?
5. How are the number of detectable events related to the baud rate and bits/second (bps)?
6. Why do high-speed modems vary more than one characteristic of a carrier wave?
7. What is the difference between full-duplex and half-duplex data transmission?
8. What is the difference between bps and baud rate?
9. What is the difference between a leased line and a dial-up line?
10. What is character encoding and why is it necessary?
11. What are the two major encoding standards?
12. Why isn't there a single encoding standard?
13. What is a bit and how is it represented within a computer?
14. How must bits be represented on a voice-grade dial-up line?
15. What are the primary differences between serial and parallel transmission?
16. Which type of transmission (serial or parallel) is most often used in data communications and why?
17. What is a UART and what role does it play in the overall process of getting data from a local PC to a remote PC?
18. List the 10 most commonly used RS-232 pins, including name, abbreviation, and DCE/DTE orientation.
19. What is the name of the device employed to monitor and manipulate RS-232 signals?
20. What is the purpose of the I-P-O model and how can it be used to model both ends of given circuit?
21. Explain in simple terms how a circuit-switched or dial-up call is established.
22. What is the bandwidth of a dial-up circuit?
23. What is the significance of the range of frequencies of a dial-up circuit?
24. What are some of the shortcomings of a dial-up circuit in terms of data communications?
25. Which two words are used in forming the contraction *modem?*

26. Complete an I-P-O chart illustrating the required functionality of a modem.
27. What role does a carrier wave play in data transmission over a dial-up line?
28. How is the fact that different modems can use carrier waves with different frequencies resolved?
29. What is the relationship between wavelength and frequency?
30. What is a signaling event?
31. How long (in seconds) is a signaling event on a 1200-baud modem?
32. How long (in seconds) is a signaling event on a 2400-baud modem?
33. Which transmission methodology requires an external clocking source? Why?
34. What are the two ways in which modems can be modified to transmit data faster?
35. How are two-wire and four-wire circuits related to full-duplex and half-duplex transmission?
36. How are handshaking and turnaround time related to full-duplex and half-duplex transmission?
37. What is a CSU/DSU and how does it differ from a modem?
38. What are the differences in functionality between a modem and a CSU/DSU when encountering line problems?
39. What is the importance of encoding standards such as Unicode/ISO 10646?
40. What is a disadvantage of encoding standards such as Unicode/ISO 10646?
41. Give an example of how physical interfaces or connectors don't necessarily imply a transmission protocol.
42. What is a constellation point?
43. What is intersymbol interference and what impact does it have on modulation scheme design?
44. What is the importance of signal to noise ratio in terms of modem design and operation?
45. What is echo cancellation and why is it important?
46. How is echo cancellation enabled?
47. Which types of transmission services are becoming popular for Internet access?
48. What are some of the shortcomings of RS-232-C and how are they overcome?
49. What are the differences between "RS" serial standards and "V" serial standards?
50. What type of device must you purchase to interface your PC to ISDN services?

ACTIVITIES

1. Gather advertisements or product specifications for modems of various types. What are the price ranges of these modems? What are the various modulation techniques employed by these modems?
2. Contact your local phone service provider. Inquire as to how many of the services listed in Figure 2-19 are available in your area? Are there other services available that are not listed? Are there any current plans to provide additional services?
3. Inquire of your local phone company how the decision is made whether or not to provide a particular data service in a given area.
4. Inquire of your local phone company the approximate time it takes to "roll out" a new service from conception, through regulatory approval, to actual deployment.
5. Contact the Electrical Engineering or Electrical Engineering Technology department at your school. Inquire as to the availability of a guest speaker who might be able to bring an oscilloscope to class to demonstrate the wave characteristics described in this chapter.
6. Inquire from your local phone company whether most local loops supplied to homes in your area are two or four wire.
7. Inquire as to the difference between ground start and loop start subscriber trunks (local loops).
8. Gather advertisements or product specifications for digital modems, CSU/DSUs, NTUs, and ISDN modems. What are the price ranges of these modems? How do these "modems" differ from POTS modems?
9. Research the deployment levels of Unicode and ISO 10646. How many operating systems support these character encoding schemes? How must application programs be modified to support them?
10. Find examples of cables or connectors used for serial transmission methods other than RS-232-C. What differences are noticeable about these cables and connectors?
11. Research advertisements for breakout boxes. Prepare a technology analysis grid detailing the technical differences and price differences among the models researched.

CASE STUDY

Stamp of Approval—ISDN for the WAN? It's Saving the Detroit Post Office Big Money

While ISDN—after a 20-year search—has finally found its corporate niche in telecommuting, Internet-access, and other modemlike applications, most businesses think It Still Doesn't Network with the wide area.

This may be changing, too.

LAN protocols are accustomed to continuously sending data to and from network segments, so dial-up media such as ISDN were rarely considered feasible candidates for LAN-to-LAN links. However, new router features that eliminate or minimize network "chattiness" are making ISDN an increasingly robust medium for LAN-to-LAN connections across the wide area.

The Detroit District Post Office is one organization getting the ISDN message. It was weighing the diffi-cult choice between high-cost dedicated lines and low-speed analog links when it decided to begin connecting its 90-plus branch offices to its central LAN and data center.

In the past, small branch offices in the Detroit postal district did not have direct access to the district headquarter's network, preventing them from sending in mail volume, zip code, budgeting, and other information.

Jerry Jamula, IS manager for the district, explained that when the time came to connect the district's remote LANs to the central network both dedicated and analog lines were, at the same time, appealing and problematic.

Frame relay provided a steady 56Kbps of throughput to branch of-fices 24 hours a day, making it a compelling means of transporting file transfers, E-mail, and print queues from hosts at the central site.

However, the Detroit district's four-person IS staff dreaded the management nightmare that would accompany a tangle of nearly 100 dedicated lines. Moreover, each dedicated line would cost about $200 a month, Jamula explained. That's a lot of 32-cent stamp sales.

Analog lines, on the other hand, did not lend themselves well to the chatty LAN traffic that flows from the remote Novell Inc. NetWare and Microsoft Windows NT-based LANs in Ann Arbor, Brighton, Monroe, and other branch offices to the central LAN and mainframe hosts in Detroit.

"What we wanted to do was reach the smaller post offices, stations, and branches in a cost-effective way and offer them services without getting [dedicated] 56Kbps lines," Jamula said.

For this reason, Jamula considered a way to digitally dialup LAN connections.

An Analog Stigma

While ISDN can be considerably less expensive than leased lines, it bears the same stigma as analog modems when it comes to connecting LANs.

LAN protocols such as AppleTalk and IPX—and even TCP/IP to an extent—want to continuously send packets between LANs. These "keep-alive" packets make sure that virtual circuits between two networks are active.

Because users usually pay for ISDN connections by the minute, it is not advantageous to have ISDN links up too often. In the past, keep-alive messages have kept ISDN connections active for 24 hours a day, seven days a week. The user often does not realize this until a $3,000 phone bill arrives in the mailbox.

To remedy this, more and more vendors are equipping their routers with spoofing and packet-filtering features that minimize network traffic and restrict transmissions to the actual transmission of data traffic.

For example, Xylogics Inc. has incorporated very robust spoofing capabilities into its Nautica line of routers. And Bay Networks Inc., through its acquisition of Xylogics, plans to include spoofing in its routers late this spring.

Ascend Communications Inc. products keep ISDN connections to a minimum by filtering out AppleTalk discovery packets, and the Veloce router from Skyline Technology Inc. lets users set a limit on the total time an ISDN line is up.

Approaches such as these are transforming ISDN into a viable solution for LAN-to-LAN connections, according to Brad Baldwin, director of remote access at International Data Corp. In Mountain View, Calif.

They let users establish an ISDN call and tear it down a minute later. Then, when users are ready to interact with the remote LAN again, routers can resume the connection in two to three seconds.

"Companies can really manage their costs by taking the line up and down," Baldwin said. "The ability to break down calls to smaller components will really be the wave of the future for how ISDN is handled," he said.

In Detroit, Jamula and his network technology staff selected two similar-sized branch post offices that they knew would require high-bandwidth access to the central LAN. In one they installed a 56Kbps leased line and in the other an ISDN link. "We wanted to know which would give us the most bandwidth and uptime at the least cost," Jamula said.

Jamula had these sites send E-mail, zip-code requests, change-of-address information, and other traffic to and from the district office. After a month he compared the performance of the links and found that ISDN provided a similar—in some cases superior—quality of service.

With compression, Jamula said that a 64Kbps ISDN line provided as much as five times the throughput as that of 56Kbps leased lines.

And the fact that ISDN is a dial-up service did not affect performance significantly, he said. "Links came up so fast you couldn't even notice [that they were dial-up connections]. Users hit a key, and the link was there," he said.

Besides comparable performance, Jamula said ISDN cost about half as much as leased lines. Ameritech Corp. charged him about $100 a month for each ISDN connection, compared with $180 a month for each leased line.

At this point, Jamula installed a Direct-Route-1—a four-line, central-office router from Symplex Communications Corp.—at the Detroit district office and Symplex Remote-Office-1 routers at four of the branch sites.

How It Works

At each of these remote sites, he had eight or nine employees operating LANs and VTs (virtual terminals) and online printers taking queues from a remote mainframe host.

When employees at branch sites send word-processing and other documents to the main office, Symplex routers open an ftp (File Transfer Protocol) connection, bring up an IP link, transfer the files over ISDN, and then drop the line. If users want to connect to send E-mail, the routers again bring up an IP connection, send the mail, and then drop the connection when the message is sent.

Printers at branch sites operate similarly. Workers at the post office's data center can either send batch jobs running on a host or initiate a mainframe print job over ISDN connections. The Symplex routers make sure the ISDN lines are up only for the length of the print session. "That was the greatest thing," Jamula said. "It gave us high-speed mainframe printing without paying the high-speed cost.

Satisfied that the ISDN routers could reliably set up and tear down connections, he began running ISDN lines out to more sites. Jamula now has 17 branch offices with about 100 users connected to the district office.

"If I can keep driving the cost down, I think we can offer the service to additional smaller offices," which are presently connected to the headquarters only through dial-up analog connections, he said.

"What we wanted to do was have high availability of bandwidth at low cost," Jamula continued. "So far, this has worked out fine."

BUSINESS CASE STUDY QUESTIONS

Activities

1. Complete a top-down model for this case by gleaning facts from the case and placing them in the proper layer of the top-down model. After having completed the top-down model, analyze and detail those instances where requirements were clearly passed down from upper layers to lower layers of the model and where solutions to those requirements were passed up from lower layers to upper layers of the model.

2. Detail any questions about the case that may occur to you for which answers are not clearly stated in the article.

Business

1. What was the effect on business processes of the small branch offices not having access to the district headquarter's network?

2. If the dedicated leased line architecture had been chosen, what would the monthly costs be?

3. How could described data layer characteristics combined with a technology choice of ISDN routers without spoofing capabilities produce drastic business layer impact?

Application

1. What were some of the on-line applications that remote branches executed with the district office?

2. What are keep-alive messages and what effect do they have on network service choice?

3. What were the mainframe-based applications and how well did ISDN service these applications?

Data

1. What were the connectivity needs of the Detroit District Post Office?

2. What characteristics of the LAN-to-LAN traffic were important to consider when considering network options?

Network

1. What is ISDN now considered as a viable option for LAN-to-LAN links?

2. What were the advantages and disadvantages of using frame relays as a WAN connectivity option?

3. What were the specific shortcomings of analog lines in meeting data layer requirements?

Technology

1. What were the connectivity options available for the Detroit District Post Office other than ISDN?

2. Why was ISDN chosen?

3. What is the relationship between 56 Kbps dedicated lines and the frame relay service?

4. How did spoofing and packet-filtering capabilities on ISDN routers influence the effectiveness of ISDN meeting the data layer requirements?

5. Describe the pilot test used to compare alternative network services.

6. What were the results of the pilot test in terms of throughput?

7. Was the fact that ISDN was a dial-up, rather than leased, service a problem? Why or why not?

8. What were the financial comparative results of the pilot test?

CHAPTER 3

BASIC DATA COMMUNICATIONS TECHNOLOGY

Concepts Reinforced

Top-Down Model	I-P-O Model
Modulation Techniques	Protocols and Compatibility
Transmission Services	Analog vs. Digital

Concepts Introduced

Modem Standards	Communications Software Analysis
Error Prevention	Data Compression
Error Detection	Error Correction
Flow Control	Dial Backup and Restoral
Modem Trends	

OBJECTIVES

After mastering the material in this chapter, you should

1. Understand modem operation, comparative modem features, the importance of modem standards, and the cost/benefit analysis of various modem purchases.

2. Understand the comparative features and proper business application of communications software.

3. Understand the implications in terms of technology and cost/benefit of the use of various carrier services.

■ INTRODUCTION

In Chapter 2, PC-to-PC communications via modems was introduced as a means of explaining many introductory concepts. In this chapter, the operation and comparative features of modems will be studied in detail. The role of communications software in the establishment, maintenance, and termination of reliable data communications will also be explored. An introduction to the world of digital carrier services will include studies of the required technology as well as the cost/benefit analysis of employing such services.

■ MODEM TECHNOLOGY ANALYSIS

**Applied
Problem
Solving**

GAUGING BUSINESS IMPACT OF TECHNOLOGY

How does one gauge the business impact of investment in modem technology? How does one justify upgrading to newer modem technology?

By first understanding business needs, one is better able to make informed technology purchase decisions. As Figure 3-1 illustrates, potential business impacts of modem technology purchases include the ability to transfer data in a manner which is

- Faster.

- More efficient.

- More reliable.

- More secure.

These four business layer characteristics become the frame of reference through which potential modem purchases are evaluated. In other words, if purchasing the technology in question will not make data transmissions faster, more efficient, more reliable, or more secure, why invest in such technology?

The concepts, standards, and technology listed in Figure 3-1 will serve as a road map for topics to be covered in this section of this chapter.

Business Layer	Concepts	Standards and Technology
Faster	• New modern standards • Digital transmission services	• V.34, older standards • DDS services, ISDN, CSU/DSUs
More efficient	• Data compression • Backward compatibility	• V.42bis, MNP 5, throughput, transmission rate • Handshaking, Hayes AT command set
More reliable	• Error prevention • Error detection • Error correction • Line-failure backup • Flow control • Error control standards	• Line conditioning, adaptive protocols, TCM • Parity, LRC, checksums, CRC • ARQ ACK/NAK • Auto-dial backup and auto restoral • RTS/CTS, XON/XOFF • V.42, MNP 4
More secure	• Unauthorized access prevention • Encryption	• Password protection, callback security • Standards, standalone vs. integrated

Figure 3-1   Gauging Business Impact of Modem Technology

Future Value of Business Analysis As new modem-related technologies are introduced in the future, their business value can be judged using such a model:

1. Does the new technology or feature fit into one of the listed supporting concept categories?

2. If not, does it represent a new category or does it not meet any currently perceived business need?

3. Does the new technology identify a new, as yet unlisted, business data communications need?

4. If so, add it to your business model layer.

5. If not, then perhaps the newly evaluated technology is either ahead of its time or not currently cost justifiable.

The entries listed on each model layer are based upon the author's experience and observations in business data communications. If your experience yields differing results, then by all means change the entries in the model. If you use *your* topdown model as a frame of reference for data communications technology evaluation, it will assist you in making sense of the current explosion of technology while maintaining an objective so-what attitude toward that technology.

Faster

Modem Standards For modems manufactured by different vendors to interoperate successfully, they must be manufactured according to common operational standards. These standards must define standardized methods of modulation, data compression, error correction, auto-dialing, and backward compatibility with older standards. Figure 3-2 summarizes significant dial-up modem standards of the past 20 years.

Modem Standard	Transmission Rate	Baud Rate	Data Compression	Error Correction	Modulation Method
V.34	28.8K	3200, 3000, 2400, 2743, 2800, 3429	V.42bis/MNP 5	V.42/MNP 4	9QAM and TCM
V.32ter	19.2K	2400	V.42bis/MNP 5	V.42/MNP 4	8QAM and TCM
V.32bis	14.4K	2400	V.42bis/MNP 5	V.42/MNP 4	6QAM and TCM
V.32	9.6K	2400	V.42bis/MNP 5	V.42/MNP 4	4QAM and TCM
V.22bis	2400	600	V.42bis/MNP 5	V.42/MNP 4	4QAM and TCM
Bell 212A	1200	600			4PSK
Bell 103	300	300			FSK

Figure 3-2 Modem Standards

Excluding V.32ter, all V-series standards featured in Figure 3-2 are officially sanctioned by ITU-T (International Telecommunications Union—Telephony Sector). The Bell standards listed in Figure 3-2 are predivestiture standards from the time when AT&T dictated modem specifications in the United States and compliance with international standards was not an option. The suffix *bis* refers to the second standard issued by a given standard committee, and the suffix *ter* refers to the third standard issued by the same committee.

Nonstandard Standards: In an effort to gain market share during the period when standards-making organizations are deliberating new standards, vendors often introduce proprietary versions of pending standards. **V.32ter,** sometimes known as V.32terbo, is not an officially sanctioned standard. It was introduced as an interim 19.2 Kbps improvement in performance over the V.32bis 14.4-Kbps modems prior to the introduction of V.34 modems. Another group of modems known alternatively as **V.FAST, V.Fast Class, or V.FC** modems were also introduced prior to the introduction of official V.34 modems. These prestandard modems were based on proprietary chip sets manufactured by AT&T and Rockwell and were not interoperable with each other or with the eventual V.34 standard.

Practical Advice and Information

One very important point to keep in mind when purchasing prestandard data communications equipment is the ability of the vendor to upgrade that equipment to meet the specifications of the official standard once it is issued. In some cases, software upgrades are possible, whereas in other cases, hardware upgrades or chip replacement is required. In some cases, these upgrades may be free and easily accomplished via a toll-free number, whereas in other cases, the upgrade may involve returning the equipment to the factory and upgrade fees of several hundred dollars. Be sure to understand all of the details regarding standards compliance upgrades before ever purchasing prestandards data communications equipment.

V.34:   **V.34** is the most current modem standard offering a transmission rate of 28.8 Kbps (28,800 bps) over dial-up lines. Note in Figure 3-2 that although modulation standards have changed to produce higher transmission rates, the associated data compression and error correction standards have remained constant. The V.34 modem standard instituted a variety of technical innovations to achieve its 28.8-Kbps transmission rate over dial-up lines of variable quality. The overall effect of these technical innovations is that the V.34 modem is better able than any previous modem standard to easily and dynamically adjust to variable line conditions to optimize transmission rate.

V.34 TECHNICAL INNOVATIONS

In Sharper Focus

Figure 3-3 (page 72) summarizes the technical innovations introduced with the V.34 modem standard and their associated importance or implication.

Practical Advice and Information

Although all of the technical innovations listed in Figure 3-3 are considered part of the V.34 standard, it is not safe to assume that they are all included in any V.34 modem. In addition, several other optional features that may or may not be supported on any given V.34 modem are as follows:

- Support of leased lines as well as dial-up lines.

- Inclusion of four-wire as well as two-wire physical interfaces.

- Password protection and callback security.

- Ability to connect to fax machines via the V.17 fax standard.

- Ability to auto-dial via the V.25bis auto-dial standard.

- Auto-dial backup for failed leased lines or lost carrier.

- Auto restoral to repaired leased lines.

This lack of assurance as to the exact features supported on any given V.34 modem can lead to interoperability problems among V.34 modems. The best solution to this dilemma is to purchase identical modems from a single manufacturer. If this is not practical, then the time invested to carefully investigate which features of the V.34 standard are implemented in a given modem would be a wise investment indeed.

MNP Standards: **Microcom networking protocols (MNP)** are error correction and data compression protocols developed by the modem manufacturer Microcom. MNP classes or groups of protocols are excellent examples of de facto standards. They are supported by most modems even though they are not mandated by any officially sanctioned standards-making organization. However, MNP classes often form the basis for officially sanctioned international standards. For example, the ITU's V.42 error correction standard incorporates MNP Classes 2, 3, and 4. Figure 3-4 (page 73) summarizes the current MNP classes. Further explanation of selected MNP classes is provided in later sections of this chapter.

Cheaper (More Efficient)

By operating more efficiently, modems are able to offer more transmitted data in a given amount of time. Although several factors can lead to increased modem efficiency, data compression can have the most significant impact in the amount of data actually delivered by a given modem in a given amount of time.

Data Compression   Simply stated, **data compression** removes repetitive patterns of characters within a raw data stream and replaces them with minimized codes that represent the larger patterns of characters. Optimally, data compression schemes can increase throughput by 400%. This means that a 28.8-Kbps (V.34) modem could optimally transfer 115.2 Kbps of data across a dial-up phone line. In this scenario, the 115,200 bps is known as **throughput** while the transmission rate is still the V.34 maximum 28.8 Kbps. Figure 3-5 illustrates the difference between throughput and transmission rate.

It is important to understand how data compression works and the fact that all of the 115,200 bits/sec do not actually travel across the phone circuit. It is equally important to understand that data compression only works if both of the modems on the circuit support the same data compression standard. Data compressed by the sending modem must be uncompressed by the receiving modem using an identical algorithm or methodology.

V.34 Technical Innovation	Importance/Implication
Multiple baud rates/carrier frequencies	The V.34 standard specifies three required baud rates (3200, 3000, 2400) and three optional baud rates (3429, 2800, 2743). Multiple potential baud rates increase the V.34 modem's ability to adapt to variable line conditions. Each baud rate supports two different carrier frequencies to optimize transmission speed on dial-up lines of variable quality.
Baud rates greater than 2400	The V.34 standard is the first to attempt baud rates of greater than 2400. The 28.8-Kbps transmission rate is achieved by interpreting 9 data bits/baud at a baud rate of 3200.
Auxiliary management channel	An auxiliary or side channel, separate from the data channel, is available for transmission of management or configuration data. This channel would be particularly important if the V.34 modem were attached to a router or similar internetworking device that might require monitoring or management without disrupting the main data traffic.
Asymmetric transmit/receive speeds	Some applications such as database queries/responses or Web requests/downloads may require wide bandwidth in one direction only. V.34 specifies a method for allocating the data with a larger bandwidth in one direction than the other.
Adaptive line probing	Adaptive line probing tests the characteristics of the transmission line not just at call initiation time but throughout the transmission. Baud rate, carrier frequency, constellation size and shape, and other parameters can be changed to optimize transmission rate.
Precoding and nonlinear encoding	Precoding and encoding reduce high-frequency line noise and increase immunity to interference on analog to digital conversion by plotting constellation points in areas with less interference.
Fallback/fallforward	Although many modem standards support fallback, V.34 supports fallforward features that allow increases in transmission rates as line conditions improve.
Trellis-coded modulation	This forward error correction methodology helps support higher baud rates on dirty phone lines by predicting the location of a given constellation point. It can add significant processing overhead.
V.8 training specification	Also known as fast training, this specification allows two V.34 modems that support V.8 training to set up and initialize a call faster than modems that do not support V.8.

Figure 3-3   V.34 Technical Innovations

MNP Class	Explanation/Importance
1	• Early error control protocol superseded by later classes
2	• Defined a method for asynchronous byte-oriented full-duplex data transmission
3	• Defined a method for synchronous bit-oriented communication between modems, even if the communication session between PCs was asynchronous; removed start bits and stop bits to increase efficiency by up to 8%
4	• Adaptive size packet assembly: Size of data packets is adjusted according to the quality of the line to avoid errors and retransmissions • Data phase packet format optimization: Eliminates the portions of the overhead or framing bytes in the data packets that do not change during data transfer • Implementation of MNP Class 4 protocols can increase transmission efficiency by up to 20%
5	• Data compression protocol that can increase throughput by up to 200% (see chapter section on data compression for further explanation)
6	• Universal link negotiation: Allows modems supporting a variety of standards to interoperate at speeds from 50 to 19.2 Kbps; eliminates incompatibilities between Bell standards and V series standards • Statistical duplexing: Also known as simulated full-duplex transmission; allows half-duplex modems to support fast turnaround time based on which direction has more data waiting to be transmitted
7	• Enhanced data compression protocol that can increase throughput by up to 300%
8	• Enhancement to MNP Class 6 simulated full-duplex by combining MNP Class 7 data compression with V.29 fast-train protocol (9600 bps, half-duplex)
9	• MNP Class 7 data compression plus V.32 (9600 bps, full-duplex) • Enhanced universal link negotiation: Allows MNP and non-MNP modems to establish optimum performance communications sessions

10	• Consists of four protocols known collectively as **adverse channel enhancements (ACE)** that were designed for inherently unreliable circuits such as cellular transmission:
	  1. Robust auto-reliable: Multiple attempts of link setup at highest common protocol level
	  2. Aggressive adaptive packet assembly: Packet size is quickly and dynamically changed in response to changing line conditions
	  3. Dynamic speed shifts: Transmission speed and modulation scheme can vary dynamically in response to changing line conditions
	  4. Negotiated speed upshifts: Transmission session is initially established at a negotiated speed that will provide the highest reliability; if line conditions improve, higher speeds will be supported

Figure 3-4   MNP Classes

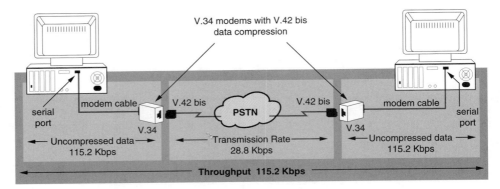

Figure 3-5   Data Compression: Transmission Rate vs. Throughput

In the case of one data compression standard known as V.42bis, the data compression software examines the raw data received from the transmitting PC, looking for repetitive patterns of characters, before it sends the data onto the circuit. Having spotted a repetitive pattern of up to 32 characters, the two modems store this pattern, along with an 11-bit code or key, in a constantly updated library. The next time this pattern of data comes along to be sent, the sending modem just sends the 11-bit code that represents the 32-byte pattern, rather than the entire data stream itself. The receiving modem then consults its library to see which "uncompressed" pattern is represented by the code character(s) received.

Obviously, the more "repetitive patterns" the data compression software can find in the data, the higher the expected compression ratio. Thus, some data is more compressible than others and would yield a higher data compression ratio.

Given the transmission of compressed data in which a single character may "uncompress" into many characters, the importance of error prevention, detection, and correction should be obvious. An erroneously transmitted character could be referenced in the receiving modem's library of repetitive patterns and incorrectly "uncompressed" into the wrong data stream.

V.42bis and MNP 5:   The two predominant data compression standards are V.42bis and MNP 5. Most modems try to negotiate with each other to implement V.42bis data compression at initialization, and use MNP 5 as a second, less powerful option.

- **V.42bis** uses a data compression algorithm known as the Lempel Ziv algorithm as described in the previous section. Ideally, it can compress files and thereby increase throughput by a 4:1 ratio. Proprietary improvements to this algorithm by modem manufacturers can be achieved in two ways:
    1. Increase the amount of memory dedicated to the library, also known as the dictionary (1.5 KB standard; some modems use up to 6 KB).
    2. Increase the size of the pattern of characters, also known as string size, that can be stored in the dictionary (32 bytes standard; some modems support strings up to 256 bytes). Proprietary improvements to standards such as V.42bis are only effective when both modems involved in a transmission are identical. It should also be noted that most independent modem testing suggests that compression ratios in the range of 2.5:1 are most likely despite higher optimal claims.

- **MNP Class 5** yields data compression ratios of between 1.3:1 and 2:1. MNP 5 uses two data compression algorithms:

    3. **Huffman encoding** is a special character encoding scheme that re-encodes ASCII characters. Frequently used characters such as *a, e,* and *s* are encoded with only 4 bits, whereas rarely occurring characters such as *x* or *z* are encoded using as many as 11 bits. Overall, the effect of Huffman encoding is that more characters are transmitted using fewer bits.

    4. **Run-length encoding** examines a data stream in search of repeating characters. When any character repeats more than three times, the run-length encoding algorithm replaces the entire string of repeated characters with only three repetitions of the character followed by a count field indicating how many times the character is actually repeated. For example, a data string containing 10 consecutive repetitions of the same character would be replaced by 3 repetitions of that character followed by a 1-byte count character. This would reduce the string in question from 10 bytes to 4 bytes for a savings of 60%. Repeated characters can include nonprinting characters such as spaces, carriage returns, and line feeds.

Principle of Shifting Bottlenecks: The potential for throughput rates of 115.2 Kbps via V.34 modems with V.42bis data compression introduces a potentially interesting dilemma. Careful examination of Figure 3-5 reveals that the serial ports of the PCs involved in the end-to-end communications session should be set to 115.2 Kbps. However, most PC serial ports are only able to support transmission speeds of 19.2 or 38.4 Kbps. These speed limits are somewhat dependent on the particular UART chip installed. This dilemma is an example of a principle of data communications common to numerous transmission systems known as the **principle of shifting bottlenecks.**

In the case of a modem-based transmission system, the modems themselves traditionally represented the bottleneck, or slowest link, of the overall end-to-end transmission. However, as modem technology advanced with the introduction of the V.34 standard, the transmission bottleneck shifted from the modem to the PC's serial port. To date, two solutions have emerged for this new bottleneck, with other potential solutions looming on the horizon.

1. Increase the speed of serial ports: One example of such an enhanced serial port is the **Hayes ESP communications accelerator.** This serial port replacement supports speeds of up to 921,600 bps by implementing two 1024-byte buffers and minimizing CPU interruption. Such serial port speeds would be necessary if one were to employ Hayes modems on both ends of a transmission that support the Hayes proprietary enhanced V.42bis data compression algorithms with potential compression ratios of 8:1.

2. Hook the modem to the parallel port rather than the serial port: The Microcom Deskporte family of modems using Microcom's **advanced parallel technology (APT)** is an example of modems that communicate with PCs via their parallel port rather than the serial port. Most PC parallel ports are capable of transmitting at 115.2 Kbps bidirectionally. One difficulty with this solution is that the PC's communications software must be able to redirect modem output to the parallel rather than serial port. Microcom claims to supply all necessary software and drivers to accomplish PC-to-modem communication via the PC's parallel port at speeds of up to 300 Kbps.

3. Fundamental changes in PC design may be the ultimate solution to the input/output (I/O) bottleneck. Some of the more significant proposals are
   - **Universal serial bus (USB)**—This external I/O port would supply throughput of up to 12 Mbps, can daisy-chain up to 126 devices, and can handle data as well as streaming traffic such as voice and video.
   - **FireWire (IEEE 1394-1995)** (otherwise known as serial bus)—This I/O specification can provide bandwidth of 100, 200, or 400 Mbps and is also being promoted as a standard interface for consumer video products such as VCRs and camcorders as well as computer peripherals such as disk drives. It supports up to 63 devices on a single copper wire bus.
   - **Serial Express (IEEE 1394.2)**—This I/O specification provides higher performance, potentially in the gigabit/second range, over longer distances than FireWire for fiber-based applications such as home or office wiring for video, audio, and climate control transmission. The development effort behind this protocol is being led by Intel, Sun, and Apple. IEEE 1394.2 is incompatible with IEEE 1394-1995, also known as 1394a or 1394.0.

More Reliable

Improving the reliability of the data transmission link between two modems will ultimately make that data transmission faster and more efficient. Fewer retransmissions due to data errors will increase the throughput of information bits, thus reducing the time necessary to transmit a given message, thereby minimizing the cost of the data transmission.

The goal of reliable transmission is to reduce the error rate of a data transmission session as close as possible to zero errors. The first category of methodologies that will be covered strives to prevent errors from happening in the first place by optimizing the condition of the transmission link **(error prevention)**. Should errors still occur, it is essential that these errors be accurately detected **(error detection)**. Once detected, the errors must be reliably corrected **(error correction).**

Error Prevention   Data transmission errors occur when received data is misinterpreted due to noise or interference on the phone lines over which the data message traveled. Errors can be prevented by

- Reducing the amount of noise or interference on a given transmission line.

- Employing modulation techniques that are able to adapt to and overcome noisy lines.

Line Conditioning, Repeaters, and Amplifiers: **Line conditioning** is a value-added service available from the phone company from whom one leases analog leased lines. Various levels of conditioning are available at prices that increase proportionally to the level of conditioning, or noise reduction, requested. Conditioning represents a promise from the phone company as to levels of noise or interference that will occur on a given analog leased line. To deliver on this promise, the phone company may have to install additional equipment to guarantee signal quality.

A **repeater** is often used by a phone company to ensure signal quality over the entire length of a circuit. As a signal travels through a medium such as copper wire, it loses some of its strength due to the resistance of the wire. This loss of signal strength or volume is known as **attenuation.**

A repeater on an analog circuit, sometimes called an **amplifier,** strengthens and repeats or retransmits the signal. Unfortunately, on analog circuits, the amplifier cannot distinguish between the voice or data signal and the background noise on the circuit and, as a result, also strengthens, repeats, and retransmits the noise of the circuit.

In contrast, repeaters on digital circuits are able to actually regenerate digital signals (remembering that digital signals are discrete voltages—Chapter 2) before repeating and retransmitting them. Thus a digital signal, including digitized voice, transmitted over a digital circuit will more reliably arrive at its destination without the need for specialized line conditioning. The repeaters in this application are primarily used only by the phone company and should not be confused with local area network repeaters, which will be covered in Chapter 8.

As analog leased lines give way to digital leased and dial-up services, the purchase of line conditioning will become a nonissue in the error prevention arena. In fact, the use of DDS or digital leased lines could be seen as an error prevention technique.

Adaptive Protocols: Another way in which errors can be prevented during data transmission is through the use of **adaptive protocols,** which are able to adjust transmission session parameters in response to varying line conditions. The MNP classes of networking protocols offer several examples of such adaptive protocols.

Adaptive size packet assembly is an MNP Class 4 protocol that can increase or decrease the amount of data sent in each packet according to the current condition of the transmission circuit. A packet that includes data and overhead information is analogous to a handwritten message (the data) plus a sealed, addressed envelope (the overhead). This protocol tries to optimize the amount of data per packet by building packets containing the greatest amount of data that can be transmitted reliably and therefore not require retransmission.

Optimization may be a moving target as line conditions change. Each packet must be processed individually, which takes time. Therefore, it would stand to reason that it would be advantageous to get as much data as possible into each packet (in our analogy, writing as long a letter as possible for each envelope). If the packet contains too little data, time is wasted processing overhead (opening envelopes in the analogy).

However, if too much data is put into each packet, retransmissions will be required, thereby consuming significant amounts of transmission time. When too much data is enclosed per packet, time is wasted retransmitting packets received in error (receiving back, rewriting, and remailing letters for insufficient postage in our analogy). Adaptive size packet assembly solves the data per packet dilemma by adapting the amount of data included in each packet according to varying line conditions.

Dynamic speed shifts is an MNP Class 10 adaptive protocol that allows two modems to change speeds up or down (faster or slower) in the midst of their data transmission in response to varying line conditions. The adaptive nature of this protocol ensures that the highest practical transmission speed will be used at all times, dependent upon current line conditions. This adaptive protocol is especially useful in cellular phone environments in which line quality can vary significantly over short periods of time.

The dynamic speed shifts adaptive protocol or any adaptive protocol can be a double-edged sword however. In the event of degraded line quality, MNP 10 modems may automatically downgrade their transmission speeds. Unless a personnel procedure is in place to take note of the lower transmission speed, the problem may go undetected and unreported to the carrier for an extended period of time.

Error Detection   Once everything possible to prevent errors has been done, the next task is to reliably detect those errors that do occur. Remembering that transmitted data, on the most elementary level, is merely a stream of 1s and 0s, the role of error detection can be defined as providing the assurance that the receiving modem receives the same 1s and 0s in the exact sequence as transmitted by the transmitting modem.

Overall Process: This assurance is achieved through the cooperative efforts of the transmitting and receiving modems. In addition to transmitting the actual data, the transmitting modem must also transmit some type of verifiable bit or character that the receiving modem can use to decide whether the transmitted data was received correctly or not. Figure 3-6 illustrates this overall process shared by all error detection techniques.

A generalized error detection process as illustrated in Figure 3-6 could be summarized as follows:

1. Both transmitting and receiving modems must agree on how the error check is to be calculated.

2. The transmitting computer calculates and transmits the error check along with the transmitted data.

3. The receiving modem recalculates the error check based on the received data and compares its newly calculated error check to the error check that was calculated and transmitted by the transmitting modem.

4. If the two error checks match, everything is fine. If the receiving modem's calculated error check does not match the transmitted error check, an error has been detected.

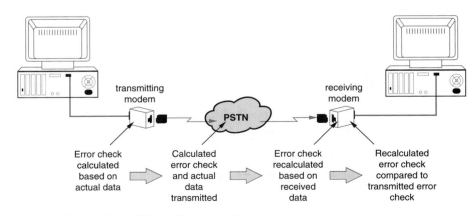

Figure 3-6   The Overall Error Detection Process

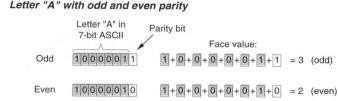

Letter "A" with odd and even parity

Figure 3-7   Odd and Even Parity

Several error detection techniques of varying degrees of complexity have been developed. The following error detection techniques, listed in order of increasing complexity and ability to detect errors reliably, will be discussed further:

- Parity.
- Longitudinal redundancy checks (LRC).
- Checksums.
- Cyclic redundancy checks (CRC).

Parity: **Parity** is the simplest of the error detection techniques. For example, since the ASCII 7-bit code for the letter *A* is 1000001, a parity bit is added as the eighth bit. Whether this bit should be a 0 or a 1 depends on whether odd or even parity has been defined or agreed upon in advance by the PCs or terminals and computer ports involved in the data transmission. These devices can also agree to data transmission with no parity. Examples of the letter *A* with odd and even parity are illustrated in Figure 3-7.

As can be seen in Figure 3-7, when the letter *A* is transmitted with odd parity, the parity bit is set to 1 so that the sum of the face value of all of the bits in the character will be odd. Conversely, when even parity is chosen by both ends of the data transmission circuit, the parity bit is set to 0 so that the face value of the transmitted data is even. If the even parity is chosen and the receiving computer adds up the face values of the bits in a character and finds that the sum is odd, then it knows that it has detected a transmission error.

Parity checking has a limitation however. Figure 3-8 illustrates parity checking's inability to detect multiple bit errors within the same character.

As can be seen in Figure 3-8, the received character has an even face value so that the receiving computer would think everything was fine; however, in fact, a letter *Q* was received even though the letter *A* was transmitted.

Multiple bit errors/even parity

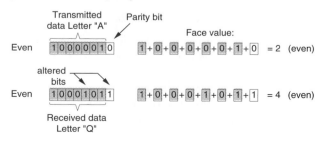
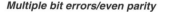

Figure 3-8   Parity Checking's Inability to Detect Multiple Bit Errors

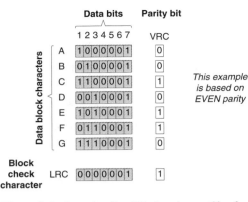

Figure 3-9   Longitudinal Redundancy Checks

Longitudinal Redundancy Checks: **Longitudinal redundancy checks (LRC)** seek to overcome the weakness of simple bit-oriented one-directional parity checking, sometimes called **vertical redundancy checking (VRC).** One can think of LRC as adding a second dimension to VRC. Figure 3-9 illustrates longitudinal redundancy checking with even parity in two dimensions.

As can be seen in Figure 3-9, LRC is a block-oriented parity checking mechanism that adds an entire parity character following a block of data characters. The bits of the parity character are set to establish property parity for each bit position within the block of data characters. In the example illustrated in Figure 3-9, both the parity bits of individual characters (VRC) and the parity bits of the longitudinal redundancy check character would be checked to be sure that even parity existed in both directions.

Checksums: **Checksums** are also block-oriented error detection characters that are added to a block of data characters. However, rather than adding binary face values of bits as was the case with the LRC, a checksum is calculated by adding the decimal face values of all of the characters sent in a given data block and sending only the least significant byte of that sum. The receiving modem generates its own checksum based on the data it has received and compares the locally calculated checksum with the transmitted checksum.

In Sharper Focus

CHECKSUM CALCULATION

The formula for calculating a checksum is as follows:

1. Add the ASCII decimal face value of each of the 128 characters in the block.

2. Divide this number by 255.

3. The remainder of this answer is the checksum character to be transmitted to and verified by the receiving modem.

To understand the inner workings of this formula, it is necessary to further understand the ASCII table, first introduced in Figure 2-2. Every value in the ASCII table has a decimal equivalent computed by transforming the 1s and 0s of any character into their base 2 column values and adding the decimal values of those base 2 columns in which 1s appear.

Example:

Capital letter *A* 7-bit ASCII code is 1000001

Now assign base 2 place values to each column

Power of 2	7	6	5	4	3	2	1	0
Decimal value	128	64	32	16	8	4	2	1
Letter *A* code		1	0	0	0	0	0	1

There is a "1" in the "64" column and a "1" in the "1" column. Adding these place values yields 64 + 1 or 65 (base 10) or decimal 65. Therefore the ASCII decimal face value of the capital letter *A* is 65. Some ASCII and EBCDIC tables supply only decimal values rather than binary values as illustrated in Figures 2-2 and 2-3.

If 128 capital *A*s were transferred as a single block of data, the total ASCII face value of the block would be 128 × 65 = 8320. Dividing the total ASCII face value by 255 yields 8320/255 = 32 r 160. So the remainder is 160. This remainder is also known as the least significant byte.

To represent the remainder (160) as a single checksum character in binary format, use the decimal values chart of the powers of 2.

Power of 2	7	6	5	4	3	2	1	0
Decimal value	128	64	32	16	8	4	2	1
Binary value of 160	1	0	1	0	0	0	0	0

Thus, the transmitted checksum character would be 10100000.

When dividing our total ASCII face value by 255, the highest remainder possible would be 254. Decimal 254 would be represented in binary and transmitted in a single checksum character (8 bits) as 11111110.

Cyclic Redundancy Checks: **Cyclic redundancy checks (CRC)** seek to improve on the error detection capability of checksums and LRCs. A CRC is really a more sophisticated form of a checksum, calculating and transmitting this checksum, or block check character, to the receiving modem for recalculation and verification. **CRC-16** (16-bit CRC) or **CRC-32** (32-bit CRC) may be seen in modem product descriptions.

To understand CRC-16 and CRC-32, binary division is required. In cyclic redundancy checking, the entire message block of 1s and 0s, even if it's 1000 bits long, is treated as a single, gigantic binary number. This gigantic string of 1s and 0s is divided by a predetermined prime binary number (a 17-bit divisor for CRC-16 and a 33-bit divisor for CRC-32). Remembering that these divisors are prime (only divisible by 1 and themselves), they will produce a 16- and 32-bit remainder, respectively.

This remainder is then attached to the actual data message (the original string of 1s and 0s to be transmitted) and transmitted to the receiving modem where the received data string is again divided by the same 16- or 32-bit divisor. The remainder calculated at the receiving modem is compared to the recently received remainder calculated at the transmitting modem.

Using this technique, a CRC-16 modem can detect error bursts of up to 15 bits 100% of the time, and a CRC-32 modem can detect error bursts of up to 31 bits 100% of the time. The CRC-16 modem can detect error bursts equal to 16 bits

$(100 - 1/2^{15})\%$ of the time, and a CRC-32 modem can detect error bursts equal to 32 bits $(100 - 1/2^{31})\%$ of the time. The CRC-16 modem can detect error bursts larger than 16 bits $(100 - 1/2^{16})\%$ of the time, and a CRC-32 modem can detect error bursts of larger than 32 bits $(100 - 1/2^{32})\%$ of the time. Computing the overall percentage for CRC-16 yields an error detection rate of 99.999984742%!

Error Correction Once it is understood how data transmission errors can be detected, they must be reliably and efficiently corrected. In simple terms, error correction amounts to

1. The receiving modem detecting an error and requesting retransmission.

2. The transmitting modem retransmitting the incorrect data.

The difference in sophistication between the various error-correcting protocols are centered around a few variables:

1. How is the retransmission requested?

2. How much data must be retransmitted?

3. How is retransmission time minimized?

Error correction could easily have been included in the "More efficient" section of the business layer model (Figure 3-1). Retransmissions take time and, in business, time is money.

Automatic Retransmission Request (ARQ): **ARQ** or **automatic retransmission request** is a general term that really describes the overall process of error detection using one of the previously described methods as well as the subsequent automatic request for retransmission of that data. As noted, the actual request for retransmission can occur in different ways.

Discrete ARQ—ACK/NAK: **Discrete ARQ** is sometimes also known as "stop and wait" ARQ. In a protocol using discrete ARQ, the transmitting device sends a block of data and waits until the remote receiving device does the following:

1. Receives the data.

2. Tests for errors using parity, LRC, checksum, or CRC.

3. Sends an **acknowledgment (ACK)** character back to the transmitting device if the transmitted data was error free or . . .

4. Sends a **negative acknowledgment (NAK)** character if the data was not successfully received.

After waiting for this **ACK/NAK,** the transmitting device does the following:

1. Sends the next block of data if an ACK was received or . . .

2. Retransmits the original block of data if a NAK was received.

This entire process repeats itself until the conclusion of the data transmission session. Obviously, the transmitting device spends a significant amount of time idly waiting for either an ACK or NAK to be sent by the receiving device. As may have been suspected, there are ARQ methodologies that take a different, more efficient approach to error detection and correction.

Continuous ARQ: A variation of ARQ known as **continuous ARQ** eliminates the requirement for the transmitting device to wait for an ACK or NAK after transmitting each block before transmitting the next block of data. This obviously eliminates a great deal of idle time and increases overall data throughput.

With continuous ARQ, sometimes known as **sliding window protocol** when implemented in a communications software package, a **block sequence number** is appended to each block of data transmitted. The transmitting device continuously transmits blocks of data without waiting for ACK or NAK from the receiving device after each block of data sent. However, there is often a sliding window block limit to prevent a modem from transmitting indefinitely without having received either an ACK or NAK. The receiving device still checks each block of data for errors just as it did with discrete ARQ. However, when the receiving device detects an error in a block of data, it sends the block sequence number along with the NAK back to the transmitting device. The transmitting device now knows which particular block of data was received in error, slides the transmission window back to the NAK'd block, and resumes transmission from that point.

Selective ARQ: Continuous ARQ's requirement to retransmit *all* blocks of data from the NAK'd block forward is more efficient than discrete ARQ but could still be more efficient. **Selective ARQ** only requires retransmission of specific blocks received in error rather than all blocks subsequent to the block in which the error was detected.

Flow Control   How does the transmitting device remember what data was in which block? Obviously, the data must be stored and saved somewhere in the block sequence order in which it was transmitted. That somewhere is in **buffer memory.** The addition of this buffer memory as well as the sophisticated programming necessary to manage the flow of data into and out of this memory adds additional costs to these devices. In making informed business decisions on technology acquisition, one must weigh the benefits of increased data throughput and resultant reduced phone circuit usage against the increased cost of this more sophisticated technology.

The constant storage and retrieval of blocks of data from this finite amount of buffer memory necessitates some type of management of the use of this memory. That management is commonly known as **flow control.** Simply stated, flow control controls the flow of data into and out of the buffer memory in order to avoid any loss of data. The flow control management software must constantly monitor the amount of free space available in buffer memory and tell the sending device to stop sending data when there is insufficient storage space. That signal to stop sending data, and the subsequent signal to resume sending data, may be either hardware or software based.

Hardware flow control—RTS/CTS: Hardware flow control was actually introduced in Chapter 2 in the section "RS-232." Pin 4, Request to Send (RTS), and pin 5, Clear to Send (CTS), are the essential elements of hardware flow control. A transmitting device will only send data into buffer memory as long as pin 5, Clear to Send, continues to be "held high" or carry an appropriate voltage. As soon as Clear to Send is "dropped", or the appropriate voltage ceases on pin 5, the transmitting device immediately ceases transmitting data.

Software flow control—XON/XOFF: Instead of using pins 4 and 5 to control flow, actual characters could be transmitted on pin 2 and received on pin 3, which would mean either "Stop Sending Data" or "Resume Sending Data." When a device cannot receive data any longer, it sends an XOFF control character to the transmitting device. The more familiar keyboard representation of XOFF is the keystroke combination CTRL-S. The transmitting device would not resume data transmission until it received an XON control character, CTRL-Q on the keyboard.

Practical Advice and Information

It has been the author's experience that hardware flow control is more reliable and probably faster than software flow control. Remember that software flow control is nothing more than transmitted characters susceptible to the same transmission problems as normal data. Occasionally, an XOFF may be transmitted in error and stop a data transmission session for no apparent reason. Secondly, because XON and XOFF are characters, they are received on pin 3 along with all the "normal" data and must be differentiated from that data. This process takes time and is subject to error.

Forward Error Correction   Sophisticated error correction techniques exist that send sufficient redundant data to the receiving modem to enable it to not only detect but also correct data transmission errors in some cases, without the need for retransmission. Forward error correction works in a similar manner to the data correction techniques previously explained. On the transmitting side, the incoming data signal is processed and redundant code bits are generated based on that incoming signal. These additional redundant bits are added to the original signal and transmitted to the receiving device. The receiving device processes the incoming data signal in the same manner as the transmitting device and regenerates the redundant code bits. The transmitted redundant code bits are compared with the redundant code bits just regenerated by the receiving modem. If they match, then no errors have occurred on the incoming signal. If they don't match, the forward error correction circuitry at the receiving device uses the transmitted redundant bits to correct the incoming data signal, thereby correcting transmission errors without the need for retransmission.

However, beware. In data communications as in life, you can't get something for nothing. To give the receiving modem sufficient redundant data to be able to correct its own detected errors, the overall throughput of informational data on the circuit is reduced. This process, known as **forward error correction,** tries to favorably balance how much redundant data can be sent "up front," thereby avoiding costly retransmissions, in order to maximize overall throughput on the circuit. It's a bit of a gamble really:

- Don't send enough redundant data and the overall throughput is reduced due to retransmissions.

- Send too much redundant data and the overall throughput is reduced because the redundant data is taking up space and processing power that could be occupied by "new," nonredundant, informational data.

Trellis-Coded Modulation: **Trellis-coded modulation (TCM)** is another way in which transmission errors can be overcome without the need for retransmission. Modems that employ TCM are able to overcome twice as much noise on a given circuit as QAM modems, which don't employ TCM. Intersymbol interference can cause a modem to detect the wrong constellation point and subsequently interpret that constellation point into an incorrect sequence of bits. Using a sophisticated technique known as **convolutional encoding.** TCM adds a redundant bit, which limits the possible valid constellation points for the current transmission. By limiting the number of possible constellation points that are potentially valid for any given symbol received, the modem is able to avoid misinterpreting symbols that would ordinarily lead to retransmissions to correct the error.

For example, if we wanted to send 6 data bits per baud, that would ordinarily require a 64-point constellation (2^6). However, by adding a seventh TCM code bit to each 6 data bits, a 128-point constellation would be generated (2^7). But remember, only 64 constellation points are required to transmit the original 6 data bits per baud, so only 64 of the 128 possible detectable constellation points are defined as valid. If one of the invalid constellation points is detected, the TCM circuitry selects the most likely valid constellation point and its associated pattern of bits. In this manner, TCM reduces errors and the need for retransmission due to line impairments. However, error detection and correction techniques must still be employed.

The sophistication of a given TCM scheme is measured by the number of potential trellis codes or states. The greater the number of TCM states, the higher the required processing power in the modems, and the higher immunity to intersymbol interference due to line noise. TCM was first introduced as part of the V.32 modem standard. V.34 modems support 16-, 32-, and 64-state trellis codes.

Error Control Standards

MNP 4:   MNP standards for error control implemented by both Microcom modems and modems of other manufacturers include MNP Classes 2, 3, and 4. These error control standards optimize the full-duplex transmission of data over dial-up lines through adaptive size packet assembly and the elimination of redundant or overhead information from transmissions.

V.42:   **V.42** not to be confused with the CCITT V.42bis standard for data compression, actually incorporates MNP Class 4 error control as the first of two possible error control protocols. In addition, a second error control produced known as **link access protocol for modems,** or **LAP-M,** adds selective ARQ to the capabilities of MNP Class 4 error control protocol. Selective ARQ, described earlier, only requires retransmission of specific blocks received in error rather than all blocks subsequent to the block in which the error was detected. V.42 also provides for negotiation during modem handshaking to allow two modems to decide whether they will implement MNP 4 or LAP-M as an error control protocol for their data transmission.

Practical Advice and Information

MNP 4 and V.42 are error control protocols implemented within modems. Using these protocols, the modems themselves ensure error-free transmission. There is no need for additional error control protocols supplied by communications software packages running as an application program on a PC.

Dial Backup/Auto Restoral   Leasing either an analog or digital dedicated circuit (leased line) from a phone company can provide high-bandwidth data transmission of guaranteed quality. That's the good news.

The bad news is that, despite what the phone company sales rep may say, *leased lines do fail.* It should stand to reason that the more complicated the circuit, the more likely it is to fail. It has been my experience that multipoint lines are more likely to fail than point-to-point leased lines.

MANAGERIAL PERSPECTIVE

Coping with leased line failure requires a business decision. The technology is available to backup failed leased lines by automatically establishing connections via dial-up lines between points on the failed circuit. However, there are at least two incremental costs involved in this automatic backup. First, there is the cost of the additional technology necessary to detect the leased line failure and establish the dial-up connection. Second, dial-up circuits must be available for the auto-dial backup unit to utilize in the event of a leased line failure. These dial-up circuits would incur both installation and monthly charges whether they are used or not. In addition, if the established dial backup connection is long distance, then per-minute usage charges for the dial-up lines could amount to a significant incremental cost. The other side of the cost/benefit equation would require the following question to be asked: "What is the cost of the business lost during the time that the leased line is down?" If that lost business can be translated into lost sales dollars in excess of the incremental cost of establishing and maintaining the dial-up backup for the failed leased line, then the acquisition of the equipment and phone lines to enable automatic backup would constitute a prudent business decision.

Some leased line modems possess sufficient technology to be able to monitor the failed leased line after establishing the **dial backup,** sense when service on the leased line has been repaired and has stabilized, and automatically restore the data transmission back onto the leased line in a process known as **auto restoral.** Sometimes this automatic backup and/or restoral capability is built into the modem (analog) of CSU/DSU (digital). These built-in features are known as integral whereas the dedicated devices that are designed to only do automatic backup and/or restoral are known as standalone devices. In this way, the automatic backup and restoral capability can be added after the initial modem or CSU/DSU purchase, if required.

CSU/DSUs used on digital leased lines can offer an additional backup option as compared with analog modems. Automatic backup and restoral features on a CSU/DSU have a choice as to which available switched or dial-up services to access when establishing the backup connection. Some digital CSU/DSUs access analog dial-up lines from the public switched telephone network (PSTN) for backup, while other CSU/DSUs access switched 56K or ISDN dial-up digital services in the event of a digital leased line failure.

One of the major functions of the CSU/DSU is to perform diagnostic tests to determine the cause of service interruption. A word of warning—If you buy your own CSU/DSUs rather than rent or buy them from the provider of the DDS service, you run the risk of being stuck between the proverbial rock and a hard place during service interruptions when

- The DDS leased line provider says the problem is in your CSU/DSU.
- The CSU/DSU provider says the problem is in your DDS service.

Many DDS providers also rent or sell the CSU/DSUs. In my experience, there is no significant difference in price between buying CSU/DSUs from the carriers and buying them from a data communications equipment distributor. By buying CSU/DSUs from the DDS provider, you will be able to make the provider totally responsible for the delivery of the service through their DCEs to your DTEs, thereby avoiding any possible fingerpointing.

More Secure

In addition to the need for reliable data communications, there exists an increasing business need for both security of transmitted data and controlled access to the corporate network over which that data is transmitted. Modem technology has been developed that provides solutions to both of these security-related issues. Although network security will be dealt with in detail in a dedicated chapter (Chapter 13), security issues related to modem-based transmission are detailed here.

Granting dial-up network access to only those individuals properly authorized is most often accomplished through either one or both of the following techniques:

- **Password protection.**
- **Dial back or callback security.**

Password Protection and Callback Units   Password protection may already be familiar as a means of controlling access to a local area network, minicomputer, or mainframe. However, it is important to understand that, in this case, it is an additional layer of password protection that is offered by certain modems or auxiliary add-on devices. Typically, a modem would answer an incoming call and require a password to allow the calling party access to the network. Failure to enter a valid password in a limited amount of time will cause the answering modem to terminate the call. However, as telecommuting and remote access have increased in popularity, the need for increased levels of dial-in security have increased proportionately.

Some modems add on additional layers of security beyond password protection. Once a valid password (and sometimes user ID also) has been entered, the answering modem

1. Terminates the call.
2. Looks up and validates the user ID and/or password in a directory.
3. Finds the phone number of the valid user in the directory.
4. Dials back the valid user and establishes the communication session.

Do not confuse this dial back unit with the dial backup unit employed for leased line failure recovery. The advantages of a dial back system include the following:

- Only valid users can gain access to the network.
- Valid users are easily maintained in one central directory. By merely eliminating terminated employees from the directory, one can prevent unauthorized network access. Of course, this assumes that users do not tell each other their passwords, either purposefully or accidentally.
- Users can also have network access restricted according to time of day or day of the week. This information would also be stored in the central directory.

- Some dial back units save and report usage information such as user ID, date and time, length of session, resources accessed, etc.

The disadvantages of a dial back system include the following:

- By always dialing back valid users, the central location of the dial back unit always incurs any long-distance phone charges.

- The fixed dial back phone number for each valid user does not work well for traveling users such as field representatives.

Only calling back users at a previously designated phone number is known as **fixed callback.** To overcome this problem, some dial back units feature **variable callback,** wherein valid users enter both a password and a phone number to which the dial back unit should return the call.

Modem Trends

As modem manufacturers search for new ways to expand market share, the new modems that they produce tend to offer customers either more speed or more convenience. In some cases, these modems require new transmission services other than POTS. While many of these new and alternative types of modems are described in Figure 3-10, their associated transmission services will be explained further in later chapters.

Modem or Access Device	Transmission Service	Transmission Speeds	Features
Enhanced V.34 modems (V.34+)	POTS	33.6 Kbps	• Extend V.34 standard to 33.6 Kbps • Provide V.80 interface for H.324 videoconferencing • Provide Ethernet LAN connectivity in a single device
56-Kbps modems	POTS	56 Kbps downstream only, 33.6 or 28.8 Kbps upstream; FCC currently limits POTS transmission to 53 Kbps	• Designed especially for connection to Internet service providers • Provides 56-Kbps download and 28.8- or 33.6-Kbps upload; standards under development • Actual speeds achieved are very debatable due to line quality constraints • Assume Internet service provider and all intermediate links are totally digital
Digital simultaneous voice data (DSVD)	POTS	28.8 Kbps	• Allows simultaneous voice and data transmission to a single location • Beware of support of emerging V.70 standard • Requires compatible communications software • Beneficial for technical support, telecommuting, and long-distance collaborative computing

Figure 3-10   Modem Trends: Faster and More Convenient

Modem or Access Device	Transmission Service	Transmission Speeds	Features
Analog simultaneous voice data (ASVD)	POTS	28.8 Kbps	• Not true simultaneous voice and data; actually switches quickly between the two • Proprietary standard • Requires compatible communications software
Cable modems	Cable TV system	10–60 Mbps	• Used as Internet access, telecommuting remote access, or alternative to T-1 leased lines • Some cable companies only support one-way broadcast; requires dial-up side channel for return path • Intercable company incompatibilities can be a problem
Cellular modems	Cellular phone network	2–3-Kbps normal throughput	• Support for cellular-specific protocols such as enhanced throughput cellular (ETC), MNP 10 (ACE), and enhanced cellular communications (ECC) • Differ in their ability to interface to a variety of different cellular phones • Differ in their ability to establish and maintain connections in spite of line impairments
Wired/wireless modems	POTS and private packet radio networks such as RAM or ARDIS	POTS: 28.8 Kbps; wireless: 8–19.2 Kbps	• Provide convenience of wireless and wireline modems in a single package • Communications software to wireless modems must be included
Asymmetric digital subscriber line (ADSL)	ADSL	Up to 8 Mbps one-way, 640 Kbps return	• Requires ADSL transmission service; only deployed in pilot tests • May replace ISDN as service of choice for home Internet access • Service called VDSL (very high bit rate digital subscriber line) may support speeds of 55 Mbps
ISDN modem	ISDN	128 Kbps	• Can provide support for simultaneous voice and data • Sometimes referred to as digital modems, terminal adapters, or NT-1 units • Requires ISDN transmission service, not universally available • Sometimes included in hybrid V.34/ISDN modems that can automatically switch between POTS and ISDN services
CSU/DSU	Switched or leased digital services	56 Kbps to 45 Mbps depending on digital service	• Will include dialing capability if interfaced to switched digital service such as switched 56K • Must be compatible with speed of digital service with which it must interface

Figure 3-10   Continued

	Transmission			Error	Data																Fax														
	Protocols				Cntrl.	Compression		Physical Characteristics											Features			Transmission Services							Support Services					
	V.34	V.FC	V.32bis	V.32	V.32terbo	V.22bis	V.42	MNP 4	V.42bis	V.42bis dictionary size	V.42bis string length	MNP 5	PCMCIA/external/internal	Maximum DCE speed	Maximum DTE speed	Serial port	Parallel port	2-wire interface	4-wire interface	Dial-up	Leased line	Group 3	Class 1	Class 2	POTS	ISDN	Cellular	Analog leased	Caller ID support	DSVD	Distinctive ring	Software included	Cables included	Flash ROM upgradeable	Warranty	Tech support options/cost
Modem A																																				
Modem B																																				
Modem C																																				
Modem D																																				
.																																				
.																																				
.																																				
Modem Z																																				

Figure 3-11　Modem Technology Analysis Grid

Modem Technology Analysis　With the functionality of modems thoroughly studied, a technology analysis grid such as the one illustrated in Figure 3-11 could be constructed. As a network analyst, you would decide which of the myriad of available modem functions listed along the horizontal axis of the technology analysis grid were most important to your business. This analysis would be accomplished using the top-down model as described at the beginning of this chapter (Figure 3-1). Next, the functional characteristics present in various modems from a variety of vendors (vertical axis; modems A–Z) would be plotted on the technology analysis grid. In this manner, you would be able to graphically see which modems met the functional requirements of your business for the best price.

■ COMMUNICATIONS SOFTWARE TECHNOLOGY ANALYSIS

The Hardware/Software Interface

Communications software interprets business data communications needs into a language that the data communications hardware can understand. Communications software is an application program that should offer easy to understand screens from which users can initiate, maintain, and terminate data communications sessions. Commands entered or menu items selected in the communications software are passed along to the operating system of the PC in question, which, in turn, interfaces directly to the PC's hardware such as an integral modem card or serial

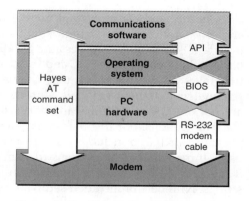

Figure 3-12   The Role of Communications Software

port. Communications software is the interface between data communications desires and the data communications hardware. Figure 3-12 graphically illustrates where communications software fits and the numerous interfaces involved in a PC-based data communications sessions. As can be seen in Figure 3-12, several interfaces are involved in the process of the communications software's interaction with a modem.

- The communications software must be compatible with the operating system of the PC. Application programs such as communications software interact with an operating system via **application program interfaces (API).** APIs are a series of commands embedded within the communications software that are understood by the installed operating system. APIs will be discussed further in later chapters.

- The operating system interacts with the PC hardware (CPU, memory, serial port, etc.) via a series of commands known as the **basic input output system (BIOS).**

- Physically, the PC is connected to the external modem via an RS-232 modem cable connected to the PC's serial port.

Hayes AT Command Set and the Modem Setup Strings   The interfaces described in the previous section establish a physical link between the communications software and the modem. But how can the communications software talk to the modem? What language or commands does the modem understand? How does the communications software wake up or initialize the modem?

The answer to all of these questions is that the de facto standard for commands that are mutually understood by both communications software and modems is the **Hayes AT command set.** The "AT" in the Hayes AT command set is itself a command that stands for "attention," a command sent from the communications software to the modem to gain its attention. Other examples of commands are ATDT followed by a number, which means tone dial the given number, or ATDP, which means pulse dial the given number. Pauses can also be inserted into a dial string to wait for a second dial tone for an outside line. Modems that understand commands from the Hayes AT command set are known as **Hayes compatible.**

One of the most important uses of the Hayes AT command set is to construct and send **modem setup strings** from the communications software to the modem to initiate a communications session. Sending the modem setup string amounts to a handshaking between the PC and the modem. Although nearly all modems support the Hayes AT command set, they can vary widely in the particular commands and parameters that must be included in their modem setup strings. These setup strings are not always straightforward nor easily written by novices to the field of data communications. For this reason, it is important that the communications software package purchased includes a setup string for the modem or modems that are to be used. If many different modems from many different manufacturers are to be used, it is essential to purchase a communications software package with numerous setup strings. Numbers of included setup strings may vary from none to several hundred.

Redirection for Local Area Network Based Modems   The previous example of a hardware/software interface assumed that a dedicated external modem was attached to the local PC's serial port. What would happen if the local PC were attached to a local area network (LAN) and the modem was attached to the LAN server rather than to the local serial port as illustrated in Figure 3-13?

Sharing modems in this way can be a very cost-effective alternative to all users having their own dedicated modems. The shared modems are hooked to a high-powered PC known as a server. In some cases, the sole job of this server is to manage modem access and other data communications related tasks, in which case it is known as a **communications server** or **remote access server.**

Even though a user's PC is hooked to a network, the communications software is still running on that individual user's PC. The difficulty arises in that the modem is not hanging off the serial port of the user's PC where the communications software would normally expect to find it. To access the modem attached to the network's communication server, the communications software must send instructions and data out through the PC's **network interface card** rather than the PC's serial port. A network interface card is a board that plugs into a PC and allows the network's cabling to attach this particular PC to other PCs on the same network.

To redirect modem output to a network interface card rather than the local serial port, a communications package must support two specialized interfaces or interrupts.

- If the local area network is using Novell's NetWare network operating system, then the communications software must be able to redirect modem output to a software interface known as **NASI (NetWare asynchronous service interface)** so that communications can be redirected by the local operating system to the local network interface card rather than the local serial port.

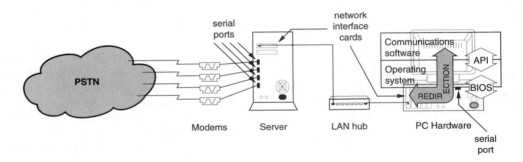

Figure 3-13   Redirection for Local Area Network Based Modems

- If the local area network is using a Microsoft network operating system, then the communications software must be able to redirect modem output to a software interface known as **Int14 (interrupt 14).**

Applied Problem Solving

Not all communications software packages support LAN redirection. If this function is required, be sure to carefully review technical specifications of communications software packages being considered.

Communications Software Functionality

Applied Problem Solving

TOP-DOWN APPROACH TO COMMUNICATIONS SOFTWARE ANALYSIS

How can a network analyst ensure that the *right* communications software package is purchased? In a manner similar to that employed for modem analysis at the beginning of the chapter, by following a top-down approach, network analysts can ensure that purchased communications software meets stated business objectives.

Business Issues: The first concerns in the top-down approach to needs analysis are the business-related needs. In Figure 3-14, the business layer model has been divided into two distinct segments, namely, business perspectives and business activities. Business perspectives are those overriding business needs that underlie specific business activities. These business perspectives are key assumptions that must be documented before business activity analysis begins. Examples of business perspectives related to communications software might be

1. Communications software must be easy to use.
2. Communications software must maximize the efficient use of available hardware and transmission services.
3. Communications software must be cost-effective (purchase prices can range from free to $400 or more).
4. Communications software must support overall business objectives such as improved customer service, more efficient operations, better and faster information to decision-makers, etc.

These themes of ease of use, maximum efficiency, cost-effectiveness, and support of overall business objectives serve as the starting point for requirements of the business layer that will be passed down to lower layers of the top-down model. It is important to note that other nonlisted business perspectives as dictated by yourself or your business should be added to this model at this layer and evaluated through subsequent layers.

Broadly speaking, the following items summarize typical business uses of communications software. Again, you should add your own unlisted business uses of communications software, if any.

1. Connect to a remote minicomputer or mainframe and login as a remote terminal.
2. Transfer files from PC to PC or from PC to minicomputer/mainframe.
3. Connect to value-added information services such as the Internet, CompuServe, Prodigy, Dow-Jones, etc.
4. Support integration with fax services.

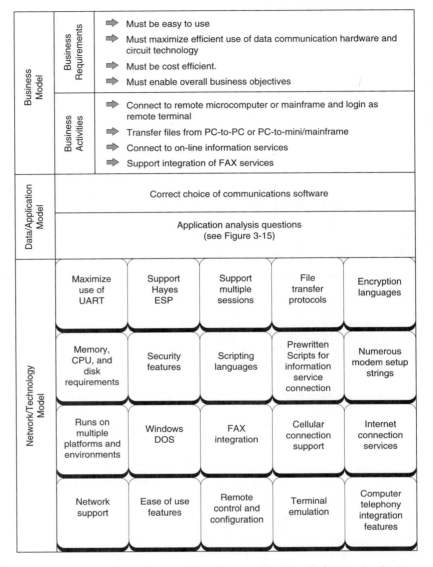

Figure 3-14   Top-Down Approach to Communications Software Analysis

Although these general statements summarize the most popular uses of communications software, additional analysis is necessary to determine the best communications software package for an individual or company based on particular required business activities and perspectives.

Analysis Questions Map Technical Features to Business Needs: Notice the placement of the "Correct Choice of Communications Software" in the top-down analysis model (Figure 3-14). It bridges the gap between the business perspectives and activities of the upper business layer and the myriad of technical features found in different communications software packages as listed in the network model or technology layer.

Figure 3-15 summarizes some key analysis questions used to assist in determining the best communications software package for a particular individual or

Analysis Question/Technical Feature	Importance/Implication
What are the hardware requirements of the communications software package?	Some packages require up to 16 MB of memory, minimum 486 chip, and 60 MB of disk space.
Which minicomputer or mainframe do you wish to log into?	Logging into minicomputers or mainframes requires terminal emulation. Variety of terminals emulated varies from 10 to 36.
Do you wish to transfer files to/from a PC, minicomputer, or mainframe?	Same file transfer protocol must run on each machine. Number of file transfer protocols ranges from 8 to 16. Some packages offer high-performance proprietary transfer protocols.
Is the modem hooked directly to your PC or to a modem server?	Not all communications packages are able to redirect output to network interface cards. Different network operating systems use different redirection interrupts.
Do you want to log onto the Internet or other information services?	Software packages vary in the number of browsers included and in the number of prewritten scripts included for automatic access to information services.
What are your security requirements? Will other users be dialing into this computer?	Security features might include password protection/encryption, data encryption, callback security support, or remote file transfer lock out.
Do your modems support V.42 and/or MNP 4 error control?	If not, the file transfer protocols included in the communications software will have to supply their own error control.
Will remote control or configuration be required?	Some packages offer remote control capabilities.
Will you be using a cellular phone network with this software?	Some packages include special enhancements to improve performance over cellular networks.
Will you be sending/receiving faxes through this software?	Some communications software packages include integrated fax functionality.
Will you need to control your phone from your PC?	Some packages offer computer telephony integration functionality such as on-screen telephone pad and dialer or support of CTI APIs.
How many different computers and operating systems does this software run on?	In a multiplatform environment, it would be nice to be able to run all of the same communications software.
Will modems of numerous manufacturers be used?	If so, you will want a communications software package with as many modem setup strings as possible.
Will you need to conduct more than one communications session simultaneously?	Some communications software packages support management of multiple simultaneous communications sessions.

Figure 3-15   Analysis Questions Map Technical Features to Business Needs

business as well as the options and implications of those questions. Analysis questions are designed to help the network analyst decide which communications software features are most important to have the purchased communications software meet stated business objectives. Again, add to the list of analysis questions as you see fit.

As the implications of each of the questions listed in Figure 3-15 are explored, each of the technical features listed in the network/technical model layer of Figure 3-14 will be explained. Few, if any communications software packages contain all of these features. Furthermore, few, if any, businesses need all of these features. The real challenge is to determine which of these technical features are truly necessary to support business activities and then to find the best-priced communications software package that offers those features.

FILE TRANSFER PROTOCOLS

In Sharper Focus

As identified on the business activities layer of our top-down model, the establishment, management, and termination of file transfers constitute one of the most common uses of communications software. Obviously, these file transfers must be free of errors. In some cases, the necessary error control is supplied as a function of the modems employed in the data transmission. MNP Class 4 and V.42, discussed earlier in this chapter, are two of the most common model-based error control protocols.

File transfer protocols, part of a communications software package, can also offer error control capabilities. As many as 15 or more file transfer protocols may be included in a given communications software package. If the modems to be used for data transmission do not supply their own error control, then be sure to purchase communications software that includes sufficient file transfer protocols with error control. Remember, for modems to furnish error control capabilities over a data transmission circuit, *both* modems must support the same error control protocol. Figure 3-16 summarizes the characteristics of popular file transfer protocols, including their error control capabilities.

As seen in Figure 3-16, file transfer protocols can differ by a relatively few criteria:

1. Error checking technique: Checksum, CRC, CRC-16, CRC-32.

2. Request for retransmit: stop and wait ACK/NAK, sliding window, none (streaming).

3. Block size in bytes: 128, 1024, variable depending on line quality.

4. Others: Batch capability, multiple platforms, auto-recovery.

File transfer protocols with the suffix of "G" (XMODEM-G, YMODEM-G) are known as **streaming protocols** because they do not stop transmitting a file until they reach an end-of-file indicator. These file transfer protocols are an appropriate choice if error control is being handled by the modems using MNP Class 4 or V.42 error control protocols. In these cases, since the error control is being handled by the hardware, there is no need for the communications software to add additional error control and its associated overhead.

Block size may be of a fixed length of either 128 or 1024 bytes, or it may vary according to the quality of the data transmission circuit. The adaptive packet length

File Transfer Protocol	Differentiating Features	Block Size	Error Control	Application Notes
XMODEM-checksum		128 bytes/block	ACK/NAK stop and wait ARQ, checksum error control	Public domain, widely used; stop and wait ARQ is not efficient
XMODEM-CRC	CRC improves error detection			
XMODEM-1K	1024 bytes (1 KB) per block	1024 bytes/block; 128 bytes/block fallback		Sometimes called YMODEM; uses CRC, may have batch capability
XMODEM-G	G implies a streaming protocol			File transfer protocol offers no error control; relies on modems with MNP 4 or V.42
YMODEM-CRC-16	Adds CRC-16 error control to YMODEM		CRC-16	
YMODEM-Batch	Batch capability			Allows transfers to be controlled by separate executable files; supports multiple file transfers at a given time
ZMODEM	Dynamically adjusts packet size as in MNP 4; automatic recovery from aborted file transfers		CRC-32 sliding window	Widely used by BBS users
Kermit	Multiple platform availability		ACK/NAK stop and wait ARQ	Great for transfers to minicomputers or mainframes; not very fast
Sliding window Kermit	Adds sliding window ARQ to Kermit		Continuous ARQ	Faster; may not be available on all of the platforms that Kermit is available on

Figure 3-16   Comparative Features of File Transfer Protocols

protocols will usually produce the greatest throughput on circuits of varying quality. Other features that may be important depending on the detailed business activities as analyzed in the top-down analysis might include

- Batch capability, which would allow multiple file transfers to take place sequentially without user intervention.

- Multiple platform capability, which is essential for those users or businesses wishing to conduct PC to minicomputer or mainframe file transfers. Kermit is an excellent example of a multiplatform file transfer protocol.

- Finally, **ZMODEM** offers a unique feature that has become especially popular with BBS (bulletin board service) users who pay by the minute for connection to online bulletin boards. An auto-recovery feature allows an aborted file transfer to resume at the point where the transfer aborted rather than starting the transfer over at the beginning of the file. Amazingly, it also doesn't matter when the transfer is resumed, assuming both files still exist.

Technology Analysis

Communications software, like most data communications technology, has undergone significant evolution in the past few years. Modem manufacturers now often include high-quality communications software at no extra cost to differentiate their products from those of competitors. Operating systems now often include communications software functionality. As a result, many of today's communications software packages are more correctly categorized as remote control or remote access products designed primarily to assist telecommuting professionals in accessing corporate data resources from their offices. Remote control and remote access software will be reviewed in Chapter 10, Remote Access and Wireless Networking. Following are a few of the currently popular communications software packages and their vendors:

Communications Software Package	Vendor
CommSuite 95	Delrina Group, Symantec Corp.
Crosstalk for Windows	Digital Communications Associates Inc.
HyperAccess 2.1A	Hilgraeve, Inc.
LapLink for Windows	Traveling Software Inc.
pcAnywhere32	Symantec Corp.
Procomm Plus 3.0 for Windows	Datastorm Technologies, Inc.
Qmodem Pro	Mustang Software, Inc.
Remotely Possible/32	Avalan Technology, Inc.
Smartcom Message Center	Hayes Microcomputer Products, Inc.

Figure 3-17 is a communications software technology analysis grid. Technical features of communications software packages are outlined along the horizontal axis. The implications or importance of these features was highlighted in Figure 3-15. Currently available communications software packages would be listed along the vertical axis. The technical features available in any given package would be plotted within the technology analysis grid. Having determined which technical features were most important in meeting stated business objectives, the network analyst could easily and objectively determine which communications software package would offer the greatest required functionality for the best price.

Communications Software Technology Analysis Grid

Category	Feature	Comm Software A	Comm Software B	Comm Software C	Comm Software D	.	.	.	Comm Software Z
System Requirements	RAM memory								
	Disk space								
	CPU chip								
	Windows 3X								
	Windows 95								
	Windows NT								
	OS/2								
	Other platforms								
File Transfer	Number of file transfer protocols								
	File transfer in background								
	Supports external protocols								
Network Redirectors	NASI								
	Int 14								
	TCP/IP support								
Internet Connectors	FTP file transfer								
	Archie search								
	Gopher browse								
	Web browser								
	News reader								
	Mail service								
Security Features	Password protection								
	Data encryption								
	Callback capability								
	Remote file transfer lock out								
	Private messages/mail								
	Log calls								
Fax and Phone Features	Fax support								
	Switch from data to voice								
	Telephone pad, dialer								
	Answering machine, voice mail								
	Audio editor								
	Import/Export ASCII phone directory								
	Import/Export from other comm software								
	Number of phone directories								
	Number of entries per directory								
Program Features	Context-sensitive help								
	Text editor included								
	Functions supplied on ICON bar								
	Direct cable connection supported								
	Maximum number of com ports supported								
	Number of terminal emulations supported								
	Number of modem setup strings								
	32-bit multithreaded design								
	Modem indicator lights								
	Unattended host mode								
Script Features	Number of prewritten scripts								
	Number of script language verbs								
	Auto-learn/scrollback buffer facility								

Figure 3-17 Communications Software Technology Analysis Grid

SUMMARY

By employing the top-down model in the analysis of currently available modem technology, any modem functionality should deliver on at least one of the following business communications requirements: faster, more efficient (cheaper), more reliable, or more secure.

By focusing on how data communications devices of any type deliver on predetermined business requirements and objectives, one can avoid purchasing technology that may be appealing or cleverly marketed but that lacks the ability to deliver a positive impact on business objectives.

Current modulation standards such as V.34 (28.8 Kbps) can deliver even more throughput over dial-up lines when compression standards such as MNP 5 or V.42bis are applied. As this increasing sophistication in dial-up modems has yielded ever faster transmission speeds over dial-up lines, the types of network services offered by carriers have also evolved. ISDN is a dial-up digital service offering 128 Kbps that has become a popular option for Internet access. Since ISDN is a digital service, it does not require a modem, but rather a device known alternatively as a terminal adapter, digital modem, or NT-1.

Reliability of data transmissions is ensured by the net effect of three related processes: error prevention, error detection, and error correction. Error prevention can be accomplished via forward error correction techniques such as TCM

or through adaptive protocols that adjust transmission characteristics in response to changing line conditions. Error detection is accomplished through a variety of techniques in which the transmitting and receiving modems transit and verify some sort of error check bit or character in addition to the transmitted data itself. Techniques such as parity, LRC, checksums, CRC-16, and CRC-32 vary in both the level of complexity of their error-checking routines and their ability to detect bursts of multiple bit errors.

Error correction is accomplished in general through retransmission of those characters received in error. Techniques such as discrete, ARQ, continuous ARQ, and selective ARQ vary in how efficiently their retransmission is accomplished.

Security is provided by a variety of techniques that can be integrated into modems or added via standalone devices. Callback access combined with password protection are typical modem-based security features.

Communications software is a key component in linking a user's communications requirements to the modems and network services that deliver on those desires. Communications software varies widely in features and price. As a result, a careful business-oriented analysis is required using a technology analysis grid such as that supplied in this chapter to objectively compare the many technological alternatives in a structured manner.

KEY TERMS

ACE, 73
ACK/NAK, 82
acknowledgment, 82
adaptive protocols, 77
adaptive size packet assembly, 77
advanced parallel technology, 75
adverse channel enhancements, 73
amplifier, 77
API, 91
application program interface, 91
APT, 75
ARQ, 82
attenuation, 77

automatic retransmission request, 82
auto restoral, 86
basic input output system, 91
Bell 103, 69
Bell 212A, 69
BIOS, 91
block sequence number, 83
buffer memory, 83
callback security, 87
checksums, 80
communications server, 92
continuous ARQ, 83

convolutional encoding, 85
CRC, 81
CRC-16, 81
CRC-32, 81
cyclic redundancy check, 81
data compression, 71
dial backup, 86
Discrete ARQ, 82
Dynamic speed shifts, 77
Error correction, 76
Error detection, 76
Error prevention, 76
FireWire (IEEE 1394-1995), 76

REVIEW QUESTIONS

1. How is a technology analysis grid employed in a business networking requirements analysis and design?
2. What is the difference between discrete ARQ and continuous ARQ?
3. What inefficiency is inherent in a data transmission session utilizing discrete ARQ over a full-duplex circuit?
4. Which modulation technique is employed in a V.34 modem?
5. What is the potential throughput of a V.34 modem with V.42bis data compression?
6. Why are standards important when it comes to data compression?
7. How can the top-down model remain useful given the rate of rapidly changing technology?
8. What is the relationship between the number of points in a constellation and the number of data bits interpreted per detectable event?
9. What effect does trellis-coded modulation have on the number of constellation points and the number of data bits interpreted per detectable events?
10. What is meant by an adaptive protocol? Give at least two examples.
11. What are the key differences between V.32 and V.32bis?
12. What does *bis* stand for?
13. What is V.Fast?
14. How does V.32terbo differ from V.32bis and V.34?
15. Explain the significance of the phrase "fully standard compliant" in terms of modem standards.
16. How does data compression work?
17. Why can't a 4:1 compression ratio always be achieved with V.42bis?
18. What is the difference between V.42 and V.42bis?
19. Why is error-free transmission so important to successful data compression?
20. In general, what are the advantages of DDS over analog leased lines?
21. How can one avoid being caught in the middle of fingerpointing when purchasing a CSU/DSU?
22. Why is a CSU/DSU different in function than a modem?
23. What are some of the most common uses of switched digital services?
24. What is handshaking and what does it have to do with modem interoperability?
25. What is the Hayes AT command set and why is it significant?
26. Elaborate on the relationship between error prevention, error detection, and error correction.
27. What are the major differences between repeaters and amplifiers?
28. Explain how multiple bit errors can remain undetected using simple parity checking.
29. Explain how LRC overcomes parity checking's inability to detect multiple bit errors.
30. Explain in simple terms how checksums and CRCs detect transmission errors.

31. What is meant by a sliding window protocol?
32. What is selective ARQ?
33. How are block sequence numbers related to sliding window protocols?
34. What role does buffer memory play in the implementation of sliding window protocols?
35. Explain the differences between hardware and software flow control.
36. Explain why hardware or software flow control may be more reliable.
37. What is forward error correction and what is the trade-off involved in such a protocol?
38. What is the difference between a dial back unit and a dial backup unit?
39. What is variable callback and when might it be required?
40. What are the potential security risks in variable callback?
41. What are the important issues to consider when purchasing communications software?
42. What are the issues when modems are to be accessed via a LAN rather than directly attached to a PC?
43. What is a UART and how does it relate to communications software choices?
44. What are the key differentiating factors between file transfer protocols?
45. What is the principle of shifting bottlenecks? Give an example.
46. Explain both a short-term and long-term solution to the current PC serial port bottleneck.
47. Explain at least three significant technical innovations introduced as part of the V.34 standard.
48. Differentiate between MNP 5 and V.42bis.
49. Differentiate between MNP 4 and V.42.
50. What are some of the dangers in buying prestandard data communications equipment?

ACTIVITIES

1. Install a modem and associated communications software. Document your installation procedure as well as any problems encountered and problem-solving techniques employed.
2. Using a modem advertisement of your choice or one chosen by your instructor, write a technical memo to a non-technically oriented manager explaining the features of the modem in terms of business layer impact. Prepare a cost/benefit analysis and make a recommendation as to whether or not the modem in question should be purchased.
3. Investigate and report on the difference between modem standards and fax modem standards. Which organizations set fax standards? Does communications software interact with the fax part of the modem or is other software required?
4. Prepare a comparative budget for a long-distance transmission between two cities of your choice. Compare the cost vs. available bandwidth of such a transmission for each of the following three scenarios:
   - V.34 modems, dial-up lines
   - CSU/DSUs, switched 56K lines
   - Digital modems, ISDN lines
5. Investigate the current status of the standardization process for the V.34bis standard. Are other modem standards in progress?
6. Using file transfer or communications software, prepare a graph showing the results of the transfer of various-sized files using different file transfer protocols as outlined in Figure 3-16. Record any error messages received as well as transfer time and file size. Abort and restart the transfer midway using different file transfer protocols and record results.
7. Research and report on the progress being made with high-speed serial ports such as USB and FireWire. Is one standard dominating? Explain your results.
8. Research product tests or buyer's guides of V.34 modems. Report on the results of performance tests regarding actual throughput. What percent of the time is the 28.8 Kbps rate maintained?
9. Research and prepare a presentation on the Hayes AT command set. How many commands are supported? What is the purpose of the registers? What are the limitations?
10. Research and report on the results of the comparative impact of the UART 16550, the Hayes ESP communications accelerator, and Microcom's APT in solving the serial port bottleneck problem.
11. Research and report on the current status of any two of the modem trends listed in Figure 3-10. Did the trends continue to materialize? Were they superseded by other trends?
12. Some communications software packages include scripting languages. What is the business application for such languages and what characteristics or features are important?

PG&E Apps Keep Lights On: Home-Grown and Oracle Applications Manage California's Gas and Electric Needs

For most people, power is a digital commodity—it is either on or off. At Pacific Gas & Electric Co., however, power is decidedly analog.

The San Francisco-based utility supplies gas and electric power to over 3 million customers with ever-changing power needs. Consequently, the company must anticipate its customers' fluctuating demand and fine-tune the power generation of its power-plant network to meet that load.

The question of how much energy to generate is not trivial. If PG&E produces too much energy, it loses money when it has to sell the excess at a discount. If the company produces too little energy, it loses money again when it has to buy energy from other utilities at a premium.

"Our objective is to operate the system at the lowest economic point we can possibly achieve in order to provide the cheapest source of power," said Marc DeNarie, Energy Management Systems (EMS) operations supervisor at PG&E's power-control department.

To meet that objective, DeNarie's department uses a number of applications to provide PG&E's internal users both historical and real-time systems data.

Real-time operational data is managed by the mainframe-based EMS. Historical data, used for load forecasting and stability analysis, is managed by a home-grown data warehouse that is updated in near-real time by the EMS.

The two systems help manage the 110 hydro-, 70 thermal-, and two nuclear-power generators and thousands of miles of transmission lines that constitute PG&E's power network.

Watts in Real Time

PG&E's primary application for power management is the EMS, which runs on redundant Control Data Corp. mainframes. The EMS was built using an ISAM (Indexed Sequential Access Method) database, which makes it difficult to offload real-time data.

To provide the EMS with real-time data, PG&E uses a process it calls telemetering. Every two seconds, more than 400 remote terminals at the company's power-generating plants, substations, and temperature monitors communicate with the mainframe at PG&E's San Francisco headquarters over leased lines and microwave communications. The mainframe then passes the data to the EMS users at four-second intervals.

Data collected from remote terminals includes information concerning line flows, power output, and circuit-breaker status. Information is also collected on ambient temperature of the remote-terminal unit's location.

Transmission-planning engineers, operations-support engineers, upper management, users in power contracts, and others who need to know the real-time status of the company's generating network access the EMS via an Enabling Tools front end.

"The company can save tens of millions of dollars a year in projects and operational expenditures," said DeNarie, "if they have the right data."

To supplement the real-time operations data, PG&E opened a data warehouse earlier this year. The goal is to give users access to historical information that can be used for day-to-day operations—for instance, using temperature histories to forecast loads—as well as for non-operational applications.

Elegant Reporting

In March the company set up an Oracle Corp. Oracle7-based data warehouse on the IBM RS/6000s it was using to run its offline EMS applications at its headquarters. Every 10 seconds, the EMS updates the data warehouse with the EMS telemetering data.

The data warehouse will replace an awkward reporting procedure that funneled user requests through DeNarie's power-management group and included hard-coded reports and Microsoft FoxPro. "It was a nightmare," said DeNarie.

The initial data-warehouse implementation presents at least one problem, however. By giving its 5,000 internal users the ability to run daily and ad hoc reports against the data warehouse, PG&E found it had inadvertently overwhelmed the RS/6000s running the data warehouse.

"The loading seems to be quite high," said DeNarie, "if we let people query directly against the Oracle7 server."

To solve the problem, PG&E plans to move the data warehouse to a dedicated Microsoft Windows NT-based machine with 20GB of disk space. This NT machine will also run Oracle7 in synchronous mode with the RS/6000 so that as updates are made to the RS/6000 they will be made simultaneously to the NT machine.

By isolating the data warehouse from the EMS, DeNarie hopes to ensure EMS' availability to those users who need the real-time data.

"The core business here is keeping the lights on," said DeNarie. "The real-time operation data is critical for us."

Source: Brent Dorshkind, "PG&E Apps Keep Lights On," *LAN Times*, vol. 13, no. 26 (November 25, 1996), p. 45. Copyright © November 25, 1996, McGraw–Hill, New York. Reprinted by permission of McGraw–Hill.

BUSINESS CASE STUDY QUESTIONS

Activities

1. Complete a top-down model for this case by gleaning facts from the case and placing them in the proper layer of the top-down model. After completing the top-down model, analyze and detail those instances where requirements were clearly passed down from upper layers to lower layers of the model and where solutions to those requirements were passed up from lower layers to upper layers of the model.

2. Detail any questions about the case that may occur to you for which answers are not clearly stated in the article.

Business

1. What was the primary business of the company described in this case study?
2. What specific business processes or procedures were described in this case study?
3. What was the financial importance of the proper support of these business processes by information systems?
4. What is the data generated by the remote telemetering application used for?

Application

1. How are applications used to meet business objectives?

Data

1. What is meant by the term "real-time" data in this article?
2. What is the importance of real-time data to this business?
3. What initial decisions as to dictate architectures have made the acquisition of real-time data difficult?
4. What is telemetering?
5. What types of data are collected from remote terminals?
6. What is the potential financial impact of the proper use of the data gathered via telemetering?
7. What is a data warehouse and what types of applications and business processes could be supported by it?
8. What data reporting procedure did the automated data warehouse replace?
9. What was one initial negative impact of the new data warehouse?

Network

1. How is the telemetering application supported by network resources?

Technology

1. Describe which applications, database management systems, and data warehouses are executing on which types of computers.
2. What technology upgrades are planned to improve system performance?

VOICE COMMUNICATIONS CONCEPTS AND TECHNOLOGY

Concepts Reinforced

Top-Down Model   Protocols and Interoperability
OSI Model

Concepts Introduced

Voice Digitization   Data/Voice Integration
Voice Compression   Voice Network Concepts
PBX Functionality and Architecture   Computer Technology Integration
Voice Transmission Alternatives   Voice over the Internet

OBJECTIVES

After mastering the material in this chapter, you should

1. Understand the underlying technical concepts for voice transmission, voice digitization, voice compression, and data/voice integration.

2. Understand currently available voice-related technology, including PBXs, voice digitizers, and voice/data multiplexers and modems.

3. Understand the functionality, concepts, standards, business impact, and technology involved with computer telephony integration.

4. Understand the functionality, concepts, standards, business impact, and technology involved with voice network services, voice transmission alternatives, and voice/data integration.

■ INTRODUCTION

Network analysts must be qualified to design networks that are capable of carrying voice as well as data. Before designing such networks, the network analyst must understand the nature of voice signals as well as how voice signals can be processed and integrated into a cohesive network with data transmissions.

In this chapter, the transmission and integration of voice into data networks is explored. Once voice transmission basic concepts such as voice digitization and compression are understood, the key piece of voice-processing technology known as the PBX or private branch exchange is studied. Increasingly, the PBX is seen as a voice server to be integrated into a client/server information system like any other server. The field of computer technology integration is dedicated to uniting PBXs with information systems.

Once the voice signal has been digitized, a wide variety of transmission services can potentially be employed to complete the transmission of the voice signal to its designated destination. In some cases, these voice transmissions can be easily integrated with a simultaneous data transmission. As is the case with any type of communications system involving the interoperability of multiple pieces of hardware and software technology, standards play an essential role in ensuring end-to-end interoperability.

■ VOICE TRANSMISSION BASIC CONCEPTS

A voice conversation consists of sound waves of varying frequency and amplitude that are represented as a continuously varying analog waveform. The POTS (plain old telephone service) network employed analog transmission methodologies to transmit the voice signals from source to destination.

But how does this analog waveform get from a person's mouth, the human transmitter, onto the analog network and subsequently into the ear, the human receiver, of the person who was called? Figure 4-1 illustrates the mechanics of a typical phone handset, which consists of both transmitter and receiver components.

The telephone handset, consisting of both a transmitter and receiver, is really a fairly simple device that works largely based on the properties of electromagnetism. The **transmitter**, or mouthpiece, consists of a movable diaphragm that is sensitive to changes in voice frequency and amplitude. The diaphragm contains carbon granules that have the ability to conduct electricity. As the human voice spoken into the transmitter varies, the amount of carbon granules striking the electrical contacts in the mouthpiece varies, sending varying analog, electrical signal out onto the voice network.

This constantly varying electrical analog wave is transmitted over the voice network to the phone of the receiving person. The **receiver**, or earpiece portion of the handset, basically works in the opposite fashion of the mouthpiece. The varying electrical waves produced by the transmitter are received at the receiver at an electromagnet. Varying levels of electricity produce varying levels of magnetism that cause the movable diaphragm to move in direct proportion with the magnetic variance. The moving diaphragm produces varying sound waves corresponding to the sound waves that were input at the transmitter. The electromagnetically reproduced sound resembles the actual sound waves input at the transmitter closely enough to allow for voice recognition by the receiving party.

Voice Bandwidth

Although the approximate range of hearing of the human ear is between 15,000 and 20,000 Hz, much less bandwidth than that is used to transmit the electromagnetic representations of analog voice signals over the analog **public switched telephone**

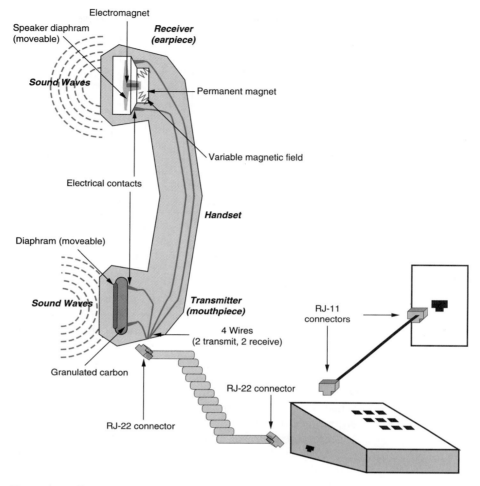

Figure 4-1   Getting Voice onto and off the Network.

network (PSTN). Plain old telephone service (POTS) uses a bandwidth of 4000 Hz including two **guardbands** to prevent interference from adjacent frequencies from interfering with the voice signal. As a result, the usable bandwidth on the local loop circuit connecting an individual's home or business to the phone company's central office for dial-up analog voice transmission is 3000 Hz, from 300 to 3300 Hz. Figure 4-2 illustrates the comparative bandwidths of human speech and the analog phone network.

Voice Digitization

Although the local loop between the local central office and a residence or place of business may be an analog circuit, it is highly unlikely that the continuously varying analog signal representing a person's voice will stay in analog form all the way to the destination location's phone receiver. Rather, it is very likely that high-capacity digital circuits will be employed to transport that call, especially between COs or carriers.

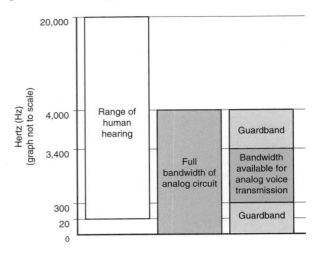

Figure 4-2   Voice Bandwidth

Converting analog voice signals for transmission over digital circuits is the exact opposite of the situation faced when digital data had to be converted into analog form for transmission over the voice network. The fact that carriers may be converting a voice conversation to digital format and reconverting it back to analog form before it reaches its destination is completely transparent to phone network users.

The basic technique for **voice digitization** is relatively simple. The constantly varying analog voice conversation must be sampled frequently enough so that when the digitized version of the voice is converted back to an analog signal, the resultant conversation resembles the voice of the call initiator. Most voice digitization techniques employ a sampling rate of 8000 samples/sec.

A device known as a coder/decoder, or **codec,** is employed to sample analog transmissions and transform them into a stream of binary digits. When a bank of codecs are arranged in a modular chassis to not only digitize analog voice conversations but also load them onto a shared high-capacity (T-1: 1.544 Mbps) circuit, the hybrid device is referred to as a **channel bank.** Codecs and channel banks may be integrated into PBXs or may be purchased separately.

Recalling that a digital signal is just a discrete electrical voltage, there are only a limited number of ways in which the electrical pulses can be varied to represent varying characteristics of an analog voice signal:

- **Pulse amplitude modulation,** or **PAM,** varies the amplitude or voltage of the electrical pulses in relation to the varying characteristics of the voice signal. PAM was the voice digitization technique used in some earlier PBXs.

- **Pulse duration modulation (PDM),** otherwise known as **pulse width modulation (PWM),** varies the duration of each electrical pulse in relation to the variances in the analog signal.

- **Pulse position modulation (PPM)** varies the duration between pulses in relation to variances in the analog signal. By varying the spaces in between the discrete electrical pulses on the digital circuit, PPM focuses on the relative position of the pulses to one another as a means of representing the continuously varying analog signal. Figure 4-3 illustrates these three voice digitization techniques.

PAM: Pulse Amplitude Modulation

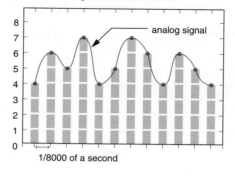

Variable: Pulse amplitude

Constants: Pulse duration, pulse position

Sampling rate = 8,000 times/second

PDM: Pulse Duration Modulation

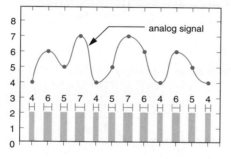

Variable: Pulse duration

Constants: Pulse amplitude, pulse position

PPM: Pulse Position Modulation

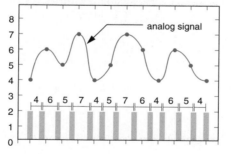

Variable: Pulse position

Constants: Pulse amplitude, pulse duration

Figure 4-3   Voice Digitization: PAM, PDM, and PPM

Pulse Code Modulation (PCM)   Although any of the previously mentioned methods may be used for voice digitization, the most common voice digitization technique in use today is known as **pulse code modulation,** or **PCM.** Figure 4-4 illustrates the basics of PCM.

As can be seen from Figure 4-4, eight bits or one byte is required to transmit the sample amplitude of an analog signal. Since an 8-bit code allows 2^8 or 256 different possible values, each time the actual analog wave is sampled, it is assigned a value from 0 to 255 depending on its location or amplitude at the instant it is sampled. Some simple mathematics will reveal the bandwidth required to transmit digitized voice using PCM. This computed required bandwidth will, by no coincidence, correspond exactly to a very common digital circuit bandwidth.

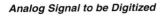

Analog Signal to be Digitized

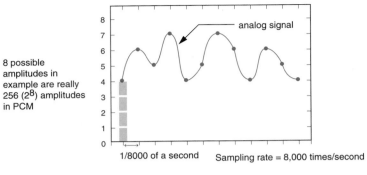

8 possible
amplitudes in
example are really
256 (2^8) amplitudes
in PCM

Step 1: Sample Amplitude of Analog Signal

Amplitude in example at sample position 1 (the gray shaded box) is   4

Step 2: Represent Measured Amplitude in Binary Notation

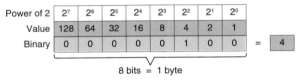

Power of 2	2^7	2^6	2^5	2^4	2^3	2^2	2^1	2^0
Value	128	64	32	16	8	4	2	1
Binary	0	0	0	0	0	1	0	0

= 4

8 bits = 1 byte

Step 3: Transmit Coded Digital Pulses Representing Measured Amplitude

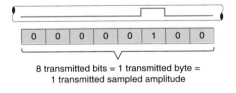

| 0 | 0 | 0 | 0 | 0 | 1 | 0 | 0 |

8 transmitted bits = 1 transmitted byte =
1 transmitted sampled amplitude

Figure 4-4   Voice Digitization: Pulse Code Modulation (PCM)

In Sharper Focus

VOICE DIGITIZATION BANDWIDTH REQUIREMENTS

Since 8000 samples/sec is required to ensure quality transmission of digitized voice and each sample requires eight bits to represent that sampled bandwidth in binary (1s and 0s) notation, the following equation reveals that 64,000 bits/sec is the required bandwidth for transmission of voice digitized via PCM. A DS-0 circuit has a transmission capacity of exactly 64 Kbps. Twenty-four DS-0s are combined to form a T-1, yielding the fact that a T-1 can carry 24 simultaneous voice conversations digitized via PCM. Following is the mathematical proof:

$$8000 \text{ samples/sec} \times 8 \text{ bits/sample} = 64{,}000 \text{ bits/sec (bps)}$$

$$64{,}000 \text{ bits/sec} = 64 \text{ Kbps} = \text{DS-0 circuit}$$

$$24 \text{ DS-0s} = 24 \times 64 \text{ Kbps} = 1536 \text{ Kbps} = 1.536 \text{ Mbps}$$

Plus: 1 framing bit/sample $\times$ 8000 samples/sec = 8000 framing bits/sec

8 Kbps + 1536 Kbps = 1544 Kbps = 1.544 Mbps

= Transmission capacity of T-1 transmission service

ADPCM   A variation of this digitization technique known as **adaptive differential pulse code modulation,** or **ADPCM,** is also very popular, employing roughly half the bandwidth for each digitized conversation relative to PCM.

ADPCM is a CCITT (ITU) standard that takes a slightly different approach to coding sampled amplitudes in order to use transmission bandwidth more efficiently. By transmitting only the approximate difference or change in amplitude of consecutive amplitude samples, rather than the absolute amplitude, only 32 Kbps of bandwidth is required for each conversation digitized via ADPCM.

Using a specialized circuit known as an adaptive predictor, ADPCM calculates the difference between the predicted and actual incoming signals and specifies that difference as one of 16 different levels using 4 bits ($2^4 = 16$). Since each voice channel can be represented by just 4 bits, ADPCM can support 48 simultaneous voice conversations over a T-1 circuit.

The ITU standard for 32-Kbps ADPCM is known as G.721 and is generally used as a reference point for the quality of voice transmission, known as **toll quality.** G.721 has been superseded by other ADPCM standards that use less than 32 Kbps per voice channel. For example, G.723 defines ADPCM for 24 and 40 Kbps whereas G.726 defines ADPCM for 40, 32, 24, and 16 Kbps.

Voice Compression

ADPCM is also known as a **voice compression** technique because of its ability to transmit 24 digitized voice conversations in half of the bandwidth required by PCM. Other more advanced techniques employ specially programmed microprocessors known as **digital signal processors (DSPs)** that process the digitized PCM code and further manipulate and compress it. In doing so, DSPs are able to transmit and reconstruct digitized voice conversations in as little as 4800 bps per conversation, an increase in transmission efficiency of more than 13 times over PCM!

Numerous voice compression technological approaches exist. Voice compression can be performed by stand-alone units or by integral modules within multiplexers. The particular method by which the voice is compressed may be according to an open standard or by a proprietary methodology. Proprietary methods require that a given vendor's equipment be present on both ends of the voice circuit in question. Each voice compression technique seeks to reduce the amount of transmitted voice information in one way or another.

Some voice compression techniques attempt to synthesize the human voice, other techniques attempt to predict the actual voice transmission patterns, and still others attempt to transmit only changes in voice patterns. Regardless of the voice compression technique employed, one thing is certain. The quality of compressed voice transmissions does not match the quality of an analog voice transmission over an analog dial-up line or a PCM-digitized voice transmission using a full 64 Kbps of digital bandwidth. The transmission quality degradation will vary from one instance to another. However, only the end-users of the compressed voice system can determine whether the reduced voice quality is worth the bandwidth and related cost savings.

■ PBX CONCEPTS

PBX Market

To provide flexible voice communications capability among people within a business organization as well as with the outside world, a switching device known as **PBX,** or **private branch exchange,** is often employed. Sales of PBXs in the United States represent approximately a $4 billion annual market, with service on these PBXs accounting for an additional $2 billion in additional revenue. The PBX market is currently dominated by Nortel (Northern Telecom) with its line of Meridian PBXs and by Lucent Technologies (formerly AT&T Global Business Communications Systems) with its line of Definity PBXs. Each of these two major players controls about 25% market share. The major players in the PBX market and their approximate market shares are displayed in Figure 4-5.

PBX Functionality and Architecture

As illustrated in the I-P-O (input-processing-output) diagram of Figure 4-6, a PBX provides an interface between users and the shared private or public network connections available for carrying users' voice and data traffic. The additional intelligent services offered by a PBX allow users to use their phones more efficiently and effectively.

A PBX is really just a privately owned, smaller version of the switch in telephone company central offices that can control circuit switching for the general public. Depending on the requested destination, switched circuits are established, maintained, and terminated on a per-call basis by a portion of the PBX known as the **switching matrix.**

Beyond the switching capabilities of a PBX, programmable features offer advanced functionality to users. These features and the overall performance of the PBX are controlled by software programs that reside in and are executed on specialized computers within the PBX in an area sometimes referred to as the **PBX, CPU, stored program control,** or **common control area.**

Phone lines to users' offices for phone connection are terminated in the PBX in slide-in modules or cards known as **line cards, port cards,** or **station cards.** To increase capacity of connections to the outside network, cards known as **trunk cards** are added to the PBX. Some trunk cards are specialized to a particular type of network line. Some PBXs allow any chassis slot to be used for any type of card or mod-

Approximate PBX Market Share	PBX Vendor
20–25%	Nortel, Lucent Technologies
10–20%	Siemens, Rolm
5–10%	NEC, Mitel
2–5%	Fujitsu, Intecom, Ericsson, Hitachi
Less than 2%	Toshiba, Executone, Tadrian, SRX, Harris Digital

Figure 4-5   PBX Vendors and Market Share

I (Input)	P (Processing)	O (Output)
Users access PBX connections and services via desktop phones or access devices	Provides necessary switching to allow connections among PBX users or to outside network services	Other local PBX users or outside local loops and PSTN connections; outside connections may also be to shared high-speed digital lines
Input traffic may be voice, data, or video	Provides additional intelligent services for tracking PBX usage, conference calling, call forwarding, least cost routing, automatic call distribution, automated attendant, and links to computer databases	

Figure 4-6   IPO Diagram of PBX Functionality

ule whereas other PBXs specify certain slots for line cards and others for trunk cards. Starting with an open chassis or cabinet with power supply and backbone or backplane, modules or cards are added to increase PBX capacity for either user extensions or connections to the outside network. Additional cabinets can often be cascaded to offer PBX expandability. Figure 4-7 illustrates the physical attributes of a representative PBX.

PBX Architecture Trends

PBX vendors must respond to the demands of their market. PBX users are demanding

- Better connectivity between phones and desktop PCs.
- Better connectivity between PBXs and LANs.
- More open PBX architectures for easier access to PBX features and services from a variety of computing platforms.
- Better integration of PBX management programs with enterprise network management packages.

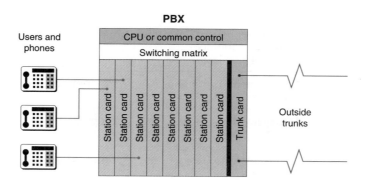

Figure 4-7   PBX Physical Architecture

In many ways, the PBX is becoming nothing more than a specialized communications or voice server that must integrate with all other servers as part of an overall enterprise network. To achieve this transparent integration as part of the enterprise network, PBXs have had to undergo a radical change in their overall design from proprietary, monolithic devices to more open architectures based on industry-standard hardware and software components. Figure 4-8 summarizes some of the transitions involved in the migration to the new open PBX architecture, and Figure 4-9 portrays a logical architecture for an open-architecture PBX.

One of the key architectural features of the open PBX architecture illustrated in Figure 4-9 is the logical separation of the call-processing functionality from the underlying switching fabric. This independence between call-processing functionality and switching functionality allows PBX vendors to introduce newer and faster switching technologies such as ATM (asynchronous transfer mode) without having to redesign their entire PBX from top to bottom.

Another important benefit of the open PBX architecture is that by supporting industry-standard APIs (application program interfaces) such as TAPI and TSAPI for telephony applications, third-party software developers are able to produce a variety of telephony applications that can interface to a variety of PBXs and computers. This frees the PBX vendors from the cost and obligation of developing proprietary telephony applications software from the PBXs. Likewise, by writing to these industry-standard APIs, third-party software developers do not need to write numerous PBX-specific versions of a particular telephony application program. TAPI and TSAPI will be discussed in more detail in this chapter's section on computer telephony integration.

PBX Attribute	Traditional PBX	New Open-Architecture PBX
Name	Private branch exchange (PBX)	Enterprise communications server (ECS)
Processor	Proprietary	Industry-standard processors
Operating system	Proprietary	UNIX
Applications software	Proprietary	Object-oriented applications written in C or C++
Design strategy	Monolithic	Modular
Transmission media	Wireline only	Integrated wireline and wireless
Computer hardware interface	Proprietary	Ethernet
Computer interface transport protocol	Proprietary	TCP/IP
Management information database format	Proprietary	Industry standard
Management interface	Proprietary	Industry standard via SNMP protocol
Application program interface	Proprietary	Industry-standard APIs: TAPI and TSAPI

Figure 4-8   Trends in PBX Architectures

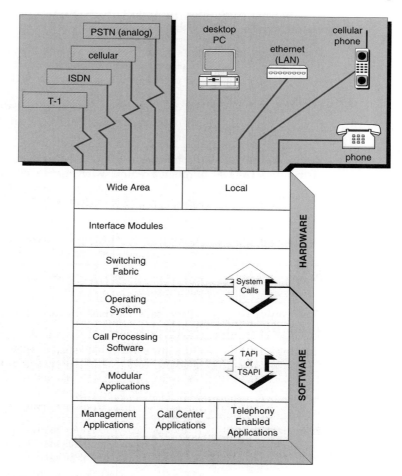

Figure 4-9   Open PBX Architecture

PBX Technology Analysis

Before reviewing PBX technology, it is essential to have performed a thorough top-down analysis beginning with the business needs and functionality that must be met by the chosen PBX technology. With those PBX features that are most important to a given business identified, the following information could be used as a representative sample of typical PBX features and services.

PBX features and services tend to fall into three broad categories:

1. Features and services that provide users with flexible usage of PBX resources.

2. Features and services that provide for data/voice integration.

3. Features and services that control and monitor the use of those PBX resources.

Voice-Based Features and Services   In the flexible-usage category, features such as conference calling, call forwarding, call transfer, speed dialing, redialing, and call hold are commonplace and shouldn't require further explanation. Other voice-based PBX features and services that support flexible usage of PBX resources are summarized in Figure 4-10.

Feature/Service	Description
Least cost routing (LCR)	Using routing and pricing information supplied by the user, PBX chooses the most economical path for any given call. This feature was especially important when WATS (wide-area telecommunications service) lines were more prevalent. These days, thanks to competition and discount programs among long-distance carriers, PBXs can access any outgoing trunk rather than trying to get certain calls onto certain trunks.
Automatic call distribution (ACD)	Incoming calls are routed directly to certain extensions without going through a central switchboard. Calls can be routed according to the incoming trunk or phone number. ACD is often used in customer service organizations in which calls may be distributed to the first available agent.
Call pickup	Allows a user to pickup or answer another user's phone without the need to actually forward calls.
Paging	Allows use of paging speakers in a building. May be limited to specific paging zones.
Direct inward dialing (DID)	Allows calls to bypass the central switchboard and go directly to a particular user's phone.
Hunting	Hunt groups are established to allow incoming calls to get through on alternate trunks when a primary trunk is busy. For example, most businesses publish only one phone number even though they may have multiple incoming trunks. If the primary trunk is busy, the PBX hunts for an open trunk transparently to the user.
Prioritization	Individual extensions can be given priority access to certain trunks or groups of trunks. In most cases, PBXs are equipped with fewer outgoing trunks than internal extensions or station lines. If certain users *must* have access to outside lines, prioritization features are important.
Night mode	Night mode is useful to companies that close their switchboard at night but still have employees working who must be able to receive and make phone calls.

Figure 4-10 Voice-Based PBX Features and Services

Data/Voice Integration Features and Services   Data/voice integration by PBXs is increasingly common although PBXs can vary significantly in the extent of support for data transmission. Differences in data interfaces and whether or not those interfaces and associated software represent an upgrade at additional cost should be investigated thoroughly before any PBX purchase. In some cases, data is transmitted through the PBX via a dedicated connection whereas in other cases, a specialized hybrid voice/data phone is used to transmit both voice and data simultaneously over a single connection to the PBX. Data and data/voice integration related features and issues are summarized in Figure 4-11.

Control and Monitoring Features and Services   Control and monitoring features range from the simple, such as limiting access to outside lines from certain extensions, to

Feature/Service	Issues
ISDN support	Are WAN interfaces for ISDN supplied or available as upgrades? ISDN BRI (basic rate interface) service is two 64-Kbps channels. ISDN PRI (primary rate interface) service is twenty-three 64-Kbps channels.
T-1 support	Are T-1 (1.544 Mbps) interfaces supported? Outside of North America, are E-1 (2.048 Mbps) interfaces supported? Are codecs included? Are channel banks included?
Data interfaces	Are computer data interfaces included on the PBX? Are hybrid voice/data phones available? Are LAN interfaces such as Ethernet and Token Ring as well as serial interfaces such as RS-232 supported? Are fax transmission, modem pooling, printer sharing, file sharing, and videoconferencing supported?
PBX-to-host interfaces	Prior to the advent of open-systems computer telephony integration APIs such as TAPI and TSAPI, each PBX vendor had its own PBX–host interface specification. How many of the following vendor-specific PBX–host interfaces are supported? Nortel: Meridian Link; Rolm: CallBridge; IBM: CallPath; AT&T: Passageway; Siemens: Applications Connectivity Link (ACL); Mitel: NeVaDa (networked voice and data).

Figure 4-11 Data and Data/Voice Integration PBX Features and Services

the complex, such as entire stand-alone **call accounting systems.** Call accounting systems are often run on separate PCs that interface directly to the PBX and execute specially written software. Accounting reports or bills sorted by department or extension can be run on a scheduled basis or on demand. Exception reports can be generated to spot possible abuses for calls over a certain length or cost or for calls made to a particular area code. Incoming as well as outgoing calls can be tracked. Call accounting systems can pay for themselves in a short amount of time by spotting and curtailing abuse as well as by allocating phone usage charges on a departmental basis.

The information on which such a call accounting system depends is generated by the PBX. In a process known as **SMDR,** or **station message detail recording,** an individual detail record is generated for each call. This data record can then be transferred from the PBX to the call accounting system computer, usually from an RS-232 DB-25 port on the PBX to the serial port on the PC. Data records can be stored and summarized on the call accounting system computer depending on available disk space. Figure 4-12 illustrates the setup of a call accounting system.

Auxiliary Voice-Related Services   Just as the previously mentioned call accounting systems are most often an add-on device for PBXs, other auxiliary systems exist to enhance PBX capability. The auxiliary nature of these systems implies that they are often not included as standard features on PBXs but may be purchased separately from either the PBX vendor or third-party manufacturers. Sometimes these services are available as a combination of specialized PC boards and associated TAPI or TSAPI compliant software. Figure 4-13 lists and describes a few of the more popular auxiliary PBX systems.

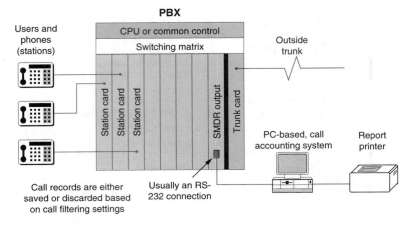

Figure 4-12   Call Accounting System Installation

Service/Device	Description
Automated attendant	A recorded message that works with a touch-tone phone that requests callers to press the number of the extension they wish to reach. Those wishing to speak to an operator are transferred.
Voice mail	Voice mail systems can vary widely in cost and sophistication. After recording an initial message for someone, voice mail systems may allow the voice mail to be handled like a written phone message. It can be forwarded, copied, attended to, saved, recalled, or deleted.
Voice response units (VRUs) Interactive voice response	Menu selections are offered to callers who use the touch pad to navigate through menu selections. Some answering machines include VRUs that allow the owner to check for messages remotely. Banks allow customers to make account inquiries and transactions via VRUs, and airlines provide arrival and departure information via VRUs.
Voice processor	Performs same basic functions as a VRU but may also provide additional services based on voice response, speech recognition, or tone detection.
Voice server	A LAN-based server that stores, processes, and delivers digitized voice messages. Often used as the processing and storage component of a voice mail system.
Music/ads on hold	When customers are put on hold, music plays or alternatively, a tape-recorded sales message interrupts periodically with messages such as "Your call is important to us; please stay on the line."

Figure 4-13   Auxiliary Voice-Related Services/Devices

PBX Trends

Multivendor Interoperability Standards   Just as open-systems architecture has become a major emphasis in the computer industry, interoperability between PBXs from various manufacturers has been receiving increased attention. An international standard sponsored by the ISO known as **Q.Sig** seeks to allow PBXs of any manufacturer to interoperate with each other and with ISDNs. As a matter of fact, Q.Sig is an extension of an ISDN standard known as **Q.931**, which allows PBX features to interoperate with public switched network features.

Q.Sig standardizes features among different PBX manufacturers and delivers those standardized features within the limitations of the feature set offered by ISDN. Among the standardized PBX features are call establishment and termination, call waiting, caller ID and caller ID blocking, and other ISDN-supported features. As with any multivendor interoperability standard, only those features common to all supported technology are implemented in the interoperability standard. This represents a least common denominator of common functionality, thereby bypassing any vendor-specific more advanced features.

PBX Integration with Wireless Phones   It seemed inevitable that with the explosion in the use of portable wireless telephones, a demand would arise for transparent integration of those wireless phones with the traditional PBX architecture. Northern Telecom, one of the world's largest and most successful PBX manufacturers, has created such a link between the wireless phones and PBXs.

Their system, called the Companion, allows wireless phones to take advantage of PBX features such as call forwarding, conference calling, speed dialing, etc. In addition, a portable phone can be "twinned" with an office phone so that both ring when the extension is called. The portable phone becomes just another PBX extension rather than an unintegrated remote phone, reachable only by dialing a full seven-digit number.

Standards support is important in wireless phones as in any other area of data communications. These PBX-integrated wireless phones support the **CT2 (cordless telephony generation 2) common air interface (CAI)** global standard for low-power wireless transmission. Such systems are especially useful in large hospitals, hotels, convention centers, and office building where key support people spend a great deal of time at various locations throughout the building.

Mini-PBXs for the Small Office Home Office Market   As the number of professionals working out of a small or home office has skyrocketed, an entire market known as **SOHO (small office home office)** has developed that demands **mini-PBXs** with all of the sophistication of large and expensive PBXs at a fraction of the cost. Also known as **multifunction telephony boards,** these PC expansion boards offer multiple workers the ability to share a small number of phone lines with integrated advanced features such as

- Auto-attendent software

- Integration with cell phones, pagers, and voice mail systems.

- ISDN support.

- Integration with auto-dialer applications, universal mailboxes, and caller ID applications.

- Integration with bundled call control software.
- Compatibility with computer telephony integration software and APIs.

■ COMPUTER TELEPHONY INTEGRATION

CTI Functionality

CTI or **computer telephony integration** seeks to integrate the two most common productivity devices, the computer and the telephone, to enable increased productivity not otherwise possible by using the two devices in a nonintegrated fashion. CTI is not a single application, but an ever-widening array of possibilities spawned by the integration of telephony and computing. Figure 4-14 briefly describes some of the subcategories of CTI applications.

CTI Architectures

Computer telephony integration is commonly implemented in one of the following three architectures:

1. **PBX-to-host Interfaces**
2. **Desktop CTI**
3. **Client/Server CTI**

Traditionally, computer telephony integration was achieved by linking mainframes to PBXs via proprietary PBX-to-host interfaces. Applications were required to be compatible with the model of both the mainframe computer and the PBX installed. In many cases, these systems actually linked to an ancillary device known as an **ACD** or **automatic call distribution** unit. These systems were very expensive and were usually only employed in large customer service call centers. In this CTI architecture, all phones are controlled by the CTI application running on the mainframe computer.

Desktop CTI, also known as **first-party call control,** is a much less expensive and simpler alternative to the PBX-to-host interface architecture. In this CTI architecture, individual PCs are equipped with telephony boards and associated call control software. Each desktop CTI-equipped PC controls only the phone to which it is directly attached. There is no overall automatic call distribution across multiple agents and their phones, and there is no sharing of call-related data among the desktop CTI PCs.

Finally, client/server CTI offers the overall shared control of the PBX-to-host CTI architecture at a cost much closer to that of the desktop CTI architecture. In this CTI architecture, a CTI server computer interfaces to the PBX or ACD to provide overall system management while individual client-based CTI applications execute on multiple client PCs. The advantage to such an architecture is that multiple CTI applications on multiple client PCs can share the information supplied by the single CTI server. Figure 4-15 illustrates the various CTI architectures.

CTI Application Category	Application Description
Call control	• Using computer-based applications, user are more easily able to use all of the features of their phone system or PBX, especially the more complicated but seldom used features. • Includes use of features like on-line phone books, auto-dialing, click-and-point conference calls, on-line display, and processing of voice mail messages.
Automated attendant	• Allows callers to direct calls to a desired individual at a given business without necessarily knowing the extension number.
Automated call distribution	• Used primarily in call centers staffed by large numbers of customer service agents; incoming calls are automatically distributed to the first available representative or, in some cases, the representative that serves a given geographic region as automatically determined by the computer based on the incoming phone number.
Audiotex	• These systems deliver audio information to callers based on responses on the touch-tone keypad to prerecorded questions. Primarily used for information hot lines.
Fax-on-demand	• By combining computer-based faxing with interactive voice response, users can dial-in and request that specific information be faxed to their fax machine.
Interactive voice response (IVR)	• Interactive voice response systems differ from audiotex systems in that IVR systems support on-line transaction processing rather than just information hot-line applications. As an example, banks use IVR systems to allow users to transfer funds between accounts by using only a touch-tone phone.
Outbound dialing	• Also known as **predictive dialing,** this merger of computing and telephony uses a database of phone numbers, automatically dials those numbers, recognizes when calls are answered by people, and quickly passes those calls to available agents.
Unified messaging	• Perhaps the most interesting for the LAN-based user, **unified messaging,** also known as the **universal in-box,** will allow voice mail, e-mail, faxes, and pager messages to all be displayed on a single graphical screen. Messages can then be forwarded, deleted, or replied to easily in point-and-click fashion. Waiting calls can also be displayed in the same universal in-box.

Figure 4-14 Computer Telephony Integration Functionality

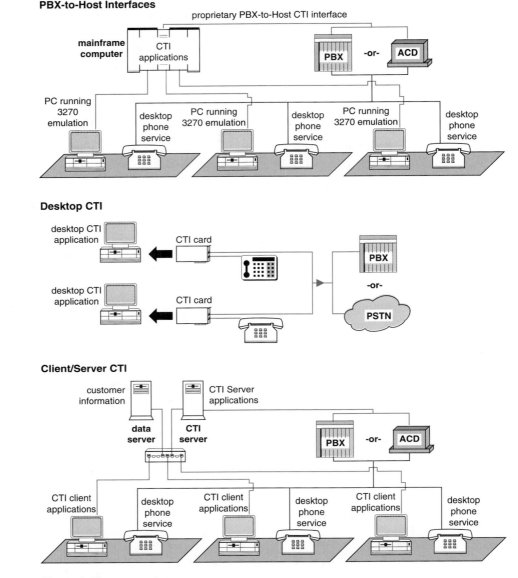

Figure 4-15   CTI Architectures

CTI Application Development and Implementation

CTI applications, like any client/server application, must be able to easily integrate with a variety of computing platforms and operating systems. Such application portability is only possible if those applications support common commands and system calls that are referred to as **application program interfaces (API).** In the case of CTI applications, two LAN-based standards for CTI API are emerging:

1. **TSAPI** or **Telephony Services API** was jointly developed and sponsored by Novell and AT&T.

2. **TAPI** or **Telephony API** was jointly developed and sponsored by Intel and Microsoft.

Applications that are written to use either of these APIs should be able to operate transparently in either a NetWare (TSAPI) or Windows (TAPI) environment. Both Novell and Microsoft are developing their own CTI application software as well. Figure 14-16 illustrates the key technology required to develop and implement a working CTI application. More specifically, an **interactive voice response (IVR)** application is illustrated. Examples of such applications are automated systems to check account balances at banks or to check arrival and departure information at airlines.

Before the CTI application can be developed, it is essential to first understand the business process that is to be automated using CTI. In addition, it is also essential to know the details of the database system to/from which data will be stored and retrieved with the CTI application.

CTI applications must first be developed using a **CTI application development tool.** Most of these tools automatically generate programming code in either Visual Basic or Visual C++ programming languages. The ease with which this code is designed and generated and the amount of programming knowledge required to use these tools can vary significantly among currently available offerings. If the CTI ap-

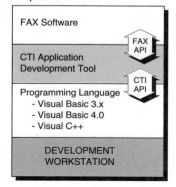

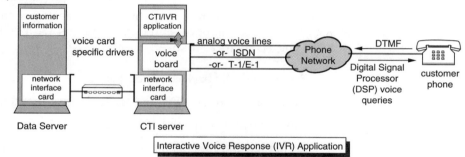

Figure 4-16   Technology Required to Develop and Implement CTI Applications

plication is to include faxback or fax-on-demand capabilities, then an optional networked faxing program may need to be integrated during the application development effort. Following are some key characteristics of CTI application development tools:

- Graphical code generators allow easy application development with a minimum of programming background.

- Debugging tools, also known as test utilities or virtual phone utilities, allow applications to be tested without the need for voice cards or phones. Log files that record all user responses and program interactions can also aid in debugging new programs.

- Interfaces to fax software for incoming and outbound fax control can add faxback or fax-on-demand capabilities.

- Sound editors are able to edit and translate between .WAV and .VOX sound files.

- Prerecorded sound bites with standard greetings and responses can lend a professional image to developed CTI applications.

- CTI applications developed with a given CTI application development tool may or may not need to pay royalties on copies of the finished application.

- Among the types of CTI applications that can be developed with such application development tools are voice mail, interactive voice response, inbound/outbound fax-on-demand, and call center CTI.

Examples of popular CTI application development tools and their respective vendors are as follows:

CTI Application Development Tool	Vendor
Visual Voice Pro	Artisoft, Inc.
CallSuite	Parity Software Development Corp.
VBVoice	Pronexus
VoysAccess for Visual Basic	Voysys Corp.

The final version of the CTI program must be deployed in a CTI server with a compatible **CTI voice card.** Compatibility between voice cards and CTI applications is assured by mutual support of CTI APIs such as TAPI or TSAPI. The key functions of a CTI voice card are as follows:

- Record and playback digitized voice.

- Create and recognize DTMF (dual-tone multifrequency) tones.

- Answer and place phone calls.

- Recognize and process incoming caller ID (automatic number identification) information.

Once the CTI application is installed, users are able to interact with the application by using a touch-tone phone to respond to voice queries generated by the CTI voice card. Authorized requests for data are passed from the voice card to the network database server. Responses to databases requests are returned to the caller via the CTI voice card. Dialogic dominates the voice card market. Other vendors include Rhetorex, Bicom, NewVoice, and Pika.

■ VOICE NETWORK CONCEPTS

The basic architecture and operation of the **PSTN,** or **public switched telephone network,** were introduced in Chapter 1. Terms such as central office (CO), local access transport area (LATA), and point of presence (POP) were introduced at that time. In this section, a more in-depth look at the operation of the PSTN will be taken, focusing on the following areas.

First, a brief look at signaling and dial tone will reveal how phones are used to signal the central office switch as to their desired destination. Second, a concept or architecture known as the **network hierarchy** and its implication on call routing and delivery will be explored. Finally, a key element in the control and management of this network hierarchy known as **signaling system 7,** or **SS7,** will be studied.

Signaling and Dial Tone

As introduced in Chapter 1, the switch at the central office routes calls from source to destination via circuit switching. Requested destinations for phone calls are indicated to the central office switch by dialing a series of numbers. These numbers tell the switch whether the call to this destination will be local, intra-LATA, or inter-LATA and subsequently which circuits must be accessed and combined to complete the call as requested.

The dialed numbers can be generated in two ways. Older style rotary phones, like the one that was taken apart to draw Figure 4-1, have a round dial that causes a certain number of pulses of electricity to be generated depending on the number dialed. Dialing a "1" produces one electrical pulse, dialing a "2" produces two electrical pulses, and so on. Many of today's phones no longer have rotary dials on them.

Instead, they contain 12 buttons that correspond to the 10 numbers on the rotary-dial plus two other characters, the star (*) and the pound sign (#). A switch is often included that can be set to pulse to emulate the dialing process of the older style of phone. This may be necessary is areas where central office switches have not been upgraded to understand tone, more commonly known as touch-tone dialing.

The tones generated during touch-tone dialing are technically known as **DTMF, or dual-tone multifrequency tones,** because the tone associated with each number dialed is really a combination of two tones selected from a matrix of multiple possible frequencies. Figure 4-17 illustrates the numbers and symbols found on a typical telephone touch panel and their associated dual-tone frequencies.

The tones generated by DTMF phones are used for much more than merely dialing. As will be seen later in the chapter, these same tones can be used to enable specialized services from PBXs, carriers, banks, information services, and retail establishments.

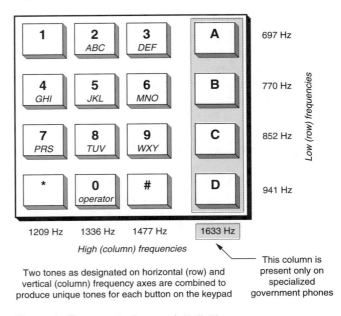

Figure 4-17   Tone Dialing with DTMF

PSTN Hierarchy

As can be seen in Figure 4-18, a residential or business call is first processed in the local central office, also known as an end office or local office. In terms of the network hierarchy, an end office is known as a **Class 5** office. This local central office contains a switch that processes incoming calls, determines the best path to the call destination, and establishes the circuit connection.

Local calls come into the local central office via a local loop and travel to their local destination via a local loop. Calls that are not local but still within the same LATA are known as intra-LATA calls and are handled by a local carrier, most often an RBOC. Technically, these are long-distance calls and a local CO may not have a direct trunk to the destination CO. In this case, the call is routed through a **tandem office** that establishes the intra-LATA circuit and also handles billing procedures for the long-distance call.

Inter-LATA calls must be turned over from a local carrier to a long-distance carrier such as AT&T, MCI, or U.S. Sprint. In most cases, the particular inter-exchange carrier (IXC) employed will have been chosen by individual residential and business subscribers. The local CO still receives such inter-LATA calls from subscribers. However, rather than routing the call themselves, the CO merely forwards the call to the local switching office of the long-distance carrier of choice.

Such a long-distance switching office is known as a POP, or point of presence, and also as a **Class 4 toll center.** The term *toll center* implies that long-distance billing calculation as well as switching activities are performed at these locations. A given local CO may have trunks to more than one toll center. As will be seen, circuit redundancy offering multiple alternative paths for call routing is a central premise of the voice network hierarchy. If the local toll center can find adequate space on a trunk headed to the destination CO, then the connection between source and destination CO is completed. If no paths to the destination are directly available to the

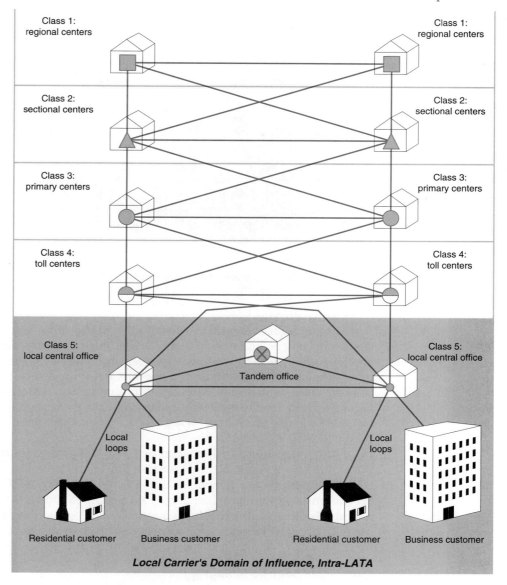

Figure 4-18   Voice Network Hierarchy

local toll center, then the call is escalated up the network hierarchy to the next level of switching office. The overall desire is to keep the call as low on the hierarchy as possible. This provides both quicker call completion for the subscriber and maximization of the cost-effective use of the lowest and least expensive switching offices possible.

Higher levels on the network hierarchy imply greater switching and transmission capacity as well as greater expense. When calls cannot be completed directly, Class 4 toll centers turn to **Class 3 primary centers** for backup which subsequently turn to **Class 2 sectional centers** which turn finally to **Class 1 regional centers.** Not all inter-LATA or long-distance carriers have a five-level network hierarchy. These categories of switching and transmission centers were originally AT&T's but have become industry-standard terminology.

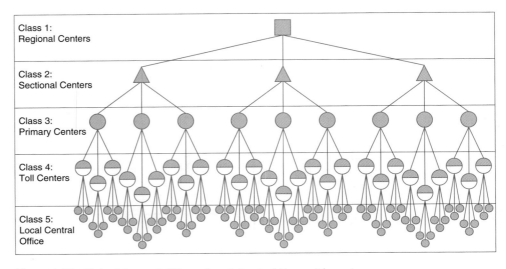

Figure 4-19   Voice Network Hierarchy: A Logical Pyramid

Although Figure 4-18 illustrates the relationship among various levels of switching centers, Figure 4-19 more clearly illustrates why higher level offices have greater routing flexibility. As can be seen in Figure 4-19, the network hierarchy is more of a logical pyramid, with numerous toll centers serviced by a single Class 3 primary center and so on. Although the numbers of centers on any given level in Figure 4-19 are for illustrative purposes only, the basic proportions may be valid. In fact, although there are over 9000 Class 5 centers, there are only 12 Class 1 regional centers in AT&T's network hierarchy.

As an interesting side note, Figure 4-18 could change in the intra-LATA or local carrier area. As a result of the passage of the Telecommunications Act of 1996, intra-LATA competition has now been allowed. Rulings from the FCC determine the exact circumstances under which intra-LATA competition is allowed within any given region. This implies that business and residential subscribers will be able to choose not only between long-distance carriers but also between local carriers as well.

Network Interoffice Signaling

As residential and business subscribers not serviced by PBXs begin to expect PBX-like intelligent services from network offerings such as ISDN, the network itself must become more "intelligent" to deliver such services. End-to-end signaling between carrier's switches and customer premises equipment **(CPE)**, regardless of what local or long-distance carrier might be involved, is the first step toward delivering intelligent services such as **ANI (automatic number identification),** better known as caller ID.

There are two key requirements of this interswitch signaling methodology. First, it must be standardized. Second, it must not travel over the same logical channel as the voice conversation itself. In other words, the signaling should travel out of the voice conversation's band or channel in a process known as **out-of-band signaling.** A more official name for out-of-band signaling is **common channel interoffice signaling (CCIS).**

Besides delivering incoming phone numbers to residential and business users, the out-of-band signaling would be used to manage the network itself by handling the routing of calls and circuit establishment as well as the monitoring of circuit status and notification and rerouting in the case of alarms or circuit problems.

Signaling System 7   The worldwide, CCITT-approved standard for out-of-band signaling is known as **signaling system 7 (SS7).** Signaling system 7 is closely related to ISDN. As an underlying architectural component of ISDN, SS7 delivers the out-of-band signaling over ISDN's D channel, delivering both intelligent services to the end-user as well as network management information to network administrators. Signaling system 7 can exist without ISDN, but transparent, interswitch services cannot be delivered via ISDN without SS7.

But what exactly *is* signaling system 7? SS7 is really nothing more than a suite of protocols, not unlike other suites of protocols examined earlier, that controls the structure and transmission of both circuit-related and non-circuit-related information via out-of-band signaling between central office switches. Like most protocol suites, SS7 can be modeled in comparison to the OSI seven-layer reference model. Figure 4-20 summarizes the major characteristics of the signaling system 7 protocols and compares the SS7 protocol suite to the OSI model.

Signaling system 7 and the intelligent services that it enables are often described as part of an all-encompassing interface between users and the PSTN known as **AIN** or **advanced intelligent network.** Among the major components of the advanced intelligent network is **SDN** or **software-defined network.** A software-defined network implies that users have some control over the flexible configuration of their wide-area telecommunications service and network. By extending SS7 out-of-band signaling to the end-users, voice networks can be reconfigured as business activities dictate.

OSI Model	Signalling System 7		
Application	O&MAP		
	TCAP		
Presentation			
Session			ISUP
Transport			
Network	SSCP		
Datalink		MTP	
Physical			

Protocol Name	Description/Function
Operations Maintenance Application Part (O&MAP)	*O&MAP* provides standards for routing and management of messages related to network operations and maintenance
Transaction Capabilities Application Part (TCAP)	*TCAP* provides standards for routing and management of noncircuit related information for transaction processing applications requiring out-of-band signaling
ISDN User Part (ISUP)	*ISUP* provides standards for routing and management of signaling messages as specifically required by ISDN and its services
Signalling Connection Control Part (SCCP)	*SCCP* provides standards for routing and management of signaling messages. Not related to call set-up between switches. A connection-oriented service providing reliable message delivery
Message Transfer Part (MTP)	*MTP* provides standards for routing of signalling messages between switches. A connectionless, datagram service

Figure 4-20   Signaling System 7 Protocols and the OSI Model

The most common application to date of SDN is customer-controlled 800 services for inbound customer service or calling center applications. For instance, with AT&Ts **intelligent call processing (ICP)** service, customers are able to reroute incoming 800 calls among multiple customer service centers in a matter of seconds. This rerouting is done completely transparent to the calling customer and is actually accomplished by the ICP user having direct access to AT&Ts switching network via SS7 out-of-band signaling. A service such as ICP allows multiple call centers geographically dispersed throughout the country to function as one logical call center, with the overall number of incoming calls distributed in a balanced manner across all centers.

User-oriented network services such as AIN and SDN are being offered in response to users' demands for in-house control over a key element of their businesses: their telecommunications systems and the links from those systems to the wide-area public switched telephone network. Catalog sales organizations are literally out of business without their phones and must have contingency plans and disaster recovery plans in place to deal with and hopefully avoid possible catastrophes.

Voice Transmission Alternatives

Although the PSTN has traditionally been seen as the cheapest and most effective way to transmit voice, alternative methods for voice transmission do exist. Several such methods are briefly explored in terms of configuration requirements, advantages, and disadvantages.

Voice over the Internet Although this alternative voice transmission methodology is often referred to as **voice over the Internet**, it is actually the underlying transport protocols of the Internet that deliver the voice conversations. These underlying transport protocols are **IP (Internet protocol)** and **UDP (user datagram protocol)** and are studied in more detail in Chapter 9. The important point about the IP and UDP is that they are not exclusively confined to use on the Internet. They can be used just as effectively in any of the following topologies:

- Modem-based point-to-point connections.

- Local area networks.

- Private internets, also known as **intranets.**

IP-based voice transmission can be successfully deployed in any of the previously mentioned topologies provided that the required technology is properly implemented. Figure 4-21 illustrates both the technology required to implement IP-based voice transmission and the alternative topologies possible.

Required client hardware and software technology for IP-based voice transmission includes the following:

- Client software for IP-based voice transmission.

- PC workstation with a sufficiently fast CPU to digitize and compress the analog voice signal (25-MHz 486 CPU minimum).

REQUIRED CLIENT TECHNOLOGY

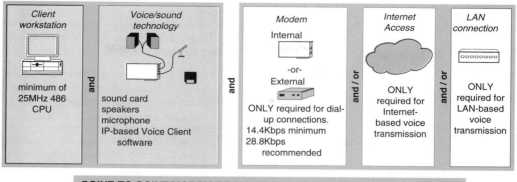

POSSIBLE IMPLEMENTATION TOPOLOGIES

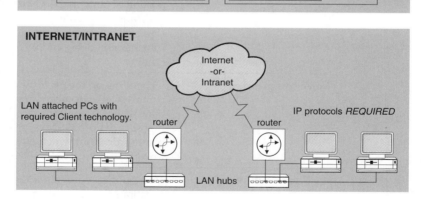

Figure 4-21   IP-Based Voice Transmission Technology and Topologies

- Sound card for local playback of received voice transmission.
- Microphone for local input of transmitted voice signals.
- Speakers for local output of received voice signals.

Figure 4-22 summarizes many of the key features and functionality of IP-based voice transmission client software.

Feature	Importance/Implication
Client platform support	Most IP-based transmission software supports Windows 95, with fewer packages supporting Windows 3.x, Windows NT, and NetWare clients.
Interoperability	The **ITU H.323** standard for interoperability among client software for low-bandwidth audio (voice) and videoconferencing is supported by some, but not all, client IP-based voice transmission software.
Transmission quality	Although transmission quality has improved thanks to improved voice compression algorithms, the fact remains that shared IP networks were designed to carry data that could tolerate delays. Voice networks are designed with dedicated circuits offering guaranteed bandwidth and delivery times to voice transmission.
Multipoint audioconferences	Some packages may employ proprietary methods whereas others may support the **T.120** conferencing standard.
Addressing for call creation	IP-based software packages employ a variety of different addressing techniques to create calls. In some cases, a directory server must be established listing all potential voice call destinations. In other cases, e-mail addresses or IP addresses may be used to initiate the IP-based voice call. Third-party directory services may also be supported.
Bandwidth reservation on shared networks	To more closely emulate the dedicated bandwidth circuits of the PSTN, an IP-based protocol known as **RSVP (resource reservation protocol)** enables routing software to reserve a portion of network bandwidth known as a **virtual circuit.** This dedicated, guaranteed bandwidth is assigned to a particular IP-based voice transmission session, thereby minimizing transmission delay and increasing overall transmitted voice quality.
Voice compression	Depending on the particular codec algorithm used, voice compression can cause a major difference in required bandwidth. Among the more popular codec standards are high-bandwidth **GSM (global systems mobile communication)** which uses 9,600–11,000 bps, and low-bandwidth **RT24**, 2400 bps.
Auxiliary features	Many IP-based voice packages support a variety of other functions that may be important to some organizations. Examples of such functions include answering machine/recorded message capabilities, on-line rolodex with photographs of called parties, text chat when sufficient voice quality cannot be maintained, electronic whiteboard for long-distance brainstorming, file transfer and application sharing, incorporation of voice transmission into HTML documents for web pages, and API to integrate voice transmission in customized applications.

Figure 4-22   Features and Functionality of IP-Based Voice Transmission Software

Some of the currently available IP-based voice transmission software and associated vendors are as follows:

IP-Based Voice Transmission Software	Vendor
CoolTalk	Netscape Communications Corp.
IBM Internet Connection Phone	IBM Corporation
Intel Internet Phone	Intel Corporation
Internet Phone	VocalTec Inc.
Microsoft NetMeeting	Microsoft Corporation
Quarterdeck WebTalk	Quarterdeck Corporation
TeleVox	Voxware, Inc.

COST/BENEFIT ANALYSIS FOR IP-BASED VOICE TRANSMISSION

Managerial Perspective

Figure 4-23 identifies many of the potential costs associated with implementing an IP-based voice transmission network. All cost categories listed will not apply in all situations. Benefits will be most significant for those organizations with large do-

Costs	
Client platforms	
Workstation (with sufficiently fast CPU) if not already available	$
Modem (14.4 Kbps minimum, 28.8 Kbps recommended)	$
Speakers	$
Microphone	$
Sound card	$
Client voice software	$
Total cost/voice client	$
Total cost for all voice clients	$
Server platforms	
Directory servers	$
Directory server software	$
Total server costs	$
Access charges	
Internet access (monthly charge to ISP)	$
Access line (paid to phone carrier)	$
Total access charges	$
Other costs	
Training and support	$
Other costs	
Total other costs	$
Total costs	$
Benefits	
Savings from reduced phone bills to phone service provider	$
Total benefits	$
Net cost/benefit	$

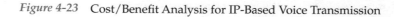

Figure 4-23   Cost/Benefit Analysis for IP-Based Voice Transmission

mestic or international long-distance calling expenses. However, it should be noted that such organizations often already have large volume discounted rate contracts with their phone service providers that minimize or negate any potential savings that might be achieved by shifting to an IP-based voice transmission network.

A more subjective criterion that must be considered is the minimum acceptable transmitted voice quality. Higher transmission quality demands higher amounts of dedicated bandwidth. Lower amounts of shared bandwidth can cause transmission delays that will be manifested as voice dropouts or clipped words.

Typical delays on voice transmission networks such as PSTN are in the 50–70-msec range whereas IP-based voice transmission networks can exhibit delays of 500 msec to 1.5 sec. Many corporations may conclude that the current generation of IP-based voice transmission technology is sufficient for internal corporate communication but is unacceptable for external communication with clients and customers.

Finally, should large amounts of revenue begin to bypass phone carriers as a result of a massive use of IP-based voice transmission over the Internet, it is very likely that the Federal Communications Commission would take steps to ensure that Internet service providers (ISP) do not have an unfair competitive advantage.

Voice over Frame Relay   IP-based voice transmission via the Internet is not the only alternative to traditional voice transmission over wide areas. **Frame relay** is another wide-area transmission service that was primarily or initially deployed for data transmission but is now capable of delivering voice transmissions as well. Although frame relay will be discussed further in Chapter 8, the implications of transmitting voice over this service will be detailed here.

To be able to dynamically adapt to transmit data as efficiently as possible, frame relay encapsulates segments of a data transfer session into variable-length frames. For longer data transfers, longer frames with larger data payloads are used and for short messages, shorter frames are used. These variable-length frames introduce varying amounts of delay due to processing by intermediate switches on the frame relay network. This variable-length delay introduced by the variable-length frames works very well for data but is unacceptable for voice payloads that are very sensitive to delay.

The **FRAD** or **frame relay access device** is able to accommodate both voice and data traffic by employing any or all of the following techniques:

- Voice prioritization—FRADs are able to distinguish between voice and data traffic and prioritize voice traffic over data traffic.

- Data frame size limitation—Long data frames must be segmented into multiple smaller frames so that pending voice traffic can have priority access. However, data must not be delayed to unacceptable levels.

- Separate voice and data queues—To more effectively manage pending data and voice messages, separate queues for data and voice messages can be maintained within the FRAD.

Voice conversations transmitted over frame relay networks require 4–16 Kbps of bandwidth each. This dedicated bandwidth is reserved as an end-to-end connection through the frame relay network known as a PVC or permanent virtual circuit. For prioritization schemes established by FRADs to be maintained throughout a voice conversation's end-to-end journey, intermediate frame relay switches within the frame relay network must support the same prioritization schemes. At this point, voice conversations can only take place between locations connected directly to a frame relay

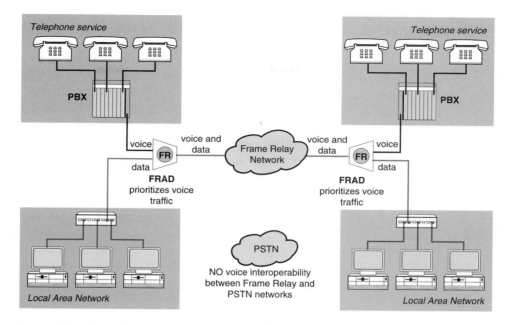

Figure 4-24   Voice Transmission over a Frame Relay Network

network. There are currently no interoperability standards or network–network interface standards defined between frame relay networks and the voice-based PSTN. Figure 4-24 illustrates voice transmission over a frame relay network.

Voice over ATM   Whereas frame relay is a switch-based WAN service using variable-length frames, **ATM (asynchronous transfer mode)** is a switch-based WAN service using fixed-length frames, more properly referred to as **cells.** Fixed-length cells assure fixed-length processing time by ATM switches, thereby enabling predictable, rather than variable, delay and delivery time. Voice is currently transmitted across ATM networks using a bandwidth reservation scheme known as **CBR** or **constant bit rate,** which is analogous to a frame relay virtual circuit. However, constant bit rate does not make optimal use of available bandwidth since during the course of a given voice conversation, moments of silence intermingle with periods of conversation. The most common method for currently transmitting voice over an ATM network is to reserve a CBR of 64 Kbps for one voice conversation digitized via PCM.

In Sharper Focus

OPTIMIZING VOICE OVER ATM

More efficient use of ATM network capacity for voice transmission can be achieved in one of the following ways:

- Voice compression—Voice compression can be achieved via the ITU-standardized voice compression algorithms using the G series of standards. Algorithms vary in the amount of bandwidth required to transmit toll-quality voice. (G.726: 48, 32, 24, or 16 Kbps; G.728: 16 Kbps; G.729: 8 Kbps). An important point to remember with voice compression is that the greater the compression ratio achieved, the more complicated and processing intensive the compression process. In such cases, the greatest delay is introduced by the voice compression algorithm with the highest compression ratio, requiring the least bandwidth.

- Silence suppression—All cells are examined as to contents. Any voice cell that contains silence is not allowed to enter the ATM network. At the destination end, the nontransmitted silence is replaced with synthesized background noise. Silence suppression can reduce the amount of cells transmitted for a given voice conversation by 50%.

- Use of **VBR (variable bit rate)** rather than CBR—By combining the positive attributes of voice compression and silence suppression, ATM-based voice conversations are able to be transmitted using variable bit rate bandwidth management. By only using bandwidth when someone is talking, remaining bandwidth is available for data transmission or other voice conversations. Use of VBR is controlled via two parameters:
    1. Peak voice bit rate controls the maximum amount of bandwidth a voice conversation can be given when there is little or no contention for bandwidth.
    2. Guaranteed voice bit rate controls the minimum amount of bandwidth that must be available to a voice conversation regardless of how much contention exists for bandwidth.

Standards for voice transmission over ATM (VTOA) networks are being developed by the ATM Forum. Among the standards available or under development are the following:

- CES (circuit emulation standard): Defines voice transport over ATM networks using CBR; equivalent to PVCs over frame relay nets.

- VTOA-ATM: For use on private or public ATM networks; defines voice transmission using
    1. ISDN as a voice source network
    2. Transport of compressed voice over ATM.
    3. Virtual tunnel groups that are able to handle multiple calls simultaneously between two locations.

- VTOA to the Desktop: Defines interoperability between ATM and non-ATM networks.

Figure 4-25 illustrates the transmission of voice conversations over an ATM network.

Voice/Data Multiplexers

As opposed to using a switch-based frame relay or ATM network for wide-area transmission of voice and data, organizations have traditionally chosen to link combined voice and data transmission over long distances via leased digital transmission services such as T-1. From a business perspective, a key difference between switched services such as frame relay or ATM and leased services such as T-1 is that switched services are usually tariffed according to usage and leased services are usually tariffed according to a flat monthly rate. As a result, leased services are being paid for 24 hr/day, 7 days/week, whether they are being used or not.

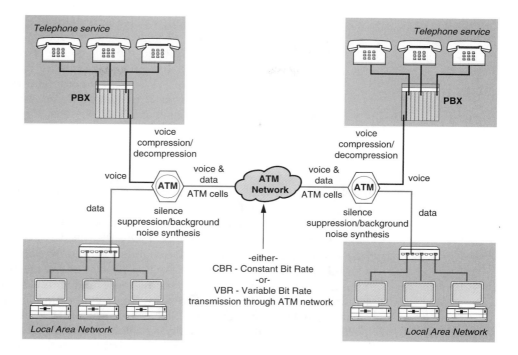

Figure 4-25   Voice Transmission over an ATM Network

Many corporations that once maintained a private network of **voice/data multi-plexers** linked via T-1 or other high-speed digital services have found that the usage-based pricing of frame relay networks can save them significant expense. A voice/data multiplexer is able to simultaneously transmit digitized voice and data over a single digital transmission service by assigning the voice and data transmissions to separate channels. Multiplexing will be explored in more depth in Chapter 8.

Voice/Data Modems

With the increase in home businesses and telecommuting, the idea of transmitting voice and data simultaneously over a single analog phone line has gathered increased interest. In this manner, a technical support specialist could be speaking with a customer while simultaneously taking over remote control of the customer's PC to run diagnostics or download files for inspection, editing, and reinstallation. Such a simultaneous conversation/data session would not require a second phone line on either end but would require modems that support simultaneous transmission of voice and data on both ends of the transmission.

Two different standards currently exist for simultaneous transmission of voice and data over a single analog phone line:

1. **ASVD (analog simultaneous voice and data)** does not transmit voice and data in a truly simultaneous manner. Instead, it switches quickly between the voice and data transmission. Voice transmission always takes priority, so that transfers are paused during data transmissions. ASVD has been formalized as ITU standard V.61 and is incorporated into VoiceView software from Radish Communications Systems that is included in Windows 95.

2. **DSVD (digital simultaneous voice and data)** digitizes all voice transmissions and combines the digitized voice and data over the single analog transmission line. The digitized voice is compressed into between 9.6 and 12 Kbps, leaving between 16.8 and 19.2 Kbps for data out of the total 28.8-Kbps transmission rate of a V.34 DSVD compliant modem. Such modems are currently available from Boca Research and U.S. Robotics. The DSVD standard has been formalized as ITU V.70.

ISDN

ISDN is a switched digital, rather than analog, service that is also capable of transmitting voice and data simultaneously. Rather than using modems, ISDN requires devices that are officially known as terminal adapters but that are frequently marketed as **ISDN data/voice modems.** ISDN BRI (basic rate interface) service offers two 64-Kbps channels. One of these channels is used for data while the other is used to simultaneously transmit voice. Analog phones or fax machines can be interfaced to the ISDN data/voice modem to allow these analog devices to access ISDN's digital transmission service. Point-to-point ISDN connections require both ends of the transmission to be able to access ISDN services via ISDN data/voice modems.

ISDN is not nearly as available as switched analog voice phone service. In addition, pricing policies for ISDN can include both a monthly flat fee and an additional usage-based tariff. ISDN will be explored further in Chapter 8. Figure 4-26 illustrates

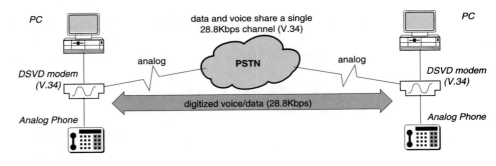

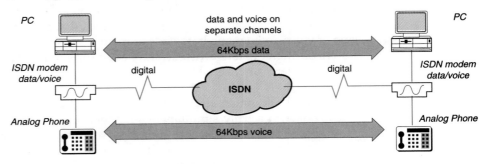

Figure 4-26   Simultaneous Voice/Data Transmission with DSVD and ISDN

the differences between simultaneous voice and data transmission using DSVD modems on analog services and ISDN data/voice modems over ISDM services.

SUMMARY

Network analysts must be qualified to design networks that are capable of carrying voice as well as data. Before designing such networks, the network analyst must understand the nature of voice signals as well as how voice signals can be processed and integrated into a cohesive network with data transmissions.

Voice bandwidth on the analog public switched telephone network (PSTN) is limited to 3100 Hz. To combine voice with data over a single transmission link, voice signals must first be digitized. Pulse code modulation and its derivatives are the most popular voice digitization techniques. Depending on the voice compression algorithms employed, digitized voice requires between 64 and 8 Kbps of bandwidth.

The PBX is the voice server or switch that links users' phones with their intended destinations. Today's PBXs have evolved from proprietary monolithic architectures to open, standards-based architectures.

PBXs are being increasingly seen as specialized servers for distributed client/server information systems. Computer telephony integration seeks to optimize the use of the telephone and the desktop computer by being able to share the information and functionality offered by each. Standardized APIs and PBX-to-host interfaces are required if CTI is to ever reach its full potential.

The voice network consists of a hierarchy of switching offices designed to offer fast, reliable service. Switches are able to communicate with each other via a common language known as signaling system 7. End-users are now able to use SS7 to monitor and control their carrier-based transmission circuits through advanced intelligent network and software-defined network services.

Alternative voice transmission architectures include voice over the Internet, voice over frame relay, voice over ATM, voice/data multiplexers, voice/data modems, and ISDN modems.

KEY TERMS

ACD, 120
Adaptive differential pulse code modulation, 111
ADPCM, 111
advanced intelligent network, 129
AIN, 129
analog simultaneous voice and data, 137
ANI, 128
API, 122
application program interfaces, 122
ASVD, 134
asynchronous transfer mode, 135
ATM, 135
audiotex, 121
automated attendant, 118
automatic call distribution, 120

automatic number identification, 128
CAI, 119
call accounting system, 117
call control, 121
call pickup, 116
CBR, 135
CCIS, 128
cells, 135
channel bank, 108
Class 1 regional center, 127
Class 2 sectional center, 127
Class 3 primary center, 127
Class 4 toll center, 126
Class 5 office, 126
client/server CTI, 120
codec, 108

common air interface, 119
common channel interoffice signaling, 128
common control area, 112
computer telephony integration, 120
constant bit rate, 135
cordless telephony generation 2, 119
CPE, 128
CT2, 119
CTI, 120
CTI application development tool, 123
CTI voice card, 124
desktop CTI, 120
DID, 116

REVIEW QUESTIONS

1. How do the sound waves of the human voice actually get transferred onto and off the voice network?
2. What is DTMF and what are its potential uses beyond assisting in completing a call?
3. What are the differences between the various voice digitization techniques?
4. How does PCM differ from ADPCM in terms of bandwidth requirements?
5. How is voice compression accomplished? What technology is involved?
6. What is the business motivation for voice compression? What is the potential trade-off?
7. What are the major architectural elements of a PBX?
8. Explain how voice transmission can be integrated

with computers to produce a service known as computer telephony integration.
9. What are some practical business applications of CTI?
10. What are some potential uses of voice processing or interactive voice response?
11. What is the voice network hierarchy and what are the fundamental implications of such a hierarchical design?
12. What is out-of-band signaling and of what importance is such a technical ability in terms of emerging network services?
13. Why might a voice conversation not be totally transmitted via analog transmission even if the source and destination loops are analog?

14. How does sampling rate in voice digitization relate to the quality of the transmitted voice signal?

15. How does ADPCM accomplish digitized voice transmission in less than 64 Kbps?

16. Why is DS-0 considered a standard circuit for transmission of digitized voice?

17. How does PCM differ from other voice digitization techniques such as PAM?

18. What are the benefits of PCM over other voice digitization methods?

19. What is the role of the codec in voice digitization?

20. What are some of the interoperability issues surrounding CTI?

21. How can the cost of call accounting systems be justified?

22. What are some of the PBX features required to support a call accounting system?

23. What are some of the issues surrounding interoperability of PBXs from various vendors?

24. What is signaling system 7 and how is it related to ISDN?

25. What is a software-defined network and what role does SS7 play in such a network?

26. Why is it important for network analysts to be qualified to design voice networks?

27. Compare the bandwidth of the PSTN with that of human hearing.

28. What is a channel bank?

29. What is toll quality and how is it related to ADPCM?

30. Show the mathematical proof of why a T-1 circuit is 1.544 Mbps.

31. Describe the basic architecture of a PBX. How is it like and unlike the switch in a CO?

32. What are some important architectural trends in PBX design and what is the driving force behind these trends?

33. What is automatic call distribution and what is an effective application of ACD?

34. Differentiate between the three major CTI architectures in terms of physical topology and delivered functionality.

35. What is predictive dialing?

36. What is a universal in-box and why might this be of benefit to its users?

37. Differentiate between TSAPI and TAPI.

38. What are some of the important functions of CTI application development tools?

39. What is the function of the CTI voice card in the CTI implementation?

40. What is a tandem office?

41. What is required to transmit voice over the Internet?

42. What are some important features of IP-based voice transmission software?

43. How is voice compression related to bandwidth requirements and delay?

44. What characteristic of frame relay must be overcome for effective voice transmission?

45. What are some of the issues surrounding voice over ATM?

46. Differentiate between ASVD and DSVD.

47. How does an ISDN data/voice modem differ from a DSVD modem?

48. What is the difference between CBR and VBR for voice over ATM?

49. Differentiate between peak voice bit rate and guaranteed voice bit rate.

50. How does a FRAD assist in optimizing voice transmission over frame relay?

ACTIVITIES

1. Suppose a normal voice-grade circuit had a bandwidth of 3000 Hz. What would be the maximum sampling rate of an analog signal on such a circuit? How much bandwidth would be required to transmit a digitized conversation from such a circuit using PCM? Using ADPCM? How many conversations could be transmitted over a T-1 using PCM? Using ADPCM?

2. Request product literature from a variety of PBX vendors. Note differences in functionality and pricing. Prepare presentations concerning PBX options and price ranges for small, medium, and large companies.

3. Investigate the level of support for CTI from the major PBX vendors. Which computing platforms are compatible with which PBXs? What impact has TAPI and TSAPI had on the CTI market?

4. What are the approximate costs of various CTI systems? Assuming a maximum payback period of 2 years, how much additional revenue would the various CTI options have to generate? Which CTI functionality is most often implemented (IVR, predictive dialing, ACD, etc.)?

5. Take apart a modern telephone handset and compare it to the handset illustrated in Figure 4-1. Draw a detailed diagram of your handset. Try to explain any differences between the two diagrams.

6. Investigate and report on which government agencies use the specialized keys illustrated in Figure 4-17 and for what purpose such keys are used.
7. Arrange a tour of a large school's or business' PBX facility. Prepare a detailed report outlining PBX functionality, installation, and architecture as well as the PBX's ability to meet business-level requirements and objectives.
8. Find out if your school or business uses a call accounting system. Speak to the person in charge of the system to investigate how it is used as well as its effectiveness at spotting and curtailing abuse of phone privileges. Report on your results.
9. Conduct a survey on how people feel about doing business with companies that employ voice processing or automated attendant systems.
10. Contact your local phone company to investigate the nearest location of each of the various classes of switching offices illustrated in Figure 4-18.
11. Investigate the current market penetration of TAPI vs. TSAPI based applications. Explain your results. What is Versit?

CASE STUDY

WAN Architecture Goes to School

A PBX maker's converged voice and data WAN architecture is finding takers among network managers for school districts.

Mitel Corp.'s Networked Voice and Data (NeVaDa) has been successfully trialed at the Stoughton Area School District here, the vendor announced last week. The school district—serving six schools, an administration building and public library—dumped its Centrex service and token-ring and Ethernet LANs for the new Mitel architecture.

Introduced at last spring's NetWorld+Interop in Las Vegas, NeVaDa is an extension of Mitel's existing fiber-distributed PBX in which all telephone calls are handled by a voice control module at the central location. To merge with a distributed data network, the voice control unit is linked to a Madge Networks, Inc. Ethernet switching hub outfitted with a new ATM/Synchronous Optical Network (SONET) module.

To make the network work, the user organization must agree to lease or install fiber capable of carrying a 155M bit/sec traffic stream into each premises building. The reason schools are taking the offer, is that they have close relationships with municipal governments that are upgrading their physical communications infrastructures, explained Dan MacDonald, Mitel's director of product marketing.

For example, with the help of the local government, the Stoughton school district installed an 18-strand hybrid fiber—12 single-mode and six multimode—to each site, following local voters' approval of a referendum last February.

And Mitel, a Canadian-based company that has a strong installed base among schools, particularly in the northern U.S., is finding that many of its educational customers are facing pressure to provide Internet access, remote library access and other new applications. To save money while doing that, they are cutting out traditional voice infrastructures, such as tie lines linking PBXs.

"By combining what were two distinctly separate operations, we were able to simplify out network and realize cost savings in the management of our overall network," said Bob Smiley, district technology director for the school district.

NeVaDa differs from other converged voice/data WANs, such as those promoted by Northern Telecom, Inc., with its Magellan Passport switches, in that an ATM/SONET module within the central Madge hub carves out a separate path for voice traffic rather than interleaving it with data traffic.

The voice control unit at the central site acts as the brains of the distributed PBX. Telephone calls originating at the remote sites travel over the fiber net through the switching hub to the voice control unit, where they are sent out to carriers.

The remote voice nodes have enough intelligence to feed traffic directly to back up originating telephone lines, he said.

BUSINESS CASE STUDY QUESTIONS

Activities

1. Complete a top-down model for this case by gleaning facts from the case and placing them in the proper layer of the top-down model. After completing the top-down model, analyze and detail those instances where requirements were clearly passed down from upper layers to lower layers of the model and where solutions to those requirements were passed up from lower layers to upper layers of the model.

2. Detail any questions about the case that may occur to you for which answers are not clearly stated in the article.

Business

1. What were the business justifications for such a network upgrade?

2. Were cost savings realized with the new network? If so, how?

Application

1. What is Centrex?
2. What is NeVaDa?
3. Did merging the voice and data traffic in this application make sense? Why or why not?

4. What types of applications are schools and local governments needing to offer?

Data

1. What was the bandwidth of the new network backbone?

2. What were the bandwidth requirements of the proposed applications?

Network

1. What were the old network architecture components (voice and data) that were replaced?
2. What were the media requirements for the network?
3. What is the difference between the voice and control unit and the remote voice nodes?

4. Do voice calls enter the PSTN on school-to-school calls? How?
5. Do voice calls enter the PSTN on long-distance calls? How?

Technology

1. How are the voice and data networks merged?
2. What types of modules were included in the switching hub?
3. How does NeVaDa differ from other PBX vendors'

data/voice integration strategies? Are these differences significant or just marketing?
4. What CTI standards (if any) are supported by NeVaDa?

LOCAL AREA NETWORK ARCHITECTURES, HARDWARE, AND OPERATING SYSTEMS

INTRODUCTION

Having gained an overall understanding of data and voice communications in Part 1, in Part 2 we study in more detail local area networking. Local area networks and client/server information systems combine to deliver productivity tools and information to locally attached users. Delivering those productivity tools and information requires a combination of local area networking hardware and software. That LAN hardware and software can be arranged and interconnected in a variety of different LAN architectures.

In Chapter 5, local area network architectures and concepts are studied. Functionality, standards, advantages, and proper business application of each alternative network architecture are addressed. The OSI model is reintroduced as a means of organizing information concerning alternative network architectures.

In Chapter 6, the hardware technology required to install a LAN is studied in detail. The numerous technological changes affecting network interface cards will be explored as will the trend toward LAN switches as a means to meet the ever increasing demands for LAN bandwidth. The hardware/software interface between network interface cards and LAN software is given particular attention as a key point for protocol compatibility.

In Chapter 7, local area network operating systems are studied from architectural and functional perspectives. Comparisons are made between currently available network operating system technologies that are representative of such network operating system categories as peer-to-peer, small business, client, and server. This chapter serves as a suitable overview of network operating systems in general.

CHAPTER 5

LOCAL AREA NETWORK CONCEPTS AND ARCHITECTURES

Concepts Reinforced

OSI Model   Top-Down Model
Hardware/Software Compatibility   Protocols and Standards

Concepts Introduced

Access Methodologies   Logical Topologies
Physical Topologies   Network Architectures
IEEE 802 Standards   High-Speed Network Architectures

OBJECTIVES

After mastering the material in this chapter, you should

1. Understand how access methodologies, logical topologies, and physical topologies combine to form alternative network architectures.

2. Understand the similarities, differences, advantages, and disadvantages to current network architectures such as Ethernet, token ring, and FDDI.

3. Understand the similarities, differences, advantages, and disadvantages of emerging high-speed network architectures such as 100BaseT, 100VG-Any-LAN, ISO-Ethernet, gigabit Ethernet, fibre channel, and LAN-based ATM.

4. Understand the value of the OSI model in the analysis of network architecture alternatives.

5. Understand how proper LAN analysis can help determine which network architecture is most appropriate in any given situation.

■ INTRODUCTION

Computers of various sizes and capabilities are able to communicate and share information thanks to the combined components of the local area network which links them. These local area network components are able to offer transparent network transmission services to attached computers due to their adherence to

147

standards and protocols. One of the key distinguishing characteristics of a particular local area network is its network architecture. In this chapter, the components of a network architecture will be first explored, followed by comparative evaluations of the numerous network architectures either currently available or emerging into the networking marketplace. The OSI model, first introduced in Chapter 1, will be reintroduced as a means in which to organize comparative information regarding alternative network architectures.

■ WHAT IS A LOCAL AREA NETWORK?

A **local area network (LAN)** is a combination of hardware and software technology that allows computers to share a variety of resources such as

- Printers and other peripheral devices.

- Data.

- Application programs.

- Storage devices.

LANs also allow messages to be sent between attached computers, thereby enabling users to work together electronically in a process often referred to as collaborative computing. The local nature of a local area network is a relative rather than absolute concept. There is no hard and fast rule or definition as to the geographic limitations of a network that qualifies to be called a local area network. In general, LANs are confined to an area no larger than a single building or a small group of buildings.

LANs can be extended by connecting to other similar or dissimilar LANs, to remote users, or to mainframe computers. This process is generally referred to as LAN connectivity or internetworking and is covered in Chapter 9. LANs of a particular company can be connected to the LANs of trading partners such as vendors and customers. These trading partners may be located in the same town or around the globe. Arrangements linking these trading partners are commonly referred to as enterprise networks. These enterprise networks are created by combining LANs with a variety of wide area network (WAN) services and are covered in Part 3.

Strictly speaking, the computers themselves are not part of the LAN. In other words, a single user could be productive on a stand-alone personal computer (PC). However, to share information, resources, or messages with other users and their computers, a LAN must be implemented to connect these computers. The LAN is the combination of technology that allows computers and their users to interact. Figure 5-1 provides a conceptual illustration of a LAN.

■ HOW IS A LOCAL AREA NETWORK IMPLEMENTED?

To begin with, appropriate networking hardware and software must be added to every computer or shared peripheral device that is to communicate via the local area network. Some type of network media must physically connect the various networked computers and peripheral devices. The various connected computers and peripheral devices will all share this media to converse with each other. As a result,

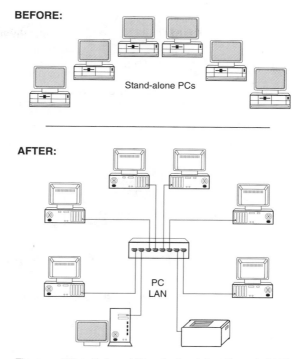

BEFORE:

Stand-alone PCs

AFTER:

PC
LAN

The same PC's with the addition of a Local Area Network (LAN.) A
LAN is a combination of hardware and software technology which
enables communication and resource sharing among attached
computers.

Figure 5-1   What Is a Local Area Network?

LANs are sometimes more specifically referred to as **shared-media LANs** or **media-sharing LANs.** Figure 5-2 provides a highly conceptual view of how a shared-media local area network might be implemented.

Don't be fooled by the apparent simplicity of Figure 5-2. All of the illustrated networking hardware and software must be compatible not only with the computer or peripheral device in which it is installed but also with the hardware and software that comprises the LAN itself and the networking hardware and software installed on all other computers and peripheral devices attached to the LAN. Compatibility refers to the ability of hardware and software, manufactured by various vendors, to work together successfully without intervention by the end-user. In other words, the combination of compatible hardware and software technology is transparent to the end-user. All that users see is that they are receiving the information they need to do their jobs effectively.

Networking Hardware

Among the types of possible networking hardware employed in implementing a LAN are

- Network interface cards, which must be installed in every linked computer and peripheral device.

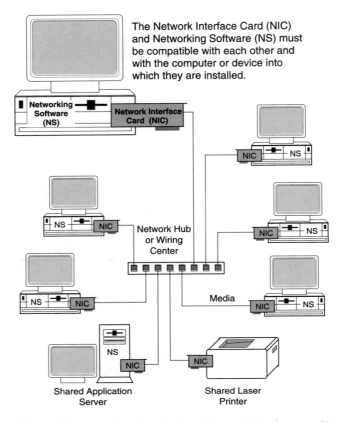

The Network Interface Card (NIC) and Networking Software (NS) must be compatible with each other and with the computer or device into which they are installed.

Figure 5-2   How Is a Local Area Network Implemented?

- Some type of network hub or wiring center into which the networked devices can be physically linked.

Most LAN-connected PCs require specialized network interface cards (NICs). Rather than using NICs, zero-slot LANs use existing serial or parallel ports of personal computers and peripheral devices for communication. Given the relatively slow speeds of the serial and parallel ports as compared to most NICs, zero-slot LANs are usually limited to two to four users.

The **network interface card** (or adapter) is appropriately named. Its job is to provide a transparent interface between the shared media of the LAN and the computer into which it is physically installed. The NIC takes messages that the computer directs it to send to other LAN-attached computers or devices and formats those messages in a manner appropriate for transport over the LAN. Conversely, messages arriving from the LAN are reformatted into a form understandable by the local computer. To ensure compatibility, all hardware and software technology interacting on the LAN must adhere to the same agreed-upon message format.

Most LANs today use some type of **hub,** also sometimes known as a wiring hub or wiring center. The hub provides a connecting point through which all attached devices are able to converse with one another. Hubs must be compatible with both the attached media and the NICs that are installed in client PCs.

Networking Software

Among the types of possible networking software employed in implementing a LAN are

- Software that allows personal computers that are physically attached to the LAN to share networked resources such as printers, data, and applications.

- Software that runs on shared network devices such as printers, data storage devices, and application servers that allows them to be shared by multiple LAN-attached users.

A stand-alone (not LAN-attached) PC requires software to operate. Commonly referred to as the operating system, this software interfaces between application programs such as a word-processing program and the client hardware (CPU, memory, disk drive).

The software that runs on personal computers and allows them to log into a LAN and converse with other LAN-attached devices is sometimes referred to as client software or client network software. A **client** PC is a computer that a user logs into to access LAN-attached resources and services. A LAN-attached client PC is sometimes characterized as a service requester. The client network software must be compatible with the network software running on all LAN-attached clients and servers. This compatibility is most easily assured by having both the clients and the servers install the same **network operating system** software. Examples of popular network operating systems are NetWare, Vines, and Windows NT (not to be confused with Windows). LAN software is discussed in Chapter 7.

Servers such as application servers and print servers are usually dedicated computers accessed only through LAN connections. Whereas a client could be considered a service requester, servers are characterized as service providers. It would stand to reason that the server's job of trying to fulfill the requests of multiple LAN-attached clients quickly and efficiently is more complicated than a single LAN-attached client making a single request for a service. Therefore, the server version of a particular network operating system is more complex, expensive, and larger than the client version of the same network operating system. Client and server versions of network operating systems are purchased separately. Client licenses are usually purchased in groups (5-user, 25-user, 100-user) whereas server licenses are most often purchased individually. Servers occasionally require software that is not supplied by the server version of a network operating system. Such software is discussed in Chapter 7.

Compatibility is again an issue as any network operating system must be compatible with the operating system and hardware of the client or server on which it is installed. Additionally, the network operating system software must be able to successfully communicate with the installed network interface card. The specifics of network operating system/network interface card compatibility will be discussed further in Chapter 7.

Networking Media

Network media can vary widely depending on required transmission speed and a variety of other factors such as network interface card type, security needs, and the physical characteristics of the environment in which the media is to be deployed.

Even the air can serve as a LAN media as evidenced by the many wireless LAN alternatives currently available.

LAN media must be installed carefully and according to industry-standard specifications. Something as innocent as pulling a cable tie too tightly can wreak havoc on high-speed LANs. LAN media must be compatible with network interface cards and hubs or wiring centers. LAN media alternatives and selection criteria will be reviewed in Chapter 6.

■ WHY ARE LOCAL AREA NETWORKS IMPLEMENTED?

Business Needs—The Underlying Motivation

Business needs as articulated by management are not inherently local area networking business needs, nor do they necessarily imply local area networks as a business solution. Only by analyzing business activities and asking business analysis questions will it be determined whether or not a local area networking solution is appropriate.

Business needs or perspectives provide the motivation for further business network analysis and design. By clearly understanding management's perspectives before beginning any technical analysis, the network analyst will have an easier time selling eventual proposals to management after completing technical analysis, assured that this proposal will meet management's business objectives. These business needs and perspectives provide the network analyst with a frame of reference within which to conduct research and evaluate options. Figure 5-3 lists a few typical business needs and perspectives that may lead to local area networking solutions.

The high-level business needs and perspectives listed in Figure 5-3 are representative examples, typical of the kinds of upper level management priorities that are often articulated. Many other possible business needs or perspectives could have been listed. Business needs and perspectives are dynamic, changing in

---

- Recognition of information as a corporate asset to be leveraged to competitive advantage

- Increased data accessibility

- Improved customer service

- Reduced expenses

- Increased productivity

- More bandwidth to the desktop for greater data accessibility

- Information systems must be
    - reliable
    - easy to install and use
    - well supported
    - affordable
    - secure

- Information systems must minimize the need for large staffs of highly trained and high-salaried technically oriented individuals

---

Figure 5-3   Business Needs and Perspectives That May Lead to Local Area Networking Solutions

response to changing economic and competitive climates as well as management teams and philosophies.

To make this exercise in business-oriented LAN analysis and design most effective, add business needs and perspectives that have been articulated to you by management. Management's business needs and perspectives should be clearly documented and understood before beginning network analysis and design. These same needs and perspectives should be referred to on a continual basis as a means of testing the feasibility of various technical networking options.

Although all business needs and perspectives will not necessarily be solved by implementing local area networks, it can be unequivocally stated that local area networks should only be implemented if they meet stated business needs. Furthermore, the analysis and design methodology that leads up to LAN implementation should be of a structured nature and should be documentable to justify final conclusions and recommendations.

The Importance of Effective LAN Analysis and Design

Given that LANs are implemented to solve real-world business needs as articulated by senior management and that recommended solutions must be both justifiable and documentable, it is essential that LAN analysis and design be conducted in a structured, effective manner. As will be seen in the following section, because of the number of possible different pieces of hardware and software technology manufactured by different vendors that may have to interoperate, effective LAN analysis and design can be an overwhelming task. From a business perspective, senior management wants assurance that money invested in technology will have the desired business impact.

Managerial Perspective

Chief executive officers seek business solutions, not technical solutions, and are concerned with making sure that information technology spending practices are properly aligned with strategic business objectives. Furthermore, senior business executives realize that the most expensive technology is not always the best at delivering business solutions and that, in fact, less expensive technology is often sufficient. Perhaps most importantly, CEOs are concerned with the inevitable, constant, accelerating rate of technological change. Dealing with this technological change by having a well-defined, strategic technology plan and infrastructure closely aligned with business strategic plans is the best way to prevent technological obsolescence from determining business outcomes. Mapping business strategic plans to technological strategic plans is the purpose of LAN analysis and design. By first understanding the challenges to effective LAN analysis and design, the network analyst will be able to propose solutions and resultant methodology that are meaningful and appropriate.

■ CATEGORIZING LAN ARCHITECTURES: THE OSI MODEL REVISITED

To effectively differentiate between various local area network architectures and the multitude of protocols associated with local area networks, some sort of standardized organizing framework or logical model is required. The OSI model, first introduced in Chapter 1, is just such a model and is a valuable tool for the network analyst.

Overall Structure and Characteristics

The **OSI model** consists of a hierarchy of seven layers that loosely group the functional requirements for communication between two computing devices. The power of the OSI model lies in its openness and flexibility. It can be used to organize and define protocols involved in communicating between two computing devices in the same room as effectively as two devices across the world from each other.

Each layer in the OSI model relies on lower layers to perform more elementary functions and to offer total transparency to the intricacies of those functions. At the same time, each layer provides the same transparent service to upper layers. In theory, if this transparency model is supported, changes in the protocols of one layer should not require changes in protocols of other layers. A **protocol** is a set of rules that govern communication between hardware and/or software components.

Physical Layer

The **physical layer,** also known as layer 1, is responsible for the establishment, maintenance, and termination of physical connections between communicating devices. These connections are sometimes referred to as **point-to-point data links.** The physical layer transmits and receives a stream of bits. There is no data recognition at the physical layer.

Specifically, the physical layer operation is controlled by protocols that define the electrical, mechanical, and procedural specifications for data transmission. The RS-232-C specification for serial transmission is an example of a physical layer protocol. Strictly speaking, the physical layer does not define the specifications for connectors and cables, which are sometimes referred to as belonging to layer 0.

Data-Link Layer

The **data-link layer** is responsible for providing protocols that deliver reliability to upper layers for the point-to-point connections established by the physical layer protocols. The data-link layer is of particular interest to the study of local area networks as this is the layer in which network architecture standards are defined. These standards are debated and established by the **IEEE (Institute of Electrical and Electronic Engineers) 802** committee and will be introduced and explained later in this chapter. The number 802 is derived from the date of the committee's formation in 1980 (80) in the month of February (2).

The data-link layer provides the required reliability to the physical layer transmission by organizing the bit stream into structured **frames** that add addressing and error-checking information. Additional information added to the front of data is called a **header,** and information added to the back of data is called a **trailer.** Data-link layer protocols provide error detection, notification, and recovery.

The data-link layer frames are built within the **network interface card (NIC)** installed in a computer according to the predetermined frame layout particular to the network architecture of the installed NIC. NICs are given a unique address in a format determined by their network architecture. These addresses are usually assigned and preprogrammed by the NIC manufacturer. The NIC provides the connection to the LAN, transferring any data frames that are addressed to it to the computer's memory for processing.

The first two layers of the OSI model, physical and data link, are manifested as hardware (media and NICs, respectively) whereas the remaining layers of the OSI model are all installed as software protocols.

Sublayers

To allow the OSI model to more closely adhere to the protocol structure and operation of a local area network, the IEEE 802 committee split the data-link layer into two sublayers.

Media Access Control   The **media access control** or **MAC sublayer** interfaces with the physical layer and is represented by protocols that define how the shared local area network media is to be accessed by the many connected computers. As will be explained more fully later in this chapter, token ring (IEEE 802.5) and Ethernet (IEEE 802.3) networks use different media access methodologies and are therefore assigned different IEEE 802 protocol numbers.

Logical Link Control   The upper sublayer of the data-link layer that interfaces to the network layer is known as the **logical link control** or **LLC sublayer** and is represented by a single IEEE 802 protocol (IEEE 802.2). The advantage to splitting the data-link layer into two sublayers and to having a single, common LLC protocol is that it offers transparency to the upper layers (network and above) while allowing the MAC sublayer protocol to vary independently. In terms of technology, the splitting of the sublayers and the single LLC protocol allows NetWare to run equally well over token ring or Ethernet NICs.

Network Layer

The **network layer** protocols are responsible for the establishment, maintenance, and termination of **end-to-end network links.** Network layer protocols are required when computers that are not physically connected to the same LAN must communicate. Network layer protocols are responsible for providing network layer (end-to-end) addressing schemes and for enabling internetwork routing of network layer data **packets.** The term *packets* is usually associated with network layer protocols whereas the term *frames* is usually associated with data-link layer protocols. Unfortunately, not all networking professionals or texts adhere to this generally accepted convention. Addressing schemes and routing will be thoroughly reviewed in the remainder of the text.

Network layer protocols are part of a particular network operating system's protocol stack. Different networking operating systems may use different network layer protocols. Many network operating systems have the ability to use more than one network layer protocol. This capability is especially important to heterogeneous, multiplatform, multivendor client/server computing environments.

Transport Layer

Just as the data-link layer was responsible for providing reliability for the physical layer, the **transport layer** protocols are responsible for providing reliability for the end-to-end network layer connections. Transport layer protocols provide end-to-end recovery and flow control. Transport layer protocols also provide mechanisms for sequentially organizing multiple network layer packets into a coherent **message.**

Transport layer protocols are also supplied by a given network operating system and are most often closely linked with a particular network layer protocol. For example, NetWare uses IPX/SPX in which IPX (Internet packet exchange) is the network layer protocol and SPX (sequenced packet exchange) is the transport layer protocol. Another popular transport/network protocol duo is TCP/IP in which TCP (transmission control protocol) provides reliability services for IP (Internet protocol).

Session Layer

The **session layer** protocols are responsible for establishing, maintaining, and terminating sessions between user application programs. Sessions are interactive dialogues between networked computers and are of particular importance to distributed computing applications in a client/server environment. As the area of distributed computing is in an evolutionary state, the session layer protocols may be supplied by the distributed application, the network operating system, or a specialized piece of additional software designed to render differences between computing platforms transparent, known as middleware.

Presentation Layer

The **presentation layer** protocols provide an interface between user applications and various presentation-related services required by those applications. For example, data encryption/decryption protocols are considered presentation layer protocols as are protocols that translate between encoding schemes such as ASCII to EBCDIC. A common misconception is that graphical user interfaces such as Windows and Presentation Manager are presentation layer protocols. This is not true. Presentation layer protocols are dealing with network communications whereas Windows and/or Presentation Manager are installed on end-user computers.

Application Layer

The **application layer,** layer 7 of the OSI model, is also open to misinterpretation. Application layer protocols do not include end-user application programs. Rather, they include utilities that support end-user application programs. Some people include network operating systems in this category. Strictly speaking, the best examples of application layer protocols are the OSI protocols X.400 and X.500. X.400 is an open-systems protocol that offers interoperability between different e-mail programs, and X.500 offers e-mail directory synchronization among different e-mail systems.

Figure 5-4 offers a conceptual view of the OSI model and summarizes many of the previous comments.

Encapsulation/De-encapsulation

The previous discussion highlighted the roles of the various OSI model layer protocols in a communications session between two networked computers. How the various protocol layers actually interact with each other to enable an end-to-end communications session is highlighted in Figure 5-5.

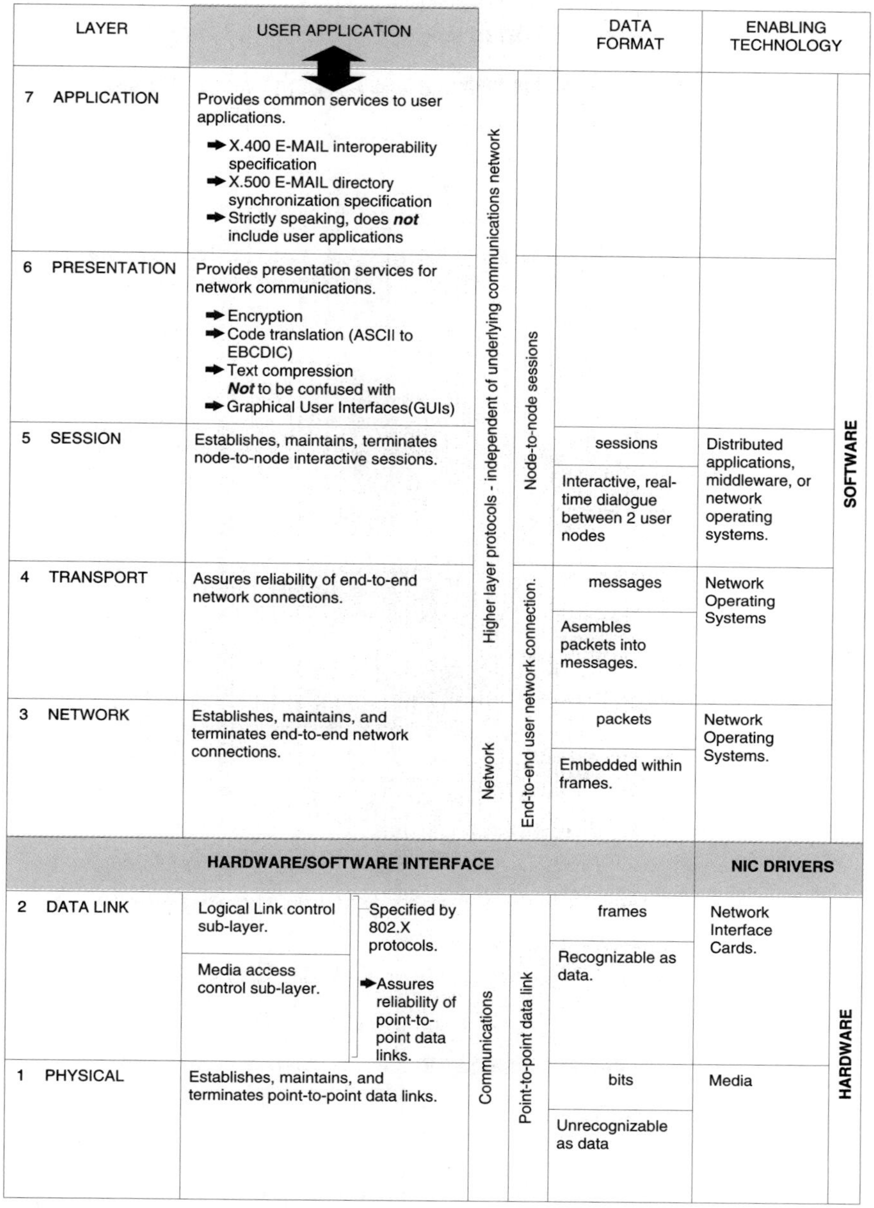

LAYER	USER APPLICATION				DATA FORMAT	ENABLING TECHNOLOGY
7 APPLICATION	Provides common services to user applications. ➡ X.400 E-MAIL interoperability specification ➡ X.500 E-MAIL directory synchronization specification ➡ Strictly speaking, does **not** include user applications	*Higher layer protocols - independent of underlying communications network*	*Node-to-node sessions*			
6 PRESENTATION	Provides presentation services for network communications. ➡ Encryption ➡ Code translation (ASCII to EBCDIC) ➡ Text compression **Not** to be confused with ➡ Graphical User Interfaces(GUIs)					
5 SESSION	Establishes, maintains, terminates node-to-node interactive sessions.				sessions / Interactive, real-time dialogue between 2 user nodes	Distributed applications, middleware, or network operating systems. *(SOFTWARE)*
4 TRANSPORT	Assures reliability of end-to-end network connections.		*End-to-end user network connection.*		messages / Asembles packets into messages.	Network Operating Systems
3 NETWORK	Establishes, maintains, and terminates end-to-end network connections.			*Network*	packets / Embedded within frames.	Network Operating Systems.
HARDWARE/SOFTWARE INTERFACE						**NIC DRIVERS**
2 DATA LINK	Logical Link control sub-layer. / Media access control sub-layer.	Specified by 802.X protocols. ➡Assures reliability of point-to-point data links.		*Point-to-point data link*	frames / Recognizable as data.	Network Interface Cards. *(HARDWARE)*
1 PHYSICAL	Establishes, maintains, and terminates point-to-point data links.		*Communications*		bits / Unrecognizable as data	Media

Figure 5-4   OSI Model—A Conceptual View

As illustrated in Figure 5-5, a data message emerges from a client front-end program and proceeds down the protocol stack of the network operating system installed in the client PC in a process known as **encapsulation.** Each successive layer of the OSI model adds a header according to the syntax of the protocol that occupies that layer. In the case of the data-link layer, both a header and trailer are added. The bit stream is finally passed along the shared media that connects the two computing devices. This is an important point. Although the OSI model may seem to imply that given layers in a protocol stack talk directly to each other on different comput-

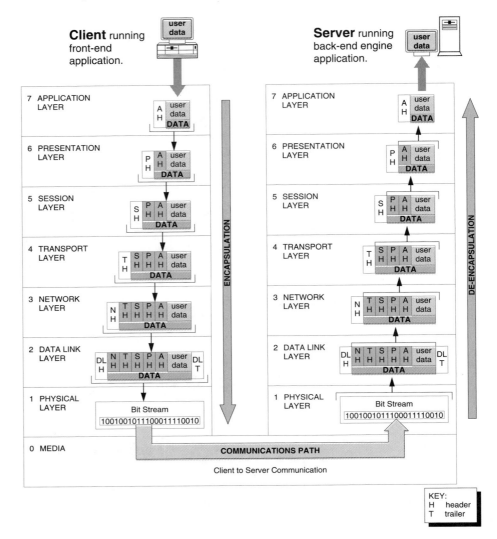

Figure 5-5   OSI Model—An Architectural View

ers, the fact is that the computers are only physically connected by the media and that is the only layer that talks directly between computers.

When the full bit stream arrives at the destination server, the reverse process of encapsulation, **de-encapsulation,** takes place. In this manner, each successive layer of the OSI model removes headers and/or trailers and processes the data that was passed to it from the corresponding layer protocol on the source client. Once the server has processed the client's request for data in the server back-end engine application, the whole process is reversed and the requested data will be encapsulated by the server's protocol stack, transmitted over the communications media, and de-encapsulated by the client PC's protocol stack before being ultimately delivered to the client front-end application that requested the data in the first place.

■ THE LOCAL AREA NETWORK ARCHITECTURE MODEL

Although not all network architectures are standardized by the IEEE or some other standards-making organization, all network architectures are made up of the same logical components. To accurately describe a given network architecture, one needs to know the following:

- Access methodology.
- Logical topology.
- Physical topology.

As numerous network architectures are evaluated later in the chapter, these three major components will be discussed in each case. The only other variable added to the network architecture of choice is the particular media over which a given network architecture can operate. As will be seen, most network architectures are able to operate over a variety of media types. The previously mentioned combinations of variables can be summarized in the following manner:

- Network architecture = access methodology + logical topology + physical topology.
- Network configuration = network architecture + media choice.

Access Methodology

Since more than one user is likely to be sending requests onto the shared local area network media at any one time, the need for some way to control which users get to put their messages onto the network and when should be obvious. If the media is to be shared by numerous PC users, then there must be some way to control access by multiple users to that media. These media-sharing methods are properly known as **access methodologies.** Sharing the media is an important concept in local area networks, which are sometimes referred to as **media-sharing LANs.**

Logically speaking, there are really only two philosophies for controlling access to a shared media. An analogy of access to a crowded freeway can provide a vivid illustration of access methodology choices.

CSMA/CD   One philosophy says, "Let's just let everyone onto the media whenever they want and if two users access the media at the exact same split second, we'll work it out somehow." Or, in the analogy, "Who needs stoplights! If we have a few collisions, we'll work it out later!"

The access methodology based on this model is known as **carrier sense multiple access with collision detection,** or **CSMA/CD** for short. A clearer understanding of how this access methodology works can be achieved if the name of this access methodology is examined one phrase at a time.

Carrier sense: The PC wishing to put data onto the shared media listens to the network to see if any other users are "on the line" by trying to sense a neutral electrical signal known as a carrier. If no transmission is sensed, then *multiple access* allows anyone onto the media without further permission required. Finally, if two user PCs should both sense a free line and access the media at the same instant, a collision occurs and *collision detection* lets the user PCs know that their data was not delivered and controls retransmission in such a way as to avoid further data collisions. Another possible factor leading to data collisions is the **propagation delay,** which is the time it takes a signal from a source PC to reach a destination PC. Because of this propagation delay, it is possible for a workstation to sense that there is no signal on the shared media, when in fact another distant workstation has transmitted a signal that has not yet reached the carrier-sensing PC.

In the event of a collision, the station that first detects a collision sends out a special jamming signal to all attached workstations. Each workstation is preset to wait a random amount of time before retransmitting, thus reducing the likelihood of reoccurring collisions. If successive collisions continue to occur, the random time-out interval is doubled.

CSMA/CD is obviously most efficient with relatively little contention for network resources. The ability to allow user PCs to access the network easily without a lot of permission requesting and granting reduces overhead and increases performance at lower network usage rates. As usage increases however, the increased number of data collisions and retransmissions can negatively affect overall network performance.

Token Passing   The second philosophy of access methodology is much more controlling. It says, "Don't you dare access the media until it's your turn. You must first ask permission, and only if I give you the magic token may you put your data onto the shared media." The highway analogy would be the controlled access ramps to freeways in which a driver must wait at a stoplight and somehow immediately get to 60 mph to merge with the traffic.

Token passing ensures that each PC user has 100% of the network channel available for data requests and transfers by insisting that no PC accesses the network without first possessing a specific packet (24 bits) of data known as a **token.** The token is generated in the first place by a designated PC known as the **active monitor** and passed among PCs until one PC would like to access the network.

At that point, the requesting PC seizes the token, changes the token status from free to busy, puts its data frame onto the network, and doesn't release the token until it is assured that its data was delivered successfully. Successful delivery of the data frame is confirmed by the destination workstation setting **frame status flags** to indicate successful receipt of the frame and continuing to forward the original frame around the ring to the sending PC. Upon receipt of the original frame with frame status flags set to "destination address recognized, frame copied successfully," the sending PC resets the token status from busy to free and releases it. After the sending PC releases the token, it is passed along to the next PC, which may either grab the free token or pass it along.

A modified form of token-passing access methodology is used in 16-Mbps token ring network architectures, in which the token is set to free and released as soon as the transmission of the data frame is completed rather than waiting for the transmitted data frame to return first. This is known as the **early token release mechanism.** The software and protocols that actually handle the token passing and token regeneration, in the case of a lost token, are usually located in the chips on the network adapter card. Figure 5-6 illustrates a simple token-passing access methodology LAN.

Token passing's overhead of waiting for the token before transmitting inhibits overall performance at lower network usage rates. However, because all PC users on a token-passing access control network are well behaved and always have the

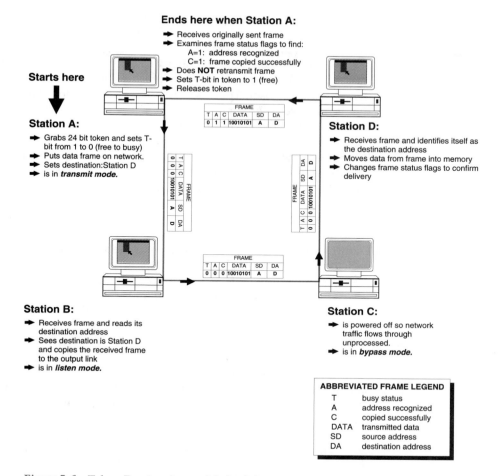

Starts here

Ends here when Station A:

➡ Receives originally sent frame
➡ Examines frame status flags to find:
    A=1: address recognized
    C=1: frame copied successfully
➡ Does **NOT** retransmit frame
➡ Sets T-bit in token to 1 (free)
➡ Releases token

Station A:

➡ Grabs 24 bit token and sets T-bit from 1 to 0 (free to busy)
➡ Puts data frame on network.
➡ Sets destination:Station D
➡ is in **transmit mode.**

Station D:

➡ Receives frame and identifies itself as the destination address
➡ Moves data from frame into memory
➡ Changes frame status flags to confirm delivery

Station B:

➡ Receives frame and reads its destination address
➡ Sees destination is Station D and copies the received frame to the output link
➡ is in **listen mode.**

Station C:

➡ is powered off so network traffic flows through unprocessed.
➡ is in **bypass mode.**

ABBREVIATED FRAME LEGEND	
T	busy status
A	address recognized
C	copied successfully
DATA	transmitted data
SD	source address
DA	destination address

Figure 5-6   Token-Passing Access Methodology

magic token before accessing the network, there are, by definition, no collisions, making token passing a more efficient access methodology at higher network utilization rates.

Logical Topology

Once a data message is onto a shared-media LAN that is connected to numerous workstations, the next thing that must be determined is how that message will be passed from workstation to workstation until the message ultimately reaches its intended destination workstation. The particular message-passing methodology employed is more properly known as a network architecture's **logical topology.** An analogy used to describe logical topologies has to do with how best to put out a fire in a PC user's wastebasket.

Sequential   The first logical topology or method of delivering data is known as **sequential.** In a sequential logical topology, also known as a **ring** logical topology, data is passed from one PC (or node) to another. Each node examines the destination address of the data packet to determine if this particular packet is meant for it. If the data was not meant to be delivered at this node, the data is passed along to the next node in the logical ring.

This is the bucket brigade logical topology method of putting out a fire in a PC user's wastebasket. A bucket of water is filled by one PC user and passed to the neighboring PC user. That user determines if his/her wastebasket is on fire. If it is, the user douses the flames with the bucket of water. Otherwise, the user passes the bucket along to the next user in the logical ring.

Broadcast The second logical topology or method of delivering data is known as **broadcast.** In a broadcast logical topology, a data message is sent simultaneously to all nodes on the network. Each node decides individually if the data message was directed toward it. If not, the message is simply ignored. There is no need to pass the message along to a neighboring node. They've already gotten the same message.

This is the sprinkler system logical topology method of putting out a fire in a PC user's wastebasket. Rather than worry about passing a bucket of water around a logical ring until it finally reaches the engulfed wastebasket, the water is just broadcast over the entire network, with the result being that the wastebasket that was on fire will know that the water was meant for it.

Physical Topology

Finally, the clients and servers must be physically connected to each other according to some configuration and be linked by the shared media of choice. The physical layout of this configuration can have a significant impact on LAN performance and reliability and is known as a network architecture's **physical topology.**

Bus The **bus** topology is a linear arrangement with terminators on either end and devices connected to the "bus" via connectors and/or transceivers. The weak link in the bus physical topology is that a break or loose connection anywhere along the entire bus will bring the whole network down.

Ring The **ring** topology suffers from a similar Achilles' heel. Each PC connected via a ring topology is actually an active part of the ring, passing data packets in a sequential pattern around the ring. If one of the PCs dies or a network adapter card malfunctions, the "sequence" is broken, the token is lost, and the network is down.

Star The **star** physical topology avoids these two aforementioned potential pitfalls by employing some type of central management device. Depending on the network architecture and sophistication of the device, it may be called a hub, a wiring center, a concentrator, a MAU (multistation access unit), a repeater, or a switching hub. All of these devices will be studied later in the text. By isolating each PC or node on its own leg or segment of the network, any node failure only affects that leg, while the remainder of the network continues to function normally.

Since all network data in a star topology is going through this one central location, it makes a marvelous spot to add system monitoring, security, or management capabilities. The other side of the coin is that since all network data is going through this one central location, it makes a marvelous networking no-no known as a **single point of failure.** The good news is, any node can be lost and the network will be fine. The bad news is, lose the hub and the whole network goes down.

Bus topology

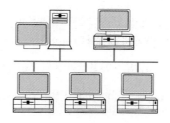

Star topology

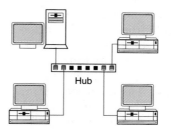

Ring topology

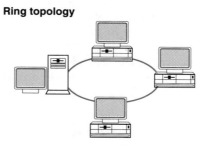

Figure 5-7   LAN Physical Topology
Choices

As we will see shortly in the study of hubs, vendors have risen to the occasion, offering such reliability extras as redundant power supplies, dual buses, and "hot-swappable" interface cards. Figure 5-7 highlights the differences between these physical topologies.

■ NETWORK ARCHITECTURES

Ethernet

Origins   The invention of **Ethernet** is generally credited to Robert Metcalfe, who later went on to become the founder of 3Com Corporation. Although, strictly speaking, Ethernet and **IEEE 802.3** are conflicting standards, the term *Ethernet* is commonly used to refer to any IEEE 802.3 compliant network. Differences between the two standards will be outlined shortly.

Functionality

- Access methodology: CSMA/CD.

- Logical topology: broadcast.

- Physical topology: traditionally, bus; currently, most often star.

Standards   The first Ethernet standard was developed by Digital, Intel, and Xerox Corporation in 1981 and was known as DIX 1.0, sometimes referred to as Ethernet I. This standard was superseded in 1982 by DIX 2.0, the current Ethernet standard, also known as Ethernet II. The frame layouts for **Ethernet II** and IEEE 802.3 are illustrated in Figure 5-8.

As illustrated in Figure 5-8, both Ethernet II and IEEE 802.3 frames can vary in length from 64 to 1518 octets.

Ethernet II   The Ethernet II frame layout consists of the following fields:

- The Ethernet II frame starts with a preamble of eight octets. The purpose of the preamble is to alert and synchronize the Ethernet network interface card to the incoming data.

- The destination and source addresses are each six octets long and are also known as MAC layer addresses. These addresses are permanently burned into the ROM (read-only memory) of the Ethernet II network interface card at the time of manufacture. The first three octets of the address identify the manufacturer of the network interface card and are assigned by the IEEE. The last three octets are assigned by the manufacturer producing unique MAC layer addresses for all Ethernet network interface cards.

- The type field identifies which network protocols are embedded within the data field. For example, if the data field contained Network IPX/SPX protocols, then the type field would have a value of 8137 (hexadecimal) and if the data field contained TCP/IP protocols, then the type field would contain a value of 0800 (hexadecimal). These type values are assigned by the IEEE. The type field is important in order to enable multiple protocols to be handled by

Ethernet II Frame Layout

Preamble	Destination Address	Source Address	Type	Data Unit	Frame Check Sequence
8 Octets	6 Octets	6 Octets	2 Octets	46 to 1500 bytes	4 Octets

The overall frame length varies from 64 to 1518 Octets

IEEE 802.3 Frame Layout

Preamble	Start Frame Delimiter	Destination Address	Source Address	Length	Logical Link Control IEEE 802.2 Data	Frame Check Sequence
7 Octets	1 Octet	2 or 6 Octets	2 or 6 Octets	2 Octets	46 to 1500 bytes	4 Octets

The overall frame length varies from 64 to 1518 Octets

NOTE: 1 Octet = 8 bits

Figure 5-8   Ethernet II and IEEE 802.3 Standards

a single network interface card that enables multiple protocol stacks to be loaded in a given client or server. Once the network interface card identifies which protocol is embedded within the data field, it can forward that data field to the proper protocol stack for further processing. Multiple protocol stacks allow communication between clients and servers of different network operating systems, which is essential to transparent distributed computing.

- The data unit field contains all of the encapsulated upper layer (network through application) protocols and can vary in length from 46 to 1500 bytes. The 46-byte minimum data field length combines with the 18 octets of fixed overhead of all of the other fields to produce the minimum frame size of 64 octets.

- The **frame check sequence (FCS)** is an error detection mechanism generated by the transmitting Ethernet network interface card. A 32-bit **cyclical redundancy check (CRC)** is generated over the address, type, and data fields. The receiving Ethernet network interface card regenerates this same CRC on the address, type, and data fields in the received frame and compares the regenerated CRC to the transmitted CRC. If they match, the frame was received error free. Error bursts of up to 31 bits can be detected with 100% accuracy with 32 CRCs.

IEEE 802.3   The IEEE 802.3 frame layout is very similar to the Ethernet II frame layout. Highlights of the IEEE 802.3 frame layout are as follows:

- The seven-octet preamble plus the one-octet starting frame delimiter perform the same basic function as the eight-octet Ethernet II preamble.

- Address fields are defined and assigned in a similar fashion to Ethernet II frames.

- The two-octet length field in the IEEE 802.3 frame takes the place of the type field in the Ethernet frame. The length field indicates the length of the variable-length **LLC (logical link control)** data field that contains all upper layer embedded protocols.

The type of embedded upper layer protocols is designated by a field within the LLC data unit and is explained more fully in the "In Sharper Focus" section that follows. The frame check sequence is identical with that used in the Ethernet II frame.

In Sharper Focus

IEEE 802.2 AND ETHERNET SNAP

In order for an IEEE 802.3 compliant network interface card to be able to determine the type of protocols embedded within the data field of an IEEE 802.3 frame, it refers to the header of the **IEEE 802.2** LLC data unit. Figure 5-9 illustrates the fields contained in the IEEE 802.2 data unit.

More specifically, the types of protocols embedded within the data unit are identified within the destination and source service access point fields (DSAP and SSAP). These fields are analogous to type field in the Ethernet frame. SAP codes that identify a particular protocol are issued by the IEEE to those companies that register their IEEE-compliant protocols. For example a SAP code of E0 identifies a Novell protocol and a SAP code of 06 identifies a TCP/IP protocol. NetWare frames adhering to this standard are referred to as NetWare 802.2 (802.3 plus 802.2).

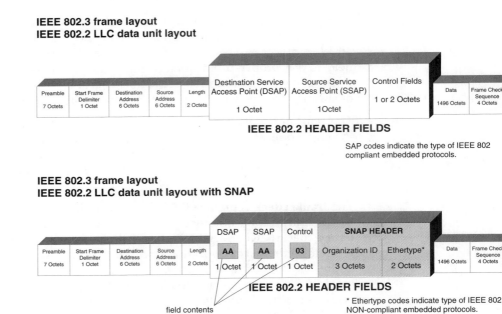

Figure 5-9   IEEE 802.2 and Ethernet SNAP

However, in some cases, rendering network protocols to be IEEE 802 compliant was not an easy task. To ease the transition to IEEE 802 compliance, an alternative method of identifying the embedded upper layer protocols was developed, known as **SNAP** or **subnetwork access protocol.** Any protocol can use SNAP with IEEE 802.2 and appear to be an IEEE 802 compliant protocol. In some cases, network operating system vendors such as NetWare used SNAP until modifications were made to bring protocols into compliance with IEEE standards. Now that NetWare is IEEE 802 compliant and has a designated SAP code, NetWare users can choose a NetWare 802.2 frame layout.

A single SAP code of AA in both the DSAP and SSAP and a control code of 03 are used to identify all noncompliant protocols. To differentiate which particular noncompliant protocol is embedded, any packet with AA in the DSAP and SSAP fields also has a five-octet SNAP header known as a **protocol discriminator** following the control field as illustrated in Figure 5-6. The first three octets of the protocol discriminator are called the organization ID and indicate to which company the embedded protocol belongs, whereas the last two octets are called the EtherType field, which indicates which protocol is embedded. If the organization ID field consists entirely of zeroes, a generic Ethernet frame, not unique to any particular company, is indicated. Examples of EtherType values include

- 08-00 for TCP/IP.

- 81-37 for NetWare.

NetWare frames adhering to this specification are known as NetWare 802.2 SNAP (802.3 plus 802.2 plus SNAP).

Media-Related Ethernet Standards   Ethernet can run over numerous media types. The unshielded twisted pair media employed in an Ethernet standard known as **10BaseT** sells for as little as 6¢/ft. The *10* in 10BaseT refers to 10-Mbps capacity, the *Base* refers to **baseband transmission,** meaning that the entire bandwidth of the media is devoted to one data channel, and the *T* stands for twisted pair, the media. Another important distinction of 10BaseT is that it specifies the use of a star topology with all Ethernet LAN segments (100-m maximum each) connected to a centralized wiring hub.

10Base5 was the original implementation of Ethernet and used thick coaxial cable (RG-11) arranged in a bus physical topology. Individual computers attached to the thick coax bus by connecting installed network adapter cards to transceivers that tapped into the thick cable using a device known as a vampire tap. A DB-15 (15-pin shell, 9 wires) attachment unit interface (AUI) cable, up to 50 m in length, connected the NIC to the transceiver. The overall bus topology had to be terminated with 50-ohm terminators. Although overall segment length is limited to 500 m, up to 100 workstations can be tapped into a single segment, placed a minimum of 2.5 m apart. Up to five segments can be joined together, yielding a total maximum network length of 2500 m with 1024 workstations.

10Base2 Ethernet replaces the thick coaxial cable with RG-58 coax, otherwise known as Thinnet, still arranged in a bus topology. Although easier to work with, the thin coax reduced overall segment length to 185 m, 30 workstations/segment, with workstations being a minimum of 0.5 m apart. 10Base2 network adapter cards offer BNC coaxial cable connectors to which T connectors are attached to allow the bus topology to be produced. The overall bus must have 50-ohm terminators on both ends. Up to five segments can be joined together, yielding an overall maximum network length of 925 m with 150 workstations.

Ethernet standards and associated media are listed in Figure 5-10. AUI connectors, BNC connectors, transceivers, and AUI cables are illustrated in Figure 6-7 in Chapter 6.

Standard	Popular Name	Speed	Media	Maximum Segment Length
10Base5	Frozen yellow garden hose	10 Mbps	Thick coaxial (RG-11) cable (0.405-in. diameter)	500-m bus
10Base2	ThinNet, CheaperNet	10 Mbps	Thin coaxial cable (RG-58)	185-m bus
10BaseT	Twisted pair Ethernet	10 Mbps	Unshielded twisted pair	100-m diameter star
10BaseF	Fiber Ethernet FOIRL (fiber optic inter repeater link)	10 Mbps	Multimode fiber optic cable	Described by IEEE 802.1j-1993 standard (1000 m)
1Base5	StarLAN	1 Mbps	Unshielded twisted pair	500 m

Figure 5-10   Ethernet Media-Specific Standards

Application   The potential for collisions and retransmission on an Ethernet network thanks to its CSMA/CD access methodology has already been mentioned. In some cases, Ethernet networks with between 100 and 200 users barely use the 10-Mbps capacity of the network. However, the nature of the data transmitted is the key to determining potential network capacity problems. Character-based transmissions, such as typical data entry, in which a few characters at a time are typed and sent over the network are much less likely to cause network capacity problems than GUI (graphical user interface) screen-oriented transmissions such as Windows-based applications. CAD/CAM images are even more bandwidth intensive.

Simultaneous requests for full-screen Windows-based transfers by 30 or more workstations on a single Ethernet LAN segment can cause collision and network capacity problems on an Ethernet network. As with any data communications problem, there are always solutions or workarounds to these problems. The point in relaying these examples is to provide some assurance that although Ethernet is not unlimited in its network capacity, in most cases, it provides more than enough bandwidth.

Token Ring

Origins   The credit for the first token ring network architecture has been attributed to Olaf Soderblum, who proposed such a network in 1969. IBM has been the driving force behind the standardization and adoption of token ring with a prototype in IBM's laboratory in Zurich, Switzerland, serving as a model for the eventual **IEEE 802.5** standard.

Functionality

- Access methodology: token passing.
- Logical topology: sequential.
- Physical topology: traditionally, ring, currently, most often star.

Standards   Unlike IEEE 802.3 Ethernet networks, which have a speed of 10 Mbps specified as part of the IEEE standard, the IEEE 802.5 token ring standard does not include a speed specification. IBM, the leading advocate of the token ring network architecture, has specified token ring network architectures that operate at 4 and 16 Mbps.

As mentioned earlier in the discussion of the token-passing access methodology, the token is actually a 24-bit formatted data packet and is illustrated in Figure 5-11 along with the IEEE 802.5 token ring MAC sublayer frame layout.

The IEEE 802.5 token ring frame layout consists of the following fields:

- The starting delimiter field alerts the token ring network interface card installed in a workstation that a token ring frame is approaching. Notice that both the token frame and the MAC sublayer frame start with the starting delimiter.

IEEE 802.5 Token Frame Layout

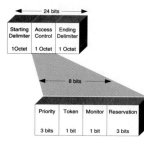

IEEE 802.5 MAC Sub-Layer Frame Layout

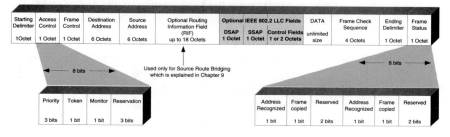

Figure 5-11   IEEE 802.5 Token Ring Token and MAC Sublayer Frame Layout

- Once the access control field is received, the workstation can distinguish between tokens and MAC sublayer frames. If the token bit within the access control field (see Figure 5-6) is set to 0, then the received frame represents a free token, in which case the access control field would be immediately followed by an ending delimiter. The workstation is welcome to receive the full token frame and change the token bit from 0 to 1 to indicate a busy token. The received starting delimiter field and the access control field with the T (token) bit now set to 1 form the first two fields of an IEEE 802.5 MAC sublayer data frame allowing the sending workstation to just append address information, data, and the remaining fields in the data frame layout and transmit this frame onto the ring.

- If the token bit on the received frame was set to 1, then the next field is the frame control field, which indicates whether this frame contains data or is a special network management frame.

- Following the frame control field are the destination and source address fields. The receiving network interface card would read the destination address to determine if it was the frame's intended recipient. If it was, then the workstation will read the rest of the frame into memory. If not, then the NIC will simply pass the rest of the bits of the frame along the ring without transferring them to the workstation's memory.

- The routing information field is used with devices known as source routing bridges, which are able to link together multiple token ring LANs. Source route bridging and other LAN-to-LAN connectivity options will be discussed in Chapter 9.

- The IEEE 802.2 header fields are used in an identical manner as they are used with IEEE 802.3 Ethernet MAC sublayer frames. Likewise, IEEE 802.2 SNAP is also supported within the IEEE 802.5 MAC sublayer frame.

- The data field contains data in the form of embedded upper level protocols if this is a data frame and network management information if this is a network management frame as indicated by the frame control field. The data field does not have a fixed maximum length as in the case of Ethernet but is effectively controlled by a timing limit as to how long any workstation can hold onto a token. The timing limit of 10 msec imposes a practical limit on the size of the data field in a 4-Mbps token ring network to about 4500 bytes and on a 16-Mbps token ring network to about 16,000–18,000 bytes.

- The frame check sequence uses a 32-bit cyclical redundancy check in an identical manner to IEEE 802.3

- The ending delimiter not only can let the workstation know that the end of the frame has arrived but also can let the workstation know if this was an intermediate frame with more related data to follow immediately behind. The ending delimiter can also indicate if another station has found an error in a frame and has indicated that it should be ignored and returned around the ring to the source address workstation for removal from the ring.

- The frame status field serves an important role in letting the sending workstation know whether or not the frame was successfully delivered. If the destination workstation recognized its address, then the A (address recognized) bits are set to 1 and if the frame was successfully copied into the destination workstation's memory, then the C (frame copied) bits are set to 1. There are two sets of A and C bits for redundancy to help eliminate errors. To be more specific, since the A and C bits are set by the destination station after the frame has been received, they are not covered by the frame check sequence error detection mechanism.

One workstation on every token ring LAN is designated as the active monitor and acts as a kind of caretaker of the token ring network architecture. Being the active monitor requires no special hardware or software, and all other workstations are designated standby monitors. Among the tasks that can be performed by the active monitor are the following:

- Removes frames from the ring that have not been removed by their sending workstations.

- Regenerates lost or damaged tokens.

- Provides a special 24-bit buffer if the physical ring is so small that it does not have enough delay or latency to hold the 24-bit token. For more information, see the "In Sharper Focus" entitled "Token Ring and Timing."

- Controls the master clock.

- Makes sure that there is only one designated active monitor on this ring.

Application   IBM's token ring network architecture, adhering to the IEEE 802.5 standard, utilizes a star configuration, sequential message delivery, and a token-passing access methodology scheme.

Remembering that the sequential logical topology is equivalent to passing messages from neighbor to neighbor around a ring, the token ring network architecture is sometimes referred to as **logical ring, physical star.**

The token ring's use of the token-passing access methodology furnishes one of the key positive attributes of this network architecture. The guarantee of no data collisions with assured data delivery afforded by the token-passing access methodology is a key selling point in some environments where immediate, guaranteed delivery is essential.

The second attribute in token ring's favor is the backing of a computer company of the magnitude of IBM. For those businesses facing integration of PCs with existing IBM mainframes and minicomputers, IBM's token ring network architecture offers assurance of the possibility of such an integration.

Although token ring is IBM's PC networking architecture, it is neither a closed system nor a monopoly. Third-party suppliers offer choices in the network adapter card and wiring hub (multiple access unit) markets, and numerous network operating systems run over the token ring architecture. Competition encourages research and development of new technology and can eventually drive prices down. Price is an important point about token ring. Network adapter cards for a token ring network tend to cost from one and one-half to two times as much as Ethernet network adapter cards.

ADDRESS BIT ORDER REVERSAL

One small but significant difference between Ethernet and token ring networks is known as **address bit order reversal.** As illustrated in Figure 5-12, both Ethernet and token ring refer to the first (leftmost) octet of the address as byte 0. Also, both Ethernet and token ring believe that bit 0 on byte 0, referred to as the **least significant bit,** should be transmitted first. However, in the case of IEEE 802.3, the least significant bit is the rightmost bit of the byte and in the case of IEEE 802.5, the least significant bit is the leftmost bit of the byte. This bit order reversal is especially troublesome for translating bridges, which must translate between token ring and Ethernet frames.

TOKEN RING AND TIMING

For the token ring network architecture to operate correctly, the 24-bit token must circulate continuously even if no workstations are in need of transmitting data. Therefore, the entire token ring network must possess enough delay or latency to hold the entire 24-bit token. This latency or required delay can be computed by dividing the length of the token (24 bits) by the ring's transmission speed (4 Mbps), yielding a required latency of 6 μsec. The next question is, how far can an electrical signal travel in 6 μsec? The answer to that question will depend on the media through which the signal is traveling, with different media possessing different propagation velocities. For example, unshielded twisted pair has a propagation velocity of 0.59 times the speed of light, denoted as c. The speed of light is equal to 300,000,000 m/sec. Finally, the minimum ring size to introduce the required 6 μsec of delay can be calculated as follows:

$$
\begin{aligned}
\text{Minimum ring size} &= \text{Required latency} \times \text{propagation velocity of media} \\
&= 0.000006 \text{ sec} \times 0.59 \times 300,000,000 \text{ m/sec} \\
&= 1062 \text{ m} \\
&= 1.062 \text{ km}
\end{aligned}
$$

Original Data Stream of 6 bytes

6 BYTES					
1 1 1 1 0 1 0 1	0 0 1 1 0 1 1 1	1 0 1 1 1 0 1 1	1 0 0 0 0 1 1 0	0 1 1 1 0 0 1 0	0 1 0 1 0 1 1 0

IEEE 802.3 Transmission

DESTINATION ADDRESS CONSISTING OF 6 BYTES					
BYTE 0	BYTE 1	BYTE 2	BYTE 3	BYTE 4	BYTE 5
1 1 1 1 0 1 0 1	0 0 1 1 0 1 1 1	1 0 1 1 1 0 1 1	1 0 0 0 0 1 1 0	0 1 1 1 0 0 1 0	0 1 0 1 0 1 1 0
bit 7 bit 6 bit 5 bit 4 bit 3 bit 2 bit 1 bit 0	bit 7 bit 6 bit 5 bit 4 bit 3 bit 2 bit 1 bit 0	bit 7 bit 6 bit 5 bit 4 bit 3 bit 2 bit 1 bit 0	bit 7 bit 6 bit 5 bit 4 bit 3 bit 2 bit 1 bit 0	bit 7 bit 6 bit 5 bit 4 bit 3 bit 2 bit 1 bit 0	bit 7 bit 6 bit 5 bit 4 bit 3 bit 2 bit 1 bit 0

Note that in the IEEE 802.3 transmission the least significant bit (BIT 0) is transmitted last.

IEEE 802.5 Transmission

DESTINATION ADDRESS CONSISTING OF 6 BYTES					
BYTE 0	BYTE 1	BYTE 2	BYTE 3	BYTE 4	BYTE 5
1 0 1 0 1 1 1 1	1 1 1 0 1 1 0 0	1 1 0 1 1 1 0 1	0 1 1 0 0 0 0 1	0 1 0 0 1 1 1 0	0 1 1 0 1 0 1 0
bit 0 bit 1 bit 2 bit 3 bit 4 bit 5 bit 6 bit 7	bit 0 bit 1 bit 2 bit 3 bit 4 bit 5 bit 6 bit 7	bit 0 bit 1 bit 2 bit 3 bit 4 bit 5 bit 6 bit 7	bit 0 bit 1 bit 2 bit 3 bit 4 bit 5 bit 6 bit 7	bit 0 bit 1 bit 2 bit 3 bit 4 bit 5 bit 6 bit 7	bit 0 bit 1 bit 2 bit 3 bit 4 bit 5 bit 6 bit 7

Note that in the IEEE 802.5 transmission the least significant bit (BIT 0) is transmitted first.

Figure 5-12   Address Bit Order Reversal in Ethernet and Token Ring

According to this calculation the minimum size of a token ring network, even for three or four workstations, would have to be over a kilometer in length. This is obviously not practical. As mentioned earlier, the active monitor station adds a 24-bit delay buffer to the ring to ensure that regardless of the size of the ring, the token will be able to continually circulate.

Managerial Perspective

TOKEN RING OR ETHERNET?

Discussions as to the relative merits of token ring or Ethernet network architectures were conducted at one time with all the fervor of a religious war. There seems to be less argument now as estimates put the ratio of Ethernet networks to token ring networks at about 3 to 1. This is not to say that Ethernet is a better network architecture. The significant advantage in terms of Ethernet market share probably has more to do with the affordability and availability of Ethernet vs. token ring hardware. Ethernet cards sell from $20 to $150 while token ring cards sell from $219 to $475. A 12-port Ethernet hub sells for around $529 whereas the equivalent token ring MAU (multistation access unit) sells for $1459.

In terms of performance, the fact is that Ethernet works just fine in most installations. Although Ethernet is said to offer 10 Mbps, when collisions and overhead are taken into consideration, actual throughputs of 6 Mbps are more the norm. There is no argument that token ring's deterministic access methodology eliminates collisions at higher traffic levels. However, due to the overhead associated with the token management, performance at lower traffic levels can suffer. Research performed on 16-Mbps token ring that features the early token release mechanism has shown conflicting results. Some studies show that network performance is not significantly greater than 10 Mbps, whereas others show nearly a full 16-Mbps throughput. If one considers cost/Mbps of throughput rather than just equipment cost differences, token ring begins to look more favorable.

At one time, token ring network architectures were more easily integrated with minicomputer and mainframe environments. This is no longer true as the mainframe/minicomputer world has evolved to embrace open systems, TCP/IP, and Ethernet.

In conclusion, the biggest difference between token ring and Ethernet continues to be the initial expense of the token ring hardware and the overwhelming market share of Ethernet. Performance is not significantly different and interoperability between the two network architectures is possible, although challenges do exist. Ethernet/token ring bridges provide transparent interoperability between the two network architectures and will be detailed in Chapter 9.

In Sharper Focus

ARCNET

ARCNet (attached resources computer network) was a popular local area network architecture that was originally developed by Datapoint, Inc. It offered 2.5-Mbps transmission speed and used a token-passing access methodology, a broadcast logical topology, and a star physical topology over RG-62 coaxial cable. Since RG-62 is the same cable used to connect IBM 3270 terminals to cluster controllers, ARCNet was often installed in downsized IBM installations where the cable could be reused. ARCNet was never standardized by the IEEE and has been largely replaced by Ethernet and token ring network architectures.

FDDI

Origins **Fiber distributed data interface (FDDI)** is a 100-Mbps network architecture that was first specified in 1984 by the ANSI (American National Standards Institute) subcommittee entitled X3T9.5. It is important to note that FDDI is not an IEEE standard. However, FDDI does support IEEE 802.2 logical link control protocols offering it transparent interoperability to IEEE-compliant upper layer protocols (layers 3–7).

Functionality

- Access methodology: Modified token passing
- Logical topology: sequential
- Physical topology: Dual counter-rotating rings

Built-in Reliability and Longer Distance FDDI supplies not only a great deal (100 Mbps) of bandwidth but also a high degree of reliability and security while adhering to standards-based protocols not associated with or promoted by any particular vendor.

FDDI's reliability comes not only from the fiber itself, which is immune to both **EMI** (electromagnetic interference) and **RFI** (radio frequency interference). An additional degree of reliability is achieved through the design of the physical topology of FDDI.

FDDI's physical topology is comprised of not one, but two, separate rings around which data moves simultaneously in opposite directions. One ring is the

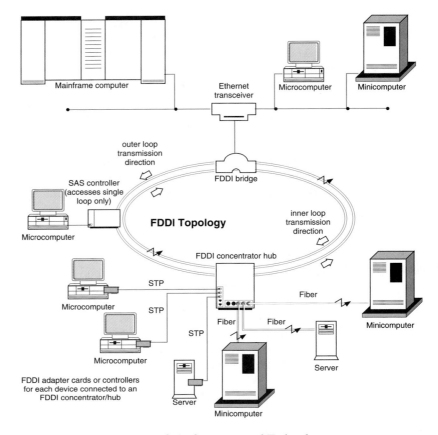

Figure 5-13   FDDI Network Architecture and Technology

primary data ring and the other is a secondary or backup data ring to be used only in the case of the failure of the primary ring or an attached workstation. Whereas both rings are attached to a single hub or concentrator, a single point of failure remains in the hub while achieving redundancy in the network media. Figure 5-13 illustrates some of the key features of the FDDI network architecture and technology whereas Figure 5-14 more specifically illustrates the self-healing capabilities of the dual counterrotating rings network architecture of FDDI.

In addition to speed and reliability, distance is another key feature of an FDDI LAN. Up to 500 nodes at 2 km apart can be linked to an FDDI network. The total media can stretch for a total circumference of up to 200 km (125 miles) if repeaters are used at least every 2 km. This increased distance capability makes FDDI an excellent choice as a high-speed backbone network for campus environments.

Another positive attribute of FDDI, illustrated in Figure 5-13, is its ability to interoperate easily with IEEE 802.3 10-Mbps Ethernet networks. In this way, a business does not have to scrap its entire existing network to upgrade a piece of it to 100-Mbps FDDI. An FDDI-to-Ethernet bridge is the specific technology employed in such a setup.

The technology involved with FDDI network architectures is similar in function to that of other network architectures and is illustrated in Figure 5-13. PCs, workstations, minicomputers, or mainframes that wish to access the FDDI LAN must be equipped with either internal FDDI network adapter cards or external FDDI controllers.

Dual-Attached Workstations in *Normal Operation*

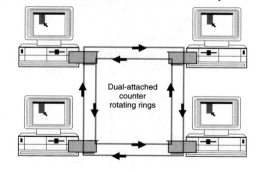

Self healed after *Link Failure*

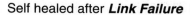

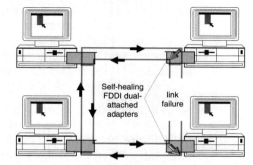

Self-healed after *Station Failure*

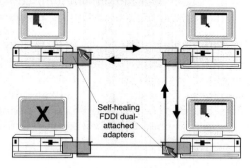

Figure 5-14   FDDI's Self-Healing Ability

One way in which some network managers cut down on FDDI's cost while still benefiting from the 100-Mbps bandwidth is to only connect to one of FDDI's two fiber rings. This type of connection is sometimes called **SAS,** or **single-attachment stations,** as opposed to **DAS,** or **dual-attachment stations,** in which both FDDI rings are accessed. Obviously, if a device is only attached to one FDDI ring, it forgoes the reliability afforded by the redundant secondary data ring.

At the heart of the FDDI LAN is the FDDI concentrator or hub. The design of these hubs is often modular, with backbone connections to both FDDI rings, management modules, and device attachment modules in various media varieties available for customized design and ease of installation.

Another key piece of FDDI technology is the FDDI-to-Ethernet bridge, which allows 10-Mbps Ethernet LANs to interface with the 100-Mbps FDDI LANs. The Ethernet LANs are very often department-based networks whereas the FDDI is more likely to be a campus-wide backbone. Bridges may be able to connect either a single Ethernet or several Ethernets to the FDDI LAN.

Standards   FDDI uses a modified token-passing access methodology. The word *modified* is used here because it is different from the IEEE 802.5 token ring type token passing in at least two key respects.

- First, because of the great potential distances on an FDDI LAN, it was impractical to turn "free" tokens into "busy" tokens and let a single station monopolize that token until it had received confirmation of successful delivery of its data. Instead, unlike token ring, which just flipped the T bit in the access control byte from 0 to 1 and appended a data frame, FDDI physically removes the token from the ring and transmits a full data frame. Upon completion of transmission, it immediately releases a new token. Recall that token ring waited until the transmitted frame returned before releasing the token. Collisions are still avoided as only one station can have the free token at a time, and stations cannot put data messages onto the network without a token.

- A second token-passing modification in FDDI is that numerous messages may be sent by a single PC before relinquishing the token as opposed to the "one message per token per customer" philosophy of the IEEE 802.5 token-passing access methodology. Frames transmitted in a continuous stream are known as **synchronous frames** and are prioritized according to a methodology known as **synchronous bandwidth allocation** or **SBA,** which assigns fixed amounts of bandwidth to given stations. While synchronous frames are being transmitted, any unused network capacity can still be used by other workstations transmitting **asynchronous frames.**

Figure 5-15 illustrates both an FDDI token layout and an FDDI data frame layout.

An alternative to fiber-based FDDI is to run FDDI over copper wiring, either shielded or unshielded twisted pair (UTP), as used in Ethernet and token ring installations. Cost savings of UTP over fiber amount to about 33%. Because running a fiber-based architecture over copper sounds a little strange, this variation of FDDI has been dubbed **CDDI** or **copper distributed data interface.** Although it will still

FDDI Token Layout

Preamble	Starting Delimiter	Frame Control	Ending Delimiter
8 Octets	1 Octet	1 Octet	1 Octet

FDDI Data Frame Structure

Preamble	Starting Delimiter	Frame Control	Destination Address	Source Address	DATA up to	Frame Check Sequence	Ending Delimiter	Frame Status
8 Octets	1 Octet	1 Octet	6 Octets	6 Octets	4500 Octets	4 Octets (32 bit CRC)	.5 Octet (4 Bits)	1.5 Octets (12 Bits)

Figure 5-15   FDDI Token and Data Frame Layouts

support 100 Mbps, distance is limited to 100 m/segment as compared with the 2 km/segment of fiber-based FDDI. The official ANSI standard for CDDI is known as **TP-PMD** (twisted pair-physical media dependent). The pinouts or wiring pattern for TP-PMD are not the same as 10BaseT Ethernet over twisted pair pinouts.

Application   To understand all the fuss about FDDI and CDDI, it is necessary to first understand why 10-Mbps Ethernet and 16-Mbps token ring may not contain sufficient bandwidth for the bandwidth-hungry applications of the not too distant future. The major bandwidth drivers fall into two major categories:

1.   Network architecture trends.

2.   Network application trends.

As far as trends in network architecture go, as more and more users are attached to LANs, the demand for overall network bandwidth increases. LANs are increasing both in size and in overall complexity. Internetworking of LANs of various protocols via bridges and routers means more overall LAN traffic. FDDI is frequently used as a high-speed backbone network architecture servicing multiple lower speed network segments, each of which supports multiple workstations.

Network applications are driving the demand for increased bandwidth as well. Distributed computing, data distribution, and client/server computing all rely on a network architecture foundation of high bandwidth and high reliability. Imaging, multimedia, and data/voice integration all require high amounts of bandwidth to transport and display these various data formats in "real" time.

In other words, if full-motion video is to be transported across the LAN as part of a multimedia program, there should be sufficient bandwidth available on that LAN for the video to run at full speed and not in slow motion. Likewise, digitized voice transmission should sound "normal" when transported across a LAN of sufficient bandwidth.

The uses of the FDDI network architecture seem to fall into three categories:

1.   Campus Backbone—Not necessarily implying a college campus, this implementation is used for connecting LANs located throughout a series of closely situated buildings. Remember that the total ring circumference can equal 200 km, and multiple FDDI LANs are always a possibility also. Building backbones would fall into this category as well, with perhaps a 100-Mbps FDDI building backbone going between floors connecting numerous 10-Mbps Ethernet LANs located on the various floors via routers. High-bandwidth devices such as servers can be connected to the FDDI backbone via concentrators. Figure 5-16 shows multiple concentrators attaching multiple devices to the FDDI rings, also known as a **dual ring of trees.** In some cases, a given server may be connected to more than one FDDI concentrator to provide redundant connections and increased fault tolerance. Dual connecting servers in this manner is known as **dual homing.**

2.   High-Bandwidth Workgroups—The second application category is when the FDDI LAN is used as a truly local area network, connecting a few (less than 20) PCs or workstations that require high-bandwidth communication with each other. Multimedia workstations, engineering workstations, or CAD/CAM workstations are all good examples of high-bandwidth workstations. As "power users" turn increasingly toward graphical user interfaces (GUI) such as Windows and OS/2, this constituency's bandwidth requirements will rise as well.

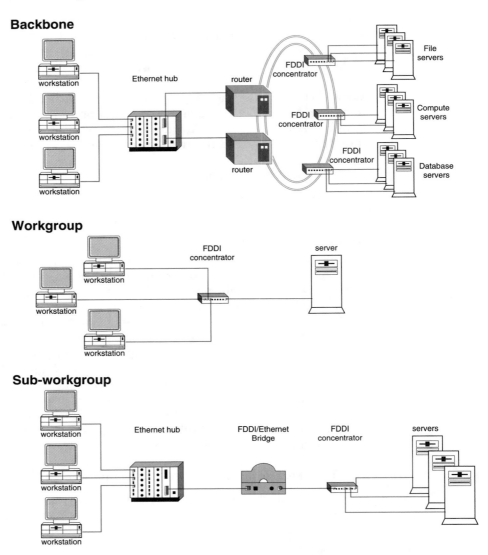

Figure 5-16   Alternative Applications of the FDDI Network Architecture

3. High-Bandwidth Subworkgroup Connections—In some cases, only two or three devices, perhaps servers, require high bandwidths. As distributing computing and data distribution increase as part of the downsizing and applications rightsizing trends sweeping the information systems industry, an increasing demand for high-speed server-to-server data transfer will be seen. Figure 5-16 illustrates alternative applications of the FDDI network architecture.

After all of these positive things to say about FDDI, surely there must be something negative about this LAN architecture. Chief among the negatives is price, although how long price will be a negative remains to be seen. As with any other shared-media network architecture, in order for a PC to access an FDDI LAN, it must be equipped with an FDDI network adapter card. These cards range from $1500 to $7500, with the "lower" priced FDDI network adapter cards able to attach to and use only one of the two FDDI data rings. Compare these prices with the average Ethernet card at $75–$200 and the average token ring card at roughly twice that price.

As FDDI gains in popularity and competition increases in the FDDI technology market, prices will undoubtedly fall, although it is doubtful that they will ever reach Ethernet price levels. The fiber media itself is seen as a negative factor by some as well. Although fiber is lightweight and can be packed more densely than copper wire, it is made of glass and can break. Also, connecting, terminating, and splicing fiber optic cables requires special tools and training. These obstacles can be overcome and, at least in some cases, the "fear of fiber" may be nothing more than the fear of the unknown.

Managerial Perspective

FDDI'S FUTURE

Occasionally in the field of data communications and networking, one technology is eclipsed or replaced by a newer technology that might be cheaper, easier to work with, or both. This may be the fate of FDDI. At one time, FDDI was the only network architecture alternative to turn to when Ethernet and token ring could no longer meet demands for bandwidth capacity. As will be seen in the next section, there now exist numerous alternative high-speed network architectures that are able to exceed FDDI in terms of price, performance, and ease of use. That is not to say that FDDI is dead, but as will be seen in the next section, the handwriting may be on the wall.

■ HIGH-SPEED NETWORK ARCHITECTURES

100BaseT

100BaseT represents a family of Fast Ethernet standards offering 100-Mbps performance and adhering to the CSMA/CD access methodology. The details of the operation of 100BaseT are in the **IEEE 802.3u** proposed standard. The three media-specific physical layer standards of 100BaseT are as follows:

- **100BaseTX**—This is the most common of the three standards and the one for which the most technology is available. It specifies 100-Mbps performance over two pair of Category 5 UTP (unshielded twisted pair) or two pair of Type 1 STP (shielded twisted pair).

- **100BaseT4**—Physical layer standard for 100-Mbps transmission over four pair of Category 3, 4, or 5 UTP.

- **100BaseFX**—Physical layer standard for 100-Mbps transmission over fiber optic cable.

Network Architecture 100BaseT standards use the same IEEE802.3 MAC sublayer frame layout and yet transmit it at 10 times faster than 10BaseT. Obviously, there must be a trade-off somewhere. The trade-off comes in the maximum network diameter:

- 10BaseT's maximum network diameter is 2500 m with up to four repeaters/ hubs between any two end nodes.

- 100BaseT's maximum network diameter is 210 m with up to only two repeaters/hubs between end nodes.

100BaseT is implemented as a shared-media LAN network architecture that links 100BaseT workstations via 100BaseT hubs and repeaters.

TIMING ISSUES AND 100BASET NETWORK DIAMETER

Collisions are a fact of life with any CSMA/CD-based network architecture. The time required for a given workstation to detect a collision is known as **slot time** and is measured in bits. When collisions occur, the transmitting station must be notified of the collision so that the affected frame can be retransmitted. However, this collision notification and retransmission must occur before the slot time has expired. The slot time for both 10BaseT and 100BaseT is 512 bits.

The speed of 100BaseT is obviously 10 times as fast as 10BaseT. To be certain that collision notifications are received by 100BaseT network attached workstations before their constant slot time expires, the maximum network diameter had to be reduced proportionately to the increase in network speed. As a result, the maximum network diameter shrinks from 2500 to 210 m.

Technology Most of the 100BaseT NICs are called **10/100 NICs,** which means that they are able to support either 10BaseT or 100BaseT, but not simultaneously. These cards cost not much more than quality 10BaseT-only cards, allowing network managers to buy 100BaseT capability now that can be enabled later when the requisite 100BaseT hubs are installed.

10BaseT and 100BaseT networks can only interoperate with the help of internetworking devices such as 10/100 bridges and routers. These types of technology will be discussed in more depth in Chapter 9.

Some Ethernet switches, which will be discussed in both Chapters 6 and 9, have the capability to support 100BaseT connections and to auto-sense, or distinguish between, 10BaseT and 100BaseT traffic. Figure 5-17 illustrates a representative 100BaseT installation.

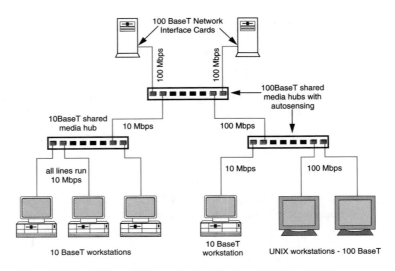

Figure 5-17 100BaseT Network Architecture Implementation

100VG-AnyLAN

100Vg-AnyLAN is a 100-Mbps alternative to 100BaseT that replaces the CSMA/CD access methodology with **demand priority access** or **DPA**, otherwise known as **demand priority protocol** or **DPP**. Details of the 100VG-AnyLAN architecture are contained in the proposed **IEEE 802.12** standard. The *AnyLAN* part of this network architecture name refers to its ability to deliver standard IEEE 802.3 or IEEE 802.5 MAC layer frames. However, both of these frame types cannot be delivered simultaneously by the same 100VG-AnyLAN network.

IEEE 802.3 and IEEE 802.5 Support   100VG-AnyLAN's ability to support IEEE 802.3 and IEEE 802.5 frame types and networks more specifically means the following:

- If current cabling for existing 10BaseT or token ring LANs meets the respective cabling specifications for those LANs, then 100VG-AnyLAN will run over the existing LAN cabling without changes to network design or cabling.

- Current network operating systems and application programs do not have to be modified to operate with the upgraded 100VG-AnyLAN interface cards.

- 10BaseT and token ring LANs can communicate with 100VG-AnyLANs by linking the respective LANs with internetworking devices such as bridges and routers.

Figure 5-18 illustrates the integration of IEEE 802.3, IEEE 802.5, and 100VG-AnyLAN architectures.

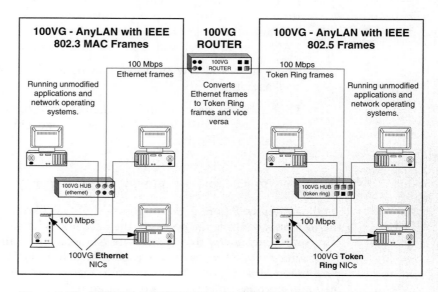

Figure 5-18   IEEE 802.3, IEEE 802.5, and 100VG-AnyLAN Architectures

Network Architecture   100VG-AnyLAN is able to match 100BaseT's speed performance and offers the following network architecture characteristics:

- Supports a network diameter of up to 2500 m between any two end notes. This is same as 10BaseT and over 10 times the maximum diameter of 100BaseT.

- Supports up to four hubs/repeaters between any two end notes whereas 100BaseT supports up to two.

Obviously, 100VG-AnyLAN cannot offer these gains in network architecture as compared to 100BaseT without some sort of trade-off.

The major difference is in the cabling requirements. Whereas 10BaseT and 100BaseT require only two pair of UTP to operate, 100VG-AnyLAN requires four pair of either Category 3, 4, or 5 UTP using a signaling methodology known as quartet signaling or channeling. Cabling standards have also been defined for two pair of Type 1 shielded twisted pair as well as single-mode and multimode fiber optic cable.

Demand Priority Access   Perhaps the most interesting aspects of the 100VG-Any-LAN architecture is the demand priority access methodology, also known as DPMA (demand priority media access). This unique access methodology eliminated the collisions and retransmissions that are characteristic of Ethernet and the token rotation delays of token ring. Key points of this access methodology are as follows:

- Specialized 100VG-AnyLAN hubs control all access to the network.

- Using a **round robin polling scheme,** the hubs scan each port in sequence to see if the attached workstations have any traffic to transmit. The round robin polling scheme is distributed through a hierarchical arrangement of cascaded hubs.

- Ports can be designated as high priority, thereby giving priority delivery status to time-sensitive types of traffic such as video or voice, which require guaranteed delivery times for smooth presentation. This makes 100VG-Any-LAN especially well suited for multimedia traffic.

- These high and low priorities can be assigned by application program as well as ports.

- High-priority ports cannot permanently monopolize the entire network. Once lower priority ports have been timed out for 250–300 msec, they are boosted to high priority.

In Sharper Focus

CASCADING HUBS AND THE ROUND ROBIN POLLING SCHEME

As illustrated in Figure 5-19, the central hub, also known as the controlling hub or the root hub, controls the access to the network, whereas all lower level hubs maintain communication with attached workstations and maintain address tables identifying which workstations are attached to which ports. When a workstation requests permission of its locally attached hub to load a message onto the network, that request for permission is passed up through the hierarchy of hubs until it reaches the designated controlling hub. The corresponding granted permission to transmit onto

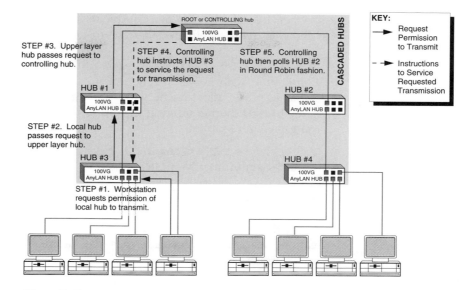

Figure 5-19   Cascading Hubs and the Round Robin Polling Scheme

the network is passed down through the hub hierarchy to the initially requesting workstation. Remember, a maximum of only four hubs or repeaters can lie between any two end nodes or workstations.

Technology   The implementation of a 100VG-AnyLAN requires compliant NICs, driver software, and hubs. 100VG-AnyLAN NICs cost between $225 and $300 whereas hubs cost about $300 per port. For ease of migration 10/100 Ethernet 100VG-AnyLAN NICs are available for generally less than $300. When it comes to technology, attention must be paid to whether this 100VG-AnyLAN technology will be transporting Ethernet frames or token ring frames. Specific NICs and hubs must be purchased for each of the two transported frame types, with Ethernet 100VG-AnyLAN technology being more readily available than token ring 100VG-AnyLAN technology.

Isochronous Ethernet

Although the ability to transport time-sensitive traffic such as voice, video, or multimedia is one of the advantages of 100VG-AnyLAN, other network architectures such as **isochronous Ethernet,** also known as **Iso-Ethernet,** can also effectively transport such traffic, although not at 100-Mbps performance. Details of the Iso-Ethernet network architecture are contained in the **IEEE 802.9a** standard, which is officially known as Isochronous Ethernet Integrated Services. The term **isochronous** refers to any signaling system in which all connections or circuits are synchronized using a single common clocking reference. This common clocking mechanism allows such systems to offer guaranteed delivery times, which are very important to streaming or time-sensitive traffic such as voice and video.

Network Architecture   One unique feature of the Iso-Ethernet network architecture is its close relationship with **ISDN (integrated services digital network)** wide area network services. Iso-Ethernet offers a combination of services by dividing the overall 16.144-Mbps bandwidth delivered to each workstation into several-specific channels:

- A 10-Mbps ISDN **P channel** is reserved for Ethernet traffic and is completely compatible with 10BaseT Ethernet. In fact, this P channel can be used by 10BaseT NICs, allowing network managers to selectively or gradually migrate to Iso-Ethernet offering the multimedia capabilities to only those workstations that require it.

- A 6.144-Mbps ISDN **C channel** is reserved for streaming time-sensitive traffic such as multimedia applications.

The 6.144-Mbps C channel is in fact further subdivided into

- 96 64-Kbps ISDN **B channels** that carry the actual multimedia traffic. Applications are able to aggregate these B channels as needed up to the 6.144-Mbps limit.

- 1 64-Kbps ISDN **D channel** that is used for management tasks such as call control and signaling.

The 6.144-Mbps C channel that carries the multimedia traffic uses the same 8-kHz clocking signal as the commercial ISDN WAN services offered by long-distance carriers, enabling a transparent interface between the Iso-Ethernet LAN and WAN segments. This "same clocking signal" is the derivation of the term *Iso* (same as) *chronous* (timing).

Network diameter of an Iso-Ethernet network is limited to 100 m from the most distant LAN workstation to the WAN interface. Iso-Ethernet runs over two pair of Category 3 or 5 UTP, allowing it to operate over existing network wiring in many cases.

Iso-Ethernet networks operate in three different service modes:

1. 10BaseT mode—uses only the 10-Mbps P channel for Ethernet traffic.

2. Multiserivce mode—uses both the 10-Mbps P channel for Ethernet and the 6.144-Mbps C channel for video/multimedia.

3. All-isochronous mode—uses all 16.144-Mbps (248×64 Kbps channels) for streaming protocols. This amount of isochronous bandwidth will support real time video or voice distribution.

Figure 5-20 illustrates an implemented Iso-Ethernet architecture including WAN links, transparent interoperability with 10BaseT workstations, and simultaneous transmission of Ethernet and multimedia traffic. Figure 5-21 illustrates the breakdown of the 16.144-Mbps Iso-Ethernet bandwidth.

Technology Iso-Ethernet hubs are known as **attachment units (AU)** and cost between $400 and $500 per port, whereas Iso-Ethernet NICs cost between $200 and $300 each. Most Iso-Ethernet attachment units include an integrated WAN port that is configured to be linked to commercial ISDN services available from long-distance carriers. A workstation with an Iso-Ethernet NIC installed is properly referred to as **integrated services terminal equipment (ISTE)**. To transmit isochronous traffic, 10BaseT NICs and hubs must be replaced. However, all 10BaseT NICs and hubs do not have to be replaced all at once.

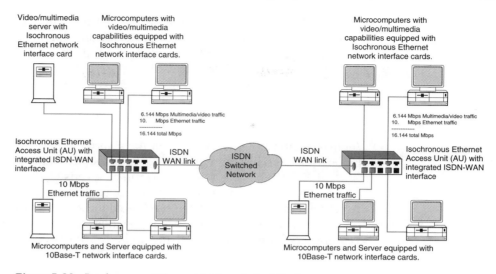

Figure 5-20   Isochronous Ethernet Network Architecture

Gigabit Ethernet

Network Architecture   **Gigabit Ethernet,** also known as 1000Base-X, is a proposed upgrade to Fast Ethernet that is being standardized as the **IEEE 802.3z** standard. An alternative gigabit Ethernet version of 100VG-AnyLAN is being developed by the IEEE 802.12 committee. If the final standard retains Ethernet's CSMA/CD access methodology, then actual throughput could be far less than 1 Gbps. Depending on the size of the packets handled by gigabit Ethernet devices, actual performance could range from 200 Mbps to 1 Gbps. Another key limitation of half-duplex CSMA/CD-based gigabit Ethernet is that it has a distance limitation of only 25 m. An alternative standard could be defined for full-duplex gigabit Ethernet that would be reserved strictly for switch-based point-to-point links. With the CSMA/CD access methodology disabled, this standard could deliver the full 1-Gbps capacity for distances of up to 2 km.

Technology   Gigabit Ethernet is implemented in switches that often include a combination of Ethernet (10 Mbps), Fast Ethernet (100 Mbps), and gigabit Ethernet ports. In such devices, users can more easily upgrade network bandwidth requirements as

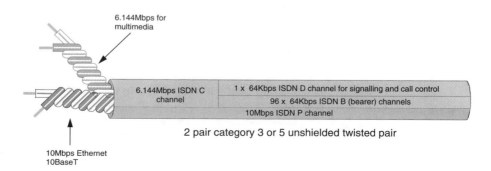

Figure 5-21   Isochronous Ethernet Bandwidth Profile

necessary. Initially, gigabit Ethernet ports will probably be reserved for connecting Ethernet switches together or to support links to high-speed servers. Servers that are to be linked to gigabit Ethernet switches must be equipped with compatible gigabit Ethernet network interface cards.

Fibre Channel

Whereas gigabit Ethernet remains in the standards proposal and technology development stage, an alternative network architecture known as **fibre channel** (ANSI standard X3T9.3) has been defined to run at speeds of 133 Mbps to 1.062 Gbps over optical fiber and copper cables. Support for speeds up to 4.268 Gbps are expected in the future. Fibre channel is often used to connect high-performance storage devices and RAID (Redundant Arrays of Independent (or Inexpensive) Disks) subsystems to computers. Fibre channel switches and NICs are also available.

LAN-Based ATM

ATM (asynchronous transfer mode) is a switched network technology that has been defined at speeds ranging from 25 Mbps to several gigabits per second. Network interface cards are available for both workstations and servers. However, for ATM-based computers to communicate with non-ATM-based computers, a process known as LAN emulation must be implemented. LAN emulation will be explored in more detail in Chapter 8. Moreover, for applications to take advantage of ATM's speed and features, they must be "ATM aware." Although desktop ATM has been implemented in such industries as animation and stock trading, many of the previously mentioned high-speed network architectures are more likely to be implemented.

Applied Problem Solving

NETWORK ARCHITECTURES IN A NUTSHELL

Many of the shared-media network architectures reviewed in this chapter are ideal in certain situations. There is no one "best" network architecture. In addition to all of the shared-media network architectures reviewed in this chapter, another entire category of network architectures known as switched network architectures will be reviewed in the next chapter. To decide which network architecture is best in any given situation, a top-down approach should be taken:

- What types of applications are required to meet business objectives?
  - Multimedia?
  - Collaborative Computing?
  - Large or frequent distributed database lookups?
  - Specialized applications such as CAD/CAM, medical imaging, or video editing?
- What are the bandwidth and network delivery requirements of the data that is produced by these applications?
  - High-bandwidth needs?
  - Guaranteed delivery times for time-sensitive or streaming traffic?
- What is the cost threshold for upgrading to a high-speed network architecture?
  - FDDI NICs traditionally cost about $1000 each and offer 100 Mbps.

- 100VG-AnyLAN NICs cost about $300 each and offer 100 Mbps. At these prices, perhaps a company doesn't even need a high-bandwidth or time-sensitive application to justify upgrading to a high-speed network architecture. Even traditional applications will be transported much more quickly.

- Which upgrade philosophy is preferred?
  - Replace all NICs, hubs, and possibly cabling?
  - Replace hubs and NICs in a gradual manner?
  - Replace just the hubs and leave the NICs and cabling alone? This option is really only available with switched network architectures, which will be studied in the next chapter.

- When an upgrade to a particular high-speed network architecture is considered, the following are just some of the issues that may require attention:
  - New NICs.
  - New NIC drivers. These can be a real problem. Where is the source of these drivers? As will be explained later, drivers must be compatible with a particular NIC and the network operating system as well as the operating system of the computer in which the NIC is installed.
  - Proper cabling to meet new cable specifications.
  - New hubs.
  - Management software.
  - New distance limitations.
  - New rules for cascading hubs or maximum number of repeaters between two end nodes.
  - Availability of internetworking hardware such as bridges and routers that are compatible with this particular high-speed network architecture. Without such hardware, the network will not be able to be extended beyond the immediate local network.

SUMMARY

Perhaps the most significant conclusion that should be drawn from this chapter is that networking analysis in general, and local area network analysis in particular, must yield business solutions, not technology solutions. Given a knowledge of what a LAN is and how a LAN is implemented, the challenge of the network analyst is to produce a documentable, justifiable network design capable of delivering stated business objectives. The key to success in this endeavor is the use of a structured methodology for LAN analysis and design. That structured methodology must assure that technology investments will yield desired productivity increases or other business objectives. In addition, the analysis and design methodology must have some way to deal with the myriad of possibilities for the combinations of hardware and software protocols yielding compatibility between communicating computers or networks.

To properly analyze and design local area networks, it is absolutely essential to have a thorough understanding of the OSI model and its constituent layers. Of particular interest is the data-link layer, which serves as the home of the IEEE LAN standards and is subdivided into the MAC and LLC sublayers for that purpose. The processes of encapsulation and de-encapsulation as OSI model processes are the basis of understanding communication between two computing devices. The importance of protocol compatibility to network communications can be modeled using the OSI model as an open framework for protocol compatibility design.

The local area network architecture model distills all network architectures into three basic components, access methodology, logical topology, and physical topology. Network architectures applied to a variety of media alternatives are known as network configurations. Key access methodologies are CSMA/CD and token passing, whereas logical topologies are either broadcast or sequential and physical topologies are most often star, but bus and ring are also possible.

Two of the most popular network architectures are Ethernet (IEEE 802.3) and token ring (IEEE 802.5). Comparisons between the two are no longer as intense as they might have once been given Ethernet's market dominance and significant price advantage. The most popular current implementation of Ethernet is 10BaseT, which uses unshielded twisted pair as media.

FDDI is the most stable traditional high-speed network architecture, offering 100-Mbps performance over dual counterrotating rings of fiber optic cable. The dual counterrotating network architecture affords FDDI exceptional fault tolerance, redundancy, and reliability.

More recent high-speed network architectures have been proposed. 100BaseT is a CSMA/CD-based 100-Mbps network architecture that operates over two pair of twisted pair but is limited to a network diameter of only 210 m. 100VG-AnyLAN is compatible with both IEEE 802.3 Ethernet and IEEE 802.5 token ring but requires four pair of unshielded twisted pair to operate and is championed primarily by a single vendor: Hewlett-Packard. 100VG-AnyLAN uses demand priority protocol as an access methodology, allowing time-sensitive traffic such as voice, video, and multimedia to be delivered effectively. An alternate method of delivering multimedia traffic is isochronous Ethernet, which is closely aligned with ISDN standards. Iso-Ethernet offers both a 10-Mbps channel for Ethernet as well as a 6.144-Mbps channel for multimedia or time-sensitive traffic.

No single network architecture can be considered the best in all situations. Top-down analysis examining business, application, and data issues is required before determining which network architecture is most appropriate in each situation.

KEY TERMS

REVIEW QUESTIONS

1. What is a local area network?
2. What are the advantages of a local area network as opposed to a group of stand-alone PCs?
3. What are the potential disadvantages or negative aspects of a local area network?
4. How would a business know when it needed a LAN?
5. What are the most popular business uses of a LAN?
6. What is the importance of the OSI model to local area network analysis and design?
7. What is a protocol?
8. What is the relationship between protocols and the OSI model?
9. What is the overall purpose of the physical layer?
10. What are the major differences between a point-to-point link and an end-to-end link?
11. Why is the data-link layer of particular interest to LAN architectures?
12. Define the relationship between the two data-link layer sublayers.
13. What does the introduction of data-link layer sublayers offer in terms of increased interoperability options.?
14. In general, what are the purposes of the header and trailer added to data-link layer frames?
15. Where are data-link frames built and why is this an appropriate place?
16. What is the relationship between the network layer and the data-link layer?
17. What is the relationship between the transport layer and the network layer?
18. Why is the session layer of more interest to client/server information systems?
19. Name at least two misconceptions as to the interpretation of layer functionality.
20. Briefly explain the purpose of encapsulation/de-encapsulation.
21. What are the three elements that make up any network architecture?
22. Compare and contrast CSMA/CD and token passing as access methodologies.
23. What are two different potential causes of collisions in Ethernet networks?
24. What does the early token release mechanism accomplish?
25. What actually is a token?
26. What is the difference between a logical and a physical topology?
27. Differentiate between the broadcast and sequential logical topologies.
28. Differentiate between the bus, star, and ring physical topologies.
29. Differentiate between Ethernet II and IEEE 802.3 Ethernet.
30. What is the relationship between IEEE 802.2 and IEEE 802.3?

31. Differentiate between IEEE 802.2 and Ethernet SNAP.
32. What is a protocol discriminator?
33. Differentiate between the various media-specific alternative configurations of Ethernet.
34. What are the unique characteristics of a token ring network architecture?
35. What is the role of the active monitor in a token ring network?
36. How are timing issues significant to token ring networks?
37. Differentiate between Ethernet and token ring in terms of performance at various traffic levels.
38. What advantages does FDDI offer over Ethernet and token ring?
39. Explain the self-healing powers of FDDI?
40. What are FDDI's primary negative attributes?
41. What are the three primary uses of the FDDI network architecture?
42. What are the advantages and disadvantages of CDDI as opposed to FDDI?
43. What is the advantage of dual homing?

44. Compare the advantages and disadvantages of 100BaseT compared to FDDI.
45. Describe the three standards defined for 100BaseT.
46. What is the advantage of buying 10/100 NICs?
47. Describe demand priority protocol?
48. How does demand priority protocol ensure that low-priority traffic does not get permanently shut out of network access?
49. Compare the advantages and disadvantages of 100BaseT vs. 100VG-AnyLAN.
50. Compare the advantages and disadvantages of isochronous Ethernet vs 100VG-AnyLAN.
51. What are some unique attributes of isochronous Ethernet when compared to other high-speed network architectures?
52. What does isochronous mean?
53. Describe the relationship between isochronous Ethernet and ISDN.
54. Describe the differences between the various gigabit Ethernet proposed standards and technology.
55. What is the common application of fibre channel?

ACTIVITIES

1. Investigate fibre channel architectures and technology. Research and report on the fibre channel five-layer model. Compare the fibre channel model with the OSI model. What types of fibre channel technology are currently available and in which types of applications is such technology typically used?
2. Investigate the standards process and technology introduction of gigabit Ethernet. Have rival standards developed? What is the price/performance ratio or gigabit Ethernet as compared to Fast Ethernet? As compared to desktop ATM?
3. Prepare a chart outlining advantages, disadvantages, and current pricing in terms of cost per user for various LAN architectures.
4. Prepare a presentation or bulletin board consisting of an empty OSI seven-layer model. As local area networks or network operating systems are encountered, place the protocols in the proper layers of the OSI model.
5. From the previous activity, determine which categories of protocols do not confirm well to a particular layer of the OSI model.
6. Design an alternative network communications protocol model to the ISO model. Justify why the new model is more effective than the OSI model.
7. Choose a particular protocol stack and outline the frame layouts for each protocol in each layer of the

OSI model. Be sure to indicate relationships between protocols as to which protocols are encapsulated by which other protocols?
8. Investigate the IEEE 802.4 token bus standard. Report on its history, implementation, available technology, and current status and give an explanation of this current status.
9. Suvey the local area network implementations in your school or business. Report on the physical topologies found. Explain your results.
10. Investigate the daisy chain physical topology. It is truly a unique physical topology or a variation of one of the three primary physical topologies?
11. Conduct a survey of Ethernet networks in your school or business. What is the media of choice in each installation? Why was each media chosen in each situation?
12. Survey schools or companies that have installed token ring networks. Report on the reasons for their choice and add you own analysis of the results.
13. Survey schools of businesses that employ FDDI network architectures. Gather information regarding motivation, installation date, satisfaction, problems, and the outcome of a similar decision on network architecture made today.
14. Investigate the availability and cost of technology

for the three standards defined for 100BaseT. Analyze your results.

15. Investigative the availability and cost of technology for 100VG-AnyLAN varieties. Analyze your results.

16. Compare the availability and cost of 100BaseT technology vs. 100VG-AnyLAN technology. Analyze your results.

17. Investigate the cost and availability of isochronous Ethernet technology. Analyze your results.

CASE STUDY

Meeting Beefier Bandwidth Goals

Remember when 10 Mbps sounded like bandwidth nirvana? And do you remember how long that feeling lasted? In the Harmon Consumer Group design and production center, nirvana lasted until the first 600MB file transfer.

That file, an Adobe Systems, Inc. Photoshop image, took 30 minutes to move from an Apple Computer Inc. Macintosh file server, across a 10Base-T network running Apple-Share, to a Macintosh workstation, according to Richard Goon, graphics designer and network manager of the design and production center (DPC) at the consumer audio manufacturer in Woodbury, N.Y.

"It froze the server because so much data was going through it," said Goon. "People had to log out from the file server just to give that machine more bandwidth.

That was in mid-1995. At that point, the DPC worked mainly with 50MB files and suffered a drag on network performance whenever a designer stored or retrieved a file.

But the 600MB file graphically foreshadowed the DPC's network future and demonstrated the inadequacy of the existing 10Mbps infrastructure. Although the DPC Macintosh network supported only 13 users, the ever-increasing bandwidth demands began to overwhelm 10Base-T.

Photoshop, Adobe Illustrator, Quark Inc. QuarkXPress, and Claris Corp. Home Page are core applications for the DPC, which is at the heart of Harmon's marketing operations. Goon and his fellow designers use the graphics packages to develop brochures, ads, posters, and other promotional materials for Harmon product lines such as JBL, Infinity, Concord, and Harmon Kardon audio products. The department needed an infrastructure boost to better deal with the large files these programs produce.

Goon did not agonize over his choice of high-speed network technology because the graphics designer-cum-network manager set one straightforward criterion for selecting the upgrade path: simplicity.

Goon, who had network-management chores dropped in his lap two years ago, was already familiar with Ethernet technology. And the DPC was wired with Category 5 UTP cable, so there was no need to rewire the department. Given his desire to stick with a infrastructure he already understood, Goon opted for a fast-Ethernet network.

Before the upgrade, the 13 DPC users, a Power Macintosh 7200 file server, and a Macintosh Quadra 950 BBS and E-mail server all shared a single 10Mbps segment. They connected to a 24-port Asanté Technologies Inc. NetStacker Intelligent Ethernet Hub.

To bring in fast Ethernet, Goon added an Asanté Fast 100 TX Hub and connected the seven graphics designers and the Power Macintosh server on that 100Mbps segment. The six copywriters, four printers, and E-mail server remained on the 10Mbps hub, and Goon linked the two environments with an Asanté Fast 10/100 Bridge.

Although managers are often loath to install new hardware because of the associated configuration work, Goon found it took about five minutes per Macintosh to install the new Asanté 10/100 adapters in the graphics designers' machines.

"It was pretty simple," said Goon. "Plug in the card, load a couple of drivers in the System Folder, and restart. Usually [the Macintosh] would select the card automatically."

Goon maintained the 10Base-T environment out of necessity. The printers have built-in 10-Mbps connections that cannot be upgraded to link at 100Mbps. And swapping adapter cards for the copywriters wasn't worth the investment.

"Those users don't really need 100Mbps," said Goon. "They're not transferring big files."

The one hitch in the migration was the AppleShare OS. In the fall of 1995, it did not support 100Mbps speeds.

The DPC runs much more smoothly with the 100Mbps segment, and while 600MB files can still cause network indigestion, 50MB files are easily digested. Still, 100Mbps will hold DPC only "until better technology comes out," said Goon.

One option Goon is looking into is a SCSI-to-SCSI network solution from Transoft Technology Corp. that promises up to 200Mbps running over SCSI cables. Given his penchant for simplicity, a solution using proprietary technology sounds like a long shot at best. Goon admits as much.

"I'm kind of leery about it," he said. "It's relatively unknown, and I'm not ready to use my site as a beta tester."

Better established high-speed technologies such as ATM, however, fail to impress Goon. "It's too expensive," he said.

How about gigabit Ethernet? "I haven't researched it," said Goon, "but it sounds pretty good."

In fact, it sounds almost like bandwidth nirvana.

Source: Brent Dorshkind, "Meeting Beefier Bandwidth Goals," *LAN Times*, vol. 13, no. 27 (December 9, 1996), p. 29. Copyright © December 9, 1996 by McGraw–Hill, New York. Reprinted by permission of McGraw–Hill, New York.

BUSINESS CASE STUDY QUESTIONS

Activities

1. Complete a top-down model for this case by gleaning facts from the case and placing them in the proper layer of the top-down model. After completing the top-down model, analyze and detail those instances where requirements were clearly passed down from upper layers to lower layers of the model and where solutions to those requirements were passed up from lower layers to upper layers of the model.

2. Detail any questions about the case that may occur to you for which answers are not clearly stated in the article.

Business

1. What were the key business activities of the business described in this case?

2. How critical were the information systems and networks to this business? Defend your answer.

Application

1. What was the application that produced the data that caused the data bottleneck?

2. What were the core applications that were used by the design and production center?

Data

1. What type of data, of what size, was being transferred when the current network bandwidth proved insufficient?

2. What were the typically sized files that were being worked with at the time?

Network

1. What was the original network architecture?
2. What network operating system was running?
3. What was the current media employed?
4. What was the key criteria for selecting the upgrade path to the new network architecture?
5. Why were both 10- and 100-Mbps architectures supported simultaneously?

6. What compatibility issue arose between the network operating system and the network architecture?
7. What are some future upgrade options if additional bandwidth is needed?

Technology

1. What new network architecture was chosen? Why?
2. Compare the technology employed in the old network architecture and the new network architecture. Highlight the new components that were added.

3. Was any upgrade work done at the workstations? Why or why not?

LOCAL AREA NETWORK HARDWARE

Concepts Reinforced

OSI Model
Network Architectures
IEEE 802 Standards
Protocols and Standards

Top-Down Model
Physical Topologies
High-Speed Network Architectures
Hardware/Software Compatibility

Concepts Introduced

LAN Technology Architecture
Network Interface Card Technology
Network Interface Card Drivers
LAN Media Alternatives

Switched LAN Architectures
Shared-Media LAN Wiring Centers
LAN Switches
Desktop ATM

OBJECTIVES

After mastering the material in this chapter, you should

1. Understand the interaction between the various hardware and software components of the local area network technology architecture.

2. Understand the differences between switched LAN architectures and shared-media LAN architectures.

3. Understand the importance of compatible network interface card drivers to overall network implementation.

4. Understand the comparative differences between and proper application of available network interface cards.

5. Understand the comparative differences between and proper application of available hubs, MAUs, switching hubs, concentrators, and similar devices.

6. Understand the comparative differences between and the proper application of the various available types of LAN media.

193

■   **INTRODUCTION**

Whereas Chapter 5 reviewed the relative merits of the various network architectures that can be implemented to link clients and servers, this chapter will focus on the hardware technology that must be employed to implement a given network architecture. The transition from shared-media network architectures to hardware-based switched network architectures is a development of major proportions of which informed network analysts must be aware. As applications demand more and more bandwidth, numerous alternatives exist for upgrading network capacity. Choosing the right upgrade path requires a thorough understanding of the local area network hardware described in this chapter.

To provide an appreciation for the interaction of all of the various LAN hardware components, this chapter begins by introducing the reader to the local area network technology architecture. To understand the role of LAN switches in network architectures, the differences between switched-based and shared-media LAN architectures are outlined prior to a detailed review of local area network hardware alternatives.

The issues, technology, and protocols involved with the management of LAN hardware are covered in Chapter 14.

■   **THE LOCAL AREA NETWORK TECHNOLOGY ARCHITECTURE**

In general terms, any local area network, regardless of network architecture, requires the following components.

- A central wiring concentrator of some type that serves as a connection point for all attached local area network devices. Depending on the particular network architecture involved and the capabilities of the wiring center, this device can be known alternatively as a hub, MAU, CAU, concentrator, LAN switch, or a variety of other names.

- Media such as shielded or unshielded twisted pair, coaxial cable, or fiber optic cable must carry network traffic between attached devices and the wiring center of choice.

- **Network interface cards (NIC)** are installed either internally or externally to client and server computers to provide a connection to the local area network of choice.

- Finally, network interface card drivers are software programs that bridge the hardware/software interface between the network interface card and the computer's network operating system.

Figure 6-1 summarizes the key components of the local area network technology architecture.

Implications of LAN Technology Choices

Within each of the major categories of LAN technology illustrated in Figure 6-1, numerous alternatives exist as to the specific make, model, and manufacturer of technology that may be chosen. It is important to note that choosing a particular tech-

Logical Diagram

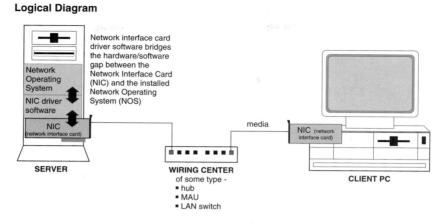

Network interface card driver software bridges the hardware/software gap between the Network Interface Card (NIC) and the installed Network Operating System (NOS)

Network Operating System

NIC driver software

NIC
(network interface card)

SERVER

media

NIC (network interface card)

CLIENT PC

WIRING CENTER
of some type -
- hub
- MAU
- LAN switch

Figure 6-1   The Local Area Network Technology Architecture

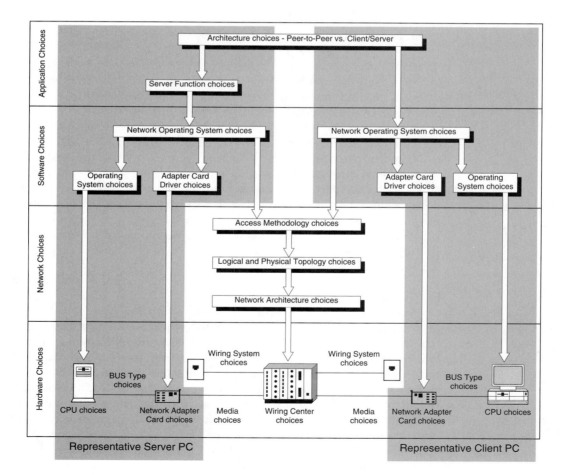

Figure 6-2   Implications of LAN Technology Choices

nology in one LAN technology category may have significant implications or limitations on available technology choices in other LAN technology categories. It is important for a network analyst to fully understand the implications of a given technology decision prior to purchase. Figure 6-2 attempts to graphically portray some of the relationships and dependencies between technology choices in a variety of LAN technology categories.

PC Hardware

As can be seen in Figure 6-2, choices of PC hardware play an especially important role in the overall LAN technology architecture. A thorough knowledge of PC hardware is required to make intelligent choices of servers and workstations. Although a detailed discussion of PC architecture issues is beyond the scope of this text, readers are encouraged to see Chapter 3, "Client Hardware," and Chapter 5, "Server Hardware and Software," in *Local Area Networks: A Client/Server Approach* by James E. Goldman.

■   MEDIA-SHARING LAN ARCHITECTURES VS. SWITCHED LAN ARCHITECTURES

As client/server information systems and distributed computing applications have put increasing demands on the local area network infrastructure in terms of the amount of data traffic to be transferred, network architects and technology providers have responded with alternative solutions.

As seen in Chapter 5, one solution to the network bandwidth crunch is to offer higher speed **shared-media network architectures** such as 100BaseT, 100VG-Any-LAN, and isochronous Ethernet. Each of these alternatives possesses the same basic shared-media structure as Ethernet and token ring, with the only difference being that the higher speed alternatives offer more bandwidth for all attached workstations to share. Media-sharing network wiring centers such as hubs offer all attached workstations shared access to a single LAN segment. If the hub happens to be a 10BaseT Ethernet hub, then all attached workstations must share access to the single 10-Mbps LAN segment, whereas 100BaseT hubs offer shared access for all attached workstations to a single 100-Mbps LAN segment. The shared-media approach is the same in both cases, the only difference being the amount of available bandwidth to be shared.

Switched LAN architectures depend on wiring centers called LAN switches or switching hubs that offer all attached workstations access to a switching matrix that provides point-to-point, rather than shared, connections between any two ports. Each port on the LAN switch is effectively a dedicated LAN segment with dedicated bandwidth offered to attached devices. Each port on the LAN switch may be assigned to a single workstation or to an entire LAN segment linked by a media-sharing network architecture (nonswitching) hub. Although shared-media LAN segments can link to a LAN switch to take advantage of its dedicated connections and guaranteed bandwidth, there is no shared media or shared bandwidth within the switched LAN architecture itself. The limiting factor in a switch-based LAN architecture is the number of simultaneous point-to-point connections that a given switch can support. Figure 6-3 contrasts the differ-

Shared Media LAN Architecture

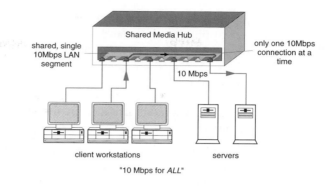

Switch-Based LAN Architecture

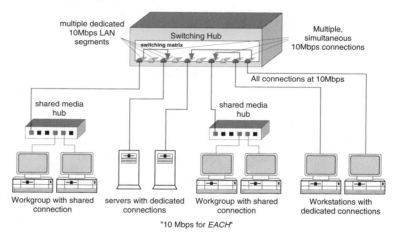

Figure 6-3 Switched LAN Architecture vs. Media-Sharing LAN Architecture Wiring Center Functionality

ences in wiring center functionality between media-sharing and switch-based LAN architectures.

ADVANTAGES OF SWITCHED LAN ARCHITECTURES

Managerial Perspective

It is important to note that switched LAN architecture implementations only change the wiring center technology and, as a result, the manner in which workstations are able to set up point-to-point communications to each other. In other words, network interface cards, network interface card drivers, and media do not change. For this reason, installing a LAN switch is often the first and easiest alternative chosen when network bandwidth demands exceed current supply. To go from an Ethernet shared-media architecture to an Ethernet switch-based architecture, it is only necessary to replace the shared-media hub with an Ethernet LAN switch. To migrate from a token ring shared-media environment to a token ring switch-based architecture, it is only necessary to replace the shared-media MAUs (multistation access units) with a token ring LAN switch.

LAN SWITCH TRAFFIC ANALYSIS

It is important to analyze the traffic patterns between attached clients and servers before swapping out hubs and installing switches. To minimize the interswitch traffic, which represents a potential bottleneck, the following are suggested:

- It is important to have those workstations and servers that communicate most often with each other attached to the same switch since switches differ in their cascadability and in the speed of the interswitch communications connection.

- Another benefit of analyzing traffic patterns before installing the switch is to identify those users and workstations that must have a dedicated switch port and those that can reside on a shared LAN segment attached to a switched port.

The following are a few general guidelines for switch port allocation:

- Servers and UNIX workstations should ideally have their own switch port.

- Distributed computing power users with frequent queries to servers should be able to be connected to switch ports via shared LAN segments of up to eight users.

- Casual or light traffic users accessing only e-mail and terminal, character-based programs can be connected to switch ports via shared LAN segments of 50 or more users.

- The ability of LAN switches to support multiworkstation LAN segments on a single switch port may vary among switches.

- The number of workstation addresses that can be supported by a given switch port may vary as well.

Furthermore, swapping a shared-media hub for a LAN switch will not necessarily improve all network traffic situations. If a server only has one 10-Mbps network interface card installed with which it must service all client requests, a LAN switch will not improve the network performance. In fact, due to the latency introduced by the switch to set up switched connections, the performance may actually degrade. The power of a LAN switch is its ability to support simultaneous connections between any combination of clients and servers. It is but one piece of a solution to network performance bottlenecks that can be effectively implemented only after a thorough network traffic analysis has been conducted.

Implementation Scenarios for Switched LAN Architectures

Depending on switch capacity and installed components, LAN switches can be implemented to fulfill a variety of different roles.

- **Stand-alone workgroup/departmental LAN switches**—Offer dedicated connections to all attached client and server computers via individual switch ports. Such an implementation is appropriate for multimedia or videoconferencing workstations and servers. In some cases, such as a distributed computing environment, dedicated ports are only necessary for servers, whereas client workstations share a switch port via a cascaded media-sharing hub. This variation is sometimes referred to as a **server front-end LAN switch.**

- **Backbone-attached workgroup/departmental LAN switches**—Offer all of the local switching capabilities of the stand-alone workgroup/departmental LAN switch plus switched access to higher speed backbone networks. This higher speed backbone connection may be to a higher capacity backbone switch or may be to a higher speed shared-media device such as a backbone router.

- **Backbone/data center switches**—Offer high-capacity, fault-tolerant, switching capacity with traffic management capabilities. These high-end switches are really a self-contained backbone network, which is sometimes referred to as a **collapsed backbone network.** These backbone switches more often offer switched connectivity to other workgroup switches, media-sharing hubs, and corporate servers that must be accessed by multiple departments/workgroups. They are often modular in design, allowing different types of switching modules such as Ethernet, token ring, Fast Ethernet, and ATM (asynchronous transfer mode) to share access to a high-capacity switching matrix or backplane.

Figure 6-4 highlights the differences between these switched LAN architecture implementation scenarios.

In Sharper Focus

FULL-DUPLEX NETWORK ARCHITECTURES

Switched LAN architectures provide dedicated point-to-point links between communicating clients and servers. In the case of Ethernet switches, for example, since the point-to-point link between two communicating PCs is dedicated, there can be no data collisions and there is no longer any need for an access methodology such as CSMA/CD, since no other workstations are contending for this dedicated bandwidth connection. As a result, communication between the two computers that serve as the end points of this switched dedicated connection could both send and receive data to and from each other simultaneously. This switch-dependent capability is known as **full-duplex Ethernet** and requires specialized full-duplex Ethernet NICs, full-duplex NIC drivers, and full-duplex Ethernet switches. Many Ethernet switches allow certain ports, such as those attached to servers, to be set for full-duplex Ethernet. In such an implementation, only the servers attached to full-duplex switch ports would require full-duplex NICs. In theory, full-duplex Ethernet should allow twice the normal Ethernet performance speed by offering a dedicated 10-Mbps communication channel in each direction for a total available bandwidth 20 Mbps.

In practice, the throughput, or actual data transferred, on full-duplex Ethernet connections is not nearly 20 Mbps. Chief among the reasons for this is that the amount of network transmission is a product of application program design. Most distributed application programs tend to exhibit short requests for services from clients to servers followed by large transfers of data from the server back to the client. However, this is not to say that the technology lacks the ability to deliver higher performance. Controlled tests involving high-bandwidth applications have produced throughput of 20 Mbps. As a result, the most likely implementation scenarios for full-duplex Ethernet are in switch-to-switch connections and switch-to-server connections.

Stand-Alone Workgroup/Departmental LAN Switches

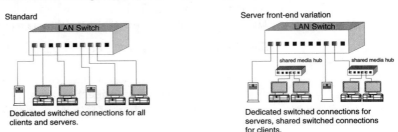

Backbone-Attached Workgroup/Departmental LAN Switches

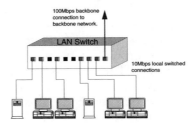

Backbone/Data Center Switches

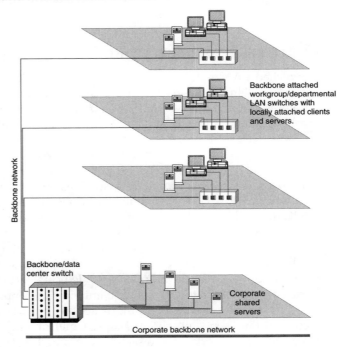

Figure 6-4   Implementation Scenarios for Switched LAN Architectures

Since the full-duplex NIC installed in the computer is both sending and receiving data simultaneously, a multithreaded operating system and network operating system are required to take full advantage of this technology. Examples of such multithreaded operating systems and network operating systems are Windows NT,

OS/2, NetWare 3.11 and 4.1, and most varieties of UNIX. Full-duplex Ethernet has gathered sufficient interest from the networking technology vendor and user communities as to warrant the formation of the **IEEE 802.3x** committee to propose standards for full-duplex Ethernet. Full-duplex technology is also either under development or available in full-duplex token ring (32 Mbps) and full-duplex FDDI (200 Mbps) varities.

■ NETWORK INTERFACE CARDS

Functionality

Network adapter cards, also known as network interface cards or NICs, are the physical link between a client or server PC and the shared media of the network. Providing this interface between the network and the PC or workstation requires that the network adapter card have the ability to adhere to the access methodology (CSMA/CD or token passing) of the network architecture (Ethernet, Fast Ethernet, token ring, FDDI/CDDI, ATM, etc.) to which it is attached. These software rules, implemented by the network adapter card, that control the access to the shared network media are known as media access control (MAC) protocols and are represented on the MAC sublayer of the data-link layer (layer 2) of the OSI seven-layer reference model.

Since these are MAC layer interface cards and are therefore the keepers of the MAC layer interface protocol, it's fair to say that it is the adapter cards themselves that determine network architecture and its constituent protocols more than any other component. Take an Ethernet adapter card out of the expansion slot of a PC and replace it with a token ring adapter card and you have a token ring workstation. In this same scenario, the media may not even need to be changed since Ethernet, token ring, and FDDI/CDDI often work over the same media.

A Network adapter card is a bit like a mediator or translator. On one side it has the demands of the client or server PC in which it is installed for network-based services, whereas on the other side it has the network architecture with its rules for accessing the shared network media or LAN switch. The network adapter card's job is to get the PC all of the network services it desires while adhering to the rules (MAC layer protocols) of the network architecture.

Technology Analysis

The following are some of the key network differences in adapter design and available features:

- Bus type.
  - ISA (8 or 16 bit).
  - EISA (16 or 32 bit).
  - MCA.
  - NuBus (Apple).
  - PCI.
  - PCMCIA.
  - SBus (Sun).
- On-board processor capabilities.

- Amount of on-board memory.

- Data transfer techniques.
  - Bus-mastering DMA.
  - DMA.
  - Shared memory.
  - Programmed I/O.

- Media interfaces.

- System memory requirements.

- Internal adapters vs. external adapters.

- Network drivers included.

- Network architecture(s) supported.

Applied Problem Solving

NETWORK INTERFACE CARD TECHNOLOGY ANALYSIS GRID

Many of these features are listed in Figure 6-5, the network interface card technology analysis grid. A technology analysis grid is a structured analysis tool for mapping functional networking requirements as identified by the logical network design of the networking layer in the top-down model to the technical capabilities and characteristics of available technology. In this manner, technology can be comparatively evaluated in an objective fashion. Recalling the basic premise of the top-down model—that each lower layer offers solutions that meet the requirements of the immediate upper layer—the chosen technology incorporated in the physical network design should meet the original business goals and objectives as identified in the business layer.

As a practical example, whereas servers will need to transfer large quantities of data more quickly than client PCs, technology analysis should be performed in order to purchase more powerful, faster NICs for servers than for clients in order to minimize potential bottlenecks.

Bus Type   The bus into which a network adapter card is attached allows many different types of add-in cards to be attached to this data transfer pipeline leading to the CPU and RAM. The expansion bus in a PC is a lot like a straight line of empty parking spaces waiting to be filled by PC expansion cards of one type or another. These expansion cards draw electricity from and transfer data to/from other system components such as the CPU or memory through the expansion bus. NICs are manufactured to physically interface to a particular type of bus.

The PCI bus offers its own clocking signal and low CPU utilization and seems to be the bus of choice for high-performance NICs. PCI bus compatible NICs are now available for a variety of network architectures, with some taking advantage of the PCI bus's ability to cascade buses by delivering four network interface ports on a single network interface card. Some PCI-based cards also have full-duplex capabilities. Such high-capacity cards are most appropriate for servers with high data transfer demands.

SBus is the type of bus included in UNIX workstations (SPARCstations) from Sun Microsystems.

The important choice related to bus architecture is that a network adapter card is chosen that not only "fits," or is compatible with, the installed bus but, more im-

		Ethernet	Token Ring (4Mbps)	Token Ring (16Mbps)	FDDI	CDDI	100Base-T	100VG-AnyLAN	ISO-ethernet	Full duplex Ethernet	ATM
Internal/external	**Bus Type**										
ISA - 8 bit/16 bit											
MCA - 32 bit											
EISA - 32 bit											
PCI - 32 bit/64 bit											
Macintosh - NUBUS											
External interface to parallel port											
PCMCIA (laptops)											
SBUS (SUN)											
NDIS	**Drivers**										
ODI											
NETBIOS											
IPX											
SOLARIS											
NT ALPHA											
NT POWERPC											
NT X86											
OS/2 WARP											
UTP	**Cabling Type (media interface)**										
STP											
Thin COAX											
Thick COAX											
Fiber											
Wireless											
BUS mastering	**Data transfer**										
DMA											
Programmed I/O											
Shared memory											
SNMP support	**Management**										
RMON support											
PROM support											
Prices											

Figure 6-5 Network Interface Card Technology Analysis Grid

portantly, takes full advantage of whatever data transfer capability that given bus may afford.

Data Transfer Method   The key job of the network adapter is to transfer data between the local PC and the shared network media. Ideally, this should be done as quickly as possible with a minimum of interruption of the PC's main CPU. Two hardware-related network adapter characteristics that can have a bearing on data transfer efficiency are the amount of on-board memory and the processing power of the on-board CPU contained on the network adapter card. Figure 6-6 summarizes four network adapter card-to-PC memory data transfer techniques:

- Programmed I/O (input/output).
- Shared memory.
- DMA (direct memory access).
- Bus-mastering DMA.

Programmed I/O

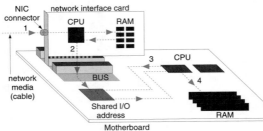

Steps
1. Data enters network interface card through the network media and connector.
2. Adapter card CPU loads network data into a specific I/O address on the motherboard.
3. Main CPU checks I/O area for data
4. If data exists, it is transferred to main memory, RAM, by main CPU.

Keynote
The motherboard's CPU has the ultimate responsibility of data transfer into RAM.

DMA (Direct Memory Access)

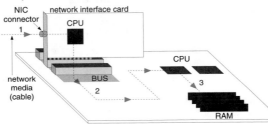

Steps
1. Data enters network interface card through the network media and connector.
2. Adapter card CPU interrupts the motherboard CPU.
3. Main CPU stops other processing and transfers the data to RAM.

Keynote
The motherboard's CPU has the ultimate responsibility of data transfer into RAM.

Shared Memory

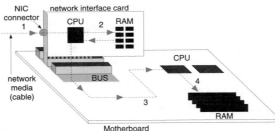

Steps
1. Data enters network interface card through the network media and connector.
2. Adapter card CPU stores data on its RAM.
3. Adapter card CPU interrupts the motherboard CPU.
4. Main CPU stops other processing and transfers data into RAM.

Keynote
The motherboard's CPU has the ultimate responsibility of data transfer into RAM.

Bus Mastering DMA

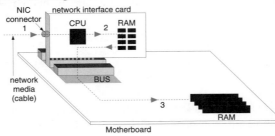

Steps
1. Data enters network interface card through the network media and connector.
2. Adapter card CPU temporarily stores data on its RAM.
3. Adapter card CPU sends data directly to motherboard RAM when network transmission completes (it does NOT interrupt the main CPU.)

Keynote
The adapter card's CPU has the ultimate responsibility of data transfer into RAM.

Figure 6-6 Network Interface Card Data Transfer Methods

Network adapter cards may support more than one of these techniques. Some of these data transfer techniques are only possible with the more sophisticated buses such as EISA, MCA, or PCI, with certain network architectures, or with a certain level of CPU power.

Remembering that one of the objectives of network-to-PC data transfer was to minimize the number of interruptions of the system CPU, it can be seen in Figure 6-6 that only the **bus-mastering DMA** data transfer technique leaves the system CPU alone to process other applications. In bus-mastering DMA, the CPU on the network adapter card manages the movement of data directly into the PC's RAM without interruption of the system CPU by taking control of the PC's expansion bus. PCI bus-based NICs also exhibit low utilization of the main CPU thanks to the intelligence of the PCI bus itself.

Bus-mastering DMA as a feature on adapter cards requires the expansion bus in the PC to support being "mastered" by the CPU on the network adapter card. Some buses are more sophisticated (MCA, EISA, and PCI) when it comes to bus mastering by maintaining more control and management over how the mastering of the expansion bus by the network adapter card CPU is handled. Also, the CPU and operating system must have the capability to relinquish control of the expansion bus for bus mastering network adapter cards to function correctly.

Media Interfaces   A network adapter card must worry about hardware compatibility in two directions. First, the card must be compatible with the expansion bus into which it will be inserted. Second, it must be compatible with the chosen media of a particular network architecture implementation. Supported media types are dependent on standards defined for a particular network architecture. All NICs do not support all media types. In addition to the type of media, the physical connector that must interface between the NIC and the media can differ.

Several network adapter cards come with interfaces for more than one media type with "jumpers" or switches enabling one media type or another. Ethernet adapter cards with interfaces for both 10BaseT (**RJ-45** or 8-pin Telco plug) and thin coax connections known as **BNC connector** or with both thick and thin coax connections are quite common. Thick coax connectors are 15-pin interfaces (DB-15), also called **AUI connectors.** AUI connectors allow Ethernet NICs to be attached to thin or thick coax Ethernet backbone networks via **transceivers** (transmitter/receivers) and AUI or transceiver cables. Figure 6-7 illustrates the three common Ethernet media interfaces and connection of an Ethernet NIC to an Ethernet backbone network via transceivers.

All of the discussion thus far regarding installation of network adapter cards has assumed that the adapters are internal or connected directly to the system expansion bus. Alternatively, network adapters can be connected externally to a PC via the PC's parallel port. This market has grown considerably with the proliferation of laptop or notebook computers lacking internal expansion capability. In these cases, **external adapters,** as small as a pack of cigarettes, are interfaced between the PC's parallel port and the network media. External adapters cannot draw electricity from the expansion bus like internal adapters and therefore require a power source of their own such as an ac adapter in most cases. Some external adapters are able to draw power from the keyboard jack on the notebook computer, eliminating the need for bulky and inconvenient ac adapters.

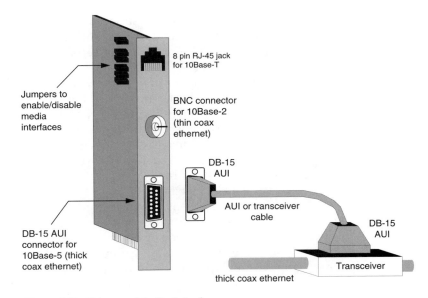

Figure 6-7   Ethernet Media Interfaces

In a good example of the principle of shifting bottlenecks, although NICs can transfer data at rates of several megabits/second, throughput on existing parallel ports hovers around 130 Kbps whereas a newer **high-performance parallel port,** also known as **EPP** or **enhanced parallel port,** delivers a throughput of up to 2 Mbps. Remember that the parallel port is a component of the laptop PC, not the external adapter. An alternative to parallel port external adapters is **PCMCIA adapters.** The top-rated PCMCIA Ethernet adapters typically deliver throughput of between 800 and 900 Kbps.

PCMCIA STANDARDS

In Sharper Focus

PCMCIA is actually a series of specifications that represent the physical and functional/electrical standards for technology adhering to these specifications. Figure 6-8 summarizes the physical specifications and Figure 6-9 summarizes the functional/electrical specifications for the PCMCIA standard.

Types I–III all must support the standard PCMCIA 68-pin interface and the 85.6 × 54 mm credit card size dimensions. Certain vendors are producing disk drives that are 16 mm thick and calling them PCMCIA Type IV. These standards are strictly proprietary as the PCMCIA Forum has not approved a Type IV specification.

The introduction of PCMCIA technology has not been without its trials and tribulations. Prior to the introduction of the V2.1 specification, incompatibility problems were very common. The card services and socket services provided a layer of transparency and compatibility between the notebook computer's hardware, the PCMCIA card, and the notebook computer's operating system software. Technical aspects of card services and socket services will be covered in the discussion of driver software later in this chapter.

Version 2.1 is currently the most widely supported version of the PCMCIA specification and has minimized, although not eliminated, many of the previous incompatibility problems. Version 2.1 also introduced hot-swappable capabilities, which allow PCMCIA cards to be inserted and removed with the notebook computer powered up.

PCMCIA Card/Slot Type	Maximum Thickness (mm)	Typical Use
Type I	3.3	Memory cards
Type II	5.5	Modems, network interface cards
Type III	10.5	Disk drives

Figure 6-8 PCMCIA Physical Specifications

Version 3.0 actually renames the cards from PCMCIA to simply PC Cards. CardBus has also been mentioned as a replacement name for the much-maligned PCMCIA. More importantly, version 3.0 vastly improves the throughput of the specification by increasing the bus width to 32 bits and the clock speed to as high as 33 MHz. The specification also adds bus-mastering capability to increase the efficiency of moving data from the card to the computer's system memory. Finally, version 3.0 defines multifunction capabilities for cards so that a single card might be a fax/modem, an Ethernet network interface card, and 4 MB of cache memory. In the interest of improving battery life on notebook computers, version 3.0 also outlined operations at 3.3 V rather than 5 V.

The future looks bright for PC Card. PC Card slots are now being included on desktop computers as well as notebooks to allow users to make the most of their investments in peripherals. Vendors are finding new uses such as dial-in servers for the PC Card. However, the reality of the situation is that presently there is no guarantee that a particular PCMCIA card will work well, if at all, with a particular computer.

Network Interface Card Trends

Among the trends in network interface cards that are either emerging or under development are the following:

- Dual-speed cards—Some 10/100 Ethernet cards feature auto-sensing, which can automatically determine whether traffic is being transmitted and received at 10 or 100 Mbps through a single media interface connector. Others, especially 100VG-AnyLAN 10/100 cards, have two separate media interface

PCMCIA Specification Version	Bus Width (bits)	Clock Speed	Comments
1.0	8	up to 6 MHz	Used for memory cards; no I/O functions or software drivers defined
2.0	8–16	up to 6 MHz	Introduced I/O but left software drivers up to card manufacturers
2.1	8–16	up to 6 MHz	Introduced card services and socket services
PC Card (3.0)	32	20–33 MHz	Up to 80-Mbps throughput

Figure 6-9 PCMCIA Functional/Electrical Specifications

connectors, one for 10-Mbps Ethernet and one for 100VG-AnyLAN. 10/100 cards are important as a means to ease migration from a 10-Mbps network architecture to a 100-Mbps network architecture.

- Integrated or on-board NICs—Some computer manufacturers such as Hewlett-Packard now include an Ethernet NIC right on the PC's motherboard, thereby saving a slot on the expansion bus.

- Multiport NICs—The cascading ability, otherwise known as the mezzanine architecture, of the PCI bus has allowed multiport NICs to be manufactured on a single card. In this manner, servers with high traffic demands can have up to four links to the network while using only a single expansion slot.

- On-NIC virus protection and security—As security and virus protection have become more important issues, focus has shifted into the NIC as the entry point for network communications. Some NICs now offer encryption, virus protection, or both as means of protection against network infiltration.

- Integrated repeater modules—Some NICs have incorporated integrated repeater modules that allow up to seven additional devices to be cascaded from the NIC and attached to the network via a single 10BaseT hub port.

- Full-duplex mode—Some Ethernet NICs have full-duplex capability that can be enabled. Recall that implementation of full-duplex Ethernet is dependent on the full-duplex Ethernet NIC being directly connected to a port on a full-duplex Ethernet switch.

- Performance improvements—Several manufacturers of Ethernet NICs have implemented **packet overlapping** or **fast packet forwarding** technology to improve overall NIC performance by as much as 50%. Traditionally, Ethernet NICs only forwarded one packet at a time from the CPU bus, through the buffer memory on the NIC, to the network media. With packet-overlapping technology, the next packet of information is immediately forwarded as soon as its start of frame is detected rather than waiting for the previous frame to be totally onto the network media before beginning transmission of the next packet.

NETWORK INTERFACE CARD DRIVERS

Role of Adapter Card Drivers

Ensuring that a purchased network interface card interfaces successfully to both the bus of the CPU and the chosen media of the network architecture will ensure hardware connectivity. Full interoperability, however, depends on compatibility between the NIC and the network operating system installed in a given computer and is delivered by **network interface card drivers.** Any driver software must be compatible with the hardware card itself, which is why many adapter card manufacturers ship numerous drivers from which to choose with the adapter cards. A given network adapter card may also be required to be compatible with a number of different network operating systems. The network operating systems use the adapter card drivers to communicate with the adapter cards and the network beyond. Without the proper adapter card drivers, there can be no communication out through the adapter card and, as a result, there is no network.

Driver Availability

Initially, drivers were written for specific combinations of a particular adapter card and a particular version of an operating system or network operating system. It was to an adapter card vendor's advantage to ship drivers for as many operating systems and network operating systems as possible. Examples of drivers typically included are:

- LANtastic.
- LANManager.
- LANServer.
- Pathworks.
- PowerLAN.
- NetWare Version 2.x, NetWare Version 3.x, NetWare 4.x, for DOS and OS/2.
- Vines.
- Windows and Windows 95.
- OS/2.
- Windows NT.
- UNIX (many varieties).

This is obviously a fairly long list and drivers may well have to be rewritten for each new version of an operating system or network operating system. Drivers written for specific adapter card/network operating system combinations are known as **monolithic drivers.** Network interface card drivers were also supplied by network operating system vendors. In these cases, the competition centered around which network operating system vendor could include drivers for the largest number of network interface cards. As the number of possible combinations of network interface cards and network operating systems continued to increase, network interface card vendors and network operating system vendors found themselves spending ever increasing amounts of time and money on driver development.

A more generic approach to the problem was for the adapter card manufacturers to supply drivers that could interact successfully with either NetBIOS or TCP/IP. The reasoning in this case is that most network operating systems, in turn, communicate with either NetBIOS (PC environment) or TCP/IP (UNIX environment). These drivers were generally successful except for the occasional incompatibilities among NetBIOS versions, so long as a given operating system supported NetBIOS or TCP/IP. Also, specifically written, monolithic drivers were more efficient and better performing in most cases.

Another approach is for the network adapter card manufacturers to emulate the adapter interface specifications of market-leading network interface cards for which drivers are most commonly available. The NE2000 adapter card, originally manufactured by Eagle Technologies and since purchased by Novell, is often emulated by other manufacturers who subsequently claim that their adapters are NE2000 compliant.

Multiprotocol Network Interface Card Drivers

Novell was the first network operating system to attempt to break the need for specially written drivers for every possible adapter card/network operating system combination. By allowing adapter card vendors to develop one file called IPX.COM which was linked with a Novell file called IPX.OBJ through a process known as WSGEN, unique drivers could be more easily created and updated. However, even these "bound" drivers were still monolithic in the sense that only a single protocol stack, Novell's IPX/SPX, could communicate with the installed network adapter card.

Thus, an industry initiative was undertaken that would develop driver software that would accomplish two major objectives.

1. Adapter card specific drivers should be developed independently from network operating system specific protocol stack drivers and the two drivers should be bound together to form a unique driver combination.

2. Driver management software should allow for installation of both multiple network adapter cards and multiple protocol stacks per adapter card.

This initiative was undertaken by two independent industry coalitions:

- Microsoft and 3Com, a major adapter card manufacturer, developed **NDIS (network driver interface specification).**

- Novell, producers of NetWare, and Apple joined forces to develop **ODI (open data-link interface).** Most adapters cards are now shipped with both NDIS and ODI drivers.

The significant operational difference that these two driver specifications offer is that they are able to support multiple protocol stacks over a single adapter card. For example, a network adapter card with an ODI driver installed could support communications both to a NetWare server via IPX protocols and to a UNIX host via TCP/IP protocols. Network operating systems and their protocol stacks will be detailed in Chapter 7.

In Sharper Focus

NDIS

NDIS is a driver specification that offers standard commands for communication between NDIS-compliant network operating system protocol stacks (NDIS protocol driver) and NDIS-compliant network adapter card drivers (NDIS MAC drivers). In addition, NDIS specifies a **binding** operation that is managed by a separate program known as the **protocol manager** (PROTMAN.DOS in DOS-based systems). As will be seen, the protocol manager program does much more than just supervise the binding of protocol drivers to MAC drivers. NDIS also specifies standard commands for communication between the protocol manager program and either protocol or MAC drivers.

Protocol drivers and MAC drivers that adhere to the NDIS specification work as follows:

1. When a DOS-based computer is first booted or powered up, a configuration file known as CONFIG.SYS is executed. One line in this file specifies that the protocol manager program (PROTMAN.DOS) should be initiated.

2. The first job of the protocol manager is to access a text file known as PROTOCOL.INI, which contains
    • Setup information about protocol drivers and MAC drivers.
    • Binding statements that link particular protocol drivers to particular MAC drivers.

3. Having read PROTOCOL.INI and parsed its contents into usable form, the protocol manager program loads the PROTOCOL.INI information into a memory-resident image.

4. As new protocol drivers or MAC drivers are loaded, they
    • Ask the protocol manager program for the location of the memory-resident image of PROTOCOL.INI.
    • Look in PROTOCOL.INI for setup information about the MAC driver or protocol driver with which they wish to bind.
    • Identify themselves to the protocol manager program, which adds their information to the PROTOCOL.INI file.

5. Binding takes place when the protocol manager program oversees the exchange of characteristic tables between protocol drivers and MAC drivers.

6. Once bound and operating, packets of a particular protocol are forwarded from the adapter card to the proper stack by a layer of software known as the **vector.**

Figure 6-10 illustrates many of the concepts and components of the NDIS specification.

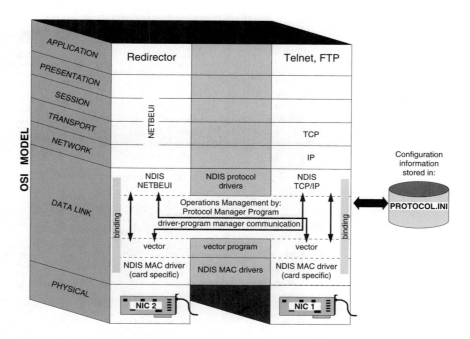

Figure 6-10   Network Device Interface Specification (NDIS) Architecture

ODI

Like NDIS, ODI allows users to load several protocol stacks simultaneously for operation with a single network adapter card and supports independent development with subsequent linking of protocol drivers and adapter drivers. In ODI, users enter configuration information regarding network adapter settings and protocol driver information into a file named NET.CFG. Operations of ODI are similar to the basic functionality of NDIS and are orchestrated by a program known as LSL.COM, where **LSL** stands for **link support layer.** Network interface card drivers are referred to as **multilink interface drivers** or **MLID** in an ODI-compliant environment. Figure 6-11 illustrates the basic architecture of an ODI-compliant environment.

PCMCIA Drivers

When network interface cards are PCMCIA based, two levels of driver software are required:

1. Drivers to interface to operating systems and network operating systems such as NDIS 2.0 for DOS and OS/2 and ODI for DOS and OS/2. Occasionally, NetWare-specific drivers may also be available with certain PC Cards.

2. Drivers to interface the PCMCIA controller to the PCMCIA card and to the aforementioned client software drivers.

As previously noted, with the introduction of PCMCIA specification version 3.0, the term *PCMCIA* has been replaced by the terms *PC Card* and *CardBus.*

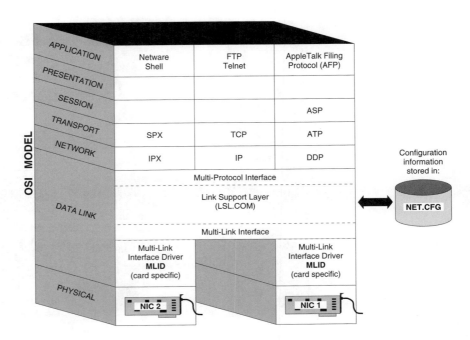

Figure 6-11   Open Data-Link Interface (ODI) Architecture

Compatibility problems and lack of standardized driver software were common occurrences with PCMCIA-based network interface cards prior to the release of PCMCIA version 2.1 with its **card and socket services (CSS)** driver specification. CSS enables the following capabilities and is supposed to be relatively self-configuring:

- Hot-swappable devices allowing PCMCIA cards to be removed and inserted while the notebook computer is powered up.

- Automatic PCMCIA card configuration.

- Multiple PCMCIA card management.

- Standby mode.

- I/O conflict management.

CSS is split into two logical sublayers:

1. The **card services** sublayer is hardware independent and interfaces to the client operating system or network operating system driver software. Card services deliver error messages and enable resource management and configuration.

2. The **socket services** sublayer is written specifically for the type of PCMCIA controller included in a notebook computer. Among the common varieties of controllers are Intel, Cirrus Logic, Databook, Vandem, Toshiba, VLSI, and Ricoh. Socket services are more hardware oriented and provide information concerning insertion and removal of cards from available slots.

If compatible CSS drivers are not available for a particular PC Card/controller combination or if the amount of memory CSS drivers require is unacceptable, then lower level drivers known as **direct enablers** must be configured and installed. Direct enablers, like the socket services of CSS, are controller specific and must be configured for each PC Card/controller combination, unlike the card and socket services drivers, which allow multiple cards to be swapped in and out of a given PCMCIA slot without the need for reconfiguration. Direct enabler drivers are often supplied on diskette along with CSS drivers by the PCMCIA card vendors.

Practical Advice and Information

It is in an adapter card manufacturer's best interests to include as many drivers as possible with their adapter cards to ensure that they will work with as many network operating systems as possible. However, before purchasing any adapter card, be sure that proven software drivers compatible with the installed or chosen network operating system(s) are included with the purchase of the adapter cards.

Remember that drivers for various cards are often supplied with the installed networking operating system as well. One of these drivers may be more efficient in terms of operation or required memory than another.

■ SHARED-MEDIA LAN WIRING CENTERS

The most common network physical topology employed today is the star topology, and the heart of the star topology is the wiring center. A wiring center may be alternatively known as a hub, a concentrator, a repeater, a MAU, or a variety of other terms. In this section, wiring center functionality, technology, management, and analysis will be examined for shared-media network architectures whereas LAN switches and switching hubs appropriate for switch-based network architectures will be covered in the next section.

Wiring Center Categories

In terms of network architectures supported, token ring wiring centers are known as **MAUs (multistation access units)** whereas wiring centers for all other network architectures are known as **hubs.** All hubs, or MAUs, are basically just multiport digital signal repeaters. They do not make logical decisions based on the addresses or content of messages. They merely repeat all digital data received among connected ports. In terms of the OSI model, repeaters or hubs are layer 1 or physical layer devices dealing only with bit streams.

In terms of functionality and features, wiring centers can be separated into three broad categories:

1. **Stand-alone hubs** are fully configured hubs offering a limited number (12 or fewer) of ports of a particular type of network architecture (Ethernet, token ring) and media. They are fully configured and include their own power supply but are not generally expandable, do not include management software, and are the least expensive of the three wiring center categories.

2. **Stackable hubs** add expandability and manageability to the basic capabilities of the stand-alone hub. Stackable hubs can be linked together, or cascaded, to form one larger virtual hub of a single type of network architecture and media. Given the larger number of ports, management software becomes essential. Most stackable hubs offer some type of local management software as well as links to enterprise management software platforms such as HP's OpenView, Sun's SunNet Manager, IBM's NetView, and Novell's NMS.

3. **Enterprise hubs,** also known as **modular concentrators,** differ from stackable hubs in both physical design and offered functionality. Rather than being fully functional self-contained units, enterprise hubs are modular by design, offering a chassis-based architecture to which a variety of different modules can be inserted. In some cases, these modules can be inserted and/or removed while the hub remains powered up, a capability known as **hot-swappable.** Among the possible modules supported by enterprise hubs are
    *   Ethernet, token ring, and FDDI port modules in a variety of port densities and media choices.
    *   Management modules.
    *   Router modules.
    *   Bridge modules.
    *   WAN link modules.
    *   Multiple power supplies for redundant power.

These broad category definitions and labels are not standards and are not universally adhered to by manufacturers. Signaling standards defined as part of the IEEE or ANSI LAN standards allow hubs and NICs of different vendors to interoperate successfully in most cases. Figure 6-12 illustrates some of the physical differ-

Stand-alone hubs

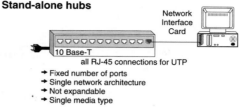

Network
Interface
Card

10 Base-T
all RJ-45 connections for UTP

→ Fixed number of ports
→ Single network architecture
→ Not expandable
→ Single media type

Stackable hubs

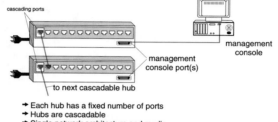

cascading ports

management
console

management
console port(s)

to next cascadable hub

→ Each hub has a fixed number of ports
→ Hubs are cascadable
→ Single network architecture and media
→ Provides management software and link
   to network management console

Enterprise hubs

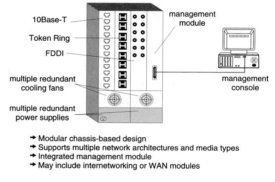

10Base-T

Token Ring

FDDI

multiple redundant
cooling fans

multiple redundant
power supplies

management
module

management
console

→ Modular chassis-based design
→ Supports multiple network architectures and media types
→ Integrated management module
→ May include internetworking or WAN modules

Figure 6-12   Major Categories of Hubs

ences between the three major categories of hubs, whereas Figure 6-13 differentiates between the functionality of the major categories of wiring centers.

Repeaters

A repeater, as its name would imply, merely "repeats" each bit of digital data that it receives. This repeating action actually "cleans up" the digital signals by retiming and regenerating them before passing this repeated data from one attached device or LAN segment to the next. Repeaters can only link devices or LAN segments of similar network architectures.

Hubs

Hubs are a subset of repeaters that allow attachment of single devices rather than LAN segments to each hub port. The terms *hub* and *concentrator* or *intelligent concentrator* are often used interchangeably. Distinctions can be made however between

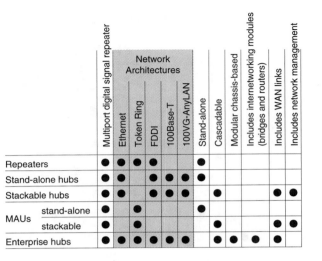

	Multiport digital signal repeater	Network Architectures					Stand-alone	Cascadable	Modular chassis-based	Includes internetworking modules (bridges and routers)	Includes WAN links	Includes network management
		Ethernet	Token Ring	FDDI	100Base-T	100VG-AnyLAN						
Repeaters	●	●	●	●			●					
Stand-alone hubs	●	●		●	●	●	●					
Stackable hubs	●	●		●	●			●			●	●
MAUs — stand-alone	●		●				●					
MAUs — stackable	●		●					●			●	●
Enterprise hubs	●	●	●	●	●	●		●	●	●		●

Figure 6-13 Wiring Center Functional Comparison

these broad classes of wiring centers, although there is nothing to stop manufacturers from using the terms as they wish.

A hub is often the term reserved for describing a stand-alone device with a fixed number of ports that offers features beyond that of a simple repeater. The type of media connections and network architecture offered by the hub are determined at the time of manufacture as well. For example, a 10BaseT Ethernet hub will offer a fixed number of RJ-45 twisted pair connections for an Ethernet network. Additional types of media or network architectures are not usually supported.

Stackable Hubs

Hubs may also be cascadable or stackable via **cascading ports,** which may be specialized ports on the hub or may be switch-configurable "normal" ports allowing repeated data to flow out of a cascading port to the next hub rather than the normal inbound-only port traffic flow. In general, cascading ports are proprietary in nature, thereby making it impossible to cascade hubs of different vendors together. Specialized hub-to-hub cascading cables may also be required and the maximum allowable distance between stacked hubs may vary as well. Stackable hubs also vary as to stackability, with the number of stackable hubs ranging from 4 to 20 and the total number of stacked ports ranging from 48 to 768. Cost per port can range from $35 to $147, with most per-port costs in the $60–70 range.

MAUs

A MAU or multistation access unit is IBM's name for a token ring hub. A MAU is manufactured with a fixed number of ports and connections for unshielded or shielded twisted pair. IBM uses special connectors for token ring over shielded twisted pair (STP) connections to a MAU known as Type 1 connectors. Some MAUs support RJ-45 connectors rather than the more bulky and difficult to work with Type 1 connectors. MAUs typically have eight ports with two additional ports labeled RI (ring in) and RO (ring out). These specialized cascading ports allow multiple MAUs to be linked in a single logical ring. MAUs may also be cascaded to each other via fiber optic cable as opposed to shielded twisted pair.

MAUs offer varying degrees of management capability. **Active-management MAUs** are able to send alerts to management consoles regarding malfunctioning token ring adapters and can also forcibly remove these misbehaving adapters from the ring. Removing malfunctioning nodes is especially critical in token ring LANs because of the possibility of one of the malfunctioning nodes becoming disabled while holding onto the token. Although such an event would be at the very least inconvenient, it would not be a catastrophe as the active monitor workstation is capable of regenerating a new token.

Enterprise Hubs

The terms *concentrator, intelligent concentrator, smart hub,* or *enterprise hub* are often reserved for a device characterized by both its flexibility and expandability. A concentrator starts with a fairly empty, boxlike device often called a chassis. This chassis contains one or more redundant power supplies and a "built-in" network backbone. This backbone might be Ethernet, token ring, FDDI, AppleTalk, 100BaseT, 100VG-AnyLAN, or some combination of these. Individual cards or modules are inserted into this "backplane."

For instance, an 8- or 16-port twisted pair Ethernet module could be purchased and slid into place in the concentrator chassis. A network management module supporting the simple network management protocol (SNMP) could then be purchased and slid into the chassis next to the previously installed 10BaseT port module. In this "mix-and-match" scenario, additional cards could be added for connection of PCs with token ring adapters, PCs or workstations with FDDI adapters, or "dumb" asynchronous terminals. These modules are most often hot-swappable, allowing modules to be added or removed without shutting down the entire enterprise hub. Obviously, the capacity of these enterprise hubs is equally as important as the flexibility afforded by the modular design. In fact, several hundred ports of varying network architectures are often supported by enterprise hubs.

This "network in a box" is now ready for workstations to be hooked up to it through twisted pair connections to the media interfaces on the network interface cards of the PCs or workstations. Allowing different media types to be intermixed in the concentrator was one of its first major selling points. Remember that Ethernet can run over UTP, STP, thick and thin coax, and fiber.

Additional modules available for some, but not all, concentrators may allow data traffic from this "network in a box" to travel to other local LANs via bridge or router add-on modules. Bridges and routers will be discussed later in the text. These combination concentrators are sometimes called internetworking hubs. Communication to remote LANs or workstations may be available through the addition of other specialized cards, or modules, designed to provide access to wide area network services purchased from common carriers such as the phone company. Whereas all local network traffic travels through this single enterprise hub, it is also an ideal location for security modules to be added for either encryption or authorization functionality.

Backplane design within enterprise hubs is proprietary and, as a result, the modules for enterprise hubs are not interoperable. Therefore, it is important to ensure that the enterprise hub to be purchased has available all required types of modules in terms of network architecture, media type, management, internetworking, WAN interfaces, or security. Vendors' promised delivery dates for required modules should not be depended on.

Hub Management

Since all local area network traffic must pass through the hub, it becomes an ideal place for installation of management software to both monitor and manage network traffic. As previously stated, stand-alone hubs rarely are manufactured with management software. In the case of stackable and enterprise hubs, two layers of management software are most often involved:

1. First, **local hub management software** is usually supplied by the hub vendor and runs under either DOS or Windows. This software allows monitoring and management of the hub from a locally attached management console.

2. Second, since these hubs are just a small part of a vast array of networking devices that might have to be managed on an enterprise basis, most hubs are also capable of sharing management information with **enterprise network management systems** such as HP's OpenView, IBM's NetView, Sun's SunNet Manager, or Novell's NMS.

Although Chapter 14 will cover network management in more detail, a small explanation here as to how this hub management information is fed to the enterprise network management system is appropriate.

Network management information transfer between multivendor network devices and enterprise network management systems must be characterized by standards-based communication. The standards that govern this network management communication are part of the TCP/IP family of protocols, more correctly known as the internet suite of protocols. Specifically, network management information is formatted according to the **SNMP** or **simple network management protocol.** The types of information to be gathered and stored have also been defined as **MIBs** or **management information bases.** There are actually numerous MIBs defined, with the most often used one for network monitoring and management known as the **RMON (remote monitoring) MIB.** Network statistics and information are gathered in the first place and packetized in SNMP format by specialized software known as **agents** that reside within the monitored network device and are supplied by the network device's manufacturer. Enterprise network management systems such as HP's OpenView are able to interpret, consolidate, and display information and alarms from a variety of different networking equipment manufactured by a variety of different vendors thanks to standards-based communication protocols. Figure 6-14 illustrates the relationship of

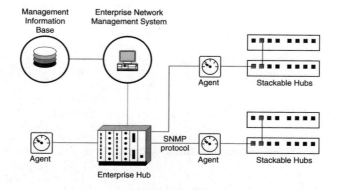

Figure 6-14 Standards-Based Network Management
Communications Protocols

the various aspects of the standards-based network management communications protocols.

Practical Advice and Information

Some hub management issues are particular to stackable and/or enterprise hubs. For example:

- Many stackable hubs offer network management capabilities as an optional hardware or software upgrade. It is important to fully understand the ease with which this upgrade can be accomplished and whether or not the hubs must be powered off while doing so.

- The network management traffic may exit the hub via a separate serial port or travel along a separate bus within the hub so as not to diminish the amount of bandwidth available for data. These options are sometimes referred to as out-of-band management connections.

- The entire stack of hubs should be viewed, monitored, and managed by the network management software as a single, virtual hub.

- The local hub management software should be simple, easy to use, and preferably Windows-based with the capability to talk to enterprise network management system platforms should that need arise.

- If at all possible, management modules or upgrades should be included with the original purchase to avoid potential upgrade hassles. Buying management modules at purchase time is often more economical than buying upgrades later thanks to vendor discount packages.

- An issue particular to token ring modules included in enterprise hubs is that the management software should possess the ability to dynamically assign ports located on the same physical module onto different logical rings to optimize network performance.

WIRING CENTER TECHNOLOGY ANALYSIS

Applied Problem Solving

Some of the major technical features to be used for comparative analysis are listed in Figure 6-15. Before purchasing a wiring center of any type, consider the implications of the various possible features listed in the wiring center technology analysis.

Wiring Center Characteristic	Implications/Options
Expandibility	Most stand-alone hubs are neither expandable nor cascadable. Stackable hubs are cascadable and enterprise hubs are expandable by adding more LAN modules. Enterprise hubs vary in the number of open slots from approximately 5 to 20. Total backplane capacity (speed) is important as this is the shared network media that must be shared by all attached modules.
Network architectures	Options: Ethernet, token ring, FDDI, AppleTalk, 100BaseT, 100VG-AnyLAN. Not all enterprise hubs have all types of network architecture modules available.
Media	Options: UTP, STP, thin coax, thick coax, fiber optic cable. Modules also differ according to supported media. Remember that a NIC is on the other end of the connection to the hub module. Is this hub module media type and connector compatible with installed NICs?
Macintosh communications	Can an Apple Macintosh be linked to the hub?
Terminal communications	Can "dumb" asynchronous terminals be connected directly to the hub? What are the physical connector and serial transmission specifications? (DB-25?, RS-232?)
Internetworking	Are bridging and/or routing modules available that can redirect traffic from module to module? Across different types of network architecture modules? Across which different network architecture modules will traffic need to be bridged?
Wide area networking	Is this hub connected to other hubs remotely through the use of carrier-based data services? If so, which WAN services are supported? Options: frame relay, ISDN, switched 56K, digital leased lines from 9.6 Kbps to 1.544 Mbps (T-1).
Management	Is a local hub management program available? Are simple network management protocols supported? Can individual ports be managed? Is monitoring software included? What security services are available? Can ports be remotely enabled/disabled? Can the hub be controlled by a port-attached workstation or only by a special management console? Can the hub be controlled remotely? Via a modem? Are management statistics and alarms graphically displayed? How are alarm thresholds set? How are faults managed? Can port access be limited by day and/or time? What operating systems can the management software run on? Options: DOS, OS/2, Windows, Windows 95, Windows NT, UNIX, Mac, etc. Can a map of the network be displayed? Which enterprise network management systems are supported? Options: HP's, Open View, IBM's, NetView, Sun's SunNet Manager, Novell's NMS.
Reliability	Is an integrated UPS included? Are power supplies redundant? Are modules hot-swappable? Are cooling fans redundant? Which components are capable of being replaced by the user?

Figure 6-15   Wiring Center Technology Analysis

■ LAN SWITCHES

The "network in a box" or "backbone in a box" offered by concentrators and hubs shrinks the length of the network backbone but doesn't change the architectural characteristics of a particular network backbone. For instance, in an Ethernet concentrator, multiple workstations may access the built-in Ethernet backbone via a variety of media, but the basic rules of Ethernet such as CSMA/CD access methodology at 10 Mbps still control performance on this "Ethernet in a box." Only one workstation at a time can broadcast its message onto the shared 10-Mbps backbone.

Switch Classification

Supported Network Architectures   A **switching hub,** or **LAN switch,** seeks to overcome this "one-at-a-time" broadcast scheme, which can potentially lead to data collisions, retransmissions, and reduced throughput between high-bandwidth-demanding devices such as engineering workstations or server-to-server communications. By adding the basic design of a data PBX to the modular-designed concentrator, numerous manufacturers have delivered "switched" Ethernet connections at 10 Mbps to multiple users simultaneously through a process known as parallel networking.

The Ethernet switch is actually able to create connections, or switch, between any two attached Ethernet devices on a packet-by-packet basis in as little as 40 msec. The "one-at-a-time" broadcast limitation previously associated with Ethernet is overcome with an Ethernet switch. Figure 6-3 illustrated the basic functionality of an Ethernet switch. Ethernet is not the only network architecture for which LAN switches are available. Either stand-alone versions or slide-in modules for enterprise switches are also available for token ring, FDDI, and Fast Ethernet.

In addition, many high-end LAN switches also support **ATM (asynchronous transfer mode),** which is a type of switching that not only allows the previously mentioned LAN architectures to be switched extremely quickly but also allows a similarly quick switching of voice, video, and image traffic. In fact, ATM can switch any type of digital information over LANs or WANs with equal ease and speeds that are currently in the 622-Mbps range and rapidly approaching the gigabit/second range.

Super-Switches or Mega-Switches support multiple different LAN architectures, ATM, and interface to WAN services.

Functional Differences   Switches can vary in ways other than just the types of network architecture frames that are switched. Significant functional differences between switches can have a dramatic effect on switch performance. The first major functional difference has to do with how the network architecture frames are processed before they are switched to their destination:

- **Cut-through switches** read only the address information in the MAC layer header before beginning processing. After reading the destination address, the switch consults an address look-up table to determine which port on the switch this frame should be forwarded to. Once the address look-up is completed, the point-to-point connection is created and the frame is immediately forwarded. Cut-through switching is very fast. However, because the frame check sequence on the forwarded frame was not checked, bad frames are forwarded. As a result, the receiving station must send a request for retransmission followed by the sending station retransmitting the original frame, leading to overall traffic increases.

- **Store-and-forward switches** read the entire frame into a shared memory area in the switch. The contents of the transmitted frame check sequence field is read and compared to the locally recalculated frame check sequence. If the results match, then the switch consults the address look-up table, builds the appropriate point-to-point connection, and forwards the frame. As a result, store-and-forward switching is slower than cut-through switching but does not forward bad frames.

- **Error-free cut-through switches** read both the addresses and frame check sequences for every frame. Frames are forwarded immediately to destination nodes in an identical fashion to cut-through switches. However, should bad frames be forwarded, the error-free cut-through switch is able to reconfigure those individual ports producing the bad frames to use store-and-forward switching. As errors diminish to preset thresholds, the port is set back to cut-through switching for higher performance throughput.

SWITCH TECHNOLOGY ISSUES

Practical Advice and Information

Switch Flow Control   Switches are very often employed to make switched connections between multiple network architectures. A common role of LAN switches is to provide switched connections between 10- and 100-Mbps network architectures. However, when servers on high-speed (100 Mbps) switched connections blast high-bandwidth data traffic back to clients on shared 10-Mbps port connections, data traffic can get backed up and data frames can be lost once buffers designed to hold overflow data become filled.

Switch vendors have attempted to respond to this situation in a variety of ways. Some switches include so-called deep buffers, which allow more overflow traffic to be buffered before it is discarded. However, the dilemma with this approach is that memory is expensive and it is difficult to determine how much buffer memory is enough while still keeping switch costs reasonable.

A second approach involves implementing a feedback mechanism known as **backpressure.** In the case of Ethernet switches, backpressure prevents lost frames during overload conditions by sending out false collision detection signals to get transmitting clients and servers to time-out long enough to give the switch a chance to forward buffered data. It is somewhat ironic that the CSMA/CD access methodology that the switch sought to overcome is being used to improve switch performance. The difficulty with backpressure mechanisms in the case of multiple-device LAN segments being linked to a single switch port is that the false collision detection signal stops all traffic on the connected LAN segment, even peer-to-peer traffic that could have been delivered directly without the use of the switch. One possible solution to this shortcoming is to only enable backpressure on those switch ports that are connected to single devices such as servers.

Switch Management   Another major issue to be faced by network managers before jumping blindly onto the LAN switch bandwagon is the matter of how to monitor and manage switched LAN connections. Unlike shared-media LAN management tools that are able to access all network traffic from a single interface to the shared-media hub, switched architecture management tools must be able to monitor numerous point-to-point dedicated connections simultaneously. In a switched LAN architecture, each port is the equivalent of a dedicated LAN that must be individually monitored and managed. Switch vendors currently offer three basic approaches to the switch management dilemma:

1. **Port mirroring** copies information from a particular switch port to an attached LAN analyzer. The difficulty with this approach is that it only allows one port to be monitored at a time.

2. **Roving port mirroring** creates a roving RMON (remote monitoring) probe that gathers statistics at regular intervals on multiple switch ports. The shortcoming with this approach remains that at any single point in time, only one port is being monitored.

3. **Simultaneous RMON view** allows all network traffic to be monitored simultaneously. Such a monitoring scheme is only possible on those switches that incorporate a shared memory multigigabit bus as opposed to a switching matrix internal architecture. Furthermore, unless this monitoring software is executed on a separate CPU, then switch performance is likely to degrade.

There is a little doubt that properly deployed LAN switches can greatly improve network performance. However, management tools for LAN switches continue to evolve and network managers should be wary of introducing technology into an enterprise network whose impact cannot be accurately monitored and managed.

LAN SWITCH TECHNOLOGY ANALYSIS

Applied Problem Solving

Some of the important analysis issues surrounding LAN switch selection are highlighted in Figure 6-16.

LAN Switch Characteristic	Implications/Options
Switching architecture	Options include cut-through, store-and-forward, and error-free store-and-forward.
Token ring switches	Some token ring switches also employ store-and-forward switching with buffering on the outbound port so that the outbound port has time to wait until the token reaches that switch port when multiple token ring devices are attached to a single switch port. Token ring switches are also able to reduce NetBIOS and source route bridging broadcast traffic by filtering. Some token ring switches also support full-duplex token ring networking, also known as DTR (dedicated token ring), (IEEE 802.5r).
Network architectures	Switches may support one or more of the following: Ethernet, token ring, FDDI, Fast Ethernet, ATM. Network architectures may be available in a variety of different media types.

Figure 6-16 LAN Switch Technology Analysis

LAN Switch Characteristic	Implications/Options
Port configuration	Switches may vary in both the number of MAC addresses allowed per port and the total number of MAC addresses supported for the entire switch. Some switches only allow single devices to be attached to each LAN switch port. How easily can devices be assigned/reassigned to switch ports? Can devices that are physically attached to different switch ports be assigned to the same virtual LAN?
Full-duplex	Some switches allow some ports to be enabled for full-duplex operation. Full-duplex switch ports will only communciate with full-duplex NICs whereas "normal" switch ports will communicate with existing NICs.
Switch-to-switch connection	Some switches use Ethernet or token ring switched ports whereas others use higher speed architectures such as FDDI or ATM. These interswitch connections are sometimes referred to as the Fat Pipe.
Internetworking	In addition to merely establishing switched connections and forwarding traffic, some switches also have the ability to examine the addressing information contained within the data frames and perform bridging and routing functions. Token ring switches may or may not perform source route bridging that is specific to the token ring architecture. Some routing models can also examine embedded protocols and make routing and filtering decisions based on that criteria.
Management	Does the switch support both SNMP and the RMON MIB? Does the switch contain a management port and management software? Which type of RMON probe is supported? Is a separate CPU provided for processing system monitoring software? Does the local management software support enterprise network management software such as HP's OpenView, IBM's NetView, and Sun's SunNet Manager? Is a port provided to which a protocol analyzer can be attached?

Figure 6-16   Continued

ATM for the LAN

ATM (asynchronous transfer mode) is a connection-oriented switched transmission methodology that holds great promise for becoming a single solution for the transmission of data, voice, and video over both local and wide area networks. The word *promise* in the previous sentence is significant. Any technology that sounds as if it is the ultimate solution to the world's transmission needs would obviously require an enormous amount of standards-making and interoperability planning effort. Such is the case with ATM.

One of the characteristics of ATM that affords it the capability of delivering a variety of traffic over both local and wide area networks is the fixed-length 53-byte cells into which all traffic is segmented. This uniform length allows timed, dependable delivery for streaming traffic such as voice and video, while simplifying troubleshooting, administration, setup, and design. Standards-making activities are divided into two major efforts:

1. **UNI** or **user–network interface** defines standards for interoperability between end-user equipment and ATM equipment and networks. These standards are well defined and equipment is fairly widely available.

2. **NNI** or **network–network interface** defines interoperability standards between various vendors' ATM equipment and network services. These standards are not as well defined as UNI.

As a result, single-vendor solutions are currently the safest bet for network managers requiring ATM's speed and flexibility. Technology supporting the cabling/speed specifications shown in Figure 6-17 is currently available for ATM.

Costs for ATM technology vary widely and should decrease significantly with increased demand. Following are some typical cost ranges:

- 25-Mbps adapter cards: $400–1500 each

- 100-Mbps and 155-Mbps adapter cards: $1200–3000 each

- Per-port cost on ATM hubs/switches: $1000–5000 each

As is the case with any high-speed network architecture, migration strategies from existing network architectures to ATM are of critical importance. Two basic migration approaches have been defined:

1. **IP over ATM,** otherwise known as **classical IP,** adapts the TCP/IP protocol stack to employ ATM services as a native transport protocol directly. This is an IP-specific proposal and is not an option for LANs using other protocol stacks such as NetWare's IPX/SPX.

2. **LAN emulation** provides a translation layer that allows ATM to emulate existing Ethernet and token ring LANs and allows all current upper layer LAN protocols to be transported by the ATM services in an unmodified fashion. With LAN emulation, ATM networks become nothing more than a transparent, high-speed delivery service. LAN emulation is most often implemented by the ATM vendor by the installation of an **address resolution server,** which provides translation between the ATM addressing scheme and the addressing scheme that is native to a particular emulated LAN.

Figure 6-18 illustrates a typical ATM implementation featuring an ATM local workgroup, connection of legacy LANs to a local ATM network, the local ATM

ATM Speed	Cabling Type
25 Mbps	STP, UTP3 or better
100 Mbps	UTP5
155 Mbps	Multimode fiber optic cable

Figure 6-17   Available ATM Speed/Cabling Specifications

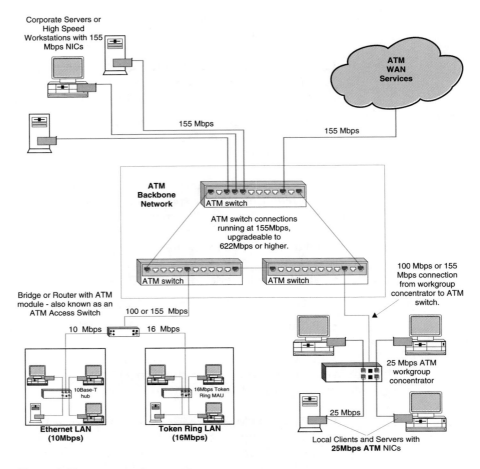

Figure 6-18 ATM Implementation

switched network itself acting as a local high-speed backbone, and access to wide-area ATM services that may be either a private network or purchased from an ATM WAN service provider.

■ LAN MEDIA ALTERNATIVES

While a variety of wire and fiber media alternatives are reviewed in this section, wireless alternatives for LAN media are explored in Chapter 10.

Not Twisted Pair

The type of phone wire installed in most homes consists of a tan plastic jacket containing four untwisted wires—red, yellow, green, and black—and is also known as **four-conductor station wire** or **RYGB.** This type of wire is not suitable for data transmission and is not the unshielded twisted pair (UTP) that is so often referred to.

Another popular type of phone wiring is referred to as **flat gray modular** wiring, also known as gray satin or silver satin. Inside this flay gray jacket are four, six, or eight wires that get crimped into either RJ-11 (four wire), RJ-12 (six wire), or RJ-45 plugs (eight wire) using a specialized crimping tool. Premises phone wiring as well as phones, crimp tools, RJ-11 plugs, and flat gray modular wire are obtainable at nearly any hardware or department store.

Flat gray modular wire is not the same as twisted pair and is only suitable for carrying data over short distances. For instance, this type of cable is often used between a PC or workstation and a nearby RJ-11 jack for access to premises wiring systems or LAN backbones. Modular adapters with RJ-11 input jacks mounted within RS-232 hoods are available to quickly construct data cables of various pin-out configurations without having to crimp RS-232 pins on individual conductors.

Unshielded Twisted Pair

Twisted pair wiring consists of one or more pairs of insulated copper wire that are twisted at varying lengths, from 2 to 12 twists/ft, to reduce interference both between pairs and from outside sources such as electric motors and fluorescent lights. Interference can cause data errors and necessitate retransmission. These individually twisted pairs are then grouped together and covered with a plastic or vinyl covering or jacket. No additional shielding is added before the pairs are wrapped in the plastic covering. Thus, the completed product is known as **unshielded twisted pair** or **UTP.** The most common numbers of pairs combined to form UTP are 2, 3, 4, and 25 pairs of twisted copper wire.

All UTP is not created equal. One of the common appeals of UTP is that it is often already installed in modern buildings for the purpose of carrying voice conversations through the voice PBX. Most often, when the twisted pair wiring for the voice PBX was installed, extra pairs were wired to each office location. Some people then jump to the conclusion that they don't need to invest in any new wiring to carry data transmission throughout their buildings; they'll just use the existing extra pairs of unshielded twisted pair wiring. The problem lies in the fact that there are five different categories of UTP as specified by **EIA/TIA 568** (Electronics Industries Association/Telecommunications Industries Association). In addition to specifying UTP specifications, EIA/TIA 568 also specifies

- The topology, cable types, and connector types to be used in EIA/TIA 568 compliant wiring schemes.

- The minimum performance specifications for cabling, connectors, and components such as wall plates, punch-down blocks, and patch panels to be used in an EIA/TIA 568 compliant installation.

Category 1 UTP, otherwise known as voice grade cable, need only carry voice conversations with reasonable clarity. Categories 3–5 (data grade) cable must meet certain predefined electrical characteristics that ensure transmission quality and speed. Before assuming that the UTP in a building is just fine for data transmission, have its transmission characteristics tested and ensure that these characteristics meet listed data-grade UTP specifications. Figure 6-19 summarizes the specifications for Categories 1–5 UTP.

Wire thickness is measured by gauge and represented with the unit **AWG** (American wire gauge). The higher the gauge number, the thinner the wire. UTP

UTP Category	Specifications/Applications
Category 1 UTP	22 or 24 AWG. Not recommended for data.
Category 2 UTP	22 or 24 AWG. Only suitable for data transmission of less than 1 Mbps.
Category 3 UTP	24 AWG. Very common in existing installations. Most often used for voice-only installations. Suitable for data up to, but not including, 16 Mbps. As a result, it can be used reliably for 4-Mbps token ring and 10-Mbps Ethernet. Tested for attenuation and near-end cross talk up to 16 MHz.
Category 4 UTP	22 or 24 AWG. Tested for attenuation and near-end cross talk up to 20 MHz. Not widely used in favor of Category 5 UTP.
Cateogry 5 UTP	22 or 24 AWG. Tested for attenuation and near-end cross talk to 100 MHz. Capable of transmitting up to 100 Mbps when strictly installed to EIA/TIA 568 specifications. Currently the most commonly installed category of UTP.

Figure 6-19   Unshielded Twisted Pair Specifications

wiring of different categories must meet specifications for resistance to different forces that interfere with signal strength. Two of the more common sources of interference or loss of signal strength are as follows:

1. **Attenuation** is the decrease in the power of signal over a distance in a particular type of wire or media.

2. **Near-end crosstalk (NExT)** is signal interference caused by a strong signal on one pair (transmitting) overpowering a weaker signal on an adjacent pair (receiving).

CATEGORY 6 CABLE?

Practical Advice and Information

Although no official Category 6 cable has become standardized, media vendors are attempting to develop cable that is capable of carrying data at frequencies of up to 600 MHz. Some such attempts are not truly unshielded twisted pair but rather are FTP or foil-twisted pair cable that is more closely related to shielded twisted pair. Buyers must be wary of so-called Category 6 cable by focusing on whether or not the cable is truly UTP and whether or not it is a specified EIA/TIA standard.

COMMON UTP INSTALLATION MISTAKES

Practical Advice and Information

As mentioned in the Category 5 UTP definition in Figure 6-19, strict adherence to EIA/TIA 568 installation standards is essential to successful transmission at 100 Mbps over Category 5 UTP. Because a less-than-perfect installation will probably transport 10-Mbps traffic without any problem, noncompliant installations may not surface until upgrades to 100-Mbps network architectures are attempted. Among the most common installation mistakes are the following:

*   Untwisting the UTP wire more than the maximum 13 mm to secure the UTP to wall plates or punch-down blocks.

- Exceeding the maximum bend radius specified for UTP. By overbending the wire, cross talk between stretched pairs of wires can be increased.

- Bundling the groups of UTP together too tightly with cable ties. By excessively pinching the UTP together, cross talk between pairs is increased.

Shielded Twisted Pair (STP)

Data transmission characteristics, and therefore the data transmission speed, can be improved by adding **shielding** both around each individual pair and around the entire group of twisted pairs. This shielding may be a metallic foil or copper braid. The function of the shield is rather simple. It "shields" the individual twisted pairs as well as the entire cable from either EMI (electromagnetic interference) or RFI (radio frequency interference). Installation of shielded twisted pair can be tricky.

Remember that the shielding is metal and is therefore a conductor. Often, the shielding is terminated in a drain wire, which must be properly grounded. The bottom line is that improperly installed shielded twisted pair wiring can actually increase rather than decrease interference and data transmission problems. STP was commonly specified for token ring installations. However, recent specifications for CDDI, Fast Ethernet, ATM, and other high-speed network architectures are using Category 5 UTP rather than STP.

Coaxial Cable

Coaxial cable, more commonly known as coax or cable TV cable, has specialized insulators and shielding separating two conductors allowing reliable, high-speed data transmission over relatively long distances. Figure 6-20 illustrates a cross section of a typical coaxial cable. Coax comes in various thicknesses and has been historically used in Ethernet network architectures. In some cases, these network architecture specifications include required characteristics of the (physical layer) coaxial cable over which the (data-link layer) MAC layer protocol is transmitted.

Ethernet 10Base5 specifies coaxial cable known as thick coax or more affectionately known as "frozen yellow garden hose," giving a hint as to how easy this media is to work with.

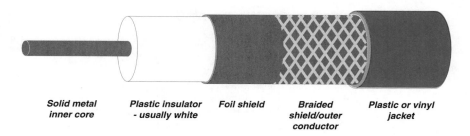

Solid metal   Plastic insulator   Foil shield   Braided   Plastic or vinyl
inner core   - usually white   shield/outer   jacket
                                          conductor

Figure 6-20   Coax Cable: Cross Section

Fiber—The Light of the Future

Coax was at one time the media of choice for reliable, high-speed data transmission. But times and technology change, and people now often turn to fiber optic cable when seeking reliable, high-bandwidth media for data transmission beyond the capabilities of Category 5 UTP. Price is still a factor however; as one can see from Figure 6-22, fiber optic cable is still the most expensive media option available. This expensive media delivers high bandwidth in the range of several gigabytes (billions of characters)/second over distances of several kilometers.

Fiber optic cable is also one of the most secure of all media as it is relatively untappable, transmitting only pulses of light, unlike all of the aforementioned media, which transmit varying levels of electrical pulses. Whereas fiber optic is really a thin fiber of glass rather than copper, this media is immune to electromagnetic interference, contributing to its high bandwidth and data transmission capabilities. Another important thing to remember is that it is, in fact, glass and requires careful handling. Fiber optic cable made of plastic is under development but does not deliver nearly the speed and bandwidth of the glass fiber cable. Fiber optic cable comes is a number of varieties. Figure 6-21 illustrates a cross section of a fiber optic cable.

Light Transmission Modes   Once a pulse of light enters the core of the fiber optic cable, it will behave differently depending on the physical characteristics of the core and cladding of the fiber optic cable. In a **multimode** or **multimode step index** fiber optic cable, some rays of light will bounce off of the cladding at different angles and continue down the core whereas others will be absorbed in the cladding. These multiple rays at varying angles cause distortion and limit the overall transmission capabilities of the fiber. This type of fiber optic cable is capable of high-bandwidth (200 Mbps) transmission but usually over distances of less than 1 km.

By gradually decreasing a characteristic of the core known as the refractive index from the center to the outer edge, reflected rays are focused along the core more efficiently, yielding higher bandwidth (3 GBps) over several kilometers. This type of fiber optic cable is known as **multimode graded index fiber.**

The third type of fiber optic cable seeks to focus the rays of light even further so that only a single wavelength can pass through at a time, in a fiber type known as **single mode.** Without numerous reflections of rays at multiple angles, distortion is eliminated and bandwidth is maximized. Single mode is the most expensive fiber optic cable but can be used over the longest distances.

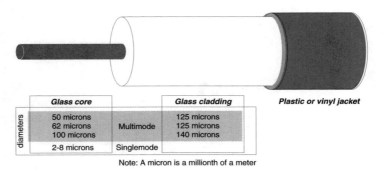

	Glass core		Glass cladding	Plastic or vinyl jacket
diameters	50 microns 62 microns 100 microns	Multimode	125 microns 125 microns 140 microns	
	2-8 microns	Singlemode		

Note: A micron is a millionth of a meter

Figure 6-21   Fiber Optic Cable: Cross Section

Core Thickness   The thickness of a fiber optic cable's core and cladding is measured in microns (millionths of an inch). The three major core thicknesses are 50, 62, and 100 microns, with their associated claddings being 125, 155, and 140 microns, respectively. The increasing core thickness generally allow transmission over longer distances at a greater expense, however.

Light Source Wavelength   The wavelength of the light that is pulsed onto the fiber optic cable is measured in nanometers (nm), with the optimal light transmitting wavelengths coming in three distinct windows of 820, 1310, and 1500 nm. Usually, 820 and 1310 nm are used for local and campus-wide networking such as FDDI, whereas 1310 and 1500 nm are used by carriers to deliver high-bandwidth fiber-based service over long distances. The higher frequency light emitting sources carry a higher price tag.

Applied Problem Solving

LAN MEDIA TECHNOLOGY ANALYSIS

Figure 6-22 illustrates LAN media technology analysis.

Media Type	Also Called	Bandwidth	Distance Limits	Connectors	Comments/Applications	Token Ring	Ethernet	FDDI	CDDI	Fast Ethernet	ATM	Price ($)
4-wire phone station wire	Quad RYGB	3 Kbps	200 feet	RJ-11 jacks	4 insulated wired-red, green, yellow, black. Home phone wiring. Voice Applications							0.09/foot
Flat gray modular	Flat satin, telephone cable, silver satin	14.4 Kbps	10-20 feet	RJ-11 or RJ-45 plugs	Comes with 4,6,8 conductors. Used for short data cables using modular (mod-tap) adapters	■	■		■	■	■	0.09-0.18/foot
Unshielded twisted pair	UTP	100 Mbps	100 feet	RJ-45	5 Designated categories. Twists prevent interference, increase bandwidth. Voice grade usually not suitable for data	■	■		■	■	■	0.10/foot
Shielded twisted pair	STP	16 Mbps	100 feet	RJ-45 or IBM data connectors	Shielding reduces interference but complicates installation	■	■		■	■	■	0.42/foot
Coax- thick	Frozen yellow garden hose	10 Mbps	500 feet	AUI (attachment unit interface)	Original Ethernet cabling		■					1.10 foot
Coax-thin	RG-58, thinnet, cheapernet	10 Mbps	200 feet	BNC connector	Looks like cable TV cable. Easier to work with than thick coax.		■					0.32/foot
Coax-thin	RG-62	2.5 Mbps	200 feet	BNC or IBM data connector	Similar to RG-58 (thinnet) but different electrical characteristics make these cables NOT interchangeable	■						0.32/foot
Fiber-optic cable	Fiber Glass	several Gbps	several kilometers	SI or SMA 905 or SMA 906	Difficult to install but technology is improving. High bandwidth, long distance, virtually error free, high security	■	■	■			■	1.00/foot

Figure 6-22   LAN Media Technology Analysis

SUMMARY

The hardware required to implement any local area network architecture falls into a relatively few broad categories: network interface cards, media, and wiring centers. Linking this hardware to the network operating system and operating system software is the network interface card driver. Advances in wiring center technology have enabled an entirely new, switch-based LAN architecture. LAN switches are extremely popular as an upgrade strategy for bandwidth-hungry networks as they do not require any changes to network interface cards, drivers, or media. However, preupgrade traffic analysis is prudent as interswitch bottlenecks can actually degrade, rather than improve, performance.

PCI-based network interface cards are emerging as the high-performance NIC of choice thanks largely to PCI's own clock, CPU, and mezzanine architecture. The key operational characteristics of network interface card drivers are the ability to support multiple protocol stacks on a single network adapter card and the need to avoid having to write monolithic drivers for every possible network interface card/network operating system combination. NDIS and ODI are the two most popular multiprotocol NIC drivers.

Shared-media wiring centers include stand-alone hubs, stackable hubs, enterprise hubs, and MAUs. These shared-media hubs merely collapse the shared-media LAN backbone into a single enclosure, while maintaining the one-at-a-time access methodologies. Hub management is especially important as numbers of users grow into the hundreds. Hub management software should be able to tie into enterprise network management software.

LAN switches offer multiple simultaneous connections to attached workstations as opposed to the one-at-a-time access schemes of the shared-media hubs. However, LAN switches are a relatively new technology and have their definite drawbacks. For one, when high-speed ports transfer large amounts of data to shared lower speed ports, data overflow and lost data can occur. Second, management of switched connections that may only last for fractions of a second is not nearly as straightforward as managing a shared-media hub. Each of these challenges is being addressed by LAN switch vendors.

LAN media can differ significantly in cost, supported speeds, ease of use, and network architectures supported. Although fiber optic cable was at one time considered to be the only media suitable for speeds of 100 Mbps and greater, Category 5 unshielded twisted pair seems to be a common media option for high-speed network standards.

KEY TERMS

active-management MAUs, 217
address resolution server, 225
agents, 218
asynchronous transfer mode, 221
ATM, 221
attenuation, 228
AUI connector, 205
AWG, 227
backbone-attached LAN switch, 199
backbone/data center switch, 199
backpressure, 222
binding, 210
BNC connector, 205
bus-mastering DMA, 205
card and socket services, 213
card services, 213

cascading ports, 216
classical IP, 225
collapsed backbone network, 199
CSS, 213
cut-through switches, 221
direct enablers, 213
enhanced parallel port, 206
EIA/TIA 568, 227
enterprise hubs, 214
enterprise network management
    systems, 218
EPP, 206
error-free-cut-through switches, 222
external adapter, 205
fast packet forwarding, 208
flat gray modular, 227

four-conductor station wire, 226
full-duplex Ethernet, 199
high-performance parallel port, 206
hot-swappable, 214
hubs, 214
IEEE 802.3x, 201
IP over ATM, 225
LAN emulation, 225
LAN switch, 221
link support layer, 212
local hub management software,
    218
LSL, 212
management information base, 218
MAU, 214
MIB, 218

REVIEW QUESTIONS

1. List the broad functions and interrelationships of each of the major categories of technology cited in the LAN technology architecture.
2. Differentiate between a shared-media network architecture and a switch-based network architecture in terms of advantages and disadvantages of each.
3. What are some of the potential drawbacks or cautions to upgrading to a LAN switch?
4. Differentiate between the three major implementation scenarios for LAN switches in terms of delivered functionality and corresponding required switch technology.
5. Describe the advantages and disadvantages of a collapsed backbone network.
6. What are the advantages and disadvantages of full-duplex network architectures?
7. What do full-duplex architectures require, in terms of both hardware and software, beyond normal switch-based LAN architectures?
8. What applications are full-duplex network architectures especially well suited for?
9. What is the meaning of the phrase "The NIC is the keeper of the MAC layer protocol"?
10. What unique advantages can PCI bus NICs offer?
11. Which NIC data transfer method is most efficient and why?
12. Why is it not safe to assume that a bus-mastering DMA NIC will work on any computer?
13. What is the disadvantage of using external adapters on notebook or laptop computers?
14. What is the functional role of a network interface card driver?
15. What are the disadvantages of monolithic drivers?
16. What are the two major advantages of multiprotocol network adapter card drivers?
17. Compare and contrast NDIS and ODI in terms of architecture and functionality.
18. What is the significance of binding in an NDIS environment?
19. Which files and programs are involved in a binding operation?
20. How are protocols actually directed to the proper protocol stack in an NDIS environment?
21. What are the differences between PCMCIA card services and socket services?
22. What are the differences between PCMCIA CSS and direct enablers?
23. Differentiate between the three major categories of hubs in terms of delivered functionality and required technology features.
24. What important advantages does an active-management MAU offer?
25. Why can't modules from one vendor's enterprise hub be used in another vendor's enterprise hub even though the modules both support the same network architecture?
26. What are the differences between the two levels of management software that hubs should support?
27. How is it possible for an enterprise network management system to compile statistics from networking equipment manufactured by a variety of different vendors?

28. What are the major functional differences between how LAN switches process and forward packets? What are the advantages and disadvantages of each method?
29. In what types of LAN switch implementations is backpressure likely to be an issue?
30. Why is traffic monitoring and management more of a challenge in LAN switches than in shared-media hubs?
31. Differentiate between the three major LAN switch traffic monitoring and management techniques.
32. What are the advantages and disadvantages of assigning multiple workstations per switch port?
33. What switching issues are unique to token ring switches?
34. What roles can ATM play in a local area network?
35. How can "legacy LANs" be integrated into an ATM network?
36. What are the unique capabilities of ATM that account for all of the interest in this technology?
37. What is LAN emulation and why is it important?
38. Why is twisted pair twisted?
39. What is the importance of EIA/TIA 568?
40. What is the most common type category of UTP installed today and why?
41. Why is Category 5 UTP favored over shielded twisted pair, coax, and fiber optic cable for many high-speed network architectures?
42. Why is shielded twisted pair considered trickier to install than UTP?

ACTIVITIES

1. Research the relative market sizes of hubs vs. LAN switches over the past 3 years. Interpret your results.
2. Find actual LAN switch implementations and analyze and compare the various implementation scenarios. What function is the LAN switch serving in each case? Are there implementation categories beyond those listed in Chapters 6, 9, and 11? Were examples found of each scenario listed?
3. Find actual implementations of full-duplex network architectures and report on the applications served by this technology. Is traffic level measured in this application? If so, report on the findings.
4. Research the network interface card market and report on those features or functions offered by the most advanced NICs.
5. Locate a computer that uses NDIS drivers. Print out the CONFIG.SYS and PROTOCOL.INI files. Trace the binding operation between MAC drivers and protocol drivers.
6. Locate a computer that uses ODI drivers. Print out the CONFIG.SYS and the NET.CFG files. Determine how multiple protocol stacks can be assigned to a single NIC.
7. Research data communications catalogs, buyers' guides, and product literature for the latest information on PCMCIA adapters. Report on the latest trends and capabilities. Are multiple functions, such as modems and NICs, being included on a single card?
8. Research data communications catalogs, buyers'
guides, and product literature for the latest information on hubs. Pay special attention to the availability of management features, especially ties to enterprise management systems.
9. Research the topic of the RMON MIB. Which standards-making organization is responsible for the definition? What types of information are collected in the RMON MIB? What are RMON probes and how do they function?
10. Research data communications catalogs, buyers' guides, and product literature for the latest information on LAN switches. Pay special attention to how the switches handle flow control issues and report on the alternative methods.
11. Research data communications catalogs, buyers' guides, and product literature for the latest information on LAN switches. Pay special attention to how the switches handle monitoring and management of LAN switch traffic and report on the alternative methods.
12. Research data communications catalogs, buyers' guides, and product literature for the latest information on ATM technology for the LAN. What is the availability and cost range for ATM NICs of various speeds? Which vendors seem to have the most complete "single-vendor solutions"?
13. Prepare a display including electrical specifications of the various types of LAN media cited in this chapter. Detail network architectures and maximum transmission speeds to which each media type is assigned.

CASE STUDY

Kodak Develops Bandwidth: Film Company Makes the Move from Shared to Switched LANs

The heat is on. A recent Gartner Group Inc. survey revealed that more than half of today's network managers are preparing to migrate from shared to switched LANs over the next year. For Eastman Kodak Co.'s Ron Huber, the reasons are straightforward: increased performance, reduced cost, and enhanced manageability.

"Our shared-media network simply wasn't capable of handling the load," said Huber, director of computing resources in the Image Science Division of Eastman Kodak in Rochester, N.Y. "We were looking for a long-term solution on which we could build a solid backbone for our network."

Huber's division is concerned with image processing: taking what was originally a photographic image and turning it into an electronic image for online storage and manipulation. Researchers rely on a 1,000GB optical jukebox and 500GB of magnetic storage. But getting images between these storage devices and their high-powered workstations was taxing the network, a 10Base-T Ethernet LAN.

"It is a very CPU-intensive, I/O-intensive type of processing," Huber said. "We were experiencing bottlenecks from routine activities, particularly to and from the file servers and between floors of the building. Our average file size is about 200MB, with some files as large as 500MB. The shared-media network simply wasn't capable of handling the load."

Fast-Switching Solution

Kodak's solution was a new switching infrastructure based on 100Mbps fast Ethernet. Huber and his colleagues evaluated switches from a

number of vendors, selecting the Catalyst 5000 switching platform from Cisco Systems Inc. primarily because of its port density and inherent manageability.

The Catalyst 5000's switching backplane operates at 1.2Gbps, using a distributed buffering and prioritization scheme to provide nonblocking performance for switched-Ethernet interfaces. Tri-level priority on the backplane ensures that delay-sensitive applications receive the necessary priority on a port-by-port basis. A 192KB buffer provides adequate port buffering for workgroup applications without dropping information during peak traffic periods.

"The Catalyst switches give us 24 full-duplex switch ports, each capable of carrying traffic at 100Mbps, along with the potential for extensive expansion," Huber said. "I can double the port density just by adding a couple of cards. Hot-swap capabilities allow us to perform repairs and upgrades without affecting the rest of the network."

Robust New Management

Switches increase performance by an order of magnitude over traditional shared hubs and also offer greater intelligence per port and new functionality not previously available, such as virtual LANs (vLANs). Intelligent ports also allow more options for port grouping, security, filtering, broadcast impression, and other important tasks.

But although LAN and ATM switches provide significant performance improvements, they also raise new challenges for network managers. Managing a switch-based network is radically different than managing a traditional hub/router-based LAN. For example, traditional

network-management tools provide network maps, that view devices by IP subnetwork and address. But as the use of switches with multiple IP addresses and vLANs grows, an IP view is no longer sufficient to view the network's virtual topology. In many cases, switches are black boxes to network probes, and other management tools, making it difficult to discern traffic patterns.

TrafficDirector

Network administration in the Image Science Division intend to use a new management application for the Catalyst 5000 called TrafficDirector, which leverages embedded RMON (remote monitoring) agents in the switches to obtain a detailed look into the switched internetwork. TrafficDirector offers monitoring and trouble-shooting capabilities at the link, network, transport, and application layers, while providing data for trend analysis and long-term planning.

"We've used switched Ethernet before but never had the same management potential," Huber said. "It can get pretty expensive to put a monitor on every network segment, and which servers connected directly to the switch, it is difficult to see the traffic load. Now we can telnet into the switch and manage it from any place on the network."

Another factor that tipped Huber's hand in favor of the Cisco solution was embedded software infrastructure within the Catalyst 5000 called Internetwork Operating System (IOS) software. Cisco IOS software resides in many types of network devices, providing a cohesive software layer among routers, switches, file servers, multiservice WAN-access switches, and ATM-capable PBXes. This could become important if Eastman Kodak adopts other Cisco devices on the corporate network because it will provide a high degree of consistency among network devices throughout the Eastman Kodak organization.

Now that the high-speed connections to key hubs and file servers are in place, Huber and his colleagues have turned their attention to installing more twisted-pair wiring to allow dedicated, 100Mbps bandwidth to the desktop for power users.

They have no immediate plans for a migration to ATM, but if the company as a whole moves in that direction, the Image Science Division is well-positioned to follow suit. ATM-backbone access is achieved on the Catalyst 5000 through an ATM LAN Emulation module that allows applications based on standard protocols, such as TCP/IP, Novell Inc. NetWare, Digital Equipment Corp. DECnet, and AppleTalk, to run unchanged over ATM networks. "We have a lot of expandability right here in our own subnet," Huber said.

Many organizations are facing growth pains as they seek to upgrade their low-bandwidth, shared-media networks to accommodate more complex information requirements. But Huber believes the primary concerns facing network managers haven't changed: the need for rock-solid stability, high-performance bandwidth, and network-management efficiencies. "We've met our needs now, and we have a lot of potential for the future," he concluded, "with plenty of dedicated bandwidth, in-cabinet expandability, and more robust network management."

Source: David Baum, "Kodak Develops Bandwidth," *LAN Times*, vol. 13, no. 10 (May 13, 1996), p. 35. Copyright © May 13, 1996 by McGraw–Hill, New York. Reprinted by permission of McGraw–Hill, New York.

BUSINESS CASE STUDY QUESTIONS

Activities

1. Complete a top-down model for this case by gleaning facts from the case and placing them in the proper layer of the top-down model. After completing the top-down model, analyze and detail those instances where requirements were clearly passed down from upper layers to lower layers of the model and where solutions to those requirements were passed up from lower layers to upper layers of the model.

2. Detail any questions about the case that may occur to you for which answers are not clearly stated in the article.

Business

1. What were the high-level goals or objectives for migrating from shared LAN media to switched LAN architecture in this case?

2. What was the problem that precipitated the network upgrade?

3. What is the business activity at this location?

Application

1. What types of applications are executed at this location to support business processes?

2. What types of management applications are run in support of the new network architecture?

Data

1. What are the data storage requirements for applications at this location?

2. What were the average and maximum file sizes?

Network

1. What are the network requirements to meet the demands of the application and data layers?

2. What types of bottlenecks and problems was the existing network causing?

3. What evaluation criteria were established to narrow the technology choices?

4. What are some of the advantages that switched LAN architectures offer over shared-media LAN architectures?

5. What are some of the disadvantages of switched LAN architectures as compared to shared-media LAN architectures?

6. How are the unique management and troubleshooting needs of switched LAN architectures being met at Kodak?

7. What is the software that runs on the Catalyst switch? Is this important? Why or why not?

8. Which types of devices were given high-bandwidth network access?

9. What are some of the migration possibilities for future network upgrades if additional bandwidth should be required in the future?

Technology

1. What switching technology was eventually chosen and why?

2. How can the Catalyst switch be managed?

3. What were some of the Catalyst 5000's technical specifications that were particularly important to meeting performance expectations for the new network?

10. Will any changes to workstations, servers, or network operating systems be required if the network backbone upgrades to ATM technology?

4. What types of expandability and reliability features were included in the Catalyst 5000?

5. What media is required to deliver 100 Mbps to the desktop?

6. Did the installed technology meet the high-level requirements set forth in the business layer? Defend your answer.

CHAPTER 7

LOCAL AREA NETWORK OPERATING SYSTEMS

Concepts Reinforced

OSI Model
Protocols and Standards
Network Architectures

Top-Down Model
Hardware/Software Compatibility

Concepts Introduced

Network Operating System
   Functionality
Peer-to-Peer Network Operating
   Systems
Network Technology Analysis
Client Network Operating Systems
LAN Software Architecture

Functional Network Analysis
Client/Server Network Operating
   Systems
Network Operating System
   Architectures
Server Network Operating Systems
Client/Server Technology Model

OBJECTIVES

After mastering the material in this chapter, you should

1. Understand the compatibility issues involved with implementing local area network operating systems.

2. Understand the basics of network operating system functionality.

3. Understand the important differences between peer-to-peer and client/server network operating system architectures.

4. Understand the emerging role of the client network operating system and the universal client.

5. Understand how to analyze functional networking requirements and match those requirements to available technology.

■ INTRODUCTION

Network operating systems, like most other aspects of data communications, are undergoing tremendous change. As a result, before examining the operational characteristics of a particular network operating system, we need to gain an overall perspective of network operating systems in general. In particular, network operating system architectures are in a state of transition from closed environments in which only clients and servers running the same network operating system could interact to open environments in which universal clients are able to interoperate with servers running any network operating system.

Network operating system functionality is examined for both client and server network operating systems. The functionality examined is representative of current network operating systems in general rather than any particular product. This review of overall network operating system functionality will serve as a basis of comparison for the more detailed analysis of particular network operating systems.

■ WHERE DO NETWORK OPERATING SYSTEMS FIT?

The network operating systems that enable communication between networked client and server computers across enterprise networks are but one type of software required to implement a secure and fully functional client/server information system. Several different categories of LAN software must be able to interoperate successfully for transparent, productive access to information to be delivered to end-users.

LAN Software Architecture

To organize and illustrate the interrelationships between the various categories of LAN software, a **LAN software architecture** can be constructed. As illustrated in Figure 7-1, LAN software is divided into two major categories:

1. Network operating systems.
2. Application software.

The **network operating systems** are concerned with providing an interface between LAN hardware, such as network interface cards, and the application software installed on a particular client or server. The network operating system's job is to provide transparent interoperability between the client and server portions of a given application program.

Applications software on a LAN is divided into **client front ends** and **server back ends** or **engines** and is concerned with accomplishment of a specific type of task or transaction. LAN applications software can be divided into two major subcategories:

1. LAN productivity software.
2. LAN resource management software.

LAN productivity software is application software that contributes directly to the productivity of its users. In other words, this is the software that people use not

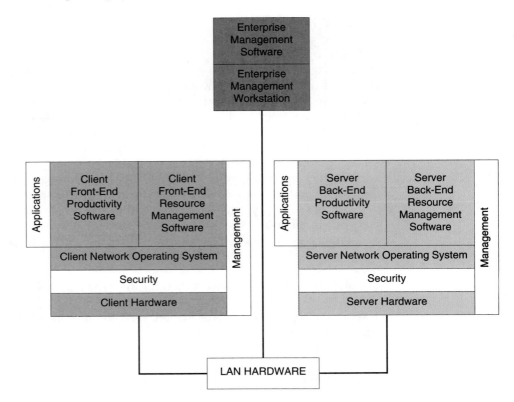

Figure 7-1   LAN Software Architecture

only to get their work done but, more importantly, to get their work done **more** quickly, effectively, accurately, or at a lower cost than if they did not have the **benefit** of this software. Examples include e-mail, scheduling software, groupware, **and a** variety of other types of software.

LAN resource management software is more concerned with providing access to shared network resources and services. Examples of such shared network-attached resources include printers, fax machines, CD-ROMs, modems, and a variety of other devices and services.

Two overlying elements that are required in any LAN software configuration are

1. Security.

2. Management.

Security is especially important in networked LAN software environments as logged-in users can be physically dispersed over large areas. Increased deployment of remote workers has led to increased need for remote access to corporate information resources. As important corporate data is transferred over network links, precautions must be taken to prevent unauthorized access to transmitted data as well as to corporate networks and computer systems.

Finally, **management software** must be incorporated to provide a single, consolidated view of all networked resources, both hardware and software. From a single location, all of the distributed elements that comprise today's client/server information systems must be able to be effectively monitored and managed. This single enterprise management platform must be able to integrate management information from not just networking components but also application programs, database management systems, and client and server hardware.

THE CLIENT/SERVER TECHNOLOGY ARCHITECTURE AND SOFTWARE COMPATIBILITY

The potential compatibility issues involved with ensuring transparent interoperability between network operating systems and the various other client and server software and hardware technology elements are outlined in more detail in Figure 7-2. The client/server technology architecture depicts the categories of software that may be present on client and server computers linked via an enterprise network. This diagram is concerned primarily with software and communications, which is why only single client and server software profiles are illustrated. The fact is, any number of clients or servers may be linked via the enterprise network, but the software compatibility issues illustrated in Figure 7-2 will still remain.

The best way to analyze software compatibility is by direction. **Vertical software compatibility** is concerned with making sure that all necessary compatible protocols are in place for all of the software and hardware within a single client or server to operate harmoniously and transparently. The most important thing to remember is that these are issues that must be analyzed in a methodical manner. It is not important to memorize potential compatible protocols. What is important is to

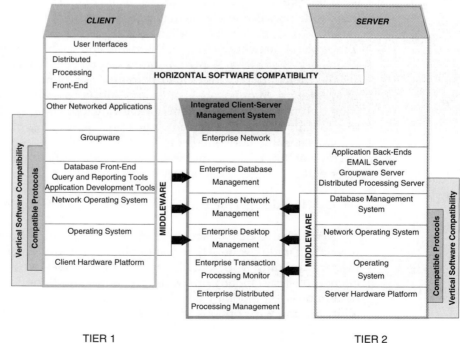

Figure 7-2 Client/Server Technology Architecture

use a structured model such as Figure 7-2 to uncover any potential incompatibilities before, rather than after, installation. For example:

1. How do I know that a particular version of UNIX (operating system layer) will work on my computer (server hardware platform layer)?

2. If I do get UNIX installed, how do I know which network operating systems and database management systems will be compatible with UNIX and with each other?

Whereas vertical software compatibility is concerned with transparency between *different* layers of software or hardware *within* the *same* client or server, **horizontal software compatibility** is concerned with transparency between *similar* software layers *between different* clients and servers.

To elaborate, one of the benefits of a client/server architecture is its ability to incorporate hardware and software technology from multiple vendors into a transparently interoperable information system. The previous statement is easier said than done. Horizontal software compatibility is most often concerned with getting different software of the same category to interoperate transparently between clients, between clients and servers, or between servers. For example:

1. How do I get a NetWare client (network operating system layer) to interoperate with a Windows NT server (network operating system layer)?

2. How do I get an Oracle database server (database management system layer) to query a Sybase SQL server (database management system layer)?

Achieving horizontal software compatibility between different types of software on different types of computers is a complicated task roughly equivalent to translating between foreign languages. As a result, although vertical software compatibility was achieved by adjacent software layers each supporting a common compatibility protocol, horizontal software compatibility is most often delivered by a category of software known as **middleware.** Middleware is an actual additional installed software program rather than just a set of mutually supported commands and messages. Middleware is often specialized by software layer: database middleware, network operating system middleware, operating system middleware, or distributed application middleware.

Occasionally, horizontal software compatibility is concerned with transparent interoperability between multiple pieces of software in the same software category layer within a single client or server. For example:

1. How do I get my Excel spreadsheet graph into my Word document?

Remember, transparency depends on the existence of compatibility protocols or translating middleware. These compatibility protocols and middleware may be proprietary and only work among one vendor's or a few vendors' software or may be open, industry-standard protocols. The important thing for the network analyst to determine is to pinpoint where the needs for horizontal or vertical software compatibility are and what options are available to deliver that compatibility.

The Enterprise Network   Connecting the client and server in Figure 7-2 is an entity entitled the **enterprise network.** The enterprise network is the transportation system of the client/server architecture. Together with middleware, it is responsible for the transparent cooperation of distributed processors and databases. In an analogy to a powerful stand-alone mainframe computer, the enterprise network would be analogous to that computer's system bus, linking the processing power of the CPU with the stored data to be processed.

The role of the enterprise network is to deliver the integration and transparent interoperability enabled by the client/server architecture. Further, the enterprise network often also incorporates host-terminal traffic, voice traffic, and videoconferencing traffic in an integrated and well-managed fashion.

What exactly does an enterprise network look like? That depends on what the business enterprise looks like. If the business enterprise is comprised of regional branches or subsidiaries widely dispersed geographically, then the enterprise network will obviously contain wide area network links. From a physical standpoint, the enterprise network is most often the combination of network devices and connections of the following categories:

- Local area network (LAN).

- LAN-to-LAN or inter-LAN, also known as internetwork.

- Wide area network (WAN).

In addition, the enterprise network plays a key role in managing a client/server information system. Due to the distributed nature of a client/server information system comprised of a multitude of widely dispersed processors, the only single location through which all traffic passes is the enterprise network. Therefore, it would stand to reason that the enterprise network is the only sensible location from which to manage the numerous shared resources of the client/server information system. A variety of management hardware and software capable of effectively supporting corporate requirements for the management of distributed information systems are connected directly to the enterprise network. The enterprise network literally serves as the backbone of the client/server information system. Hopefully, this discussion fortifies the truth of the often heard statement, "The network *is* the computer." Enterprise networks will be explored further in Chapter 11.

Management of Client/Server Information Systems   To understand the complexity of a comprehensive management system for a client/server architecture, one only needs to examine the vast array of components within that architecture that can potentially require management.

Most, if not all, of the client/server architecture elements listed in Figure 7-2 are available with some sort of management system or software. The problem is that there is little if any similarity or consistency in management system design among various vendors, even for elements of similar function. In addition, the multiple layers of management systems listed in Figure 7-2 under the enterprise network component present a management system integration problem of major proportions.

Users do not want "piecemeal" system management caused by the distributed nature of their information systems. They do not wish separate management consoles or systems for database systems, distributed applications, operating systems, network operating systems, and networking hardware. Furthermore, since the client/server architecture can feature multiple client and server operating systems and network operating systems, it can be seen how one could potentially need an entire room just for systems consoles for the management of the various client and server possibilities.

The solution to the management system integration problem comes down to a few key questions surrounding standards:

1. Can management system standards be developed that lend themselves especially well to distributed information systems?

2. More importantly, can and will these standards be adhered to by the manufacturers of the various elements of the client/server architecture?

In fact, open standards for sharing management information have been developed and integrated into several popular **enterprise network management systems.** Among the most popular of these are

- HP's OpenView.
- IBM's NetView.
- Sun's SunNet Manager.

However, it is important to distinguish between enterprise network management systems and **integrated client/server management systems.** In addition to managing a multivendor enterprise network, an integrated client/server management system must also be able to supply the following management capabilities:

- enterprise database management.
- enterprise desktop management.
- enterprise transaction processing management.
- enterprise distributed processing management.

Although there are many multivendor enterprise network management systems, most so-called integrated client/server management systems are still in the "vaporware" stage. Note that enterprise network management is only one component of the overall integrated client/server management. Enterprise network management systems and integrated client/server management systems will be discussed in detail in Chapter 14.

■ NETWORK OPERATING SYSTEM ARCHITECTURES

Now that we have gained an appreciation of where networking operating systems fit in an overall client/server architecture as well as how compatibility issues between network operating systems and various software and hardware components must be dealt with, the remainder of the chapter focuses on the architecture, functionality, and technology analysis of the client and server network operating systems themselves.

Traditional Differentiation: Peer-to-Peer vs. Client/Server

Traditionally, there were two major product categories of network operating systems:

- **Peer-to-peer network operating systems,** also known as DOS-based LAN or low-cost LANs, offered easy to install and use file and print services for workgroup and departmental networking needs.

- **Client/server network operating systems** offered more powerful capabilities including the ability to support hundreds of users and the ability to interact with other network operating systems via gateways. These client/server network operating systems were both considerably more expensive and considerably more complicated to install and administer than peer-to-peer network operating systems.

Peer-to-Peer   One of the early appeals of peer-to-peer network operating systems was their relatively minimal hardware requirements in terms of memory and disk space. In addition, the fact that they ran as a DOS-based background application made them considerably less complicated to install and administer than client/server network operating systems. When printer sharing and file sharing for less than 50 users represented the major functional requirements of a network operating system, peer-to-peer network operating systems such as Artisoft's LANtastic and Performance Technology's PowerLAN were popular choices in this technology category.

In most peer-to-peer LANs, individual workstations can be configured as a service requester (client), a service provider (server), or a combination of the two. The terms *client* and *server* in this case describe the workstation's functional role in the network. The installed network operating system is still a peer-to-peer network operating system, because all workstations in the network are loaded with the same networking software. Most peer-to-peer network operating systems lacked the ability to access servers of client/server network operating systems and suffered from diminished performance as large numbers (greater than 50) of users were added to the system. As a result, traditional peer-to-peer network operating systems were characterized as lacking interoperability and scalability.

Client/Server   In contrast, traditional client/server network operating systems require two distinct software products to be loaded on to client and server computers, respectively. The specialized client software required less memory and disk space and was less expensive than the more complicated, more expensive server software. NetWare 3.12 and Microsoft LANManager are examples of traditional client/server network operating systems. The client software was made to interact with the corresponding server software. As a result, although traditional client/server network operating systems overcame the scalability limitation of peer-to-peer network operating systems, they did not necessarily overcome the interoperability limitation. Functionally, client/server network operating systems offered faster, more reliable performance than peer-to-peer LANs as well as improved administration and security capabilities. Figure 7-3 illustrates the key differences between traditional peer-to-peer and client/server network operating systems.

Current Differentiation: Client NOS vs. Server NOS

Functional Requirements of Today's Network Operating Systems   Although traditional peer-to-peer and client/server network operating systems successfully met the functional requirements for workgroup and departmental computing, as these departmental LANs needed to be integrated into a single, cohesive, interoperable, enterprise-wide information system, the limitations of these traditional NOS (network operating system) architectures became evident.

To understand the architectural specifications of today's network operating systems, it is first necessary to understand the functional requirements that these

Peer-to-Peer

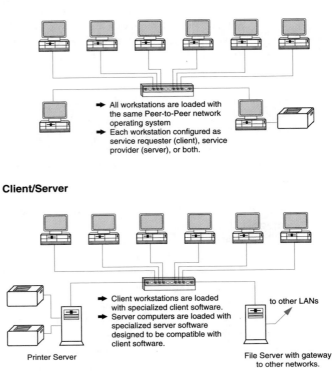

Client/Server

Figure 7-3   Peer-to-Peer vs. Client/Server Network Operating Systems

network operating systems must deliver. In taking a top-down approach to network operating system requirements analysis, one might ask, "What are users of an enterprise-wide information system demanding of a network operating system in terms of services?" The answer to this question lies in the application layer of the top-down model. Given that it is distributed applications that will enable enterprise-wide productivity and decision-making, the underlying network operating systems must support these distributed applications by supplying the message services and global directory services required to execute these applications in an enterprise-wide, multiple-server environment.

Figure 7-4 illustrates these functional requirements and contrasts them with the requirements traditionally demanded of client/server and peer-to-peer network operating systems.

As illustrated in Figure 7-4, the new or emerging demands being put on network operating systems are

- **Application services.**
- **Directory services.**
- **Integration/migration services.**

Key points about each of these emerging required services are bulleted in Figure 7-4. To successfully meet these functional requirements, network operating sys-

Traditional Requirements		Emerging Requirements		
		All services delivered seamlessly across multiple server platforms regardless of installed network operating system		
FILE SERVICES	PRINTER SERVICES	APPLICATION SERVICES	DIRECTORY SERVICES	INTEGRATION/MIGRATION SERVICES
		➡ Database back-end engines ➡ Messaging/communication back-end engines SUPPORT FOR: ➡ 32 bit symmetrical multi-processing ➡ Pre-emptive multi-tasking ➡ Applications run in protected memory mode ➡ Multithreading	➡ Global directory or naming services ➡ All network objects defined in single location and shared by all applications ➡ Directory information is stored in replicated, distributed databases for reliability, redundancy, fault tolerance	➡ Allow multiple different client network operating systems to transparently interoperate with multiple, different server network operating systems ➡ Provide easy-to-implement paths for upgrades to more recent versions or migration to different network operating systems

Figure 7-4 Required Services of Network Operating Systems: Traditional vs. Emerging

tem architectures have shifted from integrated, single-vendor client/server network operating systems, as illustrated in Figure 7-3, to independent, distinct, multivendor, client and server network operating systems. The functional characteristics of these distinct client and server network operating systems are described in detail later in this chapter. Figure 7-5 illustrates this architectural shift in network operating system development.

Client Network Operating Systems: The Universal Client   **Client network operating systems,** as illustrated in Figure 7-5, integrate traditional operating system functionality with advanced network operating system features to enable communication with a variety of different types of network operating system servers. This client workstation's ability to interoperate transparently with a number of different network operating system servers without the need for additional products or configurations is described as a **universal client** capability.

Server Network Operating Systems   **Server network operating systems** are able to be chosen and installed based on their performance characteristics for a given required functionality. For example, NetWare servers are often employed as file and print servers whereas Windows NT, OS/2, or UNIX servers are more likely to be employed as application servers. Because of the universal client's ability to communicate with any server and the server network operating system's ability to communicate with a variety of different client network operating systems, the choice of server network operating system can be based more on optimizing functional performance than on delivering required communication protocols.

Small Business Network Operating Systems   Traditional peer-to-peer network operating systems have undergone both functional and architectural transitions in response to new functional requirements. Peer-to-peer networking functionality such as file sharing, printer sharing, chat, and e-mail is now included in most client network operating systems. As a result, traditional peer-to-peer network operating system products such as LANtastic and PowerLAN had to differentiate themselves

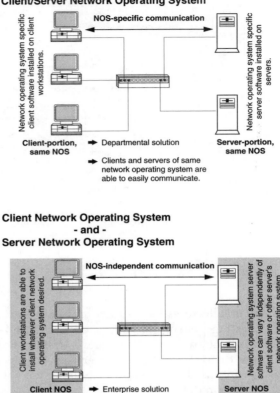

Figure 7-5 Client/Server Network Operating Systems vs. Client *and* Server Network Operating Systems

somehow from emerging client network operating systems such as Windows 95 and OS/2 Warp Connect.

Architecturally, rather than remaining as closed, identically configured, peer-to-peer environments, today's small business network operating systems offer interoperability with server network operating systems via universal client capabilities. In addition, they offer their own 32-bit server software to offer greater performance than the 16-bit peer software merely configured as a server.

One important characteristic of the latest **small business network operating systems** is that they continue to exhibit all of the positive attributes of the peer-to-peer network operating systems from which they evolved:

- DOS-based, with minimal memory and disk requirements.

- Easy installation, configuration, and management.

- High-quality file and print services.

Additionally, small business network operating systems have had to differentiate themselves from client network operating systems by offering more advanced features such as

- Dedicated 32-bit server software.

- Bundled workgroup software.

- Easy migration path to server-based network operating systems.

Small business network operating systems seem to be getting squeezed between the client and server network operating systems and are functionally situated to offer a migration path between the two markets. Figure 7-6 illustrates the architectural transition from traditional peer-to-peer network operating systems to today's small business network operating system and Figure 7-7 summarizes some of the key functional characteristics of small business network operating systems.

Peer-to-Peer Network Operating System

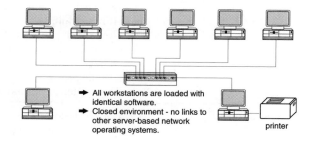

➡ All workstations are loaded with identical software.
➡ Closed environment - no links to other server-based network operating systems.

printer

Small Business Network Operating System

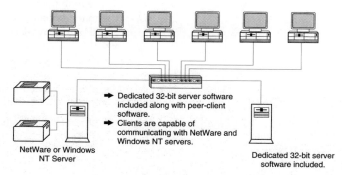

➡ Dedicated 32-bit server software included along with peer-client software.
➡ Clients are capable of communicating with NetWare and Windows NT servers.

NetWare or Windows NT Server

Dedicated 32-bit server software included.

Figure 7-6 Architectural Transition from Peer-to-Peer to Small Business Network Operating Systems

Small Business NOS Functional Category	Importance/Implication
Platform issues	• How much memory is required for client functionality? Server functionality? Both? • Are standard network interface cards supported or are proprietary NICs required? • Are multiprotocol specifications such as NDIS and ODI supported? • Which network architectures are supported? Ethernet, token ring, ARCnet, LocalTalk?
Interoperability	• Is NetWare client software included? • Is Windows client software included? • Is remote access software to enable remote clients included?
Workgroup software	• Is e-mail software included? • Is group scheduling software included? • Is fax gateway software included? • Is CD-ROM sharing software included?
File sharing	• What is the extent of security available? • Can files be hidden? • Can users share (mount) multiple remote disks? • Can applications be executed on remote shared clients?
Printer sharing	• How many printers can be attached to a given computer? • How many printers can be managed overall? • What is the extent of management capabilities available to the administrator? • How much printer management can users do on their own? • Can printers be assigned to classes based on performance characteristics with jobs queued to printer classes rather than to specific printers? • Are printer usage statistics available by user?
Scalability	• Is a 32-bit-compatible server program available? • Are any client changes necessary to interoperate with the 32-bit server? • Is there a maximum number of client nodes supported?
Management	• Is a centralized management facility available? • What is the management platform? DOS, Windows? • Does the management facility keep a log of all network events? • Is an SNMP agent available to link to enterprise management systems? • How much information is available about active users and processes? • Can logon time restrictions or password expiration dates be set?

Figure 7-7 Small Business Network Operating System Functional Characteristics

■ CLIENT NETWORK OPERATING SYSTEM FUNCTIONALITY

Now that we have gained an understanding of the new architectural arrangement of network operating systems consisting of distinct, interoperable, multivendor, client and server network operating systems (Figure 7-5), the functional aspects of client network operating systems will be explained in detail in this section whereas server network operating systems will be explained in the next major section.

Client network operating systems such as Windows 95, OS/2 Warp Connect, and Windows NT Workstation offer three major categories of functionality:

- Operating system capabilities.

- Peer-to-peer networking capabilities.

- Client software for communicating with a variety of different server network operating systems.

The logical relationship of these three distinct yet complementary categories of functionality is illustrated in Figure 7-8. Figure 7-8 also points out potential areas for compatibility and protocol consideration where the various software and hardware layers interface.

In the following sections, each of these major categories of functionality of client network operating systems is reviewed from the perspective of the network analyst. The importance of each functional category to the overall network operating system is explained as are key differences in the implementation among available technology of any given functionality. From such a review of network operating system functionality, the network analyst should be able to construct a logical network design listing that functionality that is required to meet business objectives.

This logical network design would then be used as an evaluation mechanism for comparison with the delivered functionality of available technology. Logical network design functionality can be compared to available technology's delivered functionality in a technology analysis grid such as Figure 7-15 (client network operating system technology analysis grid). As stated in previous chapters, the advantage to employing a technology analysis grid in such an endeavor is that it ensures that purchase decisions or recommendations are made based on facts rather than creative packaging or effective marketing.

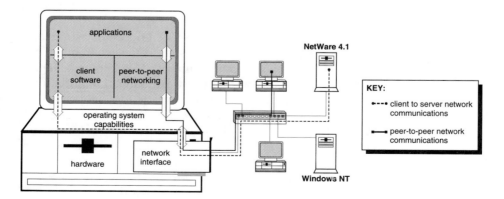

Figure 7-8 Logical Relationship of Client Network Operating System Functional Categories

Operating System Capabilities

The following desirable operating system characteristics are listed and briefly explained here from the perspective of each characteristic's importance to overall network operating system performance.

- 32-bit operating system—32-bit operating systems will allow more sophisticated and higher performance 32-bit applications to execute more quickly.

- Preemptive multitasking—Preemptive multitasking prevents misbehaving programs from monopolizing system resources at the expense of the performance of other applications.

- Protected memory space—Protected memory space prevents application programs from accidentally writing into each other's or the operating system's memory space, thereby causing general protection faults and/or system crashes.

- Support for symmetrical multiprocessing (SMP)—SMP support is especially important for server network operating systems due to the processing load imposed by multiple simultaneous requests for services from clients. Some high-powered client applications such as 3-D modeling or simulation software may warrant SMP support on client platforms as well.

- Multithreading—Multithreaded applications are only able to achieve performance increases if they are executed by an operating system that supports multithreaded applications, allowing more than one subprocess to execute simultaneously.

User Interface   **Object-oriented user interfaces** present the user with a graphical desktop on which objects such as files, directories, folders, disk drives, programs, or devices can be arranged according to the user's whim. More importantly, as objects are moved around the desktop, they retain their characteristic properties. As a result, when a desktop object is clicked upon, only legitimate actions presented in context-sensitive menus appropriate for that class of objects can be executed.

Unlike object-oriented user interfaces, Windows-based user interfaces, although graphical, do not allow icons representing directories, files, disk drives, etc. to be broken out of their particular window and placed directly on the desktop. Figure 7-9 contrasts Windows-based user interfaces and object-oriented user interfaces.

Application Program Support   A very important aspect of any migration plan to a new client network operating system is the extent of support for **backward compatibility** is terms of application support, also known as **legacy application** support. It should stand to reason that most companies cannot afford to replace or rewrite all of their application software to upgrade to a new client network operating system.

Although it was stated previously that 32-bit client network operating systems are desirable, the fact of the matter is that the vast majority or network-based applications are still 16-bit applications. In addition, many of these 16-bit application programs, commercially produced as well as "home-grown," bypass supported API calls and commands in favor of conversing directly with or controlling hardware devices. This type of programming was done initially in the interest of increased performance in most cases. Programs or subroutines that write directly to computer hardware are sometimes referred to as employing **real-mode device drivers.**

Windows-based User Interface (Windows 3.1)

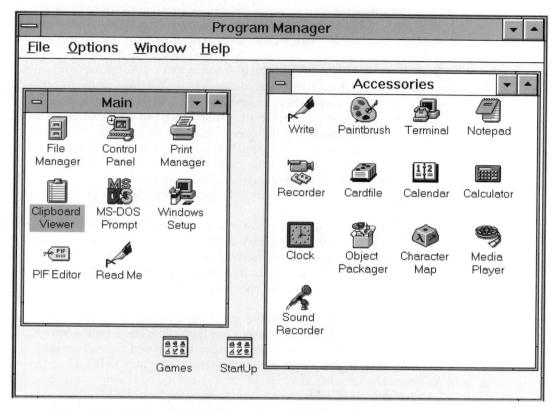

Object-oriented User Interface (Windows '95)

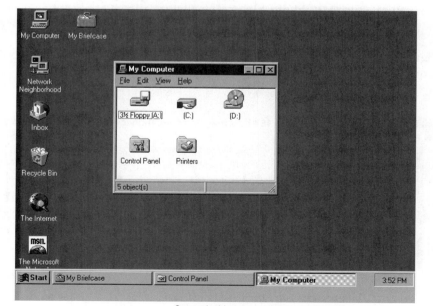

Screen shot(s) reprinted with permission from Microsoft Corporation

Figure 7-9   Windows-Based User Interfaces vs. Object-Oriented User Interfaces

Many 32-bit network operating systems do not allow application programs to address or control hardware directly in the interest of security and protecting applications from using each other's assigned memory spaces and causing system crashes. Instead, these more secure 32-bit operating systems control access to hardware and certain system services via **virtual device drivers,** otherwise known as **VxDs.** Windows NT is perhaps the best example of a 32-bit network operating system that prevents direct hardware addressing. As a result, many 16-bit applications, particularly highly graphical computer games, will not execute over the Windows NT network operating system. On the other hand, Windows NT is extremely stable.

Another issue concerning the execution of 16-bit applications is whether or not those applications execute in a shared memory address space, sometimes referred to as a **16-bit subsystem.** If this is the case, then a single misbehaving 16-bit application can crash the 16-bit subsystem and all other executing 16-bit applications. Some 32-bit operating systems allow each 16-bit application to execute in its own protected memory execution area.

When it comes to 32-bit applications, client network operating systems may execute these applications in their own address space, otherwise known as **protected memory mode.** However, all of these protected mode 32-bit applications may execute over a single 32-bit subsystem in which case a single misbehaving 32-bit application can crash the entire 32-bit subsystem and all other associated 32-bit applications.

Whether or not an application is executable over a particular network operating system is dependent upon whether or not that application issues commands and requests for network-based services in a predetermined format defined by the network operating system's **application program interface (API).** Each network operating system has its own unique API or variation. For example, Windows, Windows NT, and Windows 95 all support variations of the Win32 API.

Some client network operating systems, such as Windows NT, have the ability to support multiple APIs and multiple different operating system subsystems, sometimes known as **virtual machines.** This feature allows applications written for a variety of operating systems such as OS/2, DOS, or POSIX to all execute over a single client network operating system.

Figure 7-10 illustrates some of the concepts of application program support by client network operating systems.

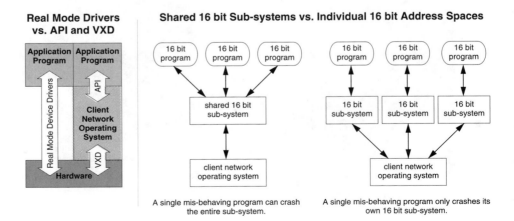

Figure 7-10   Application Program Support by Client Network Operating Systems

Plug-n-Play Features   **Plug-n-play (PnP)** features are included in varying degrees in most client network operating systems. The goal of plug-n-play is to free users from having to understand and worry about such things as IRQs (interrupt requests), DMA (direct memory access) channels, memory addresses, COM ports, and editing CONFIG.SYS whenever they want to add a device to their computer. Although that goal has not been fully realized, definite progress has been made. Ideally PnP functionality will

- Automatically detect the addition or removal of PnP devices.

- Set all of the previously mentioned settings so that they do not conflict with other devices.

- Automatically load necessary drivers to enable the particular device.

PnP standards also include support for **dynamic reconfiguration,** which will enable such things as

- PCMCIA cards being inserted into and removed from computers without a need to reboot.

- Hot docking (powered up) of laptop computers into docking bays or stations.

- Dynamic reconfiguration-aware applications software that could automatically respond to changes in system configuration.

Eventually, PnP devices will include not just network interface cards but also controllers of many types, SCSI devices, monitors, printers, and a variety of input/output devices. SCSI controllers will be configured according to a PnP standard known as **SCAM** or **SCSI configured automatically.** PnP-compliant monitors will be controlled and configured according to the PnP **DDC** or **data display channel** standard.

Compatibility issues are important to the achievement of full PnP functionality. To be specific, three distinct elements must all support PnP standards:

1. A **PnP BIOS** (basic input output system) is required to interface directly to both PnP and non-PnP-compliant hardware.

2. PnP capabilities must be supported by the client network operating system through interaction with the PnP BIOS. Windows 95 possesses the most PnP capability among currently available client network operating systems.

3. The devices that are to be installed must be PnP-compliant. This basically means that the manufacturers of these devices must add some additional software and processing power so that these devices can converse transparently with the PnP operating system and BIOS. In some cases, PnP-compliant device drivers may also need to be supplied.

To cater to the vast majority of legacy (non-PnP-compliant) devices, many PnP-compliant client network operating systems also assist in easing configuration hassles with these non-PnP-compliant devices. Using a variety of detection techniques, the client operating system detects non-PnP devices and then executes an assistant agent program, sometimes referred to as a hardware wizard, which attempts to walk the user through the configuration routine. Such programs are often capable of detecting and displaying IRQs and DMA addresses used by other devices, allowing users to often accept supplied default answers in this semiautomatic configuration scenario.

Peer-to-Peer Networking Capabilities

Many of the same functional capabilities discussed previously in the section on the evolution of the small business network operating system are included as part of the peer-to-peer capabilities of client network operating systems. In fact, it is this inclusion of workgroup application software in client network operating systems that forced the vendors of traditional peer-to-peer network operating systems such as LANtastic and PowerLAN to add new, more advanced features of their offerings.

File and Printer Sharing   Perhaps the most basic of peer-to-peer network functions is file and printer sharing. In many cases, other resources such as CD-ROM drives can also be shared. Network operating systems supporting peer-to-peer networking can vary widely in their ability to limit access to certain drives, directories, or files. How finely access can be controlled (by disk, directory, or file level) is sometimes referred to as the **granularity** of the access control scheme. In addition, access must also be able to be controlled to drives, directories, or files by user groups or individual users. Sophistication of the printer management facility can also vary from one client network operating system to another.

Not all client network operating systems include peer-to-peer networking capabilities. For example, Windows 3.1 gains its peer-to-peer networking from the Windows for Workgroups 3.11 upgrade whereas OS/2 Warp Connect, rather than OS/2 Warp, is the only version that offers peer-to-peer networking. As client network operating systems have grown in sophistication, file and printer sharing services are now available to client platforms other than those configured with identical client network operating systems. Figure 7-11 illustrates some of the cross-platform peer-to-peer file and printer sharing capabilities of Windows 95.

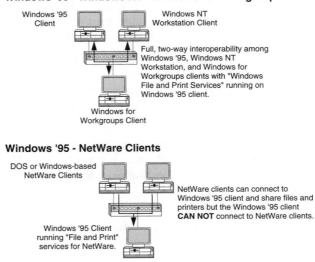

Figure 7-11   Cross-Platform File and Printer Sharing

**Practical Advice
and Information**

One very important point to be made regarding the type of cross-platform interoperability illustrated in Figure 7-11 is as follows:

- Interoperability solutions cannot be assumed to be two-way or reversible. For example, as illustrated in Figure 7-11, although NetWare clients are able to connect to a Windows 95 client running File and Print Services for NetWare, the converse is not always true. Initially, Windows 95 or NT clients and servers were not able to log in to or share the disks and files of the NetWare clients. An additional piece of software from NetWare known as the Client32 (or IntraNet-Ware Client for NT), available with NetWare 4.11, is required to link a Windows 95 or NT workstation with a NetWare server. Microsoft later introduced Client Service for NetWare and Gateway Service for NetWare. Each interoperability product offers specific interoperability options and services.

Workgroup Applications   Ever striving to find new ways to differentiate themselves from the competition, vendors are offering client network operating systems bundled with such workgroup application software as

- Terminal emulation.
- Calculator.
- Clock.
- Games.
- Paintbrush.
- Sound recorder.
- Remote access software.
- CD player.
- Backup.
- Chat.
- Phone dialer.
- Performance and network monitors.
- Diagnostic software.
- Screen savers.
- Web browsers.
- Fax access software.

Some client operating systems also offer additional more sophisticated workgroup applications in bonus packs that are sold for a modest charge. For example, IBM sells the BonusPak for OS/2 Warp Connect and Microsoft sells Win '95 Plus!.

**Managerial
Perspective**

The client network operating system that offers the greatest number of workgroup applications is not necessarily the best or most appropriate choice. Although free application software is nice, priority should be given to client network operating systems characteristics such as

- Application program support and operating system characteristics.

- Peer-to-peer networking capabilities.

- Flexibility and ease of installation and use in acting as a client to a variety of different server network operating systems.

Client network operating systems that are able to connect to a great many different server operating systems are sometimes referred to as a universal client. In support of multivendor, multiplatform, distributed information systems, this is perhaps the most important evaluation criterion of all when selecting a client network operating system.

Client Networking Capabilities

As illustrated architecturally in Figure 7-12, there are three distinct elements of networking functionality, in addition to the previously mentioned application support capabilities, that must be included in a client network operating system. In some cases, more than one alternative is offered for each of the following elements:

- Client software and network drivers that allow a particular client to communicate with a compatible server. These are MAC (media access control) protocol specifications such as NDIS and ODI.

- Network transport protocols that package and transport messages between clients and servers. These protocols correspond to the network and transport layers of the OSI model.

- Network redirectors that trap API (application program interface) calls and process them appropriately. Redirectors are concerned with providing file system related services in support of application programs.

OSI Model Layer		**Application Programs**		
APPLICATION		Network redirectors which trap API calls and forward them to proper protocol stack and file system.		Application Redirectors
PRESENTATION				
SESSION				
TRANSPORT		Responsible for end-to-end reliable transmission	TCP SPX	Network Transport Protocols
NETWORK		Responsible for end-to-end addressing	IP IPX	
DATA LINK	LLC	NIC driver software compatible with NIC and NOS	NDIS or ODI	MAC Sub-layer Specifications
	MAC SUB-LAYER			
PHYSICAL		HARDWARE	Network Interface Card	

Figure 7-12   Client Networking Functionality

As previously stated, more than one alternative protocol may be provided in a given client network operating system for each of the three network protocol categories. Figure 7-13 displays the protocol stacks for the following four different client network operating systems:

- Windows for Workgroups.

- Windows NT Workstation.

- Windows 95.

- OS/2 Warp Connect.

Rather than organize protocols in an OSI model architecture, Figure 7-13 divides the protocols into layers according to networking functionality.

Network Client to Multiple Servers   In most client network operating systems, these three elements of network functionality combine to allow client platforms to automatically find and connect to reachable, compatible servers. For example, a properly configured Windows NT client will be able to automatically display network connections and connect to Windows NT and NetWare servers that are physically reachable and to which the client has been assigned access privileges. The client software does not have to be preconfigured with any information about these servers. The server discovery and access are handled transparently by the client network operating system.

	Windows for Workgroups	Windows NT Workstation	Windows '95	IBM OS/2 Warp Connect
Application Support	WIN16 API 16-bit Windows applications supported	WIN32 API 32-bit and some 16-bit Windows applications supported	WIN32 API 32-bit and most 16-bit Windows applications supported	Supports DOS applications, 16-bit Windows applications, and native OS/2 applications
Application Re-directors and File Systems	SMB (Server Message Block Redirector (Microsoft)); FAT (File Allocation Table File System (DOS/Windows))	NCP (Netware Core Protocol Redirector (Novell)); SMB (Server Message Block Redirector (Microsoft)); FAT (File Allocation Table File System (DOS/Windows)); NTFS (NT File System)	NCP (Netware Core Protocol Redirector (Novell)); SMB (Server Message Block Redirector (Microsoft)); FAT (File Allocation Table File System (DOS/Windows))	NCP (Netware Core Protocol Redirector (Novell)); SMB (Server Message Block Redirector (Microsoft)); NFS (Network File System (UNIX)); HPFS (High Performance File System (OS/2))
Network Transport Protocols	IPX/SPX; NETBEUI (NetBIOS Extended User Interface (Microsoft)); TCP/IP	IPX/SPX; NETBEUI (NetBIOS Extended User Interface (Microsoft)); TCP/IP; Apple-Talk	IPX/SPX; NETBEUI (NetBIOS Extended User Interface (Microsoft)); TCP/IP	IPX/SPX; NETBEUI (NetBIOS Extended User Interface (Microsoft)); TCP/IP
MAC Sub-Layer Specifications	NDIS (Network Data-Link Interface Specification (Microsoft/3Com)); ODI (Open Data-Link Interface (Novell))	NDIS (Network Data-Link Interface Specification (Microsoft/3Com))	NDIS (Network Data-Link Interface Specification (Microsoft/3Com)); ODI (Open Data-Link Interface (Novell))	NDIS (Network Data-Link Interface Specification (Microsoft/3Com)); ODI (Open Data-Link Interface (Novell))

Figure 7-13   Client Network Operating System Protocol Stacks of Networking Functionality

In addition to offering network operating system client software such as Net-Ware 3.*x* and 4.*x* clients, vendors often include specialized application-oriented client software in client network operating systems. For example:

- FTP (file transfer protocol) client software.

- E-mail client software.

- Scheduling systems client software.

- Web browsers and Gopher clients.

In the case of the e-mail and scheduling clients, compatible e-mail and scheduling application servers must be available. The client portion is merely the front end to a back-end application engine executing in some other network-accessible location.

Remote Access   Specialized client software written to allow remote access to network operating systems servers is included with or available for most client network operating systems. These remote access clients must access a specialized portion of the server network operating system specifically designed to handle incoming remote access clients. The most popular server-based remote access software to which client portions are generally available are

- **Windows NT Remote Access Server (RAS)**

- **NetWare Connect**

Both of these products would execute on a typical server platform either as a dedicated communications server or in conjunction with applications server duties. An alternative to server-based remote access software is a stand-alone device alternatively known as a **dial-up server** or **remote node server.** Such a self-contained unit includes modems, communications software, and NOS-specific remote access server software in a turnkey system. Shiva is perhaps the best known vendor of dial-up servers. As a result some client operating systems include remote access client software written especially to interface to Shiva dial-up servers.

Some client network operating systems include not only remote access client software but also remote access server software. With this capability, other remote access clients can dial-in to each other for file sharing, e-mail exchange, schedule synchronization, etc. Windows NT Workstation extends this scenario by offering limited local server capability as well as remote access server capability. Figure 7-14 illustrates the relationship between remote access client and remote access server software as well as the architectural differences between applications server-based and remote-node server-based remote access.

Laptop Synchronization   As mobile computing on laptop and notebook computers has grown exponentially, the need to synchronize versions of files on laptops and desktop workstations has become apparent. Such **file synchronization software** was initially available as a stand-alone product or included as a feature on remote access or file transfer packages. Also known as **version control software** or **directory synchronization software,** this valuable software is now often included as a standard or optional feature in client network operating systems.

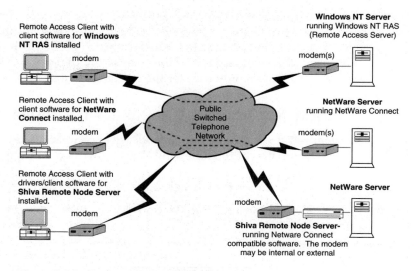

Figure 7-14   Remote Access Client Software

Laptops may be linked to their related desktop system in a number of different ways:

- The laptop and desktop computer systems may be locally linked directly via serial or parallel cables.

- The laptop and desktop computer systems may be remotely linked via modems and a dial-up line.

- The laptop and desktop computer system may be remotely linked via a local area network running a network operating system such as NetWare, Windows for Workgroups, or Windows NT.

Client network operating systems should support laptop synchronization in all of the aforementioned connectivity options, especially LAN-based alternatives. Laptop synchronization should happen automatically when the laptop computer is docked in its docking station. E-mail clients and scheduling system client software should automatically synchronize with the LAN-attached e-mail and scheduling application servers.

Some of the important functional characteristics or differences among laptop synchronization software are the following:

- Copy by date option—Files and directories can be selectively synchronized by selected data range.

- Bidirectional option—File synchronization can occur just from laptop to desktop, desktop or laptop, or both (bidirectional).

- Cloning option—This option guarantees that the contents of a directory on one system exactly match the contents of the same directory on another system.

- Refresh option—Only newer versions of files that are already located on both systems are copied from one system to another.

- **Delta file synchronization**—This is perhaps the most significant file synchronization option in terms of its potential impact on reducing required bandwidth and file transfer time to accomplish the synchronization. Rather than sending entire files across the dial-up or LAN link, delta file synchronization only transfer the changes to those files.

CLIENT NETWORK OPERATING SYSTEM TECHNOLOGY ANALYSIS

Applied Problem Solving

Figure 7-15 is a technology analysis grid comparing key architectural and functional characteristics of the following client network operating systems:

- Windows for Workgroups.
- Windows 95.
- Windows NT Workstation.
- OS/2 Warp Connect.

	Client Network Operating System			
Category	**Windows for Workgroups**	**Windows NT Workstation**	**Windows 95**	**OS/2 Warp Connect**
Hardware and platform				
Required–recommended memory	4 MB–8 MB	16 MB–32 MB	8 MB–16 MB	8 MB–16 MB
16 or 32 bit	16 bit	32 bit	32 bit	32 bit
User interface	Windows	Windows object-oriented desktop in version 4.0	object-oriented desktop	object-oriented desktop
Operating system capabilities				
Preemptive multitasking	no	yes	yes	yes
Supports SMP	no	yes	no	no
Protected memory program execution	no	yes	yes	yes
Multithreading	no	yes	yes	yes
Runs 32-bit applications	no	yes	yes	yes, but not Windows 95 or Windows NT32-bit applications
Runs 16-bit applications	yes	Some; won't support real-mode drivers	yes	Some; won't support real-mode drivers
Peer-to-peer networking				
File and printer sharing	yes	yes	yes	yes
Workgroup applications	yes	yes	yes	yes
Client networking				
Network clients	Windows NT, Microsoft Mail & Schedule	NetWare, FTP, Internet	Windows NT, NetWare, Microsoft Exchange	NetWare, Internet, Gopher, LANServer,
Network transport protocols	NetBEUI	NetBEUI, TCP/IP, IPX/SPX, AppleTalk	NetBEUI, TCP/IP, IPX/SPX	TCP/IP
Remote access	yes	yes	yes	yes
Laptop synchronization	no	yes	yes	no

Figure 7-15 Client Network Operating System Technology Analysis Grid

This grid is included as an example of how technology analysis grids can be used to effectively map networking functional requirements to available technology solutions in an objective manner. This technology analysis grid is not meant to be absolutely authoritative or all-inclusive. Its primary purpose is to provide a concrete example of the type of analysis tool used in a professional, top-down, network analysis and design methodology. It is expected that network analysts will create new technology analysis grids for each networking analysis opportunity based on their own networking functional requirements and the latest technology specifications available from buyers' guides or product reviews.

The client network operating system technology analysis grid is divided into the following major sections:

- Hardware/platform-related characteristics.

- Operating system capabilities.

- Peer-to-peer networking capabilities.

- Client networking capabilities.

■ SERVER NETWORK OPERATING SYSTEM FUNCTIONALITY

Changing Role of the Server Network Operating System

Traditionally, file and printer sharing services were the primary required functionality of server-based network operating systems. However, as client/server information systems have boomed in popularity, application services have become the criteria by which server network operating systems are judged. The distributed applications of the client server model require distinct client and server portions of a given application to interact to execute that application as efficiently as possible. It is the server network operating system that is responsible for not only executing the back-end engine portion of the application but also supplying the messaging and communications services to enable interoperability between distributed clients and servers. Figure 7-16 illustrates the evolving role of the server network operating system from an architectural perspective.

The examination of server network operating system functionality in the remainder of the chapter will focus on those aspects of functionality that are most important to the support of distributed applications and their associated distributed clients and users. In terms of currently available technology, although NetWare 3.12 is unquestionably the most widely installed server network operating system with somewhere between 60% and 70% market share, its functional strength has always been file and print services, rather than application services.

As a result, the market for the so-called "next generation" network operating systems featuring application services is more wide open. Understandably, one of the key features of these advanced server-based network operating systems is the ease of migration and upgrade from market-dominating NetWare 3.12. The two most popular next-generation server network operating systems for applications servers are

- NetWare 4.11

- Windows NT Server 4.0

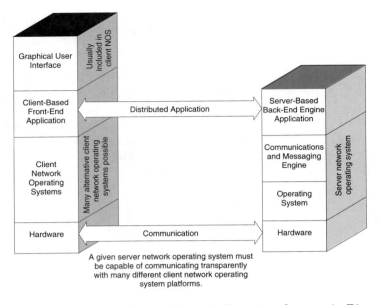

A given server network operating system must
be capable of communicating transparently
with many different client network operating
system platforms.

Figure 7-16   Role of Server Network Operating Systems in Distributed Applications

Network operating system functionality analysis in the remainder of the chapter will focus primarily on these two network operating systems.

UNIX, TCP/IP, AND NFS AS A NETWORK OPERATING SYSTEM

In Sharper Focus

Various flavors of UNIX combined with TCP/IP as a network protocol and NFS as a network-aware file system have also been a popular choice as an application server platform. However, this combination of operating system, network protocols, and file system is not as integrated or feature-rich as NetWare 4.11 or Windows NT Server 4.0 and probably does not deserve the label of "next-generation" NOS.

Nonetheless, UNIX servers are still prevalent on enterprise networks, especially as applications servers and enterprise network management servers. Although not distributed as a ready-to-run single product, UNIX as an operating system, the TCP/IP family of protocols for network communications, and NFS for a network-aware file system comprise a very common combination of elements that offer all the functionality of commercially available single-product network operating systems.

Figure 7-17 conceptually illustrates how UNIX, the Internet suite of protocols (TCP/IP), and NFS can be combined to offer full network operating system functionality to network-attached clients and servers.

UNIX   UNIX is, in fact, a large family of related operating systems that all descended from work initially done by Ken Thompson and Dennis Ritchie at Bell Laboratories in the late 1960s and early 1970s. The name *UNIX* is derived as a play on words from another Bell Labs/M.I.T. project of the same era that produced a mainframe computer utility known as Multics. Although many innovations have been

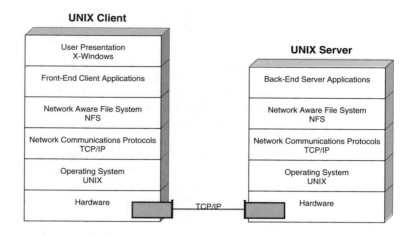

Figure 7-17   UNIX, TCP/IP, and NFS as a Network Operating System

introduced in different UNIX implementations as the UNIX evolution has continued, all variations still share much of the original UNIX architecture and its resultant functionality.

UNIX Architecture: Figure 7-18 illustrates the basic components of the UNIX operating system architecture. UNIX is a two-layered operating system consisting of

- **UNIX systems programs.**

- **UNIX system kernel.**

Most UNIX system programs and kernels are written in C, allowing for easy portability to any hardware platform with a compatible C compiler. UNIX system

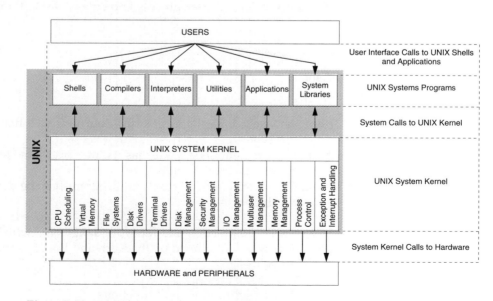

Figure 7-18   UNIX Operating System Architecture

programs and utilities deliver requested functionality to users by issuing system calls to the UNIX system kernel. The kernel then fulfills these requests by interacting with the hardware layer and returning requested functionality to the system programs and utilities. In this layered architecture, only the UNIX system kernel needs to be concerned with the particular hardware devices with which it must interact. Even within the kernel, most hardware-specific code is confined to device drivers. UNIX system programs, utilities, and end-user applications are hardware-independent and are only required to be able to issue standardized system calls to the UNIX kernel.

Most of the functionality of the UNIX kernel is concerned with managing either files or devices of some type. To simplify and standardize system calls, devices are treated just as a special type of file in UNIX.

Perhaps the most significant characteristic of the UNIX operating system is the availability of the source code, allowing individual programmers to enhance and modify UNIX over the years. The ability to enhance and modify UNIX as desired or required is due to the layered, modular design as illustrated in Figure 7-18. New utilities or system programs could be added as long as they issued standard system calls to the kernel. Modifications could be made to the kernel as long as they were compatible with the locally installed hardware including the local C compiler.

It could be concluded from the previous discussion of the major architectural characteristics of UNIX that the operating system's two chief positive attributes are

- Portability—Portability is a characteristic of UNIX on two distinct levels. First, UNIX itself is portable across numerous hardware platforms. Second, application programs written for UNIX are also inherently portable across all UNIX platforms.

- Modularity—UNIX is a viable, dynamic operating system to which functionality can be added in the form of new system utilities or system programs. Even modifications to the UNIX kernel itself are possible.

UNIX Shells: In UNIX, the command interpreter, which is the user's interface to the system, is a specialized user process known as a **shell.** Popular UNIX shells include

- Bourne shell.

- C shell.

- TC shell.

- Korn shell—combines features of the Bourne and C shells.

Each of the aforementioned shells has its own associated shell script, and users are also able to write their own shells.

Cross-shell, cross-platform scripts and programs can be developed using either of the following languages:

- **Perl** (practical extraction and reporting language), which adds the following functionality to that offered by the Korn and Bourne shells:
  - List processing.
  - Associative arrays.
  - Modern subroutines and functions.

- More control statements.
- Better I/O.
- Full function library.
- In addition, Perl is free via download from the Internet. On the negative side, Perl is similar in syntax and commands to the more cryptic UNIX shells it sought to improve upon. As a result, for UNIX nonexperts, Perl may still not be the answer.

- The **Rexx** scripting language, which is an easier to learn and use alternative that supports structured programming techniques such as modularity while still offering access to shell commands.

UNIX File System: UNIX implements a hierarchical, multilevel tree file system starting with the root directory as illustrated in Figure 7-19. In fact, UNIX is able to support multiple file systems simultaneously on a single disk. Each disk is divided into multiple **slices,** each of which can be used to accommodate a file system, a swap area, or a raw data area. A UNIX slice is equivalent to a partition in DOS. Each disk has one and only one root file system, and each file system has one and only one root directory.

In UNIX, files are treated by the kernel as just a sequence of bytes. In other words, although application programs may require files of a particular structure, the kernel merely stores files as sequenced bytes and organizes them in directories. In the UNIX file system, directories are treated as specially formatted files and contain information as to the location of listed files. The basic job of the file system in UNIX is to offer file services as a consistent interface without requiring user application programs to worry about the particulars of the physical storage hardware used.

Path names are used in UNIX to identify the specific path through the hierarchical file structure to a particular destination file. **Absolute path names** start at the root directory in the listing of the path to the destination directory whereas **relative path names** start at the current directory. The difference between absolute and relative path names is also illustrated in Figure 7-19.

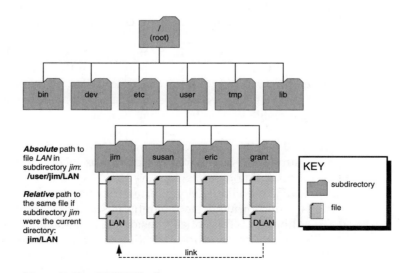

Figure 7-19   UNIX File System

Links are another unique aspect of the UNIX file system and allow a given file to be known by and accessed by more than one name. A link is nothing more than an entry in a directory that points to a file stored in another directory or another whole directory. Links are also illustrated in Figure 7-19.

TCP/IP   **TCP/IP (transmission control protocol/Internet protocol)** is the term generally used to refer to an entire suite of protocols used to provide communication on a variety of layers between widely distributed different types of computers. Strictly speaking, TCP and IP are just two of the protocols contained within the family of protocols more properly known as the **Internet suite of protocols.** TCP/IP was developed during the 1970s and widely deployed during the 1980s under the auspices of **DARPA** (Defense Advanced Research Projects Agency) to meet the Department of Defense's need to have a wide variety of different computers be able to interoperate and communicate. TCP/IP became widely available to universities and research agencies and has become the de facto standard for communication between heterogeneous networked computers.

Overall Architecture: TCP/IP and the entire family of related protocols are organized into a protocol model. Although not identical to the seven-layer OSI model, the **TCP/IP model** is no less effective at organizing protocols required to establish and maintain communications between different computers. Figure 7-20 illustrates the TCP/IP model and its relationship to the seven-layer OSI model. TCP/IP and other members of the Internet suite of protocols will be explored further in Chapter 9.

As can be seen in Figure 7-20, the OSI model and TCP/IP model are functionally equivalent, although not identical, up through the transport layer. Whereas the OSI model continues on with the session, presentation, and application layers, the TCP/IP model has only the application layer remaining, with utilities such as Telnet (terminal emulation) and FTP (file transfer protocol) as examples of application layer protocols. As illustrated in Figure 7-20, the functionality equivalent to the OSI model's session, presentation, and application layers is added to the TCP/IP model by combining it with the Network File System (NFS) distributed by Sun Microsystems. As a result, to offer equivalent functionality to that represented by the full seven-layer OSI model, the TCP/IP family of protocols must be combined with NFS, sometimes known as the open network computing (ONC) environment.

NFS   **NFS** or **Network File System** was originally developed by Sun Microsystems as part of their open network computing (ONC) environment. NFS allows multiple, different computing platforms to share files. To all of the heterogeneous computers that support NFS, NFS appears as a transparent extension to their local operating system or file system by making remote disk drives appear as local. Print jobs can also be redirected from local workstations to NFS servers. Although originally developed for the UNIX operating system and TCP/IP transport protocols, NFS is now supported on a variety of platforms including PCs. This fact has allowed network operating systems such as NetWare and Windows NT to transparently support NFS, as well, thereby offering transparent interoperability with UNIX workstations, minicomputers, and mainframes.

Although NFS is often considered functionally equivalent to the file systems of fully integrated network operating systems such as NetWare or Windows NT, in fact, NFS derives much of its functionality from the native operating system of the platform on which it is installed. Additionally, although NFS is capable of support-

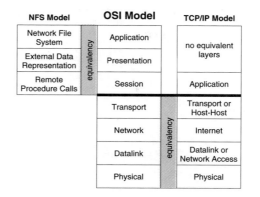

Figure 7-20   The TCP/IP Model

ing file sharing between different computing platforms, more advanced file management features such as user and group access rights, file and record locking, and conversion between different file types may not be universally supported. In other words, in some cases, NFS is only able to implement those features that are common to all linked file systems and computing platforms as opposed to the most advanced file management functionality of any particular computing platform.

NFS Architecture: The term *NFS* is generally used to refer to a collection or suite of three major protocols:

- NFS or Network File System.

- **XDR** or external data representation.

- **RPC** or remote procedure call.

Strictly speaking, NFS is only the API portion of a collection of programs and utilities that offer the transparent file management interoperability typically associated with the NFS suite of protocols. Transparency is a key point as the client application requesting files does not know that the NFS client software will be used to communicate with a remote NFS server to deliver the requested files. Each NFS client protocol stack interacts with the native operating system and file system of the computing platform on which it is installed and translates requests and responses for NFS services into standardized NFS protocols for communication with similarly configured NFS servers. NFS could be considered an example of an OSI layer 7 protocol.

XDR is a presentation layer protocol responsible for formatting data in a consistent manner so that all NFS clients and servers can process it, regardless of the computing platform or operating system on which the NFS suite may be executing.

RPC is a session layer protocol responsible for establishing, maintaining, and terminating communications sessions between distributed applications in an NFS environment. NFS protocols may use either UDP or TCP for transport layer services. The architectural relationship between the NFS suite of protocols and the TCP/IP suite of protocols is illustrated in Figure 7-21.

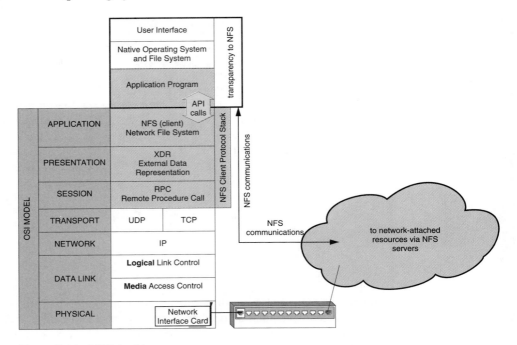

Figure 7-21   NFS Architecture

Comparative Network Operating System Functionality

Directory Services   Network operating systems have always depended on some sort of naming service or directory in which to store information about users as well as system resources such as disks, servers, and printers. NetWare 3.*x* servers stored this type of information in a **bindery.** NetWare 4.1 employs a **global directory service** known as **NDS** or **NetWare Directory Services** whereas Windows NT uses a **domain directory service.**

Global Directory Services vs. Domain Directory Services: Global and domain directory services differ primarily in the organization of information concerning network users and resources. Global directory services organize all network user and resource data into a single hierarchical database, providing a single point of user and resource management. The hierarchical database is based on an organizational hierarchical tree structure of the network that must first be designed. All servers that are part of this global hierarchical network can see all other parts of the hierarchical network. In this sense, the hierarchical directory database is merely a reflection of the hierarchical network itself.

This global directory database may well be **distributed,** implying that different portions of the data are physically stored on multiple distributed servers linked via the network. In addition, this global directory database may be **replicated,** implying that multiple copies of identical data may also be stored on multiple servers for redundancy and fault tolerance purposes. In terms of a logical view of the network, global directory services provide a view of a single, enterprise network.

In contrast, domain directory services see the network as a series of linked subdivisions known as **domains.** Domain delivery services associate network users and resources with a primary server known as a **PDC** or **primary domain controller.**

Each domain's directory must be individually established and maintained. Domains can be individually maintained and controlled in terms of how much of other domains can be seen.

Directory services can also vary in what types of information are stored in the directory services database. In some cases, all users and network resources are considered **network objects** with information concerning them stored in a single database, arranged by object type. Object attributes can be modified and new network objects can be defined. In other cases, network users and network resources are kept in separate databases. Frequently, separate databases are maintained for network user account information and e-mail user account information.

In Sharper Focus

DIRECTORY SERVICES COMMUNICATION

In a global directory service such as NetWare 4.1's NDS, when a user wants to access resources on a remote or foreign server, that server performs a look-up in the NDS database to authenticate the user's right to the requested service. This NDS database look-up is repeated for every request for service from remote users. Recalling that the NDS database is distributed, the physical location of the server that contains the rights information of the requesting user may be located anywhere in the hierarchical distributed network.

In the case of a domain directory service such as Windows NT 3.51, the remote of foreign server receives the user authentication from the user's primary domain controller (local server) in a process known as **interdomain trust (IT).** By having servers act on behalf of their local users when verifying authenticity with remote and foreign users, every user ID does not have to be entered and maintained in every domain's directory service. In addition, once the interdomain trust has been established for a particular user, the remote domain server does not repeat the request for authentication.

As enterprise networks become more heterogeneous comprised of network operating systems from a variety of different vendors, the need will arise for different network operating systems to share each other's directory services information. This is especially true for user information and e-mail addresses from various e-mail systems. A directory services specification known as **X.500** offers the potential for this directory services interoperability. NetWare 4.1's NDS is based on X.500 with proprietary extensions.

Another potential protocol for directory interoperability is known as **lightweight directory access protocol (LDAP).** LDAP is basically a simplification of X.500's directory access protocol that allows computers executing LDAP client software to manage a hierarchical directory database using TCP/IP as a transport protocol. LDAP is not a directory service but a protocol for exchanging information between different vendors' directory systems. Companies such as Netscape, Banyan, Novell, IBM, Microsoft, and Lotus have expressed support for LDAP. Microsoft is also promoting its own directory interoperability standard known as **open directory services interface (ODSI).** Still another possibility for open directory standards is DCE (Distributed Computing Environment) Cell Directory Services that has been included in the latest release of OS/2 Warp Server.

NOS-Independent Enterprise Directory Services: Beginning with Windows NT 4.0, a beta version of a distributed file system known as **Dfs** has been available to provide a more global or logical view of all accessible files, rather than providing a view in which users have to know in which server a particular file is physically stored. Dfs service must be added to Windows NT or Windows 95 clients to access Dfs services.

The lack of a native enterprise directory service for a very popular network operating system such as Windows NT has spawned an opportunity for other software vendors to offer their own enterprise directory services that are compatible with Windows NT. Figure 7-22 lists some of these enterprise directory services and their key characteristics.

Application Services   Recalling that the primary objective of the next-generation server NOS is to provide high-performance application services, the most important enabling NOS characteristic delivering that objective is the NOS' ability to support symmetrical multiprocessing. As the number of users and sophistication of application programs continue to increase, the only real solution is for the application to be able to utilize more processing power simultaneously. Not all server network operating systems support symmetrical multiprocessing and those that do may vary in the maximum number of processors supported. Other server network operating system characteristics that are essential to optimization of application program performance are

- Preemptive multitasking.
- 32-bit execution.
- Multithreaded application support.
- Program execution in protected memory space.

Enterprise Directory Service	Vendor	Functionality
StreetTalk for Windows NT	Banyan Systems	TCP/IP-based version of Vines StreetTalk that identifies enterprise network objects by unique names, stored in a distributed database.
Netscape Directory Server	Netscape Communications Corp.	Uses LDAP to let users and administrators browse and manage LDAP-compliant directories.
Synchronicity for NT	NetVision Inc.	Enables NT domains to be controlled exclusively by NDS administration utility (NWADMIN).
NDS for NT	Novell	Full NDS port to Windows NT expected some time in 1997. Novell also plans NDS ports to SCO UNIX and HP-UX.

Figure 7-22   NOS-Independent Enterprise Directory Services

File Services   Application programs are stored in a particular file system format. In addition, when these application programs execute, they may request additional services from the resident file system via API calls. Server network operating systems vary in the types and number of supported file systems. Some network operating systems, such as Windows NT, can have multiple partitions on a disk drive, with one partition supporting the FAT (file allocation table) file system and another partition supporting the NTFS (NT file system) file system. Figure 7-23 lists some possible file systems supported by server network operating systems.

Other file services offered by some server network operating systems include file compression utilities and **data migration** utilities that manage the migration of data among different types of storage devices as part of a comprehensive hierarchical storage management (HSM) program. Finally, just as client network operating systems were either bundling or offering optional workgroup software as part of their package, server network operating systems are offering a variety of bundled back-end engines as part of their offerings. For example, as an option or add-on to Windows NT Server, a bundled product known as Microsoft Back-Office offers the following suite of server applications:

- System Management Server.
- SQL Server.
- Mail & Schedule (Exchange) Server.
- SNA Gateway to IBM mainframe networks.

Networking and Connectivity Services

Network Clients Supported: In addition to the client network operating systems that were previously reviewed, server network operating systems may also have to communicate with client platforms with only the following operating systems installed:

- DOS.
- Windows.
- Macintosh.
- OS/2.
- UNIX (implies support for NFS).

File System Name	Associated Network Operating System
FAT (file allocation table)	Windows NT Server
HPFS (high-performance file system)	OS/2 LANServer
NetWare file system	NetWare 3.12 and 4.1
NFS	UNIX (native); Most other NOS: optional
NTFS (NT file system)	Windows NT Server
Vines file system	Banyan Vines 5.54

Figure 7-23   File Systems and Associated Server Network Operating Systems

In these cases, because the previously listed operating systems possess no native networking functionality, the server network operating system must possess the ability to generate diskettes with the necessary operating system-specific network communications capabilities. These diskettes are then loaded on the intended networking client, and the required network communication capabilities are merged with the native operating system.

Network Protocols Supported: The key question concerning network protocols and server network operating systems is not just how many different network protocols are supported but, more importantly, how many network protocols can be supported simultaneously. In these days of heterogeneous multivendor enterprise networks, it is essential that server network operating systems possess the ability to support multiple network protocols simultaneously to maximize not only the different types of clients but also the number and type of other servers with which a given server can communicate. The ease with which multiple network protocols can be supported or whether multiple network protocols can be supported at all can vary among different server network operating systems.

Related to the ability of a server network operating system to simultaneously support multiple protocols is the ability of a server network operating system to support multiple network interface cards. If a single NIC is the bottleneck to network communications, additional NICs can be added so long as multiple NICs can be supported by the computer's bus and can be communicated with by the server network operating system. As PCI buses and PCI-based NICs have increased in popularity, PCI cards containing up to four NICs are being produced. Unless the server network operating system has the ability to communicate with four NICs simultaneously, this four-NIC PCI card would be of little use.

Multiprotocol Routing: Underlying a server network operating system's ability to process multiple protocols simultaneously is the presence of **multiprotocol routing** software. This multiprotocol routing software may be either included, optional, or not available, depending on the server network operating system in question. Multiprotocol routing provides the functionality necessary to actually process and understand multiple network protocols as well as translate between them. Without multiprotocol routing software, clients speaking multiple different network protocols cannot be supported. Routing in general and multiprotocol routing in particular will be covered in great detail in Chapter 9. Figure 7-24 illustrates the relationship between multiple network protocols, multiple network interface cards per server, and multiprotocol routing software.

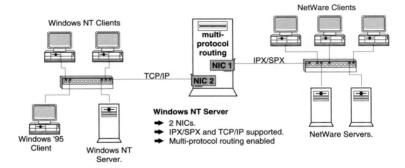
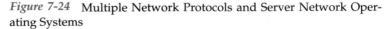

Figure 7-24 Multiple Network Protocols and Server Network Operating Systems

Remote Access and Gateway Services: Just as client network operating systems supplied the client portion of a remote access communication, server network operating systems may or may not supply the server side of the remote access communication. These remote access servers may be included with the server NOS or may be available for an additional fee. It is important that these remote access servers are well integrated with the server network operating system to ensure remote users both reliable performance and the full functionality offered locally connected users. Windows NT RAS (Remote Access Server) is integrated with Windows NT Server 3.51 and NetWare Connect is the remote access server that integrates with NetWare 4.1.

In some cases, it may be necessary for either clients or servers to access IBM mainframe computers or AS/400s that are linked on IBM's proprietary network architecture known as **SNA (systems network architecture).** In such cases, it makes more sense for the translation software necessary to access the SNA network to reside on a single server than on multiple clients. In this scenario, the server with the SNA translation software installed becomes a **gateway** to the SNA network. Windows NT's product for IBM mainframe access is called SNA Gateway while NetWare's is called NetWare for SAA (Systems Application Architecture).

Management and Administration Services

Installation, Configuration, and Administration: Recent reviews of server network operating systems consistently list **auto-detection and auto-configuration** of installed controllers, interface cards, and peripherals as the most important installation-related feature. The ability of a server network operating system to automatically configure a controller, adapter, or peripheral is dependent on the network operating system possessing a compatible driver for that device. It should stand to reason that the greater the number of drivers supported by a given network operating system, the greater the probability that auto-configuration will be successful.

Another hardware compatibility issue related to installation is the number of different CPUs on which a given server network operating system can operate. For example, although NetWare 4.1 can only operate on Intel chips, Windows NT Server can operate on Intel chips, DEC Alpha chips, PowerPC chips, and MIPs RISC chips.

To appreciate the differences in ease of administration offered by server network operating systems, it is important to scale the vision of the network to be administered to a multiserver enterprise network serving hundreds if not thousands of users. With this scenario in mind, some pertinent questions might be

- How many steps are involved in creating a new user account?

- What is involved in giving a user access to remote servers?

- How easily can a user profile be copied and used as a template to automatically generate other user profiles? This feature is particularly important in academic settings where user profiles must be constantly generated in large numbers.

- What tools are available to assist in managing multiple servers simultaneously?

Server network operating systems can vary widely in the sophistication of the **performance monitoring** software included or available as an add-on. Ideally, the monitoring software should offer the ability to set thresholds for multiple system performance parameters. If these thresholds are exceeded, alerts or alarms should notify network management personnel of the problem and offer advice as to possible diagnoses or solutions. Event logging and audit trails are often included as part of the performance monitoring package.

In multiple-server environments, it is particularly important that all servers can be monitored and managed from a single management console. Desktop and server management software offers capabilities beyond the monitoring software included in server network operating systems. For example, performance statistics are often gathered and stored in databases known as **MIBs (management information bases).** In addition, this performance management information can be communicated to enterprise management systems such as HP's OpenView or IBM's SystemView in the proper **SNMP (simple network management protocol)** format. Microsoft's desktop and server management product is known as SMS or System Management Server and Novell's is known as ManageWise.

Integration and Migration: Integration and migration features of next-generation network operating systems are clearly aimed at one audience: the 60+% of servers currently running NetWare 3.12. **Integration** refers to that transitionary period of time in the migration process when both network operating systems must be running simultaneously and interacting to some degree. **Migration** features are aimed at easing the transition from NetWare 3.12 to either NetWare 4.1 or Windows NT. Key among the migration concerns is the conversion of the directory services information stored in the NetWare 3.12 bindery into either NetWare 4.1 NDS or Windows NT domain directory services. Utilities are available from third-party software vendors as well as from Novell and Microsoft to at least partially automate the bindery conversion.

Following are among the more important incompatibilities between NetWare and NT that must be overcome:

- Interoperability issues will differ dependent on which version of NetWare is involved. For example, NetWare's VLMs are not interoperable with NT.

- Communications protocol incompatibilities are fairly easily solved thanks to Windows NT's ability to run IPX/SPX as its native communications protocol.

- File systems and directory services incompatibilities must be overcome.

- NT's integration utilities do not fully support NetWare's NDS although NetWare plans to release a version of NDS that runs over NT. An NDS-enabled version of Windows 95 is available but it does not support advanced functionality such as NetWare Application Manager.

Figure 7-25 summarizes some of the NetWare/NT interoperability solutions currently available. In evaluating any interoperability solution, one should ask several key questions:

1. What level of interoperability is offered?

2. Is this service included in the NOS or is it a separately purchased product?

3. Is the product installed on every client or just on servers?

4. How difficult is the product to install, configure, and manage?

Product Name	Funtionality/Explanation
NW Link	Windows NT's IPX/SPX protocol stack is NDIS compliant and allows Windows NT servers to be accessed by NetWare clients without requiring any additional hardware or software on the NetWare clients. Such a scenario is especially appropriate when the NT server is required to function as a powerful applications or database server.
Client Service for NetWare	This service allows a Windows NT client to access file and print services from a NetWare server. Clients can only access NetWare 4.1 servers in bindery emulation mode.
Migration Tool for NetWare	Available from Microsoft, this product migrates the user and group accounts of a NetWare 3.x bindery to NT server.
Gateway Service for NetWare	This service allows a Windows NT server to access file and print services from NetWare servers and also offers these NetWare services to attached NT clients that are not running their own Client Service for NetWare software. NT servers can only access NetWare 4.1 servers in bindery emulation mode.
NetWare Requestor for Windows NT	Available from Novell, this product allows NT clients to access NetWare servers. This product allows NT clients to access NetWare 4.1 NDS databases through NT's File Manager utility. Allows NT clients to login to NetWare 4.1 servers as NetWare users.
Directory Service Manager for NetWare	Available from Microsoft, this product is intended for networks transitioning from NetWare 3.x to NT rather than ongoing network interoperability. Requires Gateway Service for NetWare. This product is able to import NetWare bindery files and transform them into databases on NT primary and backup domain controllers. From this point forward, all of the former bindery information can be maintained from Windows NT.
File and Print Service for NetWare	Available from Microsoft, this service allows a Windows NT server to offer file and print services to NetWare clients. The NetWare clients are unmodified and think that they are interacting with a native NetWare server. Such a product is aimed at allowing NetWare users who wish to use NT as an application server to also use NT for file and print services as well.
BW-Multiconnect for Windows NT	Available from Beame & Whiteside, a traditional TCP/IP client developer, this product offers similar functionality to Microsoft's File and Print Service for Net Ware. It has slightly less functionality than the Microsoft product such as a lack of support for NetWare login scripts and client print utilities.

Figure 7-25   NT/NetWare Interoperability Alternatives

5. Is the product designed to offer interoperability or is it actually designed to provide a transition or migration path from one product or platform to another?

Managerial Perspective

By examining the array of products available from Microsoft, it should become clear that although interoperability with NetWare is certainly achievable with these products, the fact remains that their primary purpose is to form a suite of products that make the transition from NetWare to NT as painless as possible.

Security: Several important security enhancements have been added to NetWare 4.1. Due to a well-publicized security hole in NetWare 3.*x* that allowed imposters to gain supervisory privileges, **authentication** is perhaps the most important of the security innovations. Using a combination of private encryption keys and passwords, the VLM requester security agent on the client workstation and NDS file server combine to ensure that users are properly authenticated before being logged in. Should even higher security be required, every packet transmitted from a particular client workstation can have a unique, encrypted digital signature attached to it that can only be authenticated by the server in a process known as **packet signing.** However, a performance price of 5 to 7% is paid for the increased security as valuable CPU cycles are spent encrypting and decrypting digital signatures.

Whereas authentication and packet signing ensure that only valid users are accessing system resources, an extensive **auditing system** monitors and reports on what those valid users are doing. The auditor acts independently of the supervisor in an effort to ensure a proper system of checks and balances in which no single person could remain undetected while performing harmful acts. The auditing system separately monitors activity on both the file system as defined by volumes and the NetWare Directory Services database as defined by container units. Figure 7-26 illustrates the organization and capabilities of the NetWare auditing system.

Security is an integral part of the Windows NT operating system rather than a shell or subsystem. As a result, security in Windows NT offers not only user authorization services typically associated with network operating system security but also an assurance that the programs and processes launched by those authorized users will only access system resources to which they have the appropriate level of permission. In Windows NT, no interprocess communication takes place without the knowledge and approval of the Windows NT security system.

The overall security system is organized around the concept of objects, not unlike NetWare 4.1's view of the NetWare Directory Services object-oriented database. In Windows NT, examples of objects are files, directories, print queues, and other networked resources. All objects are assigned permission levels which are then associated with individual users or user groups. Examples of permission levels are

- Read.
- Delete.
- Write.
- Change permission level.
- Execute.

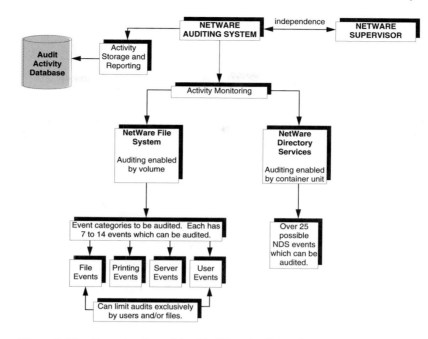

Figure 7-26 Organization of the NetWare Auditing System

- Take ownership.
- No Access.

By monitoring permission levels, NT security can monitor and control who accesses which objects as well as how those objects are accessed. In addition to monitoring and control, NT security can also audit and report on these same object accesses by users according to permission level. The components of the Windows NT security model are illustrated in Figure 7-27.

A logical start for introducing the interacting components of the Windows NT security model might be the **logon process** which is responsible for the interaction with the user on whatever computer platform that user may wish to log in on. This is really a client presentation layer function, identified as a separate component to allow login processes for a variety of different computer platforms to all interact with the Windows NT security model in a standardized manner.

The platform-specific login process interacts with the **local security authority,** which actually provides the user authentication services. Specifically, the local security authority generates a **security access token** for authorized users that contains **security IDs (SID)** for this user and all of the user groups to which this user belongs. This security access token accompanies every process or program launched by this user and is used as a means to reference whether or not this user and this user's spawned processes have sufficient permissions to perform requested services or access requested resources. The local security authority also controls the security model's audit policy and generates audit messages that are stored in the audit log.

All of the user and user group ID and permission level information is stored in and maintained by the **security account manager,** which interacts with the local security authority to verify user IDs and permission levels. The **user accounts database** is physically stored on the primary domain controller except in those cases

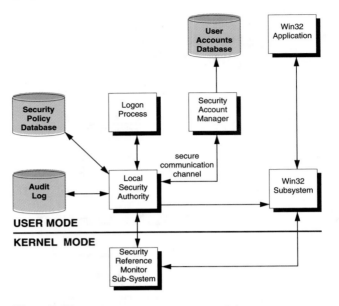

Figure 7-27   Windows NT Security Model

when an individual workstation may have a need to verify specific user IDs for re-mote access to that workstation. The links between components of the NT security model involved in the logon process are designed as secure communication chan-nels to ensure that traffic that is supposedly received from a given workstation or computer is actually from that computer. This authentication is accomplished in Windows NT by a process very similar to the challenge handshake authentication protocol (CHAP) that is employed in NetWare 4.1 for a similar purpose. Passwords are encrypted before being transmitted during the logon process.

The only kernel mode portion of the NT security model is the **security refer-ence monitor (SRM),** which really serves as the security engine or back-end appli-cation for all of the previously mentioned security client applications. It is the secu-rity reference model that has the ultimate responsibility for ensuring that users have the proper authority to access requested network resources. The SRM is able to meet this responsibility by comparing the requested object's security description as docu-mented in **access control lists (ACL)** with the requesting user's security information as documented on the user's security access token. Besides access validation, the SRM is also responsible for audit checking and generating audit messages.

Applied Problem Solving

SERVER NETWORK OPERATING SYSTEM TECHNOLOGY ANALYSIS

A network analyst's job is to always seek out the latest information that the industry has to offer before making recommendations for purchases that could have a signifi-cant bearing on both the company's prosperity and the analyst's personal job secu-rity. The server network operating system technology analysis grid shown in Figure 7-28 is given as an example but is not meant to be either authoritative or all-inclu-sive. The technology analysis grid is divided into the following major categories:

- Hardware/platform characteristics.
- Installation and configuration.

Server Network Operating System Characteristic	Windows NT Server 4.0	NetWare 4.11
Hardware/platform		
Min/max memory	16 MB–4 GB	16 MB–4 GB
Min/max disk space	90 MB–1700 TB	75 MB–32 TB
CPUs	Intel, DEC, Alpha, MIPs RISC, PowerPC	Intel
Symmetrical multi-processing	yes	yes
Preemptive multitasking	yes	yes
Multithreading	yes	yes
Protected memory applications execution	yes	yes, but not with NLMs
Installation and configuration		
Automatic detection and configuration of adapters, and peripherals	yes	no
Requires a separate administrator console	no	yes
Number of included NIC drivers	98	68
Networking and connectivity		
Clients supported	DOS, Windows, Windows for Workgroups, OS/2, Windows NT, Windows 95, Mac, UNIX	DOS, Windows, Windows for Workgroups, Windows 95, UNIX, OS/2, Windows NT, Mac
Network protocols supported	TCP/IP, IPX, NetBEUI, AppleTalk, TCP/IP encapsulated NetBIOS	TCP/IP, IPX, AppleTalk, TCP/IP encapsulated IPX, encapsulated NetBIOS
Routing supported	TCP//IP, IPX	TCP/IP, IPX, AppleTalk
Supports DHCP, WINS, and DNS integration	yes	no
Multiprotocol routing software included	yes	yes
Remote access services	Windows NT RAS included	NetWare Connect optional
E-mail gateways	Mail server optional	MHS included
Clients able to access remote resources	yes	yes
Web browser and server included	yes	yes
Messaging services	Requires Exchange Server	Requires GroupWise
Management and Administration		
Can act as SNMP agent for enterprise management system	yes	optional
Can set performance thresholds and alerts	yes	yes with ManageWise (optional)
Central management of multiple servers	yes	yes
Audit trails and event logs	yes	yes
Security level supported	C2	C2
RAID levels supported	0, 1, 5	0, 1

Figure 7-28   Server Network Operating System Technology Analysis Grid

- Networking and connectivity.

- Management and administration.

NT VS. NETWARE

Network managers, analysts, and consultants are constantly asked, "Which is the better network operating system, NT or NetWare?" The fact of the matter is that there is no single network operating system that is best in all cases. The best network operating system in any given situation depends on a variety of factors including business needs and objectives, current and planned applications, and current and planned network infrastructure.

Windows NT is being installed in corporations for use as web servers, database servers, applications servers, SNA servers that act as gateways to mainframe computers, DHCP servers that lease IP addresses to attached workstations, messaging servers that support Microsoft Exchange, and as a workstation or server operating system. In general, NT's greatest strength is as a back-end or application engine platform.

NetWare has always been known as a good file and print service system. With the release of NetWare 4, Novell introduced NetWare Directory Services (NDS). NDS can be managed either centrally or in a distributed fashion and has the ability to allow all network resources (printers, users, groups, and servers) to be viewed as a single entity. NDS is very scaleable with its ability to effectively manage hundreds of thousands of network resource objects. However, NDS does not currently support non-NetWare environments that are often part of an enterprise's computing resources.

NetWare and Windows NT each have unique strengths. Which is the best network operating system? The answer is: whichever one provides the required functionality as defined in a thorough top-down analysis for the best price.

■ SERVER NETWORK OPERATING SYSTEM TRENDS

Overall, network operating systems are evolving into interoperable suites of network infrastructure services that could potentially be purchased from a variety of vendors. Network operating system vendors such as Banyan and Novell have already unbundled their fully integrated network operating systems and are selling their directory services platforms in a variety of versions compatible with application engine operating systems such as NT and various flavors of UNIX.

In addition, to support mission-critical applications, network operating systems will be called upon to deliver the kind of performance and reliability that was formerly associated with mainframe computers. Symmetrical multiprocessing, clustering, and fault tolerance all contribute to these reliability and high-performance capabilities.

Symmetrical Multiprocessing, Clustering, and Fault Tolerance

Symmetrical Multiprocessing   **Symmetrical multiprocessing (SMP)** is a system architecture in which multiple CPUs are controlled by the SMP operating system and individual threads of application processes are assigned to particular CPUs on a first-available basis. In this manner, all CPUs are kept equally busy in a process known as **load balancing.** In SMP systems, the multiple CPUs generally share system memory and devices such as disk controllers. This is by far the most popular multiprocessor server system architecture, with close to 90% of all multiprocessor servers employing this option.

Windows NT supports SMP and is able to run on as many as 32 processors simultaneously. NetWare 4.11 includes SMP capability, whereas NetWare 4.1 required a separate product known as NetWare 4.1 SMP.

In Sharper Focus

NETWARE 4.1 SMP

Since the original NetWare 4.1 did not have SMP capability, some way was needed to be found to support SMP while still ensuring backward compatibility with all existing NLMs. This was done by having **NetWare 4.1 SMP** load a second operating system kernel, known as the **SMP kernel,** which works cooperatively with the first or native operating system kernel. The native kernel works on processor one while the SMP kernel works on processors two through four. Since the SMP kernel has to be able to take full advantage of multiple processors, it also must support multithreading, although the native kernel does not.

The two kernels must cooperate when data must be shared between threads executing on the two kernels. If data needed by a thread executing in the SMP kernel belongs to code executing in the native kernel, then that thread must be migrated from the SMP kernel to the native kernel to retrieve the required data. Once the required data has been retrieved, the thread is returned to the SMP kernel for further processing on CPUs two through four.

Practical Advice and Information

SMP scalability refers to the percentage of increased performance achieved for each additional CPU. For example, 100% SMP scalability implies that adding a second CPU will double the original performance or computing power of a computer and that adding a third CPU will triple the original performance of a computer. In reality, due to the operating system overhead caused by having to coordinate the efforts of multiple CPUs, something less than 100% is the highest achievable SMP scalability.

Clusters and Fault Tolerance   Fault tolerance is another characteristic that is increasingly important to corporate application services. NetWare supports fault tolerance through a separate product known as NetWare SFT III whereas Microsoft supports **automatic failover** via clustering. Automatic failover implies that a clustered server will automatically and transparently take over for another failed server in the same cluster. Microsoft is developing a series of clustering APIs for NT servers known as Wolfpack.

PC cluster hardware is available from such vendors as Intel, Compaq, Tandem, Stratus, and Hewlett-Packard. UNIX is also a popular operating in many clustered environments. The numbers of servers that can be clustered together can vary from as few as two to several hundred.

NetWare 4.1 SFT III offers an automatic failover version known as **server duplexing.** In such a case, not only are the contents of the disks synchronized but the contents of the server's memory and CPUs are also synchronized. In case of the failure of the primary server, the duplexed server takes over transparently. The synchronization of the servers is accomplished through a dedicated link known as the **mirrored server link (MSL).** The use of the dedicated MSL and dedicated MSL adapters prevents the server duplexing from adversely affecting LAN traffic.

Besides providing automatic failover capabilities, clustering can also imply using the CPU power of multiple CPUs located in separate computing platforms to produce a single, more powerful, virtual computer in a process known as **dynamic scalability.** Clusters are also sometimes referred to as **virtual parallel machines (VPM).** Clustering is neither a new concept nor unique to PCs. Digital Equipment Corporation (DEC) produced software to link multiple VAX minicomputers together in a VAXcluster during the 1980s. Future versions of NetWare will support clustering through a systems architecture that Novell refers to as **distributed parallel processing (DPP).**

Practical Advice and Information

Before rushing out and establishing a clustered server environment, be sure to investigate the availability of applications that have been specially written to run in a clustered environment.

SUMMARY

Network operating systems have traditionally provided shared file and print services among networked clients. With the increased implementation of client/server architectures and the associated increase in distributed applications, network operating systems are being called upon to provide application services, directory services, and messaging and communications services in support of these distributed applications.

Network operating systems were once categorized as either peer-to-peer or client/server. The network operating system evolution shows peer-to-peer network operating systems evolving to small business network operating systems and client/server network operating systems evolving to distinct, independent, client and server network operating systems.

Client network operating systems functionality can be categorized into operating system capabilities, peer-to-peer networking capabilities, and client networking capabilities. Client networking capabilities are largely measured by the number of different server network operating systems with which the client can transparently interoperate. Remote access capability is also important.

Server network operating systems are now primarily concerned with high-performance application services for back-end application programs. Enterprise-wide directory services must also be provided. The two major approaches to enterprise directory services are global directory services and domain directory services. To communicate with numerous client platforms, server network operating systems must support a variety of different network clients as well as a variety of different network transport protocols. Multiprotocol routing and remote access services are also essential to deliver transparent interoperability to the greatest number of client platforms. In the multiple-server environments of the enterprise network, monitoring, management, and administration tools play a critical role.

KEY TERMS

16-bit subsystem, 254
absolute path names, 267
access control lists, 280
ACL, 280
API, 254
application program interface, 254
application services, 246
applications software, 239
auditing system, 278
authentication, 278
auto-detection and auto-configuration, 275
automatic failover, 283
backward compatibility, 252
bindery, 270
client front ends, 239
client network operating systems, 247
client/server network operating systems, 245
DARPA, 268
data display channel, 255
data migration, 273
DDC, 255
delta file synchronization, 262
Dfs, 271
dial-up server, 260
directory services, 246
directory synchronization software, 260
distributed, 270
distributed parallel processing, 284
domain directory services, 270
domains, 270
DPP, 284
dynamic reconfiguration, 255
dynamic scalability, 284
engines, 239
enterprise network, 242
enterprise network management systems, 244
file synchronization software, 260
global directory service, 270
granularity, 256
horizontal software compatibility, 242
integrated client/server management systems, 244
integration, 276
integration/migration services, 246

interdomain trust, 271
Internet suite of protocols, 268
IT, 271
LAN productivity software, 239
LAN resource management software, 240
LAN software architecture, 239
LDAP, 271
legacy application, 252
lightweight directory access protocol, 271
links, 268
load balancing, 283
local security authority, 279
logon process, 279
management information base, 276
management software, 240
MIB, 276
middleware, 242
migration, 276
mirrored server link, 283
MSL, 283
multiprotocol routing, 274
NDS, 270
NetWare 4.1 SFT III, 283
NetWare 4.1 SMP, 283
NetWare Connect, 260
NetWare Directory Services, 270
Network File System, 268
network objects, 271
network operating system, 239
NFS, 268
object-oriented user interfaces, 252
ODSI, 271
open directory services interface, 271
packet signing, 278
path names, 267
PDC, 270
peer-to-peer operating systems, 244
performance monitoring, 275
Perl, 266
plug-n-play, 255
PnP BIOS, 255
PnP, 255
primary domain controller, 270
protected memory mode, 254
RAS, 260
real-mode device drivers, 252
relative path names, 267

remote node server, 260
replicated, 270
Rexx, 267
RPC, 269
SCAM, 255
SCSI configured automatically, 255
security, 240
security access token, 279
security account manager, 279
security IDs, 279
security reference monitor, 280
server back ends, 239
server duplexing, 283
server network operating systems, 247
shell, 266
SID, 279
simple network management protocol, 276
slice, 267
small business network operating systems, 248
SMP, 282
SMP kernel, 283
SMP scalability, 283
SNA, 275
SNMP, 276
SRM, 280
symmetrical multiprocessing, 282
systems network architecture, 275
TCP/IP, 268
TCP/IP model, 268
transmission control protocol/Internet protocol, 268
universal client, 247
UNIX system kernel, 265
UNIX systems programs, 265
user accounts database, 279
version control software, 260
vertical software compatibility, 241
virtual device drivers, 254
virtual machines, 254
virtual parallel machines, 284
VPM, 284
VxDs, 254
Windows NT Remote Access Server, 260
X.500, 271
XDR, 269

REVIEW QUESTIONS

1. What effect has the adoption of client/server architectures and distributed applications had on network operating system architectures?
2. Differentiate between peer-to-peer network operating systems and client/server network operating systems.
3. Differentiate between today's client network operating system and the client portion of client/server network operating systems.
4. How does the combination of today's client and server network operating systems differ from a client/server network operating system implementation?
5. What is a universal client?
6. Why is a universal client important to enterprise computing?
7. What new demands for services are being put on today's server network operating systems?
8. Describe the importance of the following service categories in more detail: directory services, application services, integration/migration services.
9. Differentiate between peer-to-peer NOS and small business NOS.
10. What forces have caused the transition from peer-to-peer to small business NOS?
11. Describe the major categories of functionality of client network operating systems.
12. What are the major differences between an object-oriented user interface and a graphical user interface?
13. Explain the difficulty in supporting legacy applications while offering protected memory mode execution.
14. What are real-mode device drivers and how do they differ from applications that interact with the operating system via APIs?
15. Why do many computer games use real-mode device drivers?
16. Why don't some client and server network operating systems support real-mode device drivers?
17. Describe how 16-bit or 32-bit applications running in their own protected memory space can still cause system crashes.
18. What is the objective of PnP standards?
19. Describe the components required to deliver a PnP solution and the relationship of the described components.
20. Which client network operating system is most PnP-compliant?
21. What is meant by the statement, "Interoperability is not two-way."

22. Describe the three elements of networking functionality belonging to client network operating systems, paying particular attention to the relationship between the elements.
23. Why is it important for a client network operating system to be able to support more than one network transport protocol?
24. Describe the importance of laptop synchronization as a client network operating system feature.
25. Describe the major differences between global directory services and domain directory services in terms of architecture and functionality.
26. What is accomplished by having directory services databases be both distributed and replicated? Differentiate between the two techniques.
27. What is interdomain trust?
28. How does interdomain trust save on network administration activity?
29. What is X.500?
30. What is the relationship between file systems, APIs, and application services?
31. Why might it be important for a network operating system to support more than one file system?
32. What is the role of NCP and SMB redirectors in offering application services?
33. What is the difference in terms of functionality and communication between a client running only an operating system such as Windows and a client running a network operating system such as Windows 95?
34. What is the role of multiprotocol routing in a server network operating system?
35. What is the role of gateway services such as Microsoft SNA Server?
36. What are some important functional characteristics of server network operating systems related to installation and configuration?
37. What are some important functional characteristics of server network operating systems related to integration and migration?
38. How is the combination of UNIX, TCP/IP, and NFS functionality equivalent to a fully integrated network operating system such as Windows NT?
39. What is the relationship between the UNIX system programs, UNIX system kernel, UNIX shells, and UNIX application programs?
40. Describe some of the unique features of the UNIX file system.
41. What is the relationship between the UNIX file system and NFS?
42. What is the relationship between TCP/IP, the Internet suite of protocols, and the TCP/IP model.

43. Explain the relationship between the various layers of the NFS architecture.
44. Differentiate between vertical and horizontal software compatibility. How is each achieved?
45. What is middleware and what is its role in distributed processing systems?
46. What is the role of the enterprise network in client/server information systems?
47. What elements or subnetworks might make up an enterprise network?
48. What types of traffic might an enterprise network carry?
49. Differentiate between enterprise network management systems and integrated client/server management systems.
50. Evaluate the pros and cons of server duplexing.

ACTIVITIES

1. Using back issues of a publication such as *PC Magazine*, prepare a presentation tracing the functionality of peer-to-peer LANs from 1992 to the present. Prepare a graph detailing price, number of supported users, and required memory over the research period.
2. Using back issues of a publication such as *PC Magazine*, prepare a presentation tracing the functionality of client/server LANs from 1992 to the present. Prepare a graph detailing price, number of supported users, and required memory over the research period.
3. Gather current market share statistics for the following market segments and prepare a presentation: peer-to-peer NOS, small business NOS, client NOS, server NOS.
4. Analyze the results of the previous activity. Which products are gaining market share and which are losing market share? Relate the market shifts to product functionality. Present your results in a top-down model format.
5. Prepare a presentation on the comparative functionality of Windows 95 vs. OS/2 Warp Connect. Compare marketing campaigns and current market share.
6. Conduct a survey of users of object-oriented user interfaces (Windows 95, OS/2 Warp) and graphical user interfaces (Windows). What are users' impressions of the two? Does one really make users more productive than the other? Is this increase in productivity measurable?
7. Review advertisements and catalogs for devices that support the PnP standard. Prepare a listing detailing which types of devices have the most PnP offerings. Which network operating system (if any) do devices claim to be compatible with?
8. Prepare a product review of dial-up or remote node servers, paying special attention to the source and compatibility of client software. Are most dial-up servers NOS specific? Why or why not?
9. Research and prepare a presentation on X.500. What software categories supported X.500 specs originally? Currently? What key vendor groups or standards bodies (if any) support X.500? What is your prediction as to the widespread adoption of X.500?
10. Compare the performance monitoring capabilities of various server network operating systems. Which are best at monitoring a single server? Multiple servers? Which are best at setting thresholds and alerts? Which are best at linking to enterprise management systems such as HP's OpenView or IBM's NetView?
11. Compare the functionality of Microsoft's Systems Management Server and Novell's ManageWise. Contrast these programs with enterprise management systems such as HP's OpenView and IBM's SystemView in terms of functionality and price.
12. Investigate and compare the structures of NetWare 3.12 bindery and NetWare 4.1 NDS database.
13. Prepare a product review of software tools designed to automate the migration from the 3.12 bindery to the 4.1 NDS database.
14. Research the planned functionality of the following "next-generation" network operating systems. Present the results of your research as well as your opinions as to the importance of the planned features of each product: Microsoft: Cairo (NT 5.0), Nashville, Memphis; Apple: Copland; NetWare: Moab, Park City.

CASE STUDY

Hospital Weighs NT Move

As the merits of Novell Inc. NetWare vs. Microsoft Windows NT continue to be debated, network managers are facing real-life decisions between the two. Lance Colyer, director of operations and network systems at Harlem Hospital Center in New York, is one of those managers.

Across the six buildings on its main campus and eight satellite clinics, the hospital maintains 35 NetWare LANs and a handful of NT-based LANs, but none of these networks is connected to the others. A few Artisoft Inc. LANtastic and Apple Computer Inc. Macintosh networks, some legacy systems, and one Sun Microsystems Inc. Solaris server are also sprinkled around the area (see "Network Prescription," above).

Of the NetWare networks, only five have their own LAN administrators. Plans are being made for overdue enterprisewide upgrades that would result in the migration of some of the NetWare servers to NetWare 4.x and 30 of the NetWare servers to NT 4.0 in the coming year.

Whence They Came

"When I first got here, it was like walking into Bedrock," said Colyer, who added that healthcare providers are notoriously slow at adopting new technology.

Many end users have no E-mail and can perform only DOS-based word processing, but beyond providing for these basic needs looms the greater issue of connectivity: Not one of the networks can talk to any other. And with systems running under protocols as wide ranging as Digital Equipment Corp. LAT (Local-Area Transport), Appletalk, Stratus Computer Inc. Virtual Operating System, and Hewlett-Packard

Co. MPE/iX, Colyer wants to implement an OS with native TCP/IP when he establishes the backbone to connect them all.

"With native IP, NT will make it easier because we don't want to worry about protocol conversion with [NetWare's use of] IPX," he said.

IP also produces less overhead than IPX in communications between clients and servers, he said, and that helps in the effort to reduce network traffic. With that goal in mind, Colyer is also investigating Citrix Systems Inc. WinFrame thin clients, another capability inherent in NT.

Because all the NetWare servers except one run versions 3.x and lower, they would have to be upgraded to the current 4.11 to take advantage of Novell's IPX-to-IP gateway.

"We'll have to get the systems up and running quickly, and we don't have enough NetWare experience to take a chance with problems," Colyer said. The current budget will not allow for more NetWare-certified personnel, he said, adding that the IPX gateway was delivered too late to be properly tested before the migration plans are submitted for final approval.

The hospital doesn't have the staff or the budget to maintain every NetWare server. Many of the original administrators are no longer around, so the networks are run by part-time administrators who have other responsibilities and must find the time to trouble shoot when problems arise.

"If the people who are forced to manage these networks now are familiar with Windows, they can grasp the concepts and make the connections better with NT," said Colyer.

In addition to ease of administration, Colyer also anticipates ease of adoption by end users when Windows 95 is deployed on most of the systems. Many of the hospital's approximately 500 users are not extremely computer literate, he said, and they can get easily tripped up by DOS prompts or arcane command messages when things go wrong under NetWare.

Because of Windows 95's similarity to and tighter integration with Windows NT, users will encounter error messages they may be familiar with and so are more likely to work through the problems themselves.

Getting users up to speed quickly at a large hospital also requires a comfortable and flexible environment for applications use and development. Many departments at Harlem Hospital Center will be using products in the Microsoft BackOffice Suite, including SQL Server, Exchange, Systems Management Server, and Visual Basic. Colyer is more comfortable with the way these applications integrate into NT.

Furthermore, certain users at the hospital needed specialized applications, which are more likely to be available on the NT or Solaris sides than on NetWare. The radiology department, for example, is investigating picture-archiving and -retrieval systems, which couldn't be found in a NetWare version, said Colyer.

"We also have new apps coming in that need to interface with other hospitals currently running UNIX systems," said Colyer. "Because of the similarity between UNIX and NT and because so many other hospitals are moving to NT, having NT [at Harlem Hospital] will make it easier—espeically with the capability to avoid protocol conversions."

Tools of the Trade

For the actual migration, Colyer plans to first connect a NetWare 4.x server to the other NetWare LANs and clean up their directory structures. Then additional services such as E-mail, groupware, and a document-management repository will be passed through the 4.x server.

At that point, Colyer will undertake the physical process of moving user IDs and translating NetWare bindery structures to NT domains—with the help of the migration tool in NT 4.0. "That's where it can get hairy," he said.

Because of users' relative inexperience with shared services beyond their departments, only one user per group will initially be entrusted with all other relevant domains. Further combinations of domains will occur as users become accustomed to network operations and data sharing.

Colyer eagerly looks forward to that day and will have few regrets about abandoning NetWare. "I can see a place for NetWare for a long time," he said. "It's very stable and does what it does well, but with NT our users will be much more comfortable, and so will I."

Source: Brett Mendel, "Hospital Weighs NT Move," *LAN Times,* vol. 13, no. 25 (November 11, 1996), p. 29. Copyright © November 11, 1996 by McGraw–Hill, New York. Reprinted by permission of McGraw–Hill, New York.

BUSINESS CASE STUDY QUESTIONS

Activities

1. Complete a top-down model for this case by gleaning facts from the case and placing them in the proper layer of the top-down model. After completing the top-down model, analyze and detail those instances where requirements were clearly passed down from upper layers to lower layers of the model and where solutions to those requirements were passed up from lower layers to upper layers of the model.
2. Detail any question about the case that may occur to you for which answers are not clearly stated in the article.

Business

1. What are the major business activities of the organization in this case?
2. How did budget constraints and the availability of network management personnel influence the network operating system purchase decision?
3. What policies will be enforced to limit access afforded inexperienced users? Why?
4. Do you think that NT was the best choice in this case? Was the decision based on valid evaluation criteria?

Application

1. What types of applications are being executed on the current network?
2. What types of general productivity applications will be executed on the new enterprise network?
3. What types of specialized business process-specific applications will be executed?
4. How did the ability of these applications to integrate with network operating systems affect the choice of network operating system?

Data

1. What types of data sharing with other hospitals will be required?
2. What types of network protocols and operating systems do these enterprise partners have and how might this affect the choice of network operating system?

Network

1. What is the current mix of network operating systems serving the hospital?
2. What is the current mix of network protocols being supported?
3. Is there currently a high-bandwidth network backbone connecting all servers?
4. What are some of the problems with the current network setup?
5. What are the requirements for the new enterprise backbone?
6. What network protocol was chosen as the standard for the enterprise backbone? Why?
7. What will be the client platform of choice? Why?

Technology

1. Why was NT the preferred choice of network operating system technology in this case?
2. Why was it necessary to upgrade the NetWare 3.x to 4.11?
3. What is the role of the IPX-to-IP gateway? Why is it required?
4. How will technology ease the migration from NetWare to NT?

ENTERPRISE NETWORKING

INTRODUCTION

Having gained an understanding of local area networks in Part 2, we study in Part 3 the techniques required to access these local area networks remotely and to interconnect them to each other over long distances. These connections may be via traditional wide area network services, wireless transmission, or the Internet.

In Chapter 8, "Wide Area Networking Concepts, Architectures, and Services," the reader is introduced to a broad foundation of information concerning wide area networking. This information is critical to an appreciation of the issues involved with linking local area networks over long distances.

In Chapter 9, "Internetworking," the hardware and software protocols involved to actually link disparate local area networks together are studied in detail. This chapter provides a broad introduction to this complex topic on which entire texts have been written.

In Chapter 10, "Remote Access and Wireless Networking," the proper design of remote access solutions based on a thorough understanding of user needs, network architecture alternatives, available technology, and available WAN services is studied, with significant emphasis on the increasingly important field of wireless data communications.

Finally, Chapter 11, "Enterprise Networks and the Internet," introduces the reader to the numerous issues surrounding enterprise network design through the exploration of alternative enterprise network architectures, topologies, and technologies including the use of the Internet as an enterprise network backbone.

By the end of Part 3, the reader should have a thorough understanding of how networking components can interact to effectively deliver networking services to an entire enterprise.

WIDE AREA NETWORKING CONCEPTS, ARCHITECTURES, AND SERVICES

Concepts Reinforced

OSI Model   Internet Suite of Protocols Model
Top-Down Model

Concepts Introduced

Wide Area Network Architecture   Switching Architectures
Transmission Architectures   Multiplexing
Packetization   Local Loop Transmission Alternatives
Broadband Transmission   Wide Area Network Services

OBJECTIVES

After mastering the material in this chapter, you should

1. Understand the concept of multiplexing in general as well as several multiplexing techniques and related technology and applications in particular.

2. Understand the relationship between business motivation, available technology, and carrier services in creating wide area networking solutions.

3. Understand the advantages, limitations, and technology of current and forthcoming packet-switching networks.

4. Understand the importance of standards as applied to wide area networking.

5. Understand the interrelationships and dependencies between the components of any wide area network architecture.

6. Understand the impact of the evolution in switching methodologies as it applies specifically to frame relay and cell relay.

■ INTRODUCTION

One of the most significant differences between wide area networks and the local area networks that were studied in Part 2 is the dependency, in most cases, on

293

third-party carriers to provide wide area transmission services. The ability to understand the transmission and switching architecture that underlies and enables the variety of wide area transmission services that are offered by these carriers is of critical importance to successful wide area network managers.

To understand wide area switching and transmission architectures, one must first understand some basic principles or concepts of wide area networking such as multiplexing, packet switching, and circuit switching. Once switching and transmission architectures are understood, the wide area network services, both wireless and wireline, that are enabled by these architectures can be more effectively understood.

■ BASIC PRINCIPLES OF WIDE AREA NETWORKING

Underlying Business Issues

To understand the basic technical principles of wide area networking, one must really start by looking at the basic business principles of wide area networking. In wide area networking as in most areas of business, the desire to maximize the impact of any investment in technology is a central focus. Figure 8-1 illustrates the underlying business motivation of wide area networking principles. Given five systems (LANs, computers, terminals to mainframes) that need to be linked over long distances, there are basically two choices of physical configurations. A dedicated wide area link can be provided for each system-to-system connection or somehow both the principles and technology necessary to share a single wide area link among all five system-to-system connections can be found. The basic principles, architectures, and services involved in establishing, maintaining, and terminating multiple wide area system-to-system connections constitute the topics covered in the remainder of the chapter.

Underlying Technical Concepts

The two most basic principles involved in sharing a single data link among multiple sessions as illustrated in Figure 8-1 are **packetizing** and **multiplexing.** Packetizing is the segmenting of data transmissions between devices into structured blocks or packets of data that contain enough "overhead" or management information in addition to the transmitted data itself to ensure delivery of the packet of data to its intended destination. Multiplexing then takes this packetized data and sends it over a shared wide area connection along with other packetized data from other sources. At the far end of the single wide area network link, the multiple-source, multiplexed data packets are demultiplexed and sent to their respective destination addresses. A long-distance parcel shipping analogy may clarify the underlying technical concepts of packetizing and multiplexing. Figure 8-2 illustrates this analogy.

As can be seen in Figure 8-2, multiple packages of several presents each are transported over a long distance via a single transport mechanism and subsequently delivered to their individual destinations. The equivalent wide area data transmission events are listed along the top of Figure 8-2, illustrating several packets of data from multiple sources being transmitted over a single, shared wide area communications link and subsequently demultiplexed and delivered to their individual destination addresses.

A. Dedicated Multiple Wide Area System to System Connections

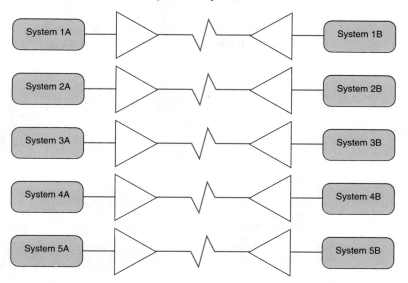

B. Single Wide Area Link Shared to Provide Multiple System to System Connections

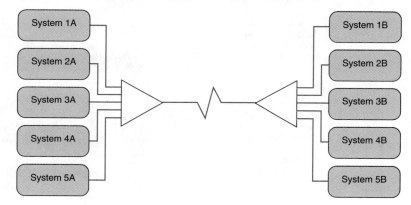

Figure 8-1   WAN Technical Principles Are Motivated by Business Principles

Packetizing

A **packet** is a group of data bits organized in a predetermined, structured manner, to which overhead or management information is added to ensure error-free transmission of the actual data to its intended destination. These generalized packets may be alternatively known as frames, cells, blocks, data units, or several other names. The predetermined, structured nature of a packet should not be overlooked. Recall that all of the raw data as well as any address information or error control information is nothing more than bits of data, 1s and 0s, that will be processed by some type of programmed, computerized communication device. This programmed data communication device must be able to depend on exactly where certain pieces of key information, such as destination address and error check numbers, are located within a packet containing both raw data and overhead information.

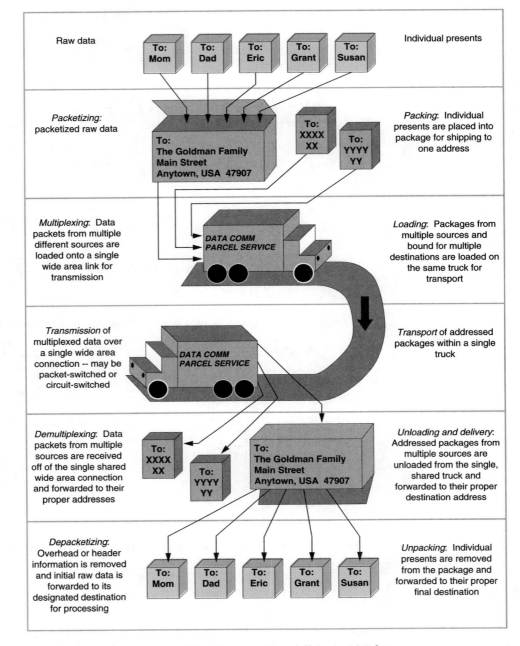

Figure 8-2   Packetizing and Multiplexing: A Parcel Shipping Analogy

By knowing exactly which bits within a packet represent a destination address and which bits represent data to be forwarded, the data communications device can process incoming data packets more quickly and efficiently. Ethernet and token ring frame layouts, examined in Chapter 5, illustrate the need for and use of predetermined structured packet organization. In a WAN environment, similar information is also needed. See Figure 8-24 as an example of a WAN-based packet format.

The parcel shipping analogy also illustrates the need for predetermined, structured packets. When shipping a parcel with nearly any parcel shipping company, one must fill out one of their standardized "structured" shipping forms, putting all data in the properly marked spaces. By doing so, the wide area transport mechanism, the parcel shipping company, can process packages more quickly and efficiently by only reading one type of form and knowing where specific data is located on that form. Regulations pertaining to maximum and minimum package size as well as packaging techniques also serve to allow the parcel shipping company to perform more efficiently. As will be seen, maximum and minimum packet lengths in wide area data transmission are important to overall transmission efficiency as well.

Multiplexing

Two basic techniques are employed in multiplexing digitized traffic:

- **Frequency division multiplexing (FDM).**
- **Time division multiplexing (TDM).**

A variation of TDM known as **statistical time division multiplexing (STDM)** is also commonly employed for digital data.

The previous three multiplexing techniques are limited to digitized traffic in which bits of data are transmitted as discrete voltages of electricity. In the optical transmission world, in which bits of data are represented by bursts of light energy of varying wavelengths, a relatively new multiplexing technique known as **wavelength division multiplexing (WDM)** has been developed. WDM technology is deployed primarily by telecommunications carriers with extensive long-distance fiber optic networks to increase transmission capacity up to 10-fold without the need to install additional fiber. In WDM, multiple bits of data can be transmitted simultaneously over a single fiber by being represented by different wavelengths of light.

Frequency Division Multiplexing   In frequency division multiplexing, multiple input signals are modulated to different frequencies within the available output bandwidth of a single composite circuit, often a 3000-Hz dial-up line, and subsequently demodulated back into individual signals on the output end of the composite circuit. Sufficient space in between these separate frequency channels is reserved in **guardbands** to prevent interference between the two or more input signals that are sharing the single circuit. Figure 8-3 illustrates a simple frequency division multiplexing configuration.

The communications device that employs frequency division multiplexing is known as a frequency division multiplexer or FDM. At one time, FDMs were employed to transmit data from multiple low-speed (less than 1200 bps) terminals over dial-up or leased lines. As the speed of frequency division multiplexed terminals increases, the guardband width between channels in the shared composite circuit must increase also. As terminal speeds and demand for more bandwidth per terminal have risen, frequency division multiplexing is no longer the most practical multiplexing method employed.

Although FDM is seldom if ever still used to multiplex data from multiple terminals, it is still employed in devices known as **data over voice** units or DOV units. DOV units are most often employed where data transmission is desired to a location that is currently wired for phones but that cannot be easily or affordably also be

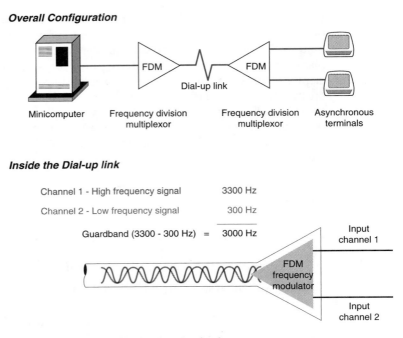

Figure 8-3   Frequency Division Multiplexing

rewired for data. In these cases, both the data and the voice transmission are simultaneously transmitted over the existing phone wiring. What's more, the data and voice transmissions are independent of one another. A person can be talking to someone else across the country while being on-line with a data transmission to the local computing center. It is important to point out that DOV units cannot be used over the PSTN (public switched telephone network). They must be used in environments that are served by a local PBX. College campuses are probably the most popular environment for DOV unit usage.

In FDM, the total bandwidth of the composite channel is divided into multiple subchannels by frequency. With FDM, from a connected terminal's point of view, a portion of the total bandwidth is available 100% of the time, yielding the appearance of a dedicated circuit. As a result, the timing of signals between a connected terminal or device and the centralized processor is not affected.

Time Division Multiplexing   In time division multiplexing (TDM), just the opposite is true. With TDM, from a connected terminal's point of view, 100% of the bandwidth is available for a portion of the time. The portion of time that is available to each connected input device is constant and controlled by the time division multiplexer. A key point to understand about time slots in a TDM environment is that a fixed portion of time, measured in milliseconds, is reserved for each attached input device whether the device is active or not. As a result, efficiency is sacrificed for the sake of simplicity.

There are times in a TDM environment when a terminal with nothing to say is given its full time allotment while other busy terminals are waiting to transmit. A TDM is really a fairly simple device employing many familiar elements such as buffer memory and flow control. Figure 8-4 illustrates simple time division multiplexing.

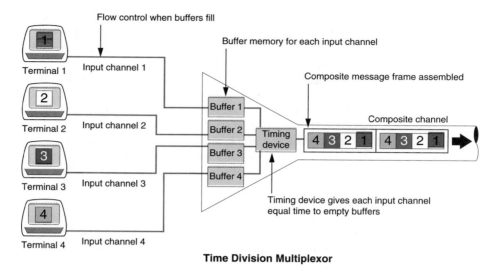

Time Division Multiplexor

Figure 8-4   Time Division Multiplexing

As can be seen in Figure 8-4, each input channel has a fixed amount of buffer memory into which it can load data. Flow control, either XON/XOFF or CTS/RTS, tells the terminal to stop transmitting to the buffer memory when the buffer memory fills. A **central clock** or timing device in the TDM gives each input device its allocated time to empty its buffer into an area of the TDM where the combined data from all of the polled input devices is conglomerated into a single message frame for transmission over the composite circuit. This process of checking on each connected terminal to see if any data is ready to be sent is known as **polling.**

If a terminal was inactive and had nothing in its input buffer to contribute to the consolidated message frame, that input terminal's allotted space in the **composite message frame** is filled with blanks. The insertion of blanks, or null characters, into composite message links is the basis of TDMs' inefficient use of the shared composite circuit connecting the two TDMs. Although the data from the various input terminals is combined into a single message frame, each individual terminal's data is still identifiable by position within that composite message frame. This fact is important since once the composite message frame has finished its journey down the transmission link, it must be resegmented back into the individual terminal's original data format.

Statistical Time Division Multiplexing   Statistical time division multiplexing (STDM) seeks to offer more efficient use of the composite bandwidth than simple TDM by employing increased monitoring and manipulation of input devices to accomplish two major goals:

1.   Eliminate "idle time" allocations to inactive terminals.

2.   Eliminate padded blanks or null characters in the composite message blocks.

In a Stat MUX, allocation time is dynamically allocated to input devices. As terminals become more active, they get more time to send data directly to the Stat MUX. As terminals become less active or inactive, the Stat MUX polls them for input less frequently. This dynamic time slot allocation takes both processing power and additional memory. Statistics are kept as to terminal activity over time and hence the name: statistical time division multiplexers. Specially programmed microprocessors and additional buffer memory are key upgrades to STDMs and contribute to their increased costs over the simpler TDMs.

To increase the efficiency of use of the composite link, padded blanks and null characters are not inserted into message frames for inactive terminals. Remember the purpose of the blanks: to occupy the space in the composite message frame assigned to that particular device. In an STDM, rather than assign space to input devices in the composite message frame by position regardless of activity, the STDM adds control information to each terminal's data within the composite message frame that indicates the source terminal and how many bytes of data came from that terminal. Figure 8-5 illustrates composite message block construction in STDMs.

Practical Advice and Information

The following important points about Stat MUXs should be noted:

- The time allocation protocols and composite message frame building protocols are proprietary and vary from one manufacturer to the next. As a result, multiplexers from different manufacturers are not interoperable.

- The dynamic allocation of time afforded to individual terminals or devices by the STDM can interfere with any timing that might have been previously set up between the remote device and the central processor. This is particularly important in manufacturing or process control operations.

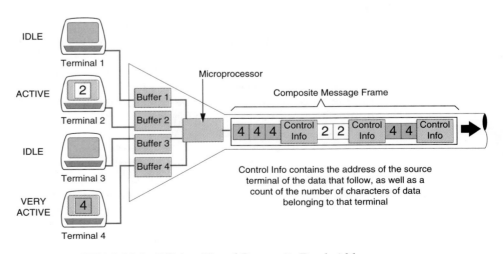

Figure 8-5   STDMs Make Efficient Use of Composite Bandwidth

STDM COST/BENEFIT ANALYSIS

From a business standpoint, what does a cost/benefit analysis of an STDM reveal? The STDM's increased costs are due to increased buffer memory, more sophisticated programming, and an integral microprocessor. On the benefits side of the equation, STDMs produce increased efficiency in time slot allocation and composite bandwidth usage. Some STDMs also include proprietary data compression techniques as well. These increased efficiencies in STDMs seem to produce "something for nothing."

For example, it is not unheard of for STDMs to seemingly transmit data for four or even eight times the speed of the composite link. For instance, I have installed 16-port STDMs with four printers running at 2400 bps and 12 asynchronous terminals running at 4800 bps for an apparent bandwidth requirement of 67.2 Kbps $[(2400 \times 4) + (4800 \times 12)]$. The fact of the matter is these 16 devices ran just fine over a 9600-bps leased line! This apparent discrepancy is largely due to the "statistical" nature of data transmission from terminals, which demonstrates the likelihood that only a relatively small percentage of terminals will be transmitting data at any split second in time. It is the STDM's sophisticated dynamic time slot allocation capabilities that take advantage of this relatively large "idle time." Figure 8-6 illustrates the STDM's apparent ability to offer something for nothing.

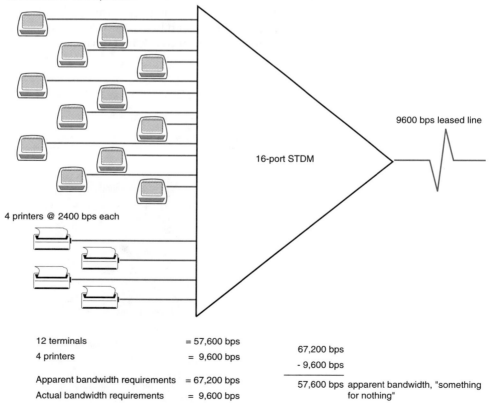

Figure 8-6   STDMs Seem to Offer Something for Nothing

Wide Area Network Architecture

To better understand how packetizing, multiplexing, and other wide area networking principles combine to create all of the current and emerging wide area networking technologies and services, a simple model defining the major segments and interrelationships of an overall wide area network architecture are included in Figure 8-7.

As can be seen in Figure 8-7, **user demands** are the driving force behind the current and emerging wide area **network services** that are offered to business and residential customers. Companies offering these services are in business to generate profits by implementing the underlying architectures that will enable them to offer the wide area networking services that users are demanding at the lowest possible cost.

For users to take advantage of network services, standardized **interface specifications** must be developed to ensure interoperability among different manufacturer's end-user equipment. As an example, the X.25 interface specification ensures that users can purchase packet assembler/disassemblers from any manufacturer and be able to successfully interface to a packet-switched network service. Having packetized user payloads according to standard interface specifications, carrier network services must be accessed via an appropriately sized **access line** running from the user's residence or business to the entry or gateway to the carrier's network service.

To assure transparent delivery of network services to users regardless of location, several carriers may need to cooperatively hand-off user payloads to each other. The transparent interoperability of network services from different carriers requires predefined **network-to-network interfaces.**

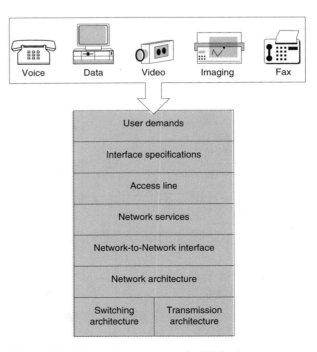

Figure 8-7   Major Components of a Wide-Area Network Architecture

Network services cannot be offered unless the underlying infrastructure of the carriers and companies wishing to offer these services is technically capable of doing so. The combination of sophisticated switches **(switching architecture)** and transmission facilities **(transmission architecture)** that comprise this infrastructure is known as the **network architecture.** Switching architectures or methods, such as circuit switching or packet switching, ensure the proper routing of information (data, voice, video, etc.) from the data's source to its destination. Transmission architectures or methods are the circuits or data highways over which the information is actually delivered.

To return to the parcel shipping analogy, switching is the activity that takes place inside depots and warehouses, whereas transmission takes place in the trucks on the highways and in the planes in the air. By adjusting depot organization, manpower, floor space, or equipment, a parcel shipping company could adjust its switching capacity or sophistication. By utilizing varying numbers of planes or trucks or by changing truck or plane routes, the same parcel shipping company could adjust its transmission capacity or sophistication.

In the case of wide area or packet-switched networks, the copper, fiber, microwave, and satellite links and the protocols that control access to and monitoring of these circuits constitute the transmission architecture of wide area networks. The central office switches and packet switches that build connections from source to destination utilizing these transmission circuits constitute the switching architecture of the wide area or packet-switched network. The importance of the relationship between the two architectures is well illustrated by the parcel shipping company analogy. If the parcel shipping company were to increase switching capacity and sophistication by building several new depots but did not upgrade its transmission capacity by increasing numbers of trucks and planes, the result would be less than optimal. Similarly, providers of wide area network services are in the process of upgrading both their switching and transmission facilities to be able to meet future user demands for sophisticated and reasonably priced wide area network services.

■ WIDE AREA NETWORKING SWITCHING

Switching of some type or another is necessary in wide area network architectures because the alternative is unthinkable. To explain: Without some type of switching mechanism or architecture, every possible source of data in the world would have to be directly connected to every possible destination of data in the world, not a very likely prospect. Switching allows temporary connections to be established, maintained, and terminated between message sources and message destinations, sometimes called **sinks** in data communications. There are two primary switching techniques employed in switching architectures:

- **Packet switching.**
- **Circuit switching.**

In packet-switched networks, users' packetized data is transported across circuits between packet switches along with the data of other users of the same packet-switched network. In contrast, in circuit-switched networks, users get dedicated bandwidth on circuits created solely for their use.

Packet Switching

In a **packet-switched network,** packets of data travel one at a time from the message source to the message destination. A packet-switched network, otherwise known as a **public data network (PDN),** is represented in network diagrams by a symbol that resembles a cloud. Figure 8-8 illustrates such a symbol as well as the difference between circuit switching and packet switching. The cloud is an appropriate symbol for a packet-switched network since all that is known is that the packet of data goes in one side of the PDN and comes out the other. The physical path that any packet takes may be different from that of other packets and, in any case, is unknown to the end-users. What is beneath the cloud in a packet-switched network is a large number of **packet switches** that pass packets among themselves as the packets are routed from source to destination.

Remember that packets are specially structured groups of data that include control and address information in addition to the data itself. These packets must be assembled (control and address information added to data) somewhere before entry into the packet-switched network and must be subsequently disassembled before delivery of the data to the message destination. This packet assembly and disassembly is done by a device known as a **PAD** or **packet assembler/disassembler.** PADs may be stand-alone devices or may be integrated into specially built modems or multiplexers. These PADs may be located at an end-user location or may be located at the entry point to the packet-switched data network. Figure 8-8 illustrates the latter scenario in which the end-users employ regular modems to dial-up to the packet-switched network that provides the PADs to properly assemble the packets

Circuit Switching

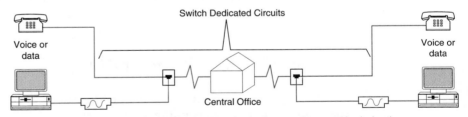

All data or voice travel from source to destination over the *same* physical path

Packet Switching

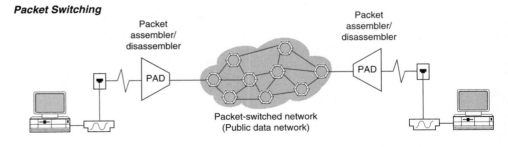

Data enter the packet-switched network one packet at a time;
Packets may take *different* physical paths within packet-switched networks.

Figure 8-8   Circuit Switching vs. Packet Switching

prior to transmission. This setup is often more convenient for end-users as they can still employ their modem for other dial-up applications as well.

The packet switches illustrated inside the PDN cloud in Figure 8-8 are generically known as **DSEs** (data-switching exchanges) or **PSEs** (packet-switching exchanges). DSE is the packet-switching equivalent of the DCE and DTE categorizations that were first encountered in the study of modems and dial-up transmission.

Another way in which packet switching differs from circuit switching is that as demand for transmission of data increases on a packet-switched network, additional users are not denied access to the packet-switched network. Overall performance of the network may suffer, errors and retransmission may occur, or packets of data may be lost, but all users experience the same degradation of service. This reason for this is that, in the case of a packet-switched network, data travels through the network one packet at a time, traveling over any available path within the network rather than waiting for a switched dedicated path as in the case of the circuit-switched network.

Connectionless vs. Connection-Oriented Packet-Switched Services For any packet switch to process any packet of data bound for anywhere, it is essential that packet address information be included on each packet. Each packet switch then reads and processes each packet by making routing and forwarding decisions based upon the packet's destination address and current network conditions. The full destination address uniquely identifying the ultimate destination of each packet is known as the **global address.**

Because an overall data message is broken up into numerous pieces by the packet assembler, these message pieces may actually arrive out of order at the message destination due to the speed and condition of the alternate paths within the packet-switched network over which these message pieces (packets) traveled. The data message must be pieced back together in proper order by the destination PAD before final transmission to the destination address. These self-sufficient packets containing full source and destination address information plus a message segment are known as **datagrams.** Figure 8-9 illustrates this packet-switched network phenomenon.

A switching methodology in which each datagram is handled and routed to its ultimate destination on an individual basis resulting in the possibility of packets traveling over a variety of physical paths on the way to their destination is known as a **connectionless** packet network. It is called connectionless because packets do not follow one another, in order, down a particular path through the network.

There are no error detection or flow control techniques applied by a datagram-based or connectionless packet-switched network. Such a network would depend on end-user (PCs, modems, communications software) to provide adequate error control and flow control. Because datagrams are sent along multiple possible paths to the destination address, there is no guarantee of their safe arrival. This lack of inherent error detection or flow control abilities is the basis for connectionless packet networks also being known as **unreliable** packet networks.

Virtual Circuits In contrast to the connectionless packet networks, **connection-oriented** or **reliable** packet networks establish **virtual circuits** enabling message packets to follow one another, in sequence, down the same connection or physical circuit. This connection from source to destination is set up by special packets known as **call set-up packets.** Once the call set-up packets have determined the best path from the source to the destination and established the virtual circuit, the message-bearing packets follow one another in sequence along the virtual circuit from

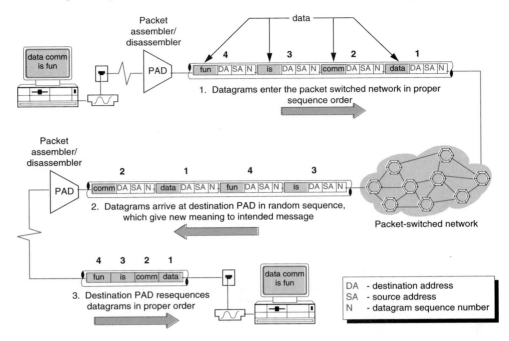

Figure 8-9   Datagram Delivery on a Packet-Switched Network

source to destination. Unlike a connectionless service, a connection-oriented service, because of the establishment of the virtual circuit, can offer check sum error detection with ACK/NAK retransmission control and flow control. These services can be offered by the packet network itself rather than depending on the end-user devices. Because connection-oriented packets all follow the same path, or **logical channel,** from source to destination, they do not require the full global addressing on each packet as in the case of the connectionless datagram networks. Instead, connection-oriented network packets have an abbreviated **logical channel number,** or **LCN,** included with each packet. The details that relate the LCN to a physical circuit consisting of an actual series of specific packet switches within the packet-switched network are stored in a **virtual circuit table.**

Connection-oriented packet-switching networks actually define two types of virtual circuits: **switched virtual circuits (SVC)** and **permanent virtual circuits (PVC).** The switched virtual circuit connection is terminated when the complete message has been sent and a special **clear request packet** causes all switched virtual circuit table entries related to this connection to be erased. The virtual circuit table of the permanent virtual circuit is not erased, making the PVC the equivalent of a "virtual" circuit-switched leased line.

Although the use of LCNs as opposed to full global addressing reduces overhead in connection-oriented packet networks, the following elements add to that overhead:

1.   Connection setup.

2.   Network-based, point-to-point error detection and flow control.

Figure 8-10 contrasts the overhead of connectionless vs. connection-oriented packet-switched networks as well as several other key differentiating criteria.

	Overhead	Greatest Strength	Call Set-up	Addressing	Also Known As...	Virtual Circuit	Error Correction	Flow Control
Connectionless	Less	Ability to dynamically reroute data	None	Global	Datagram unreliable	None	Left to end-user devices	Left to end-user devices
Connection-oriented	More	Reliability	Yes	Local logical channel number	Reliable Virtual circuit	Created for each call, virtual circuit table established	By virtual circuit	By virtual circuit

Figure 8-10　Connection-Oriented vs. Connectionless Packet-Switched Networks

The truth is that unless a company plans to set up their own packet-switched network, decisions regarding the relative merits of connectionless vs. connection-oriented packet-switched networks will not have to be considered. It is more likely that a company will access a major commercial packet-switched network service. In that case, what goes on "inside the cloud" is invisible to the users of that packet-switched network. In such a case, an end-user's only concern is how to interface to "the cloud."

Circuit Switching

In a **circuit-switched network,** a switched dedicated circuit is created to connect the two or more parties, eliminating the need for source and destination address information such as that provided by the packetizing techniques explored earlier. The switched dedicated circuit established on circuit-switched networks makes it appear to the user of the circuit as if a wire has been run directly between the phones of the calling parties. The physical resources required to create this temporary connection are dedicated to that particular circuit for the duration of the connection. If system usage should increase to the point where insufficient resources are available to create additional connections, users would not get a dial tone.

A BUSINESS PERSPECTIVE ON CIRCUIT SWITCHING VS. PACKET SWITCHING

If the top-down model were applied to an analysis of possible switching methodologies, circuit switching and packet switching could be properly placed on either the network or the technology layer. In either case, to make the proper switching methodology decision, the top-down model layer directly above the network layer, namely, the data layer, must be thoroughly examined. The key data layer question becomes:

- What is the nature of the data to be transmitted and which switching methodology best supports those data characteristics?

The first data-related criterion to examine is the data source.

- What is the nature of the application program (application layer) that will produce this data?

- Is it a transaction-oriented program or more of a batch update or file-oriented program?

A transaction-oriented program, producing what is sometimes called interactive data, is characterized by short bursts of data followed by variable-length pauses due to users reading screen prompts or pauses between transactions. This bursty transaction-oriented traffic, best categorized by banking transactions at an automated teller machine, must be delivered as quickly and reliably as the network can possibly perform. In addition to data burstiness, time pressures and reliability constraints are other important data characteristics that will assist in switching methodology decision-making.

Applications programs more oriented to large file transfers or batch updates have different data characteristics than transaction-oriented programs. Overnight updates from regional offices to corporate headquarters or from local stores to regional offices are typical examples. Rather than being bursty, the data in these types of applications is usually large and flowing steadily. These transfers are important, but not often urgent. If file transfers fail, error detection and correction protocols such as those examined in the study of communications software can retransmit bad data or even restart file transfers at the point of failure.

From a business perspective the two switching techniques vary as well. Although both circuit-switched and packet-switched services usually charge a flat monthly fee for access, the basis for usage charges differs. In general, circuit-switched connections are billed according to time connected to the circuit. Leased lines are billed with a flat monthly fee that varies according to circuit mileage. Packet-switched networks usually charge according to packet transfer volume.

To analyze further, if a company gets charged for connection time to the circuit-switched circuit whether they use it or not, they had better be sure that while they are connected, their data is steady and taking full advantage of available bandwidth.

One other switching difference is worth noting before some conclusions are drawn. In terms of the need to deliver bursty, transaction-oriented data quickly and reliably, call set-up time can be critical. With circuit-switched applications, a dial tone must be waited for and the number must be dialed and switched through the network. With connection-oriented packet-switched networks, call set-up packets must explore the network and build virtual circuit tables before the first bit of data is transferred. Datagrams don't require call set up but offer no guarantee of safe delivery.

By first carefully examining the characteristics of the data traffic to be transported, a network analyst can more reliably narrow the choices of possible network services to consider.

■ WIDE AREA NETWORKING TRANSMISSION

WAN transmission technologies and services fall into two overall categories. This categorization is based largely on WAN services as they are organized by and purchased from carriers.

- **Local loop transmission** provides bandwidth to users' residences and businesses, generally offering connectivity between these end points and the carrier network service of choice. Strictly speaking, the term *local loop* is a geographic designation.

- **Broadband transmission** usually refers to transmission services offering greater than 1.544-Mbps transmission rates that offer connectivity between network switches or between different carriers' network services. Large consumers of bandwidth may require broadband transmission services to their various corporate locations as access lines.

Local Loop Transmission Alternatives

Local loop transmission, sometimes referred to as "the last mile," provides a means for users' residences or businesses to connect to the voice or data services of their choice. As indicated in the wide area network architecture diagram (Figure 8-7), local loop services must be properly sized to provide sufficient bandwidth to deliver user payloads efficiently and cost-effectively. Although a wide variety of local loop transmission services are possible, among the most popular current or emerging local loop technologies are the following:

- POTS (plain old telephone service).
- ISDN (integrated services digital network).
- ADSL (asymmetric digital subscriber line).
- Cable TV.

POTS   **POTS** (plain old telephone service) was introduced in Chapter 4 as the default local loop technology. Users employ V.34 (28.8 Kbps) or V.34+ (33.6 Kbps) modems for transmitting data over the analog POTS network. Research indicates that optimal transmission rates are seldom achieved and rarely maintained due to line impairments and interference on analog transmission lines. POTS architecture and technology were detailed in Chapter 4.

ISDN   **ISDN** is somewhat of a phenomenon in the telecommunications industry. A constant topic of discussion, opinions on it range from consideration of it as a revolutionary breakthrough to absolute conviction that it won't ever materialize. ISDN has brought more humor to telecommunications than nearly any other topic with the various interpretations of the ISDN acronym such as **I**t **S**till **D**oes **N**othing or **I Still D**on't **N**eed it. ISDN has been described as a solution in search of an application. The need for dial-up access to Internet services at transmission rates greater than those available via POTS has significantly increased the interest in ISDN as a local loop transmission alternative.

Architecture: ISDN, sometimes known as **narrowband ISDN,** is a switched digital network service offering both voice and nonvoice connectivity to other ISDN endusers. Voice, video, and data are all transportable over a single ISDN connection. Depending on bandwidth requirements, voice, video, and data may even be transported simultaneously over a single network connection. The fact that ISDN is a switched service allows temporary connections to be constructed and terminated dynamically among a variety of ISDN sites unlike other digital services of similar bandwidth that are only available as static point-to-point circuits. Figure 8-11 illustrates a high-level view of possible ISDN use.

Narrowband ISDN is deliverable in two different service levels or interfaces. **Basic rate interface,** or **BRI,** is also referred to as **2B+D.** This 2B+D label refers to the channel configuration of the BRI service in which 2 **B**earer channels (64 Kbps each) and one **D**elta or data channel (16 Kbps) are combined into a 144-Kbps interface. The **bearer channels** are intended to "bear" or carry services such as voice, video, or data transport, while the **D channel** is intended for network management data for call set up and teardown, calling number identification and other ISDN-specific network signals. In some cases, 9.6 Kbps of the D channel may be used for additional X.25 packed-based transmissions in a service known as ISDN D Channel Packet service.

The use of this side D channel for carrying signal data is known as **out-of-band signaling** and is one of the key features of ISDN. The "out of band" refers to the fact that the signal control information does not have to be intermingled with the user data, thereby maximizing the available bandwidth for user data. Prior to ISDN, control information was passed over the network within the user channels in a technique known as **in-band signaling.** This is why many so-called ISDN services such as **automatic number identification** can be offered without ISDN.

A second ISDN service label known as **PRI** or **primary rate interface,** also known as **23B+D,** consists of 23 64-Kbps bearer channels and one 64-Kbps data channel for a combined bandwidth of 1.536 Mbps. With a small amount of additional overhead, PRI maps nicely onto the 1.544-Mbps **T-1** circuit. In Europe, ISDN is offered in a **30B+D** configuration yielding 1.984 Mbps. Additional overhead in this case maps nicely to the **E-1** (European Digital Signal Level 1) of 2.048 Mbps. Figure 8-12 summarizes the narrowband ISDN architectural information.

In some cases, users may want variable amounts of bandwidth depending on specific applications and circumstances. In such cases, **multirate ISDN** may be employed. Multirate ISDN uses a technique known as **inverse multiplexing** in which a

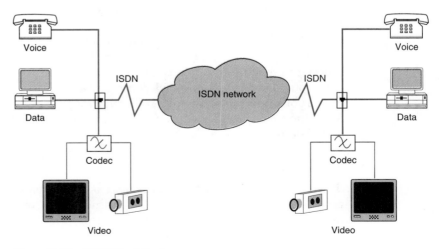

Figure 8-11   ISDN Architecture

Services	Video freeze-frame Voice Data	LAN Interconnect Full motion video Voice Data
Transport category	BRI (Basic Rate Interface)	PRI (Primary Rate Interface)
Transport capacity	2 B + D 2 · 64 Kbps 128 Kbps + 16 Kbps 16 Kbps 144 Kbps	23 B + D 23 · 64 Kbps B channels + 64 Kbps D channels 1.536 Mbps
Transport architecture	2-wire Dial-up	T-1
Inter-switch protocol and switching architecture	Signalling System 7 (SS7)	

Figure 8-12 Narrowband ISDN Architectural Information

collection of 64-Kbps B channels are dialed-up and combined together into a single logical channel of sufficient bandwidth to meet application needs such as videoconferencing. To ensure interoperability among inverse multiplexing devices, a standard known as **BONDING (bandwidth on demand interoperability group)** is supported by most ISDN inverse multiplexers.

Services: Earlier in its history, ISDN was widely criticized for spotty deployment leading to "islands of isolation" for those ISDN pioneers that decided to adopt the service. The ISDN coverage situation has improved significantly. In 1996 in the United States, roughly 75% of RBOC customers were able to access ISDN services, with a goal of 100% accessibility set for 1997. However, technical issues may keep this goal from fruition. Signaling requirements limit ISDN installations to residences and businesses within 18,000 ft, about 3.4 mi, from the ISDN switch. Another often overlooked service-related issue of ISDN is that ISDN customer premises equipment requires external ac power, unlike today's analog phones. Whereas today's POTS customers have grown accustomed to having phone service even during power failures, this would not be the case with ISDN-based phone service. Charges for ISDN vary from carrier to carrier although most charge a flat monthly rate plus a per-minute usage charge.

The heart of an ISDN network is the **ISDN switch.** Prior to 1992, two competing ISDN switches, **AT&T's 5ESS switch** and **Northern Telecom's DMS100 switch,** had slightly different specifications as to interfaces with **customer premises equipment (CPE).** Customer premises equipment that supported the AT&T specification would not operate on Northern Telecom switches and vice versa. In 1992, the Corporation for Open Systems International and the North American ISDN Users Forum launched an effort entitled Transcontinental ISDN Project 1992 (TRIP '92) to define necessary specifications to eliminate incompatibilities between ISDNs. The interoperability specifications developed is known as **NISDN-1 (National ISDN-1)** and defines a national standard for ISDN switches as well as interswitch communication.

Managerial Perspective

Although deployment and technology incompatibility difficulties may have been overcome, that is not to say that ISDN ordering and implementation is either easy or foolproof. To properly interface an end-user's ISDN equipment to a carrier's ISDN services, desired ISDN features must be specified. In some cases, end-user equipment such as remote access servers must be programmed with **service profile identifier numbers (SPID)** to properly identify the carrier's equipment with which the user equipment must interface. Depending on what combinations of voice, video, or data traffic a user wishes to transmit over ISDN, up to 20 or more **ISDN ordering codes (IOCs)** are possible. To try to further simplify this process, an alternative ordering code scheme known as **EZ-ISDN** has been proposed by the National ISDN Users Forum. However, some of the EZ codes duplicate IOCs whereas others do not correspond to existing IOCs, leaving network administrators to do their best to work with carrier personnel to see that required ISDN features are implemented.

Technology: Uses of ISDN fall into two broad categories of connectivity:

- Single user-to-office or Internet connectivity.
- Office-to-office connectivity.

Applications for single user-to-office or Internet connectivity include telecommuting, Internet services access, simultaneous voice and data technical support, and collaborative computing. Applications for office-to-office connectivity include remote office routing, LAN-to-LAN connectivity, and disaster recovery through the use of ISDN lines as a backup to failed leased lines.

To get voice or data onto the ISDN, the equivalent of an ISDN modem known as an **ISDN terminal adapter** must be employed. A terminal adapter is a type of ISDN CPE (customer premises equipment) that allows analog devices such as phones and fax machines to interface to the all-digital ISDN. Without the terminal adapter, special digital ISDN phones would have to be purchased to interface directly to the ISDN service. These ISDN terminal adapters are available both as PC cards for installation into a PC's expansion bus and as stand-alone units or are integrated into ISDN data/voice modems.

Practical Advice and Information

Software compatibility issues should not be overlooked. Just as asynchronous modems required compatible communications software with appropriate modem set-up strings, to have ISDN terminal adapters automatically dialing-up switched ISDN connections, compatible software and drivers must also be available. This software and drivers must be compatible with installed network operating systems as well as with the purchased terminal adapter. Most often this software complies with NDIS and ODI driver specifications and is supplied by the terminal adapter vendor.

A **network termination unit-1 (NTU-1)** or **(NT-1)** is required to physically connect the ISDN line to a user's ISDN CPE. Most integrated ISDN equipment includes built-in NT-1s, although stand-alone models are available.

To support office-to-office connectivity needs, ISDN terminal adapters and NT-1s are often integrated with internetworking technology such as routers and access servers. Although these devices will be explored further in Chapter 9, it is impor-

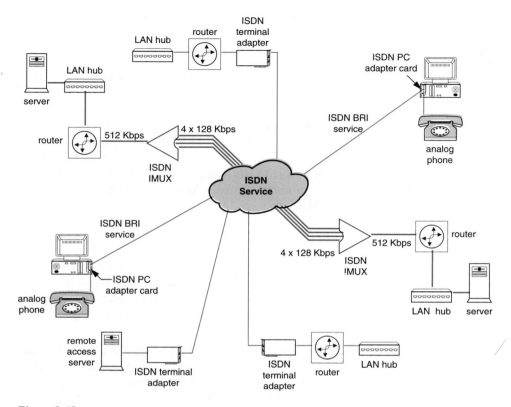

Figure 8-13   ISDN Technology

tant at this point to understand why ISDN is well suited to such applications. For occasional communications between offices for LAN-to-LAN connectivity or database updates, ISDN routers can be much more cost-effective than leased line routers. Although rates may vary according to location, a general rule of thumb is that ISDN access for office-to-office connectivity is cheaper than leased lines of equivalent bandwidth when connectivity needs are 4 hr/day or less. Figure 8-13 illustrates the installation and interaction of a variety of ISDN technology.

ADSL   An alternative digital local loop transmission technology is known as **asymmetric digital subscriber line** or **ADSL.** Unlike ISDN, ADSL works along with POTS for traditional voice services. In fact, ADSL works over POTS, at higher frequencies, on the same copper pair that currently carries voice transmission. Unlike using a modem on a voice line, ADSL does not interfere with voice services. That is to say, one could be connected to the Internet via ADSL and still make and receive voice phone calls on the same line.

Architecture: The term *asymmetric* in ADSL refers to the service's differing upstream (away from the user) and downstream (toward the user) bandwidths. The bandwidths and associated distance limitations from the carrier's central office of two of the most common ADSL implementations are listed in Figure 8-14. Other transmission speeds and distance limitations are possible.

To transmit high-bandwidth data simultaneously with circuit-switched voice conversation, ADSL employs frequency division multiplexing as described earlier in

ADSL Upstream	ADSL Downstream	Distance Limitation
150 Kbps	1.5 Mbps	18,000 ft
640 Kbps	6.0 Mbps	12,000 ft

Figure 8-14   ADSL Bandwidth Comparison

this chapter. While POTS occupies the lowest frequencies from 0 to 4 kHz, upstream data uses from about 25 to 200 kHz, whereas downstream data uses from about 250 kHz to 1.1 MHz.

There are currently two competing standards for how ADSL units manage bandwidth for data transmission:

- **Carrierless amplitude and phase (CAP)** treats the frequency range as a single channel and uses a technique similar to quadrature amplitude modulation to build constellations and avoid interference. CAP is a de facto standard, deployed in many trial ADSL units, and was developed by AT&T Paradyne.

- **Discrete multitone (DMT)** divides the 1 MHz of usable bandwidth in 4-kHz channels and adjusts the usage of any of the 4-kHz channels to minimize interference and noise. DMT has been approved as an ADSL standard (ANSI Standard T1.413) by the ANSI T1E1.4 working group.

At least three other DSL solutions are currently in various stages of development. All DSL solutions support simultaneous POTS:

- **VDSL (very high speed digital subscriber line)** provides 52 Mbps downstream and between 1.6 and 2.3 Mbps upstream over distances of up to only 1,000 ft. It is being explored primarily as a means to bring video-on-demand services to the home.

- **RADSL (rate-adaptive digital subscriber line)** is also able to adapt its data rate to the level of noise and interference on a given line. Currently, it is not able to support this adaptive rate on a dynamic basis, however.

- **SDSL (symmetric digital subscriber line)** differs from ADSL in that it offers upstream and downstream channels of equal bandwidth.

Technology: ADSL is an attractive alternative from a carrier's perspective because it does not require carriers to upgrade switching technology. Separate ADSL units, about the size of a modem, are deployed at customer sites and at the central office where voice frequencies are stripped off and passed to existing voice switching equipment and data frequencies are separated off and forwarded to an Internet service provider. The ADSL units provide an Ethernet 10BaseT interface for data that may be connected to the 10BaseT interface in the user's PC, to a shared 10BaseT hub, or to a 10BaseT router.

Carriers may need to recondition or replace some lines within the 18,000-ft distance limitation to provide ADSL services. ADSL equipment cannot work through bridge taps and loading coils that carriers have installed over the years to boost voice signals to residences beyond 18,000 ft from the closest central office. Figure 8-15 illustrates a typical installation of ADSL technology.

Practical Advice and Information

The author participated in an ADSL trial with GTE in West Lafayette, IN, from November 1996 through April 1997. ADSL really works very well. Downstream rates from the Internet were consistently at the expected 1.5-Mbps level and the data transmission had no effect on existing voice services.

Cable TV as a WAN Service   At first glance, it might seem that cable TV providers have ample bandwidth available for wide area data and voice transmission. When all of the facts are known, however, cable TV as a WAN service may not have such a distinct advantage over carrier-based services such as ADSL.

Architecture: Most cable TV systems were built for one-way broadcast transmission, downstream from the cable head end to the user's residences. To provide the necessary upstream bandwidth, cable providers have two basic options:

- Provide upstream bandwidth over POTS while providing downstream bandwidth in a coordinated fashion over the installed cable plant. This architecture does not deliver simultaneous voice capability as in ADSL architectures.

- Modify cable architecture to support simultaneous upstream and downstream transmission. Current implementations of such as architecture provide up to 30 Mbps downstream and 768 Kbps upstream.

However, providing upstream bandwidth is only one of the architectural obstacles that cable providers must overcome. Whereas phone carriers provide voice service via a switched-media architecture (circuit switching), cable companies provide

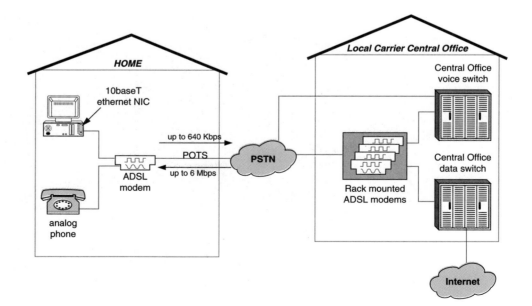

Figure 8-15   ADSL Technology Implementation

cable service via a shared-media architecture in which an entire neighborhood may be served by the same shared coaxial cable. Therefore, although 30-Mbps downstream bandwidth may sound impressive, one needs to really know among how many users that 30 Mbps will be shared. The access methodologies for sharing cable bandwidth are being standardized as **IEEE 802.14** cable network specifications.

Cable companies, like voice-service carriers, must either develop their own Internet access services or buy these services from an existing Internet service provider to provide transparent Internet access to their customers.

Technology: Cable modems will be provided by cable companies and will connect to standard RG-59 coax for the network connection while offering a 10BaseT Ethernet connection for users' local data access. Figure 8-16 illustrates a typical cable modem network implementation.

Broadband Transmission

T-1   To effectively establish and manage long-distance telecommunications links between end-user locations as well as between multiple vendors, standards were required to outline both the size and organization of high-capacity digital communications links between carriers. The standard high-capacity digital transmission circuit in North America is known as **T-1** with a bandwidth of 1.544 Mbps. In other parts of the world, the standard high-capacity digital circuit is known as an **E-1** with a bandwidth of 2.048 Mbps.

T-1 Framing: The T-1 circuit is divided into twenty-four 64-Kbps channels to allow more flexible use of the 1.544 Mbps of bandwidth. In this manner, some of the 24 channels can be used for voice while others are used for data. Differentiating between channels is accomplished through a technique known as **framing,** which is

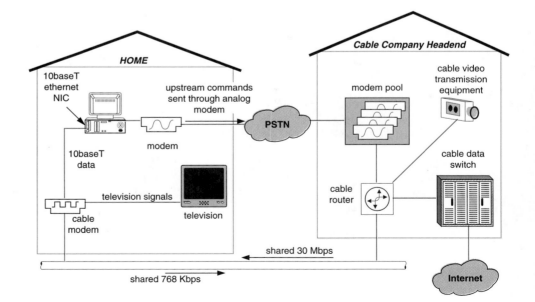

Figure 8-16   Cable Modem Installation

really an adaptation of the TDM (time division multiplexing) techniques that were explored earlier in this chapter.

Recalling the voice digitization technique known as pulse code modulation that was introduced in Chapter 4, eight bits are required to transmit the PCM sampled amplitude of an analog signal. Since 8000 samples/sec are required to ensure quality transmission of digitized voice and each sample requires eight bits to represent that sampled bandwidth in binary (1s and 0s) notation, 64,000 bits/sec is the required bandwidth for transmission of voice digitized via PCM. A DS-0 circuit has a transmission capacity of exactly 64 Kbps. Twenty-four DS-0s are combined to form a T-1, yielding the fact that a T-1 can carry 24 simultaneous voice conversations digitized via PCM. However, it is important to note that any or all of these 64-Kbps channels could just as easily carry data traffic or any other type of digitized traffic.

In a technique known as **periodic framing** or **synchronous TDM,** 24 channels of eight bits each (192 bits total) are arranged in a **frame.** Each group of eight bits represents one sampling of voice or data traffic to be transmitted on its associated channel. Each group of eight bits is known as a **time slot.** Twenty-four time slots are grouped into a frame, sometimes also known as a **D-4** frame. Each frame is terminated with a **framing bit** in the 193rd position. Such a frame, sometimes known as a D-4 frame, is illustrated in Figure 8-17.

Rather than just using the 193rd bit as a simple frame marker, techniques have been developed to combine the values of sequential framing bits into meaningful arrangements that provide management and error control capabilities for the T-1 transmission service. A group of 12 frames is known as a **superframe** and a group of 24 frames is known as an **ESF** or **extended superframe.** Superframes and extended superframes are illustrated in Figure 8-18.

Digital Service Hierarchy: The 1.544-Mbps standard is part of a hierarchy of standards known as the **Digital Service Hierarchy** or **DS** standards. These standards are independent of the transmission services that may deliver the required bandwidth of one of the standards. For instance, technically speaking, DS-1 is not the same as T-1 but the two terms are very often used interchangeably. To be exact, a **T-1** transmission service delivers **DS-1** equivalent bandwidth. Figure 8-19 summarizes

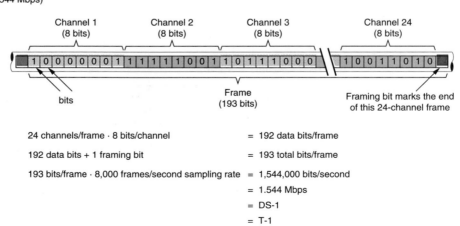

T-1 Transmission Service
(1.544 Mbps)

24 channels/frame · 8 bits/channel = 192 data bits/frame

192 data bits + 1 framing bit = 193 total bits/frame

193 bits/frame · 8,000 frames/second sampling rate = 1,544,000 bits/second
= 1.544 Mbps
= DS-1
= T-1

Figure 8-17 T-1 Frame Layout

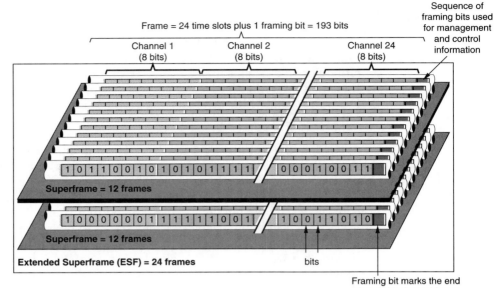

Figure 8-18   Superframes and Extended Superframes

Digital service (DS) hierarchy.

Digital Service Level	Number of Voice Channels	Transmission Rate	Corresponding Transmission Service
DS-0	1	64 Kbps	DS-0 or switched 64K
DS-1	24	1.544 Mbps	T-1 or switched T-1
DS-1C	48	3.152 Mbps	T-1C
DS-2	96	6.312 Mbps	T-2
DS-3	672	44.736 Mbps	T-3
DS-4	4032	274.176 Mbps	T-4

CCITT digital hierarchy.

Digital Service Level	Number of Voice Channels	Transmission Rate	Corresponding Transmission Service
1	30	2.048 Mbps	E-1
2	120	8.448 Mbps	E-2
3	480	34.368 Mbps	E-3
4	1920	139.264 Mbps	E-4
5	7680	565.148 Mbps	E-5

Figure 8-19   Digital Service Hierarchy and CCITT Standards

the Digital Service Hierarchy for North America as well as the CCITT standards for international digital service. Although numerous transmission service designators may be listed, T-1 and T-3 are by far the most common service levels delivered. T-1 service is most often delivered via four copper wires (two twisted pair), and T-3 service is most commonly delivered via optical fiber media.

T-1 Architecture: T-1 lines are examples of leased or private lines, also known as dedicated lines, and differ from circuit-switched line usage in several ways:

With leased lines there is no dial tone. The circuit is always open and available. The end-user is billed for the circuit 24 hr/day, 7 days/week. With leased lines, it is even more imperative than with circuit-switched lines to have sufficient data traffic to utilize as close to 100% capacity as possible 100% of the time to assure cost-justification of circuit costs. Higher bandwidth leased lines cost more per month than lower bandwidth leased lines.

Before the advent of high-speed packet services and high-speed modems that worked over dial-up (circuit-switched) lines, leased lines were the only available means of high-speed data transfer over a wide area network. Network managers did their best to get the most out of these relatively expensive leased lines through the use of STDMs, explained earlier in this chapter.

Leased lines do not get set up in a matter of seconds in a manner such as circuit-switched lines. In most cases, 4–6 week lead time is required for the installation of a leased line. Leased lines are constructed to circumvent central office switch facilities so as not to monopolize limited circuit-switching capacity.

In some cases the multiple 64-Kbps channels within a T-1 transport circuit can be manipulated or utilized on an individual basis. A service that offers such capability is known as **fractional T-1** or **FT-1.** The fact of the matter is that the full T-1 circuit must be physically delivered to the customer premises, but only a given number of 64-Kbps channels within the T-1 are enabled. Fractional T-1 is really just a creative marketing practice on the part of the carriers as a means of increasing sales of digital transmission services.

T-1 Technology: To access T-1 service offered by carriers users may use a variety of T-1 technology. The most basic piece of T-1 technology is the **T-1 CSU/DSU** (channel service unit/data service unit) that interfaces directly to the carrier's termination of the T-1 service on the customer premises. Physically, a T-1 is delivered as a four-wire service (two for transmit, two for receive) most often terminated in an **RJ-48c** jack. Most T-1 CSU/DSUs have a corresponding RJ-48c jack to connect to the carrier's RJ-48c jack. The CSU/DSU will transfer the 1.544 Mbps of T-1 bandwidth to local devices such as routers, PBXs, or channel banks via V.35, RS-530, or RS-449 high-speed serial connectors or RJ-45 connectors for direct connection to 10BaseT or 100BaseT Ethernet networks. Because these T-1 CSU/DSUs play such an important role in a corporation's wide area network, they are often able to communicate status and alarm information to enterprise network management systems via SNMP (simple network management protocol).

T-1 multiplexers are able to aggregate several lower speed data or voice channels into a single composite T-1 link. T-1 MUXs often have CSU/DSUs built in and require all data input channels to be in digital format adhering to such transmission standards as RS-232, RS-449, or V.35. Voice input to T-1 muxes must already be digitized in a digital voice PBX and output in a transmission format known as DSX-1. **Fractional T-1 multiplexers** are able to use less than the full 1.544 Mbps of composite T-1 output bandwidth. Obviously, FT-1 multiplexers make good business sense if less than 1.544 Mbps of composite bandwidth is sufficient, thereby saving on monthly carrier charges. A **T-1 IMUX** or **inverse multiplexer** is able to combine multiple T-1 output lines to provide high-bandwidth requirements for such application as LAN-to-LAN communication via routers or high-quality videoconferencing.

A **T-1 channel bank** is similar to but more flexible than a T-1 MUX. A T-1 channel bank is an open-chassis-based piece of equipment with a built-in CSU/DSU to which a variety of data and voice input channel cards can be flexibly added. Input data channels may be synchronous or asynchronous at a variety of different speeds and serial transmission protocols. Voice channels may accept analog voice traffic to be digitized by a variety of voice digitization techniques. Output of a T-1 channel bank is typically just a single T-1. Finally **T-1 switches** can be employed by companies wishing to build their own private wide area networks. T-1 switches are able to switch entire T-1 or particular DS-0s among and between other T-1 switches to flexibly deliver voice and data to a variety of corporate locations. Figure 8-20 illustrates the implementation of a variety of T-1 technology.

SONET   **SONET (synchronous optical network)** is an optical transmission service delivering multiple channels of data from various sources thanks to periodic framing or TDM much like T-1 transmission service. The differences between T-1 and SONET transmission services lie chiefly in the higher transmission capacity of

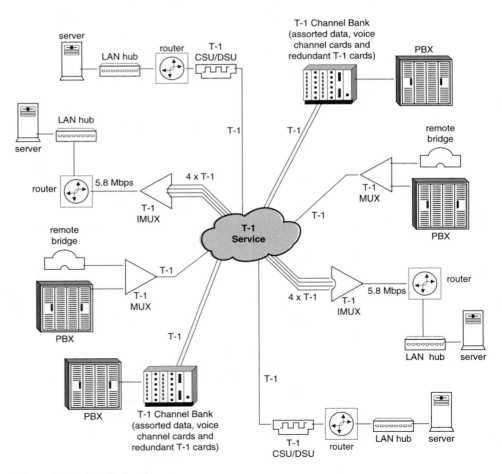

Figure 8-20   T-1 Technology

SONET due to its fiber optic media and the slightly different framing techniques used to channelize this higher transmission capacity.

Just as the Digital Service Hierarchy defined levels of service for traditional digital service, optical transmission has its own hierarchy of service levels. Rather than being designated as DS levels, optical transmission is categorized by **OC** or **optical carrier** levels and illustrated in Figure 8-21. Because SONET will eventually carry voice, video, and image as well as data, the basic unit of measure is referred to as an **octet** of 8 bits rather than a byte of 8 bits. Byte is usually reserved for referring to data only and is often synonymous with a character.

SONET Framing: In many ways, SONET framing is the same as T-1 framing. The basic purpose of each is to establish markers with which to identify individual channels. Because of the higher bandwidth of SONET (51.84-Mbps OC-1 vs. 1.544-Mbps T-1) and potential for sophisticated mixed-media services, more overhead is reserved surrounding each frame than the single bit reserved every 193rd character in a T-1 frame.

Rather than fitting 24 channels per frame delineated by a single framing bit, a single SONET frame or **row** is delineated by 3 octet of overhead for control information followed by 87 octets of **payload.** Nine of these 90 octet rows are grouped together to form a **SONET superframe.** The 87 octets of payload per row in each of the time rows of the superframe is known as the **synchronous payload envelope** or **SPE.** The electrical equivalent of the **OC-1,** the optical SONET superframe standard, is known as the **STS-1** or synchronous transport signal. The SONET frame structure is illustrated in Figure 8-22.

Virtual Tributaries in SONET: Unlike the T-1 frame with its 24 predefined 8-bit channels, SONET is flexible in its definition of the use of its payload area. It can map DS-0 (64 Kbps) channels into the payload area just as easily as it can map an entire T-1 (1.544 Mbps). These flexibly defined channels within the payload area are known as **virtual tributaries** or **VTs.**

For instance, a T-1 would be mapped into a virtual tributary standard known as **VT-1.5,** with a bandwidth of 1.728 Mbps, the difference between that figure and the 1.544 Mbps T-1 being accounted for by the additional SONET overhead.

The virtual tributaries of SONET are equivalent to circuit-switched transmission

SONET's OC (Optical Carrier) standards

Digital Service Level	Transmission Rate	
OC-1	51.84	Mbps
OC-3	155.52	Mbps
OC-9	466.56	Mbps
OC-12	622.08	Mbps
OC-18	933.12	Mbps
OC-24	1.244	Gbps
OC-36	1.866	Gbps
OC-48	2.488	Gbps

Figure 8-21 Optical Carrier Levels

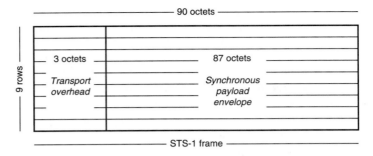

90 octets/row · 8 bits/octet = 720 bits/row

720 bits/row · 9 rows/frame = 6,480 bits/frame

6,480 bits/frame · 8,000 frames/second (sampling rate) = 51,840,000 bits/second

Transfer Rate of 51.84 Mbits/second

Figure 8-22   SONET Framing

services. In addition to the 3 octets/row of transport overhead in OC-1, there is also a variable amount of path overhead embedded within the SPE to keep track of which virtual tributaries start where within the SPE payload boxcar. This path overhead brings the total overhead to about 4% before any additional overhead embedded within the SPE payload boxcar is considered.

SONET Deployment: SONET services are currently available within many major metropolitan areas. Accessing such services requires the local carrier to bring the fiber-based ring directly to a corporate location and to assign dedicated bandwidth to each SONET customer. Because of the limited geographic scope of most SONET services, it is most appropriate for those organizations with very high bandwidth needs (OC-1 to OC-48) between multiple locations within the limited SONET service area. Such companies would typically be employing multiple T-3s and looking at SONET as an attractive upgrade path.

Add-drop multiplexers, sometimes referred to as broadband bandwidth managers, are the customary type of hardware used to access SONET services. Such devices are often capable of adding several T-1 or T-3 digital signals together and converting those combined signals into a single, channelized, optical SONET signal. In some cases, ATM switches are equipped with SONET interfaces for direct access to either a local SONET ring or commercial SONET services.

Another key advantage of SONET is the fault tolerance and reliability afforded by its fiber-based architecture. In the event of a network failure, traffic can be rerouted. The two principal architectures for SONET deployment are

- Unidirectional path-switched rings (UPSR) in which all users share transmission capacity around the ring rather than using dedicated segments.

- Bidirectional line-switched rings (BLSR) in which each user's traffic is specifically rerouted in the case of a fiber failure.

Conclusion: So What Is SONET?   SONET is a service-independent transport function that carry the services of the future such as B-ISDN (broadband ISDN) or HDTV (high-definition television) as easily as it can carry the circuit-switched traffic of today such as DS-1 and DS-3. It has extensive performance monitoring and fault location capabilities. For instance, if SONET senses a transmission problem, it can switch traffic to an alternate path in as little as 50 msec (1000ths of a second). This network survivability is due to SONET's redundant or dual-ring physical architecture. Based on the OC hierarchy of standard optical interfaces, SONET has the potential to deliver multigigabyte bandwidth transmission capabilities to end-users.

Managerial Perspective

SONET availability is currently limited to large metropolitan areas in most cases. SONET availability implies that a high-capacity, dual-ring, fiber optic cable based transmission service is available between the customer premises and the carrier central office. SONET services cost about 20% more than conventional digital services of identical bandwidth. The benefit of the 20% premium is the network survivability offered by SONET's dual-ring architecture. Unless a corporation has identified mission-critical network transmission requiring fault-tolerant circuits, SONET's benefits may not be worth the added expense.

■ WIDE AREA NETWORK SERVICES

As illustrated in Figure 8-7, the foundation of any wide area network architecture is dependent upon the particular switching and transmission architectures employed therein. Wide area network services that are offered to consumers are dependent upon these underlying transmission and switching architectures. Switching architectures and transmission architectures have already been reviewed in this chapter. In this section, different wide area network services will be reviewed while explaining the business aspects of these services, the underlying switching and transmission architectures required, and the technology employed to interface to such services.

X.25

X.25 is an international CCITT standard that defines the interface between terminal equipment (DTE) and any packet-switched network (the cloud). It is important to note that X.25 does *not* define standards for what goes on *inside* the cloud. One of the most common misconceptions is that the X.25 standard defines the specifications for a packet-switching network. On the contrary, X.25 only assures that an end-user can depend on how to get information into and out of the packet-switched network.

X.25 is a three-layer protocol stack corresponding to the first three layers of the OSI model. The total effect of the three-layer X.25 protocol stack is to produce packets in a standard format acceptable by any X.25-compliant public packet-switched network. X.25 offers network transparency to the upper layers of the OSI protocol stack. Figure 8-23 illustrates the relationship of the X.25 protocol stack to the OSI model.

Architecture   The X.25 standard consists of a three-layer protocol that ensures transparent network access to OSI layers 4–7. In other words, applications running on one computer that wish to talk to another computer do not need to be concerned with anything having to do with the packet-switched network connecting the two computers. In this way, the X.25-compliant packet-switched network is nothing more than a transparent delivery service between computers.

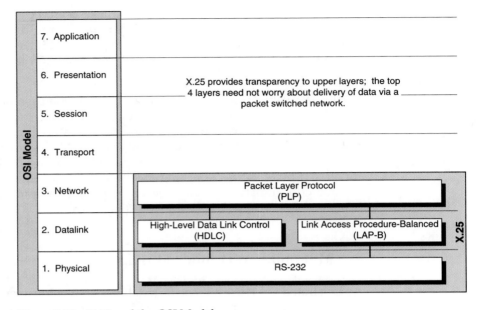

Figure 8-23 X.25 and the OSI Model

The physical layer (layer 1) protocol of the X.25 standard is most often RS-232 or some other serial transmission standard. The data-link layer (layer 2) protocol is known as **HDLC** or **high-level data-link control.** HDLC is very similar to IBM's SDLC in structure. Functionally, HDLC accomplishes the same things as any other data-link layer protocol, such as Ethernet or token ring:

- Organizes data into structured frames that may contain more than one packet.

- Ensures reliable delivery of data via error checking.

- Provides point-to-point data delivery between adjacent nodes.

Figure 8-24 illustrates a HDLC frame. In the case of HDLC and X.25, error checking is achieved via a 16-bit frame check sequence, whereas the control field transports important management information such as frame sequence numbers and requests for retransmission. Newer implementations of X.25 use **LAP-B,** or **link access procedure-balanced,** a subset and functional equivalent of the full HDLC frame, as a data-link layer protocol. The network layer (layer 3) X.25 protocol is known as **PLP** or **packet-layer protocol.** Remembering that the job of any OSI layer 3, network layer protocol is the establishment, maintenance, and termination of

Flag	Address field	Control field	Information field	Frame check sequence	Flag
8 bits	8 bits	8 bits	Variable	16 bits	8 bits

Figure 8-24 X.25 Data-Link Layer Protocol: HDLC

Standard	Explanation/Importance
X.121—global addressing scheme	As packet-switching networks have become gobal in nature, a global addressing scheme is necessary to allow transparent global access to these networks. X.121 defines zone codes, country codes, and PSN codes within countries. This four-digit global addressing prefix is followed by up to ten digits to uniquely identify the destination address node.
X.28 and X.32—dial-up access directly into PADs	X.28 (asynchronous) and X.32 (synchronous) define standards that allow users to dial-up a PAD and subsequently place a call over the packet-switched network.
X.75—internetworking packet-switched networks	X.25 defined the interface from the end-user device into the packet-switched network cloud. A standard was required to define a standardized interface between different packet-switched networks. X.75 is that standard and has been referred to as the packet-switched network gateway protocol.

Figure 8-25   X.25-Related Standards

end-to-end connections, PLP's main job is to establish, maintain, and terminate virtual circuits within a connection-oriented packet-switched network.

Figure 8-25 lists important standards related to X.25 and a brief explanation of their importance.

Technology   X.25 requires data to be properly packetized by the time it reaches the cloud. Terminals and computers that do not possess the X.25 protocol stack internally to produce properly formatted packets employ a **PAD** or **packet assembler/disassembler** to packetize their output data into X.25 format for entry into the cloud. Such devices usually have several (4–16) RS-232 serial ports for input from PCs, terminals, or host computer ports that wish to transmit traffic via a carrier's X.25 service. These input ports are typically asynchronous. The single composite output port is synchronous and is most often limited to 2 Mbps although most X.25 carrier services are limited to about 9.6 Kbps. This seemingly excess composite output capacity is due to the fact that many X.25 PADs are also capable of accessing higher speed packet-switched network services such as frame relay, which is explained in the next section. Inside the carrier's X.25 cloud, X.25 switches are connected together in a mesh topology and are most often connected to each other via high-speed digital transmission services such as T-1. Figure 8-26 illustrates X.25 technology implementation.

Frame Relay

Figure 8-27 illustrates the relationship between a packet-switched network service such as X.25 and other packet-switched and circuit-switched network services. While the differences between circuit switching and packet switching have already been explained, the differences among the various packet-switched network services are based largely around transmission speed and overhead.

To understand how these packet services could be made faster, the source of the overhead or slowness of the existing X.25 packet-switching networks must first be

X.25 Implementation

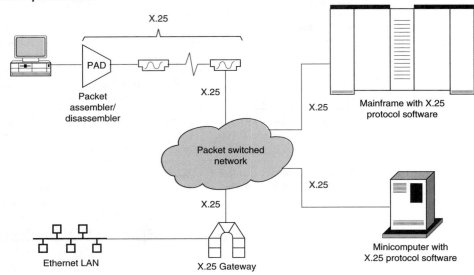

Figure 8-26   X.25 Technology Implementation

examined. Recall from the previous discussion of connection-oriented packet-switched networks that error checking and retransmission requests were done on a point-to-point basis between adjacent packet switches. This point-to-point oriented error checking is sometimes also called hop-by-hop error checking.

At the time X.25 was first introduced about 20 or so years ago, the long-distance circuits connecting the X.25 packet switches were not nearly as error free as they are today. Transmission errors are measured by **bit error rate (BER).** As a result, to guarantee end-to-end error-free delivery, it was necessary to check for errors and re-quest retransmissions on a point-to-point or hop-by-hop basis at every X.25 packet switch in the network. Although necessary, this constant error checking and correc-tion added significant overhead, and therefore delay, to the X.25 packet transmis-sion process.

Today's long-distance digital transmission systems are largely fiber based and far less error prone than those of 20 years ago. As a result, new packet-switching

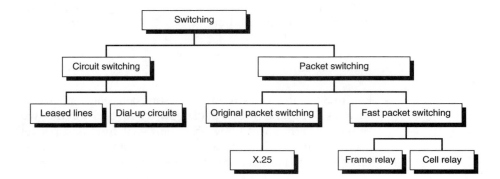

Figure 8-27   Switched Network Services Hierarchy

methodologies such as **frame relay** were introduced that sought to take advantage of the decreased bit error rate on today's transmission systems. The basic design philosophy is simple:

- Given the quality of the transmission system, stop all point-to-point error correction and flow control within the network itself and let the end nodes worry about it!

The end nodes, such as PCs, servers, mainframes, etc., would use higher level (layers 4–7) protocols to perform their own error checking. In the case of a PC, this would likely be a sliding window file transfer protocol. This philosophy works fine as long as the basic assumption, the low bit error rate of today's transmission system, holds true. If not, then retransmissions are end-to-end, spanning the entire network, rather than point-to-point between adjacent packet switches.

Architecture

Error Detection and Correction: It is important to distinguish between **error detection** and **error correction.** Both frame relay and X.25 perform point-to-point error detection by comparing generated **CRCs (cyclic redundancy checks)** with transmitted CRCs, also known as **FCSs (frame check sequences).** The difference and resultant processing time savings for frame relay occur in the action taken upon the detection of an error.

An X.25 switch will always send either a positive ACK or negative NAK acknowledgment upon the receipt of each packet and will not forward additional packets until it receives an ACK or NAK. If a NAK is received, the packet received in error will be retransmitted. Packets are stored in X.25 switches in case a NAK is received, necessitating retransmission. This is why X.25 packet switching is sometimes called a **store-and-forward** switching methodology.

On the other hand, if a frame relay switch detects an error when it compares the computed vs. transmitted FCSs, the bad frame is simply discarded. The correction and request for retransmission of bad frames are left to the end node devices—PCs, modems, and computers—and their error correction protocols. Technically speaking, in frame relay, there is point-to-point error detection, but only end-to-end error correction. Although X.25 networks were typically limited to 9.6 Kbps, frame relay network typically offer transmission speeds of T-1 (1.544 Mbps) and occasionally T-3 (44.736 Mbps). Figure 8-28 illustrates point-to-point vs. end-to-end correction.

In terms of the OSI model, the difference between X.25 packet switching and frame relay is simple. Frame relay is a two-layer protocol stack (physical and data link) whereas X.25 is a three-layer protocol stack (physical, data-link, and network). There is no network layer processing in frame relay, accounting for the decreased processing time and increased throughput rate.

Flow Control: Although end node devices such as PCs and modems can handle the error detection and correction duties shed by the frame relay network with relative ease, **flow control** is another matter. End nodes can only manage flow control between themselves and whatever frame relay network access device they are linked to. There is no way for end nodes to either monitor or manage flow control within the frame relay network itself. Some frame relay switch vendors have implemented their own flow control methodologies, which is sufficient if only that vendor's switches are being used.

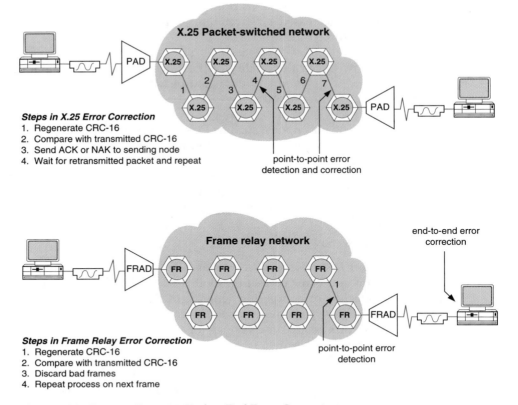

Steps in X.25 Error Correction
1. Regenerate CRC-16
2. Compare with transmitted CRC-16
3. Send ACK or NAK to sending node
4. Wait for retransmitted packet and repeat

point-to-point error
detection and correction

Steps in Frame Relay Error Correction
1. Regenerate CRC-16
2. Compare with transmitted CRC-16
3. Discard bad frames
4. Repeat process on next frame

point-to-point error
detection

end-to-end error
correction

Figure 8-28   Point-to-Point vs. End-to-End Error Correction

Referring to the frame relay frame structure diagram in Figure 8-29, there are three bits in the frame definition known as **BECN, FECN,** and **DE,** which stand for **backward explicit congestion notification, forward explicit congestion notification,** and **discard eligibility.** BECN is sent back to the original source user to tell the FRAD to throttle back its transmission onto the frame relay network whereas FECN warns the destination recipient of this frame of the congested network conditions. If the discard eligible field is set, then the carrier managing the frame relay network is granted permission to discard such frames to relieve network congestion. These bits are the elements of a scheme to allow frame relay devices to dynamically adjust flow control. Some frame relay devices even have the ability to read or write to these fields.

**Practical Advice
and Information**

The only problem is, what action should be taken by a given device in the event that any of these bits indicate a flow control problem has not necessarily been agreed upon or uniformly implemented by frame relay technology manufacturers. Unless you were responsible for setting up your own frame relay network, you might not think much of this problem. On the other hand, it represents the need to have a healthy dose of cynicism when shopping for data communications devices, even when those devices "support all applicable standards." If standards are not uniformly implemented by technology manufacturers, they are of little use.

HEADER									TRAILER	

(Figure diagram)

FLAG	unique bit sequence that indicates beginning of frame
EA	extended address -- standard address is two octets, this bit setting can extend address to 3 or 4 octets
C or R	command or response -- application specific -- not used by standard frame relay protocol
DLCI	data-link connection identifier (address) -- identifies particular logical connection over a single physical path
EA	extended address -- standard address is two octets, this bit setting can extend address to 3 or 4 octets
DE	discard eligibility -- used by frame relay switches for flow control
BECN	backward explicit congestion notification -- used by frame relay switches for flow control
FECN	forward explicit congestion notification -- used by frame relay switches for flow control
DLCI	data-link connection identifier (address) -- identifies particular logical connection over a single physical path
INFORMATION	minimum number of octets - enough to make total frame at least 7 octets long. Maximum number of octets is 8000. Carries upper layer data
FRAME CHECK	frame check sequence for error detection - also called cyclic redundancy check
FLAG	unique bit sequence that indicates end of frame

Figure 8-29 Frame Relay Frame Layout

In a similar manner to X.25 packet formation, frame relay frames are formatted within the FRAD or in computers or PCs that have frame relay protocol software loaded to build frame relay frames directly. The **frames** that a frame relay network forwards are variable in length, with the maximum frame transporting nearly 8000 characters at once. Combining these potentially large, variable-length frames with the low overhead and faster processing of the frame relay switching delivers a key characteristic of the frame relay network: High throughput with low delay.

Figure 8-29 illustrates the frame definition for frame relay networks. This frame definition is said to be a subset of the LAP-D protocol. **LAP-D** stands for **link access procedure-D channel,** where the D channel refers to the 16-Kbps Delta channel in BRI ISDN.

The variable-length frames illustrated in Figure 8-29 can be a shortcoming however. Because there is no guarantee as to the length of a frame, there can be no guarantee as to how quickly a given frame can be forwarded through the network and delivered to its destination. In the case of data, this lack of guaranteed time delivery or maximum delay is of little consequence.

However, in the case of more time-sensitive information such as voice or video, it could be a real issue. Digitized voice or video can be packetized or put into frames like any other data. The problem arises when framed voice and video do not arrive in a predictable timed fashion for conversion back to understandable voice and video. As a result, frame relay is often described as a data-only service. That's not exactly true. Options do exist to transport digitized, compressed voice transmissions via a frame relay network. However, most voice over frame relay technology is proprietary, requiring all FRADs and/or switches that support voice over frame relay to be purchased from the same vendor.

Virtual Circuits: Frame relay networks most often employ **PVCs (permanent virtual circuits)** to forward frames from source to destination through the frame relay cloud. **SVC (switched virtual circuit)** standards have been defined but are not readily available from all carriers. Remembering that an SVC is like a dial-up call, to transport data over an SVC-based frame relay network, a LAN NOS such as Net-Ware or Windows NT would have to communicate call set-up protocol information to the frame relay network before sending a data request or transaction update to a remote server.

Frame relay transmission rates are commonly as high as a 1.544 Mbps and occasionally as high as 44.736 Mbps. Remembering that multiple PVCs can exist within the frame relay network cloud, another key advantage of frame relay over circuit-switched options such as leased lines is the ability to have multiple PVCs supported from only one access line. From a cost justification standpoint, this would allow a frame relay user to replace multiple leased line connections with a single access line to a frame relay network. Remember also that frame relay network charges are based on usage, whereas circuit-switched leased lines charges are based on flat monthly fees whether they are used or not. Figure 8-30 illustrates the concept of multiple PVCs per single access line.

Dynamic Bandwidth Allocation: Another important characteristic afforded by the many transmission options available with the mesh network of the frame relay cloud is the ability to allocate bandwidth dynamically. In other words, up to the transmission limit of the access line and the circuits between the frame relay

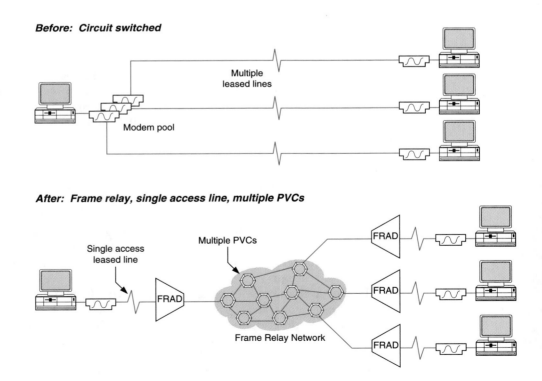

Figure 8-30   Multiple PVCs per Access Line

switches, the frame relay network will handle bursts of data by simply assembling and forwarding more frames per second onto the frame relay network, over multiple PVCs if required.

This ability to handle bursty traffic is especially appealing for LAN interconnection. Inter-LAN communication tends to be bursty with intermittent requests for data and file transfers. Remembering that this inter-LAN communication should be as transparent as possible, frame relay's ability to handle bursty traffic by dynamic bandwidth allocation is especially appealing. In the case of frame relay network access for LAN interconnection, the internetwork bridge or router is often integrated with a frame relay assembler/disassembler or frame relay protocol software.

A word of caution however. "Bursty" traffic is not easy to define. How large a burst, in terms of maximum bandwidth demand, and of what duration is the frame relay network expected to be able to handle? An attempt has been made to structure burstiness with the following two terms:

- **CIR** or **committed information rate** refers to the minimum bandwidth guaranteed to users for "normal" transmission.

- **CBS** or **committed burst size** defines the extent to which a user can exceed their CIR over a period of time. If a user's CBS is exceeded, the frame relay network reserves the right to discard frames in order to deliver guaranteed CIRs to other users.

Protocol Independence and Network-to-Network Interface: Another frame relay feature that is appealing for LAN interconnection is the fact that frame relay merely encapsulates user data into frames and forwards it to the destination. Frame relay is merely a delivery service. It does not process user data and is therefore protocol independent or protocol transparent. It can forward SNA/SDLC traffic just as easily as it can forward TCP/IP or Novell IPX traffic.

An issue hindering widespread global use of frame relay is the need for better coordination among the different frame relay network vendors in order to offer transparent access between them in a manner similar to the standard interfaces developed by phone companies for voice traffic. A conceptual standard known as **NNI** or **network-to-network interface** would be the functional equivalent of the X.75 internetwork standard for X.25 packet-switched networks.

Technology As can be seen in Figure 8-28, the technology configuration for the X.25 packet-switched network and the frame relay network is amazingly similar. In the case of the frame-relay network, the access device is known as a **FRAD** or **FAD** (frame relay or frame assembler/disassembler) rather than a PAD, and the switching device is known as a **frame relay switch** rather than a packet or X.25 switch. FRADs are also known as **frame relay access devices.** FRADs and frame relay switches are available in numerous configurations and integrated with numerous other internetworking devices such as bridges, routers, multiplexers, and concentrators.

Conclusion: What Is Frame Relay? First and foremost, frame relay is an interface specification. The LAP-D data-link layer protocol defines a frame structure that contains destination address, error checking, control information, and user data all in a single protocol layer frame. It is this interface specification that allows faster processing to take place within the frame relay network.

Secondly, frame relay is also a network service, offered by several regional and long-distance phone companies primarily for the purpose of LAN interconnection. Frame relay's ability to dynamically allocate bandwidth over a single access line to the frame relay network makes it particularly well suited for the bursty nature of inter-LAN traffic. Private frame relay networks can be established as well.

Finally, frame relay could also be considered a switching architecture. What goes on inside the frame relay network cloud remains transparent to end-users as long as the interface specification causes frame relay frames to enter the cloud and frame relay frames to exit the cloud. However, there are true frame relay switches designed specifically to forward frame relay frames at an optimal rate. A mesh network comprised of these "native" frame relay switches could legitimately be considered a switching architecture.

SMDS

SMDS, switched multimegabit data service, is a connectionless network service delivering switched LAN internetworking and data dial tone in a metropolitan area network deployment while adhering to the **IEEE 802.6** and **DQDB (distributed queue dual bus)** protocols by delivering fixed-length cells of data to their destinations via a SONET transmission system at speeds up to T-3 (45 Mbps). Architecturally, it differs from frame relay primarily in the fact that it is a connectionless service and does not support virtual circuits.

Managerial Perspective

Practically speaking, SMDS is losing the WAN services battle to frame relay. In 1996, 27% of WAN services customers purchased frame relay services whereas only 1% purchased SMDS. Projections for 1999 call for frame relay usage to increase to 47% whereas SMDS is projected to increase to only 6% of WAN service customers, although some studies predict no market growth whatsoever. Part of the reason for the small market share has to do with a lack of support from carriers. Among the local service providers, only Ameritech, Bell Atlantic, Bell South, PacTel, GTE, and Southwestern Bell offer SMDS services and MCI is the only long-distance carrier offering SMDS.

The service advantage that SMDS possesses over frame relay due to its connectionless architecture is its ability to broadcast to multiple sites by sending data only once to the SMDS service provider. SMDS is best suited for highly interconnected or meshed networks carrying high-capacity data traffic. SMDS advocates have submitted proposals to the ATM Forum proposing protocols that will allow SMDS to be transmitted over ATM networks. In this manner, SMDS popularity may stand a better chance of improvement by piggybacking on the increasing popularity of ATM.

Cell Relay—ATM

Architecture   As seen in Figure 8-27, **cell relay** is another "fast packet" switching methodology and a key part of future network architectures. **ATM** or **asynchronous transfer mode** is the widely accepted standardized cell relay transmission service. The key physical difference between cell relay and frame relay is that, unlike the variable-length frame relay frames, all cells in ATM networks are of a fixed length, 53 octets long (an octet is 8 bits). Forty-eight of the octets per cell are reserved for user data or information from higher layer protocols and the remaining five octets are used for header information.

ATM Protocol Model: Because of the constant-length cells, cell relay switches can perform much faster than frame relay switches by being able to depend upon constant cell length, since more instructions for processing can be included in firmware and hardware. The constant-sized cells also lead to a predictable and dependable processing rate and forwarding or delivery rate. The lack of a predictable maximum delivery delay was a key weakness in frame relay.

This predictable delivery time of each and every cell makes cell relay a better choice for transmission of voice or video applications as well as data. Cell relay switching can provide switching capability on a scale similar to that of the highest capacity transmission alternatives such as T-3s (45 Mbps) and fiber optic transmission circuits with capacity of up to 2.4 GB/sec.

ATM is presently defined by two different cell formats. One is called **UNI (user-network interface)** and carries information between the user and the ATM network. The second cell standard is known as **NNI (network-network interface)** and carries information between ATM switches. Figure 8-31 depicts the ATM UNI protocol model that conceptually illustrates how inputs of data, voice, or video can all be processed and transmitted as homogeneous ATM cells whereas Figure 8-32 relates the layers of the ATM model to the layers of the OSI model.

ATM Cell Structures: User inputs of data, video, or voice must be processed into fixed-length ATM cells before they can be forwarded and delivered by ATM switches. This processing is done on the **AAL** or **ATM adaptation layer.** Depending on the type of input (voice, video, or data), a different type of adaptation process may be used and different types of delivery requirements or priorities can be assigned within the ATM network. After emerging from the ATM adaptation layer, all cells are in an identical format as illustrated and explained in Figure 8-33.

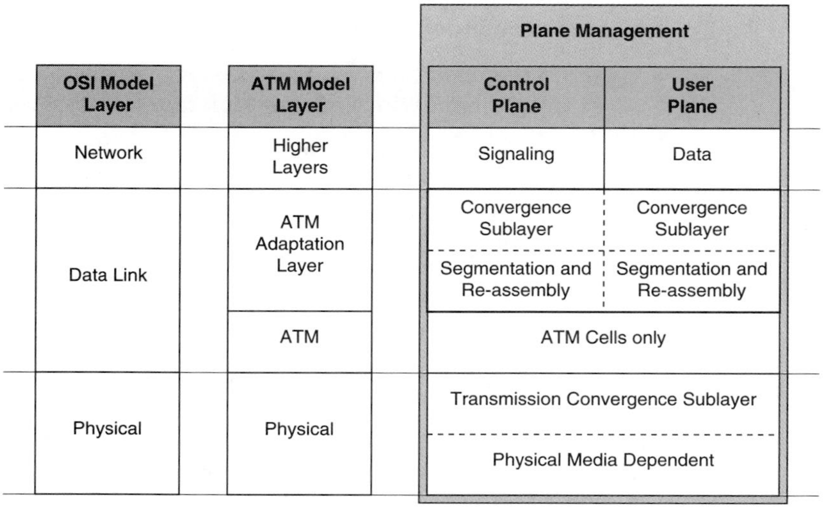

| OSI Model Layer | ATM Model Layer | | Plane Management | |
			Control Plane	User Plane
Network	Higher Layers		Signaling	Data
Data Link	ATM Adaptation Layer		Convergence Sublayer	Convergence Sublayer
			Segmentation and Re-assembly	Segmentation and Re-assembly
	ATM		ATM Cells only	
Physical	Physical		Transmission Convergence Sublayer	
			Physical Media Dependent	

Figure 8-31 ATM UNI Protocol Model

OSI Layer	ATM Layer	Explanation
Network	Signaling	Fault management, performance management, connection management
	Data	User data, voice, or video input that must be adapted into ATM cells
Data link	AAL (ATM adaptation layer)	Divided further into CS (convergence sublayer) and SAR (segmentation and reassembly sublayer); converts input data, video, and voice into ATM cells
	ATM (asynchronous transfer mode)	ATM cell processing layer; flow control, address assignment and translation
Physical	TCS (transmission convergence sublayer)	Cell delineation, header error check, path overhead signals, multiplexing
	PMD (physical medium dependent)	Physical transport and connectivity, framing, bit timing, line coding, loopback testing

Figure 8-32   ATM Model vs. OSI Model

AAL Protocols: ATM adaptation layer protocols are designed to optimize the delivery of a wide variety of possible types of user inputs or traffic. However, all of these different types of traffic vary in a relatively small number of ways:

- Delay sensitivity—Can the traffic tolerate variable delay or must end-to-end timing be preserved?

- Cell loss sensitivity—Can the traffic tolerate the occasional cell loss associated with connectionless transmission services or must connection-oriented transmission services be employed to avoid cell loss?

- Guaranteed bandwidth—Must the traffic receive a constant amount of guaranteed bandwidth or can it tolerate variable amounts of bandwidth?

- Additional overhead required—In addition to the five octets of overhead in the ATM cell header, some AAL protocols require additional overhead to properly manage payloads. This additional overhead is taken from the 48-octet payload. This can raise overhead percentages to as high as 13%.

To date, four different types of AAL protocols have been defined and are summarized in Figure 8-34.

ATM Bandwidth Management: As illustrated in Figure 8-34, the type of bandwidth required for a given type of traffic varies according to which AAL protocol was employed. There are currently three different categories of bit rates or bandwidth management schemes supported by ATM standards:

- **CBR** or **constant bit rate** provides a guaranteed amount of bandwidth to a given virtual path, thereby producing the equivalent of a leased T-1 or T-3

ATM Cell Field Name	Explanation
GFC: generic flow control	Multiple devices of various types (voice, video, or data) can gain access to an ATM network through a single access circuit. These different devices may require different flow control signaling.
VPI: virtual path identifier	The virtual path identifier uniquely identifies the connection between two end nodes and is equivalent to the virtual circuits of X.25 or frame relay networks. A VPI consists of several VCIs (see next entry).
VCI: virtual channel identifier	Because ATM can carry multiple types of information (voice, video, or data), serveral channels of information could be traveling along the same end-to-end connection simultaneously. The VCI uniquely identifies a particular channel of information within the virtual path.
PT: payload type	Payload type indicates whether the cell contains user information or network control information.
CLP: cell loss priority	If an ATM transmission exceeds its allotted bandwidth, including concessions for burstiness, a cell can be marked by the ATM network in a process known as policing. If congestion occurs on the network, these marked cells are the first to be discarded.
HEC: header error control	Header error control ensures that header information contains no errors. The biggest concern is that the VPI and VCI are correct.

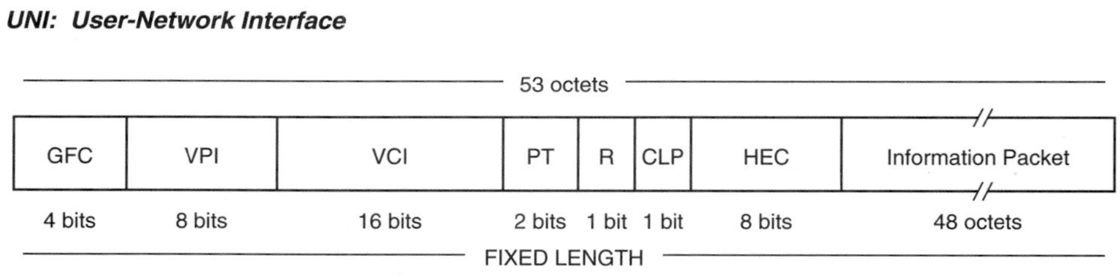

UNI: *User-Network Interface*

Figure 8-33   ATM Cell Structure

line. The negative side of CBR is that if this guaranteed amount of bandwidth is not required 100% of the time, no other applications can use the unused bandwidth.

- **VBR** or **variable bit rate** provides a guaranteed minimum threshold amount of constant bandwidth below which the available bandwidth will not drop. However, as bursty traffic requires more bandwidth than this constant minimum, that required bandwidth will be provided.

- **ABR** or **available bit rate** provides leftover bandwidth whenever it is not required by the variable bit rate traffic.

Figure 8-35 illustrates the relationship between CBR, VBR, and ABR.

AAL Protocol	Timing	Cell Loss	Bandwidth	Payload	Application/Notes
AAL-1	Preserved end-to-end	Connection oriented	Constant bit rate	47 octets	Used for mapping TDM services such as T-1 and T-3
AAL-2	Preserved end-to-end	Connection oriented	Variable bit rate	45–47 octets	Variable-rate compressed video
AAL-3/4	Variable delay acceptable	Connectionless	Variable bit rate	44 octets	Compatible with connectionless WAN data services such as SMDS
AAL-5	Variable delay acceptable	Connection oriented	Variable bit rate	48 octets	Currently most popular AAL protocol. Also known as SEAL (simple and efficient adaptation layer)

Figure 8-34   AAL Protocols

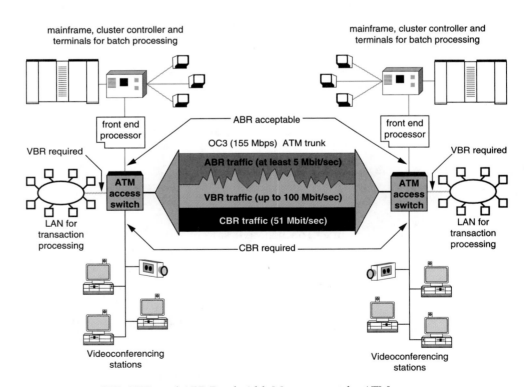

Figure 8-35   CBR, VBR, and ABR Bandwidth Management for ATM

Technology   The key benefits that the ATM architecture affords actual implementations of ATM technology are as follows:

- Constant cell length affords faster, predictable delivery times.

- Constant cell length and predictable delivery times allow voice, video, and data to all be transported effectively via ATM.

- ATM protocols are supported from the LAN to the WAN, from network interface cards to ATM WAN switches, thereby removing the necessity for multiple protocol conversions from the desktop across enterprise networks.

ATM on the LAN: ATM network interface cards are currently available at speeds from 25 to 155 Mbps. Workstations equipped with ATM NICs would be linked to each other via an ATM hub that would usually have a higher speed ATM up-link to a higher speed ATM enterprise switch. Workstations with Ethernet or token ring NICs do not have to have those NICs replaced to access ATM enterprise networks. **ATM gateway switches,** otherwise known as **ATM access switches,** can provide switched access for an entire legacy shared-media LAN to an ATM enterprise network. Ethernet switches with ATM uplinks are a common example of an ATM gateway switch.

A virtual LAN refers to a group of workstations that appear to be all locally connected to each other but that, in fact, are geographically dispersed. Virtual LANs can be created across an enterprise-wide ATM network among geographically distributed workstations via an ATM capability known as **ATM LAN emulation.** In ATM LAN emulation, LAN MAC layer addresses are converted to ATM network addresses and forwarded via switched ATM connections across the enterprise network to their destination workstation. This capability allows workstations and legacy LANs to take advantage of ATM's speed without having to make any hardware or software modifications to the LAN workstations themselves.

ATM across the WAN: An implementation of an ATM-based enterprise network would consist of ATM access devices as well as a "cloud" of ATM switches. The ATM access devices would take user information in the form of variable-length data frames from a LAN or workstation, digitized voice from a PBX, or digitized video from a video codec and format all of these various types of information into fixed-length ATM cells. The local ATM switch could route information to other locally connected ATM devices as well as to the wide area ATM network.

In a sense, the general makeup of the ATM network is not unlike the X.25 or frame relay networks. Access devices ensure that data is properly formatted before entering "the cloud" where the data is forwarded by switches specially designed to handle that particular type of properly formatted data. However, the functionality that an ATM network can offer far exceeds that of either the X.25 or frame relay networks. Figure 8-36 illustrates a possible implementation of a variety of ATM technology.

Broadband ISDN

SONET is the optical transmission interface and mechanism that will deliver **broadband ISDN** services. ATM is the switching architecture that will ensure that video,

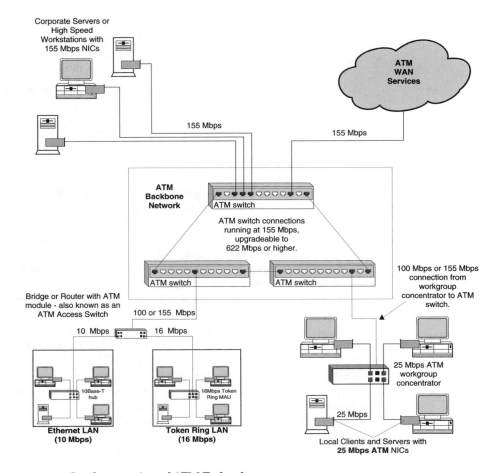

Figure 8-36   Implementation of ATM Technology

voice, data, and image packets delivered by **B-ISDN** services are delivered to the proper destination. Together, ATM and SONET form the underlying network architecture of the B-ISDN of the future. ATM provides the cell relay switching fabric providing bandwidth on demand for bursty data from any source (voice, video, etc.) whereas SONET's synchronous payload envelope provides empty boxcars for ATM's cargo. Simply stated, SONET possesses the flexibility to carry multiple types of data cargo (voice, video, etc.) simultaneously whereas ATM has the ability to switch multiple types of data simultaneously. The fact that the complementary nature of the two architectures produces a network service known as B-ISDN should come as no surprise.

Much of the excitement concerning B-ISDN is due to its ability to support existing services (T-1, T-3), emerging services (SMDS, frame relay) as well as future services (HDTV, medical imaging), and services as yet undiscovered. B-ISDN should be the service that finally delivers true bandwidth on demand in a uncomplicated, transparent, and hopefully affordable manner.

SUMMARY

To understand the basic technical principles of wide area networking, one must really start by looking at the basic business principles of wide area networking. In wide area networking as in most areas of business, the desire to maximize the impact of any investment in technology is a central focus.

The two most basic principles involved in sharing a single data link among multiple sessions are packetizing and multiplexing. Packetizing is the segmenting of data transmissions between devices into structured blocks or packets of data that contain enough "overhead" or management information in addition to the transmitted data itself to ensure delivery of the packet of data to its intended destination. Multiplexing then takes this packetized data and sends it over a shared wide area connection along with other packetized data from other sources.

An overall wide area network architecture is a simple model defining how packetizing,

multiplexing, and other wide area networking principles combine to create all of the current and emerging wide area networking technologies and services. Switching architectures and transmission architectures combine to enable network services.

Packet switching and circuit switching are the two major categories of switching architectures. Transmission architectures include local loop transmission alternatives such as POTS, ISDN, ADSL, and cable, whereas broadband transmission alternatives include T-1, T-3, and SONET. Among the network services enabled by these switching and transmission architectures are X.25, frame relay, SMDS, ATM, and broadband ISDN.

It is important to note that there is no single best network service for all applications. Network analysis must carefully match business applications to appropriate network services through careful and thorough analysis of data traffic as well as business objectives.

KEY TERMS

REVIEW QUESTIONS

1. Differentiate between the following multiplexing techniques in terms of mechanics, technology, and application: (a) frequency division multiplexing; (b) time division multiplexing; (c) statistical time division multiplexing.

2. Are multiplexers from different manufacturers interoperable? If not, why not?

3. What limitations in network design or operation would a lack of interoperability cause?

4. What are some of the technological differences between an X.25 network and a frame relay network?

5. What are some of the performance or architectural differences between an X.25 network and a frame relay network?

6. What are frame relay's underlying assumptions regarding transmission media and bit error rates?

7. What types of information are included in packets other than the actual data message itself?

8. How is it possible with a DOV unit that the voice and data don't necessarily have to share the same destination?

9. What are the key shortcomings of TDM and how does STDM seek to overcome these?

10. What is polling and what does it have to do with multiplexer efficiency?

11. What is the difference between switching and transmission and how do the two architectures complement each other?

12. What is the difference between circuit switching and packet switching?

13. What is the difference between a packet assembler/disassembler and a packet switch?

14. What are the positive and negative aspects of a datagram delivery service?

15. What is the difference between connectionless and connection-oriented packet services in terms of overhead, physical transmission path, and reliability?

16. What do connection-oriented services use in place of global addressing?

17. What overhead is involved with the establishment and maintenance of logical channel numbers?

18. What are the differences between PVCs and SVCs in terms of establishment, maintenance, and termination?

19. Which part of the packet-switched network does X.25 actually define?

20. What is meant by the term *bursty data* and what unique transmission challenge does it pose?

21. What is the most common source of bursty data?

22. Name the major components of the wide area network architecture and the significance of each.

23. Give examples of switching and transmission architectures in today's network architectures.

24. Differentiate between X.25 and frame relay in terms of error control.

25. How is flow control handled in a frame relay network?

26. What is the significance of frame relay's variable-length frames in terms of types of payloads that can be effectively delivered?

27. Why is dynamic allocation of bandwidth an important feature of frame relay?

28. Why is multiple PVCs per access line an important feature of frame relay?

29. What are the primary differences between frame relay and cell relay in terms of architecture and network performance?

30. What is the relationship between cell relay and ATM?

31. Differeniate between CBR, VBR, and ABR in terms of architecture and applications.

32. What is the purpose of the AAL protocols?

33. What are the differences between ISDN and B-ISDN?

34. What are the differences between POTS and ISDN?

35. What have been the traditional stumbling blocks to widespread ISDN deployment and what progress has been made in overcoming these?

36. What is SONET and where does it fit in the wide area network architecture?

37. What unique performance characteristics does SONET offer and what type of application might require such characteristics?

38. What is the difference between a T-1 and an E-1?

39. Differeniate between the following: time slot, frame, superframe, ESF.

40. What is the significance of NISDN-1?

41. What is the difference between DS-1 and T-1?

42. What is fractional T-1 and what is the business motivation behind such a service?

43. What is ADSL and what performance characteristics does it offer subscribers?

44. Why might carriers be especially interested in deploying ADSL services?

45. What are some other potential DSL services and how do they differ from ADSL?

46. What are some of the limitations facing the widespread use of cable modems?

47. What are the roles of the virtual tributaries in SONET?

48. What is B-ISDN and what switching and transmission architectures does it require?

49. What are some of the services that may be supported by B-ISDN?

50. What is the purpose of the D channel in ISDN?

51. What is the difference between BRI and PRI ISDN?

52. What is inverse multiplexing and what applications are well suited to it?

53. What is SMDS and why has it not been adopted as widely as frame relay?

ACTIVITIES

1. Contact your local phone carrier. Is ISDN available in your area? What are the nonrecurring and monthly charges for service? What are the performance guarantees? What special equipment is required? What is the cost of such equipment and must it be purchased from the carrier? Are both PRI and BRI services available? What intelligent services are available via ISDN? Can all 128 Kbps be used?

2. Contact your local phone carrier. Is ADSL available in your area? What are the nonrecurring and monthly charges for service? What are the performance guarantees? What special equipment is required? What is the cost of such equipment and must it be purchased from the carrier? Is Internet access available? At an additional cost?

3. Contact your local cable TV provider. Is cable modem service available in your area? What are the nonrecurring and monthly charges for service? What are the performance guarantees? What special equipment is required? What is the cost of such equipment and must it be purchased from the carrier? Is Internet access available? At an additional cost?

4. Gather articles on ATM from trade journals. Create a bulletin board or prepare a research topic summarizing the current issues facing ATM, focusing particularly on obstacles to widespread deployment, such as the pace of the standards development process.

5. Contact the ATM Forum and request literature concerning current standards development activities.

6. Investigate the installation and ongoing costs of an X.25 packet-switched service. What are the performance limitations?

7. Investigate the installation and ongoing costs of a frame relay packet-switched service. What are the performance limitations?

8. How are frame relay service tariffed in your local area? How are committed information rates and committed burst size negotiated? Is zero CIR available? What happens if you exceed your CIR? How do frame relay CIRs compare with X.25 transmission speeds?

9. Choose two cities within your LATA. Contact your local carrier for a quote on the cost of a leased line between these two cities. Compare pricing for both analog and digital lines of various sizes. Are switched digital services available? What are the installation and recurring costs?

10. Now choose another city just outside your local LATA. Contact multiple long-distance carriers for quotes similar to the previous question. How do the quotes from the various long-distance companies compare? How do the long-distance carrier quotes compare to the local carrier quotes? What was the impact on cost of leaving your LATA? Did recurring or nonrecurring costs increase more? Explain your results?

11. Find out if your local carrier can now offer inter-LATA data services thanks to the Telecommunications Act of 1996.

12. Research the wavelength division multiplexing technology market. How large is the market currently? What are the expected growth rates over the next 5 years? Who are the major vendors and who are the major customers? How exactly does WDM work? Report on the results of your research.

CASE STUDY

Leased Lines Traded In

It's 9:30 a.m. Monday morning, and with an 80 percent load on its primary wide-area link, the MIS department at brokerage company J. W. Charles Group Inc. should be pulling its hair out. But for this company, it's just another day at the office.

Credit the company's recent migration from leased lines to a frame-relay WAN based on switches for the reigning calm. As brokers in 16 branch offices and 50 affiliate sites simultaneously check the morning's stock prices, update their portfolios, and buy and sell stocks, the MIS director, Thomas Terpko, isn't worried about the link's rate of use.

The migration has enabled Terpko to accommodate rapid growth rates on J. W. Charles' network while reducing WAN costs and increasing manageability at the same time.

The Way It Was

J. W. Charles' frame-relay migration began as an effort to simplify the network. Each of the company's brokers tracks 50 to 100 stocks. As prices rise or fall throughout the day, brokers request stock quotes from a central site server, as well as news stories and other information pertaining to their traded companies.

In the past, J. W. Charles provided much of this information by connecting remote sites in the southeastern states to its headquarters in Boca Raton, Fla., via point-to-point, 9,600-baud lines leased from BellSouth Corp. Offices outside the BellSouth territory were tied in by similar lines from interexchange carrier LDDS WorldCom, now MFS WorldCom.

This WAN infrastructure required J. W. Charles to run two leased lines to each remote site, one for stock quotes and the other for back-office applications such as accounting, payroll, and billing.

But each leased line that connected a branch to J. W. Charles' headquarters cost as much as $1,200 a month. Moreover, 28.8Kbps dial-up connections, used to connect affiliate brokers, could cost as much as $450 a month per location.

Ready for a Switch

So about a year ago, J. W. Charles, with the help of Omnico, a systems integrator in Fort Lauderdale, Fla., began looking for a way to avoid the expensive leased lines.

The changeover to frame relay, which J. W. Charles completed this spring, reduced line costs to between $250 and $350 for dedicated 56Kbps connections.

But unlike many IS shops that outfit themselves with frame-relay access devices (FRADs) and routers, J. W. Charles is taking advantage of a switched enterprise WAN infrastructure. A switch-based WAN provides greater scaleability, according to Terpko, letting him quickly connect remote LANs and PCs to J. W. Charles' rapidly growing network.

At both its headquarters and Atlanta disaster-recovery site, J. W. Charles uses an Athena enterprise switch from WAN equipment developer Develcon Electronics Ltd. In Saskatoon, Saskatchewan.

A single 1,544Mbps, or T-1, connection from MCI Telecommunications Corp., public frame-relay network terminates at each switch, and each switch then connects to three routers. These devices support a stream of quote requests and responses that continue until after the trading floor closes.

The switch has provided J. W. Charles a level of flexibility that would have been impossible with leased lines or even with a traditional router-based, frame-relay infrastructure. Rather than connect three separate T-1s or fractional T-1s to the three different routers, he connects a single T-1 to the switch. The switch then directs traffic to the routers, which forward the traffic appropriately.

For example, Terpko is now in the process of hooking up an independent broker in Issaquah, Wash., to the central office. J. W. Charles will provide this broker, and other affiliate contractors like him, with back-office quotes and other stock-related information and services.

"In the past we could not have provided service to that guy," Terpko said, because bringing up new leased-line connections was an expensive and time-consuming process.

But in the new frame-relay environment, the Washington affiliate occupies only one port on the 15-port Develcon 4000 router, which itself occupies only one of the Athena's 18 ports.

Because the routers support so many ports, and because more can be added by connecting additional routers to the switch, Terpko said the headquarters' incoming T-1 will run out of bandwidth long before the switch runs out of ports.

Management Advantage

In addition to providing a flexible infrastructure that accommodates J. W. Charles' rapidly growing WAN—the company adds five remote sites each month— the use of frame-relay switches also simplifies management, Terpko said.

"The switch gives us more flexibility in moving [connections]," Terpko said, comparing his switch-based wide-area network to one based on a router.

Because Terpko's use of both routers and switches has provided a plethora of ports, frame-relay connections that are not performing properly can be switched to a new port while Terpko's MIS staff trouble shoots the network.

This design has helped Terpko deal with the finger-pointing that telephone companies and equipment vendors are often guilty of during times of network crisis.

For example, shortly after Terpko completed the migration to frame relay, one of the connections stopped transmitting data.

MCI blamed the failed connection on an equipment problem and suggested that Terpko contact his hardware vendors. Terpko decided to create point-to-point connections between the switch's ports. He saw that all ports were working well and so could prove to MCI that the problem resided in the carrier's network.

"We can take my PVC [permanent virtual circuit] in our network, establish a point-to-point connection to the switch, and trouble shoot it," he said. "Since we've had the switch, we've been able to easily correct any problem that's come up."

Source: Brian Riggs, "Leased Lines Traded In," *LAN Times,* vol. 13, no. 22 (September 30, 1996), p. 29. Copyright © September 30, 1996, by McGraw–Hill, New York. Reprinted by permission of McGraw–Hill, New York.

BUSINESS CASE STUDY QUESTIONS

Activities

1. Complete a top-down model for this case by gleaning facts from the case and placing them in the proper layer of the top-down model. After completing the top-down model, analyze and detail those instances where requirements were clearly passed down from upper layers to lower layers of the model and where solutions to those requirements were passed up from lower layers to upper layers of the model.

2. Detail any questions about the case that may occur to you for which answers are not clearly stated in the article.

Business

1. What were the primary activities of the organization in this case?
2. What types of activities might an individual broker be involved with during the business day?
3. How many branch offices and affiliate sites were connected to the wide area network in this case?
4. What were the monthly costs of the original network?
5. What was the motivating factor to begin looking at frame relay?
6. What was the monthly cost savings from the frame relay network?
7. What was the overall financial impact of the WAN migration?
8. What is the growth rate of the business (number of new remote sites per month)?

Application

1. What were the primary types of applications executed in support of business processes?
2. What applications other than stock quotes were run at each location?

Data

1. What was the bandwidth of the original leased lines?
2. How many leased lines were run to each location? Why?

Network

1. Why did the J. W. Charles Group migrate from leased lines to frame relay?
2. What was the bandwidth of the frame relay connections to branch offices and independent brokers?
3. What was the bandwidth of the frame relay connections to corporate headquarters in Boca Raton?
4. What was the bandwidth of the frame relay connections to the disaster recovery site in Atlanta?

Technology

1. What were the overall benefits of the migration?
2. What type of device was chosen to interface to the frame relay service? Why?
3. What benefit does the chosen network design offer over FRADs connected to individual routers?
4. Describe the expandability of the new network architecture.
5. What is the relationship between the routers and the WAN switch in this architecture?
6. What impact has the new architecture had on ease of management?
7. How did the new architecture ease troubleshooting and avoid fingerpointing?

CHAPTER 9

INTERNETWORKING

Concepts Reinforced

OSI Model
Protocols and Standards
Network Operating Systems
   Architecture
Network Addressing

Internet Suite of Protocols Model
Interoperability
Network Operating Systems
   Functionality
TCP/IP Protocols

Concepts Introduced

Internetwork Design
Bridging
Switching vs. Routing
Bridges
Repeaters
SNA/SDLC

Internetworking Technology
Routing
Routing Protocols
Routers
Bridging Protocols
SNA/LAN Integration

After mastering the material in this chapter, you should

1. Understand why an organization would want to implement LAN-to-LAN internetworking.

2. Understand the basics of internetwork design including decisions as to bridging, routing, or switching.

3. Understand the importance of protocols to successful internetworking design and implementation.

4. Understand the functionality and proper application of the following types of internetworking technology: repeaters, bridges, branch office routers, edge routers, boundary routers, route servers, distributed routers, dial-up routers, ISDN bridges and routers, wireless bridges, source routing bridges, and software-only routers.

5. Understand the options available for integrating LAN traffic with SNA/SDLC mainframe traffic.

■ INTRODUCTION

There are two basic purposes for this chapter:

- To introduce the reader to the complexities and basic principles of internetwork design.

- To introduce the reader to the available technology with which to implement designed internetworking solutions.

These internetwork design and technology issues will be explored for both LAN-to-LAN internetworking and LAN-to-mainframe internetworking. To understand the importance of internetworking in general, it is first necessary to understand the business motivation for seeking internetworking solutions.

■ INTERNETWORKING DESIGN

BUSINESS MOTIVATION AND INTERNETWORKING CHALLENGES

Managerial
Perspective

Local area networks tend to grow by a natural process until the shared-media network architecture (Ethernet, token ring, FDDI, etc.) becomes too congested and network performance begins to suffer. This scenario is one of the two primary reasons for investigating **internetworking** solutions. The other situation that often leads to internetworking design is when independently established and operated LANs wish to begin to share information. These scenarios really boil down to business issues. The poor performance of the overloaded shared-media LAN leads to a decrease in worker productivity, with potential ripple effects to decreases in customer satisfaction, sales, market share, etc.

The ability to provide decision-makers with instantaneous access to the right information at the right place and time, regardless of the location of that information, is really the key motivation for internetworking. The key challenge or stumbling block to achieving transparent information access is the numerous incompatibilities caused by the multiple vendor hardware and software technologies that comprise the individual LANs to be linked. The operational characteristics of LANs are defined by protocols, which when organized into a layered model such as the OSI model, are referred to as a protocol stack. A LAN's protocol stack is really a definition of that LAN's personality. In other words, if transparent LAN-to-LAN interoperability is to be achieved, each protocol in a given LAN's protocol stack must be either matched or converted to transparently interoperate with the corresponding protocol in the neighboring LAN to which the given LAN is to be linked. Overall LAN-to-LAN transparent interoperability is only achieved when corresponding protocols are able to achieve transparent interoperability.

Overall Internetworking Design Strategies

To improve performance on overburdened shared-media LANs, several proven design strategies can be followed:

- **Segmentation** is usually the first approach to reducing shared-media congestion. By having fewer workstations per segment, there is less contention for the shared bandwidth. Segmentation improves performance for both CSMA/CD (Ethernet) and token-passing (token ring) access methodologies. Some type of internetworking device, such as a bridge or router, will be required to link the LAN segments.

- When segmentation is taken to the extreme of limiting each LAN segment to only a single workstation, the design strategy is known as **microsegmentation.** A microsegmented internetwork requires a LAN switch that is compatible with the NICs installed in the attached workstations. Both Ethernet and token ring switches are readily available.

- Instead of assigning all workstations to their own LAN segment as in microsegmentation, only selected high-performance devices such as servers can be assigned to their own segment in a design strategy known as **server isolation**. By isolating servers on their own segments, guaranteed access to network bandwidth is assured.

- **Hierarchical networking** isolates local LAN traffic on a local network architecture such as Ethernet or token ring while transmitting internetwork traffic over a higher speed network architecture such as FDDI, Fast Ethernet, or ATM. Servers are often directly connected to the **backbone network** whereas individual workstations access the backbone network only as needed through routers.

Figure 9-1 illustrates these overall internetworking design strategies.

Bridging, routing, and switching are the three primary internetworking processes that offer LAN segmentation and isolation of network resources. All three internetworking processes are basically address processors, making decisions as to how to forward internetwork traffic based on data-link layer and network layer addresses. The three processes differ in their use of network addresses, in their overall sophistication, and in their advantages and limitations. The bridging, routing, and switching internetworking processes are reviewed here, whereas differences between their associated internetworking technologies are reviewed later in the chapter.

Bridging

Bridging is often the first internetworking or LAN segmentation strategy employed due to its ease of installation and effective results. Dividing a single overburdened LAN into two LAN segments linked by a bridge must be done with some forethought to minimize the amount of internetwork traffic and thereby avoid having the bridge become an internetwork bottleneck. The 80/20 rule is often used in deciding which workstations and servers should be assigned to each side of the bridge. The goal should be that 80% of all LAN traffic should stay on the local LAN, with no more than 20% of overall traffic requiring processing and forwarding by the bridge.

Addressing   Bridging is a data-link layer process, making forwarding decisions based on the contents of the MAC layer or data-link layer addresses. Bridges are passive or transparent devices, receiving every frame broadcast on a given LAN. Bridges are known as **transparent** due to their ability to only process data-link layer addresses while transparently forwarding any variety of upper layer protocols

Segmentation

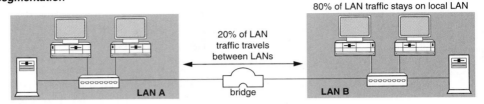

Micro-Segmentation

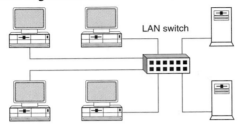

Server Isolation

Hierarchical Networking

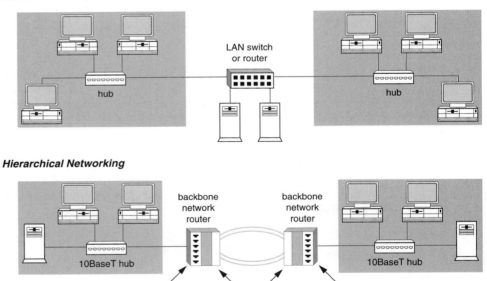

Figure 9-1 Overall Internetworking Design Strategies

safely embedded within the data field of the data-link layer frame. Rather than merely transferring all data between LANs or LAN segments, a bridge reads the **destination address** (MAC layer address of destination NIC) of each data frame on a LAN, decides whether the destination is local or remote (on the other side of the bridge), and only allows those data frames with nonlocal destination addresses to cross the bridge to the remote LAN.

Data-link protocols such as Ethernet contain **source addresses** as well as the destination addresses within the predefined Ethernet frame layout. A bridge checks the source address of each frame it receives and adds that source address to a table of **known local nodes.** In doing so, the bridge is learning, without having to be manually reconfigured, about new workstations that might have been added to the local LAN. Some bridges broadcast requests to all locally attached workstations, thereby forcing responses that can then be stored in the known local nodes table.

After each destination address is read, it is compared with the contents of the "known local nodes" table to determine whether the frame should be allowed to cross the bridge or not (whether the destination is local or not). Since only frames with destination addresses not found in the known local nodes table are forwarded across the bridge, bridges are sometimes known as a **"forward-if-not-local"** devices. Figure 9-2 illustrates the use of data-link layer frame addresses by bridges.

Advantages   Due to their ability to learn, bridges are relatively easy to install and configure, providing quick, cost-effective relief for overburdened network segments. In addition to providing logical segmentation of LAN traffic, bridges also are able to extend network segment length by repeating, retiming, and regenerating received signals before forwarding them across the bridge. Bridges are also able to translate between different network architectures (token ring to Ethernet) and between different media types (UTP to fiber).

Bridges are most often used to either segment traffic between LANs or segment traffic between a LAN and a higher speed backbone network.

Limitations   The primary limitation of bridges is also one of their strengths. Because bridges learn and do not require ongoing configuration, they only know to forward all packets that are addressed to nonlocal nodes. In the case of a destination node that is many LANs and connecting bridges away from its source workstation, all workstations on all LANs between the source and destination workstation will be broadcast with the frame bound for the distant destination. Forwarding messages to all workstations on all intermittent LANs is known as **propagation.** In the case of improperly addressed frames or frames destined for nonexistent addresses, frames can be infinitely perpetuated or flooded onto all bridged LANs in a condition known as a **broadcast storm.** Bridges are generally not able to support networks containing redundant paths since the multiple active loops between LANs can lead to the propagation of broadcast storms.

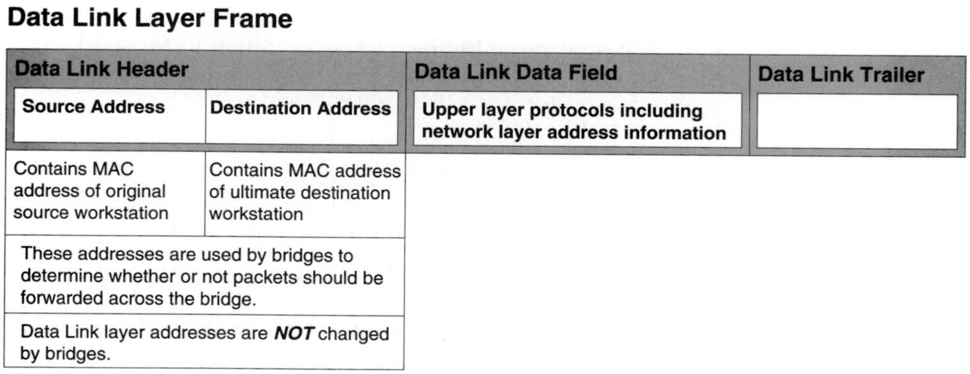

Data Link Layer Frame

Data Link Header		Data Link Data Field	Data Link Trailer
Source Address	**Destination Address**	**Upper layer protocols including network layer address information**	
Contains MAC address of original source workstation	Contains MAC address of ultimate destination workstation		
These addresses are used by bridges to determine whether or not packets should be forwarded across the bridge.			
Data Link layer addresses are **NOT** changed by bridges.			

Figure 9-2   Use of Data-Link Addressing by Bridges

Routing

Although both processes examine and forward data packets discriminately, routing and bridging differ significantly in several key functional areas:

- Although a bridge reads the destination address of every data packet on the LAN to which it is attached, a router only examines those data packets that are specifically addressed to it.

- Unlike the bridge, which merely allows the data packet access to the internetwork, a router is both more cautious and more helpful.

Before indiscriminately forwarding a data packet, a router first confirms the existence of the destination address as well as the latest information on available network "paths" to reach that destination. Next, based on the latest network traffic conditions, the router chooses the best path for the data packet to reach its destination and sends the data packet on its way.

Addressing   Whereas bridges make their forwarding decisions based on the contents of the MAC layer addresses contained in the header of the data-link layer frame, routers make their forwarding decisions based on the contents of the network layer addresses embedded within the data field of the data-link layer frame.

The router itself is a data-link layer destination address, available to receive, examine, and forward data packets from anywhere on any network to which it is either directly or indirectly internetworked.

How do data packets arrive at a router? The destination address on an Ethernet or token ring packet must be the MAC address of the router that will handle further internetwork forwarding. Thus, a router is addressed in the data-link layer destination address field. The router then discards this MAC sublayer "envelope" that contained its address and proceeds to read the contents of the data field of the Ethernet or token ring frame. Data-link layer addressing is functionally referred to as point-to-point addressing.

Just as in the case of the data-link layer protocols, network layer protocols dictate a bit-by-bit data frame structure that the router understands. What looked like just "data" and was ignored by the data-link layer internetworking device, the bridge, is "unwrapped" by the router and examined thoroughly to determine further processing.

After reading the network layer destination address, which is actually the network address of the ultimate destination workstation, the router consults its **routing tables** to determine the best path on which to forward this data packet. Routing tables contain at least some of the following fields upon which to base their "best path" decisions:

- Network number of the destination network. This field serves as the key field or look-up field used to find the proper record with further information concerning the best path to this network.

- MAC address of the next router along the path to this target network.

- Port on this router out of which the readdressed data-link layer frame should be sent.

- Number of hops, or intermediate routers, to the destination network.

• The age of this entry in order to avoid making routing decisions based on outdated information.

Having found the best path, the router has the ability to repackage the data packet as required for the delivery route (best path) that it has chosen. Although the network layer addresses remain unchanged, a fresh data-link layer frame is created. The destination address on the new data-link layer frame is filled in with the MAC address of the next router along the best path to the ultimate destination, and the source address on the new data-link layer frame is filled in with the MAC address of the router that just completed examination of the network layer addresses. Network layer addressing is functionally referred to as end-to-end addressing.

Unlike the bridge, which merely allows access to the internetwork (forward-if-not-local logic), the router specifically addresses the data packet to a distant router. However, before a router actually releases a data packet onto the internetwork, it confirms the existence of the destination address to which this data packet is bound. Only once the router is satisfied with both the viability of the destination address and the quality of the intended path will it release the carefully packaged data packet. This meticulous processing activity on the part of the router is known as **forward-if-proven-remote** logic. Figure 9-3 illustrates the router's use of data-link and network layer addresses, whereas Figure 9-4 illustrates a simple logic flow diagram for the addressing aspects of the routing process.

Advantages   In comparison with bridging, routing is able to make more efficient use of bandwidth on large networks containing redundant paths. The effective use of a network's redundant paths allows routers to perform **load balancing** of total network traffic across two or more links between two given locations. Choice of "best path" by routers can be determined by a variety of factors including number of hops, transmission cost, and current line congestion. Routers are able to dynamically maintain routing tables, thereby adjusting performance to changing network conditions. Thanks to the "forward-if-proven-remote" logic, routers are more able

Data Link Layer Frame

Header		Data (Embedded Network Layer Packet)			Trailer
Source Address	Destination Address	Source Address	Destination Address	Network layer data field containing upper layer protocols and user data	
MAC Layer addresses		Network Layer (IP, IPX) addresses			
Used for point-to-point connections		Used for end-to-end connections			
MAC address of router which last processed this packet	MAC address of next HOP router	Network layer address of original workstation	Network layer address of ultimate destination workstation	Used by router to determine best path according to information contained in routing table.	
Addresses change with each HOP		Addresses do NOT change			

Figure 9-3   Router's Use of Data-Link and Network Layer Addresses

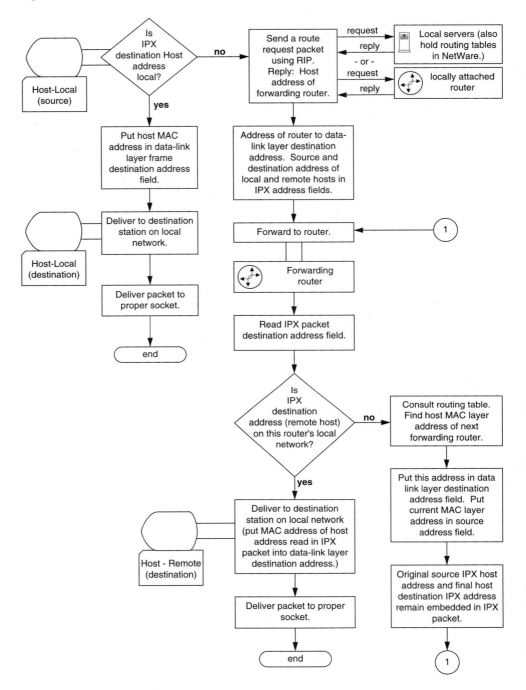

Figure 9-4   Logic Flow for Address Processing by Routers

to keep misbehaving or misaddressed traffic off of the network through filtering of network layer addresses. In this role, routers can be considered as firewalls between connected networks. Router-based networks are much more scaleable than bridge-based networks. Routers are able to forward more sophisticated and informative management information to enterprise network management systems via SNMP.

When LANs are connected over a long distance via WAN links, it is more likely that routers rather than bridges should be employed to interface to the WAN link. Thanks to the router's ability to more accurately identify upper layer protocols, unnecessary or unwanted traffic can be kept off of the relatively low-speed, high-cost WAN links.

Perhaps the most significant advantage of routers is their ability to process multiple network layer protocols simultaneously. A properly configured router could process IP, IPX, and AppleTalk packets simultaneously while forwarding each protocol type to the proper destination network. In addition, some routers are also able to handle nonroutable protocols such as NetBIOS, LAT, or SNA/SDLC that don't possess any network layer addressing scheme. In these cases, either the data-link layer frames are bridged or the upper layer protocols are encapsulated in a network layer envelope such as IP.

To summarize, routers provide the following services to the internetwork:

- Create firewalls to protect connected LANs.
- Filter unwanted broadcast packets from the internetwork.
- Discriminate and prioritize processing of packets according to network layer protocol.
- Provide security by filtering packets by either data-link or network layer addresses.
- Provide transparent interconnection between LANs.

Limitations   Due to the sophisticated processing offered, routers are considerably more complicated to configure and manage than bridges. As the number of routers increases in a router-based network, the complexity level of network management increases proportionately. If routers are expected to be able to process multiple network layer protocols, then they must have all supported protocol stacks installed and properly configured.

The router's sophisticated processing also has an impact in terms of the sophistication and cost of the router technology in comparison to bridging technology.

Switching

Switching, otherwise known as LAN switching, is very similar in function to bridging. The key difference between switching and bridging is that switching is done in hardware, or ASIC (application-specific integrated circuit), chips and is extremely fast in comparison to bridging. The primary purpose for employing a switch is to increase available bandwidth within a shared-media LAN by implementing microsegmentation on the local LAN. Since the switch creates point-to-point connections for each packet received, shared-media LANs that employ switches become switched media LANs.

Addressing   Switching uses addresses in a manner similar to bridging. LAN switches read the destination MAC addresses on incoming data-link layer frames and quickly build a switched connection to the switched LAN segment that contains the destination workstation. The switch ports for LAN segments that contain multiple workstations are able to discriminate between traffic between locally attached workstations and traffic that must be switched to another LAN switch port.

Switches work best when traffic does not have to leave the LAN segments linked to a particular LAN switch. In other words, to minimize the use of expensive WAN links or filter the traffic allowed onto high-speed backbone networks, layer 3 protocols will need to be examined by a router. In some cases, this routing functionality is being incorporated into the LAN switch. Basic LAN switches are layer 2 devices that must be complemented by either external layer 3 routers or by internal layer 3 routing functionality.

Much like a bridge would handle "nonlocal" traffic, when a LAN switch receives a data-link frame bound for a destination off of the local network, it merely builds a switched connection to the switch port to which a router is connected or to a virtual router within the switch where the switch's routing functionality can be accessed.

Practical Advice and Information

In discriminating between the proper roles of switching and routing, the best advice may be: Switch for bandwidth; route for filtering and internetwork segmentation.

Advantages   LAN switches are able to produce dramatic increases in bandwidth in comparison to shared-media LANs if sufficient thought has gone into organizing workstations and servers on LAN switch segments in a logical manner.

Virtual LANs, which will be thoroughly explored in Chapter 11, are enabled by the LAN switch's ability to quickly make any two workstations or servers appear to be physically attached to the same LAN segment. Virtual LANs take advantage of this switching capability by logically defining those workstations and computers that belong to the same virtual LAN regardless of the physical location of those workstations and servers. A given workstation or server can belong to more than one virtual LAN.

Limitations   A LAN switch's limitations are largely a result of its bridging heritage. Switching cannot perform sophisticated filtering or security based on network layer protocols because LAN switches are unable to read network layer protocols. Switches are not able to discriminate between multiple paths and make best path decisions. Management information offered to enterprise network management systems by LAN switches is minimal in comparison to that available from routers.

Perhaps more importantly, because switched LAN connections may only exist for a matter of microseconds, monitoring and management of traffic within the LAN switch are considerably more challenging than performing similar tasks on routers. Traditional LAN analyzers constructed for use on shared-media LANs are of no use on switched-media LANs. Potential solutions to this and other switching limitations such as buffering between high- and low-speed network architectures within a single switch are covered in the LAN switch technology analysis section of the chapter on LAN hardware (Chapter 6).

■ INTERNETWORKING TECHNOLOGY

Internetworking Technology and the OSI Model

Internetworking technology can be categorized according to the OSI model layer corresponding to the protocols that a given internetworking device is able to process. In this way, the following internetworking devices can be categorized with the following OSI layers:

- Repeaters: OSI layer 1   physical layer
- Bridges: OSI layer 2   data-link layer
- Routers: OSI layer 3   network layer

Each of these categories of internetworking devices will be explored in more detail in the following sections. Although switching was dealt with in this chapter as an internetworking design issue based on future directions such as virtual LANs and integrated routing, LAN switch technology was previously explored in the chapter on LAN hardware due to its current deployment largely in local area networks rather than in internetworks.

A few characteristics are true of all internetworking devices in relation to the protocols of the OSI layer with which they are associated.

- Any given network device can translate or convert protocols associated with OSI layers lower than or equal to the OSI layer of the internetworking device.

- Any given network device is unable to process protocols associated with OSI layers higher than the OSI layer of the internetworking device.

The relationship between the OSI model and internetworking devices is illustrated in Figure 9-5.

Repeaters

Functionality   All data traffic on a LAN is in a digital format of discrete voltages of discrete duration traveling over one type of physical media or another. The only

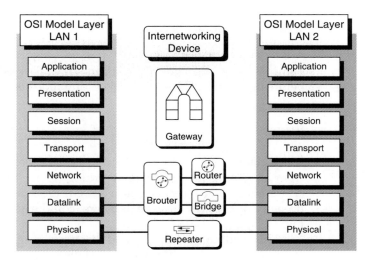

Figure 9-5   Relationship between the OSI Model and Internetworking Devices

exception to this statement would be in the case of wireless-based LANs, in which case the transmission would be through the air in an analog format. Given this, a **repeater's** job is fairly simple to understand:

- Repeat the digital signal by regenerating and retiming the incoming signal.

- Pass all signals between all attached segments.

- Do not read destination addresses of data packets.

- Allow for the connection of and translation between different types of media.

- Effectively extend overall LAN distance by repeating signals between LAN segments.

A repeater is a nondiscriminatory internetworking device. It does not discriminate between data packets. Every signal that comes into one side of a repeater gets regenerated and sent out the other side of the repeater. Repeaters are available for both Ethernet and token ring network architectures for a wide variety of media types. A repeater is a physical layer device concerned with physical layer signaling protocols relating to signal voltage levels and timing. The primary reasons for employing a repeater are as follows:

- Increase the overall length of the network media by repeating signals across multiple LAN segments. In a token ring LAN, several MAUs can be linked together by repeaters to increase the size of the LAN.

- Isolate key network resources onto different LAN segments to ensure greater survivability.

- Translate between different media types supported for a given network architecture.

Figure 9-6 illustrates typical installations of repeaters.

Technology Analysis

Figure 9-7 outlines some of the technology analysis issues that should be considered before purchasing Ethernet or token ring repeaters.

Applied Problem Solving

Bridges

Functionality   When users on one LAN need occasional access to data or resources from another LAN, an internetworking device that is more sophisticated and discriminating than a repeater is required. From a comparative outlook on the functionality of **bridges** vs. repeaters, one could say that bridges are more discriminating.

This reading, processing, and discriminating indicates a higher level of sophistication of the bridge, afforded by installed software, and also implies a higher price tag than repeaters (repeaters: $250–2500; bridges: $2000–6000). Bridges come in many varieties as determined by the characteristics of the two LANs joined by a

Installation - Ethernet Fiber-Optic Multiport Repeater

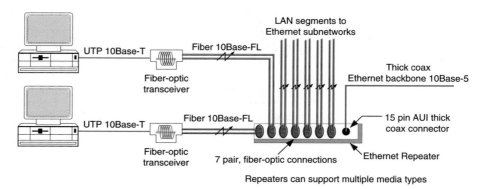

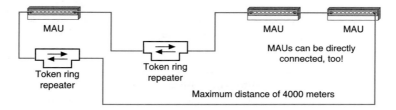

Repeaters can support multiple media types

Installation - Token Ring Repeaters

Figure 9-6   Repeater Installations

particular bridge. Physically, bridges may be network interface cards that can be plugged into an expansion slot of a PC along with additional bridging software or they may be stand-alone devices.

Bridge performance is generally measured by two criteria:

- **Filtering rate:** Measured in packets/sec or frames/sec. When a bridge reads the destination address on an Ethernet frame or token ring packet and decides whether or not that packet should be allowed access to the internetwork through the bridge, that process is known as **filtering.** Filtering rates for bridges range from 7,000 to 60,000 frames/sec.

- **Forwarding rate:** Also measured in packets/sec or frames/sec. Having decided whether or not to grant a packet access to the internetwork in the filtering process, the bridge now must perform a separate operation of **forwarding** the packet onto the internetwork media whether local or remote. Forwarding rates range from as little as 700 packets/sec for some remote bridges to as much as 30,000 packets/sec for RISC-based high-speed local bridges.

Although bridging functionality has already been reviewed in the section on internetwork design, two issues specific to bridging deserve further explanation:

- Dealing with redundant paths and broadcast storms.
- Source route bridging.

Network Architecture	Technology Analysis Issue	Importance/Implications
Ethernet	Media type/interface support	• 10BaseT: UTP, RJ-45 • 10Base2: Thin Coax, BNC • 10Base5: Thick Coax, AUI • 10BaseFL: fiber optic cable, ST or SMA connectors
	Long extended distance repeaters	• Work over single-pair telephone wire • Extend Ethernet LANs up to 1250 ft • Must be used in pairs • Fiber optic links yield distances of up to 1.2 mi
	Local repeaters	• Used to extend and segment local LANs
	Modular repeaters	• Hot-swappable modules allow flexible use for a variety of different media types and interfaces
	Workgroup repeaters	• Used for media conversion • All possible media combinations are available
	Auto-partitioning	• An important feature that prevents failure of one connected segment from affecting other segments • Auto-restoral upon segment re-establishment is often also included
	Number of segments per repeater	• Repeaters vary in segment capacity • Typical segment capacities range from 2 to 8
	Cascadability	• Some repeaters can be daisy-chained or cascaded to increase overall LAN length
	Price range	• $250–2500
Token ring	Transmission speed	• Token ring is available in 4 Mbps and 16 Mbps • Some repeaters are able to convert between speeds • Repeaters must support proper speed
	MAU ring length vs. lobe length	• Token ring repeaters can extend either the overall ring length as measured by the distance between MAUs or the lobe length, which is the distance from the workstation to the MAU
	Fiber optic repeaters	• Token ring fiber optic repeaters can extend ring length to 8200 ft
	Media type/interface support	• Type 1 cabling: STP, Type 1 connectors • Type 3 cabling: UTP, RJ-45 connectors
	Price range	• $815–2300

Figure 9-7   Repeater Technology Analysis

Spanning Tree Algorithm   The **spanning tree algorithm (STA)** has been standardized as **IEEE 802.1** for the purposes of controlling redundant paths in bridged networks and thereby reducing the possibility of broadcast storms. When multiple bridges are installed in a complex internetworking arrangement, a looping topology containing multiple active loops could be accidentally introduced into the internetwork architecture. The spanning tree algorithm (IEEE 802.1), which is implemented as software installed on STA-compliant bridges, can sense multiple paths and can disable all but one. In addition, should the primary path between two LANs become disabled, the spanning tree algorithm can re-enable the previously disabled redundant link, thereby preserving the inter-LAN link. STA bridges accomplish this path management by communicating with each other via **configuration bridge protocol data units** (configuration BPDU). The overall effect of STA-compliant bridges is that they enable the positive aspects of redundant paths in bridged networks while eliminating the negative aspects.

Source Route Bridging   **Source routing bridges** are not to be confused with routers since the capture of the routing information that delineates the chosen path to the destination address is done by the source device, usually a LAN-attached PC, and not by the bridge. The PC sends out a special **explorer packet** that determines the best path to the intended destination of its data message. The explorer packets are continually propagated through all source routing bridges until the destination workstation is finally reached by the explorer packet. Along the journey to the destination workstation, each source routing bridge enters its address in the routing information field (RIF) of the explorer packet. The destination workstation sends the completed RIF back directly to the source workstation. All subsequent data messages include the suggested path to the destination embedded within the header of the token ring frame. Having determined the best path to the intended destination, the source PC sends the data message along with the path instructions to the local bridge, which forwards the data message according to the received path instructions.

Data messages arrive at a source routing bridge with a detailed map of how they plan to reach their destination. One very important limitation of source routing bridges as applied to large internetworks is known as the **7 hop limit**. Because of the limited space in the **RIF (router information field)** of the explorer packet, only 7 hop locations can be included in the path to any remote destination. As a result, routers with larger routing table capacity are often employed for larger internetworks.

To avoid constantly flooding the network with explorer packets seeking destinations, source routing bridges may employ some type of **address caching** or RIF caching, so that previously determined routes to known destinations are saved and reused.

Technology Analysis

Applied Problem Solving

Bridges can be categorized in a number of different ways. Perhaps the major criterion for categorizing bridges is the network architecture of the LANs to be joined by the bridge.

First and foremost, are the two LANs that are to be bridged Ethernet or token ring? Bridges that connect LANs of similar data-link format are known as **transparent bridges.** Transparent bridges exhibit the following characteristics:

- **Promiscuous listen** means that transparent bridges receive all data packets transmitted on the LANs to which they are connected.

- Store-and-forward bridging between LANs means that messages that are not destined for local workstations are forwarded through the bridge as soon as the target LAN is available.

- Learning is achieved by examining all MAC source addresses on data-link frames received to understand which workstations are locally attached to which LANs through which ports on the bridge.

- The IEEE 802.1 spanning tree algorithm is implemented to manage path connectivity between LANs.

A special type of bridge that includes a **format converter** can bridge between Ethernet and token ring. These special bridges may also be called **multiprotocol bridges** or **translating bridges.**

A third type of bridge, somewhat like a translating bridge, is used to bridge between Ethernet and FDDI networks. Unlike the translating bridge, which must actually manipulate and rewrite the data-link layer frame, the **encapsulating bridge** merely takes the entire Ethernet data-link layer frame and stuffs it in an "envelope" (data frame) that conforms to the FDDI data-link layer protocol.

Source-routing bridges are specifically designed for connecting token ring LANs that have source routing enabled. Not all token ring LANs are source-routing LANs but only token ring LANs can be source-routing LANs. Bridges that can support links between source-routing token ring LANs or transparent LANs are known as **source-routing transparent (SRT) bridges.** These bridges are able to identify whether frames are to be bridged transparently or source routed by reading the flag's setting in the data-link frame header.

Figure 9-8 illustrates typical bridge installations whereas Figure 9-9 identifies some of the technology analysis issues that should be considered prior to purchasing bridge technology.

Wireless Bridges   When corporate LAN locations are located up to 3 mi apart, remote bridges linked by WAN services such as 56-Kbps or faster lines are a common internetworking solution. This design implies monthly recurring expenses of approximately $500 for the WAN services in addition to fixed costs for the acquisition of the remote bridges and associated transmission equipment. An increasingly popular alternative for bridging remote LANs within 3 mi of each other are **wireless bridges.** Wireless bridges use spread spectrum radio transmission between LAN sites and are primarily limited to Ethernet networks at this time.

Like most Ethernet bridges, most wireless bridges support the spanning tree algorithm, filtering by MAC addresses, protection against broadcast storms, SNMP management, encryption, and a variety of different Ethernet network media. Like other remote bridges, wireless bridges must be used in pairs. List prices can range from $2700 to $13500 with the majority of wireless bridges in the $4000 to $5000 range. These prices make wireless bridges comparable to remote WAN bridges in initial cost but have the added advantage of not requiring ongoing monthly expense for WAN services.

Routers

Functionality   Among the advanced functionality offered by routers, perhaps the most important is their ability to discriminate between multiple network layer pro-

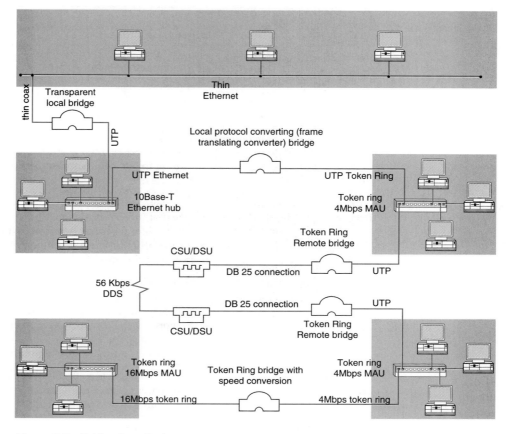

Figure 9-8   Bridge Installations

tocols. For instance, remembering that multiple protocols can be "sealed" within Ethernet data-link layer "envelopes," a router may be programmed to open the Ethernet envelopes and forward all NetWare (IPX) traffic to one network and all TCP/IP (IP) or AppleTalk (AFP) to another. In some cases, a certain protocol may require "priority" handling due to session time-out restrictions or the time sensitivity of the embedded data.

Routers are made to read specific network layer protocols to maximize filtering and forwarding rates. If a router only has to route one type of network protocol, then it knows exactly where to look for destination addresses every time and can process packets much faster. However, realizing that different network layer protocols will have different packet structures with destination addresses of various lengths and positions, some more sophisticated routers known as **multiprotocol routers** have the capability to interpret, process, and forward data packets of multiple protocols.

In the case of an Ethernet data-link frame, the multiprotocol router knows which network layer protocol is embedded within the data-link frame's information field by the contents of the type field in the Ethernet frame.

Bridge Technology Analysis Issue	Importance/Implication
Network architectures to be connected	• Bridges for Ethernet and token ring are common • Bridges for FDDI, 100BaseT, and 100VG-AnyLAN are less common • Network architecture determines LAN speed • Network architecture determines supported network media
Transparent bridges	• Used for connecting Ethernet to Ethernet or non-source-routing token ring to non-source-routing token ring • Must be able to support promiscuous listen, store-and-forward bridging, learning, and spanning tree algorithm
Translating bridges	• Ethernet/token ring is the most common translating bridge • Can become a serious network bottleneck due to incompatibilities between Ethernet and token ring frame layouts, transmission speeds, and frame lengths
Source-routing bridges	• Used to connect two or more source-routing-enabled token ring LANs • Source routes are determined by explorer packet broadcasts • Explorer packet broadcasts can negatively effect network performance • Routes are limited to 7 hops (intermediate bridges)
Source-routing transparent bridges	• An intelligent bridge that is able to distinguish between transparent bridge traffic and source-routing bridge traffic and is able to bridge each appropriately

Bridge performance testing	• Bridge performance can be measured in any of the following ways:
	  • Throughput: Maximum sustained transmission rate with zero errors or lost packets
	  • Packet loss rate: percent of packets lost at maximum theoretical transmission speed of the bridge
	  • Latency: The time it takes for a bridge to process a single packet or, in other words, the delay per packet introduced by the bridge

Local bridges	• Local bridges connect two or more LANs directly via network media • Local bridges contain two or more network interface cards • Local bridges are used to translate between media types
Multiport bridges	• Multiport bridges contain more than two network interface cards • If the bridge has learned which ports a destination workstation is attached to (by building known local nodes table for each port), it will forward the data-link layer frame to that port • If the bridge does not know which port a destination workstation is attached to, it will broadcast the data-link layer frame to all ports except the one from which it came

Figure 9-9   Bridge Technology Analysis

Remote bridges	• Remote bridges contain network interface cards as well as serial ports for connection to WAN links via modems or CSU/DSUs • Most remote bridges contain one network interface card, specific to a particular network architecture, and one serial interface (RS-232 or V.35) • A compatible remote bridge must be used on the far end of the WAN link to complete the LAN-to-LAN connection • Data compression is particularly important to remote bridges as the WAN links possess significantly less bandwidth than the LANs (compression rates depend on the file being compressed; 3:1 compression ratios are possible) • SNMP management information from remote bridges is important to allow these bridges to be monitored and managed by an SNMP- compliant enterprise network management system • To be able to configure remote bridges from a centralized support location, the remote bridges must support Telnet login
WAN services for remote bridges	• Among the WAN services available for remote bridges are 56-Kbps DDS, ISDN, and T-1 (1.544 Mbps).
Hot-swappable modules	• Some bridges may support hot-swappable modules, allowing users to flexibly configure the network interfaces in a bridge without disabling the network
RISC processors	• Bridge performance is directly related to the speed of the processor within the bridge • RISC processors produce superior performance results
Price range	• $2000–6000

Figure 9-9   *(Continued)*

The following are some common network layer protocols and their associated network operating systems or upper layer protocols:

- IPX   NetWare
- IP   TCP/IP
- VIP   Vines
- AFP   AppleTalk
- XNS   3Com
- OSI   Open Systems

Other protocols processed by some routers are actually data-link layer protocols without network layer addressing schemes. These protocols are considered **non-routable**. Nonroutable protocols can be processed by routers either by having the routers act as bridges or by encapsulating the nonroutable data-link layer frame's upper layer protocols in a routable network layer protocol such as IP. At one time, specialized devices that could either bridge or route were referred to as **brouters**; however, today most advanced routers include bridging functionality. The following are some of the more common nonroutable protocols and their associated networking environments:

- LAT   Digital DECNet
- SNA/SDLC   IBM SNA
- NetBIOS   DOS-based LANs
- NetBEUI   LAN Manager

ROUTING PROTOCOLS

In Sharper Focus

Routers manufactured by different vendors need a way to talk to each other to exchange routing table information concerning current network conditions. Every network operating system contains an associated routing protocol as part of its protocol stack. Figure 9-10 lists common routing protocols and their associated protocol suites or network environments.

RIP, routing information protocol, at one time the most popular router protocol standard, is largely being replaced by **OSPF, open shortest path first.** OSPF offers several advantages over RIP including its ability to handle larger internetworks as well as a smaller impact on network traffic for routing table updates.

A major distinction between routing protocols has to do with the method or algorithm by which up-to-date routing information is gathered by the router. For instance, RIP uses a **distance vector** algorithm that only measures the number of hops to a distant router, to a maximum of 16, whereas the OSPF protocol uses a more comprehensive **link state** algorithm that can decide between multiple paths to a given router based on variables other than the number of hops such as delay, capacity, throughput, and reliability of the circuits connecting the routers. Perhaps more importantly, OSPF uses much less bandwidth in its efforts to keep routing tables up-to-date.

Distance vector routing requires each router to maintain a table listing the distances in hops, sometimes referred to as link cost, between itself and every other reachable network. These distances are computed by using the contents of neighboring routers' routing tables and adding the distance between itself and the neighboring router that supplied the routing table information. Routing tables must be kept up-to-date to reflect any changes in the network. The key problem with dis-

Routing Protocol		Network Environment
RIP	(routing information protocol)	XNS, NetWare, TCP/IP
OSPF	(open shortest path first)	TCP/IP
NLSP	(NetWare link state protocol)	NetWare 4.1
IS-IS	(intermediate system to intermediate system)	DECnet, OSI
RTMP	(routing table maintenance protocol)	AppleTalk
RTP	(router table protocol)	Vines

Figure 9-10   Router-to-Router Protocols

tance vector routing protocols is that changes in the network are not always known by all routers immediately due to the delays in having routers recalculate their own routing tables prior to retransmitting updated information to neighboring routers. This phenomenon is referred to as **slow convergence.**

Link state protocols such as OSPF (TCP/IP) and NLSP (NetWare) are able to overcome slow convergence and offer a number of other performance enhancements as well. One important distinction between distance vector and link state routing protocols is that distance vector routing protocols only use information supplied by directly attached neighboring routers, whereas link state routing protocols employ network information received from all routers on a given internetwork.

Link state routing protocols are able to maintain a complete and more current view of the total internetwork than distance vector routing protocols by adhering to the following basic processes:

- Link state routers use special datagrams known as **link state packets (LSP)** to determine the names of and the cost or distance to any neighboring routers and associated networks.

- All information learned about the network is sent to all known routers, not just neighboring routers, using LSPs.

- All routers have all other routers' full knowledge of the entire internetwork via the receipt of LSPs. The collection of LSPs are stored in an LSP database. This full internetwork view is in contrast to only a view of one's immediate neighbors using a distance vector protocol.

- Each router is responsible for compiling the information contained in all of the most recently received LSPs to form an up-to-the-minute view of the entire internetwork. From this full view of the internetwork, the link state routing protocol is able to calculate the best path to each destination network as well as a variety of alternate paths with varying costs.

- Newly received LSPs can be forwarded immediately whereas distance vector routing protocols had to recalculate their own routing tables before forwarding updated information to neighboring routers. The immediate forwarding of LSPs allows quicker convergence in the case of lost links or newly added nodes.

Technology Analysis

Applied Problem Solving

The most significant distinguishing factor among routers is directly related to the location and associated routing requirements into which the router is to be deployed. As a result, **central site routers,** otherwise known as **enterprise** or **backbone routers,** are employed at large corporate sites, whereas **boundary** or **branch office routers** are employed at remote corporate locations with less routing requirements and fewer technical support personnel. For branch offices whose amount of internetwork traffic does not warrant the constant bandwidth and higher cost of leased lines, **dial-up routers** are often employed. Figure 9-11 illustrates the installation of various types of routers.

Boundary Routers and Branch Office Routers   In the case of boundary or branch office routers, all routing information is kept at the central site router. This allows the

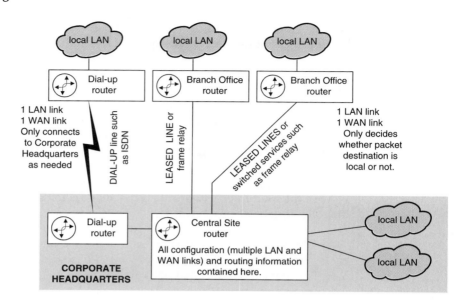

Figure 9-11 Router Installations

boundary router to require less technical configuration and to be available for a lower cost than central site routers. Boundary routers generally have just two interfaces: one WAN link and one LAN link. A boundary router's logic is fairly simple. All locally generated packets are either destined for the local LAN, in which case they are ignored, or they are forwarded over the single WAN link to the central site router for further processing.

The obvious limitations of such a topology are that there is no direct communication between boundary routers and that the central routers must include redundancy since all internetwork communication depends on them. Also, a particular vendor's boundary routers must be matched with that vendor's central office routers as there are no interoperability standards for this configuration. Figure 9-12 outlines some of the technical analysis issues to be considered with boundary routers.

Dial-Up Routers In those cases where the amount of inter-LAN traffic from a remote site does not justify the cost of a leased line, dial-up routers may be the appropriate choice of internetworking equipment. This is especially true if the dial-up digital WAN service known as ISDN (integrated services digital network) is available at the two ends of the LANs to be linked. ISDN BRI (basic rate interface) provides up to 128 Kbps of bandwidth on demand, and ISDN PRI (primary rate interface) provides up to 1.536 Mbps of usable digital bandwidth on demand. There are currently no interoperability standards for dial-up routers. As a result, dial-up routers should always be bought in pairs from the same manufacturer.

In addition to all of the technical features that are important to boundary routers, perhaps the most important feature of dial-up routers is **spoofing.** Spoofing is a method of filtering chatty or unwanted protocols from the WAN link while assuring that remote programs that require ongoing communication from these filtered protocols are still reassured via emulation of these protocols

Technical Analysis Issue	Importance/Implication
Ability to deal with nonroutable traffic	• Must be able to deal with nonroutable protocols such as SNA/SDLC and NetBIOS • Must be able to deal with timing requirements such as SDLC's session time-out limitation
Remote configuration support	• Must be able to be configured remotely • Software upgrades must be able to be performed remotely from central site • What happens if the transmission line or power fails during a remote update?
SNMP compatibility	• Must be able to output SNMP compatible management information for interaction with enterprise network management systems
WAN services supported	• May be any of the following: 56-Kbps, DDS, T-1, Frame relay
Frame relay support	• If frame relay is to be used as the WAN service, can the device interact properly with frame relay's congestion control mechanism to avoid packet loss?
Backup WAN services	• Are switched WAN services available for backup if the leased line fails? • Examples: ISDN, Dial-up asynchronous, switched 56K
WAN protocols supported	• Examples: HDLC, X.25, frame relay, PPP
LAN architectures supported	• Examples: Ethernet, token ring; Others?
LAN protocols routed	• Examples: IP, IPX, DECnet, AppleTalk, Vines, XNS, OSI
LAN protocols filtered	• Some LAN protocols are very chatty and can waste precious WAN bandwidth • Boundary routers should be able to filter these protocols to keep them off the WAN link: SAP, RIP, NetBIOS broadcasts, source-routing explorer packets

Figure 9-12 Boundary Router Technology Analysis

by the local dial-up router. Among the chatty protocols that are most in need of filtering are:

- RIP (routing information protocol): NetWare and TCP/IP.

- SAP (service advertising protocol): NetWare.

- Watchdog, otherwise known as keep-alive messages: NetWare.

- Serialization, looking for duplicate license numbers: NetWare.

The reason filtering is so important to dial-up routers is that these unwanted protocols can easily establish or keep a dial-up line open, thereby unnecessarily leading to excessive line charges. Spoofing as a combination of filtering and emulation is illustrated in Figure 9-13.

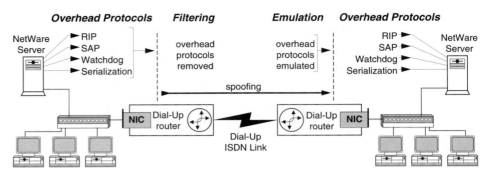

Figure 9-13   Dial-Up Router Spoofing

Occasionally, updated information such as session status or services availability must be exchanged between dial-up routers so that packets are not routed in error and sessions are not terminated incorrectly. The manner in which these required updates of overhead information are performed can make a significant difference in the efficiency of the dial-up routers and the size of the associated charge for the use of dial-up bandwidth. It is important to remember that these routers only communicate via dial-up connections and that it would be economically unwise to create or maintain immediate dial-up connections for every update of overhead information. Different dial-up routers use different update mechanisms. Three primary methods for efficient updating are as follows:

- **Timed updates** are performed at regular predetermined intervals.

- **Triggered updates** are performed whenever a certain programmable event, such as a change in available services, occurs.

- **Piggyback updates** are performed only when the dial-up link has already been established for the purposes of exchanging user data.

Routing Evolution   Although no one knows for sure what the future of internetworking design and technology holds, most people seem to agree that some combination of switching and routing will be the likely scenario in the foreseeable future. Although switching is excellent at providing large amounts of switched LAN bandwidth, it is a layer 2 technology and is unable to offer advanced filtering, security, and internetwork segmentation associated with layer 3 routing technology.

Three different possible internetwork design evolutionary scenarios are as follows:

- **Distinct layer 2 switching and layer 3 routing** in which separate layer 2 switches and layer 3 routers cooperatively contribute what each does best to deliver internetwork traffic as efficiently as possible.

- **Distributed routing** in which layer 2 switching and layer 3 routing functionalities are combined into a single device sometimes referred to as a **multilayer switch.**

- **Route servers** will provide a centralized repository of routing information whereas **edge switches** deployed within the LANs will be programmed with minimal routing information. Edge switches will consult distributed route servers for "directory assistance" when they encounter routing situations that they are not equipped to handle. In this scenario, routing information and processing overhead is kept to a minimum at the switches, which are primarily responsible for providing local bandwidth.

Practical Advice and Information

In differing manners, each of these scenarios implements the future of internetwork design as described by the currently popular phrase, "Switch when you can, route when you must." These three internetworking design scenarios combining switching and routing are illustrated in Figure 9-14.

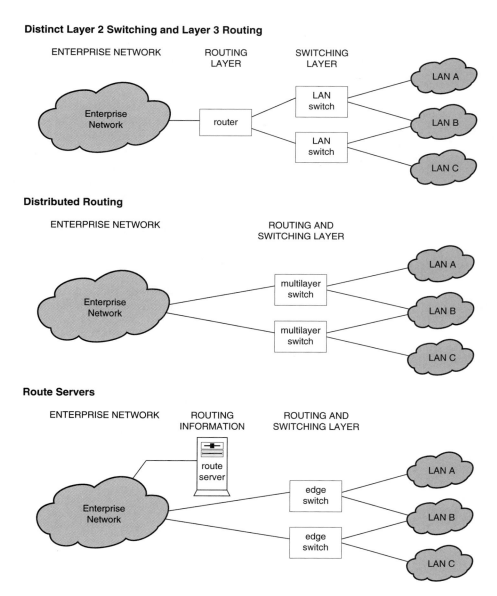

Figure 9-14   Routing Evolution Scenarios

IP Switching   Another possible evolutionary scenario combining switching and routing is known as **IP switching.** By implementing IP routing software directly on ATM switching hardware, IP switching combines switching and routing capabilities into a single device and discriminates between which traffic should be switched and which should be routed. For streaming data such as file transfers or multimedia sessions, ATM switched virtual circuits are established and the traffic is allowed to flow through the virtual circuit without the typical packet-by-packet processing associated with routers. For connectionless datagrams and shorter transmissions, IP routing software is implemented. Protocols to distinguish which traffic should be switched and which should be routed have been proposed by at least three different companies and will eventually be considered by the IETF. The early entries for IP switching management protocols are flow management protocol from IPsilon Networks, tag distribution protocol from Cisco, and aggregate route-based IP switching from IBM.

■ LAN-TO-MAINFRAME INTERNETWORKING

Introduction

Micro–Mainframe Connectivity vs. Peer-to-Peer Internetworking   Strictly speaking, micro–mainframe connectivity and internetworking are two different concepts. In **micro–mainframe connectivity,** the micro (stand-alone or LAN-attached PC) pretends to be or "emulates" a mainframe terminal such as an **IBM 3270** attached and logged into the mainframe. Although file transfer utilities may allow more capability than mere remote login, this is not the peer-to-peer networking implied by the term internetworking.

With full **peer-to-peer internetworking,** the PC can exchange data with any mainframe or any other PC on a host-to-host level rather than acting like a "dumb" terminal as in the case of micro–mainframe connectivity. Although these two mainframe connectivity alternatives have their differences, they still have much in common. The truth is that most "IBM Shops" have a mixture of 3270 terminal connections, mainframes, and LANs that must communicate with each other on a number of different levels.

Hierarchical Networks and Peer-to-Peer Communications Networks   A hierarchical network structure such as the "classic" SNA (systems network architecture) centers around the mainframe. If two devices other than the mainframe on an SNA network wanted to communicate, they would have to establish, maintain, and terminate that communication through the mainframe. This model is in direct contrast to a peer-to-peer network communications structure, typical of most LANs, in which any device may communicate directly with any other LAN-attached device.

Classic SNA Architecture

Figure 9-15 illustrates a simple SNA network and introduces some key SNA network elements.

Two devices in a classic SNA environment as illustrated in Figure 9-15 are

- **Front-end processor** (FEP) (IBM 3745, 3746)—A front-end processor is a computer that offloads the communications processing from the mainframe,

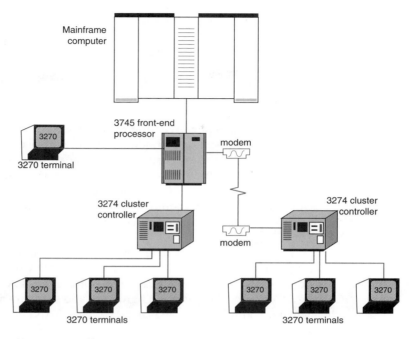

Figure 9-15   Classic SNA

allowing the mainframe to be dedicated to processing activities. A high-speed data channel connects the FEP to the mainframe locally although FEPs can be deployed remotely as well. The FEP, also known as a communications controller, can have devices such as terminals or printers connected directly to it, or these end-user devices may be concentrated by another device known as a cluster controller. There are two options for high-speed data channels between FEPs and IBM mainframes:

- **Bus and tag** has a transmission rate of 4.5 Mbps and has been available since 1967.
- **ESCON II (enterprise system connection)** has a maximum transmission rate of 70 Mbps, has been available since 1990, and is able to transmit up to 30 mi over fiber optic cable.

- **Cluster controller** (IBM 3174, 3274)—A cluster controller is a device that allows connection of both 3270 terminals and LANs with possible wide area links to packet-switched networks (X.25) or high-speed leased lines. A cluster controller concentrates the transmissions of its numerous input devices and directs this concentrated data stream to the FEP either locally or remotely.

The hierarchical nature can be seen in Figure 9-15 as data received from the lowly terminals is concentrated by multiple cluster controllers for a front-end processor that further manages the data for the almighty mainframe. As additional processors and minicomputers such as an IBM AS/400 are added, the hierarchical nature of classic SNA can be seen even more clearly.

The network illustrated in Figure 9-15 will be modified one step at a time until the goal of an architecture that seamlessly transports SNA as well as LAN traffic is reached.

Micro–Mainframe Connectivity

PCs as 3270 Terminals   The first step of PC or LAN integration with classic SNA is allowing a stand-alone PC to emulate a 3270 terminal and conduct a communications session with the mainframe. To accomplish this, **protocol conversion** must take place to allow the PC to appear to be a 3270 terminal in the eyes of the mainframe.

A **3270 protocol conversion card** is inserted into an open expansion slot of a PC. Additional protocol conversion software, which may or may not be included with the protocol conversion card, must be loaded onto the PC to make the PC keyboard behave like a 3270 terminal keyboard (keyboard remapping). The media interface on the card is usually RG-62 Thin Coax for local connection to cluster controllers. Synchronous modems could also be employed for remote connection. Figure 9-16 illustrates possible configurations for stand-alone PC 3270 terminal emulation.

LAN-Based SNA Gateways   The next scenario to be dealt with is how to deliver mainframe connectivity to LAN-attached PCs. One way would be to mimic the method for attaching stand-alone PCs. That is, for every LAN-attached PC, buy and install the 3270 protocol conversion hardware and software and provide a dedicated link to a cluster controller. Whereas most of these LAN-attached PCs only need mainframe connectivity on an occasional basis, this would not be a very cost-effective solution. This would be wasteful in terms of not only the number of PC boards purchased but also the number of cluster controller ports monopolized but underutilized.

Instead, it would be wiser to take advantage of the shared resource capabilities of the LAN to share a protocol conversion attachment to the mainframe. Such a LAN server based, shared protocol converted access to a mainframe is known as a

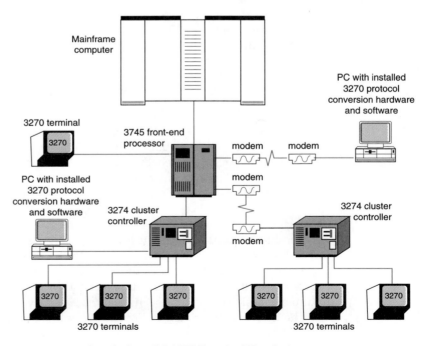

Figure 9-16   Stand-alone PC 3270 Terminal Emulation

gateway. Two popular SNA gateway software packages associated with LAN operating are as follows:

- Microsoft SNA Server for linking to Windows NT LANs.

- NetWare for SAA for linking to NetWare LANs.

Figure 9-17 illustrates both a LAN-based local gateway and a remote gateway. As can be seen in Figure 9-17, a gateway configuration can allow multiple simultaneous 3270 mainframe sessions to be accomplished via a single gateway PC and a single port on the cluster controller. A remote PC-based LAN gateway needs additional hardware and software to emulate not only the 3270 terminal but also the 3274 cluster controller. Such remote 3274 cluster controller boards and software are as readily available as 3270 terminal emulation hardware and software. As a slight variant on the PC-based emulation hardware and software previously mentioned, stand-alone protocol conversion devices for both 3270 terminal and 3274 cluster controller emulation are available as illustrated in Figure 9-17.

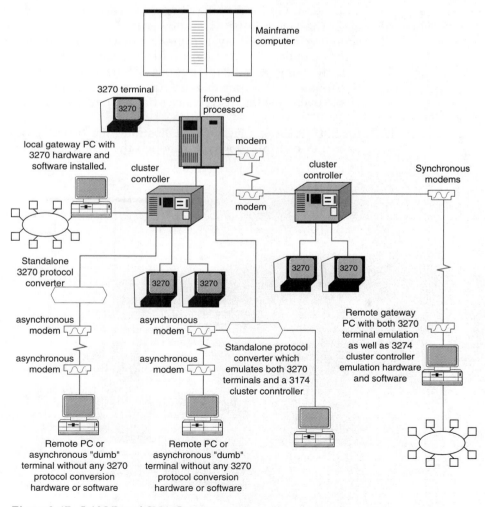

Figure 9-17   LAN-Based SNA Gateways

Mainframe Channel-Attached Gateways   As an alternative to LAN-based gateways, **channel-attached gateways** are able to interface directly to the mainframe's high-speed data channel, thereby bypassing the FEP entirely. Physically, the channel-attached gateways are often modules that are added to enterprise routers. Depending on the amount of actual 3270 terminal traffic required in a given network, the use of channel-attached gateways either may preclude the need for additional FEP purchases or may allow FEPs to be replaced altogether.

The price difference between channel-attached gateways and FEPs is significant. An ESCON-attached IBM 3745 FEP costs approximately $225,000 whereas an equivalent router-based Cisco channel interface processor costs approximately $69,000. Figure 9-18 illustrates the installation of channel-attached gateways for linking LAN-based PCs as 3270 terminals to mainframes.

The SNA Model

Figure 9-19 illustrates a seven-layer model of the SNA hierarchy. Like the OSI model, the SNA model starts with media issues in layer 1, the physical control layer, and ends up at layer 7, the transaction services layer, which interfaces to the end-user. The layers in between, however, do not match up perfectly with the corresponding numbered layer in the OSI model although general functionality at each layer is similar. "Similar general functionality" will not suffice when it comes to internetworking. As a result, options will be seen for merging SNA (SDLC) and OSI (LAN-based) data transmissions on a single internetwork involving various methods to overcome the discrepancies between the two architectures.

The SDLC Protocol   Figure 9-20 illustrates the structure of the **SDLC (synchronous data-link control)** protocol. Although the protocol structure itself does not look all

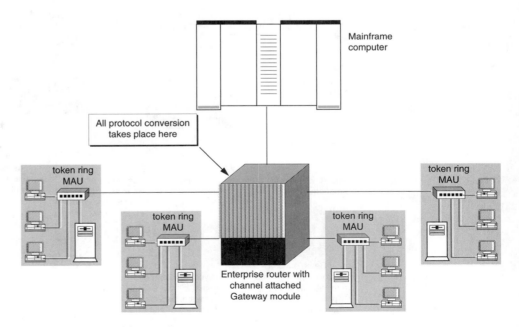

Figure 9-18   Channel-Attached LAN/SNA Gateways

Layer number	Sublayer number	Layer/Sublayer Name	Function
7		Transaction Services	Provide network management services. Control document exchange and distributed database access.
6		Presentation Services	Formats data, data compression, and data transformation.
5		Data Flow Control	Synchronous exchange of data supports communications session for end-user applications, assures reliability of session.
4		Transmission Control	Matches the data exchange rate, establishes, maintains, and terminates sessions. Guarantees reliable delivery of data between end points. Error control, flow control.
3		Path Control	Overall layer: Creates the link between two end-points for the transmission control protocols to manage. Divided into 3 sublayers.
	3	Virtual Route Control	Create virtual route (virtual circuit), manage end-to-end flow control.
	2	Explicit Route Control	Determines actual end-to-end route for link between end nodes via intermediate nodes.
	1	Transmission Group Control	If multiple possible physical paths exist between the end-points, this protocol manages to use these multiple lines to assure reliability and load balancing.
2		Data Link Control	Establishes, maintains, and terminates data transmission between two adjacent nodes. Protocol is SDLC.
1		Physical Control	Provides physical connections specifications from nodes to shared media.

Figure 9-19 The SNA Model

that unusual, it is the fact that the information block of the SDLC frame does not contain anything equivalent to the OSI network layer addressing information for use by routers which makes SDLC a **nonroutable protocol.** SDLC is nonroutable because there is simply no network layer address information available for the routers to process. This shortcoming can be overcome in a number of different ways. However, it is important to understand that this nonroutability is one of the key challenges facing SNA/LAN integration.

Given that SDLC cannot be routed, network managers had no choice but to implement multiple networks between corporate enterprises. One network would carry SDLC traffic between remote cluster controllers and FEPs to local cluster controllers, FEPs, and mainframes, whereas a second network would support remote bridged/routed LANs linking with local LANs between the same corporate locations. Such an implementation is sometimes referred to as a **parallel-networks model.** Obviously, it would be advantageous from both business and network management perspectives to somehow combine the two traffic streams into a single network. Figure 9-21 illustrates this multiple-network scenario.

Flag 1 byte	Address 1 byte	Control 1 byte	Information	Frame Check Sequence 2 bytes	Flag 1 byte

Figure 9-20 SDLC Data-Link Control Frame Layout

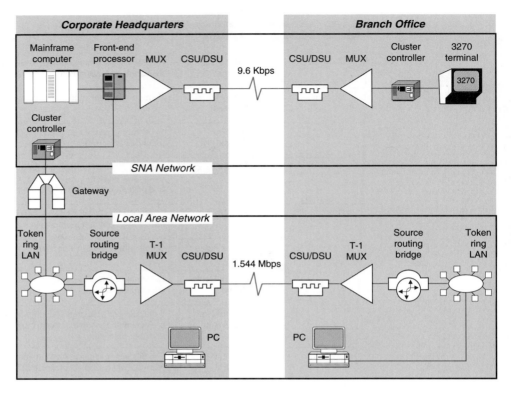

Figure 9-21   SNA/LAN Incompatibilities Yield Multiple Networks

Challenges to SNA/LAN Integration

To understand how SNA and LAN traffic can be integrated, the incompatibilities between SNA networks and local area networks must first be delineated.

- The first SNA characteristic that can cause trouble on a LAN is the great amount of **acknowledgment and polling traffic** between SNA processors and SNA end-user devices. This constant chatter could quickly monopolize the better part of the LAN bandwidth.

- The second SNA characteristic that can cause problems when run over a shared LAN backbone is that SNA has **timing limitations** for transmission duration between SNA hosts and end-user devices. Thus on wide area, inter-networked LANs over shared network media, SNA sessions can "time-out," effectively terminating the session.

- Another traffic contributor that can easily monopolize internetwork bandwidth comes from the LAN side of the house. As described earlier in this chapter, token ring LANs use an internetworking device known as a source-routing bridge. To define their source-routed internetworking paths, source PCs send out numerous explorer packets as a means of gaining a sense of the best route from source to destination. All of these discovery packets mean only one thing—significantly more network traffic.

- As previously stated, SDLC is a nonroutable protocol. To maximize the efficiency of the integrated SNA/LAN network, some way must be found to route SDLC or otherwise transparently incorporate it with LAN traffic.

Given the aforementioned incompatibilities, it would seem clear that there are three major challenges to allowing SNA and LAN traffic to share an internetwork backbone:

- Reduce unnecessary traffic (source-routing explorer packets and SDLC polling messages).

- Find some way to prioritize SNA traffic to avoid time-outs.

- Find a way to allow internetwork protocols to transport or route SDLC frames.

SNA/LAN Integration Solutions

Several major categories of SNA/LAN integration solutions are currently possible. Each varies in both approach and the extent to which SNA/LAN incompatibilities are overcome:

- Add a token ring adapter to a compatible cluster controller.
- TCP/IP Encapsulation.
- SDLC conversion.
- APPN (advanced peer-to-peer networking).

Token Ring Adapter into Cluster Controller The first method, as illustrated in Figure 9-22, is the least expensive and, predictably, also the least effective in terms of meeting the SNA/LAN integration challenges. A token ring network adapter is attached to an available cluster controller port and attached to a token ring network. The SNA traffic is transported using the standard source route bridging (SRB) to its destination.

However, that is only one of the three challenges to be met. The failure to deal with unnecessary traffic and prioritization of SNA traffic make this a less than ideal solution. This is a bridged approach, dealing only with OSI layer 2 protocols. Notice, however, the significant potential reduction to hardware and networking costs by this simple approach.

TCP/IP Encapsulation The second method is known alternatively as **TCP/IP encapsulation,** passthrough, or tunneling. Simply stated, each upper layer SNA packet is "stuffed" into an IP "envelope" for transport across the network and processing by routers supporting TCP/IP internetworking protocol. This IP passthrough methodology for SDLC transport is a common feature or option on internetworking routers. In this methodology IP is supplying the network layer addressing that was lacking from the native SDLC protocol, thereby enabling routing. Figure 9-23 illustrates a passthrough architecture. Upon close examination of Figure 9-23, it may become obvious that, in fact, there is no SNA/LAN integration. What the SNA and LAN traffic share is the T-1 wide area network between routers. The SNA traffic

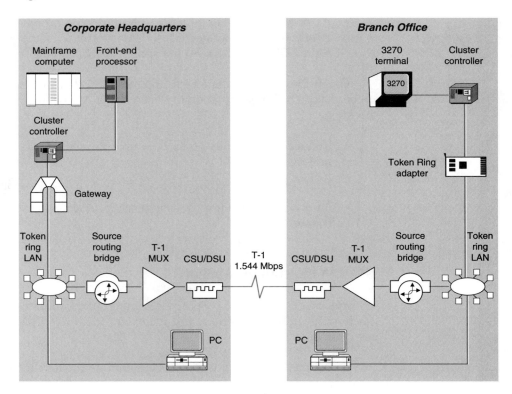

Figure 9-22   Token Ring Adapter into Cluster Controller

never travels over shared LAN media. Cost savings as compared to the parallel-networks model (Figure 9-21) includes eliminating one wide area link and associated internetworking hardware. The actual TCP/IP encapsulation may take place in either a gateway or a router.

IBM's version of TCP/IP encapsulation is known as **data-link switching** or **DLSw** and has been proposed as a standard to the IETF (Internet Engineering Task Force) as RFC (Request for Comment) 934. DLSw does not propose anything radically new but incorporates many vendor-specific TCP/IP encapsulation features into a single standard that will hopefully be widely supported. DLSw is implemented as a software feature on supported routers.

In addition to encapsulating SNA packets in IP addressed envelopes, DLSw also deals with the polling traffic and session time-out issues of SDLC traffic. **Poll spoofing** is the ability of an internetworking device, such as an SDLC converter or router, to respond directly to, or acknowledge, the FEP's constant polling messages to the remote cluster controller. By answering these status check messages locally, the inquiry and its answer never enter the wide area link portion of the internetwork. **Proxy polling,** on the other hand, emulates the FEP's polling messages on the remote side of the network, thereby assuring the remote cluster controller that it is still in touch with an FEP.

Broadcast filtering addresses a bad habit of the LAN side of SNA/LAN integration. In token ring source route bridging, individual PCs send out multiple broadcast packets or explorer packets, causing potential congestion on the internetwork links. Instead of allowing these packets onto the internetwork, routers can filter these broadcast packets out of the traffic, read the destination address to which

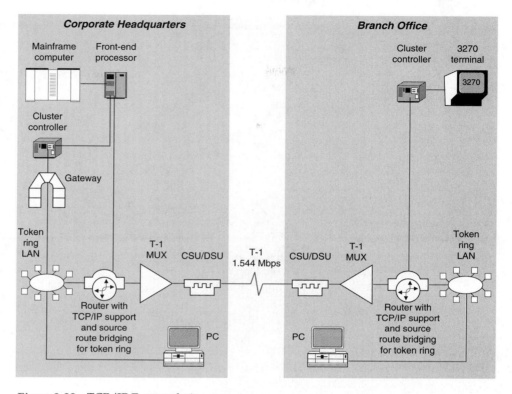

Figure 9-23   TCP/IP Encapsulation

the PC is seeking a route, and supply the PC directly with that information after consulting its own routing tables.

SDLC Conversion   The third possible solution to SNA/LAN traffic integration is known as **SDLC conversion** and is characterized by SDLC frames actually being converted to token ring frames by a specialized internetworking device known as a **SDLC converter.** The SDLC converter may be a stand-alone device or may be integrated into a bridge/router. As can be seen in Figure 9-24, in the SDLC conversion configuration, the cluster controller is attached to the token ring LAN via a stand-alone or integrated SDLC converter.

SDLC frames are converted to token ring frames, transported across the token ring internetwork, and routed to a gateway that transforms the token ring frames back into SDLC frames and forwards them to the mainframe. Also notice the absence of the FEP from the illustration, a potential savings of several thousand dollars. Eliminating the FEP assumes that all 3270 traffic could be routed through attached LANs and gateways.

APPN: IBM's Alternative to LAN-Based SNA/LAN Integration   **APPN (advanced peer-to-peer network)** is IBM's answer to multiprotocol networking on a peer-to-peer basis using SNA rather than a LAN-based network architecture. Simply put, attached computers, whether PCs, AS/400s, or mainframes, are welcome to talk directly with each other without having the communications session established, maintained, and terminated by the almighty mainframe as was required in classic SNA. Recent

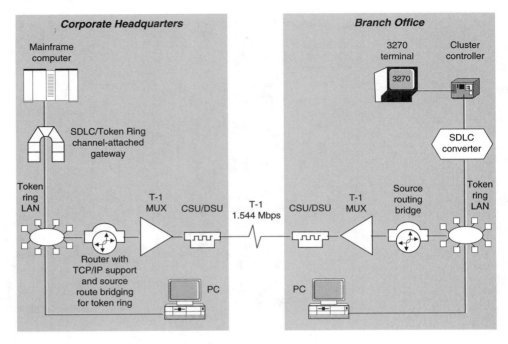

Figure 9-24   SDLC Conversion

enhancements to APPN known as **HPR (high-performance routing)/AnyNET** now allow multiple transport protocols such as IP and IPX to travel over the APPN network simultaneously with SNA traffic. In such an implementation, APPN rather than TCP/IP serves as the single backbone protocol able to transport multiple LAN protocols as well as SNA traffic simultaneously. The specific APPN protocol that deals with SNA/LAN integration is known as **DLUR/S (dependent logical unit requester/server).**

APPN is a software-based solution that consists of only three basic components:

- **End nodes** are end-user processing nodes, either clients or servers without any information on the overall network, available internetwork links, or routing tables.

- **Network nodes** are processing nodes with routing capabilities. They have the ability to locate network resources, maintain tables of information regarding internetwork links, and establish a session between the requesting end node and the internetwork service requested.

- The **central directory server** can save time as well as network traffic for the network nodes. Instead of each network node on an internetwork doing their own information gathering and internetwork exploration and inquiry, they can simply consult the central directory server.

A simple example of an APPN with HPR/AnyNET is illustrated in Figure 9-25.

If the functionality of APPN sounds a lot like what was just reviewed in the other SNA/LAN integration solutions, that should come as no surprise. IBM is not proposing any radical new methodologies. Rather, they are offering an IBM-backed

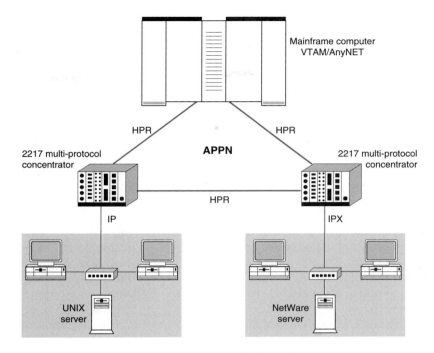

Figure 9-25   APPN with HPR/AnyNET for SNA/LAN Integration

migration from the hierarchical SNA network to a more effective peer-to-peer environment. Alternatively stated, rather than running SNA over a TCP/IP-based LAN internetwork, APPN runs TCP/IP, and other protocols, over an SNA mainframe-based internetwork.

Managerial Perspective

Although it now supports multiple protocols, APPN should not be misconstrued as an open architecture. APPN is a single-vendor solution with only limited support from third-party internetworking hardware vendors.

SNA/LAN Integration and Frame Relay   Although all of the SNA/LAN integration solutions illustrated thus far have used a leased T-1 (1.544 Mbps) as their WAN service, this is by no means the only option. A WAN packet-switched network service known as **frame relay** has become a popular alternative SNA/LAN integration WAN service. The key positive attribute of frame relay is that charges are based on actual amounts of traffic transmitted rather than fixed monthly rates. The key negative aspect of using frame relay as a WAN service for SNA/LAN integration is that the frame relay network is being shared with numerous other subscribers and is subject to congestion. At such times, the access device to the frame relay network, known as a **frame relay access device** or **FRAD,** must be able to respond to requests from the frame relay network to "throttle back" or slow down the input to the network or risk losing transmitted packets due to network overload.

Specifications for the transmission of integrated SNA/LAN traffic over frame relay networks, including proper reaction to congestion notification, is contained in IETF RFC 990.

SUMMARY

Internetworking represents an evolutionary stage of LAN development brought on by either poor network performance or a need to share information between two different LANs. Internetworking design includes techniques such as segmentation and hierarchical networking as well as processing methodologies such as bridging, routing, and switching.

Bridging is an OSI layer 2 process that makes forwarding decisions based on the contents of data-link layer addresses. Routing is an OSI layer 3 process that makes forwarding decisions based on the contents of network layer addresses. Switching is actually an implementation of microsegmented bridging designed to supply ample bandwidth to a local area network.

Switching and routing functionality must be combined to deliver optimal performance on the internetwork. Switching is used for supplying bandwidth whereas routing is used for security, filtering by network layer protocols, and internetwork segmentation.

Repeaters are a physical layer internetworking device used to extend LAN segment length and to convert between media types. Bridges are a data-link layer internetworking device used to logically segment LANs, thereby supporting fewer workstations and more bandwidth on each LAN. Division of workstations onto bridged LANs should be done with some forethought to avoid having the bridge become an internetwork bottleneck.

Routers are network layer devices that are able to deal with larger internetworks than bridges and are able to determine best paths to destination workstations. Routers must keep routing tables up-to-date with the latest internetwork status through the use of routing protocols. Routing protocols can add significantly to bandwidth usage.

LAN–mainframe connectivity can be as simple as 3270 terminal emulation or as sophisticated as SNA/LAN integration via a single backbone protocol. In either case, alternatives are available that vary in their ability to meet the challenges of SNA/LAN integration as well as in their cost and complexity.

KEY TERMS

3270 protocol conversion card, 372
7 hop limit, 359
acknowledgment and polling
   traffic, 376
address caching, 359
advanced peer to peer networking,
   379
APPN, 379
backbone network, 347
boundary router, 365
bridge, 356
broadcast filtering, 378
broadcast storm, 349
brouters, 364
bus and tag, 371
central directory server, 380
central site router, 365
channel-attached gateways, 374
cluster controller, 371
configuration bridge protocol data
   unit, 359

data-link switching, 378
destination address, 348
dial-up router, 365
distance vector, 364
distinct layer 2 switching and layer
   3 routing, 368
distributed routing, 368
DLSw, 378
edge switches, 368
encapsulating bridges, 360
end nodes, 380
ESCON, 371
explorer packet, 359
FEP, 370
filtering, 357
filtering rate, 357
format converter, 360
forward if not local, 349
forward if proven remote, 351
forwarding, 357
forwarding rate, 357

FRAD, 381
frame relay, 381
frame relay access device, 381
front-end processor, 370
gateway, 373
hierarchical networking, 347
HPR/AnyNET, 380
IBM 3270, 370
IEEE 802.1, 359
internetworking, 346
IP switching, 370
known local nodes, 349
link state, 364
link state packets, 365
load balancing, 351
LSP, 365
micro–mainframe connectivity, 370
microsegmentation, 347
multilayer switch, 368
multiprotocol bridges, 360
multiprotocol routers, 361

REVIEW QUESTIONS

1. What is internetworking?
2. What are some of the factors that can lead an organization to seek internetworking solutions?
3. Differentiate between the four basic internetwork design strategies in terms of proper application.
4. Describe the use of data-link layer addresses by bridges.
5. What is meant by the phrase "forward-if-not-local"?
6. What are some of the key limitations of bridges?
7. How do routers overcome some of the key limitations of bridges?
8. Describe the use of data-link layer addresses by routers.
9. Describe the use of network layer addresses by routers.
10. What is meant by the phrase "forward-if-proven-remote"?
11. What are some of the key services that routers are able to provide to the internetwork?
12. Is switching more like bridging or routing? Explain.
13. What types of functionality are switches not able to deliver?
14. What can be said of all internetworking devices in relation to the OSI model layers and protocols?
15. Describe the types of functionality a repeater is able to deliver.
16. What is auto-partitioning and why is it important to repeaters?
17. What is the difference between ring length and lobe length in token ring networks?
18. What is the difference between filtering and forwarding in bridge functionality?
19. What is the importance of the spanning tree algorithm?
20. What are the advantages and disadvantages of source route bridging?
21. Name and describe the functional characteristics of transparent bridges.
22. Differentiate between translating bridges and encapsulating bridges.
23. Differentiate between source-routing bridges and source-routing transparent bridges.
24. What implementation scenario is particularly well suited for wireless bridges?
25. What makes a protocol nonroutable?
26. What is slow convergence and why is it a problem?
27. Differentiate between distance vector and link state routing protocols in terms of delivered functionality.
28. From a business standpoint, when should boundary routers and dial-up routers be employed?
29. What functionality is of particular importance to boundary or branch office routers? Why?
30. What functionality is of particular importance to dial-up routers? Why?
31. What is spoofing and why is it important?
32. Differentiate between the three major methods for updating spoofed protocols on dial-up routers.
33. Differentiate between the three major alternatives for combining routing and switching functionality.
34. Differentiate between micro–mainframe connectivity and peer-to-peer internetworking in terms of where presentation, data management, and application processing take place in each alternative.
35. Why is classic SNA considered hierarchical?
36. What is the difference in terms of functionality

between a front-end processor and a cluster controller?

37. Differentiate between LAN-based SNA gateways and channel-attached SNA gateways in terms of cost and functionality.

38. What is SDLC?

39. Why is SDLC considered nonroutable?

40. What is the parallel-networks model and what is its cause?

41. Describe each of the challenges to SNA/LAN integration introduced by either SDLC or LAN protocols.

42. Differentiate between the four major SNA/LAN

integration solutions in terms of their ability to meet the previously identified SNA/LAN integration challenges.

43. What is DLSw? Describe its functionality.

44. What is the importance of poll spoofing and proxy polling to DLSw?

45. Differentiate between TCP/IP encapsulation and SDLC conversion in terms of functionality, advantages, and disadvantages.

46. What are some of the major differences between APPN and TCP/IP encapsulation?

47. What is IP switching and how does it differ from conventional switching and routing?

ACTIVITIES

1. Find an organization that has implemented internetworking solutions. Interview the individuals who initiated the internetwork design. What were the motivating factors? Were they primarily business-oriented or technology-oriented?

2. Survey a number of organizations with internetworks to determine how many use primarily bridges vs. routers. Explain your results.

3. Research the expected market forecast for bridges, routers, and other internetwork technology. Many professional periodicals publish such surveys in January. Report on the results of your study.

4. Research broadcast storms and the spanning tree algorithm. Draw diagrams depicting how broadcast storms are created and how the spanning tree algorithm controls multiple active loops.

5. Print out the contents of a routing table from two different routers on the same internetwork. Trace the logical path that a packet would take from a local workstation on a LAN connected to either router.

6. Conduct a survey among organizations with internetworks. Research how many organizations are currently employing or plan to implement LAN switches. What do all of the situations have in common? How do they differ?

7. Research the topic of source route bridging. What

percentage of token ring LANs employ source route bridging? Is this percentage increasing or decreasing? How is source route bridging being dealt with in multiprotocol internetworks by either bridges or routers?

8. Conduct a survey of organizations with router-based internetworks as to the router-to-router protocol currently employed and planned within the next year. What percentage use RIP vs. OSPF? What percentage are planning a change? Analyze and present your results.

9. Review trade magazines, professional periodicals, and product literature to determine the alternative methods for combining switching and routing technology. Is one method dominant? Report on and explain your results.

10. Conduct a survey of organizations with both SNA/SDLC traffic and LAN internetwork traffic. What percentage run parallel networks? What percentage have achieved SNA/LAN integration? How was SNA/LAN integration achieved? What are the plans for the 1-year horizon? Report on and explain your results.

11. Research IP switching technology and protocol development efforts. Have protocols been standardized? Who are the technology market leaders? How widespread is the deployment of IP switching technology? What are the projected growth rates for the IP switching market? Report on and explain your results.

CASE STUDY

Taking Standards to Heart

While other companies embrace a multivendor computing environment, one division of Rockwell International Corp. has bucked the trend and simplified its network infrastructure by standardizing on Sun Microsystems Inc. software and hardware.

A little more than a year ago, Bill Quayle's boss challenged him to find a way for employees in the field—among them engineers and sales representatives—to quickly access customer and product information. Quayle was told that obtaining the data should take no longer than the time a traveling sales representative might have between flights, roughly about a half-hour.

As senior systems administrator at Rockwell Switching Systems Division in Downers Grove, Ill., Quayle knew the company's existing infrastructure, which spread information across a variety of systems, couldn't support those demands. "Our information base was split between environments," said Quayle. A 400-node Novell Inc. NetWare 4.1 network accommodated personnel and nonengineering employees, but the engineering group, key to the division's livelihood, operated on a TCP/IP network with Sun SPARC servers and workstations. The company's IBM mainframe housed legacy business and financial applications and the company's parts-inventory and order-entry applications. Employees in the six major field offices, engineers out in the field, and sales reps on the road had to dial in to the Novell network to gain remote access to local information.

Speed Requirement Failed

"You couldn't get information in a half-hour when you had to dial in

three times," said Quayle. "My task was to bring it all together." After a significant search process and a cost/benefits analysis, Quayle's team decided to toss out the Novell network in favor of a TCP/IP-based networking solution that would provide seamless access to a central Sun Solaris 2.5-based data repository; Sun technology had worked well for the company's engineering department. Rockwell chose a large Oracle Corp. Oracle7 7.1 database to store financial, engineering, human-resources, order-entry, and inventory data. The company stuck with the SPARC servers already used by engineering.

Rockwell also turned to Sun's PC-NFS-pro 2.0, which lets Microsoft Windows users access Unix resources across a TCP/IP network. The software includes file-transfer and Internet-access capabilities and a MAPI (Messaging API) E-mail system.

The company also has placed a Solaris 2.4 server in all six field offices; each server supports between a dozen and two dozen users. Those sites are connected to the home office by a frame-relay connection.

Although the current trend is for companies to move toward multivendor environments rather than away from them, Quayle feels confident that Rockwell's strategy is the best way to simplify its network infrastructure and management. "We think it's a good idea to stay as much as possible with one single vendor because, at least in theory, their products should work together," he said.

Scattered data in disparate systems had "created a large number of problems for Rockwell—the most important being flow of informa-

tion between people who needed to be working together," Quayle explained. "We had this large brick wall between support people in the field, marketing, human resources, and engineering."

Piecing It Together

Until Rockwell underwent standardization, there was no such thing as a typical PC. "Everyone's got something a little different," Quayle explained. "We go from low-end 486es to multiprocessing [Intel Corp.] Pentiums" running Windows 3.1 and Windows for Workgroups. And, those PCs are just as likely to be outfitted with IBM adapter cards as with 3Com Corp. adapter cards or the like, which has made connecting users to the new network more tedious and time-consuming, Quayle said.

In an attempt to sidestep these woes in the future, Rockwell has vowed for homogeneity among its PCs, restricting which adapter cards and bells and whistles users can have on their systems. "We're standardizing on PC configuration so everyone will have access to the same set of applications on the network," said Quayle.

To ease the conversion process, Quayle's team began moving through the organization one division at a time, maintaining the data structure that the groups have grown accustomed to in the Novell environment. "We take a whole Novell server and put it in one partition in the Sun server," said Quayle. A PC runs dual protocol stacks, and each night Quayle transfers the Novell server to the Sun server as read-only files.

Working in his favor is the relative independence of the Rockwell Switching Systems Division. "Unlike other companies I've worked for, this division of Rockwell International is very self-contained," said Quayle. "Human resources, marketing, engineering, and finance are all in one spot. Manufacturing is the only thing not contained, but we have a high-speed link to it."

Rockwell has already switched over its technical-support group, quality-assurance system, and engineering to the new network with positive results.

"The flow of information between technical support and engineering is now open," said Quayle. "We've blocked IPX from everyone and run one protocol. Standardizing on one network protocol makes life a lot simpler."

Rockwell plans to convert the rest of the division—sales, marketing, and the remainder of human resources—by the beginning of this month, with the financial group following under a separate conversion.

But the systems administrator's plans don't end there. Already, many of the users he services are clamoring for Internet access, and he intends to provide it.

Source: Teri Robinson, "Taking Standards to Heart," *LAN Times*, vol. 13, no. 5 (March 4, 1996), p. 29. Copyright © March 4, 1996, by McGraw–Hill, New York. Reprinted by permission of McGraw–Hill, New York.

BUSINESS CASE STUDY QUESTIONS

Activities

1. Complete a top-down model for this case by gleaning facts from the case and placing them in the proper layer of the top-down model. After completing the top-down model, analyze and detail those instances where requirements were clearly passed down from upper layers to lower layers of the model and where solutions to those requirements were passed up from lower layers to upper layers of the model.
2. Detail any questions about the case that may occur to you for which answers are not clearly stated in the article.

Business

1. What was the primary business activity of the organization described in this case?
2. What the business issue/problem/opportunity that needed to be addressed?
3. How did the company in this case justify its single-vendor approach?
4. How was data access adversely effecting business processes?

Application

1. What applications were required to meet the specified business opportunity?
2. Which types of applications ran on which platforms in the original network environment?
3. What new application environment was chosen? Why?
4. What are some possible future applications?

Data

1. What types of information did field employees need to access?
2. How quickly did field employees need to access this information?
3. Since the corporate data was now on a UNIX server, how were Windows clients able to access that data?

Network

1. Describe the original or existing network.
2. What was the original remote access setup?
3. What effect did the original network design have on the ability of field engineers to retrieve information?
4. What WAN service is employed to link the six field offices with headquarters?

Technology

1. Describe the proposed network architecture including network protocols, server hardware and software, and client platform hardware and software configuration.
2. What types of standards for desktop PCs have been implemented? Why?
3. How was the migration organized?

CHAPTER 10

REMOTE ACCESS AND WIRELESS NETWORKING

Concepts Reinforced

OSI Model
Top-Down Model
Internetwork Design
Network Operating Systems

Internet Suite of Protocols Model
Protocols and Compatibility
Internetworking Technology

Concepts Introduced

Remote Access
Remote Node
Remote Access Security
Wireless WAN Services
Remote Access Network Design

Remote Control
Mobile Computing
Wireless LANs
Remote Access Technology

OBJECTIVES

After mastering the material in this chapter, you should

1. Understand the difference between and proper application of remote node vs. remote control computing.

2. Understand the business motivation behind the need for remote access network design.

3. Understand the importance of and networking implication of mobile computing.

4. Understand how to successfully design logical and physical topologies for remote access networks, including wireless LAN and WAN services.

5. Understand how to evaluate remote access technology, including hardware, software, and WAN services.

6. Understand the unique security issues introduced by remote access and mobile computing.

■ INTRODUCTION

To understand the importance of remote access and wireless technology, it is first important to appreciate the business forces that have created the increased demand for such technology.

One of the most important things to understand about LAN remote access is the relatively limited bandwidth of the wide area network links that individuals will use to connect to corporate information resources. Although the goal of LAN remote access may be to offer transparent remote LAN connectivity, decreases in bandwidth by a factor of 100 on WAN links as compared to LAN links cannot be ignored.

The overall goal of this chapter is to outline a methodology for the proper design of remote access solutions based on a thorough understanding of user needs, network architecture alternatives, available technology, and available WAN services.

Managerial Perspective

BUSINESS ISSUES OF REMOTE ACCESS

As information has come to be seen as a corporate asset to be leveraged to competitive advantage, the delivery of that information to users working at remote locations has become a key internetworking challenge. Corporate downsizing has not only increased remaining employees' responsibilities but pushed those responsibilities ever closer to the corporation's customers. As a result, the voice mail message "I'll be virtual all day today" is becoming more and more common. The business-oriented motivations for remote access to local LAN resources fall into three general categories.

The first category of remote LAN access is often referred to as **telecommuting,** or, more simply, working from home with all the information resources of the office LAN at one's fingertips. This category of connectivity and computing is often referred to as **SOHO,** or **Small Office Home Office.**

Studies have indicated that some of the ways in which telecommuting can increase overall worker productivity are the following:

- Better, quicker, more effective customer service.

- Increased on-time project completion and quicker product development.

- Increased job satisfaction among highly mobile employees, leading to both greater productivity and employee retention.

- Decreased worker turnover, leading to decreased training and recruiting budgets.

- Increased sales.

A variation of telecommuting, **mobile computing,** addresses the need for field representatives to be able to access corporate information resources to offer superior customer service while on the road. These field representatives may or may not have a corporate office PC into which to dial.

Although some of the positive results of enabling remote access to corporate data for mobile workers are similar to those of telecommuters, the increased customer focus of the mobile worker is evident in the following benefits:

- Faster responses to customer inquiries.

- Improved communications with co-workers and support staff at corporate offices.

- Better, more effective customer support.

- Increased personal productivity by the mobile workers such as being able to complete more sales calls.

- Increased ability to be "on the road" in front of customers.

- More efficient service from service personnel.

The third major usage of remote computing is for **technical support** organizations that must be able to dial-in to client systems with the ability to appear as a local workstation, or take control of those workstations, to diagnose and correct problems remotely. Being able to diagnose and solve problems remotely can have significant impacts such as

- Quicker response to customer problems.

- Increased ability to avoid having to send service personnel for on-site visits.

- More efficient use of subject matter experts and service personnel.

- Increased ability to avoid revisits to customer sites due to a lack of proper parts.

- Greater customer satisfaction.

The market for remote access technology is expected to grow by 600% between 1994 and 1998 to a yearly revenue level of $4.4 billion.

Managerial Perspective

THE HIDDEN COSTS OF TELECOMMUTING

To fully understand the total costs involved in supporting telecommuters, it is first essential to understand which employees are doing the telecommuting. Telecommuting employees generally fall into one of the following categories:

- Full-time, day-shift, at-home workers.

- After-hours workers who have a corporate office but chosen to extend the workday by working remotely from home during evenings and weekends.

Most studies indicate that more than 75% of telecommuters are of the occasional, after-hours variety. However, corporate costs to set up and support these occasional users are nearly equal to the costs for setting up and supporting full-time at-home users, over $4000/year. Among the hidden costs to be considered when evaluating the cost/benefit of telecommuting are the following:

- Workers may not be within the local calling area of corporate resources, thereby incurring long-distance charges.

- It may be necessary to add wiring from the street to the home or within the home to support additional phone lines.

- If existing phone lines are used, personnel time is used to sort personal calls from business calls.

- To provide sufficient bandwidth, more expensive ISDN lines are often installed, if available.

- Some applications, especially those not optimized for remote access, run very slowly over dial-up lines, leading to decreased productivity.

■ ARCHITECTURAL ISSUES OF REMOTE ACCESS

There are basically only four steps to designing a dial-in/dial-out capability for a local LAN:

- Needs analysis.

- Logical topology choice.

- Physical topology choice.

- Current technology review and implementation.

Logical Design Issues

Needs Analysis   As dictated by the top-down model, before designing network topologies and choosing technology, the network analyst must first determine what is to be accomplished in terms of LAN-based applications and use of other LAN-attached resources. Among the most likely possibilities for the information-sharing needs of remote users are the following:

- Exchange e-mail.

- Upload and download files.

- Run interactive application programs remotely.

- Utilize LAN-attached resources.

The purpose in examining information-sharing needs in this manner is to validate the need for the remote PC user to establish a connection to the local LAN that offers all of the capabilities of locally attached PCs.

In other words, if the ability to upload and download files is the extent of the remote PC user's information-sharing needs, then file transfer software, often included in asynchronous communications software packages, would suffice at a very reasonable cost. A network-based bulletin board service (BBS) package is another way in which information can be shared by remote users easily. Likewise, if e-mail exchange is the total information-sharing requirement, then e-mail gateway software loaded on the LAN would meet that requirement.

However, to run LAN-based interactive application programs or utilize LAN-attached resources such as high-speed printers, CD-ROMs, mainframe connections, or fax servers, a full-powered remote connection to the local LAN must be established. From the remote user's standpoint, this connection must offer transparency. In other words, the remote PC should behave as if it were connected locally to the LAN. From the LAN's perspective, the remote user's PC should virtually behave as if it were locally attached.

Logical Topology Choice: Remote Node vs. Remote Control In terms of logical topology choices, two different logical methods for connection of remote PCs to LANs are possible. Each method has advantages, disadvantages, and proper usage situations. The two major remote PC operation mode possibilities are

- Remote node.
- Remote control.

The term **remote access** is most often used to generally describe the process of linking remote PCs to local LANs without implying the particular functionality of that link (remote node vs. remote control). Unfortunately, the term *remote access* is also sometimes more specifically used as a synonym for remote node.

Figure 10-1 outlines some of the details, features, and requirements of these two remote PC modes of operation whereas Figure 10-2 highlights the differences between remote node and remote control installations.

Remote node or remote client computing implies that, in theory, the remote client PC should be able to operate as if it were locally attached to network resources. In other words, the geographic separation between the remote client and the local LAN resources should be transparent. That's a good theory, but, in practice, the comparative bandwidth of a typical dial-up link (28.8 Kbps for a V.34 modem) as compared with the megabit/second bandwidth of the LAN is anything but transparent. Whereas a NIC would normally plug directly into an expansion slot in a computer, a remote node connection merely extends that link via a relatively low-speed dial-up link. Client applications run on the remote client rather than a local LAN-attached client.

Client/server applications that require large transfers of data between client and server will not run well in remote node mode. Most successful remote node applications are rewritten to minimize large data transfers. For example, modified

Functional Characteristic	Remote Node	Remote Control
Also called	Remote client Remote LAN node	Modem remote control
Redirector hardware/ software required?	Yes	No
Traffic characteristics	All client/server traffic	Keystrokes and screen images
Application processing	On the remote PC	On the LAN-attached local PC
Relative Speed	Slower	Faster
Logical role of WAN link	Extends connection to NIC	Extends keyboard and monitor cables
Best use	With specialty written remote client applications that have been optimized for execution over limited-bandwidth WAN links	DOS applications; graphics on Windows applications can make response time unacceptable

Figure 10-1 Remote Node vs. Remote Control Functional Characteristics

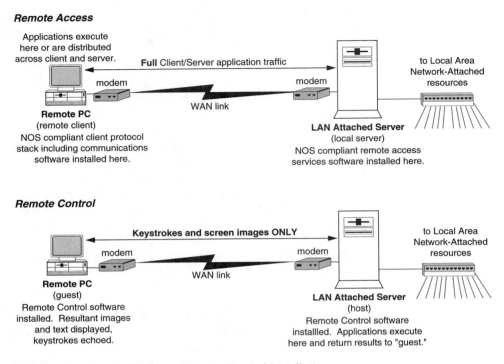

Figure 10-2   Remote Node vs. Remote Control Installations

remote node e-mail client software allows just the headers of received messages, which include sender, subject, and data/time, to be transferred from the local e-mail server to the remote client. The remote client selects which e-mail messages should have the actual e-mail message body and attachments transferred. Local e-mail client software, which assumes plenty of LAN bandwidth, does not bother with such bandwidth-conserving modifications. Other client/server applications must be similarly modified if they are to execute acceptably in remote node mode.

Although transparent interoperability was discussed as one of the goals of remote access, that does not necessarily mean that a worker's mobile computer programs must be identical to those running on one's desktop at the price of terrible performance. One of the most commonly overlooked aspects in deploying remote access solutions is the need to customize applications for optimal performance in a remote access environment.

Remote node mode requires a full client network operating system protocol stack to be installed on the remote client. In addition, wide area network communication software must be incorporated with the remote client NOS protocol stack. Remote node software often also includes optional support of remote control functionality.

Remote control differs from remote node mode in both the technology involved and the degree to which existing LAN applications must be modified. In remote control mode, the remote PC is merely supplying input and output devices for the local client, which interacts as normal with the local server and other locally attached LAN resources. Client applications still run on the local client, which is able to communicate with the local server at native LAN speeds, thereby precluding the need to rewrite client applications for remote client optimization.

Remote control mode requires only **remote control software** to be installed at the remote PC rather than a full NOS client protocol stack that is compatible with the NOS installed at the local LAN. The purpose of the remote control software is only to extend the input/output capabilities of the local client out to the keyboard and monitor attached to the remote PC. The host version of the same remote control package must be installed at the host or local PC. There are no interoperability standards for remote control software.

One of the most significant difficulties with remote control software is confusion by end-users as to logical disk assignments. Recalling that the remote PC only supplies the keyboard and monitor functionality, remote users fail to realize that a C: prompt refers to the C: drive on the local LAN-attached PC and not the C: drive of the remote PC that they are sitting in front of. This can be particularly confusing with file transfer applications.

Protocols and Compatibility   At least some of the shortcomings of both remote node and remote control modes are caused by the underlying transport protocols responsible for delivering data across the WAN link.

In the case of remote control, the fact that proprietary protocols are used between the guest and host remote control software is the reason that remote control software from various vendors is not interoperable.

In the case of remote node, redirector software in the protocol stack must take LAN-based messages from the NDIS or ODI protocols and convert them into proper format for transmission over asynchronous serial WAN links.

Some remote node software uses TCP/IP as its protocol stack and PPP as its data-link layer WAN protocol. In this manner, remote node sessions can be easily established via TCP/IP, even using the Internet as the connecting WAN service should that connection satisfy the security needs of the company in question. Once the TCP/IP link is established, the remote control mode of this software can be executed over TCP/IP as well, overcoming the proprietary protocols typically associated with remote control programs. In addition, due to PPP's ability to transport upper layer protocols other than TCP/IP, these remote node clients can support communications with a variety of different servers.

Figure 10-3 illustrates the protocol-related issues of typical remote control and remote node links as well as TCP/IP-based links.

Security   Although security from an enterprise-wide perspective will be dealt with in Chapter 13 security issues specifically related to remote access of corporate information resources are introduced here. Security-related procedures can be logically grouped into the following categories:

- Password assignment and management—Change passwords frequently, even considering single-use passwords. Passwords should not be actual words found in a dictionary but should ideally be a random or meaningless combination of letters and numbers.

- Intrusion responses—User accounts should be locked after a preset number of unsuccessful logins. These accounts should only be able to be unlocked by a system administrator.

- Logical/physical partitioning of data—Separate public, private, and confidential data onto separate physical servers to avoid users with minimum security clearances from gaining unauthorized access to sensitive or confidential data.

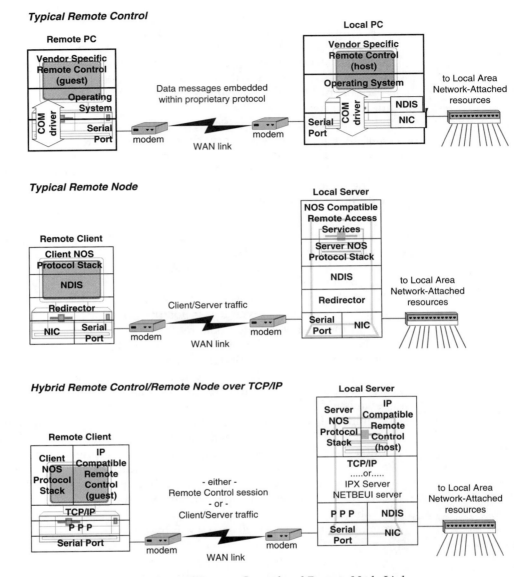

Figure 10-3 Protocol Issues of Remote Control and Remote Node Links

- Encryption—Although it is important for any sensitive or proprietary corporate data to be encrypted, it is especially important that passwords be encrypted to avoid interception and unauthorized reuse.

- Dial-back systems—After a remote user enters a proper user ID and password, these systems terminate the call and dial back the authorized user at a preprogrammed phone number.

- Remote client software authentication protocols—Remote client protocol stacks often include software-based authentication protocols such as PAP (password authentication protocol) or CHAP (challenge handshake authentication protocol).

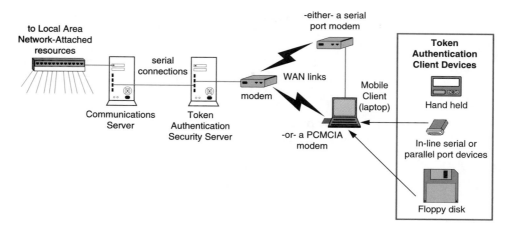

Figure 10-4   Token Authentication Physical Topology

One remote access security category that deserves further explanation is hardware-based **token authentication.** Although exact implementation details may vary from one vendor to the next, all token authentication systems include server components linked to the communications server and client components that are used with the remote access clients. Physically, the token authentication device employed at the remote client location may be a hand-held device resembling a calculator or a floppy disk or it may be an in-line device linked to either the remote client's serial or parallel port. Figure 10-4 illustrates the physical topology of a typical hardware-based token authentication remote access security arrangement.

In Sharper Focus

TOKEN AUTHENTICATION

Logically, token authentication schemes work in either of two different ways:

- **Token response** authentication schemes work as follows:
  1. Remote user dials-in and enters a private identification number (PIN).
  2. Authentication server responds with a challenge number.
  3. Remote user enters that number into a hand-held authentication unit or it is received automatically by an in-line client authentication unit.
  4. Client authentication unit generates a challenge response number that is either automatically transmitted back to the authentication server or entered manually by the remote user.
  5. Transmitted challenge response is received by the authentication server and compared to the expected challenge response number that was generated at the server. If they match, the user is authenticated and allowed access to network-attached resources.

- **Time-synchronous authentication** schemes work as follows:
  1. Random authentication numbers are generated in time-synchronous fashion at both the authentication server and client.
  2. Remote user enters PIN and the current random authentication number displayed on the client authentication unit.

3. Due to time synchronization, the server authentication unit should have the same current random authentication number, which is compared to the one transmitted from the remote client.

4. If the two authentication numbers match, the authentication server authenticates the user and allows access to the network-attached resources.

A few other important operational issues concerning token authentication security systems for remote access are as follows:

- Most authentication servers have a management console that provides supervisory access to the authentication security system. Transmission between the management console and the authentication server should be encrypted.

- Valid passwords and user IDs may be stored on either the management console or the authentication server. In either case, security-related data such as user IDs and passwords should be stored in encrypted form.

- The authentication server's response to failed attempts at remote login should include both account disabling and the ability to generate an alarm, preferably both audible and as a data message to the management console. Ideally, the authentication server should pass alarms seamlessly to enterprise management systems via SNMP to avoid having separate management consoles for every management function.

- Although this functionality is also supplied by remote access server products such as Windows NT RAS, the authentication server should also be able to limit access from remote users to certain times of the day or days of the week.

- As can be seen in Figure 10-4, the authentication server must be able to transparently interoperate with the communications or remote access server. This fact should not be assumed, but demonstrated or guaranteed by the authentication server vendor.

Physical Design Issues

Physical Topology: Alternative Access Points   As Figure 10-5 illustrates, there are three basic ways in which a remote PC user can gain access to the local LAN resources.

- Serial port of a LAN-attached PC—Perhaps the simplest physical topology or remote access arrangement is to establish a communications link to a user PC located in the corporate office. However, many field representatives or mobile computing users no longer have permanent offices and workstations at a corporate building and must depend on remote access to shared computing resources.

- Communications server—As an alternative to having a dedicated PC at the corporate office for each remote user to dial into, remote users could attach to a dedicated multiuser server known as an **access server** or **communications server** through one or more modems. Depending on the software loaded on the communications server, it may deliver remote node functionality, remote control functionality, or both.

Access Point 1: Serial Port of LAN-Attached PC

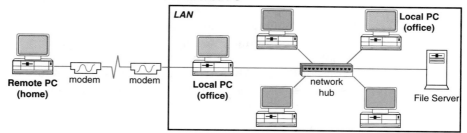

Access Point 2: Communications Server

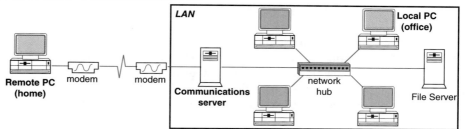

Access Point 3: LAN Modems

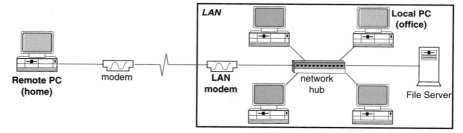

Figure 10-5   Physical Topology: Alternative Access Points

- LAN modem—Another alternative is to install a specialized device known as a **LAN modem,** also known as a **dial-in server,** to offer shared remote access to LAN resources. LAN modems come with all necessary software preinstalled and therefore do not require additional remote control or remote node software. LAN modems are often limited to a single network architecture such as Ethernet or token ring and/or to a single network operating system protocol such as IP, IPX (NetWare), NetBIOS, NetBEUI, or AppleTalk.

The physical topology using the communication server (Figure 10-5, Illustration 2) actually depicts two different possible remote LAN connections. Most communications servers answer the modem, validate the user ID and password, and log the remote user on the network. Some communications servers go beyond this to allow a remote user to access and/or remotely control a particular networked workstation. This scenario offers the same access capabilities as if the networked workstation had its own modem and software but also offers the centralized management, security, and possible financial advantage of a network-attached communications server.

The three access arrangements illustrated are examples of possible physical topologies and do not imply a given logical topology such as remote node, remote control, or both. It is important to understand that the actual implementation of each of these LAN access arrangements may require additional hardware and/or software. They may also be limited in their ability to utilize all LAN-attached resources or to dial out of the LAN through the same access point.

■ REMOTE ACCESS TECHNOLOGY

Hardware

Communications Services and Remote Access Servers   As is often the case in the wonderful but confusing world of data communications, communications servers are also known by many other names. In some cases these names may imply, but don't guarantee variations in configuration, operation, or application. Among these varied labels for the communications server are

- Access servers
- Remote access servers.
- Remote node servers.
- Telecommuting servers.
- Network resource servers.
- Modem servers (usually reserved for dial-out only).
- Asynchronous communications servers.

A communications server offers both management advantages and financial payback when larger numbers of users wish to gain remote access to/from a LAN. Besides the cost savings of a reduced number of modems, phone lines, and software licenses, perhaps more important are the gains in control over the remote access to the LAN and its attached resources. By monitoring the use of the phone lines connected to the communications server, it is easier to determine exactly how many phone lines are required to service those requiring remote LAN access.

Multiple remote users can dial into a communications server simultaneously. Exactly how many users can gain simultaneous access will vary with the sophistication and cost of the communications server and the installed software. Most communications servers service at least four simultaneous users.

Figure 10-6 provides an I-P-O (input-processing-output) diagram illustrating options for the key functional components of a communications server.

As can be seen from Figure 10-6, the key hardware components of the communications server are

- Serial ports.
- CPU(s).
- Network interface card(s).

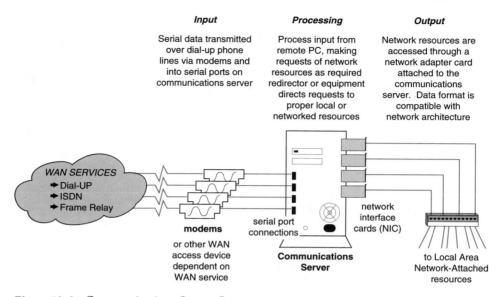

Figure 10-6   Communications Server Components

The relative number of each of these three components included in a particular communications server is a key differentiating factor in communications server architectures of configurations. Although not guaranteed, the differentiation between communications servers and remote node servers is generally considered the following:

- Communications servers include several CPU boards inside a single enclosure. These servers combine both applications server functionality and remote node server functionality. Applications are physically loaded and executed on the communications server. Communications servers are often used for remote control functionality as an alternative to having several separate desktop PCs available for remote control. Consolidating the CPUs into a single enclosure provides additional fault tolerance and management capabilities over the separate-PCs model. Examples of communications servers and vendors are as follows:

Communications Server	Vendor
J&L Chatterbox	J&L Information Systems
CubixConnect Server	Cubix Corp.
CAPServer	Evergreen Systems

- **Remote node servers** are strictly concerned with controlling remote access to LAN-attached resources and acting as a gateway to those resources. Applications services are supplied by the same LAN-attached applications servers that are accessed by locally attached clients.

The functional differences between communications servers and remote node servers are illustrated in Figure 10-7.

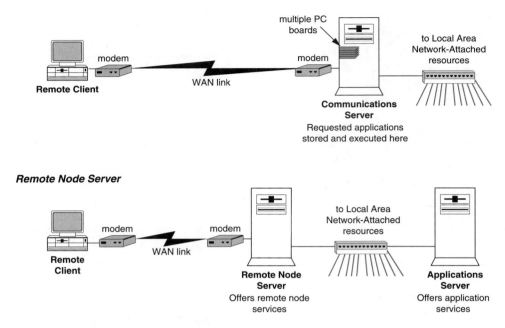

Figure 10-7   Communications Servers vs. Remote Node Servers

Currently, remote node server solutions fall into three major categories:

- Software-only solutions in which the user supplies a sufficiently powerful server and adds a remote node server software package such as Windows NT RAS or NetWare Connect or other third-party remote node software package. In some cases, a multiport serial board may be included with the software to add sufficient serial ports to the user's server. More information about software-only solutions is offered in the section on remote node software.

- Turnkey or hardware/software solutions in which fully configured remote node servers are compatible with existing network architectures and operating systems. Integrated modems may or may not be included. The remote node server software included on these turnkey systems must be compatible with the installed network operating system. Among the more popular remote node servers are the following:

Remote Node	Vendor
LANexpress 4000	Microcom
RLN Turnkey Server	Attachmate
LAN Rover/E Plus 3.5	Shiva
NetBlazer	Telebit
AccessBuilder 2000	3Com
Remote Annex 2000	Xylogics

- LAN modems, also occasionally known as dial-up servers, could be thought of as a remote node server with one or more integrated modems. Included security and management software are also installed on the LAN modem. Given the rapid increase in modem transmission speeds due to evolving modem transmission standards, integrating a modem that cannot be upgraded within a remote node server may be less beneficial than using external modems, which can be more easily upgraded. Perhaps in a response to this need for convenient modem upgrades, some remote node servers now come with four or eight PC Card (PCMCIA) slots into which the latest modem technology can be easily inserted. LAN modems are generally included in reviews of remote node servers rather than being looked upon as a distinct product category.

When a self-contained remote node server including both hardware and software is employed, compatibility with existing network resources on a number of different levels must be taken into account. These compatibility issues as well as key functional issues of remote node servers are outlined in Figure 10-8.

Remote Node Server Compatibility/Functional Issue	Importance/Implication
Network architecture compatibility	• Since the remote node server includes network interface cards, these must be compatible with the architecture (Ethernet, token ring) of the network in which it is to be installed. • Most all remote node servers have Ethernet models whereas fewer offer token ring models. • Media compatibility must also be assured. For example, Ethernet may use AUI, BNC, or RJ-45 interfaces.
Network operating system compatibility	• The remote node server software installed in the server must be compatible with the network operating system installed in the network-attached applications servers. • Since these are third-party hardware/software turnkey systems, the remote node server software is not the same as the native software-only solutions such as Windows NT RAS or NetWare Connect which imply guaranteed compatibility with their respective network operating systems. • The remote node server must also be compatible with the underlying transport protocols used by the installed network operating system. • Can the remote node server access the network operating system's user authorization files to avoid having to build and maintain a second repository of user IDs and passwords? • In the case of NetWare LANs, integration with NetWare Bindery (3.12) or NDS (4.1) should be provided.

Figure 10-8   Compatibility and Functional Issues of Remote Node Servers

Remote Node Server Compatibility/Functional Issue	Importance/Implication
Remote client software compatibility	• The remote node server software must be compatible with the remote node software executed on the remote clients. • This remote client software must be compatible with the native operating system on the remote client. • If compatible remote client software is not supplied with the remote node server, is compatibility with third-party PPP client or remote client software guaranteed? • The cost of the remote client software may be included in the remote node server purchase cost or may be an additional $50/client.
Physical configuration	• Number of serial ports: Most models start at 8; some are expandable up to 128. • Serial port speed: Most support serial port speeds of 110.2 Kbps; some support speeds of 230.4 Kbps.

Transmission optimization	• Use of the limited-bandwidth WAN link can be optimized in a variety of ways:
	  • Compression—Are both headers and data compressed?
	  • Spoofing—Are chatty protocols restricted from the WAN link?
	  • Are users warned before launching remote applications that may bog down the WAN link and offer poor performance?

Routing functionality	• Routing functionality would allow LAN-to-LAN or remote server-to-local server connectivity rather than from a single client to the local server. • Routing functionality allows the remote node server to also act as a dial-up router. Dial-up routers must be used in pairs.
WAN services supported	• Are connectivity to ISDN, X.25, frame relay, and dial-up lines supported? • Some remote node servers have high-speed serial ports for connection to higher speed WAN services such as T-1 (1.544Mbps)
Call management	• Are dropped calls automatically redialed? • Can connect-time limits be enforced? • Can status of all remote access calls be viewed and controlled from a single location? • Are event logs and reports generated? • Are status and alarm messages output via SNMP agents? • Is fixed and variable callback supported? • Is encryption supported?

Figure 10-8   *Continued*

DIALING-OUT FROM THE LAN

Normally, when a modem is connected directly to a PC, the communications software expects to direct information to the local serial port to which the modem is attached. However, in the case of a pool of modems attached to a remote node server, the communications software on the local clients must redirect all information for modems through the locally attached network interface card, across the local LAN, to the remote node server, and ultimately to an attached modem. This ability to redirect information for **dial-out** modem applications from LAN-attached PCs is a cooperative task accomplished by the software of the remote node server and its corresponding remote client software. Not all remote node servers support dial-out functionality.

The required redirection is accomplished through the use of industry-standard software redirection interrupts. The interrupts supported or enabled on particular remote node servers can vary:

- **Int14,** or Interrupt 14, is one of the supported dial-out software redirectors and is most often employed by Microsoft network operating systems. Int14 is actually an IBM BIOS serial port interrupt used for the purpose of redirecting output from the local serial port. A TSR (terminate-and-stay-resident) program running on the client intercepts all of the calls and information passed to Int14 and redirects that information across the network to the modem pool.

- **NASI,** or NetWare asynchronous service interface, is a software interrupt that links to the NetWare shell on NetWare clients. As with the Int14 implementation, a TSR intercepts all of the information passed to the NASI interrupt and forwards it across the network to the dial-out modem pool.

Figure 10-9 illustrates some of the issues involved in dialing-out from the LAN.

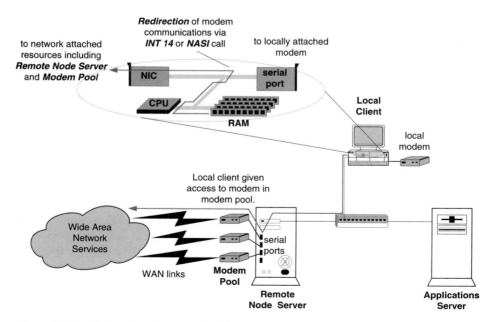

Figure 10-9   Dialing-Out from the LAN

Wireless LANs   Although not limited to use strictly in a remote access setting, wireless LANs do play a role in the overall objective of untethering workers to increase productivity and customer satisfaction. Although wireless LANs may have been initially marketed as a means of replacing wire-bound LANs, that marketing strategy has not been reflected in their applied uses to date.

Mobile computing can be performed within the confines of a corporate or campus environment as well as over longer distances with the assistance of wireless bridges or WAN services. Portable or notebook PCs equipped with their own wireless LAN adapters can create an instant LAN connection merely by getting within range of a server-based wireless LAN adapter or wireless hub. In this way, a student or employee can sit down anywhere and log into a LAN as long as he/she is within range of the wireless hub and has the proper wireless adapter installed in his/her portable PC. These implementations are especially helpful in large warehouse or inventory settings.

Meeting rooms could be equipped with wireless hubs to allow spontaneous workgroups to log into network resources without running cables all over the meeting room. Similarly, by quickly installing wireless hubs and portable PCs with wireless adapters, temporary expansion needs or emergency/disaster recovery situations can be handled quickly and with relative ease—no rerunning of wires or finding the proper cross-connects in the wiring closest.

Finally, wireless LAN technology allows entire LANs to be preconfigured at a central site and shipped "ready to run" to remote sites. The nontechnical users at the remote site literally just have to plug the power cords into the electrical outlets and they have an instant LAN. For companies with a great number of remote sites and limited technical staff, such a technology is ideal. No preinstallation site visits are necessary. Also voided are costs and supervision of building wiring jobs and troubleshooting building wiring problems during and after installation.

Wireless LANs are a relatively new technological phenomenon. Although they have been called a technology looking for a market or, perhaps more aptly, a solution looking for a problem, they do offer significant flexibility and spontaneity not possible with traditional wire-bound LANs. It is important to note that, in general, wireless LANs cannot match the speed of their wired equivalent network architectures. For example, most Ethernet wireless LANs are limited to around 2 Mbps in comparison to Ethernet's 10-Mbps wire-based capacity.

There are currently two popular wireless transmission technologies in the local area network technology area. They are

- **Spread spectrum transmission.**

- **Infrared transmission.**

In Sharper
Focus

FREQUENCY-HOPPING VS. DIRECT-SEQUENCE SPREAD SPECTRUM TRANSMISSION

Spread spectrum transmission, as its name implies, spreads a data message across a wide range or spectrum of frequencies. This technique was originally employed as a security measure since a receiver would need to know exactly how the message was spread across the frequency spectrum to intercept the message in meaningful form. Spread spectrum transmission for wireless LANs is most often limited to two frequency ranges:

- 902–928 MHz.

- 2.4–2.4835 GHz.

In addition, only two spread spectrum techniques are allowed by the FCC for wireless LANs:

- **Frequency-hopping spread spectrum (FHSS).**
- **Direct-sequence spread spectrum (DSSS).**

As can be seen in Figure 10-10, DSSS is more commonly employed in wireless LAN technology and, in general, is capable of delivering higher data throughput rates than FHSS. DSSS transmits at a particular frequency within the allowable range. To distinguish between transmissions from multiple wireless workstations, DSSS adds at least 10 bits to the data message to uniquely identify a particular transmission. DSSS receivers must be able to differentiate between these bits, known as chips, to properly distinguish transmissions. The addition, removal, and interpretation of chips in DSSS add complexity, cost, and processing overhead. Nonetheless, DSSS generally delivers superior throughput to FHSS.

FHSS hops from one frequency to another throughout the allowable frequency range. The pattern of frequency hopping must be known by the wireless receiver so that the message can be reconstructed correctly. A given wireless transceiver's signal is on a given frequency for less than 1 sec. Another desirable effect of all of the

Wireless LAN	Manufacturer	Network Architecture	Wireless Transmission Technology	Data Throughput	Maximum Distance
AirLAN	Solectek Corp.	Ethernet	DSSS, 902–928 MHz	2 Mbps	800 ft
ArLAN	Aironet Wireless Communications Inc.	Ethernet or token ring	DSSS, 902–928 MHz	860 Kbps	1000 ft
			DSSS, 2.4–2.4835 GHz	2 Mbps	500 ft
Collaborative	Photonics Corp.	Ethernet	Diffuse infrared	1 Mbps	30-ft radius
FreePort	Windata	Ethernet	DSSS, 902–928 MHz	5.7 Mbps	260 ft
Infranet	JVC	Ethernet	360° infrared	10 Mbps	16.5-ft radius
InfraLAN	InfraLAN Wireless	Ethernet	Line-of-sight infrared	10 Mbps	90 ft
NetWave	Xircom Inc.	Ethernet	FHSS, 2.4–2.4835 GHz	1.6 Mbps	750 ft
RangeLAN2	Proxim Inc.	Ethernet	FHSS, 2.4–2.4835 GHz	1.6 Mbps	100 ft
Roamabout	Digital Equipment Corp.	Ethernet	DSSS, 2.4–2.4835 GHz	2 Mbps	800 ft
WaveLAN	AT&T G.I.S.	Ethernet	DSSS, 902–928 MHz	2 Mbps	800 ft

Figure 10-10 Wireless LAN Functional and Technical Analysis

hopping from one frequency to another is that the transmission tends to be less affected by interference, an especially desirable characteristic for mobile computing applications.

Practical Advice and Information

Interference with wireless LANs using the 2.4–2.4835-GHz frequency range can be generated by microwave ovens. Other electronic devices such as cordless phones and wireless scanners are also licensed to use the 902–928-MHz frequency range.

Although spread spectrum and infrared are the primary wireless transmission methods today, Motorola produced a wireless LAN product known as Altair until 1995 using microwave transmission on frequencies that it had licensed with the FCC. A new wireless Ethernet offering from RadioLAN, Inc., operates in the 5.8-GHz microwave frequency and claims to offer 10-Mbps performance at distances of 120–300 ft, depending on obstacles.

Some of the technical and functional differences between these wireless LAN technologies are summarized in Figure 10-10. Internetworking devices that are able to link wireless LANs with wire-based LANs are known as wireless bridges or wireless access points and were reviewed in Chapter 9.

Some functional issues of wireless LANs not addressed in Figure 10-10 are as follows:

- Network interface cards—Since wireless LAN technology seems to be shifting toward an emphasis on mobile computing via laptops and portables, it should come as no surprise that most wireless LAN interface cards area available as PC Cards (PCMCIA). In such a case, card and socket services compatibility should be verified. Parallel port adapters that can also be attached to portable computers are also available on some wireless LANs, as are ISA adapters.

- Encryption—Since data is being sent through the air, it is especially important to consider security with wireless LANs. Some wireless LANs support DES (data encryption standard) encryption directly on the network interface card, usually through the installation of an optional encryption chip.

WIRELESS LAN STANDARDS: IEEE 802.11 MOBILE IP

In Sharper Focus

One of the key shortcomings to date of wireless LANs has been a lack of interoperability among the wireless LAN offerings of different vendors. In an effort to address this shortcoming, a proposal for a new wireless LAN standard known as **IEEE 802.11** has been proposed. Key points included in the standard are as follows:

- Physical layer: The standard defined physical layer protocols for each of the following transmission methods:
- Frequency-hopping spread spectrum.
- Direct-sequence spread spectrum.

- Pulse position modulation infrared (diffuse infrared rather than line of sight).

- Medial access control layer: The standard defined **CSMA/CA (carrier sense multiple access with collision avoidance)** as the MAC layer protocol. The standard is similar to CSMA/CD except that collisions cannot be detected in wireless environments as they can in wire-based environments. CSMA/CA avoids collisions by listening to the network prior to transmission and not transmitting if other workstations on the same network are transmitting. Before transmitting, workstations wait a predetermined amount of time to avoid collisions and set up a point-to-point wireless circuit to the destination workstation. Data-link layer header and information fields such as Ethernet or token ring are sent to the destination workstation. It is the responsibility of the wireless LAN access device to convert IEEE 802.3 and 802.5 frames into IEEE 802.11 frames. The wireless point-to-point circuit remains in place until the sending workstation receives an acknowledgment that the message was received error free.

- Data rate: Either 1 or 2 Mbps selected either by the user or by the system dependent upon transmission conditions.

One important issue not included in the IEEE 802.11 standard is **roaming** capability, which allows a user to transparently move between the transmission ranges of wireless LANs without interruption. Proprietary roaming capabilities are currently offered by many wireless LAN vendors. **Mobile IP,** under consideration by the IETF, may be the roaming standard that wireless LANs require. Mobile IP, limited to TCP/IP networks, employs two pieces of software to support roaming:

- A mobile IP client is installed on the roaming wireless client workstation.

- A mobile IP home agent is installed on a server or router on the roaming user's home network.

The mobile IP client keeps the mobile IP home agent informed of its changing location as it travels from network to network. The mobile IP home agent forwards any transmissions it receives for the roaming client to its last reported location.

Practical Advice and Information

In January 1997, the FCC set aside an additional 300 MHz of bandwidth for a new class of wireless LANs and other wireless devices. The frequencies, from 5150 to 5350 MHz and from 5725 to 5825 MHz are collectively known as the Unlicensed National Information Infrastructure (U-NII). Compliant devices could include PCs and laptops with built-in or external radio receivers.

Software

Remote Control Software **Remote control software,** especially designed to allow remote PCs to "take over" control of local PCs, should not be confused with the asynchronous communications software used for dial-up connections to asynchronous host via modems. Modem operation, file transfer, scripting languages, and terminal emulation are the primary features of asynchronous communications software.

Taking over remote control of the local PC is generally only available via remote control software. Remote control software allows the keyboard of the remote PC to control the actions of the local PC, with screen output being reflected on the remote PC's screen. The terms *remote* and *local* are often replaced by **guest** (remote) and **host** (local) when referring to remote control software.

Operating remote control software requires installation of software programs on both the guest and host PCs. Various remote control software packages do not interoperate. The same brand of remote control software must be installed on both guest and host PCs. Both the guest and host pieces of the remote control software may or may not be included in the software package price. Remote control software must have modem operation, file transfer, scripting language, and terminal emulation capabilities similar to those of asynchronous communications software. However, in addition, remote control software should possess features to address the following situations unique to its role:

- Avoid lockups of host PCs.

- Allow the guest PC to disable the keyboard and monitor of the host PC.

- Additional security precautions to prevent unauthorized access.

- Virus detection software.

Additionally, Windows-based applications pose a substantial challenge for remote control software. The busy screens of this graphical user interface can really bog down even with V.32bis or V.34 modems. Some remote control software vendors have implemented proprietary Windows screen transfer utilities that allow Windows-based applications to run on the guest PC as if they were sitting in front of the host PC, while others do not support Windows applications remotely at all.

Figure 10-11 summarizes the important features of remote control software as

Feature Category	Feature	Importance/Implication
Protocol compatibility	Windows support	• How are Windows applications supported? Are full bit-mapped screens transmitted or only the changes? • Proprietary coded transmission of Windows screens?
	Windows 95 support	• Are Windows 95 applications supported?
	Network operating system protocols	• Which network operating system protocols are supported (IP, IPX, NetBIOS)?
LAN compatibility	LAN versions	• Are specific multiuser LAN server versions available or required?
	Host/guest	• Are both host and guest (local and remote) versions included?
	Operating system	• Some remote control packages require the same operating system at host and guest PCs whereas others do not.

Figure 10-11 Remote Control Software Technology Analysis

Feature Category	Feature	Importance/Implication
Operational capabilities	Printing	• Can remote PC print on local or network-attached printers?
	File transfer	• Which file transfer protocols are supported (Kermit, XModem, YModem, ZModem, proprietary)?
		• **Delta file transfer** allows only changes to files to be transferred.
		• Automated file and directory synchronization is important to mobile workers who also have desktop computers at home or at the office.
	Drive mapping	• Can guest (remote PC) drives be mapped for host access?
		• Can local (host PC) drives be mapped for guest access?
	Scripting language	• Allows repetitive call setups and connections to be automated.
	On-line help system	• Context sensitive, which gives help based on where the user is in the program, is preferable
	Color/resolution limitations	• Different packages vary from 16 to 16 million colors and 800 × 600 to 2048 × 1280 pixel resolution.
	Terminal emulation	• How many different terminals are emulated? Most common are VT100, VT102, VT320, and TTY.
	Simultaneous connections	• Some packages allow more than one connection or more than one session per connection, for example, simultaneous file transfer and remote control.
Security	Password access	• This should be the minimum required security for remote login.
	Password encryption	• Since passwords must be transmitted over WAN links, it would be more secure if they were encrypted.
	Keyboard disabling	• Since the local PC is active but controlled remotely, it is important that the local keyboard be disabled to prevent unauthorized access.
	Monitor blanking	• Similar to rationale for keyboard disabling, since output is being transmitted to the remote PC, it is important to blank the local monitor so that processing cannot be viewed without authorization.
	Callback system	• Added security, although not hacker-proof, hangs up on dial-in and calls back at preprogrammed or entered phone number.

Figure 10-11   Continued

Feature Category	Feature	Importance/Implication
Security	Access restriction	• Are remote users able to be restricted to certain servers, directories, files, or drives? Can the same user be given different restrictions when logging in locally or remotely?
	Remote access notification	• Can system managers or enterprise network management systems be notified when remote access or password failures have occurred?
	Call logging	• Can information about all calls be logged, sorted, and reported?
	Remote host reboot	• Can the remote PC (guest) reboot the local host if it becomes locked up?
	Limited logon attempts	• Are users locked out after a given number of failed login attempts?
	Virus protection	• This feature is especially important given file transfer capabilities from remote users.
		• Can remote users be restricted to read-only access?
	Logoff after inactivity time-out	• To save on long-distance charges, can users be logged off (and calls dropped) after a set length of time?

Figure 10-11   Continued

well as their potential implications. The following are among the more popular remote control software packages:

Software	Vendor
CO/Session for Windows 3.0	Triton Technologies
PCAnywhere for DOS 5.0	Symantec
PCAnywhere for Windows 2.0	Symantec
Close Up 6.0	Norton/Lambert
Carbon Copy for Windows 3.0	Microcom

Price ranges from $65 to $199 with most in the $99 range.

The remote control software loaded onto a communications server for use by multiple simultaneous users is not the same as the remote control software loaded onto single remote (guest) and local (host) PCs. Communications servers' remote control software has the ability to handle multiple users and, in some cases, multiple protocols. Because of this, it is considerably more expensive than the single-PC variety. Prices range from $399 for 2 users to $6,850 for 16 users. Examples of LAN remote control software are

Software	Vendor
Remote LAN Node (RLN)	Digital Communication Associates
Close Up/LAN Pro	Norton/Lambert
WinView For Networks 2.3	Citrix Systems

Remote Node Software   Traditionally remote node client and server software were supplied by the vendor of the network operating system on the server to be remotely accessed. **Windows NT RAS** and **NetWare Connect** are two examples of such NOS-specific **remote node server software.** Third-party software vendors have also offered remote node server products which vary as to operating system or network operating system compatibility. It is important to note that these are software-only solutions, installed on industry-standard, Intel 486 or higher application servers as opposed to the proprietary hardware of specialized remote access or communications servers. A representative list of remote node server software, required operating system or network operating system, and vendors is given in Figure 10-12.

Some of the important functional characteristics of remote node server software other than operating system/network operating system compatibility are listed in Figure 10-13.

Most of the remote node server software packages also include compatible **remote node client software.** A problem arises, however, when a single remote node client needs to log into a variety of different servers running a variety of different network operating systems or remote node server packages. What is required is some sort of universal remote access client. In fact, such remote node clients are available. These standardized remote clients with the ability to link to servers running a variety of different network operating systems are sometimes referred to as **PPP clients.** In general, they can link to network operating systems that support IP, IPX, NetBEUI, or XNS as transport protocols. Those that support IPX are generally installable as either NetWare VLMs (virtual loadable modules) or NLMs (NetWare loadable modules). In addition, these PPP client packages include sophisticated authentication procedures to ensure secure communications, compression to ensure optimal use of the WAN link, and most of the important features of remote control software. The inclusion of remote control software allows users to choose between remote node and remote control for optimal performance.

Among the specialized compression and authentication algorithms included with a majority of these PPP clients are

- **CIPX**—For compression of IPX headers.

Remote Node Server Software	Required Operating System or Network Operating System	Vendor
Windows NT RAS	Windows NT 3.5, 4.0	Microsoft
NetWare Connect	NetWare 3.12 or 4.1	Novell
IBM LAN Distance	OS/2	IBM
Remote Office Communications Server	DOS	Stampede Technologies
Enterprise Wide Foray PPP Server	DOS	TechSmith
WanderLink	NetWare 3.1x or 4.1	Funk Software

Figure 10-12   Remote Node Server Software Operating System Compatibility

Remote Node Server Software Functional Characteristic	Importance/Implication
NOS protocols supported	• Although most remote node server software supports IP and IPX, support of NetBIOS, NetBEUI, AppleTalk, Vines, LANtastic, and SNA is more limited. • If IP is supported, is the full IP protocol stack including applications and utilities supplied?
WAN data-link layer protocol	• Most remote node server software now supports PPP, while others support proprietary protocols. Proprietary protocols are fine in single-vendor environments.
Modem support	• How many serial ports can be supported simultaneously? Numbers vary from 32 to 256. • How many modem setup strings are included? If the setup string for a particular type of modem is not included, configuration could be considerably more difficult. Numbers vary from 75 to over 400. • Does the remote node server software support modem pools or does there have to be a modem dedicated to every user? • Does the remote node server software support dial-out functionality over the attached modems?
Management	• How is the remote node server managed? Via a specialized console or any attached workstation with proper software? • Does the remote node server software output management information in SNMP format? • Can remote users be limited as to connect time or by inactivity time-out?
Security	• Is forced password renewal (password aging) supported? • Are passwords encrypted? • Is the remote node server software compatible with third-party security servers such as token authentication servers? • Does the remote node server support callback (dial back) capabilities?
Client support	• Which types of client platforms are supported (DOS, Mac, Windows, Windows for Workgroups, Windows 95, Windows NT, OS/2)? • Are both NDIS and ODI driver specifications supported?

Figure 10-13   Remote Node Server Software Functional Characteristics

- **VJ**—For compression of IP headers.

- **CHAP MD5**—For PPP encrypted authentication.

- **CHAP MD80**—Authentication for Windows NT RAS.

- **SPAP**—Shiva's proprietary authentication protocol which includes password encryption and callback capability.

Some of the available PPP clients and their vendors are as follows, although not all include both fully functional remote control software and full TCP/IP stacks and utilities:

Software	Vendor
Remotely Possible	Avalan Technology
Timbuktu Pro	Farallon Computing
WanderLink PPP Client	Funk Software
PPP	Klos Technologies
LAN Express PPP Client	Microcom
TCP Pro	Network TeleSystems
ShivaPPP	Shiva Corp.
Remote Office Gold	Stampede Technologies

Mobile-Aware Operating Systems   The mobile computer user requires flexible computing functionality to easily support at least three possible distinct computing scenarios:

- Stand-alone computing on the laptop or notebook computer.

- Remote node or remote control computing to corporate headquarters.

- Synchronization of files and directories with desktop workstations at home or in the corporate office.

Operating systems that are able to easily adapt to these different computing modes with a variety of included supporting accessory programs and utilities are sometimes referred to as **mobile-aware operating systems.** Windows 95 is perhaps the best current example of such as operating system. Among the key functions offered by such mobile-aware operating systems are the following:

- Auto-detection of multiple configurations—If external monitors or full-size keyboards are used when at home or in the corporate office, the operating system should automatically detect these and load the proper device drivers.

- Built-in multiprotocol remote node client—Remote node software should be included that can automatically and transparently dial-in to a variety of different network operating systems including Windows NT RAS or NetWare Connect. The remote node client should support a variety of network protocols including IP, IPX, and NetBEUI as well as open data-link WAN protocols such as SLIP and PPP.

- Direct cable connection—When returning from the road, field representatives should be able to easily link to their portable desktop workstations via direct connection through existing serial or parallel ports. The software utilities to initiate and manage such connections should be included.

- File transfer and file/directory synchronizations—Once physical connections are in place, software utilities should be able to synchronize files and directories between either the laptop and the desktop or the laptop and the corporate LAN server.

- Deferred printing—This feature allows printed files to be spooled to the laptop disk drive and saved until the mobile user is next connected to corporate printing resources. At that point, instead of having to remember all of the individual files requiring printing, the deferred printing utility is able to automatically print all of the spooled files.

- Power management—Since most mobile computing users depend on battery-powered computers, anything that the operating system can do to extend battery life would be very beneficial. The demand for higher resolution screens has meant increased power consumption in many cases. Power management features offered by operating systems have been standardized as the **advanced power management (APM)** specification.

- Infrared connection—To avoid the potential hassle of physical cable connections, mobile-aware operating systems are including support for infrared wireless connections between laptops and desktops. To ensure multivendor interoperability, the infrared transmission should confirm to the **IrDA (Infrared Data Association)** standard. The IrDA standard defines line-of-sight infrared transmission parameters rather than diffuse infrared transmission as defined by IEEE 802.11 IR. IrDA is currently limited to point-to-point distances of only 3 ft.

Mobile-Aware Applications   Beyond the shortcomings of remote node applications already delineated, mobile applications that are dependent on inherently unreliable wireless transmission services must be uniquely developed or modified to optimize performance under these circumstances.

Oracle Mobile Agents, formerly known as Oracle-in-Motion, is perhaps the best example of the overall architecture and components required to produce **mobile-aware applications.** As illustrated in Figure 10-14, the Oracle Mobile Agents architecture adheres to an overall **client-agent-server** architecture, as opposed to the more common LAN-based client/server architecture. The overall objective of such an architecture is to reduce the amount of client-to-server network traffic by building as much intelligence as possible into the server-based agent so that it can act on behalf of the client application. Oracle's testing of applications developed and deployed in this wireless architecture have produced performance improvements of up to 50:1.

The agent portion of the client/agent/server architecture consists of three cooperating components:

- The **message manager** executes on the mobile client and acts as an interface between client applications requesting services and the wireless link

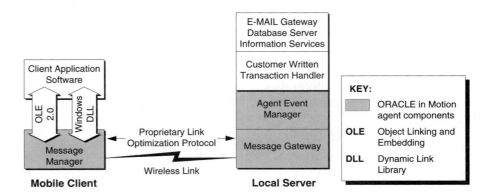

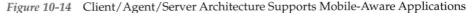

Figure 10-14   Client/Agent/Server Architecture Supports Mobile-Aware Applications

over which the requests must be forwarded. It keeps track of requests pending on various servers that are being handled by intelligent agents. Oracle Mobile Agents also operates over LAN links or PPP-based dial-up links.

- The **message gateway** can execute on the local server or on a dedicated UNIX or Windows workstation and acts as an interface between the client's message manager and the intelligent agent on the local server. The gateway also acts as a holding station for messages to and from mobile clients that are temporarily unreachable. The client-based message manager and the message gateway communicate with each other via a communications protocol developed by Oracle that provides reliable message delivery over wireless transmission services while minimizing acknowledgment overhead.

- The **agent event manager** is combined with a customer-written transaction handler to form an entity known as the **intelligent agent** which resides on the local server. Once the agent event manager receives a request from a mobile client, it acts on behalf of that client in all communications with the local server until the original client request is totally fulfilled. During this processing time in which the intelligent agent is representing the mobile client, the wireless connection can be dropped. Once the original client request has been fulfilled, the entire response is sent from the intelligent agent to the client-based message manager in a single packet, thereby conserving bandwidth and transmission time. Having received the response to a pending request, the client-based message manager deletes the original request from its pending request queue.

Mobile Middleware An emerging category of software that seeks to offer maximum flexibility to mobile computing users while optimizing performance is known as **mobile middleware.** Although specific products within this software category can vary significantly, the ultimate goal of mobile middleware is to offer mobile users transparent client/server access independent of the following variables:

- Client or server platform (operating system, network operating system).
- Applications (client/server or client/agent/server).
- Wireless transmission services.

Figure 10-15 illustrates the basic components and interactions of mobile middleware.

As can be seen in Figure 10-15, the primary purpose of mobile middleware is to consolidate client/server traffic from multiple applications for transmission over a variety of potential wireless (or wire-based) transmission services. By consolidating client requests from multiple applications into a single transmission, overall transmission time and expense can be reduced. In some cases, the mobile middleware has sufficient intelligence to inform clients or servers if the intended destination is currently reachable or not, thereby saving wasted time and transmission expense. Some mobile middleware also has the ability to evaluate among available wireless service between the mobile client and the local server and to

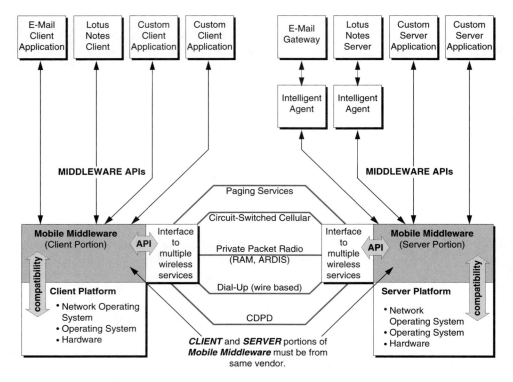

Figure 10-15   Mobile Middleware

choose an optimal wireless transmission service based on performance and/or expense.

Mobile middleware is an emerging category of software characterized by proprietary APIs and a resultant lack of interoperability. As a result, applications written to interact with one vendor's mobile middleware probably won't interact with another vendor's mobile middleware. As can be seen in Figure 10-10, mobile middleware interacts with two sets of APIs: one between the mobile middleware and the applications, and one between the middleware and the wireless transmission services. In an effort to standardize wireless APIs for mobile middleware, two standardization efforts are currently underway:

- The Winsock 2 Forum is developing standardized Winsock 2 APIs for linking mobile middleware with Windows-based applications. This API would be able to deliver transmission-related information such as signal strength and transmission characteristics to the application themselves. Such information could make the applications more intelligent and responsive to changing transmission quality.

- The PCCA (Portable Computer and Communications Association) is developing the standardized API for linking mobile middleware to a variety of wireless transmission services. This API will provide extensions to existing multiprotocol data-link layer device specifications such as NDIS and ODI.

Among the currently available mobile middleware packages and their vendors are the following:

Software	Vendor
MobileSync	Adaptive Strategies
MobileWare	MobileWare
Worldlink	Technology Development Systems
RemoteWare	XcelleNet
Transnet II	Teknique
Mobilera	Business Partners Solutions
Via	Moda Systems

Management and Configuration of Remote Access Technology

Practical Advice and Information

OPTIMIZING REMOTE NODE AND REMOTE CONTROL SOFTWARE PERFORMANCE

As previously described in the section on the remote node logical topology, suitable performance of remote client applications is severely hampered by the limited transmission speed of the WAN links combined with the high bandwidth demands of client/server applications. Besides rewriting the client/server application to minimize the amount of remote client to local server traffic, several other opportunities to improve remote access performance are available. These optimization techniques will also improve performance of remote control applications as well:

- Use V.34 modems. This new modem specification can support transmission speeds of up to 28.8 Kbps over dial-up lines, while V.34⁺ modems can achieve speeds up to 33.6 Kbps.

- Use ISDN services, if available, as an alternative to asynchronous dial-up with the V.34 modem. ISDN BRI delivers up to 144 Kbps of switched digital bandwidth. Using ISDN requires ISDN terminal adapters, the equivalent of an ISDM modem, and compatible communications software.

- Use 16550 UARTs and matching serial port drivers. The UART (universal asynchronous receiver transmitter) transmits and receives data to and from a PC's serial port which interfaces to the modem. The 16550 UART includes increased buffering capacity to match the performance of faster modems such as the V.34. Transmission via serial ports and UARTs is controlled by operating system software known as serial or COM drivers. Some of these COM drivers have limitations of 19.2 Kbps. More recent operating systems, such as Windows 95, and many asynchronous communication packages support serial transmission rates of at least 110.2 Kbps.

- Use data compression software/hardware and set communication software transmission speed to/from the modem to the PC (DTE rate) high enough to take full advantage of the compression software's capabilities. V.34 modems include V.42bis built-in compression capabilities that can yield compression ratios of up to 4:1 dependent on file content. Since V.34 modems have a maximum transmission speed of 28.8 Kbps and V.42bis supplies 4:1 data compression, maximum serial transmission rates of 110.2 Kbps (28.8 × 4) should be supported by PC hardware and software.

- Make sure that the remote control or remote node software being used supports **screen caching,** which allows only changes to screens rather than entire screens to be transmitted over the limited-bandwidth WAN links. Screen caching will reduce the amount of actual traffic transmitted over the WAN link.

- Not to be confused with screen caching software, **network caching** or **LAN caching** software is able to improve overall remote node performance up to five times by caching repetitive application commands and system calls. These add-on packages consist of both client and server pieces that work cooperatively to cache application commands and reduce network traffic over relatively low-speed WAN links. Network caching software is network operating system and protocol dependent, requiring that compatibility be assured prior to purchase. Two network caching software packages and their vendors are

Software	Vendor
Powerburst	AirSoft, Inc.
Shared LAN Cache	Measurement Techniques, Inc.

Mobile MIB   To integrate the management of mobile computing users into an overall enterprise network management system such as HP's OpenView or IBM's SystemView, a specialized MIB was required to store configuration and location information specific to remote users. The Mobile Management Task Force (MMTF) has proposed a **mobile MIB** capable of feeding configuration and location information to enterprise network management systems via SNMP. A key to the design of the mobile MIB was to balance the amount of information required to effectively manage remote clients while taking into account the limited bandwidth and expense of the remote links over which the management data must be transmitted. From the enterprise network management system's side, controls will need to be installed as to how often remote clients are to be polled via dial-up or wireless transmission for the purpose of gathering up-to-date management information. Among the fields of information included in the proposed mobile MIB are the following:

- Current user location.

- Type and speed of connection device.

- Type of remote client or remote control software installed on remote device.

- Battery power.

- Memory.

■ NETWORK SERVICES

Wireless WAN Services

Whereas wireless LANs offer mobility to users across a local scope of coverage, a variety of wireless services are available for use across wider geographic spans.

These **wireless WAN services** vary in many ways, including availability, applications, transmission speed, and cost. Among the available wireless WAN services that will be explained further are the following:

- Circuit-switched analog cellular.

- CDPD (cellular digital packet data).

- Private packet radio.

- Enhanced paging and two-way messaging.

- ESMR (enhanced specialized mobile radio).

- Microcellular spread spectrum.

- PCS (personal communications services).

Applied Problem Solving

A TOP-DOWN APPROACH TO WIRELESS WAN SERVICES ANALYSIS

Due to the many variable factors concerning these wireless WAN services, it is important to take a top-down approach when considering their incorporation into an organization's information systems solution. Questions and issues to be considered on each layer of the top-down model for wireless WAN services are summarized in Figure 10-16.

As a practical example of how to use the top-down model for wireless WAN services analysis, start with the business situation that requires wireless support and examine the applications and data characteristics that support the business activity in question. For example, which of the following best describes the data to be transmitted by wireless means?

- Fax.

- File transfer.

- E-mail.

- Paging.

- Transaction processing.

- Database queries.

The nature of the content, geographic scope, and amount and urgency of the data to be transmitted will have a direct bearing on the particular wireless WAN service employed. Unfortunately, no single wireless WAN service fits all application and data needs. Once a wireless WAN service is chosen, compatibility with existing local area network architectures and technology must be assured. Typical uses of the currently most widely available wireless WAN services are as follows:

- Transaction processing and database queries: CDPD.
    - Advantages: Fast call setup, inexpensive for short messages.
    - Disadvantages: Limited availability but growing, expensive for large file transfers.

Top-Down Layer	Issues/Implications
Business	• What is the business activity that requires wireless transmission? • How will payback be calculated? Has the value of this business activity been substantiated? • What are the anticipated expenses for the 6-month, 1-year, and 2-year horizons? • What is the geographic scope of this business activity? Localized? National? International?
Application	• Have applications been developed especially for wireless transmission? • Have existing applications been modified to account for wireless transmission characteristics? • Have training and help-desk support systems been developed?
Data	• What is the nature of the data to be delivered via the wireless WAN service? Short bursty transactions, large two-way messages, faxes, file transfers? • Is the data time-sensitive or could transmission be batched during off-peak hours for discounted rates? • What is the geographic scope of coverage required for wireless data delivery?
Network	• Must the WAN service provide error correction? • Should the WAN service also provide and maintain the access devices?
Technology	• Which wireless WAN service should be employed? • What type of access device must be employed with the chosen WAN service? • Are access devices proprietary or standards-based?

Figure 10-16   Top-Down Analysis for Wireless WAN Services

• Large file transfers and faxes: Circuit-switched cellular.
  • Advantages: Widely available, call duration pricing is more reasonable for longer transmissions than per-kilopacket pricing.
  • Disadvantages: Longer call setup time than CDPD (up to 30 sec vs. less than 5 sec), expensive for short messages.
• Short bursty messages and e-mail: Private packet radio.
  • Advantages: Wide coverage area and links to commercial e-mail systems.
  • Disadvantages: Proprietary networks, expensive for larger file transfers.

The key characteristics of these and other wireless WAN services are summarized in Figure 10-17.

Two-Way Messaging

Two-way messaging, sometimes referred to as enhanced paging, allows short text messages to be transmitted between relatively inexpensive transmission devices

Wireless WAN Service	Geographic Scope	Directionality	Data Characteristics	Billing	Access Device	Standards and Compatibility
Circuit-switched analog cellular	National	Full-duplex circuit switched	14.4 Kbps	Call duration	Modems with specialized error correction for cellular circuits	MNP-10 (adverse channel enhancements) and ETC (enhanced throughput cellular)
Private packet radio	Nearly national, more cities than CDPD but less than circuit-switched cellular	Full-duplex packet-switched digital data	4.8 Kbps	Per character	Proprietary modem compatible with particular private packet radio service	Proprietary; two major services: RAM Mobile Data and Ardis.
CDPD	Limited to large metro-politan areas	Full-duplex packet-switched digital data	19.2 Kbps max	flat monthly charge plus usage charge per kilopacket	CDPD modem	Compatible with TCP/IP for easier internetwork integration
Enhanced paging	National	One or two way, relatively short messages	100 characters or fewer	Flat monthly charges increasing with coverage area	Pagers	
ESMR	Currently limited	One or two-way, voice, paging or messaging	4.8 Kbps	Unknown, service is under de-velopment	Proprietary integrated voice/data devices	
Microcell spread spectrum	Limited to those areas serviced by microcells, good for college and corporate campuses	Full-duplex	10–45 Mbps	Monthly flat fee	Proprietary modem	Most provide access to Internet, e-mail services
PCS	Under de-velopment, should be national	Full-duplex, all digital voice and data services	up to 25 Mbps		Two-way pagers, personal digital assistants, PCS devices	Standards-based should ensure device/service interoperability

Figure 10-17   Wireless WAN Services Technology Analysis

such as PDAs (personal digital assistants) and alphanumeric pagers. Two distinct architectures and associated protocols have the potential to deliver these services.

One such architecture is based on **CDPD (cellular digital packet data)** and is being proposed and supported by AT&T Wireless Services, formerly known as McCaw Cellular. CDPD is a service that uses idle capacity in the circuit-switched cellular network to transmit IP-based data packets. The fact that CDPD is IP-based allows it to easily interface to IP-based private networks as well as to the Internet and other e-mail services.

By adding a protocol known as **LSM (limited size messaging),** CDPD will be able to transport two-way messaging, which will offer the following key services beyond simple paging:

- Guaranteed delivery to destination mobile users even if those devices are unreachable at the time the message was originally sent.

- Return receipt acknowledgments to the party that originated the message.

An alternative two-way messaging architecture is proposed by the PCIA (Personal Communicator Industry Association). Rather than building on existing IP-based networks as the CDPD/LSM architecture did, the **TDP (telocator data protocol)** architecture is actually a suite of protocols defining an end-to-end system for two-way messaging to and from paging devices. Figure 10-18 illustrates the differences between the LSM and TDP two-way messaging protocols.

Analog Cellular

The current circuit-switched cellular network is more properly known by the transmission standard to which it adheres—**advanced mobile phone service (AMPS)** and operates in the 800-MHz frequency range. Transmitting data over analog cellular networks requires modems that support specialized cellular transmission protocols on both ends of the cellular transmission to maximize throughput. Examples of such protocols are **MNP-10 adverse channel enhancements** and **enhanced throughput cellular (ETC).** In some cases, cellular service providers are deploying modem pools of cellular enhanced modems at the **mobile telephone switching office (MTSO),** where all cellular traffic is converted for transmission over the wireline public switched telephone network (PSTN). Figure 10-19 illustrates data transmission over the circuit-switched analog cellular network.

Digital Cellular/Personal Communications Services

PCS, or **personal communications services,** is a visionary concept of an evolving all-digital network architecture that could deliver a variety of telecommunications services transparently to users at any time regardless of their geographic location. PCS is not a totally new "from the bottom up" telecommunications architecture. In fact, it is the integration of a number of existing telecommunications environments. PCS seeks to combine the capabilities of the PSTN, otherwise known as the **landline telephone network,** with a new all-digital cellular network along with paging networks and satellite communications networks.

The need for seamless delivery of a combination of all of these services is easily illustrated by the plight of today's mobile professional. A single person has a phone

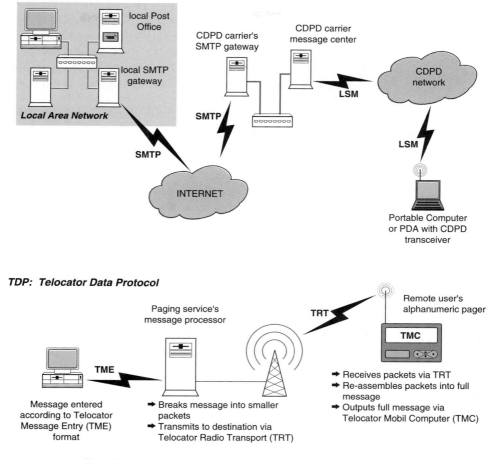

LSM: Limited Size Messaging

TDP: Telocator Data Protocol

Figure 10-18   Two-Way Messaging Protocols: LSM and TDP

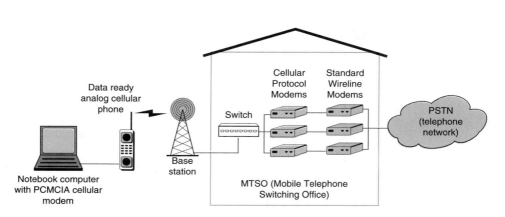

Figure 10-19   Data Transmission over the Circuit-Switched Analog Cellular Network

number for a home phone, a voice and fax number for an office phone, a phone number for a cellular phone, a pager phone number for a pager, and perhaps even another phone number for a satellite service phone for use outside of cellular phone areas. The premise of PCS is rather straightforward: one person, one phone number.

This **personal phone number,** or **PPN,** would become the user's interface to PCS and the vast array of transparently available telecommunications services. This personal phone number is a key concept to PCS. It changes the entire focus of the interface to the telecommunications environment from the current orientation of a number being associated with a particular location regardless of the individual using the facility to a number being associated with particular individual regardless of the location, even globally, of the accessed facility. Figure 10-20 illustrates the basic elements of PCS.

Digital Cellular Standards   Given the limited bandwidth (only about 140 MHz from 1.85 to 1.99 GHz, referred to as the 2-GHz band) allocated to PCS and the potentially large number of subscribers needing to share that limited bandwidth, a key challenge for PCS is the ability to maximize the number of simultaneous conversations over a finite amount of bandwidth. Just as multiplexing was originally introduced in the study of wide area networks as a means of maximizing the use of wire-based circuits, two variations of multiplexing are being field tested as a means of maximizing the use of the allocated bandwidth of these air-based circuits.

TDMA (time division multiple access) and **CDMA (code division multiple access)** are the two methodologies currently being researched in PCS field trials.

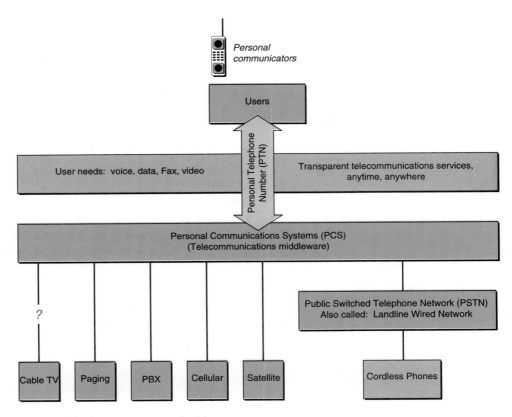

Figure 10-20   Basic Elements of PCS

TDMA-based digital cellular may be able to support three times (some tests indicate six or seven times) the transmission capacity of analog cellular whereas CDMA could offer as much as a tenfold increase. Note that the names of each of these techniques end in the words "multiple access" rather than "multiplexing." The "multiple access" refers to multiple phone conversations having access to the same bandwidth and yet not interfering with each other.

TDMA achieves more than one conversation per frequency by assigning time slots to individual conversations. Ten times slots per frequency are often assigned, with a given cellular device transmitting its digitized voice only during its assigned time slot. Receiving devices must be in synch with the time slots of the sending device to receive the digitized voice packets and reassemble them into a natural-sounding analog signal. TDMA should be able to transmit data at 9.6 Kbps. TDMA digital standards to handle call setup, maintenance, and termination have been defined by the Telecommunications Industry Association (TIA) as follows:

- IS-130: TDMA Radio Interface & Radio Link Protocol 1.
- IS-135: TDMA Services, Async Data and FAX.

CDMA is the newest and most advanced technique for maximizing the number of calls transmitted within a limited bandwidth by using a spread spectrum transmission technique. Rather than allocate specific frequency channels within the allocated bandwidth to specific conversations as in the case with TDMA, CDMA transmits digitized voice packets from numerous calls at different frequencies spread all over the entire allocated bandwidth spectrum.

The *code* part of CDMA lies in the fact that to keep track of these various digitized voice packets from various conversations spread over the entire spectrum of allocated bandwidth, a code is appended to each packet indicating which voice conversation it belongs to. This technique is not unlike the datagram connectionless service used by packet-switched networks to send packetized data over numerous switched virtual circuits within the packet-switched network. By identifying the source and sequence of each packet, the original message integrity is maintained while maximizing the overall performance of the network. CDMA should be able to transmit data at up to 14.4 Kbps. The CDMA standard defined by the TIA is IS-99: Data Services Option for Wideband Spread Spectrum Digital Cellular Systems. Figure 10-21 illustrates both TDMA and CDMA.

TDMA and CDMA are being pursued and implemented primarily by cellular carriers in North America. In Europe and much of the rest of the world, **Global System for Mobile Communication (GSM)** is either currently deployed or planned for implementation, whereas **Personal Handyphone System (PHS)** is the digital cellular standard being implemented in Japan. At the present time, these various digital cellular transmission standards are not interoperable, thereby precluding the possibility of transparent global access to digital cellular services.

Digital cellular systems will be deployed on an as-needed basis in the most congested metropolitan areas. As a result, existing analog cellular networks will be required to coexist and interoperate with newer digital cellular networks. Transmission protocols such as TDMA and CDMA must be compatible with analog transmission protocols, and next-generation cellular phones must be able to support both analog and digital transmission.

Transmitting digital data from a notebook computer over digital cellular networks will not require modulation as was required with analog cellular networks. As a result, notebook computers should be able to interface directly to TDMA- or

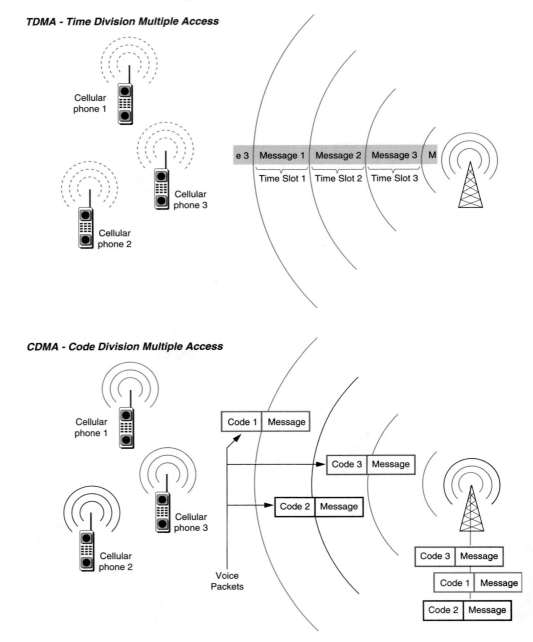

Figure 10-21   Maximizing Minimum Bandwidth: TDMA and CDMA

CDMA-based digital cellular phones via serial ports. Figure 10-22 illustrates data transmission over a digital cellular network.

THE FUTURE OF PCS

Managerial Perspective

PCS faces significant challenges on its way to worldwide deployment. Required changes in thinking and behavior on the part of PCS users should not be overlooked. For instance, if a person can be called anywhere thanks to the PPN, who

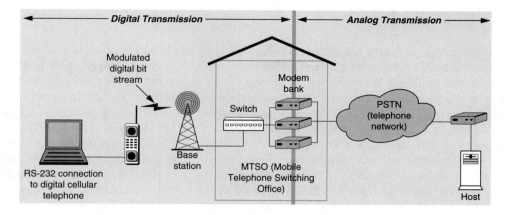

Figure 10-22   Data Transmission over a Digital Cellular Network

should pay for that call, the called party or the calling party? Caller ID services will now display the calling party's name or personal number rather than the number of the phone from which that person is calling. Remember, with PCS, numbers are associated with people, not with equipment and phone lines.

If callers are to be responsible for payment, they would probably like to know where they are calling before placing calls. However, as a potentially called party, would you want just anybody knowing your location? Vandals or your supervisor could pinpoint your location without even placing a call. Advanced call screening services could allow only certain PPN calls to be received on a person's personal communicator, while forwarding others to voice mail. As with any dramatically new technology, societal impact and changes will result. PCS should be no exception.

Perhaps the most significant hurdles are the individual and, at times, conflicting business missions of the various industries that must somehow achieve a metamorphosis that will produce a comprehensive, seamless, global, transparent personal communications service for subscribers. Another industry with its own distinct mission and on a possible collision course with the telecommunications industry is the cable television industry. PCS spread-spectrum communicators have been successfully demonstrated on CATV networks.

PCS vendors bid $7.7 billion for auctioned spectrum in 1995/1996. It is estimated that somewhere between an additional $10 billion and $50 billion will needed to be spent on PCS infrastructure before services can be deployed. The dilemma is that PCS vendors must price their services attractively enough to gain market share while maintaining enough cash flow to surrender a tremendous amount of debt.

Finally, future PCS deployment levels may be determined by simple market demand. There is always the possibility that a seamless, comprehensive, location-independent communications system such as PCS is of more interest to the companies that stand to profit from it than to the buying public who are supposedly demanding it.

SUMMARY

Remote access to LANs has taken on increased importance in response to major changes in business conditions. As indicated by the top-down model, network functionality must respond to changing business conditions. Expectations of LAN remote access are significant. Remote users expect the same level of data accessibility, application services, and performance on the road as they receive at the office. Delivering this equivalent functionality is the challenge faced by networking professionals today. The major obstacle to this lofty objective is the bandwidth, availability, and quality of the wide area network services that are expected to deliver remote connectivity to mobile users. Increasingly, wireless WAN services are at the forefront of remote access solutions.

In designing remote access solutions, one must start with a thorough understanding of the needs of remote users. These needs will dictate both the logical and physical topologies of the remote access network.

There are two basic logical topologies for remote access. Remote control allows a remote PC to take over or control a local PC. Processing occurs on the local PC and only keyboard strokes and screen images are transported over the WAN link. Remote node allows the remote PC to act as a full-fledged LAN client to the local LAN server. In this case, full client/server traffic travels over the WAN link as the application executes on the remote client PC. One of these logical topologies is not preferable in all cases. Each situation must be analyzed on an individual basis.

Physical topologies include accessing a local LAN-attached PC directly via a modem, accessing a shared communications server that might include PC boards for embedded shared computing power, or accessing a LAN modem that would provide access to local LAN computing resources.

Mobile computing requires specialized software included mobile-aware operating systems, mobile-aware applications, and mobile middleware to interface between multiple applications and multiple possible wireless WAN services.

Wireless WAN services vary widely in terms of availability, bandwidth, reliability, and cost. No single wireless WAN service is appropriate for all mobile computing applications. It is important to understand the application needs and data characteristics of mobile applications before choosing a wireless WAN service. Digital cellular and personal communications services may hold the promise of higher bandwidth, reliable wireless transmission. However, substantial infrastructure development remains before such services will be universally available.

KEY TERMS

access server, 396
advanced mobile phone service, 422
advanced power management, 414
adverse channel enhancements, 422
agent event manager, 415
AMPS, 422
APM, 414
carrier sense multiple access with collision avoidance, 407
CDMA, 424
CDPD, 422
cellular digital packet data, 422
CHAP MD5, 412
CHAP MD80, 412

CIPX, 411
circuit-switched cellular, 419
client/agent/server, 414
code division multiple access, 424
communications server, 396
CSMA/CA, 407
delta file transfer, 409
dial-in server, 397
direct-sequence spread spectrum, 405
DSSS, 405
enhanced paging, 421
enhanced throughput cellular, 422
ESMR, 421

ETC, 422
FHSS, 405
frequency-hopping spread spectrum, 405
Global System for Mobile Communication, 425
GSM, 425
guest, 408
host, 408
IEEE 802.11, 406
Infrared Data Association, 414
infrared transmission, 404
Int14, 403
intelligent agent, 415

REVIEW QUESTIONS

1. What are some of the key business trends that have led to an increased interest in LAN remote access?
2. What is the importance of needs analysis to LAN remote access design?
3. Differentiate between remote node and remote control in terms of functionality and network impact.
4. What is the major limitation in terms of delivering transparent access to remote LAN users?
5. Describe how it is possible to run remote control software via a remote node connection. What are the advantages of such a setup?
6. What are some of the security issues unique to remote access situations?
7. What added security capability can token authentication systems offer?
8. What advantages does a communications server offer over separate remote access links to multiple PCs? Disadvantages?
9. What is the common differentiation between communications servers and remote node servers?
10. Differentiate between the three major categories of remote node servers.
11. Why are dial-out solutions for remote node servers different from dial-in solutions?
12. How can dial-out solutions be implemented on LANs equipped with remote node servers?
13. Differentiate between the two spread spectrum transmission techniques approved by the FCC in terms of functionality and application.

14. Why are wireless LAN NICs most often PCMCIA?
15. Differentiate between CSMA/CD and CDMA/CA.
16. What is roaming and why is it important to remote access users?
17. How does mobile IP work?
18. What is the relationship between the guest and host remote control software?
19. Why is remote control software not interoperable?
20. Differentiate between remote control and remote node software in terms of transport protocols and client protocol stacks.
21. Differentiate between LAN (multiuser) remote control software and point-to-point remote control software.
22. What are some of the unique functional requirements of remote control software beyond being able to control local (host) PCs?
23. What are some of the unique functional requirements of remote node server software?
24. What advantage do PPP clients offer?
25. What are some of the unique functional requirements of mobile-aware operating systems?
26. Differentiate between the client/agent/server architecture and the client/server architecture.
27. How do mobile-aware applications need to adjust to or compensate for wireless transmission services?

28. Describe the interaction between the components of Oracle Mobile Agents.
29. What two distinct interfaces do mobile middleware products transcend?
30. What are the functional objectives of mobile middleware?
31. How can the proprietary nature of mobile middleware products be overcome?
32. Describe standards development efforts that may affect mobile middleware.
33. What are some of the ways in which remote node or remote control applications can be optimized?
34. What is the difference between screen caching and network caching?
35. What unique information is required in a mobile MIB and why?
36. What are the conflicting objectives or limitations of mobile management software and the mobile MIB?

37. Why is CDPD of such interest to circuit-switched cellular vendors?
38. What standards are important to a person wishing to purchase a "cellular-ready" modem?
39. Match each of the following to the most appropriate wireless WAN service and justify your answer: transaction processing, short messages, large file transfers.
40. What are the advantages of two-way messaging systems for data transfer?
41. Differentiate between analog and digital cellular transmission systems in terms of data transfer capabilities and equipment requirements.
42. How is the notion of a personal phone number central to PCS and what changes in thinking about phone systems does it require?
43. Differentiate between TDMA and CDMA.
44. What are some of the obstacles to the vision of universal PCS?

ACTIVITIES

1. Gather articles regarding business trends that have contributed to the rise in LAN remote access. Relate these business trends to market trends for remote access technology and wireless WAN services. Use graphical presentation wherever possible.
2. Find an organization currently supporting LAN remote access. Analyze the situation from a business perspective. Which business activities are being supported? Was cost/benefit or payback period analysis performed or considered?
3. In the organization being studied, what is the physical topology employed? Links to multiple PCs? Communications servers? LAN modems? Prepare a diagram of the physical topology including all software components such as network operating systems and transport protocols.
4. In the organization being studied, is remote node functionality supported? If so, which remote client software is installed? Are remote users able to access servers with multiple different network operating systems? Are PPP clients installed?
5. In the organization being studied, are dial-out capabilities supplied? If so, how?
6. In the organization being studied, have any efforts

been made to optimize the performance of remote node or remote control applications? If so, what were those adjustments, and what impact did they have?
7. What types of additional security precautions, if any, are instituted for remote users?
8. Investigate infrared wireless LANs. What is the difference between line-of-sight and diffuse infrared? Where are infrared wireless LANs being deployed? What is the percentage market share of infrared wireless LANs vs. spread spectrum wireless LANs?
9. Why did the FCC choose the frequency bands that they did for spread spectrum transmission?
10. What devices other than wireless LANs use the 902–928-MHz frequency range? Could this be a problem?
11. What is the difference between the CSMA/CA employed in IEEE 802.11 and that employed in AppleTalk networks?
12. What is the current status of IEEE 802.11? What are the perceived shortcomings of the standard?
13. Research current PCS or digital cellular pilot tests. Compare how many use TDMA and how many use CDMA. What have been the results of these pilots tests?

CASE STUDY

Biotech Firm Finds a Winner in Wireless

Two years ago, start-up Univax Biologics, Inc. had no need of a sales force, let alone a sales force automation system. Then in 1994, the biotechnology firm got Federal Drug Administration approval for its first product—a drug that help prevent blood clotting in pregnant women.

The company hired 20 salespeople to push the product to hospitals and clinics, and Jack Dausman, assistant director of information systems, got the job designing and implementing a wireless system to support them.

In a nascent mobile computing industry with a reputation for unsettled standards and immature products and services, some networking managers might have been daunted by the task.

But Dausman saw it as an opportunity to build a system from scratch—tailored to user specifications and free of migration constraints.

Today, Univax salespeople are on the road armed with NEC America, Inc. Versa V laptops equipped with circuit-switched cellular wireless modems. They use Lotus Development Corp.'s cc:Mail Remote to exchange messages over wireless links, and keep records and generate reports about their dealings with clients using Symantec Corp.'s Act for Windows contact management application. Reports are sent to a supervisor via Act MobileLink.

The application has simplified paperwork for the sales force, says Larry Lynam, regional manager for Univax's western division. "They can generate a report in minutes, send it in seconds," he says.

Another key piece of laptop software is the client portion of MobileWare, a client/server remote access

management package from Dallas-based MobileWare Corp. The server portion, running on Microsoft Corp.'s NT 3.5 at the home office, coordinates laptop user's access to cc:Mail post offices, and NetWare 4.1 file, print and fax services.

Univax chose wireless to ensure that salespeople can communicate with the home office from places where phone jacks are out of reach, such as a cars and airports.

"We wanted a messaging backbone with broad geographic coverage" that would enable salespeople to report in whenever they have a spare minute, Dausman says, instead of playing phone tag or waiting until they get back to the office.

Lynam says he's seen increased detail and frequency of reports sent from the field. Those reports range from summaries of a week on the road to brief notes about a new contact or any immediate circumstances about a customer or prospect.

Getting that information right away means someone at the home office can quickly fax over product information to a potential customer, forward an order to a distributor, respond to a customer's service issue or answer a query on how to use the product correctly.

Under the old scenario, a customer might have waited a week until a salesperson keyed in a report at the end of a trip, Lynam says.

In addition, senior managers sometimes use the wireless links to access files from the NetWare servers. IS installed an RSA Data Security, Inc. encryption system on the NT server "so that senior staff can be comfortable it they are sending a five-year budget analysis," Dausman says.

What are the damages?

The whole system costs $58,000, or about $2,900 per user, including MobileWare client and server software, laptop hardware and software, and a Microsoft NT 3.5 server with 18M bytes of RAM and a 1G-byte hard drive.

Wireless service bills range from $70 to $100 per month per user, with a few users who roam a lot racking up $350 monthly bills, Dausman says.

According to Lynam, one potential area for improvement would be to bring Univax's outside distributors into the wireless electronic mail loop so they can be notified immediately of a new or changed order.

"Right now, I have to fax them," Lynam says.

Overall, however, the new system hits all the right buttons. The system is "easy to use and fast to get into," and does not suffer from reliability or response-time problems, Lynam says.

Involving the users

IS got the sales force automation system right the first time, Lynam says, primarily because users were brought into the design process at the outset.

Users helped IS design a system "without a lot of cumbersome manipulation," he says.

Even sales managers with little or no computing experience were comfortably transmitting and receiving within two weeks, according to Lynam.

Dausman began gathering user input 18 months ago with a study asking sales people to list all the features they'd like to see in an ideal automation system. Their wish lists included:

■ Broad geographic coverage

because salespeople visit clinics and hospitals all over the country.

■ Reliability and confirmation that messages are received.

■ Ease of use because end users "don't want to futz around with modern connections," Dausman says.

Univax fulfilled many of these requests through MobileWare. The software often provides key services to ensure that applications run over the link reliably, efficiently and securely. For example, MobileWare provides an acknowledgment system to let senders know a message got through.

MobileWare client software on the laptop enables users to set up a series of dialing sequences and then call one up at the touch of a button, depending on whether they are using a hotel phone, their home phone or the wireless connection.

Once a user is validated and logged on to the MobileWare server, the server transparently takes care of hooking up to the right LAN resource.

MobileWare also secures Univax's home office LAN from unauthorized access by blocking users from directly calling up a file on a NetWare server.

Instead, they call up a replication of their directory rights and request a particular file, then disconnect, Dausman says.

The system calls them back five minutes later and sends the file. This procedure is more often used by telecommuting executives than by mobile salespeople, he says.

The system includes an MCI Mail gateway, enabling salespeople to communicate with Univax customers at university medical facilities who are on the Internet, Dausman says.

End users also helped IS identify ways to cut overall platform costs. User feedback helped IS determine that it didn't have to purchase an expensive turnkey sales automation package because they tend to come bundled with an abundance of features Univax found unnecessary.

Univax had no need for direct order entry, for example, since orders are filled by an outside distributor.

Turnkey systems also often require the vendor's own middleware and connectivity software, Dausman says.

Such software tends to become out-of-date much more quickly than a third-party middleware package such as MobileWare's, he adds.

MobileWare's willingness to function as a partial systems integrator was necessary to get the mobile system off the ground, Dausman says. "They stepped us through some of the pieces, sent us out a brand-new copy of their new NT-based server" and helped set up the software drivers, he says.

Sound advice

Dausman has some advice for users embarking on similar projects:

■ Start with a detailed needs study with plenty of user input.

■ Tailor the system closely to users' needs, taking into account what they don't need, as well.

■ If you have limited in-house IS resources, bring in a systems integrator or a vendor willing to act as one.

■ Training is crucial—be prepared to go full blast with it. While Univax IS originally set up a half-day of training, this was expanded to a day and a half. The reason: Users tended to exaggerate their PC expertise initially.

Dausman's people are now looking to enhance the wireless messaging system to serve the needs of an expanded company of 2,000 employees and three sites, formed from a recent merger between Univax and North American Biologicals, Inc.

The firm intends to migrate to a standardized client/server messaging and groupware platform to facilitate collaboration among tethered and untethered sites.

Dausman's group remains satisfied with circuit-switched analog cellular and has no plans to migrate to one of the newer digital technologies. Analog cellular has improved over the months with more robust handshaking and speeds close to 9.6K bit/sec.

"A decent wireless data connection seems to have a practical limit of 9.6K bit/sec," Dausman says. "For our applications, that's not too bad."

BUSINESS CASE STUDY QUESTIONS ···

Activities

1. Complete a top-down model for this case by gleaming facts from the case and placing them in the proper layer of the top-down model. After completing the top-down model, analyze and detail those instances where requirements were clearly passed down from upper layers to lower layers of the model and where solutions to those requirements were passed up from lower layers to upper layers of the model.

2. Detail any questions about the case that may occur to you for which answers are not clearly stated in the article.

Business

1. What is the primary business activity of the organization featured in this case?
2. How has the adoption of the applications affected business processes?
3. How has the choice of wireless networking affected business processes?
4. Give an example of how wireless networking could improve customer service in this case.
5. What were the total costs and costs per user of the new system?

6. What are the recurring monthly costs of the system?
7. What opportunities exist for wireless network expansion to include enterprise partners?
8. Describe the design process that produced the wireless network and applications.
9. What aspects of the design process do you think helped ensure a successful implementation?
10. What major changes in the business may force changes in the application choice and network design?

Application

1. Which business process was supported by the applications and network in this case?
2. Which applications were chosen to support the chosen business processes?
3. What are some of the important functions supplied by MobileWare?

4. Which types of applications were deemed unnecessary?
5. What types of applications are now being considered in view of recent business developments?

Data

1. What security features were introduced regarding data transfers?
2. How much data transfer bandwidth is possible with analog circuit-switched cellular?

3. What is replication and why is it of particular concern in a wireless environment?

Network

1. Which remote access management software was chosen?
2. What types of functionality does the remote access management software offer?
3. Why was wireless networking chosen?

4. How did wireless networking uniquely support identified business processes?
5. What type of network expansion is anticipated in the near future?

Technology

1. Decribe the technology employed to implement the designed network. Include client and server platforms and all known protocols.

CHAPTER 11

ENTERPRISE NETWORKS AND THE INTERNET

Concepts Reinforced

OSI Model	Internet Suite of Protocols Model
Internetwork Design	Internetworking Technology
Switching vs. Routing	Top-Down Model

Concepts Introduced

ATM	Virtual LANs
LAN Emulation	Middleware
Enterprise Network Logical Design	Enterprise Network Physical Design
Internet Connectivity Services	Internet/Web Client Hardware
Internet/Web Client Software	Internet/Web Server Software
Internet/Web Server Hardware	Internet Client/Server Design
Internet Business Considerations	

OBJECTIVES

After mastering the material in this chapter, you should

1. Understand the business motivation for the analysis, design, and implementation of enterprise networks.

2. Understand the issues surrounding the analysis, design, implementation, and management of virtual LANs.

3. Understand the differences between, as well as the advantages and disadvantages of, alternative physical topologies for enterprise networks.

4. Understand the importance of ATM to virtual LANs and enterprise networks.

5. Understand how Internet clients and servers are able to connect to the Internet.

6. Understand available hardware and software technology for building client/server connections to the Internet and the World Wide Web.

7. Understand the business implications of Internet use.

■ INTRODUCTION

Having gained an appreciation of the type of services that can be delivered by well-designed LANs as well as the business-related benefits of those services, network managers wanted to extend these benefits to the entire business enterprise including, in some cases, vendors and customers. Although LANs may be local in geographic scope, the data that is generated and stored on LANs is an enterprise-wide asset that must be quickly and easily accessible by the entire enterprise. Beyond the obvious challenges of building networks of international geographic scope, more important network design hurdles such as the following needed to be overcome before the competitive advantage of enterprise networks could be realized:

- A relative lack of affordable wide area network bandwidth required to carry integrated voice, data, video, and multimedia applications.

- The multivendor, multiplatform, multiprotocol reality of the numerous nodes of a typical enterprise network would need to be transparently integrated.

- Due to the quickly changing nature of the competitive business environment combined with downsized human resources, enterprise networks would need to be extremely flexible allowing individuals to cooperatively collaborate on projects regardless of geographic location.

- Data required for decision-making would need to be able to be quickly and easily accessed regardless of physical location or data management system. This ease of access was especially critical for data locked away in mainframe computers.

These are just some of the challenges that must be addressed to effectively analyze, design, and implement enterprise networks. The purpose of this chapter is to introduce the reader to the numerous issues surrounding enterprise network design through the exploration of alternative enterprise network architectures, topologies, and technologies including the use of the Internet as an enterprise network backbone.

Applied Problem Solving

BUSINESS MOTIVATIONS FOR ENTERPRISE NETWORKS

As dictated by the top-down model, to understand the functionality required of an enterprise network, the network analyst must first understand the business-related issues and requirements that the enterprise network will be expected to fulfill. Figure 11-1 (on page 436) uses the top-down model to summarize the factors influencing the required functionality of enterprise networks.

A business phenomenon known as the **virtual corporation** implies a business partnership among cooperating business entities that is electronically enabled via an **enterprise network.** In most cases, the virtual corporation implies that these business entities are sufficiently distant from one another that constant travel between locations to accomplish business objectives would not be possible. In other words, without the enterprise network, the virtual corporation would not exist.

Top-Down Model Layer	Enterprise Network Implications
Business	• Dawn of the virtual corporation • Dynamic work teams, virtual workgroups • Matrix management, centers of excellence • More workers telecommuting or working on the road with increased customer contact • Extending the enterprise to include customers and vendors • Minimize expenses to increase profits
Application	• Remote users require full access to corporate information resources • Remote users require intelligent agent based software to act on their behalf when they are not logged in • Virtual workgroups require specialized collaborative software for cooperative development and design projects
Data	• Remote users require data and files to be automatically synchronized each time they log in to corporate information resources • Collaborative application software often transmits video, image, and voice as well as traditional data • Collaborative application software often requires database replication across numerous geographically distributed databases
Network	• Collaborative application software has high bandwidth demands and time-sensitive delivery constraints • Distributed database replication imposes high bandwidth demands on the network • Enterprise network services have become mission-critical, requiring absolute 7 day/week, 24 hr/day availability • Because of constant relocation of workers in virtual workgroups, the network services must be more active and intelligent by being able to provide appropriate services for each workgroup member regardless of physical location • Virtual LANs are required to provide the flexible, dynamic workgroup connections for virtual workgroups
Technology	• More powerful SMP servers • LAN switches for local bandwidth • ATM for high-speed backbone switching • SONET for high-speed WAN transmission • Open, standards-based technology helps to ensure multivendor, multiplatform, multiprotocol interoperability • Use of Internet as enterprise network backbone • Tunneling protocols to allow virtual private networks

Figure 11-1   Top-Down Model for Enterprise Networks

If the virtual corporation is considered a strategic business initiative, then the tactical fulfillment of that strategic objective is accomplished through the establishment and support of **virtual workgroups.** By dynamically allocating people to projects based on expertise rather than location, organizations can more easily assign the most qualified people to appropriate projects without concern for the expense and wasted productivity caused by extensive travel or frequent relocation.

Virtual workgroups require specialized application software that will allow them to cooperatively function as if they were all in the same geographic location. Collaborative computing software such as groupware is required to support the need for multiple simultaneous forms of communication (voice, video, data, image, multimedia).

The enterprise network that must support these virtual workgroups consisting of numerous remote computing users must be able to be dynamically defined to mirror the dynamic definition of the virtual workgroups themselves. In other words, although virtual workgroup members may be geographically dispersed, when they log into corporate information resources, the enterprise network must treat them as if they are all connected to the same LAN. Networks that can make geographically distributed users appear to be connected to the same LAN are known as **virtual LANs.**

◾ OVERALL ENTERPRISE NETWORK ARCHITECTURE

Figure 11-2 presents a logical model for how an enterprise network supports a virtual corporation.

As can be seen in Figure 11-2, the virtual corporation requires a **distributed information system** consisting of a number of major interacting components or subsystems. The application layer functionality of the top-down model is delivered by a **distributed computing** solution that is able to interact successfully with the numerous virtual workgroups. Data from this distributed computing environment is distributed and replicated as needed through the functionality delivered by the **data distribution** or data management subsystem. The client-to-server messaging from the distributed computing subsystem must be transparent to differences in computing platforms, operating systems, network operating systems, or data management systems. This messaging transparency is delivered by an important category of software known as **middleware.** All client-to-server and server-to-server messages are actually delivered via the **enterprise network.** This enterprise network could be privately implemented and managed by a corporation or could use the Internet for its connectivity, in which case it would be referred to as a **virtual private network (VPN).**

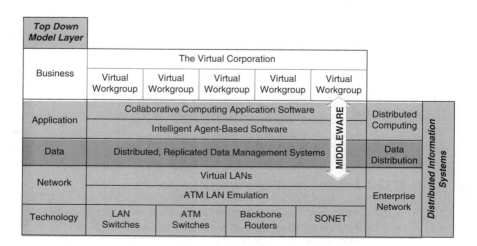

Figure 11-2   Overall Enterprise Network Architecture

■ ENTERPRISE NETWORK LOGICAL DESIGN

The logical design of the enterprise network must deliver the required functionality to allow businesses to respond to rapidly changing business requirements by supporting the rapid formation of dynamic workgroups and project teams. Organizations must be able to bring together in-house knowledge and resources on an as-needed basis in a quick and efficient manner. Rather than having to physically rewire network connections for each change in workgroup configurations, a **virtual LAN** allows for flexible assignment of dedicated network resources to virtual workgroups by grouping users logically rather than according to physical network connections.

Virtual LANs

Basic Functionality The logical network design known as a virtual LAN is dependent on a physical device, the LAN switch, for its functionality. Although the original LAN switches delivered abundant bandwidth to locally attached workstations and segments, they lacked the ability to partition the switch into multiple segregated broadcast zones and to segment users into corresponding separate workgroups.

Virtual LANs are software definable through configuration software contained within the LAN switch. The use of virtual LANs allows workgroup members to be assigned to more than one workgroup quickly and easily, if necessary. Subsequently, each virtual workgroup is assigned some portion of the LAN switch's backplane capacity. LAN switches that support virtual LANs use OSI layer 2 bridging functionality to logically segment the traffic within the switch into distinct virtual LANs.

Any message received by a LAN switch destined for a single workstation is delivered to that destination workstation via an individual switched network connection. The key difference between a LAN switch that does not support virtual LANs and one that does is the treatment of broadcast and multicast messages. In a virtual LAN, broadcasts and multicasts are limited to the members of that virtual LAN only, rather than to all connected devices. This prevents propagation of data across the entire network and reduces network traffic. To simplify, virtual LANs are nothing more than logically defined broadcast/multicast groups within layer 2 LAN switches since point-to-point traffic is handled by switched dedicated connections.

Limitations A key limitation of virtual LANs is that when members of the same virtual LAN are physically connected to separate LAN switches, the virtual LAN configuration information must be shared between multiple LAN switches. Currently, no interoperability standards exist for transmitting or sharing virtual LAN information between layer 2 LAN switches. As a result, only proprietary switch-to-switch protocols between a single vendor's equipment are possible for multiswitch virtual LANs.

Management and monitoring of virtual LANs are more difficult than management and monitoring of traditional LANs due to the virtual LAN's dependence on LAN switches for physical connectivity. Because the switched LAN connections are established, used, and terminated in a matter of microseconds for most transmissions, it is difficult if not impossible to monitor these transmissions in real time by traditional means. One solution to this dilemma is known as **traffic duplication** in which traffic between two switch ports is duplicated onto a third port to which traditional LAN analyzers can be attached.

Figure 11-3 illustrates the differences between a LAN switch, a virtual LAN, and a multiswitch virtual LAN.

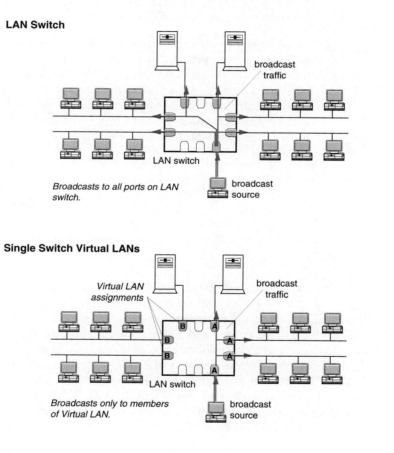

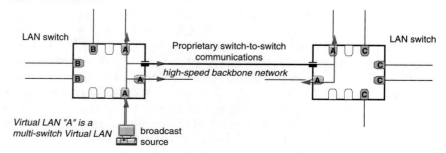

Figure 11-3   LAN Switches and Virtual LANs

TRANSMISSION BETWEEN LAYER 2 LAN SWITCHES

Among the alternative methods used by switch vendors to share virtual LAN information across layer 2 LAN switches are the following:

- Signaling message—Switches inform each other whenever new workstations come on line as to the MAC address and virtual LAN number of that workstation. To keep all switches' information synchronized, each switch's virtual LAN tables are broadcast periodically to all other switches. In larger switched networks, this virtual LAN table transfer can introduce significant amounts of broadcast traffic.

- Frame tagging—A tag indicating the virtual LAN number of the source workstation is appended to every data-link layer frame which must travel between LAN switches. In this way, the recipient switch knows immediately to which virtual LAN workstations the received frame must be forwarded. One difficulty with frame tagging is that the added bits may exceed the maximum frame length of the data-link layer protocol, thereby requiring additional proprietary methods to cope with this limitation.

- Time division multiplexing—Each virtual LAN is assigned a specific portion of the bandwidth available on the LAN switches' backplanes. Only the assigned virtual LAN is allowed to use designated bandwidth. In this way, each virtual LAN has a virtual private backplane and traffic from one virtual LAN does not interfere with traffic from another virtual LAN. However, assigned but unused bandwidth cannot be shared among other virtual LANs.

One possibility for standardization of switch-to-switch communication in support of virtual LANs that span multiple switches is **IEEE 802.10.** Originally conceived as a standard for secure data exchange on LANs that would allow workstations to set encryption and authentication settings, this standard is of interest to virtual LAN switch vendors because of the addition of a 32-bit header to existing MAC sublayer frames. Instead of just holding security information, this additional 32-bit header could hold virtual LAN identifiers. To overcome the limitation on maximum data-link layer frame length, IEEE 802.10 also includes specifications for segmentation and reassembly of any frames that should exceed maximum length due to the addition of the 32-bit header.

Transmission between Virtual LANs   Virtual LANs are built using LAN switches, which are OSI layer 2 devices only able to distinguish between MAC layer addresses. As a result, LAN switches are only able to offer the "forward-if-not-local" internetworking logic of bridges. To selectively transmit traffic between virtual LANs, routing functionality is required. This routing functionality may be supplied by an external router or by specialized router software included in the LAN switch. LAN switches with built-in routing capabilities are sometimes referred to as layer 3 switches. Since traffic cannot move between virtual LANs without the benefit of routing, the virtual LAN logical design has been credited with offering firewall functionality due to the filtering capabilities of intermediary routers.

Classification of Virtual LANs   Virtual LANs are often classified in terms of the OSI layer that represents their highest level of functionality:

Layer 2 virtual LANs are built using LAN switches that act as microsegmenting bridges. A LAN switch that supports a layer 2 virtual LAN distinguishes only between the MAC addresses of connected workstations. No differentiation is possible based on layer 3, network layer, protocols. One or more workstations can be connected to each switch port.

Layer 3 virtual LANs are built using LAN switches that are able to process layer 3 network addresses. Such devices may be called **routing switches.** Since these devices are able to perform filtering based on network layer protocols and addresses, they are able to support multiple virtual LANs using different network layer protocols.

In other words, one virtual LAN might support only TCP/IP whereas another might only support IPX/SPX. Since layer 3 switches understand layer 3 addressing schemes, they are able to use the subnetwork numbers embedded within layer 3 addresses to organize virtual LANs. Since these subnetwork numbers are previously assigned to workstations, some layer 3 switches are able to query all connected workstations and auto-configure or automatically assign workstations to virtual LANs based on these subnetwork numbers. Workstations using nonroutable protocols such as LAT, NetBEUI, or NetBIOS are likewise segregated into their own virtual LANs.

Figure 11-4 illustrates the architectural differences between layer 2 and layer 3 virtual LANs whereas Figure 11-5 details the functional differences between the two virtual LAN designs.

Managerial
Perspective

VIRTUAL LAN REALITIES

Depending on which network expert one listens to, virtual LANs are either a passing fad or the greatest thing to happen to networking in the past 10 years. As is most often the case, the truth probably lies somewhere in between. Virtual LANs are not the ultimate network architecture for all organizations. It is important to differentiate between the switched bandwidth capabilities delivered by the LAN switch and the broadcast domain limitation added by virtual LAN definitions. The lower cost of moves, adds, and changes most often credited to virtual LANs will only be significant if a given organization is constantly moving, adding, and changing users among workgroups and from LAN to LAN. Virtual LANs remove the architectural constraint that all members of a given local area network must exist in close physical proximity to each other. This property allows all servers to be maintained at a secure, centralized location with technical support personnel, while users of that LAN server may be physically located at another location. As virtual LANs grow in sophistication, configuration and management become more of an issue. The trend toward auto-configuring LAN switches and more sophisticated monitoring and management reporting tools should allow virtual LANs to be more easily integrated into an enterprise network. From a management perspective, perhaps the biggest stumbling block to widespread acceptance of virtual LANs and the LAN switches upon which they are deployed is the current lack of open, industry-wide standards for multivendor LAN switch and virtual LAN interoperability.

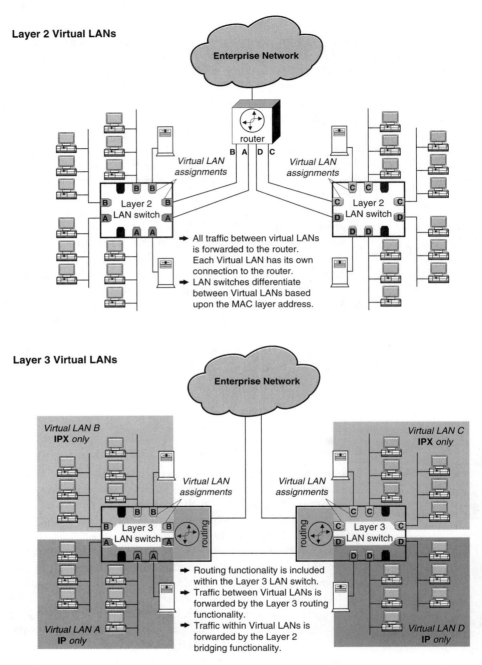

Enterprise Network

Figure 11-4   Layer 2 vs. Layer 3 Virtual LANs: An Architectural Comparison

Bandwidth Hierarchy

One of the overriding principles of the logical design of enterprise networks is the creation and management of a structured **bandwidth hierarchy.** By creating a bandwidth hierarchy as part of a strategic network design, required bandwidth can be upgraded incrementally in a planned fashion rather than facing wholesale replace-

Virtual LAN Characteristic	Layer 2 Virtual LAN Functionality	Layer 3 Virtual LAN Functionality
Configuration	Simpler	More difficult
Expense	Less expensive, but may require external routers	More expensive, but includes internal routing capability
Performance	Faster since only layer 2 addresses are processed	Up to 30% slower since layer 3 protocols must be processed
Nonroutable protocols	No problem since this is a layer 2 only device	May be able to segregate into a separate VLAN or may not be able to handle
Routable protocols	No ability to differentiate between layer 3 protocols	Can differentiate between layer 3 protocols and can build separate virtual LANs based on layer 3 protocol; layer 3 switches vary in the number of routable protocols supported
Multiswitch virtual LANs	Must use proprietary switch-to-switch communication, which adds to network traffic congestion in most cases	Able to use subnetwork numbers in network layer addresses to keep track of virtual LANs that span multiple switches without the need for proprietary switch-to-switch protocols
Broadcasts	Broadcasts to all segments that belong to a particular virtual LAN	Can broadcast to only appropriate subnetwork within a virtual LAN
Filtering	No filtering on network layer addresses or protocols possible	Filtering on network layer addresses and protocols for security and virtual LAN segmentation by protocol
Routing capabilities	Must be supplied by external router	Included with built-in routing software that provides traffic management and protocol isolation; some layer 3 switches are able to communicate with routers via RIP or OSPF whereas others are not able to

Figure 11-5   Layer 2 vs. Layer 3 Virtual LANs: A Functional Comparison

ment of networking technology in reaction to a crisis of crippling network performance.

Adherence to the top-down model should produce anticipated bandwidth requirements as an outcome of the analysis of the applications and their associated data that must traverse various levels of the enterprise network. As application and data requirements for each location and groups of locations on the enterprise network are calculated, the required bandwidth necessary to produce required response times should fall into one of the available network services contained in an

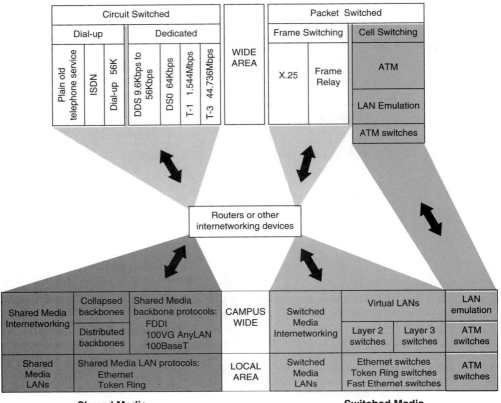

Figure 11-6 Enterprise Network Bandwidth Hierarchy

enterprise networks' bandwidth hierarchy. Figure 11-6 illustrates one example of an enterprise network hierarchy.

Other bandwidth hierarchies for other enterprise networks are possible and are equally correct. There is no single correct bandwidth hierarchy that would apply universally to all enterprise networks. As a result, it is absolutely essential to take a top-down approach to each enterprise networking opportunity.

As illustrated in Figure 11-6, the bandwidth needs of local area networks are often initially met by a shared-media LAN architecture such as Ethernet or token ring. Once local area network traffic begins to burden given network segments, logical segmentation through the use of bridges will reduce the amount of traffic on each segment. Bridges are an example of shared-media internetworking. Physically, shared-media internetworking can be accomplished via two different backbone architectures:

- **Distributed backbones,** in which individual LAN segments are linked to a backbone LAN media via bridges and transceivers, were once the norm. These backbone networks often ran vertically between floors of a building with multiple, horizontal LAN segments were distributed throughout the building and attached to the backbone via bridges.

- **Collapsed backbones,** a more recent innovation, collapse the entire network backbone, which once spanned several floors of a building, into the backplane of a single internetworking device such as a router. The backplane of the router, which is shared by numerous internetworking modules, has enormous bandwidth capacity, usually in the gigabits/sec range.

Figure 11-7 contrasts distributed and collapsed backbone architectures for shared-media internetworking.

Higher speed backbone network architectures such as FDDI, 100BaseT, or 100VGAnyLAN can offer incremental upgrades to overburdened LAN segments as well as serving as a backbone protocol for linking internetworking devices such as routers. Servers can be linked directly to the higher speed backbone network rather than to a LAN segment of Ethernet or token ring.

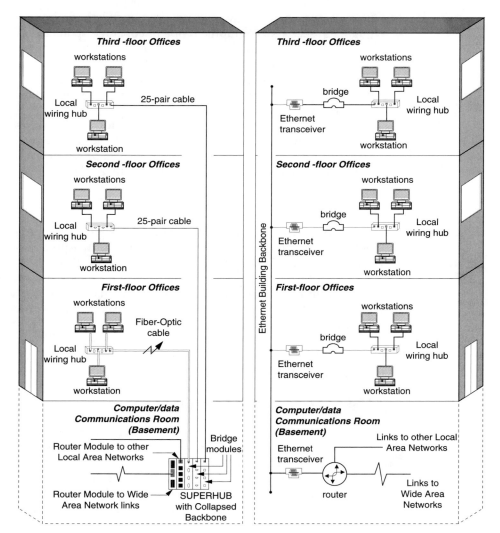

Figure 11-7   Collapsed vs. Distributed Backbones

Another upgrade alternative when shared LAN segments running Ethernet or token ring become overburdened is to install switched LAN media technology such as a LAN switch. As described in the previous section, LAN switches can also support virtual LANs which can be linked via layer 2 or layer 3 LAN switches. In some cases, LAN switches support proprietary higher speed switch-to-switch transmission links. Ethernet switches are by far the most common LAN switch although token ring and FDDI switches are also available. Some LAN switches also support more than one network architecture, with Ethernet switches supporting both 10- and 100-Mbps speeds being the most common example of this type of switch.

If the switched bandwidth offered by traditional LAN switches is not sufficient, then a faster switching technology known as **ATM,** or **asynchronous transfer mode,** is also available. One of the real benefits of ATM is it ability to switch LAN traffic without the need to make any hardware or software changes to LAN clients or servers. This transparent delivery of LAN information via ATM is known as **LAN emulation** and is explained in more detail later in this chapter. Another key benefit of ATM is its scalability both in terms of transmission speed and geographic scope of coverage. While ATM transmission speeds have been defined up to 2.4 Gbps (gigabits/sec), its geographic scope of coverage spans from LAN-based switches to wide area ATM network services offered by long-distance carriers. The net effect of ATM's availability from the LAN to the WAN is that virtual LANs can be established over long distances using ATM switches as the virtual LAN bandwidth provider. In addition, ATM can transmit voice, video, data, and image simultaneously between network locations.

Alternatively, as local area network information needs to be shared over the wide area, more traditional circuit-switched and packet-switched WAN services can be purchased from a variety of WAN service providers. As a network analyst, it is important to know which WAN services are available at each corporate location, including remote branches and telecommuting sites.

Managerial Perspective

The importance of a bandwidth hierarchy as part of a strategic network plan is that network segments can be offered required bandwidth as needed without having to rewrite or modify the applications that will use those network segments. In addition, due to the availability of incrementally increasing levels of bandwidth in a bandwidth hierarchy, bandwidth requirements can be met with a minimum of service disruption, an ever increasingly important issue as networks become mission critical to corporate survival.

■ ENTERPRISE NETWORK PHYSICAL DESIGN

ATM as a Common Switching Platform

Although different vendors of enterprise networking equipment may each be promoting their own view of the enterprise network of the future, one view shared by all of these vendors is that ATM will serve as the high-speed switched backbone network service used to connect geographically dispersed corporate networks. As was previously discussed in the section on virtual LANs, layer 2 switching, no matter how fast, is not by itself a sufficient enterprise network platform. As a result, routing capabilities must be added to the underlying switching capabilities offered by ATM. How the routing capabilities are added to the ATM switching fabric and the subsequent enterprise network performance characteristics exhibited as a result of those routing capabilities are the basic differences between alternative enterprise network physical topologies.

ATM LAN Emulation   Since ATM acts as a layer 2 switching service and since layer 2 LAN switches support virtual LANs, it would stand to reason that ATM switches ought to be able to support virtual LANs as well. In fact, through a process known as **ATM LAN emulation,** virtual LANs are able to be constructed over an ATM switched network regardless of the geographic scope of that network. ATM LAN emulation is considered a bridging solution, like LAN switch-based virtual LANs, since traffic is switched based on MAC layer addresses. Unlike LAN switch-based virtual LANs, however, MAC layer addresses must be translated into, or resolved into, ATM addresses in a process known as **ATM address resolution.** In ATM LAN emulation, the ATM switching fabric adds an entire layer of its own addressing schemes which it uses to forward virtual LAN traffic to its proper destination.

In Sharper Focus

ATM LAN EMULATION ARCHITECTURE

How MAC layer addresses are resolved into ATM addresses is defined by an ATM Forum specification known as LAN emulation or more formally as L-UNI (LAN emulation user-to-network interface) or LANE (LAN emulation). The ATM LAN emulation specification actually defines an entire architecture of interacting software components to accomplish the ATM-to-MAC layer address resolution. Among the interacting components that cooperate to accomplish ATM LAN emulation as illustrated in Figure 11-8 are the following:

- **LAN emulation client (LEC)** software may physically reside within ATM-to-LAN conversion devices or may be included within a router that supports ATM interfaces. The job of the LEC is to appear to be an ATM end station on behalf of the LAN clients it represents. As a result, the LEC is sometimes referred to as a proxy ATM end station. The LEC is also responsible for converting the LAN's data-link layer protocols (Ethernet, token ring, FDDI) into fixed-length ATM cells. Once the local LEC knows the ATM address of the remote LEC that is acting as an ATM proxy for the remote LAN destination, it sets up a switched virtual circuit, or switched network connection, to the remote LEC that subsequently delivers the information payload to the remote LAN workstation in a **unicast** (point-to-point) transmission.

- **LAN emulation server (LES)** software resides on a server or workstation that is directly attached to the ATM network and has a unique ATM address. The LES software performs three major tasks or services that can actually be accomplished by separate software programs executed on separate servers:
  - LES **configuration services** are responsible for keeping track of the types of virtual LANs that are being supported over the ATM switching fabric and which LECs belong to which type of LAN. MAC addresses and corresponding ATM addresses of attached workstations are stored by the configuration server. LAN type (Ethernet, token ring, FDDI) is important to keep track of due to the variability of the maximum frame length accepted by workstations attached to each type of LAN.
  - LES **broadcast and unknown services (BUS)** are responsible for handling requests for broadcasts and multicasts within the virtual LANs that

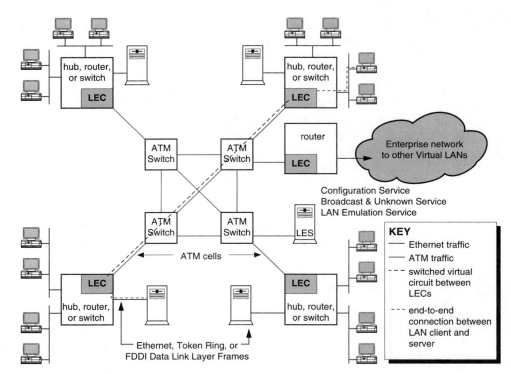

Figure 11-8   ATM LAN Emulation Architecture

exist across the ATM switching fabric. In addition, should a LEC not know the destination ATM address of a destination LAN workstation, it will forward that frame to the broadcast and unknown server, which will broadcast that frame throughout the virtual LAN on behalf of the LEC.

- LES **LAN emulation services** receive address resolution protocol (ARP) requests from LECs seeking the ATM addresses of destination LAN workstations for which the MAC address is known. Once the LES responds to the LEC with the requested ATM address, the LEC is able to set up the point-to-point connection to the destination LEC. If the LES does not respond right away, the LEC continues to use the BUS to broadcast the destination frame throughout the virtual LAN.

Managerial Perspective

It is important to understand that ATM LAN emulation, like other virtual LAN architectures built on layer 2 switching, is basically a bridge topology that suffers from the same limitations as other layer 2 switched networks:

- Flat network topology.

- Broadcast storms (although limited to a particular virtual LAN).

- No layer 3 filtering for security or segmentation.

On the other hand, because it does not discriminate between network layer (layer 3) protocols, ATM LAN emulation is able to support, or transport, multiple network layer protocols between virtual LANs.

Perhaps more importantly, however, ATM LAN emulation offers no routing capability. As a result, each virtual LAN that is emulated using ATM emulation, must still have a dedicated connection to a router that is able to process layer 3 addresses and make appropriate route determination and forwarding decisions between virtual LANs.

Layer 3 Protocols over ATM Networks   A variety of initiatives are underway by both the IETF (Internet Engineering Task Force) and the ATM Forum to somehow integrate layer 3 functionality with ATM networks. IETF RFC (request for comment) 1577 is known as **Classical IP over ATM.** The goal of Classical IP over ATM is to allow IP networks, as well as all upper layer TCP/IP protocols, utilities, and APIs encapsulated by IP, to be delivered over an ATM network without requiring modification to the TCP/IP protocols. Using Classical IP over ATM, the ATM network is treated by IP like just another subnet or data-link protocol such as Ethernet or token ring. IP routers see the entire ATM network as only a single hop, regardless of the actual size of the ATM network. IP subnets established over ATM networks using this protocol are known as **logical IP subnets,** or **LIS.**

A significant limitation of Classical IP over ATM is that it only works within a given subnet. As a result, to use IP addresses to properly route data between Classical IP subnets, an IP router must still be employed. Just as with ATM LAN emulation, Classical IP over ATM also requires address resolution. In this case a new protocol known as **ATMARP (ATM address resolution protocol)** runs on a server in the logical IP subnet and provides address resolution between IP addresses and ATM addresses. ATM addresses may actually be the virtual circuit ID numbers of the virtual circuits or connections that are established between two ATM end points on the ATM network.

Understandably, Classical IP over ATM only supports IP as a network layer protocol over ATM networks. Other initiatives are underway to support multiple network layer protocols over ATM. The ATM Forum is currently working on **MPOA (Multiprotocol over ATM),** which will not only support IP, IPX, AppleTalk, and other network protocols over ATM, but also be able to route data directly between virtual LANs, thereby precluding the need for additional external routers. Routing implemented on switches using protocols such as MPOA is sometimes referred to as **cut-through routing** and uses ATM LAN emulation as its layer 2 switching specification. Like ATM LAN emulation, MPOA operates transparently to end devices and does not require any hardware or software changes to those end devices or their applications. Multiprotocol over ATM is actually an entire architecture as illustrated in Figure 11-9 consisting of the following key components:

- **Edge Devices,** which might be a kind of hybrid hub, switch, and router, would act as interfaces or gateways between LANs and the ATM network. Once the ATM address is known, edge devices would be capable of establishing new virtual circuits over the ATM network.

- A **route server** would supply edge devices with their routing information including ATM addresses and virtual circuit IDs. The route server may actually be located within one of the ATM switches in the ATM backbone. Routing tables within the route server are organized according to layer 3 protocol specific subnets referred to as **Internet address summarization groups (IASG).**

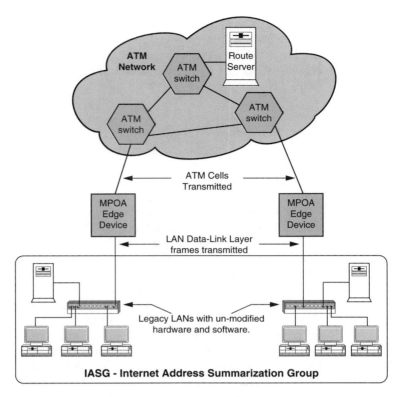

Figure 11-9   Multiprotocol over ATM Architecture

Whereas MPOA defines multiprotocol communications between ATM end stations and a given route server, another ATM Forum specification known as **integrated private network-to-network interface (IPNNI)** defines how route servers are able to communicate path and address information to each other and to/from ATM switches over an ATM network. If multiple route servers are required on a given enterprise network, then a protocol such as IPNNI must be implemented to share the layer 3 information between ATM switches and route servers to allow the best path through the network to be selected dynamically.

The IETF is currently working on RFC 1483, **Multiprotocol Encapsulation over ATM Adaptation Layer 5.** One of the significant contributions of this proposal is that it defines two different ways in which multiple network layer protocols can be transmitted simultaneously over an ATM network. The first method, LLC/SNAP encapsulation, places indicators in the ATM data-link layer frame to identify which network layer protocols are embedded within that data-link layer frame. The second method, virtual channel-based multiplexing, establishes a separate virtual circuit, or connection, through the ATM network for each network layer protocol transported from one workstation to another.

Another alternative to add routing capabilities to ATM switching fabrics is known as **IP switching.** IP switching technology distinguishes between the length of data streams and switches or routes accordingly on a case-by-case basis. In the case of long data streams associated with file transfers or voice or video transmissions, the IP switch sets up a virtual circuit through the ATM switching fabric and then forwards packets immediately via layer 2 switching to that virtual circuit. In the case of datagram-oriented, short messages, each message is forwarded through the layer 3 routing software located in the IP switch. Protocols to distinguish between the types of transmissions and to decide whether to switch or route are under development. IPsilon Networks has proposed **flow management protocol (FMP),** and Cisco Systems has proposed as alternative protocol known as **tag switching.**

■ THE INTERNET AS AN ENTERPRISE NETWORK BACKBONE

The **Internet** is a wide area network linking over 4,000,000 host computers. Originally developed as a means for the research, education, and scientific communities to share information, the Internet has been opened up in recent years to more commercial uses as well as to access by individuals. The purpose of this section is to explore the use of the Internet from a business perspective. Specifically, this section will deal with the following:

- What does the Internet have to offer business?

- What are the various ways in which businesses can access Internet services?

- How can a business integrate the Internet with its local area networks in a client/server architecture?

- How can a business safely and securely use the Internet as an enterprise network backbone?

This section will not deal with how to "surf the Net" or "navigate the Web." Many books have been written on the best ways to travel through cyberspace on the Internet. Rather, this section will offer business-oriented network analysts and management a top-down approach to objectively evaluate the merits of connecting to the Internet as well as a methodology to develop the logical and physical network designs to do so.

More specifically, after a review of the potential advantages and disadvantages offered by the Internet to business, the section will continue with a study of the use of the Internet as a client/server platform or enterprise network backbone.

■ BUSINESS PERSPECTIVE ON THE INTERNET

Why Connect to the Internet?

From a business perspective, the Internet is currently being used primarily as a marketing tool rather than a sales tool. Millions of dollars in sales transactions are not presently taking place on the Internet. Most companies currently using the Internet for marketing purposes are doing so for image building rather than direct profit increases.

A recent survey of businesses currently using the Internet for marketing purposes produced the following results:

- 72% of companies surveyed said the purpose of their Internet usage was to enhance their company's image.

- 22% said their Internet usage was financially rewarding.

- 40% didn't expect financial rewards for 12–24 months.

- Less than 6% of companies conduct credit card transactions over the Internet.

From the potential customer perspective, 4–5 times more people use the Internet for browsing rather than buying.

Managerial Perspective

Strategically speaking, when should a company start to think about developing a presence on the Internet?

- If existing or potential customers are Internet users, then it would probably be advantageous, for public relations reasons if nothing else, to look into establishing a presence on the Internet.

- If enterprise partners such as key vendors or suppliers have an Internet presence, then it may be advantageous for a company to also be connected.

The Internet customer market is small in comparison to other, more general markets. For example, there are an estimated 11 million Internet users in the United States whereas there are over 200 million television viewers. Internet users are a highly specialized, technically knowledgeable market segment. At the present time, the Internet offers a means to develop specially targeted marketing for this relatively small but significant market segment. It does not at the present time or in the short term however, for a variety of reasons to be discussed in the remainder of the chapter, provide a lucrative untapped market for on-line electronic commerce and credit card transactions.

What Are the Available Services/Resources?

The Internet is currently in a state of major transition from a government-funded entity designed for a research and education audience to a privately funded entity catering increasingly to commercial concerns. The Internet offers three major service categories:

1. The World Wide Web.

2. Information servers.
   - FTP servers.
   - Gopher servers.
   - WAIS servers.
   - USENET servers.

3. Global e-mail.

The World Wide Web   The **World Wide Web (WWW)** is a collection of servers accessed via the Internet that offer graphical or multimedia (audio, video, image) presentations about a company's products, personnel, or services. WWW servers are accessed via client-based front-end software tools commonly referred to as **Web browsers.** Companies wishing to use the World Wide Web as a marketing tool establish a **Web site** on the Internet and publicize the address of that Web site. Web presentations can be interactive, inviting visitors to the Web site to register their visit, complete marketing surveys, watch product demos, download available software, and participate in a variety of other multimedia activities. The Web site and Web server presentation design, implementation, and management can be done in-house or can be contracted out to professional Web site development and management services.

Information Servers   Text-based information stored in Internet-connected servers can be accessed by remote users logging into these servers via a TCP/IP protocol known as **Telnet.** Once they are successfully logged into an Internet-based information server using either previously assigned user accounts and passwords or general access "anonymous" user accounts, users are able to execute programs on the remote computer as if they were locally attached.

To download, or transfer, information back to their client PCs, users would access another TCP/IP protocol known as **FTP** (file transfer protocol). Servers that support such activity are often called **FTP servers** or anonymous FTP servers. Users can access FTP servers directly or through Telnet sessions. The difficulty with searching for information in this manner is that users must know the Internet address of the specific information server (Telnet or FTP) that they wish to access.

A menu-based client/server system that features search engines that comb through all of the information in all of these information servers is referred to as the **Gopher** system, named after the mascot of the University of Minnesota where the system was developed. The key difference between Gopher and the World Wide Web is that Gopher's information is text-based whereas the World Wide Web is largely graphical. Also, Web sites tend to be more interactive whereas the Gopher subsystem is more analogous to searching for information in a library and then extracting or checking out that desired information. Gopher client software is most often installed on a client PC and interacts with software running on a particular **Gopher server,** which transparently searches multiple FTP sites for requested information and delivers that information to the Gopher client. Gopher users do not need to know the exact Internet address of the information servers that they wish to access.

A third type of information server offers a text-searching service known as **WAIS** or **wide area information services.** WAIS indexers generate multiple indexes for all types of files that organizations or individuals wish to offer access to via the Internet. **WAIS servers** offer these multiple indexes to other Internet-attached WAIS servers. WAIS servers also serve as search engines that have the ability to search for particular words or text strings in the indexes located across multiple Internet-attached information servers of various types.

USENET servers or newsgroup servers share text-based news items over the Internet. Over 10,000 newsgroups covering selected topics are available. USENET servers update each other on a regular basis with news items that are pertinent to the newsgroups housed on a particular server. USENET servers transfer news items between each other using a specialized transfer protocol known as **NNTP (network news transport protocol)** and are also known as NNTP servers. Users wishing to access NNTP servers and their newsgroups must have NNTP client software loaded on their client PCs.

Global E-Mail   Millions of users are connected worldwide to the Internet via the **global e-mail** subsystem. From a business perspective, Internet e-mail offers one method of sending intercompany e-mail. Most companies have private networks that support e-mail transport to fellow employees but not necessarily to employees of other companies. By adding Internet e-mail gateways to its private network, a company can potentially send e-mail to users all over the world. However, Internet e-mail gateways are a double-edged sword. Unauthorized access from the Internet into a company's private network is also possible unless proper security precautions are taken. Such security issues as firewall servers will be discussed later in the chapter.

Global e-mail users can subscribe to e-mail mailing lists of their choice on various topics of interest. Companies can easily e-mail to targeted audiences by sending a single e-mail message to a list server and allowing the list server to forward that e-mail message to all subscribed users. Targeted list servers provide the best commercial use of global e-mail for marketing or sales purposes. Global e-mail also affords access to specifically targeted electronic magazines (**E-zines**) and topical discussion groups often referred to as "frequently asked question" groups or **FAQ groups.** FAQ groups are similar to ListServe groups that users can subscribe to via e-mail.

What Are the Potential Advantages?

To gain the maximum benefit from Internet connectivity, a company would probably wish to avail itself of the services of all three of the previously mentioned Internet subsystems rather than choosing just one. By combining the benefits offered by the World Wide Web, Gopher, and global e-mail, a company could have access to highly focused marketing campaigns, almost limitless research data, and access to peers, partners, and customers throughout the world. More specific examples of benefits, advantages, or trends supporting increased Internet access by business are highlighted in Figure 11-10 and will be elaborated upon in the chapter.

What Are the Potential Disadvantages?

From a business perspective, the current major concern of widespread business use of the Internet is probably a perceived lack of adequate security. As will be seen later in the chapter, several alternate methods have been proposed to deal with this perception. If the Internet is to succeed as a viable commercial communications link for business, then financial transactions of any magnitude must be able to be conducted in an absolutely secure and confidential manner. Figure 11-11 summarizes some of the other potential disadvantages or obstacles to widespread use of the Internet by business.

■ A CLIENT/SERVER APPROACH TO INTERNET CONNECTIVITY

Before deciding which combination of technology and network services must be employed to provide the desired Internet access, it must first be determined what the nature of that Internet access by a business will be. When it comes to Internet access, companies can be either **information consumers** or **information providers** or a combination of the two functions. Depending on the nature of the desired access to the Internet, technology requirements can vary dramatically.

Overall Client/Server Architecture for Internet Connectivity

Figure 11-12 illustrates an overall view of some of the ways in which businesses can access Internet services as either information consumers or providers. Elements of the overall architecture are explained in the following paragraphs.

Benefit/Advantage/Supporting Trend	Implication/Explanation
More readily accessible internet access	Local, regional, and national Internet access providers are now plentiful, leading to competitive pricing. AT&T, Sprint, and MCI as well as most RBOCs (regional Bell operating companies) offer Internet access services of some type.
Realistic bandwidth	Mere access to the Internet is not enough. The "pipe" (bandwidth) into the Internet must be wide enough to accommodate desired traffic. Graphical traffic from the WWW is especially bandwidth intensive. Advances in modem technology support 28.8 Kbps over dial-up lines whereas ISDN offers up to 144 Kbps and is becoming more widely available.
Improved front-end tools	Improved front-end tools or browsers mean that even novices have a reasonable chance of finding what they're looking for on the Internet. Many of these tools will be integrated into more familiar products such as word processors and presentation graphics packages.
Improved server tools	Internet access gateways and internet server software will be increasingly integrated into mainstream server operating systems from companies such as IBM, Novell, and Microsoft. This will make the software easier to use, more tightly integrated, and more reliable.
Improved information services	The types of information and services that can be accessed on the Internet continue to improve and broaden in scope. Airline reservations, stock trading and quotations, weather forecasts, publishers, government agencies, and high-tech companies are but a few of the types of information and services available.

Figure 11-10   Benefits, Advantages, and Supporting Trends of Internet Access for Business

As will be explained further in the section on Internet connectivity services, a company should be able to purchase as much or as little Internet connectivity assistance as it deems appropriate. Although there are no hard and fast rules, Internet service providers are often categorized as follows:

- **Internet access providers (IAP)** (also known as Internet connectivity providers (ICP)) are primarily concerned with getting a subscriber company physically hooked up to the Internet. The IAP may provide for additional hardware acquisition and maintenance but is unlikely to provide programming services. IAPs may be the local or long-distance phone company or may be a business entirely independent of established phone companies. IAPs are most concerned with the infrastructure required to provide Internet access for subscriber companies.

Disadvantage/Obstacle	Implication/Explanation
Bandwidth availability	Although ISDN is becoming more widely available, it is still not universally available. Bandwidth must be reasonably priced as well. Also, local providers of Internet access bandwidth vary in their financial backing and commitment to provide adequate bandwidth as user traffic demands grow.
Search abilities	The information on the Internet is rather loosely organized. If it is to be commercially viable, information must be organized and catalogued in such a way that it is easier to find. Busy businesspeople do not have a lot of time to "surf" for information. Sophisticated search agents and global search engines would suggest best and/or nearest sources of desired information. Although front-end tools are improving, they are still new and largely unproven.
Internet ownership	The management and funding of the Internet is transitioning from government to the private sector. Questions remain as to who is (and will be) responsible for network maintenance, upgrades, management, and policy development and enforcement.
Internet regulation	The Internet is unregulated. Questions are being raised in the U.S. Congress as to what represents acceptable use of and behavior on the Internet. It is uncertain whether or not the Internet will remain unregulated. Certain information available on the Internet may be considered offensive to certain people. The Internet is accessed by millions of users, most of them "surfers," not buyers.

Figure 11-11   Disadvantages and Obstacles to Widespread Use of the Internet by Business

- **Internet presence providers (IPP)** are primarily concerned with designing, developing, implementing, managing, and maintaining a subscriber company's presence on the Internet. IPPs may depend on IAPs for the actual physical access to the Internet. If a company wanted a Web page on the World Wide Web but did not want to invest in the required hardware and personnel to launch such a venture in-house, that company would be likely to contract with an IPP.

Clients, servers, and local area networks are connected to the Internet via a **network access device** such as a modem, an ISDN access device, or a router. Which particular network access device is required in each case is a function of the type and bandwidth of the access line and the characteristics of the client or server to which the network access device must interface.

Those companies that only wish to be Internet information consumers only require a properly configured client PC to be connected to the Internet. Companies wishing to be only information providers on the Internet only require a properly configured server to be connected to the Internet, whereas companies wishing to both consume and provide Internet information must have both client(s) and server(s) properly attached.

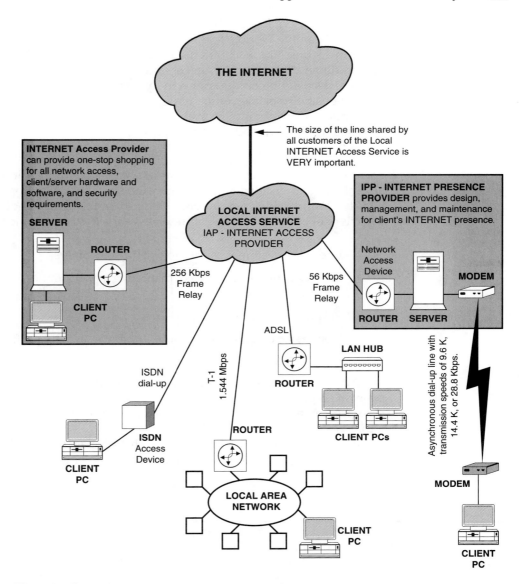

Figure 11-12   Overall Client/Server Architecture for Internet Connectivity

Service-Specific Client/Server Architectures for Internet Connectivity

Configurations of client and server hardware and software will vary depending on which Internet services a company wishes to access. Alternative configurations for each major category of Internet services are explained in the following section.

World Wide Web Connectivity Alternatives   Internet information consumers wishing to access the World Wide Web will require a client PC configured with a front-end software tool or Web browser such as **Mosaic, Internet Explorer,** or **Netscape.** Several connectivity alternatives exist for those companies that wish to establish a presence or Web site on the World Wide Web. The characteristics of these alternatives are detailed in Figure11-13. Each alternative connectivity option listed in Figure 11-13 is broken down into the major processes involved in establishing and maintaining a Web site. Depending on the connectivity alternative chosen, these processes may be the responsibility of the company (C) wishing to establish the Web presence or of the vendor (V) providing the Web connectivity service. Approximate costs are also included for each connectivity alternative.

Managerial Perspective

Each of the alternatives for establishing a Web site outlined in Figure 11-13 has its advantages and disadvantages. There is no single best way for all businesses to establish a World Wide Web presence. A company must first understand the business objectives of establishing such a presence. Some possibilities include

- Improved customer service to existing customers.
- Increased or more focused marketing opportunities toward potential customers.
- Response to competitive pressures.
- Web presence should (or should not) be financially profitable.

Although the first alternative listed in Figure 11-13, "post customer-designed page on access provider's server," is relatively inexpensive, the sophistication of the Web presentation will not match those of the more expensive Web connectivity alternatives.

For example, it is less likely that such Web pages would be highly interactive and possess the ability to prompt and store customer responses.

Connectivity Alternative	Design, Develop, and Maintain Web Page	Establish and Maintain Internet Node	Establish, Maintain, and Manage Network Access	Configure and Maintain the Web Server	Approximate Cost, both Recurring (RC) and Nonrecurring (NRC)
Post customer-designed page on access provider's server	C	V	V	V	$20–40/month (RC)
Hire Web service provider	V	V	V	V	$100–1000 (NRC) $25–10,000/month (RC)
In-house development and deployment	C	C	C	C	$1,000's/month (RC); depends on number of staff assigned

Figure 11-13 Web Server Connectivity Alternatives

Hiring a Web service provider to perform all aspects of establishing and managing a Web site is certainly a quicker and more certain way to get on the Web but obviously can run into a substantial financial investment. The experience offered by at least some of these providers enables the production of professional-quality presentations that can then be incorporated into **cybermalls** with other professional-quality Web pages adhering to the standards established by the cybermall management.

Hiring, training, and keeping an in-house staff to maintain a company's Web site constitute a distinct third alternative. Hiring experienced Web site developers can be costly, whereas waiting out the learning curve of new-hires will delay the establishment of a Web site. Operation costs for maintaining the Web server and access to the Internet need to also be considered as does the security concerns of anonymous access to corporate network facilities.

Finally, a mix of the previous three approaches is also possible. Perhaps a Web service provider could be hired on a fixed-length contract to quickly establish a quality Web site. Depending on customer response and potential profitability of the Web site, in-house staff could be hired and trained as management of the Web site is gradually transitioned into their realm of responsibility.

Practical Advice and Information

It is important not to confuse the World Wide Web with **electronic commerce.** Electronic commerce, in the forms of **electronic data interchange (EDI)** and **electronic funds transfer (EFT),** preceded the existence of the World Wide Web. The expansion of the industry-specific electronic commerce programs into a more universal **electronic market** offering global financial interaction between consumers and vendors as well as among industrial trading partners will result from a merging of electronic commerce and World Wide Web technologies.

■ CLIENT/SERVER TECHNOLOGY FOR INTERNET CONNECTIVITY

Web browser software, otherwise known as Web client software, is executed on client hardware for the purpose of accessing previously developed Web pages that are available on Internet-attached Web servers. These Web servers run specialized Web server software that supports **HTTP (hypertext transport protocol)** to handle the organization of servicing the multiple Web client requests for Web pages. These Web pages are collections of text, graphics, sound, and video elements and are programmed in the first place by using Web publishing software that may run on either client or server platforms. The Web pages are programmed using text formatted with **HTML (hypertext markup language).** Since HTML is text based, any text editor could be used to generate the HTML code, which would then be interpreted by the HTTP server software.

When a Web client running Web browser software requests a Web page or constituent element from a Web server by clicking on a hyperlink, a TCP/IP message is sent to the Web server identified in the **URL (uniform resource locator).** Included in this message is the identity of the requested Web page file noted with a .HTML extension and a version indicator identifying which version of HTML the requesting client understands. In response, the Web server retrieves the requested file and transfers it to the Web client. Figure 11-14 distinguishes between Web browsers, Web servers, and Web publishers.

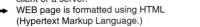

WEB PAGE PUBLISHING

- ➡ WEB page is published using WEB publishing software running either on a client or a server.
- ➡ WEB page is formatted using HTML (Hypertext Markup Language.)

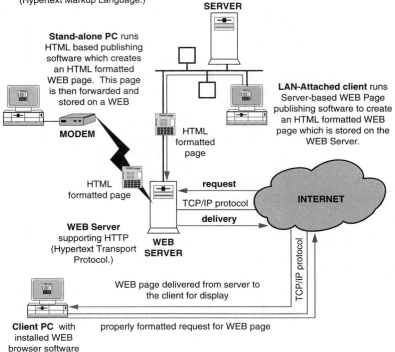

Figure 11-14   Web Clients, Web Servers, and Web Publishers

Internet/Web Clients

Web Browsers   Web browsers are a client-based category of software that is undergoing tremendous development due to the vast interest in the World Wide Web. The scope of Web browser software is expanding horizontally to include access to not only Internet-attached resources but also

- Local client attached resources.
- Local area network attached resources.
- Enterprise or corporate network attached resources.

The latest Web browser products display all reachable resources, from the local PC to the worldwide Internet, on a single hierarchical file tree display. The scope of Web browser software is also expanding vertically as well by including access to all Internet-attached resources and services and not merely to the World Wide Web. By combining navigation features of traditional Web browsers and search features of information server front ends, some of the resources that are now directly accessible from the latest Web browsers include

- Global e-mail.

- Search agents.

- FTP.

- Gopher.

- WAIS and other index and search engines.

- USENET newsgroups.

Web browsers' transition to managing locally attached hardware resources means that they must be more closely integrated with client operating systems than before. Whereas in the past Web browsers were merely just another application program executing over a particular operating system via APIs and operating system calls, they are now more like a single integrated piece of software with a particular client operating system embedded within the Web browser software. This is an interesting phenomenon to observe as Web browser software vendors such as Netscape and Wollongong attempt to embed operating systems within their Web browsers and traditional operating system vendors such as Microsoft, IBM, and Novell attempt to embed Web browsers within their operating systems. For example Windows 95 features an add-on known as the Internet Explorer Browser and OS/2 Warp includes the Web Explorer.

It should be noted that many high-quality browsers can be downloaded from the Internet and are available at little or no charge. In general, all Web browsers offer transparency to users from the following concerns and compatibility issues:

- Geography—Users do not need to know the Web address or physical location of the destination Web server.

- Storage file format—Users do not need to know the file format of the target Web page feature regardless of whether the Web page feature is text, sound, video, or image.

- Hardware characteristics and operating system of the destination Web server.

- Type of network or transport protocol involved with the destination Web server.

Figure 11-15 summarizes the key comparative criteria when evaluating Web browser software.

One thing to bear in mind about Web browsers and their ability to search the World Wide Web for a particular Web page or topic is that Web browsers still require a master Web index service or home page. The LYCOS home page at Carnegie-Mellon University is an example of such a master Web indexing service. Indexed Web pages that may be located throughout the Internet are accessible through LYCOS via hot-clickable links known as **URLs** or **uniform resource locators.**

URLs are also used within a given Web page to allow **hypertext** links to other related Web pages, documents, or services such as e-mail. The term hypertext merely refers to documents that have the ability to link to other documents. In Web pages, hypertext is usually highlighted in a different color and hot-clickable for instant access to the linked document.

Web Browser Characteristic	Explanation/Implication
Vertical integration	• Does the Web browser software supply access to all Internet-attached resources including global e-mail?
Ease of Setup and use	• How easy is the software to install and configure? • Is technical support available and helpful? • Can the Web browser handle dial-up connections using SLIP/PPP as well as LAN-attached connections using TCP/IP?
Performance	• Can multiple sessions be executed simultaneously? • Can the Web browser be easily customized with user bookmarks that remember paths to particular Internet resources? • Can graphics be partially displayed while they are still being downloaded? • Can the Web browser link easily to other programs such as word processing, spreadsheet, or presentation graphics programs? • Can downloaded material be easily transferred into other applications programs? • Can the Web browser support a variety of sound and video compression and storage formats? • Can URL's for new resources be added easily? • Can hot lists (local lists of bookmarks for favorite Web pages) be annotated with user notes? • Which versions of HTML does the browser support?
Horizontal integration	• Does the Web browser only organize access to Internet-attached resources or are locally and network-attached resources also accessible through the browser?

Figure 11-15   Web Browser Differentiating Criteria

Internet/Web Gateways

Internet E-Mail Gateways   LAN-based mail servers act as post offices delivering mail to intended LAN-attached recipients and forwarding nonlocal destination mail onto other distant mail servers (post offices) for eventual delivery to clients. Mail servers run a particular type of mail server software such as Microsoft Mail or cc:Mail. When clients on the LANs to which these mail servers are attached run the same type of e-mail client software, no translation between mail systems is necessary. However, when a Microsoft Mail client wants to send e-mail via the Internet to a cc:Mail client, translation is required. This translation is supplied by an **Internet e-mail gateway.** The Internet e-mail gateway acts as a translator, speaking a LAN-specific e-mail software protocol on one side and speaking the Internet's **SMTP (simple mail transport protocol)** on the other. Depending on the transport protocol used by the local area network, the Internet e-mail gateway may also have to translate between transport protocols since the Internet uses strictly TCP/IP.

Figure 11-16 illustrates the relationship between LAN-based e-mail servers, Internet e-mail gateways, and the Internet.

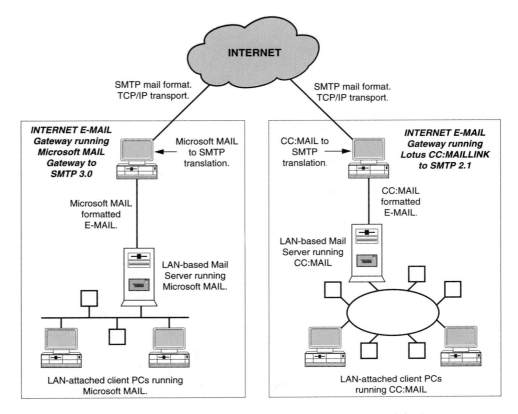

Figure 11-16   LAN-Based Mail Servers, Internet E-Mail Gateways, and the Internet

A key differentiating factor among Internet e-mail gateway products is their ability to support document attachment through support of protocols such as MIME. Some e-mail gateways also limit the number of attachments per e-mail message. Whether or not the Internet e-mail gateway software can be monitored by the local area network's system monitoring or performance monitoring is also important. Gateways are a likely location for system bottlenecks due to the amount of processing involved with translating between mail protocols, especially at high traffic levels.

The Internet e-mail gateway product itself is actually strictly software. It is installed like any other application over a particular operating system, most often DOS or OS/2. The required power of the hardware on which the gateway software must execute is a product of the amount of Internet e-mail that must be translated by the gateway. In some cases, the gateway software may be physically installed on the same server as the LAN-based e-mail server software. In other cases, increased Internet-bound e-mail traffic warrants a dedicated server.

Internet Gateways vs. Internet Servers   Whereas Internet e-mail gateways offer translation strictly between different LAN-based e-mail packages, **Internet gateways** offer a LAN-attached link for client PCs to access a multitude of Internet-attached resources including e-mail, FTP/Telnet, newsgroups, Gopher, and the World Wide Web. An Internet gateway is a software product that includes multiuser versions of the client front ends for each supported Internet-attached resource. The Internet gateway also translates between the local area network's transport protocol and TCP/IP. A common type of Internet gateway is an **IPX/IP gateway,** capable of translating between a NetWare LAN's IPX/SPX transport protocols and the TCP/IP transport protocols of the Internet. An Internet gateway is an *access*-oriented product.

An Internet gateway offers no Internet-attached services for users from distant corners of the Internet to avail themselves of. An Internet gateway is strictly an on-ramp to the Internet. LAN-attached client PCs accessing the Internet through the Internet gateway must seek the Internet services they desire from an **Internet server.** An Internet server runs a server application and offers e-mail services, Gopher services, newsgroup services, or World Wide Web services to all Internet-attached users.

As an alternative to an Internet gateway, LAN-attached client PCs can also set up individual links to Internet servers via a shared router. Each client PC must be loaded with TCP/IP software and Internet client software for whatever Internet services the user wishes to access. Figure 11-17 differentiates between the connectivity

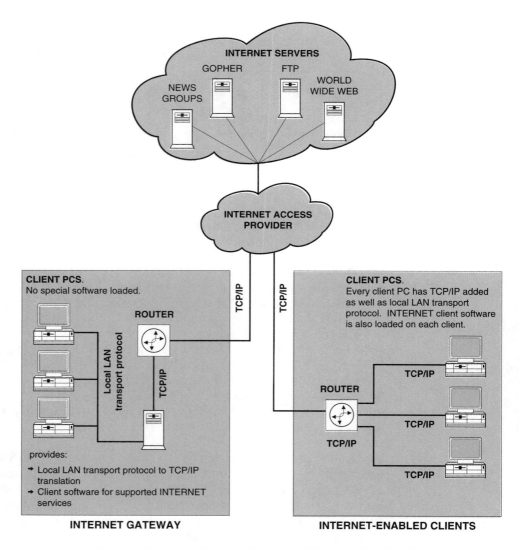

Figure 11-17   Internet Gateways, Internet Servers, and Internet-Enabled Clients

	Internet Gateway	Internet-Enabled Clients
Advantages	• Single location of TCP/IP and client front ends is easier to implement and manage than multiple client locations	• Eliminates gateway as potential bottleneck
Disadvantages	• Gateway can become a bottleneck with large number of users	• Every client requires its own TCP/IP software and Internet client front ends • Each client PC must be individually configured and managed • Client PCs also need to be able to use local LAN transport protocol as well

Figure 11-18   Internet Gateways vs. Internet-Enabled Clients

of Internet gateways, Internet servers, and Internet-enabled clients whereas Figure 11-18 highlights the advantages and disadvantages of Internet gateways vs. Internet-enabled clients.

Internet Transport Protocols   TCP/IP (transmission control protocol/Internet protocol) is the transport protocol used within the Internet that allows different types of computers and network access devices to exchange messages and deliver data and e-mail. The network access devices, most often routers, that connect to Internet services package their messages according to the Internet-standard TCP/IP protocols. The phone lines connecting the network access devices to the Internet are direct or leased lines that are constantly connected. In this way, it is as if the remote network access device is directly connected to the devices on the Internet and therefore can converse with the Internet-attached computers (nodes, hosts) using the native transport protocol, TCP/IP.

However, it is not cost-effective for individual client PCs to have expensive leased line connections to Internet access providers. Instead, these stand-alone PCs, which need only occasional access to the Internet, use dial-up circuits of one type or another. Transport protocols belonging to the TCP/IP family of protocols, more properly known as the Internet suite of protocols, that support communication over serial or dial-up lines are **SLIP (serial line Internet protocol)** and the more recently released and more functional **PPP (point-to-point protocol).**

To provide virtual private networking capabilities using the Internet as an enterprise network backbone, specialized **tunneling protocols** needed to be developed that could establish private, secure channels between connected systems. Two rival standards are examples of such tunneling protocols:

- Microsoft's **point-to-point tunneling protocol (PPTP).**

- Cisco's **layer two forwarding (L2F).**

An effort is underway to have the Internet Engineering Task Force (IETF) propose a unification of the two rival standards known as **layer 2 tunneling protocol (L2TP).** One shortcoming of the proposed specification is that it does not deal with

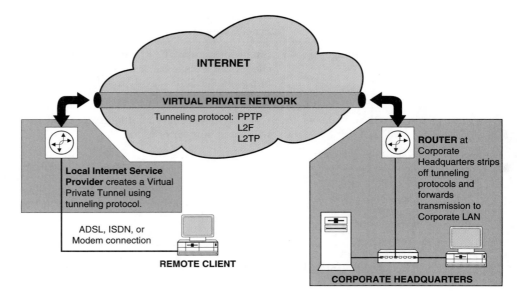

Figure 11-19   Tunneling Protocols Enable Virtual Private Networks

security issues such as authentication. Internet security issues will be discussed in Chapter 13. Figure 11-19 illustrates the use of tunneling protocols to build virtual private networks using the Internet as an enterprise network backbone.

Internet/Web Servers

An **Internet server** requires a combination of hardware and software to offer

- Web services.
- Global e-mail.
- FTP/Telnet services.
- USENET newsgroup services.

A **Webserver** combines hardware and software components to offer primarily Web services, but increasingly Web servers are also offering links to Gopher, FTP, and news services, making the terms *Web server* and *Internet server* more and more synonymous. Web servers may or may not also contain software to develop or program Web pages and Web applications.

Server Hardware/Software Analysis   Any Internet or Web server implementation requires four basic components:

1. A link to the Internet via an appropriately sized (sufficient bandwidth) access transmission line.

2. An IP address that uniquely identifies the intended server among all Internet-attached servers.

3. The server hardware that will connect to the Internet and fulfill client requests.

4. The server software that will run on the server hardware. In the case of a Web server, this server software is usually based on the HTTP (hypertext transfer protocol) server from NCSA (National Center for Supercomputing Applications).

The link to the Internet would be purchased from a local telecommunications company and would be terminated at a chosen Internet access provider (IAP). In some cases, the IAP will make the arrangements for the access line with the local telecommunications vendor. The IP address to uniquely identify an Internet or Web server could be provided by either the IAP or the InterNIC, which is the sole official authority in charge of issuing Internet IP addresses.

To understand the types of hardware and software required to successfully implement an Internet or Web server, one must first examine intended objectives of the server, focusing especially on the server's intended audience and what services will be offered to that audience. As stated above, the server may strictly offer access to Web pages or may also offer gateway services to file transfer and search resources such as FTP, Gopher, USENET, and WAIS.

For example, a company that wishes to offer only product information could suffice with a Web server, whereas a gateway to file transfer and search engines would be required for a company wishing to offer on-line technical support as well. Since proposals for implementing security protocols to ensure the confidentiality of financial transactions over the Internet are pending, companies should be wary of implementing widespread financial dealings via the Internet. Web security will be discussed shortly in the section on Internet/Web application development. Some companies may only wish to display product information on Web pages whereas others may want customer input for demographic or product development purposes. The ability to handle customer-input forms is a Web server software capability that cannot be assumed.

Server Software   Internet/Web server software differs in its ability to deliver any or all of the following capabilities:

- Web page display and management.

- Gateway to Internet file transfer and search engines such as FTP, Gopher, USENET, and WAIS.

- Level of security supported.

- Ability to develop and manage customer-input forms.

- Ability to monitor and report on Web page or Internet resource usage. This feature is important to be able to cost justify the investment in server hardware and software. Is the intended customer audience responding in the intended fashion?

- Ability to integrate management functions with the enterprise management system of the server's operating system?

Besides just displaying Web pages, Web servers may also possess the ability to execute interactive Web applications such as the previously mentioned customer-input forms. Some servers offer a standardized API known as **CGI,** or **common gateway interface,** which allows Web applications to be written and potentially executed on multiple different Web servers.

Some Web server software supports **proxy servers,** which act as holding bins or repositories for previously requested Web pages from distant Internet servers. If a request from a local client is received for a previously requested Web page that is still in the local proxy server, that Web page can be delivered quickly to the local client without the normal delay associated with downloading the Web page again in its entirety across the Internet.

Perhaps most significant among the differentiating characteristics of server software is the supporting operating system. Due to the high processing demands of a Web server, UNIX in its many variations has been the standard operating system, although Windows NT based Web server software is now available. For lower-end applications, Web server software is also available for Macintosh computers.

Server Hardware   Retrieving and transmitting the highly graphical Web pages with a good response time to multiple users simultaneously calls for high-performance server hardware. To know a recommended hardware configuration, a Web server manager (Web Master) must really know how many inquiries per day are anticipated on the Web server. In general, the following minimum recommendations are generally agreed upon for Web server hardware configuration:

- CPU: 120 MHz (or faster) Pentium is acceptable but higher speed RISC chips such as the DEC Alpha or Mips R4600 will be required for high-performance servers.

- Storage: Graphical images and digitized voice and video take up a lot of space so provision should be made for numerous drive bays or attachment to a RAID subsystem.

- Bus: PCI bus for fast internal transfer of images.

- Memory: 128 MB installed is not unusual for Web servers, with potential capacities up to 1024 MB desirable.

- Network interface cards: 100-Mbps Ethernet or multiple 10-Mbps Ethernet cards should be sufficient. Remember, Internet-attached users will be accessing this server via telecommunications lines of various bandwidths. These transmission lines are most often the least bandwidth of the entire system.

As demands for server performance increase to 250,000 or more inquiries per day, high-end UNIX workstations with over 128 MB of RAM and 1 GB of disk space are recommended.

Server Trends   The Web server software market is very young and changing rapidly. Although many of the original Web server software offerings were shareware or offered by third-party vendors, mainstream software vendors such as IBM, Microsoft, NetScape, and Novell are aggressively pursuing this market. The advantage of Web server software produced by the leaders in software development will be increased integration with that vendor's enterprise management system and application suites.

Internet Connectivity Services

A Top-Down Approach to Internet Connectivity Needs Analysis

Applied Problem Solving

Internet service providers vary widely in their levels of provided services and in the fees charged for these services. To ensure that purchased Internet services meet the business objectives of a given company, it is essential that a top-down approach to Internet connectivity needs analysis be executed. By starting with business objectives and detailing, in writing, all of the performance requirements associated with each layer of the top-down model, the network analyst will possess detailed documentation that can serve as the basis for negotiations with Internet service providers. In this manner, there is no doubt as to what is expected of the Internet service provider and that provided Internet services will meet stated business objectives. Figure 11-20 divides the numerous issues surrounding Internet connectivity needs analysis into their respective top-down model layers.

Top-Down Model Layer	Internet Connectivity Needs Analysis Issues

Business	• What are the business objectives for Internet connectivity?
	  • Increased market exposure
	  • Improved customer service
	  • Response to competitive pressures
	  • Increase market share
	  • New market entry
	  • Improved market research capabilities
	  • Improved intra- and intercompany communications
	• What are the budgetary limitations of this connectivity, if any?
	• Does senior management have a preference for outsourcing vs. in-house development, support, and management?
	• What are the availability requirements? (24 hr/day?)
	• What are the reliability requirements? (length of acceptable downtime?)
	• What are the security requirements regarding this Internet connection?
	• What are the acceptable uses of the Internet by employees?

Application	• What applications are required to support identified business objectives?
	  • Global e-mail
	  • World Wide Web
	  • Information/news services
	  • FTP/Telnet
	  • Gopher
	• Will the company be offering Internet services (Web pages) for Internet users or strictly accessing Internet services?
	• How many users will be offered access to which services?
	• What is an acceptable response time for the various required Internet services? Remember—there are literally millions of

Figure 11-20   Internet Connectivity Needs Analysis

Top-Down Model Layer	Internet Connectivity Needs Analysis Issues
Data	• Depending on the application required, how much data (in kilobytes) is likely to be required? • Graphical applications (WWW) have much higher bandwidth demands than text-based services.

Network	• Complete a logical network design outlining the required functionality of the network that will successfully support the data, application, and business layer requirements of the top-down model.
	• Depending on the amount of data required to be transferred and the acceptable response time, what is the minimum size (Kbps or Mbps) of the access line to the Internet services provider required?
	• What is the anticipated growth of bandwidth demand for Internet connectivity access?
	• What will be the Internet connectivity network configuration?
	    • Internet (TCP/IP)-enabled clients
	    • Internet gateway
	    • Dial-up links into Internet service provider's Internet server
	• Reliability issues:
	    • What kind of redundant circuits are required?
	    • What kind of redundant or hot-swappable networking hardware is required?

Technology	• Produce a physical network design that will support the logical network design completed in the network layer of the top-down model.
	• Depending on the choice of Internet connectivity services provider, any or all of these technology issues may or may not be handled by that provider.
	    • Installation, management, troubleshooting of access line
	    • Size of access line between Internet provider and the Internet
	    • Choice of Internet front-ends, Web browsers
	    • Choice of Web page development software
	    • Choice of Web/Internet server software
	    • Use of proxy servers and/or local domain name servers
	    • Choice of network access devices, routers
	    • Development of firewalls and other security capabilities
	• Who is responsible for ensuring integration and compatibility of all of the hardware and software technology?
	• Who is responsible for ensuring a reasonable migration and upgradability path for acquired technology?
	• What types of data transmission services are available from local telecommunications providers at each corporate site? (ISDN?, T-1?, T-3?, ATM?)
	• What are the local telecommunications provider's plans for deploying high-speed data services?

Figure 11-20   (Continued)

As is always true of top-down analysis, if business objectives of Internet connectivity are clearly stated and verified by senior management and each successive layer of the top-down model successfully meets the requirements of the preceding layer, then the physical network design produced on the technology layer will produce an Internet connectivity network capable of meeting initial business objectives.

Differences between Internet Connectivity Service Providers Once the Internet connectivity needs analysis has been completed and documented using the top-down model, the next step is to find the Internet connectivity service provider that best matches the business objectives and technological needs of the company. Although the range of services offered by potential Internet service providers is constantly changing, there are basically three categories of vendors involved in this market:

- Internet presence providers.
- Internet access providers.
- Telecommunications companies.

Internet presence providers are full-service organizations offering everything from Web page setup to 24 hr/day monitoring of Internet links.

Practical Advice and Information

Numerous local and regional Internet access providers have emerged since the recent explosion of interest in the Internet in general and the World Wide Web in particular. It is important to evaluate the financial stability of Internet service providers. Many such newly formed operations may not be sufficiently capitalized to be able to afford necessary upgrades to maintain satisfactory service levels. Especially important is the bandwidth of the access line between the Internet access provider and the Internet itself. That access line is shared by all subscribers of a particular Internet access provider. If the access line between the Internet access provider and the Internet becomes a bottleneck, then the size of a company's access line to the Internet access provider is irrelevant. Such companies may lack sufficient technical expertise to diagnose or troubleshoot compatibility or technology integration issues. It is important to have written agreements as to the division of user and Internet service provider responsibilities in terms of technology integration.

If the development, installation, and management of Internet access and services is to be handled by an in-house operation, then arranging the installation of a data line for Internet access with the local telecommunications vendor may be the only interaction with outside vendors required. Outside of large metropolitan areas, the availability of data transmission services from local telecommunications vendors can vary widely. Increased deregulation of the local access market may have a dramatic effect on the availability of local data transmission services. Some local and regional telecommunications companies have developed Internet presence provider and Internet access provider services in addition to their basic data transmission services. Ameritech and PacTel are two of the more aggressive RBOCs (regional bell operating companies) in the Internet presence provider market.

Figure 11-21 lists the typical types of activities required to complete a connection to the Internet and which of those activities are typically provided by Internet presence providers, Internet access providers, and local telecommunications ven-

Internet Connectivity Activity	Internet Presence Provider	Internet Access Provider	Local Telecommunications Provider
Provide local access line for Internet connectivity	•	•	•
Monitor and manage local access	•	•	
Provide terminating equipment for local access	•	•	•
Security services offered	•		
Design and develop Web page	•		
Manage and monitor Web/Internet activity	•		
Guarantee sufficient bandwidth/growth path	•		
Provide Web server hardware	•		
Provide Web server software	•		
Provide client front-end software	•		
Provide Internet (IP) address	•	•	
Resolve incompatibility issues	•		
Manage global e-mail addressing issues	•		

Figure 11-21   Internet Connectivity Activities and Providers

dors. The term *local telecommunications vendors* in this case refers to those companies or divisions that offer only basic data transmission services, without any Internet-related value-added services.

Beyond Internet Connectivity   Connectivity to the Internet does not necessarily meet all the wide area communications needs of a global enterprise. Another category of services commonly known as **business communications services** goes beyond Internet connectivity to include additional services such as

- Videoconferencing.
- Simultaneous document sharing.
- Electronic data interchange (EDI).
- Global fax service.
- Electronic document distribution.
- Paging.
- E-mail.
- News and information services.

These additional services enable globally dispersed enterprises to function as if all network-attached users were physically located in the same building. In other words, anything that co-workers in the same building can accomplish ought to be able to be accomplished via the business communications services network. The deliverance of this capability is sometimes referred to as a **virtual corporation.** Some of these business communications services include access to global e-mail via the Internet. It is likely that these business communications services will be integrated with Internet presence provider services offered by the same vendor at some time in the future.

SUMMARY

As competitive pressures have caused businesses to accomplish more with fewer employees, distributed information systems and the underlying enterprise networks that link businesses with their trading partners, as well as with telecommuting and remote employees, have taken on mission-critical roles. The analysis, design, and implementation of enterprise networks must deal not only with the wide area geographic scope of such networks but also with the multiplatform, multiprotocol, multivendor reality of the distributed information systems that must be delivered by these enterprise networks.

The most significant trend in the logical design of enterprise networks is the virtual LAN. By adding configuration capabilities to existing LAN switches, virtual LANs are able to offer switched bandwidth on demand while confining broadcasts and multicasts to designated workstations.

Nearly all enterprise network physical designs include ATM as the basic underlying switching fabric of the enterprise network. Designs differ primarily in how routing capabilities are added to ATM's switching capabilities. Virtual private networks utilize the Internet as the enterprise network backbone rather than implementing and maintaining a private network. Specialized tunneling protocols are required to build private tunnels through the public Internet.

The Internet is a wide area network linking over 4,000,000 host computers. Originally developed as a means for the research, education, and scientific communities to share information, the Internet has been opened up in recent years to more commercial uses as well as to access by individuals. Before investing in the required technology to link to the Internet, a business should first have a thorough understanding of the types of services available on the Internet and what business objectives are to be achieved by such a link.

The World Wide Web is a fully graphical Internet service that has generated a great deal of interest recently. Other Internet services include global e-mail, FTP servers, Gopher servers, and USENET groups. Depending on how much support is required, a company may choose to enlist the services of either an Internet presence provider or an Internet access provider. These Internet connectivity services differ dramatically in the level of services offered and, in some cases, level of technical expertise and financial stability.

With the Internet itself acting like a global LAN, an Internet-based client/server architecture would require specialized client hardware and software and server hardware and software. The particular software required depends on which Internet service a company wishes to access or offer. Clients are Internet services consumers and servers are Internet services providers.

To develop a presence on the Internet, a company needs four basic elements: an access transmission line of sufficient bandwidth, an IP Internet address, server hardware, and appropriate server software designed for particular Internet service.

KEY TERMS

asynchronous transfer mode, 446
ATM, 446
ATM address resolution, 447
ATM address resolution protocol,
  449
ATMARP, 449
ATM LAN emulation, 446
bandwidth hierarchy, 442
broadcast and unknown services, 447
BUS,447
CGI, 468
Classical IP over ATM, 449
collapsed backbone, 444
common gateway interface, 468
configuration services, 447
cut-through routing, 449
cybermalls, 459
data distribution, 437
distributed backbone, 444
distributed computing, 437
distributed information systems, 437
E-zines, 454
edge devices, 449
EDI, 459
EFT, 459
electronic commerce, 459
electronic data interchange, 459
electronic funds transfer, 459
electronic market, 459
enterprise network, 435
FAQ group, 454
flow management protocol, 451
FMP, 451
FTP, 453
FTP servers, 453
global e-mail, 453
Gopher, 453
Gopher server, 453
HTML, 459
HTTP, 459

hypertext, 461
hypertext markup language, 459
hypertext transport protocol, 459
IAP, 455
IASG, 449
IEEE 802.10, 440
information consumers, 454
information providers, 454
integrated private network-to-
  network interface, 450
Internet, 451
Internet access providers, 455
Internet address summarization
  group, 449
Internet e-mail gateway, 462
internet gateways, 463
Internet presence providers, 456
Internet servers, 464
IP switching, 450
IPNNI, 450
IPP, 456
IPX/IP gateways,464
L2F, 465
L2TP, 465
LAN emulation, 447
LAN emulation client, 447
LAN emulation server, 447
LAN emulation services, 448
layer 2 virtual LANs, 441
layer 3 virtual LANs, 441
layer two forwarding, 465
layer 2 tunneling protocol, 465
LEC, 447
LES, 447
LIS, 449
logical IP subnets, 449
middleware, 437
Mosaic, 457
MPOA, 449
Multiprotocol Encapsulation over

ATM Adaptation Layer 5, 450
Multiprotocol over ATM, 449
Netscape, 457
network access device, 456
network news transport protocol,
  453
NNTP, 453
point-to-point protocol, 465
point-to-point tunneling protocol,
  465
PPP, 465
PPTP, 465
proxy servers, 468
route server, 449
routing switches, 441
serial line interface protocol, 465
simple mail transport protocol, 462
SLIP, 465
SMTP, 462
tag switching, 451
Telnet, 453
traffic duplication, 439
tunneling protocols, 465
unicast, 447
uniform resource locator,459
URL,459
USENET servers, 453
virtual corporation, 435
virtual LANs, 437
virtual private network, 437
virtual workgroups, 436
VPN, 437
WAIS, 453
WAIS servers, 453
wide area information services, 453
Web browsers,452
Web server, 466
Web site, 452
World Wide Web, 452
WWW, 452

REVIEW QUESTIONS

1. Describe some of the business motivations for the development of enterprise networks.
2. Describe the relationship between virtual corporations, virtual workgroups, and virtual LANs.
3. What is middleware and what is its relationship to distributed applications and the enterprise network?

4. How does the functionality of a virtual LAN differ from that offered by a simple LAN switch?
5. What are the advantages of a virtual LAN over a shared-media LAN?
6. What are some of the key limitations of virtual LANs?
7. What are some of the ways in which the limitations of virtual LANs can be overcome?

8. Why is transmission between layer 2 switches important and what is the current status of protocol standardization for such communications?

9. What is IEEE 802.10?

10. Why must routing be used to transmit between virtual LANs?

11. What are some of the alternative ways in which routing can be used to transmit between virtual LANs?

12. What are the key functional differences between layer 2 and layer 3 virtual LANs?

13. What is the importance of developing a bandwidth hierarchy to enterprise network design?

14. Differentiate between distributed and collapsed backbones.

15. What are some of the advantages of ATM?

16. What is ATM LAN emulation and what are its advantages and limitations?

17. How is ATM LAN emulation actually implemented?

18. How are ATM addresses mapped to LAN addresses?

19. What is the purpose of the configuration service?

20. What is the purpose of the broadcast and unknown service?

21. Compare the alternatives being developed for routing over ATM in terms of advantages, disadvantages, and limitations.

22. What is the difference between routing and cut-through routing?

23. What is IP switching and what advantage does it have over other combined switching and routing alternatives?

24. What are some of the protocols unique to IP switching?

25. What are some of the reasons why a business might be interested in connecting to the Internet?

26. What are some bad reasons for a company to connect to the Internet?

27. Distinguish between the available Internet services in terms of information available, ease of access, and most probable uses/users.

28. What is the World Wide Web?

29. How does the World Wide Web differ from other Internet services in terms of information offered and hardware/software requirements?

30. Distinguish between the major types of information servers available on the Internet.

31. What are some of the trends that have combined to produce this increased interest in corporate access to the Internet?

32. What are some of the potential pitfalls of corporate access to the Internet?

33. Differentiate between IAP and IPP.

34. When are transport protocols such as SLIP or PPP used?

35. What is the difference between HTTP and HTML?

36. What is a Web browser?

37. Name two popular Web browsers.

38. Differentiate between Web client, Web browser, Web page, and Web server.

39. Describe and differentiate between hypertext links and URLs.

40. Differentiate between Internet gateways and Internet e-mail gateways.

41. What are the advantages and disadvantages of an Internet gateway?

42. Differentiate between accessing Internet services via an Internet gateway as opposed to Internet-enabled clients.

43. Differentiate between an Internet server and a Web server.

44. What is the potential value of CGI?

45. What is the impact of proxy servers on network performance?

ACTIVITIES

1. Research and report on the results of the relationship between business trends and enterprise network design. Cite specific examples of how enterprise networks have taken on increasingly mission-critical roles.

2. Research virtual corporations and describe the technology required to enable such corporations.

3. Using buyers' guides and product specifications, prepare a comparative analysis of the middleware market. What are the product categories and market leaders within each category? What are the important functional trends in middleware?

4. Prepare a survey of businesses or organizations in your area. How many are employing LAN switches? Of this number, what percentage are employing virtual LANs? What was their reason for implementing virtual LANs? What kinds of benefits have the virtual LANs offered? Were there any complications either anticipated or unanticipated?

5. Research and report on the results of your investigation into the development of the IEEE 802.10 standard or other standards development efforts for layer 2 switch communication.

6. Research the IP switching market. Who are the key vendors? What is the status of protocol standardization? Which vendors are actually shipping the most product? What are the initial reactions from implemented systems? Is this market set to explode or a passing fad?

7. Prepare a position paper or organize a debate on any or all of the following questions: What should a company's policy be regarding employee use of corporate Internet accounts after business hours? Should employees have to distinguish, disclaim, or otherwise identify personal opinions and messages posted to the Internet from corporate accounts?

Should an official company spokesperson be designated to represent a company's on-line position and image? Should employees be able to upload or download software of their choice to/from the Internet via corporate Internet accounts? Should "cyberporn" sites be declared off-limits or restricted from corporate Internet accounts regardless of time of day? Should the federal government regulate the use of the Internet?

8. Gather statistics and prepare a graph, chart, or presentation regarding the growth of the Internet in general and the WWW in particular.

CASE STUDY

Long Road to Online Commerce

Before Burlington Coat Factory Warehouse Corp. could sell even a single overcoat on its World Wide Web site, it faced a much tougher transaction—selling its own buyers on the Web concept.

Burlington's IS department spent months trying to pique the merchants' interest by touting the benefits of selling items such as coats and baby furniture on the Web. Their support was key to transforming Burlington's bare-bones Web site into a virtual storefront. But compared with the buyers' long tradition of big revenue generated off racks and shelves, it was no surprise that they weren't nearly as enthused about the Web, which at best represented only about 1 percent of their sales prospects.

It took Burlington chairman Monroe Milstein's stamp of approval to get the buyers aboard. Earlier this year, Milstein began pushing the IS department to beef up the company's Web site as a way to capture some of the home-shopping market and expand globally.

For Burlington, like other businesses exploring Web commerce, bridging the knowledge and culture gap within the company can be more difficult than ringing up an online sale. And it can slow plans to hang out an electronic shingle. "I would like to have had more merchant backing for the Web sooner," says Percy Young, the company's Web-master and manager of store systems. "We could have gotten it out the door and produced revenue faster."

The Accidental Merchant

The Burlington Web launch probably wouldn't serve as a model strategy because it happened, well, by accident. "This is more of a study in what not to do," admits Burlington's chief information of-ficer, Michael Prince, whose IS department is spearheading the Web effort.

The company began experimenting with a prototype Web server in the spring of 1994, after Young conceived of the idea during an industry conference. By June of that year, Burlington's external Web site was up and running on a Sun Microsystems Inc. SPARCstation server with Web-server software from the NCSA (National Center for Supercomputing Applications). By default, this experimental server eventually became an intranet server (see "It's Browsers for Burlington,"

opposite page). IS was encouraged to tinker with the intranet server and Web site, but preferably not on company time.

For the IS team, of which many members consider themselves "children of the Internet" given Burlington's long history with Internet E-mail and TCP/IP, electronic commerce on the Web was the logical next step. "It was natural for us to use the Web as a catalog medium," says Prince. "You didn't have to be a futurist to see [the Web] was taking off."

The turning point in Burlington's Web push came when Milstein got behind it. Although not a technologist by trade, Milstein has an impressive track record in this area: He was the driving force behind Burlington abandoning mainframes for a client/server setup in the late 1980s when many companies were only talking about making the move. Now, thanks to the Web, he is facing off with the likes of L.L. Bean Inc. and Spiegel Inc., in addition to Burlington's regular competitors such as J.C. Penney Company Inc.

www.coat.com

With Milstein now behind the project, the real work has just begun. IS must evolve the experimental Web site from a static information booth to an interactive sales entity (see "Evolution of a Web Site," this page). So when Web users visit http://www.coat.com, not only do they find the Burlington Coat Factory store nearest them, but they can also purchase a coat, jacket, shoes, and more.

The idea is to make the Web site a way to draw customers into stores, as well as generate online sales of merchandise that could easily be purchased through a catalog. The Burlington Web site would particularly benefit stores that don't have enough space to carry certain items, such as baby furniture, says Young.

Prince hopes to also use the Web for personalized advertising. Regular shoppers, for instance, would be greeted at the Burlington Web-site door with ads catering to their buying patterns.

Basic Web technology, such as Web-conversion tools, is the easy part of the whole endeavor: It simplifies setting up and implementing a Web site, according to the Burlington IS team. Startup costs, too, are typically low.

When Burlington first began dabbling with Web technology two years ago, the company downloaded NCSA's Web-server software for free. The company also used its existing Cisco Systems Inc. firewall router software and SPARCstation server. "We didn't have to buy a thing," says Young.

At press time Burlington was deciding among several off-the-shelf Web-server packages. They are all better equipped for electronic commerce than the NCSA software because they offer security features and room to grow.

Online-Commerce Hurdles

The real challenge for Burlington is the corporate re-engineering necessary to support Web commerce. The company is not equipped to fill orders from the Web. Its operations rely largely on its warehouse and main distribution center, both in

Burlington, N.J., for its roughly 250 stores nationwide. The two buildings are not set up for ordering specific merchandise, according to Prince.

No one knows for sure just how Burlington will stock, ship, and track merchandise for the shop-at-home crowd. The two possibilities are for Burlington to either set up a makeshift catalog outlet at what it calls Store One, its flagship first store, or hire a third-party distributor to oversee it all, says Ginger Atwater, a special-project analyst in Burlington's IS department.

The company will initially employ a toll-free number to handle all financial transactions; this is a method many businesses are using today for the delicate process of taking credit-card numbers. Burlington eventually plans to deploy a financial-transaction model where credit-card data is handled directly by a bank, not by Burlington.

Perhaps the biggest gap in Burlington's Web site is the lack of an order-fulfillment system—the link from the customer's electronic order on the Web to Burlington's inventory and billing operations. Most likely, the system Burlington selects will work with its Novell Inc. Tuxedo transaction-processing software to log and update sales.

Then there are the operational issues associated with filling orders. "You'd need to train workers, set aside space, and man the handling and packing of the merchandise—a real change in our business," says Prince.

Other concerns include questions of who will manage Store One's catalog-warehouse function or whether Store One, if it runs out of an item, should get the item from another store or have the other store ship it directly to the customer. Most likely, Burlington will ship products from the store nearest the customer, says Prince, but that begs another question: How do you ring up that sale?

Burlington must also decide how it will update or make changes to its online catalog of merchandise.

"If we have several thousand items on the Web, we need to dynamically maintain them from our Oracle [Corp.] database," says Atwater. So if Burlington were to mark down the price of a baby crib, for instance, this change must immediately be reflected on the Web. Some fashion items, such as dresses, sell and change very rapidly, so these will be particularly challenging to keep up-to-date.

The Web also puts a new spin on some of Burlington's sales policies. Its return policy, for instance, requires that shoppers receive a store credit, not cash. "This might not necessarily work for Web buyers," notes Prince.

So how is Burlington dealing with such major changes? A small group within the IS department is handling the effort—without the luxury of any new staff. With the pressure on from the executive suite, the IS team is scrambling to get Burlington's existing Web site ready for electronic commerce.

This entails gathering all the merchandise data, scanning hundreds of photos, and creating numerous Web pages. Most of the IS staffers involved in the project work on the Web site on the side. "Many are still major players in other projects," says Atwater.

The only formal body that actually convenes on the Web projects is the MIS Steering Committee, which is made up of top managers in the buying, distribution, financial, and other areas. But the Web is just one of many topics they discuss.

It's still unclear just what the potential sales will be for Burlington. Few if any businesses bother to estimate their return on investment in Web technology, mostly because it just doesn't cost that much to invest in. "No one expects us to put a big dent in sales" initially, says Prince.

The closest thing to gauging sales prospects was a promotional campaign that Burlington held on its Web site last year. It offered 2,000 coupons for $5 off any purchase of $50 or more in its stores. Young estimates that the company generated some $100,000 in sales from the promotion, and more important, buyers were required to travel to a store.

Burlington executives don't expect virtual shopping to replace the social interaction associated with in-store shopping. Nor do they expect the company to realize any major revenue from the site, at least not in the near term.

"We should be using the Web to promote the stores more aggressively," says Prince. "This way, we are using the Web as a personalized vehicle to advertise products, in addition to offering products at the push of a button."

Source: Kelly Jackson Higgins, "Long Road to Online Commerce," *LAN Times,* vol. 13, no. 13 (June 17, 1996), p. 18. Copyright © June 17, 1996 by McGraw–Hill, New York. Reprinted by permission of McGraw–Hill, New York.

BUSINESS CASE STUDY QUESTIONS

Activities

1. Complete a top-down model for this case by gleaning facts from the case and placing them in the proper layer of the top-down model. After completing the top-down model, analyze and detail those instances where requirements were clearly passed down from upper layers to lower layers of the model and where solutions to those requirements were passed up from lower layers to upper layers of the model.
2. Detail any questions about the case that may occur to you for which answers are not clearly stated in the article.

Business

1. In what type of business was the organization described in the case engaged?
2. What were the business layer objectives that the company hoped to meet with the deployment of the electronic commerce application?
3. How did the Burlington Coat Factory see on-line sales affecting in-store sales?
4. How many stores are currently supported by how many distribution centers?
5. Did the current order fulfillment business process lend itself to fulfilling Web-based on-line ordering? Why or why not?
6. What are some store-based sales policies that may not work as well in an electronic commerce mode?
7. What level of manpower was committed to the electronic commerce project?
8. What level of senior management support was committed to the electronic commerce project?
9. What are the expectations of objectives of the electronic commerce project?
10. Do you think the electronic commerce project will meet its stated objectives? Defend your answer.

Application

1. What strategic application was the business trying to deploy?
2. Whose support was critical to a successful deployment of this application?
3. What is the biggest application gap between the on-line ordering system and the current inventory and billing system?
4. What is Tuxedo and what role might it play in deploying on-line commerce at the Burlington Coat Factory?

Data

1. What is the intended evolution of the Burlington Coat Factory's Web site?
2. How will sensitive credit card data be handled both immediately and eventually?

Network

1. What was the configuration (hardware and software) of the Burlington Coat Factory's original Web site?
2. What benefits were offered by the company's intranet?
3. What technology was employed by the company's intranet?
4. How did the company's intranet differ from its electronic commerce Web site?

Technology

1. What were the impending technological requirements as the Web site moved from supplying static information to serving as an electronic commerce outlet?

NETWORK ADMINISTRATION

INTRODUCTION

Having gained an overall understanding in Parts 1, 2, and 3 of how network components can be integrated to produce an effective enterprise network, we study in Part 4 how such networks can be effectively designed, secured, and managed.

In Chapter 12, "The Network Development Life Cycle," all of the concepts and technology mastered in previous chapters will serve as background knowledge for the actual network development process outlined in this chapter. Simply stated, this chapter should tie together much of the material covered to this point in the text which talked *about* data communications by explaining how to *do* data communications.

In Chapter 13, "Network Security," the various processes, concepts, protocols, standards, and technology associated with network security are reviewed. Maintaining a realistic approach, the importance of people and their basic honesty and integrity as the underlying foundation for any successful network security implementation are stressed.

Finally, Chapter 14, "Network Management," stresses that the successful implementation of a network management strategy requires a combination of policy, process, people, and technology. Merely throwing network management technology in a vacuum at a network management opportunity will not produce the desired results. This final chapter introduces the reader to the business issues as well as the technology and underlying concepts concerning the effective management of enterprise networks.

CHAPTER 12

THE NETWORK DEVELOPMENT LIFE CYCLE

Concepts Reinforced

Top-Down Model   Cost/Benefit Analysis
Business Process Re-engineering

Concepts Introduced

Network Development Life Cycle   Network Analysis and Design
Comprehensive Systems and   Methodology
   Networking Budget Model
Integrated Computer-Assisted
   Network Engineering

OBJECTIVES

After mastering the material in this chapter, you should

1. Understand how the network development life cycle relates to other systems development architectures and life cycles and consequently how the network analyst/designer must interact with analyst/designers involved in these related processes.

2. Understand the network development life cycle including overall issues, process structure, detailed activities for each step of the process, and coping with the reality of today's multiprotocol, multivendor environments.

3. Understand how one remains focused with a business perspective throughout the network development life cycle.

4. Understand what automated tools are available to assist in the network development life cycle process as well as the cost justification necessary for the acquisition of such tools.

5. Understand the current shortcomings of these automated tools as well as possible proposals for solutions to these shortcomings.

6. Understand the role of vendors at various stages of the network development life cycle and how to maximize the effectiveness of these vendors.

■ INTRODUCTION

This chapter is perhaps the most important chapter in this entire book. Although a process-orientation and top-down approach have been taken throughout the entire text as data communications concepts and technology have been introduced, the focus of this chapter is solely on the data communications process known as the network development life cycle. All of the concepts and technology mastered in previous chapters will serve as available resources for the actual network development process outlined in this chapter. Simply stated, this chapter should tie together much of the material covered to this point in the text which talked *about* data communications by explaining how to *do* data communications.

This chapter will not include instruction in network traffic engineering. Whereas this is an introductory text, an appropriate level of complexity will be presented for the more technical aspects of network design. Re-emphasizing the practical aspect of this chapter, techniques for effective interaction with consultants and vendors who possess the technical expertise to perform network traffic engineering are stressed.

■ WHERE DOES NETWORK DESIGN FIT IN OVERALL INFORMATION SYSTEMS DEVELOPMENT?

To be able to fully understand the importance of a properly designed network to a smoothly operating information system, one must first understand how the network design process relates to other information system development processes. The top-down model, which has been a constant strategic framework throughout the text, serves as an appropriate means for portraying the relationship between the network development process and other information systems related development processes. This relationship is illustrated in Figure 12-1.

Top Down Model	Information Systems Development Process
Business	• Strategic business planning • Business process re-engineering
Application	• Systems development life cycle • Systems analysis and design • Application development life cycle
Data	• Database analysis and design • Database distribution analysis
Network	• Network development life cycle • Network analysis and design • Logical network design
Technology	• Physical network design • Network implementation • Technology analysis

Figure 12-1   The Top-Down Model and the Network Development Life Cycle

As can be seen in Figure 12-1, the network development life cycle depends upon previously completed development processes such as strategic business planning, application development life cycle, and data distribution analysis. If an implemented network is to effectively deliver the information systems that will, in turn, fulfill strategic business goals, then a top-down approach must be taken to the overall information systems development process as well as to the network development life cycle.

Although the previous statement may seem to be obvious or self-evident, it is by no means a given in the information systems development community. Network analysts who begin their analysis by asking about strategic business plans are likely to be asked, "What does that have to do with networking?"

■ UNDERSTANDING SYSTEMS DEVELOPMENT: PROCESS AND PRODUCT

Two key components to any systems development effort are the **process** and the **product** of each stage of that development life cycle. Simply stated, the process describes activities that should be taking place at any point during the development cycle, and the product is the outcome or deliverable from a particular stage of the overall cycle.

A focus on the process allows one to visualize what he or she will be or should be doing at any point in the development life cycle. The product, meanwhile, could be interpreted as a milestone or deliverable indicating completion of one stage of the development cycle and a readiness to proceed with subsequent stages.

A focus on product and process will facilitate the understanding of any systems development life cycle, not only the network development life cycle. Identification of process and product can be beneficial on high-level or summarized development cycle as well as more detailed methodologies. Figure 12-2 takes the high-level processes identified in Figure 12-1 and lists possible products, or outcomes, from each of the corresponding processes.

Information Systems Development Process	Product or Milestone
Strategic business planning Business process re-engineering	• Strategic business plan • Long range business goals • Business process models, methods, or rules
Systems development life cycle Systems analysis and design Application development life cycle	• Information systems design • Applications program design
Database analysis and design Database distribution analysis	• Database design • Database distribution design
Network development life cycle Network analysis and design Logical network design	• Network requirements document • Network design proposal
Physical network design Network implementation Technology analysis	• Detailed network diagram • Network product specifications • Network circuit diagrams

Figure 12-2 Understanding Systems Development: Process and Product

Figure 12-2 clearly points out the need for significant analysis and design, and associated products or deliverables, prior to the commencement of any network analysis and design activities. As has been stated many times previously in this text, network analysis and design cannot be successfully performed in a vacuum. Rather, network analysis and design is but one step in an overall comprehensive information systems development cycle, commencing with business layer analysis and concluding with an analysis of the technology currently available to implement the system as designed.

■ THE NETWORK DEVELOPMENT LIFE CYCLE

The key model behind the network design process is known as the **network development life cycle (NDLC)** as illustrated in Figure 12-3.

The word *cycle* is a key descriptive term of the network development life cycle as it clearly illustrates the continuous nature of network development. A network designed "from scratch" clearly has to start somewhere, namely with an analysis phase.

Existing networks, however, are constantly progressing from one phase to another within the network development life cycle. For instance, the monitoring of existing networks would produce management and performance statistics perhaps using a network management protocol such as SNMP. These performance statistics of this existing network would then be analyzed by qualified network analysts. Design changes may or may not be implemented based on the analysis of these performance statistics. Many times, proposed network design changes are first simulated using sophisticated network simulation software packages or prototyped in a test environment, safely removed from a company's production network, before being deployed or implemented.

This cycle of monitoring, management, analysis, design, simulation, and implementation is of an ongoing nature. Just as demands on a network are in a constant state of change due to changes in business, application, or data requirements, so must the network design itself be of a dynamic nature to successfully support these changing requirements. The network development life cycle serves as a logical framework in which this dynamic network design is able to thrive.

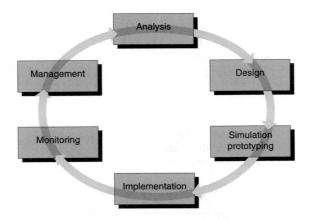

Figure 12-3   Network Development Life Cycle

■ NETWORK ANALYSIS AND DESIGN METHODOLOGY

Although the network development life cycle is useful as a logical model of the overall processes involved in network development, it is not at all specific as to how the various stages within the life cycle are to be accomplished. What is required is a more detailed step-by-step methodology that complements the overall logical framework as outlined by the network development life cycle.

The **network analysis and design methodology** is a practical, step-by-step approach to network analysis and design and is illustrated in a summarized fashion in Figure 12-4.

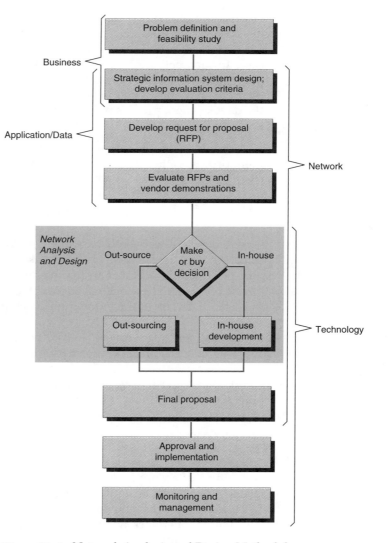

Figure 12-4   Network Analysis and Design Methodology

Overall Characteristics

Before the major categories of the methodology as illustrated in Figure 12-4 are described in detail, a few important characteristics of the overall methodology are worth noting.

- First, the network analysis and design methodology is consistent with previous information systems development models in that business, application, and data requirements definition is required prior to network design activities.

- Second, this methodology treats both in-house personnel and outside consultants as potential service providers by clearly documenting requirements in a formalized RFP (request for proposal) and expecting compliance with those requirements by whomever may be eventually chosen to perform network development duties.

- Finally, although any diagram of a systems development methodology would indicate that activities are of a serial nature, occurring one after another, with discrete starting and ending points, such is very often not the case. In fact, activities from various stages of the methodology often take place simultaneously. In addition, network analysts often must backtrack to previous activities when new or contradictory information is uncovered as the development process progresses.

- Thus, the network analysis and design methodology as illustrated in Figure 12-4 should be looked upon as an overall guideline to the network development process rather than a step-by-step cookbook-style set of instructions.

Critical Success Factors of the Network Development Life Cycle

Also associated with the overall network development process, rather than with any specific step of the process, are several key behaviors or things to remember that can be of critical importance to the overall successful outcome of the network development life cycle. These **critical success factors** are summarized in Figure 12-5 and each is elaborated on in the following paragraphs.

Identification of All Potential Customers The people who must use the system most frequently are the best source of information for system performance requirements. However, all user groups and levels of management must be consulted during the analysis and design phase to assure that no individuals or groups feel left out of the development process. Although one would like to think it isn't true, the best designed systems can be doomed to failure due to the effective internal sabotage of disenchanted users.

Political Awareness At the very least, it is imperative to be aware of the so-called corporate culture of an organization. Corporate culture is sometimes described in terms related to network design. For instance, corporate cultures can be described as "hierarchical" or as "distributed" or "open." If the corporate culture of the organization in which a network analyst is working is hierarchical, then it would be a mistake to make an appointment to interview an end-user without first interviewing and seeking approval of the required levels of management. On the other hand,

Critical Success Factor	Explanation
Identification of all potential customers and constituencies	No one likes to feel left out or that his or her input does not matter. It is better to include too many as representative user groups than to inadvertently exclude anyone.
Political awareness	Awareness of the corporate political environment as well as the overall corporate culture can have a large impact on a project's success.
Buy-in	As each stage is concluded, buy-in, or agreement as to conclusions from all affected customer groups, is of critical importance.
Communication	Do not assume others know what is going on with the project. Write memos, distribute newsletters, send e-mail, or communicate with key people in person.
Detailed project documentation	Document every phone call and every meeting. Keep the project well organized from day one with copies of all correspondence.
Process/product awareness	As a simple means of staying focused and on track, keep in mind what is the process and product for each step in the network analysis and design methodology.
Be honest with yourself	Be your own harshest critic. Identify weak points in your proposal and address them accordingly. Play "devil's advocate" with your proposal and prepare for possible objections.

Figure 12-5   Critical Success Factors of the Network Development Life Cycle

"open-door" corporate cultures are less concerned with hierarchies of authority, thereby allowing quicker and simpler access to end-users.

Unfortunately, so-called "backroom" politics can play an important role in systems design as well. The best researched and planned network design may go unimplemented if the company president's brother-in-law is in the computer business and has a different idea. Sad, but true. The best way to defend against such situations is to first be aware of any such possible political situations. Specific strategies for ensuring the objectivity of the analysis and design process will be highlighted as the overall network analysis and design methodology is described further.

Buy-in   All of the critical success factors listed in Figure 12-5 are important. However, one of the most important, yet easiest to accomplish, is **buy-in.** After all potential customers and constituencies have been identified, it is imperative to gain buy-in from each of these groups for the deliverable, or product, of each stage of the overall network analysis and design methodology.

By reaching consensus on the acceptability of the results or deliverables of each and every stage, one avoids having initial assumptions or work on earlier stages brought into question during the presentation of the final proposal. In other words, the approved results of one stage become the foundation or starting point for the next stage. If buy-in from all affected parties is assured at each stage, the presentation of the final proposal should be much smoother with a minimum of backtracking or rework required.

Communication Many of the other critical success factors listed in Figure 12-5 depend upon effective communication, both verbal and written. Oftentimes in network or systems development projects, it is assumed that because network analysts and designers are aware of the project status, everyone must be fully informed as well. Unfortunately, this is not the case. As previously pointed out, no one likes to feel left out. More importantly, networks often cross the "territory" or authority of numerous individuals. To keep these people supportive of the project, it is imperative to keep them informed and to make them feel that they are an important part of the process.

Communication can take many forms. Newsletters, project status reports, and e-mail are all suitable means of keeping people informed and up-to-date. More ambitious communications schemes such as videoconferencing or the production of a VCR tape might be appropriate for critical tasks, public relations, or training opportunities.

Detailed Project Documentation As a project manager, it is required not only to manage the overall network analysis and design project effectively with task schedules, project lists, and to-do lists but also to document every aspect of the project. Every conversation, by phone or in person, should have notes entered into a log book indicating such things as date, time, persons involved, topics of conversation, and required follow-up. E-mail messages should be printed and filed. Meetings should be documented in a similar fashion, with agendas and action item assignments included in a project binder as well as being sent to responsible parties and key managers.

Organization of this project documentation is of equal importance. A large binder with several sections for different portions of the project can be a very effective way to be able to quickly access any piece of project documentation required.

This documentation is of particular importance in the latter stages of the project when consultants and vendors become a part of the project. Document everything in writing and take no action on any agreement until it has been presented in writing.

Process/Product Awareness As a facilitator in meetings of end-users trying to define system requirements, it is the network analyst's job to keep the participants focused and the meeting on track. To accomplish that, it is important to have a clear understanding of the process involved at that particular stage of the network analysis and design methodology as well as the nature of the product or deliverable that is to be the outcome of this process.

Meetings can easily get off on tangents and aggressive users can easily sway meetings toward personal agendas. By remaining focused on the proper topics of discussion and a clear visualization of the product of that discussion, a facilitator can maximize the effectiveness of the analysis and design process. As the leader of the meeting, it is important not to go overboard on controlling the discussion of the meeting however. With practice and patience, experienced facilitators can direct meetings that foster imaginative solutions and proposals without either stifling creativity or allowing discussion to wander ineffectively.

Be Honest with Yourself One of the greatest advantages of being totally honest with yourself is that no one else knows the potential weaknesses or areas for improvement in your proposal better than you. The difficulty comes in forcing yourself to be totally honest and acknowledging the potential weaknesses in your proposal in order to either correct them or defend them.

Peer review and egoless programming are other systems development techniques employed to identify potential weaknesses in programs or proposals prior to implementation. Not all weaknesses can necessarily be corrected. Financial or time constraints may have restricted potential solutions. If that is the case, an honest self-review of the proposal will give one the opportunity to have an objective explanation to such weaknesses prepared in advance.

Critical Success Factors Are Learned Behaviors   Although many of the critical success factors listed in Figure 12-5 may seem to be nothing more than common sense, it has been the author's experience that more network analysis and design projects suffer from difficulties caused by a failure to address one or more of these critical success factors than from any other cause of failure. These critical success factors must be applied throughout the entire life of the network development project and are therefore best seen as habits or behaviors, rather than discrete events to be scheduled or planned.

Start with a Clearly Defined Problem

A network cannot very well provide effective solutions to problems that have not been clearly defined in objective terms. To attempt to implement networks before everyone agrees to (buy-in) the exact nature of the problem to be solved is somewhat akin to hitting a moving target. The network will never satisfy all constituencies' needs because not everyone agreed what those needs were in the first place. All network development efforts start with a problem as perceived by someone, be they management or end-users. At some point, management agrees that a problem exists that is worth expending resources to at least investigate. The responsibility for conducting the investigation may be given to in-house personnel or to an outside consultant or facilitator.

The first job of the facilitator is to identify all parties potentially affected by the perceived problem. Next, representatives of each of these constituencies are selected and convened for brainstorming sessions to determine the nature of the problem and, perhaps, the requirements of a solution. To make these problem definition sessions as productive as possible, it is important that representatives do their "homework" prior to the meetings. Figure 12-6 shows an excerpt of a letter the author has sent to user group representatives prior to problem definition brainstorming sessions.

Understand Strategic Business Objectives

Once the group has been assembled, it is time to remember the top-down model. To keep the problem definition session and the subsequent solution proposal session on track, it is vital to start with the strategic business goals of the organization as articulated by senior management. Whenever the author consulted as a user group facilitator, he always strived to have either the chief executive officer or chief financial officer (or both) present at the initial meeting to say a few words about the importance of the user group's work and the strategic direction of the corporate business

Goldman Consulting and Development
101 Hickory Drive
Goodsville, ME 11321

Unautomated Materials Corporation
213 Old Way Avenue
Pastview, FL 32911

Nathan Investigator:

When we meet in November, we will *not* be talking about computers. We will be talking about your job, the decisions you have to make in your job, and the information you need to make those decisions.

Some questions that we might address to which you might want to give some thought:

1. If you had to break down your job into major functions or categories, what would they be?
2. When are you most buried in paperwork?
3. When do you find yourself saying, "A computer ought to be able to do this"?
4. What questions from customers or supervisors involve long searches through files or stacks of paper?
5. Where in your operation do you see possible increases in productivity if a computer could keep track of something that is tracked manually now?
6. Where in your operation do you see opportunities for improved customer service or improved bottom-line contribution?

I am looking forward to working with you. If you have any questions in the meantime please feel free to call me.

Sincerely,

James E. Goldman

Figure 12-6   Productive Problem Definition Sessions Require Advance Preparation (Sample Letter)

goals. In addition, if strategic corporate goals had been prepared in writing, these were shared with the group, as allowed by company policy. In this way, the whole group starts off with the same focus and strategic business direction with the proper attitude about the overall process.

Importance of Baseline Data

To measure the eventual impact, hopefully positive, of the installed network, one has to have baseline data, or the current status of the system and network, from which to measure that eventual network impact. This baseline data can often be collected from the various customer groups or constituencies of the information system and network who are chosen to attend the problem definition sessions. Depending on the extent, in terms of both geography and sophistication, to which current systems have been implemented, a structured framework may be required to record this systems information in a standardized manner. Fortunately, the top-down model is an excellent example of such a framework.

Top-Down Model Organizes Baseline Data   Using the top-down model as a framework for organizing the baseline data to reflect the current system and network status does not necessarily imply that a separate top-down model must be completed for every corporate location attached to the network or that every layer of the top-down model must be filled in for every location. Just enough data should be collected at this point in the network analysis and design methodology to clearly define the problem in measurable terms.

Information that is gathered in the top-down model at this stage should relate directly to the problems as perceived by the user groups. Hopefully, the problems have some business layer impact; otherwise this whole process may be a waste of time. In other words, although the source of the problem may be in the application, data, network, or technology layer, if it has no impact on the business layer, why should time be spent studying it?

Notice how most of the questions in Figure 12-6 deal with business problems or situations. Once these business problems are identified, the sources of these business problems within the lower layers of the top-down model would be subsequently investigated as part of the problem definition process. Conversely, these same lower layers of the top-down model will be redesigned to become the source of business solutions as delivered by the new network.

Feasibility Studies and Buy-in

Once sufficient information has been gathered to document the current status of the systems and networks in objective, measurable terms, the required product for this process, the problem definition, has been completed and it is time to assure buy-in. The problem definition and its associated alternative recommendations for further study are sometimes referred to as a **feasbility study.**

The need for buy-in on a problem definition or feasibility study will vary from one case to another. Much of the need for management buy-in and the associated approval to proceed will depend on the nature of the original charge from management.

In other words, if management's initial charge was, "Look into this problem and get back to me," then a feasibility study followed by management buy-in and approval prior to further study is clearly appropriate. Conversely, if management's charge was, "Figure out what's wrong and fix it," then a formalized feasibility report with formal presentation may not be called for. However, remember one of the key critical success factors—communications. Even if a formal feasibility report is not required, timely management reports should be completed and submitted on a regular basis to keep management abreast of progress and in tune with overall project strategic direction. Figure 12-7 summarizes the key points (process and product) of the problem definition phase.

■ STRATEGIC INFORMATION SYSTEM DESIGN

The primary mission of a network is the delivery of the right information at the right time to the right decision-maker in the right place. The determination as to what or who is the right information, time, decision-maker, or place is the responsibility of the strategic information system (application and data layers) design, which lies above the network layer in the top-down model. Although this textbook cannot and should not give a comprehensive coverage of the applications development and database development methodologies, it is still important to understand

Process		
	1.	Problem is perceived
	2.	Management perceives problem as worth investigating
	3.	Management delegates responsibility for problem definition
	4.	User/constituency groups are identified and representatives chosen
	5.	Representative groups are convened.
	6.	Senior management commitment and priorities are conveyed to representative group
	7.	Representative groups produce baseline data of current system status
	8.	Depending on the extent of the current system and network implementation, the top-down model may be used to organize this baseline data into a standardized format
	9.	Buy-in
Product		
	1.	Baseline data describing current system status in objective, measurable terms. Can be organized into multiple top-down models
	2.	A formalized feasibility study may be required depending on the initial charge/direction from management

Figure 12-7   Key Points of Problem Definition and Feasibility Study

the process of strategic information system design as it relates to the network analysis and design methodology.

The product of this entire phase of the network analysis and design methodology, in addition to the **strategic information system design** itself, is the **evaluation criteria** by which the proposed new system and its underlying network will be judged.

Importance of Establishing Evaluation Criteria

The problem definition phase provided a starting point of baseline data for the new system whereas the strategic information system design provides the operational goals for the new system to attain. Just as the baseline data has to be objective and measurable, so must the evaluation criteria associated with these operational goals.

These goals may have a direct impact on network design when defined in terms such as maximum response time, transactions per second, or mean time between failures. By producing objective, measurable goals or performance evaluation criteria and getting subsequent management buy-in on those goals, one helps to assure the objectivity of the entire network analysis and design process. For example, should a substandard system be suggested due solely to "back-room" politics, it is simply evaluated against the evaluation criteria as previously agreed upon by all appropriate levels of management. Figure 12-8 summarizes the key points of the strategic information system design phase in terms of both process and product.

Identify Overall System Characteristics

The word *strategic* is used in the context of information system design to portray the top-down strategic business goal orientation of the entire information design process. As can be seen in Figure 12-8, the strategic information system design process starts with a review of the strategic business goals as articulated by senior management.

Process		
	1.	Review strategic corporate objectives
	2.	Define the overall characteristics of an information system that can successfully support/achieve these objectives
	3.	Break the overall business down into major functional areas
	4.	List the business processes performed under each functional area
	5.	Highlight the decision points in the listed business processes and list information required to make informed decisions at each decision point
	6.	Highlight the opportunities for improvement in listed business processes and list information required to take advantage of these opportunities for improvement
	7.	Prepare performance evaluation criteria
	8.	Prioritize the various aspects of the strategic information system as designed
	9.	Buy-in
Product		
	1.	Strategic information system design
	2.	Performance evaluation criteria in objective measurable terms

Figure 12-8 Key Points of Strategic Information System Design

With these strategic business goals in mind, the next step in the process is to describe the overall characteristics of an information system that could fulfill these strategic business goals. The following are some examples:

To fulfill our corporation's strategic business goals, this information system must

1. Enable delivery of improved customer service.

2. Enable improved inventory control.

3. Allow for more flexible pricing.

4. Enable shorter shelf restocking cycles.

5. Allow for more efficient use of manpower.

Many other examples could have been easily included. The point of these overall characteristics, in terms of the top-down model, is to assure and specify that the application layer solutions will deliver on the business layer requirements. As can be seen from Figure 12-8, one of the key products of this strategic information system design phase is the performance evaluation criteria. The foregoing overall required system characteristics serve as one set of evaluation criteria for proposed information systems designs. Other more objective evaluation criteria will be developed further along in the overall design process. However, the importance of the strategic system performance evaluation criteria lies in their ability to measure the extent to which proposed information system designs deliver on strategic business goals.

Identify Major Business Functional Areas

Once overall system performance characteristics have been established, the overall business can be broken down into large functional areas. These functional areas may correspond to corporate departments or divisions. Example might include manufacturing, inventory control, project management, customer service, accounting and payroll, and human resources.

In practice, each of these identified major **business functional areas** can be written on a separate large sheet of flip chart paper and taped up all over the walls of the room in which the user groups meet. It is not important to argue about which functional areas deserve their own sheet of paper at this point. Consolidation and editing take place at a later time in the process.

Identify Business Processes Associated with Each Business Functional Area

Once the major functional areas of the business have been established, the business processes that take place in each major functional area are listed. This presents a wonderful opportunity for **business process re-engineering.** Oftentimes, user groups are made up of individuals from various business units who have not had the time to really understand each other's jobs and responsibilities. As business processes are described, brainstorming quickly takes over and problems that seemed deeply embedded in current systems are solved as new or modified business processes are defined for the new strategic information system design. This process is repeated for every major business functional area identified in the previous step.

It is important for the facilitator of this process to keep the discussions on a fairly strategic level, thereby avoiding lower level implementation issues such as screen design, report layouts, etc. Continuing with the flip chart scenario, each major business functional area should now have its own flip chart(s) with detailed business processes described for each large business functional area.

Managerial Perspective

THE NETWORK ANALYST AND BUSINESS PROCESS RE-ENGINEERING

As current business processes are discussed during the network development life cycle, opportunities abound for improvement of these business processes. It is important, however, to take an organized approach to business process improvement, more popularly known as business process re-engineering. Part of that required organized approach hinges on maintaining one's common sense. For example:

- If it isn't broken, don't fix it—In searching for opportunities for improvement, concentrate on the processes that are in the greatest need of improvement.

- How will you know if the new process is better if you never measured how bad the old process was?—Baseline data must be gathered to document the performance of current processes before redesign takes place. These same evaluation criteria and methods must be used to evaluate the new processes to objectively evaluate improvement levels.

- Learn from other's mistakes—Pay attention to other business process re-engineering efforts, especially those in closely related industries that have failed. What lessons can be learned and what mistakes can avoid being repeated?

- Don't be afraid to admit mistakes—If the re-engineered business process does not produce anticipated results based on objective evaluation criteria, don't be afraid to admit the mistakes early and make corrections as soon as possible to minimize negative impact.

As information systems and networking professionals are increasingly called upon to justify their budgets and corporate contributions in the face of outsourcing alternatives, it is imperative that network analysts understand the importance of a realistic approach to business process re-engineering.

Identify Decision Points and Opportunities for Improvement

Recalling that one of the primary goals of a well-designed strategic information system is to deliver the right information to the right decision-maker, the next logical step in the design process is to identify the key **decision points** in all of the documented business processes where decision-makers must make decisions.

Once identified, each decision point is then analyzed as to what information (the "right" information) is required for the decision-maker to make an informed decision at each respective decision point. This analysis process often brings out the fact that decision-makers are getting much more information than they need to make informed decisions. Entire reports hundreds of pages long may contain only one or two pieces of information that are of critical importance to a decision-maker at any given decision point.

Figure 12-6 highlighted some of the "homework" analysis questions to which user group representatives were to have given some thought. One of the key areas in which user group members can contribute is in the identification of **opportunities for improvement** that can be enabled by this strategic information system design. Opportunities for improvement may imply improvement in any one of a number of areas: financial, productivity, inventory control, accounts receivable collections, customer service, customer satisfaction, repeat customers, employee retention, etc.

The important thing to remember is that if these opportunities for improvement support the strategic business goals of the corporation, then they should be identified along with the information required to turn these opportunities into reality. Figure 12-9 illustrates the relationship of the various processes described thus far in the strategic information system design.

Develop Specific Evaluation Criteria

Once the strategic information system has been designed as described, more specific evaluation criteria can be created from the business process descriptions, decision points, and opportunities and their associated information requirements. This is not a difficult process. In reality, a checklist or report card is being prepared consisting of all of the system requirements (automated business processes, decision points, opportunities) as defined in the strategic information system design process. These specific evaluation criteria are then combined with the overall required performance characteristics as previously defined to produce an unbiased, objective evaluation mechanism with which to judge prospective systems.

Prioritization

Priorities can then be assigned to each of the major functional areas, business processes, decision points, and opportunities. These priorities may assist in the evaluation process by identifying those systems that exhibit the most important ele-

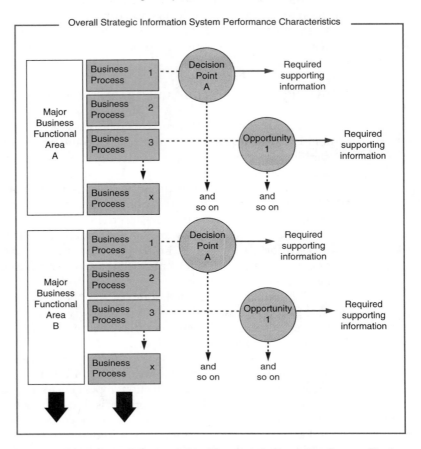

Figure 12-9   Process Relationship of Strategic Information System Design

ments of the strategic information system design. A simple yet effective approach to systems design prioritization is known as the **three-pile approach.** In this prioritization scheme, there are only three priorities, defined as follows:

- Priority 1 items are so important that the system is simply not worth implementing without them.

- Priority 2 items can be lived without or "worked around" but really need to be implemented as soon as possible.

- Priority 3 items would be nice to have but can be lived without.

One important point to remember is that these priorities should be considered in terms of business impact. At this point, a strategic, or high-level, information system design has been completed. Many details need to be added to this requirements document before proposals can accurately reflect their ability to meet not only the business and application layer system requirements but the data and networking requirements that must support this strategic information system as well.

Producing the Request for Proposal (RFP)

By organizing the strategic information system design information into an understandable format and by adding detailed information concerning performance evaluation criteria for the data and network layers, a document known as **RFP (request for proposal)** is produced. It is important to understand the benefits of a RFP to be able to justify the work that goes into it.

By taking the time to prepare a detailed RFP, a company assures that its priorities and unique business processes and requirements are fulfilled by the information system and network that is eventually installed. All vendor proposals are measured against the users' predefined requirements regardless of whom the vendor may be related to. If a vendor's proposal does not meet minimum standards for meeting the requirements of the RFP, it is dropped from further consideration regardless of how nice the screens look or how colorful the brochures are. The RFP assures that the delivered system, whether developed in-house or purchased from an outside vendor, will be flexible enough to change as business needs and requirements change. Unfortunately, the alternative is all too often the case, in which businesses are forced to mold their business practices according to the constraints of the purchased information system and network. Figure 12-10 summarizes both the processes and products involved in the RFP preparation phase of the network analysis and design methodology.

Examine Each Corporate Location   Now that the strategic information system design has been completed, the next step is to carefully examine each corporate location at which the information system will be eventually deployed. The purpose of gathering all of this data about each of the corporate locations is to compile an accurate representation of the scope and requirements of the network over which this strategic information system will be implemented.

As each location is examined, the information gathered will help determine the unique data and processing requirements for those locations. This detailed location-specific information is distinct from the high-level information gathered in top-down model format as part of the problem definition phase.

Process		
	1.	Examine each corporate location
	2.	Produce evaluation criteria for application and data layer consideration as required
	3.	Survey all existing system resources: people, hardware–software–media, data, network, physical plant
	4.	Prepare preliminary overall project schedule
	5.	Determine information required from vendor
	6.	Determine potential vendors
	7.	Determine percent-of-fit goal
	8.	Compile and distribute RFP to selected vendors
Product	1.	Formalized request for proposal
	2.	Percent-of-fit goal

Figure 12-10   Preparing the Request for Proposal

Some corporate locations may be regional offices, concentrating data or transactions from several branch offices. These, along with many other facts, must be recorded to accurately define data and network layer requirements for the overall information system. Although each company may differ in what location-specific statistics are important in terms of strategic network design, many of the points in Figure 12-11 may warrant consideration.

The information gathered in such location-by-location surveys adds to the evaluation criteria of any potential system proposal. Any need identified must be met by a proposed system solution in accordance with the determined priority of each of these requirements. It is of critical importance that this survey is done as accu-

Category	Questions/Issues
People	• Number of total employees • Number of employees performing each business function as listed in strategic information system design • Feeling about the "new" system • Key political situations • Number of network-oriented/technically-oriented employees • Training needs

Hardware–software media	• Current level of computerization
	• Current applications software
	• Current networking status
	• Local phone company
	• Availability of data services from local phone company
	• Software performance requirements
	    • Maximum time for customer look-up
	    • Maximum time for part number or pricing look-up
	    • Maximum time for order entry
	• How "mission-critical" is each application?
	• Must backup systems be ready at a moment's notice?

Data	• Number of customers • Number of inventory items • Number of open orders • Need for sharing data with other locations, regional offices, corporate headquarters • Special security needs for data or transmission
Network	• Current network configuration • Network traffic volumes • Network protocols • Network monitoring and management technology • Current problems with network to be corrected • Expected growth of network, traffic volume, user community
Physical Plant	• What is the condition of each remote site? • Will additional electrical, heating, data wiring, space, or security systems be required at any sites to accommodate the new systems?

Figure 12-11   Possible Location-Specific Statistics

rately as possible since this is the data upon which the initial network design will largely be based. Buy-in by all affected groups at this stage is especially important as outside vendors and in-house staffs will be using this data to prepare detailed application, database, and network designs.

Final RFP Preparation   The two major components of the RFP that should have been completed at this point are

1.   Strategic information system design.

2.   Corporate location survey results.

To put the finishing touches on the RFP, a few more pieces of information must be either supplied to or requested from potential system and network suppliers. This additional information is often included in a section of the RFP known as the **management abstract.** Figure 12-12 illustrates a sample table of contents from an RFP including the items that might be included in a management abstract.

Information Supplied *to* Vendors   Among the information included in the management abstract that should be supplied to potential vendors to give them as accurate a description as possible of the opportunity are the following items:

- Company profile—A brief description of the company issuing the request for proposal. Number of corporate locations, approximate yearly sales, anticipated growth rate, and a brief statement concerning the current state of computerization or networking could all be elements of this section.

- Statement of the problem—From a business perspective, what was the source of the initiation of the problem definition process and what did the problem definition team conclude?

- Overall system characteristics—It is important to include overall system characteristics at the beginning of the RFP as some of these requirements may be beyond the capabilities of possible vendors and their systems. In this way, these vendors won't waste their time or yours in submitting a proposal that can't meet these basic overall requirements. Figure 12-13 lists some possible overall system characteristics that might be included in an RFP. Al-

Management abstract	• Company profile • Statement of the problem • Overall system characteristics • Project phase prioritization • Proposed project schedule summary • Information requested from vendor: system development experience; hardware, software, networking experience; references; pricing; support; training and documentation; vendor background
System design	• Summary review • Details of geographic locations • System requirements of each software module

Figure 12-12   Sample RFP Table of Contents

1. Source code must be owned by the client company.
2. The system must be easy to use and maintain and must contain on-line help as well as extensive input editing and verification to help prevent errors.
3. The system must require a minimum of training.
4. The system must be easy to install (hardware and software) to expedite installation throughout all corporate locations.
5. The system must allow multiple users simultaneous access to information. The system must have the capability to assure information integrity through record locking and must have adequate security to ensure against unauthorized access to information.
6. The system must have windowing capabilities allowing drop-down menus and screens to allow simultaneous access to multiple files and/or modules.
7. The system must be easily transportable to numerous hardware and operating system platforms on both minicomputers and microcomputers.
8. The system must have the ability to output and input ASCII data files to assure necessary informational ties to regional centers.
9. The system must have database/file rollback capabilities to assure data integrity in the event of a system failure or power outage.

Figure 12-13   Possible Required Overall System Characteristics

though some of the requirements listed in Figure 12-13 may seem obvious or unnecessary, it is important not to assume anything when shopping for information systems.

- Project phase prioritization—If some modules (business area computerization plans) of the overall strategic information system design are more critical than others, this prioritization should be conveyed to potential vendors. Often, a vendor may be able to supply some, but not all, of the information system modules. If the vendors have a sense of which modules are most important they will be better able to know whether to submit a proposal or not.

- Proposed project schedule summary—Figure 12-14 illustrates a sample proposed project schedule with key events that may be of concern to potential vendors listed. Before taking the time to prepare detailed proposals, many vendors appreciate knowing the implementation timetable of the proposed

Event	Proposed Completion Date
Requests for proposals sent to selected vendors	07/29/98
Proposals due to consultant from vendors	08/29/98
Selection and notification of vendor finalists	09/14/98
Presentation/demonstration by vendor finalists	09/21/98–10/07/98
Make or buy decision	10/14/98
Pilot test	12/14/98
Projected system implementation date	04/01/99

Figure 12-14   Proposed Project Schedule Summary

project. If the vendor already has projects underway or anticipated, they may lack sufficient manpower to meet this RFP's proposed implementation schedule.

Information Requested *from* Vendors   At least as important as the information supplied to potential vendors is the information required from potential vendors. To avoid being sent standard proposals with preprinted product literature and brochures, it is advantageous to list specific information required from vendors and to evaluate only those proposals that supply the requested information.

Figure 12-15 lists some of the information that may be requested of vendors although the list is by no means authoritative or exhaustive. Information requested

System development	• Vendor's experience in client's industry • Number of installed systems • Date of first installation • Integration with related manufacturing and financial modules • Scope of installed systems
Hardware/operating systems/software	• Which hardware platforms does system run on? • Multiuser? • Operating systems • Programming languages • 4GL/DBMS experience • Ease of/availability of customization • Source code availability
References	• Names, addresses, and phone numbers of three customers with similar systems implemented
Pricing	• Hardware: If vendor will supply hardware, list cost by component including manufacturer and model number • Software: List cost per module, additional per-user license costs, source code costs, cost for software customization, cost for maintenance and support agreements, cost for operating or run-time systems
Training	• Include information regarding facilities, courses, materials, instructor availability, schedule, media used, and cost
Support	• Hours—hotline available? • Cost—800 number? • Experience of support personnel • Software guarantees • Bug fixes—turnaround time • Software updates—maintenance
Vendor background	• Number of employees • Yearly sales (approximate) • Growth pattern • Strategic direction • Research and development

Figure 12-15   Information Requested from Vendor

should satisfy corporate policies as well as business layer concerns from initial problem definition analysis. The overall purpose of this section is to ensure that

1. The vendor has significant experience in developing and implementing systems of a similar nature to the one described in the RFP.

2. The vendor has a sufficiently large organization to support the smooth and successful implementation of such a system.

3. The vendor is financially solvent so as not to be likely to declare bankruptcy in the middle of the project implementation.

Percent-of-Fit Goal   The RFP should now be fairly complete and ready to send to prospective system vendors. In addition to the RFP itself, one other important product of this phase of the overall network analysis and design methodology is known as the **percent-of-fit goal.** This is an especially important element if in-house development of the system and network is a possibility. The percent-of-fit goal is a rather arbitrary percentage that is determined by the user representative group preparing the RFP and is subject to the same overall buy-in as the RFP itself.

The purpose of the percent-of-fit goal is to set a minimum threshold of compliance for vendor proposals to warrant further consideration and invitations for demonstrations. As an example, perhaps the users group feels that any proposal that meets at least 50% of the priority 1 features deserves further consideration.

This percent-of-fit goal offers an element of objectivity to the proposal evaluation process. The percent-of-fit goal combined with the specific descriptions of required features in the RFP constitutes an objective, comprehensive evaluation mechanism for evaluating proposals according to what is important to the corporation. By having this evaluation mechanism clearly defined before receipt of the first proposal, evaluators are less likely to be swayed by fancy brochures or systems' "bells and whistles."

If an in-house systems development group feels that they should rightfully be developing and/or implementing this system, they must submit a proposal in compliance with the requirements outlined in the RFP. Their proposal will be evaluated along with all of the outside vendors' proposals.

The percent-of-fit of a particular proposal can be easily calculated. Recalling that all features or requirements of the RFP were given a priority of 1, 2, or 3, by merely counting how many features of each priority are present in a given proposal, an overall objective "score" can be determined for each proposal. The process is fair, is objective, and, to a large extent, eliminates politics from the proposal evaluation process.

Proposal Evaluation and the Make or Buy Decision   Having determined a percent-of-fit score for each proposal as well as a percent-of-fit goal for proposals to warrant further consideration, invitations to selected vendors might be the next logical step. However, before selected vendors are invited for demonstrations, it is important once again to gain buy-in from all affected parties, especially management, on not only the selected vendors but, perhaps more importantly, the vendor selection process. Only when all groups agree that the vendor screening and proposal process has been fair and objective should the overall process move forward to the vendor demonstration stage.

At vendor demonstrations, it is important once again for the users, rather than the vendors, to be in charge. Have a copy of the vendor's proposal at the demonstration and ask to see each and every feature demonstrated that was described as included or supported in the vendor's initial proposal. Score should be kept on those features successfully demonstrated and this score should be compared to the score received based on the proposal evaluation.

Following all of the vendor demonstrations comes time for the **make or buy decision.** Were any of the vendors' systems worth further consideration or should the system be developed in-house? Once again, before proceeding, buy-in of the vendor demonstration evaluation and the make or buy decision should be assured.

Managerial Perspective

OUTSOURCING

Outsourcing allows information systems and networking administrators to hire outside contractors to operate and maintain corporate information systems and networks. This option has become increasingly popular with companies whose primary business is not related to information systems or networking. Early ventures into outsourcing were not always ideal, as corporations and outsourcing vendors wrestled with where one entity's control terminated and the other's began.

As corporations have gained more experience with outsourcing, the delineation of control has become clearer. Corporations should maintain control over which services can be subcontracted by the outsourcing vendor and should maintain the right to exclude certain subcontractors. The relationship between the corporation and the outsourcing company should be viewed as a strategic partnership rather than as a typical supplier–customer relationship. Partnership agreements can be written to include mutual benefits for mutually achieved goals or shared successes. In this manner, both the client and the outsourcing company stand to gain by working together to reach mutually beneficial goals—a truly win–win situation.

■ IN-HOUSE NETWORK ANALYSIS AND DESIGN

Although it may seem as if a great deal of analysis and design has been done already, it is important to note that the network layer requirements are now ready to be addressed, having designed satisfactory solutions for business, application, and data requirements. As stated several times before, a network cannot be designed in a vacuum but rather must be designed to deliver solutions and performance in response to specific, well-defined, data, application, and business layer requirements.

The overall network analysis and design summary process diagram illustrated in Figure 12-4 shows both in-house and outsourcing options for the network analysis and design phase of the project based on the make or buy decision. The term *network analysis and design* really refers more specifically to wide area network analysis and design. LAN design considerations and internetworking (LAN to LAN) connectivity issues were covered in their respective chapters. In this chapter, a more corporate-wide view of networking will be taken by designing a network that will effectively support the strategic information system design across geographically dispersed corporate locations. Figure 12-16 illustrates the key points, both process and product, of the in-house network analysis and design phase. Each of these steps will be explained in detail.

Process	1.	Data traffic analysis
		• Payload type analysis
		• Transaction analysis
		• Protocol stack analysis
		• Time studies
		• Mission-critical analysis
		• Traffic volume analysis
	2.	Circuit analysis and configuration alternatives
	3.	Network hardware analysis and configuration alternatives
Product	1.	Data traffic analysis report for each geographic location
	2.	Alternative network configuration diagrams including circuit and network hardware details

Figure 12-16   In-House Network Analysis and Design

The overall network analysis and design process can be broken down into three major steps:

1. **Data traffic analysis** examines all aspects and characteristics of the traffic that will be passed between corporate locations over the proposed network. Since this data traffic is what the network must carry effectively, it is important to start with a thorough analysis of the data traffic to design an effective network. As an analogy, it would be equally wise to understand the driving patterns and transportation needs of an urban area before designing a new highway system.

2. Once the nature of the data traffic is thoroughly understood, **circuit analysis and configuration alternatives** explores the possibilities for delivering that data traffic in a reliable and effective manner. Whereas there are often alternative ways to transport data from point A to point B, it is important to document alternative network configurations along with an understanding of the advantages and disadvantages of each alternative.

3. Finally, given the nature of the data traffic, especially its protocol-related characteristics, and the possible circuit configurations over which that data may be transported, **network hardware analysis and configuration alternatives** explores the possible data communications hardware devices that may be required to tie the various circuit configurations together into a reliable, manageable, network.

Data Traffic Analysis

The exact types of analysis performed in the major step known as data traffic analysis may vary from one networking design to another. Figure 12-17 details some of the possible types of data traffic analysis. The required outcome from this step is a data traffic analysis report, which will form the basis for circuit and networking hardware selection. It is the obligation of the network analyst to perform whatever types of data traffic analysis are necessary to assure that the data traffic analysis report is as complete as possible while forming the foundation on which to build a network design.

Data Traffic Analysis Category	Description
Payload type analysis	Most locations will require at least voice and data service. Videoconferencing and multimedia also may need to be supported. All payload types should be considered and documented prior to circuit and networking hardware selection.
Transaction analysis	Use process flow analysis and document flow analysis to identify each type of transaction. Analyze detailed data requirements for each transaction type.
Time studies	Once all transaction types have been identified, analyze when and how often each transaction type occurs.
Traffic volume analysis	By combining all known types of transactions with the results of the time study, a time-sensitive traffic volume requirements profile can be produced. This is a starting point for mapping bandwidth requirements to circuit capacity.
Mission-critical analysis	Results of this analysis phase may dictate the need for special data security procedures such as encryption or special reliability/fault tolerance features such as redundant circuits and networking components.
Protocol stack analysis	Each corporate location's data traffic is analyzed as to protocols that must be transported across the corporate wide area network. Many alternatives for the transport of numerous protocols exist, but first these protocols must be identified.

Figure 12-17   Data Traffic Analysis

Payload Type Analysis   For the most cost-effective network design, voice as well as data requirements should be considered during the network analysis and design phase. Videoconferencing, imaging, and multimedia requirements should also be considered due to their bandwidth-intensive transport demands. Digitized video and voice represent streaming data and often require isochronous transmission whereas inter-LAN data tends to be of a more bursty nature. These data characteristics may have a major impact on network design decisions.

Transaction Analysis   To determine the actual data traffic requirements from a given corporate location, the network analyst has to examine the source of that data: transactions of one type or another. Examples might include customer entry or inquiry, order entry, inventory receipt, order fulfillment, part number or pricing look-up, etc.

Each of these different transaction types should be identified from the business process definitions of the strategic information system design. **Process flow analysis** and **document flow analysis** are also employed as ways to identify and analyze transaction types. Once each transaction type has been identified, the amount of data required to complete that transaction is calculated and documented. Some transactions such as credit card verifications or automated teller machine transactions are comprised of short bursts of data that must be handled quickly and accurately. Some nightly backup or file transfer applications may not require the same type of high-speed, high-priority transmission. The difference in the characteristics of these transactions may warrant a difference in the network design in each case. Perhaps one type of transaction is better suited to a packet-switched approach whereas the other may require a leased line.

Time Studies   Once all transaction types have been identified, the next step is to analyze when and how often these transactions are executed. One method of determining both the frequency and the time distribution of these transactions is through a time study. Simply stated, a time study merely counts how often and at what time of day, week, or month a given transaction or process is executed. For instance, a retail store's daily close-out procedure is executed once per day. However, is it the same time each day and are all stores executing the same process at the same time each day? What are the network implications of month-end closing procedures? The answers to these types of questions can have a major bearing on bandwidth requirements and the resultant network design.

Traffic Volume Analysis   Traffic volume analysis could be looked upon as the product of transaction analysis and time studies. By knowing the data and network requirements of every transaction type and by further knowing the frequency and time distribution of the execution of a given transaction type, one should be able to construct a time-sensitive traffic volume requirements profile. Such a profile would show average network bandwidth requirements as well as peak or maximum requirements. Seasonality of transaction volume should not be overlooked. The transaction frequency of retail businesses can easily double or even triple during the Christmas shopping season. An undersized network must not be the cause of poor customer service during important periods of increased customer activity. As another example, power companies must design voice and data networks that can easily accommodate higher than normal demand to provide adequate customer service during power outages or other emergencies.

Traffic volume analysis should also be viewed from a location-oriented perspective. To have an accurate representation of overall traffic volumes, one must consider the average and peak traffic volume levels between all identified corporate locations or network nodes. Such point-to-point traffic volume analysis data can then be fed into network design and simulation software packages for further analysis and what-if scenario development.

Mission-Critical Analysis   Although all data could be considered important, some transactions are so important to a business that they are known as mission critical. Electronics funds transfer is a good example of a mission-critical transaction. The mission-critical nature of some transactions can spawn further analysis and design in two other areas. Data security may require investigation. Encryption of data transmitted over wide area networks may be a requirement. If so, this fact should be stated as part of the overall data traffic analysis report.

Secondly, it is a fact of life that data circuits do fail from time to time. If certain mission-critical transactions cannot tolerate an occasional faulty data circuit, then redundant links may need to be designed into the initial network design configuration.

Protocol Stack Analysis   As has been seen in both the LAN and internetworking design processes, protocol stack analysis is of critical importance. Some protocols, such as SNA, are extremely time sensitive. Some protocols are routable whereas others are not. Others, such as SNA and some LAN protocols, are very "chatty," sending constant status-checking and keep-alive messages onto the network and occupying precious bandwidth. As each corporate location's data traffic is analyzed, special attention must be paid to the various protocol stacks of that data.

Will the wide area network be required to support more than one protocol? What are the bandwidth and network hardware implications of a multiprotocol WAN? Is TCP/IP encapsulation an option or is SDLC conversion a more appealing alternative? Before reaching any conclusions as to how various protocols are to be transported over the corporate network, one must accurately identify and document those protocols. This is the role of the protocol stack analysis.

Circuit Analysis and Configuration Alternatives

A thorough data traffic analysis should produce sufficient information to configure various network design alternatives that will effectively support the strategic information system design to all corporate locations. Evaluating alternative network configurations and computing circuit capacity are beyond the reasonable expectations of a person who may be using this textbook in support of a first course in data communications. Upper level courses in wide area networking or network analysis and design would better prepare a person to perform such a task.

Wide area network design software has greatly simplified the design process but is relatively expensive. In most cases, even using the software requires a great deal of network design expertise. As a result, in most cases, only companies that can afford to have full-time network analysts and designers on staff are likely to own copies of network design software. The various categories of network design software will be explored in greater detail later in this chapter.

A second alternative for circuit analysis and network configuration would be to hire a data communications/networking consultant. This too may be a very expensive alternative. Furthermore, there is little or no regulation as to the level of expertise required to call oneself a telecommunications consultant.

Thirdly, telecommunications companies, both local carriers and inter-exchange carriers, have the ability to design networks according to customer data requirements. The network design process is part of preparing a quote and is done at no charge. Therefore, it may be advisable for the small company or novice data communications person to let the experts design the network. Talk to several carriers and get a network design proposal with associated costs from each. By allowing the carriers to design the network and quote a price, they can consequently be held accountable for delivering service at a quoted price in accordance with the data traffic analysis and performance evaluation criteria.

Consideration of Network Alternatives

It is important to consider more than just the data traffic analysis when evaluating network configuration alternatives. The detailed survey of existing system resources should also be considered. For instance, local carriers servicing some remote corporate locations may be limited in their ability to offer certain data transmission services. This should be documented in the survey of existing system resources.

Regardless of who actually designs the network configuration alternatives, it is important to ensure that sufficient bandwidth has been allocated to handle sudden increases in demand. More gradual increases in bandwidth demand due to expanding business opportunities can usually be accommodated with upgrades to higher capacity lines and their associated data communications equipment.

A second performance evaluation criterion for network configurations has to do with reliability. Based on the data traffic analysis study, sufficient redundancy should be implemented in the network to properly support mission-critical applications. Thirdly, is the data transmission provided by these circuits sufficiently secure? Truthfully, the goal is

- to find a network configuration that has sufficient bandwidth to reliably deliver the data as described in the data traffic analysis report in a secure manner at a reasonable cost.

Alternative configurations must be understood in terms of both performance and costs. Comprehensive methodologies for project budgeting will be presented shortly. However, the point remains that the choice of a given network configuration may come down to a business decision. That decision may be that a given network configuration is all a company can afford and, as a result, that company will have to live with the associated performance and reliability. Conversely, the business decision may be that the business requires optimum network performance, regardless of the cost.

In any case, it is not the role of the network analyst to dismiss network design alternatives on the basis of cost. The network analyst's job is to deliver network design alternatives capable of delivering required network functionality. Only senior management should determine the feasibility of any particular network design in terms of its affordability. In any case, the person presenting the various network configurations to senior management for buy-in must know the pros and cons of each configuration. The ability of each configuration to handle expansion or business growth should be anticipated.

Network Hardware Analysis and Configuration Alternatives   Before the process of network hardware analysis is described, it is important to first reiterate the information gathered thus far that will assist in the decision-making process. Two key products of earlier analysis form the basis of the supporting material for selection of the particular networking devices that will be placed throughout the corporate wide area network. These two key products are

1.   Data traffic analysis reports for each corporate location.

2.   Circuit configuration alternatives diagrams.

Recall briefly the process involved in producing each of these products. The data traffic analysis report was based upon a detailed study of numerous aspects of the data traveling to or from each corporate location. The circuit configuration alternatives were designed, in turn, based on a careful study of the required bandwidth and delay sensitivity of the transactions performed at each corporate location as identified in the data traffic analysis study. If the results of these two analysis efforts are valid, then the networking devices chosen to tie the network together that are based on these results should be valid as well.

Use of the I-P-O Model   The actual decision-making process for network device selection utilizes a model of data communications that was first introduced very early in the text. By compiling the results of the data traffic analysis report and the circuit

Input	Processing	Output
	Required Network Device	**Wide Area Network Circuit**
Local Data Characteristics	**Characteristics**	**Characteristics**
Host-terminal data	Host-terminal data	Circuit-switched WAN services
IBM 3270 (synchronous)	Cluster controllers	POTS
VT-100 (asynchronous)	STDMs	ISDN
Transport protocols	T-1 MUXs and switches	Switched 56K
SNA	X.25 MUXs and switches	Leased WAN services
DECNet	Frame relay MUXs and	DDS
TCP/IP	switches	T-1
IPX/SPX	ATM access devices and	T-3
Payload Types	switches	Packet/cell-switched services
LAN data	LAN data	X.25
Terminal data	Bridges	Frame relay
Voice	Routers	ATM
Video	Switches	
Imaging/multimedia	Voice	
Internet Access	T-1 channel banks	
	Video	
	Inverse MUXs	
	Internet access	
	Modems	
	ADSL devices	

Figure 12-18   I-P-O Diagram as a Tool for Network Device Analysis

configuration diagram in an I-P-O diagram, the required processing ability of the sought-after device can be documented. With the performance characteristics of the required network device identified, product specifications can be reviewed and vendor presentations can be scheduled to find the proper networking device for each location.

Just as the data traffic analysis and circuit analysis were done on a location-by-location basis, so must the network device analysis be done. Figure 12-18 shows a sample use of an I-P-O diagram as a tool for network device analysis.

Figure 12-18 is not meant to be all-inclusive by any means. What Figure 12-18 is attempting to portray is that by knowing that data characteristics of the local data, with particular attention paid to the protocol stack, and by knowing the circuit alternatives available for carrying that data over the wide area network, the choices among network devices that can join the two are relatively limited.

Careful analysis of the available alternatives that can join the input and output characteristics can then be further analyzed from a business or strategic planning objective. Additional information to assist in this evaluation may come from the detailed reports of each corporate location that were prepared as part of the preparation of the RFP.

Review of Overall Network Analysis and Design Process

With the network hardware analysis, the circuit analysis, and the data analysis completed, the finishing touches can now be put on the final proposal. Before doing so, a brief review of the network analysis and design process may be in order.

Notice that the network design process did not start with a discussion of network hardware device alternatives. To do so would have been to ignore the importance of the top-down model, a central theme of this book. Many so-called data communications experts still start with their favorite hardware alternative and adjust data and circuit characteristics to match the chosen network hardware.

In this case, just the opposite approach was taken:

- Determine data characteristics based upon a thorough examination of the transactions that generate the data.

- Determine circuits based upon required bandwidth and delay sensitivity as determined by the data analysis study.

- Determine the networking hardware devices capable of transporting this data over these circuits while remaining responsive to business and location-specific influences.

Preparing the Final Proposal

Figure 12-19 summarizes the key points of wrapping up the network analysis and design methodology. After the final proposal is presented, buy-in is sought from all affected constituencies, hopefully followed by final approval and funding by senior management. One element of the final proposal process deserves further explanation.

Final Proposal	Process	1.	Prepare a detailed comprehensive budget
		2.	Prepare a detailed implementation timetable
		3.	Prepare project task detail
		4.	Prepare formal presentation
		5.	SELL!
	Product	1.	Comprehensive systems and networking budget model
		2.	Project management details
		3.	Presentation graphics
Approval	Process	1.	Final buy-in by all affected parties
		2.	Contract negotiation—outsourcing only
		3.	Executive approval
Implementation	Process	1.	Pilot test
		2.	In-house trial—outsourcing only
		3.	Performance evaluation
		4.	Prepare deployment schedule
		5.	Roll-out
	Product	1.	Detailed list of tasks and responsible parties with due dates
		2.	Identify and satisfy needs for management, support, and training on new system/network

Figure 12-19   Final Proposal, Approval, and Implementation

Preparing a Comprehensive Budget

It has been the author's experience that senior management can accept well-organized, comprehensive budgets representing large sums of money. What has been found to be unacceptable are the so-called hidden or forgotten costs of network and systems implementation often left out of budgets.

As a result, a comprehensive budget format needed to be developed that would help to identify as many elements of potential implementation and operation costs as possible. Figure 12-20 illustrates a sample budget page from the **comprehensive systems and networking budget model.** Along the vertical axis, major budget categories are listed including

- Hardware/equipment.
- Software.
- Personnel.

Proposal Number:		Description:		
	Acquisition	Operation	Incremental Change Anticipated Growth	**TOTALS**
Hardware	Data center: Network operations: Application Development:	Data center: Network operations: Application Development:	Data center: Network operations: Application Development:	Data center: Network operations: Application Development:
Software	Data center: Network operations: Application Development:	Data center: Network operations: Application Development:	Data center: Network operations: Application Development:	Data center: Network operations: Application Development:
Personnel	Data center: Network operations: Application Development:	Data center: Network operations: Application Development:	Data center: Network operations: Application Development:	Data center: Network operations: Application Development:
Communications	Data center: Network operations: Application Development:	Data center: Network operations: Application Development:	Data center: Network operations: Application Development:	Data center: Network operations: Application Development:
Facilities	Data center: Network operations: Application Development:	Data center: Network operations: Application Development:	Data center: Network operations: Application Development:	Data center: Network operations: Application Development:
TOTALS	Data center: Network operations: Application Development:	Data center: Network operations: Application Development:	Data center: Network operations: Application Development:	Data center: Network operations: Application Development:

Figure 12-20   Comprehensive Systems and Networking Budget Model

- Communications (carrier services).

- Facilities.

There is nothing sacred about these categories. Change them to whatever best reflects your situation. The important point is to organize the budget grid in such a way that all possible costs are identified in advance.

The horizontal axis has three columns representing the major categories of costs with respect to time. Networking and systems budgets typically focused only on the **acquisition costs** of the new system. Even within the acquisition category, costs associated with personnel additions, changes, and training were often omitted. Likewise, costs involved with facilities upgrades or changes such as electrical wiring, cabinets, wiring closets, or security systems were also likely to be overlooked or unanticipated. Preventing surprises such as these requires a two-step approach:

1. Required or anticipated facilities upgrades and personnel needs are identified during the location-by-location survey as part of the final preparation of the RFP.

2. Any legitimate need that was identified in the location-by-location survey should be budgeted for in the comprehensive systems and networking budget model.

Even a budget that identifies all acquisition costs is still neither complete nor accurate. Two other major categories of costs must be accounted for:

1. Operations.

2. Incremental change/anticipated growth.

Operations Costs   **Operations costs** would include estimated monthly costs for leased line or dial-up line usage as well as the estimated cost for the additional electricity required to run new equipment. If additional cooling, heating, or environmental control will be required as a result of system implementation, these costs should be included as well. Service contracts, maintenance agreements, or budgeted time and materials for repairs should also be considered as operation costs.

ANTICIPATING AND BUDGETING FOR NETWORK GROWTH

Practical Advice and Information

Another aspect of project budgeting often overlooked at proposal time is the cost associated with the anticipated growth of the system during the first 3–5 years after implementation. These **incremental change costs** may be significant if certain elements of the system or network design are not expandable or only moderately so. As an example, perhaps a remote site starts with a four-port STDM as its networking device. To add four more users, an upgrade kit could be installed for $1300. However, to add a ninth user would require replacing the entire STDM with a higher capacity unit at a cost of $5000. Although the costs in this example may not be precise, the point of the example remains. Anticipated growth should be budgeted. In some cases, this budgeting process of the anticipated growth may cause changes in the equipment choices at acquisition time.

To accurately budget for anticipated systems and network growth, the network analyst must have access to strategic business plans that outline the anticipated growth of the business. After all, the implemented system and network are a direct result of the business requirements, including the required ability to respond to changing business conditions, in accordance with the overall business vision as articulated in a strategic business plan. Depending on the corporate culture, network analysts may not be allowed access to such strategic business planning information.

As shown in Figure 12-20, each budget category that is formed by an intersection of a column and row can be further subdivided if such department budgeting is required within the overall project budget. In Figure 12-20, the three categories shown correspond to three typical departments within an overall M.I.S. operation: Data Center, Network Operations, and Application Development. Make this budget grid fit your business. If departmental or cost center budgeting is not required for your business, ignore these subcategories. If other departmental designations are more appropriate, substitute them.

Managerial
Perspective

RETURN ON INVESTMENT, TOTAL COST OF OWNERSHIP, AND TOTAL BENEFIT OF OWNERSHIP

Increasingly, networking and information systems professionals are being called upon to quantify the positive impact of their projects and implemented systems in financial terms. A variety of options exist for this quantification. **Return on investment (ROI)** is perhaps the most traditional approach to measuring cost/benefit and is well suited to incremental upgrades of existing systems. However, for entirely new or innovative projects, although costs may be accurately projected, projected benefits are more intangible and are far more difficult to quantify in real terms. **Total cost of ownership (TCO)** is another popular measure for objectively comparing the relative costs of alternative approaches or potential technology strategies. However, there are no universally accepted methods for calculating TCO and, as a result, the factor has become widely used as a marketing tool by vendors trying to convince corporations to migrate to a particular technology platform. Furthermore, TCO ignores the benefit side of the equation. Consequently, **total benefit of ownership (TBO)** tries to quantify the usability and associated benefits of technological options. TBO attempts to quantify productivity increases as well as cost reduction. However, to properly quantify increased productivity, one must first measure current levels of productivity by developing evaluation criteria so that baseline data can be gathered.

■ THE NETWORK IMPLEMENTATION PROCESS

Although specific details of an implementation process will vary from one project to the next, there are a few general points worth making. Perhaps most importantly, regardless of how well designed an information system or network may be, it is still essential to test that design in as safe a manner as possible. "Safe" in this case could be defined as the least likely to have a tragic effect on production systems or networks.

Pilot tests are a popular way to safely roll out new systems or networks. For example, bring one retail store on-line and monitor performance, fix unanticipated problems, and gain management experience before deploying the system on a wider scale. Honest feedback and performance evaluations are essential to smooth system implementations. User groups can be a helpful feedback mechanism if managed skillfully to prevent degeneration into nothing more than gripe sessions.

Project Management

Another important skill to a smooth implementation process is effective project management. Detailed task lists including task description, scheduled start and finish dates, actual start and finish dates, and responsible parties are at the heart of good project management. Some systems and network professionals use project management software. The author has used project management software on occasion but has found that, in general, that loading and maintaining all of the project detail in the project management software were more work than managing the project manually. Although perhaps overly simplistic, the general rule of thumb as to when to use project management software goes something like this:

- When a project is too complicated to manage manually, then you may benefit from the use of project management software.

People Are Important

Despite this book's focus on networking hardware and software, people are the most important element of any systems implementation. Buy-in at every stage by all affected parties was stressed throughout the network analysis and design process to assure that everyone gets behind the new system and network and that all parties feel that they had an opportunity to make their thoughts known. The best designed network will fail miserably without the support of people.

Therefore, a key element of system and network implementation is to assure that people-related needs such as management, support, and training have been thoroughly researched and appropriately addressed.

■ AUTOMATING THE NETWORK DEVELOPMENT LIFE CYCLE

Sophisticated software packages now exist to assist network analysts in the analysis and design of large and complicated networks. These software tools can vary greatly in sophistication, functionality, scope, and price.

Managerial Perspective

THE BUSINESS CASE FOR COMPUTER-ASSISTED NETWORK ENGINEERING

The entire network development life cycle is sometimes referred to as **network engineering.** The use of software tools of one type or another to assist in this process is known as **computer-assisted network engineering (CANE).** Companies must be able to make a strong business case for the payback of this computer-assisted network engineering software since the prices for the software generally range from $10,000 to $30,000 per copy. Besides the obvious use of the software for designing new networks "from scratch," several other uses of computer-assisted network engineering software can offer significant paybacks.

By using analysis and design software to model their current network, companies are able to run **optimization routines** to reconfigure circuits and/or network hardware to deliver data more efficiently. In the case of optimization software, "efficiently" can mean maximized performance, minimized price, or a combination of both.

When current networks have grown over time in a somewhat helter-skelter manner without any major redesigns, network optimization software can redesign networks, which can save anywhere from thousands of dollars per month to millions of dollars per year depending on the size of the network.

Another important use of analysis and design software on a corporation's current network is for **billing verification.** Most analysis and design packages have up-to-date tariff information from multiple regional and long-distance carriers. By inputting a company's current network design in the analysis and design software and by using the tariff tables to price individual circuits within that network, prices generated from the tariff tables can be compared to recent phone bills. Such verification often uncovers discrepancies in billing amounts, which can be significant.

Either of the two previous uses of computer-assisted network engineering software could pay back the cost of that software within 6 months to 1 year. Another very common use of this type of software with a less tangible short-term financial payback but significant future benefits is **proactive performance assurance.** For the rapidly growing network, the ability of this software to simulate different possible future combinations of traffic usage, circuits, and networking equipment can avoid costly future network congestion problems or failures.

Figure 12-21 illustrates the various categories of computer-assisted network engineering software along with a few examples of each type. There are many other software packages available in each category offering a range of features at a range of prices. The differentiation between network design tools and network simulation tools is not as definitive as Figure 12-21 might imply. In fact, most network design tools now include at least some network simulation capabilities as well as network design intelligence to actively assist in the network design.

Analysis and Design Tools

Figure 12-22 lists some of the more common elements of network design tools in an input-processing-output model format. The following is a listing of some of the important features to look for when considering network analysis and design tools:

- Tariff databases—How current are they? How many carriers and types of circuits are included? How often are the tariff databases updated? Is there an

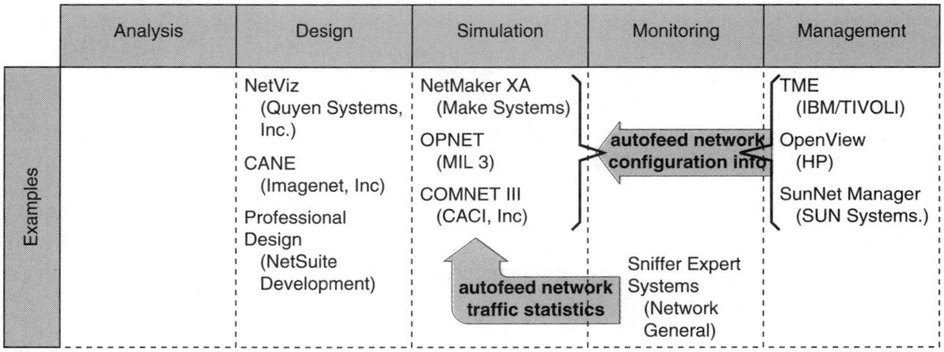

Figure 12-21   Computer-Assisted Network Engineering Software

Phase	Network Design Tool Features
Input	• Input requirements definitions • Drop network objects • Auto-discovery on existing networks from enterprise network management packages such as HP's OpenView, IBM's NetView, or Sun's SunNet Manager • Assign traffic characteristics and distribution • Link objects with circuits • Assign attributes and protocols to network devices and circuits • Build a computer-assisted network model
Processing	• Validate the design (which objects can be connected to which other objects) • Roll up and simulate a fully loaded network • Assure protocol compatibility • Assess reliability and security • Test alternative configurations for cost and performance optimization • Conduct what-if testing
Output	• Detailed network equipment requirements by vendor • Detailed transmission circuit requirements • Detailed protocol design • Bill of materials listing all items to be purchased

Figure 12-22   Input-Processing-Output Model for Network Design Tools

additional charge for tariff database updates? Tariff structures have become very complicated and are calculated in a variety of different ways. Confirm that the tariff database in the analysis and design software includes all necessary tariffs.

• Response time calculation—Does the software take into consideration the processing time of the particular host computer that may be a part of the network? Can user-defined elements, e.g., applications programs of various types or different types of networking equipment, be taken into account in the response time calculation?

• Multiple transport protocols—Can the software take into consideration the effect of various transport protocols on response time? How many protocols are included? SNA, DECNet, ISDN, TCP/IP, X.25, frame relay, ATM, satellite, microwave, cellular?

• Multiple topologies—How many different topologies can the software model? Examples: hierarchical, hub and spoke, mesh, point-to-point, multipoint, concentrated, packet-switched, multiple host.

• Circuit design—Can the software configure circuits for a combination of simultaneous voice and data traffic or must voice and data circuits be designed separately? Can multiplexers be cascaded? Are tail circuits allowed?

• Financial—Can the software roll up costs for network equipment as well as for circuits? Can costs as well as performance be optimized simultaneously? Can costs be compared across multiple carriers for comparison shopping?

- Input/output—Can protocol analyzers or network monitoring or management systems be interfaced directly to the analysis and design software for automatic input of current system performance data? Can analysis and design results be output directly to spreadsheet, database, and word processing packages?

- Operating platforms—What platform does the design software run over? NT, UNIX, SunOS, Win '95?

- Design platforms—What types of networks can the software design? LAN only, WAN only, LAN/WAN and internetworking?

- Product library—Different network design packages can contain varying numbers of network device objects that contain manufacturer-specific information and specifications.

- Design validation—The software should validate that all devices are accounted for, all segment lengths conform to standards, and all hardware is properly matched according to protocols.

Simulation Tools

Simulation software tools are also sometimes known as **performance engineering** software tools. All simulation systems share a similar trait in that the overall network performance that they are able to model is a result of the net effect of a series of mathematical formulas. These mathematical formulas represent and are derived from the actual performance of the circuits and networking equipment that comprise the final network design.

The value of a simulation system is in its ability to predict the performance of various networking scenarios, otherwise known as **what-if-analysis.** Simulation software uses the current network configuration as a starting point and applies what-if scenarios. The benefits of a good network simulation package include

- Ability to spot network bottlenecks such as overworked servers, network failures, or disk capacity problems.

- Ability to test new applications and network configurations before actual deployment. New applications may run well in a controlled test environment but may perform quite differently on the shared enterprise network.

- Ability to re-create circumstances to reproduce intermittent or occasional network problems.

- Ability to replicate traffic volume as well as traffic transaction type and protocol mix.

The key characteristics that distinguish simulation software are as follows:

- Network types—Which different types of networks can be simulated? Circuit-switched, packet-switched, store-and-forward, packet-radio, VSAT, microwave?

- Network scope—How many of the following can the simulation software model either individually or in combination with one another? Modems and multiplexers, LANs, NetWare only, internetworks, WANs, MANs?

- Network services—How many of the following advanced services can be modeled? Frame relay, ISDN (BRI and PRI), SMDS, X.25?

- Network devices—Some simulation systems have developed performance profiles of individual networking devices to the point where they can model particular networking devices (bridges, routers, MUXs) made by particular manufacturers.

- Network protocols—In addition to the network transport protocols listed in the analysis and design section, different router-to-router protocols can have a dramatic impact on network performance. Examples: RIP, OSPF.

- Different data traffic attributes—As studied in previous chapters, all data traffic does not have identical transmission needs or characteristics. Can the software simulate data with different traits? For example: bursty LAN data, streaming digitized voice or video, real-time transaction-oriented data, batch-oriented file transfer data.

- Traffic data entry—Any simulation needs traffic statistics to run. How these traffic statistics may be entered can make a major difference in the ease of use of the simulation system. Possibilities include manual entry by users of traffic data collected elsewhere, traffic data entered "live" through a direct interface to a protocol analyzer, and a traffic generator, which generates simulated traffic according to the user's parameters or auto-discovery from enterprise network management systems.

- User interface—Many simulation software tools now offer easy-to-use graphical user interfaces with point-and-click network design capability for flexi-ble "what-if" analysis. Some, but not all, produce graphical maps that can be output to printers or plotters. Others require users to learn a proce-dure-oriented programming language.

- Simulation presentation—Some simulation tools have the ability to animate the performance of the simulated network in real time whereas others per-form all mathematical calculations and then play back the simulation when those calculations are complete.

Object-Oriented Technology Meets Network Engineering   As network simulation soft-ware has shifted its intended audience from network engineers well versed in the intricacies of network performance optimization to network analysts most familiar with networking requirements, the designers of that software have had to make some fairly radical changes in the ease of use as well as the sophistication of the software.

The mathematical formulas representing the performance characteristics of individual networking elements become the methods of the network objects, whereas the attributes describe the details such as manufacturer, model, price, capacity, etc. By merely clicking on one of these network objects representing a particular network device or circuit, the user automatically adds all of the associ-ated methods and attributes of that network object to the network simulation. Particular applications programs or transport protocols can also be represented as network objects and be clicked upon to be added to the overall network simu-lation. In this way, all seven layers of the OSI model can be included in the final simulation run.

Management: Proactive LAN Management

Sophisticated proactive network management software has the ability to monitor network performance on an ongoing basis and to report unusual network conditions or activities to a network management workstation. The term *unusual network conditions* is really user definable. **Thresholds,** or desired limits, of certain performance characteristics are set by the user. In some cases, the user may have no idea what to set these thresholds at. To aid in such a situation, some management systems can record "normal" performance characteristics over an extended period of time to gather valid **baseline data.**

Some management software systems even have the ability to feed this "alarm data" back to certain simulation systems that can simulate the "threshold crossing" and allow what-if analysis to be performed to diagnose the cause of the problem and propose a solution.

■ THE FUTURE OF THE AUTOMATED NETWORK DEVELOPMENT LIFE CYCLE

Some of the trends mentioned in the previous sections will continue as computer-assisted network engineering software tools continue to evolve and mature. The key word in terms of the future of these various tools that comprise the automated network development life cycle is integration. The real potential of network engineering software integration has just barely scratched the surface and only in a few vendor-specific cases.

For instance, as can be seen in Figure 12-21, certain protocol analyzers such as Network General's Distributed Sniffer have the ability to interface directly into certain network simulation systems such as Comnet III and LANSim. In such a scenario, actual traffic statistics from the current network configuration are fed directly into the mathematical engines underlying the simulation software. Such vendor-specific, product-specific integration is significant. However, to have true transparent integration of all computer-assisted network engineering tools, a more open and standardized approach must be undertaken.

Horizontal Integration

Figure 12-23 illustrates, on a conceptual level, how such a standardized open architecture offering seamless **horizontal integration** might be constructed. Rather than having to know the intricacies, and, in some cases, the trade secrets, of how each other's products work, vendors of computer-assisted network engineering software merely pass the output from their particular software product to a "neutral" data platform known as **CNIP,** or **common network information platform.** Any other CANE tool that could use that output to provide transparent integration with other CANE tools would import the standardized, formatted data from the common network information platform. The end result of the use of such a standardized platform for CANE tool data output and retrieval is the seamless integration of a variety of CANE tools spanning all phases of the network development life cycle.

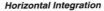

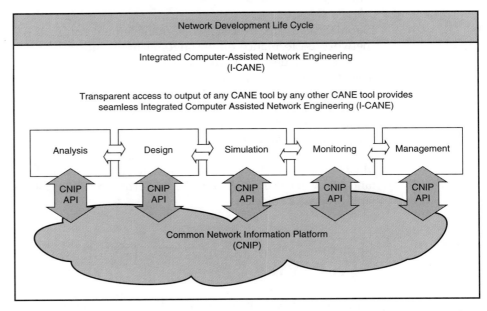

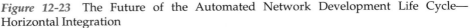

Figure 12-23 The Future of the Automated Network Development Life Cycle—Horizontal Integration

The Final Frontier: Vertical Integration

Integration implies not only horizontal integration with software from other categories of the CANE family but also **vertical integration** with applications development platforms such as CASE (computer-assisted software engineering) tools. Integrated CASE (I-CASE) tools could generate code for a new corporate-wide client/server application and could download key information concerning that new application to the CANE suite of software products to predict network impact of the new proposed application.

Proactive network management is the result when the network implications of the deployment of new network-intensive applications are known before the actual release of the software.

As can be seen in Figure 12-24, the actual gateway between the I-CASE and **I-CANE** tools may not be a simple API. Due to the sophistication of the interface between these two platforms, expert systems may be required to dynamically model the relationships between the objects underlying the CASE tools and those underlying the CANE tools.

Extending the vertical integration above the CASE tools and the strategic information systems that they produce, expert systems could again maintain the relationships between major software platforms. Applications layer objects used by the CASE tools could be dynamically linked via expert systems to the objects representing the business rules and processes which, in turn, support strategic business goals and objectives.

Thus, although current technology may not possess the capability, the business information system of the future may interface to the strategic business planning person who amends strategic business goals and objects via a graphical user inter-

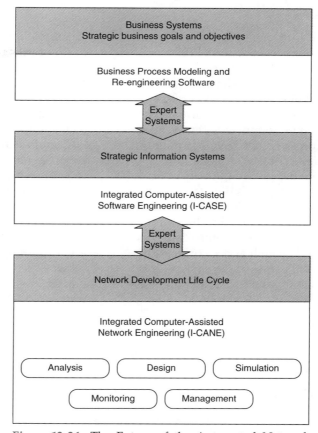

Figure 12-24 The Future of the Automated Network Development Life Cycle—Vertical Integration

face and point-and-click manipulation of business process objects. The changes caused by this business process re-engineering are immediately forwarded via an expert system interface to the strategic information systems design which supports these business processes. Applications program changes are automatically generated by integrated CASE tools.

Resultant changes in the applications programs produced by the CASE tools are immediately forwarded via expert systems to the integrated computer-assisted network engineering platform. Finally, network objects, circuits and networking devices, are amended as necessary due to the impact of the new applications programs. Network simulation programs are automatically run to access network impact while network design optimization programs automatically reconfigure the network design to adjust most appropriately to the new network impacts. The amazing part of this whole process is that it was initiated originally by a change in strategic business objectives. The future of computer-assisted network engineering software represents one of the most exciting opportunities in data communications and networking while adhering to the overall top-down model philosophy of network design.

SUMMARY

As has been stated throughout the text, network design cannot be done in a vacuum. Effective network designs will only result from strict adherence to the top-down model by beginning with an analysis of business objectives rather than networking technology. Strategic information system design must be conducted after business objectives and processes have been thoroughly examined. The importance of strategic information system design lies not only in its delivery of business objectives but also in its role as a template for network design.

Information systems may be developed in-house or may be outsourced. In either case, it is essential to have a thorough and accurate RFP (request for proposal). Data traffic analysis is a multistep process that ensures that all potential sources of network traffic are identified and accurately quantified. Circuit analysis and configuration alternatives matches the proper WAN service to each location's data delivery needs, whereas network hardware analysis and configuration alternatives matches the proper networking hardware with the location's input data and the installed WAN service.

Comprehensive budgets go beyond the typical proposal focus of acquisition costs to include categories for operations and anticipated network growth for a variety of cost centers and categories. Finally, although network design has been a manual process for many years, automated network design and simulation tools are beginning to become more popular as network scope and complexity make "back of the napkin" network design both impractical and unwise.

KEY TERMS

acquisition costs, 512
baseline data, 519
billing verification, 515
business functional areas, 494
business process re-engineering, 494
buy-in, 487
CANE, 514
circuit analysis and configuration
   alternatives, 504
CNIP, 519
common network information
   platform, 519
comprehensive systems and
   networking budget model, 511
computer-assisted network
   engineering, 514
critical success factors,486
data traffic analysis, 504
decision points, 495
document flow analysis, 505
evaluation criteria, 492
feasibility study, 491

horizontal integration, 519
I-CANE, 520
incremental change costs, 512
make or buy decision, 503
management abstract, 499
mission-critical analysis, 506
NDLC, 484
network analysis and design
   methodology, 485
network development life cycle, 484
network engineering, 514
network hardware analysis and
   configuration alternatives, 504
operations costs, 512
opportunities for improvement, 495
optimization routines, 514
payload type analysis, 505
percent-of-fit goal, 502
performance engineering, 517
pilot tests, 513
proactive performance assurance,
   515

process, 483
process flow analysis, 505
product, 483
protocol stack analysis, 506
request for proposal, 497
return on investment, 513
RFP, 497
ROI, 513
strategic information system
   design, 492
TBO, 513
TCO, 513
three-pile approach, 496
thresholds, 519
time studies, 506
total benefit of ownership, 513
total cost of ownership, 513
traffic volume analysis, 506
transaction analysis, 505
vertical integration, 520
what-if analysis, 517

REVIEW QUESTIONS

1. Where does the network development life cycle fit in the overall systems development life cycle?
2. How can one ensure that a network design will meet strategic business requirements?
3. How can a company cost justify the expense of network analysis and design software?
4. What does optimization accomplish in network design software?
5. What are the two major characteristics on which networks are optimized?
6. Can these two optimization characteristics conflict with each other?
7. How is horizontal integration of CANE tools likely to be enabled?
8. How is vertical integration of CANE tools likely to be enabled?
9. What is so significant about the comprehensive systems and networking budget model?
10. What is meant by the term *critical success factor?* Discuss three.
11. What is the significance of process and product in the network analysis and design methodology?
12. What are the important elements of data traffic analysis?
13. Explain the relationship of data traffic analysis, circuit analysis, and network hardware analysis.
14. Explain the importance of evaluation criteria and percent-of-fit goals to the overall network design process.
15. What is the purpose of an RFP?
16. What are the major components of an RFP?
17. How can the RFP process be kept as objective and nonpolitical as possible?
18. What types of information must be gathered about each corporate location?
19. How can a network analyst assure widespread support of new systems or network implementations?
20. What is cyclic about the network development life cycle?
21. How can computer-assisted network engineering software products exhibit the same cyclic nature?
22. Why are seasonal or occasional differences in transaction volumes or processes so important to network design?
23. What are some of the potential advantages and disadvantages of outsourcing network analysis and design functions?
24. How can so-called back-room politics affect network development and how can a network analyst minimize such effects?
25. What does corporate culture have to do with the method in which a network development project is carried out?
26. What does buy-in imply beyond simple agreement and why is it important to the network development life cycle?
27. How can responses to RFPs be objectively evaluated to determine those vendors worthy of further consideration?
28. What is the role of protocol analyzers in the network development life cycle and in the functionality of network optimization tools?
29. How do network analysts assure that they have a clear understanding of a business problem before proceeding to a network solution?
30. What is the importance of baseline data to the ability to articulate the eventual success or failure of a network development effort?
31. How can too much information be as detrimental as too little information for decision-makers? What effect on network design might this have?
32. What is the danger in not starting the network development life cycle with an examination of business layer issues but merely networking business operations as they currently exist?
33. How can the amount of work invested in the development of an RFP be justified?
34. Why is the customer's proposed project schedule important to potential vendors?
35. What is the importance of the corporate location-by-location survey?
36. Although specific questions asked of vendors in an RFP may vary, what are the overall objectives in asking for this information?
37. How can a network analysis project leader assure that vendor demonstrations are objective and useful and don't revert to "dog and pony" shows?
38. What are some of the difficulties in transporting voice and data simultaneously?
39. What are some of the promising network technologies for transmission of video and data on both the LAN and WAN?
40. How can an I-P-O diagram be used to assist in the proper selection of network hardware devices?
41. Describe those items beyond acquisition costs that should be included in a network budget as well as the importance of those items.
42. What impact has object-oriented programming had on network design and simulation tools?
43. What is so proactive about proactive LAN management? What is the likely business impact of proactive LAN management?
44. Differentiate between ROI, TCO, and TBO in terms of methodology as well as appropriateness for network development projects.

ACTIVITIES

1. You have been asked to design a network for a state lottery commission connecting between 1500 and 2000 outlets to lottery headquarters. Without knowing any further details, what might some of the strategic requirements for such a network be? In other words, from a business perspective, if the state lottery is to prosper as a business, what characteristics must the network supporting this business venture exhibit?

2. Concerning the state lottery example, how important are seasonality or peak transaction periods to network design and performance? What network characteristics might reflect this level of required performance?

3. You have been asked to be project leader of a network design team. Rumor has it that the company president's goal partner already has been hired to install the network and that this network design project is intended to give the appearance of an objective process. Prepare a detailed outline of your approach including long-range project plan, detailed task list, meetings to schedule, and alternative courses of action based on the results of those scheduled meetings.

4. You are in charge of a nationwide voice and data network that has grown in a piecemeal fashion and may benefit from design optimization using automated network design software. It is essential to demonstrate a relatively short payback period for the software investment. The software must contain current tariff information from a number of different carriers so that actual installation and operating costs are generated along with various network design scenarios. Use buyer's guides found in professional periodicals or the Internet to find product information and pricing information. Determine which packages might best meet your needs and write a memo to your company president outlining your recommendation.

5. Modify the requirements in the previous question to include a need to model all seven layers of the OSI model rather than the more typical ability of network design/simulation packages to model only layers 1–3. By modeling all seven layers, you should be able to model the impact of a given application or transport protocol. This package must allow you to define your own objects for any layer of the OSI model.

6. Modify the requirements in question 4 to include a need to model the performance of network devices from a particular manufacturer. For example, it may be a requirement to differentiate

between network performance using switches and routers manufactured by Cisco and Bay Networks.

7. Prepare a technology analysis grid for network design and simulation software that shows the difference in features to justify the differences in software costs.

8. Investigate an opportunity to perform a network analysis and design project within your department or business. By dividing the entire project into sections to be performed by various teams, more can be accomplished in a shorter time. Perhaps your instructor, supervisor, or department chairperson has such an opportunity in mind. If not, consider one of the following scenarios:
   a. Develop a network to deliver local and remote e-mail interoperability.
   b. Develop a network to deliver transparent database distribution.
   c. Develop a network to support remote access and transparent telecommuting.
   d. Develop a network to support Internet access and a corporate Web site.
   e. Develop a network to support desktop videoconferencing.
   f. Develop a network to deliver CAD/CAM engineering drawings to a manufacturing environment or shop floor.
   g. Develop a network that can handle electronic funds transfer between banks on an international basis.
   h. Develop a network with a bandwidth hierarchy scheme including frame relay, T-1, and ATM.
   The outcome of such studies may not be a physical network design. A great deal of meaningful learning can take place on the way to a physical design. Take a top-down approach by starting with strategic business layer concerns. Try to get through the development of the RFP and the data traffic analysis stages.

9. Choose a networked application for your department or business.
   a. Gather baseline data on this process.
   b. What is the nature of the transactions involved?
   c. How much data is transmitted per transaction?
   d. Perform a time study to produce a traffic volume requirements profile.
   e. What networking resources are currently involved?

10. Describe how a network analyst might cope with a "Because that's the way we've always done it" attitude during the business process analysis phase of the network development life cycle.

11. Develop a corporate location survey covering people, hardware, software, media, data, networking, and physical plant. Use this survey on at least five corporate locations or academic departments. Re-evaluate the survey and modify and/or improve it as necessary.

12. Prepare a data traffic analysis report on the data transmitted between these five locations by performing as many types of data traffic analysis as possible from the types listed in the chapter. Protocol stack analysis must be completed for each location.

13. Contact your local or long-distance carrier to determine how one gets a quote for various types of data services. Are there different contacts for
   a. Analog leased lines.
   b. DDS services.
   c. ISDN.
   d. Switched 56K.
   e. X.25.
   f. Frame relay.
   g. ATM.
   h. ADSL.

14. One of the vendors that responded favorably to the RFP has been in business less than 3 years. What are your concerns and should these concerns be addressed?

15. Invite a local vendor of data communications equipment to present a guest lecture or demonstration. Notice how the vendor responds to questions.

16. Prepare a comprehensive budget proposal for one of the networks proposed in question 8.

CASE STUDY

Navigating the Corporate Tempest

As companies energetically plow millions of dollars into IS to fund everything from elaborate client/server applications to enterprise-wide intranets, managing these new projects has naturally gotten tougher and tougher.

True, network administrators who are laying out backbones, managing multiple protocols, and expanding their user base by leaps and bounds have to juggle hefty budgets and allocate resources just like their counterparts in applications development. But they also have to shoulder burdens their software brethren need not worry about.

For starters, there's nothing sexy about network infrastructure. Because you can't flash it on-screen like a sporty new GUI, it's the kind of thing upper management finds perplexing. Second, teams working on various network projects often span the globe, with members on several continents. These projects also tend to include several ven-dors, who can be testy about accepting responsibility for system misfires, says Bill Munson, senior consultant for Keane Inc., a software-services and -consulting company in Boston.

"It's easy for hardware vendors to say their product isn't the problem," Munson says. "They often blame the software or the architecture."

Such challenges are now part of everyday network-project management, which has become very demanding, very quickly. As a result, many LAN managers are finding themselves assigned to high-stakes projects and carrying out work that is dramatically different from what they're used to. But after early mistakes, IS is finally learning how to chart smooth courses on rough project-management seas.

LAN Managers Can't Juggle

Fueling the rising concern over the dearth of project-management skills is IS's continuing evolution from specialty shop to business department. At most companies, the techies who once stoked the mainframe have been recast as business analysts, trading nebulous titles such as "systems operator" for such buttoned-down versions as "customer account manager."

This new focus is generating project opportunities on a scale most departments have never seen, says Ann Senn, a partner in the IT practice at Deloitte & Touche Consulting Group in Minneapolis. Stuck in maintenance mode as they tended to legacy applications, IS staffs simply didn't need to know how to shepherd complex, 18-month projects to completion or handle huge budgets.

Computer downsizing changed all that. As senior management uttered the client/server mantra, network managers and others in IS were pressed—untrained—into service as project managers. Not surprisingly, many of the results have been dismal.

Recent research by The Standish Group International Inc., a consulting company in Dennis, Mass., showed that one-third of applications-development projects were canceled. Of those that saw completion, a scant 16 percent finished on time and on budget. The cost of such corporate bungling? Standish estimates that in 1995 U.S. companies and government agencies racked up $81 billion in costs for canceled software projects.

Those poor scores undoubtedly reflect all technology sectors. "Whether it's robotics, hardware, software, or biochemistry, project management is not a practiced skill," says Orion Kopelman, president of Global Brain Inc., a consultancy in Palo Alto, Calif. "People don't think of project management as a science."

One company Kopelman met with proudly pointed out its informal project-management process: "They called it the 'pizza theory'—order enough pizzas for the team, and it'll come up with something."

Professional project managers wince at such attitudes. Face it, they say: Just because someone can set up a WAN in his or her sleep doesn't mean that person has what it takes to keep a raucous meeting from falling apart.

In the Madison, Wis., offices of TDS Computing Services, Bob Kranz supervises a team of project managers that oversees everything from infrastructure to applications development to training plans. "As a project manager, you get work done through others," says Kranz, manager of development support services at TDS, the information-services division of Telephone and Data Systems Inc., a provider of telecommunications services and products. "That's very different from working in task-specific situations."

Indeed, beyond project-management basics such as critical path and resource allocation, a network manager's ability to usher in all of a project's elements on time is a key talent. More often than not, this can mean serving as taskmaster for unruly team members and even vendors.

Keane's Bill Munson was recently called in to assist a client installing a LAN. An unresponsive telecommunications provider had slowed the installation process, and the project manager was having little success reining in the vendor. "Getting the hardware vendors to put this client higher on their list of priorities was an issue," says Munson. "A lot of project managers see those kinds of issues as being outside of their control," but they're very much a part of the job, he says.

Recognition and Some Help

While software-development teams typically work out of offices at the same site, hardware and network projects often include far-flung members. The migratory effort required to upgrade Microsoft Windows 3.1 to Windows NT, for example, means not only redesigning the network but also coordinating the procurement of new hardware and software through multiple sites. And this can require a planning ability on a par with, say, the recent Olympic Games' opening ceremonies in Atlanta.

But hardware and software projects actually share many characteristics. One is the tentativeness by both IS and upper management to apply project management to client/server and network projects. "There still isn't strong recognition of project management or a lot of maturity in using it," says Denys Mueller, a project manager at Northrop Grumman Corp.'s Data Systems and Services Division in Pico Rivera, Calif.

Mueller recently oversaw the implementation of a $28 million, three-tier client/server project for the U.S. Air Force. At "Grumman, we don't use advanced tools [such as] groupware and ABT [Corp. Workbench]. As a result, we keep falling back on pencil and paper to manage projects," he says.

Tools and methodologies are available, however. TDS' Kranz uses Microsoft Project Manager and Workbench to develop schedules, and he has also developed in-house work breakdown plans and templates. In addition, TDS uses Andersen Consulting's Method/1. Network-integrator Vanstar Corp. has standardized on Lotus Notes 4.0 to facilitate communication among it project teams.

What's the best criterion for choosing project-management aids? Common sense, according to most project pros. "Methodologies don't vary a lot from one place to another," says Deloitte & Touche's Senn. "It doesn't matter what you use; it matters that it fits the situation."

More companies are making project management a permanent IS and network process. When the IS department at United Services Automobile Association's Investment Management Co. began implementing project management in its San Antonio office two years ago, "we had a lot of resistance," says Magda Santos, a systems planner at IMCO. Time-strapped IS members said they were too busy for planning meetings, "but users were telling us we were always late with projects," says Santos. "It was a major culture shock."

Project planning at IMCO had always been informal: "Everyone knew there was a plan, but no one knew what it was," says Santos, who acts as the liaison between IS and upper management. Eventually, the idea took off, and since then project-management policies have been adopted by other USAA divisions. In fact, many USAA and IMCO personnel are now taking the Project Management Institute's official certification exam.

TDS is experimenting with project-management solutions, including the establishment of a central project office, staffed by strong managers with at least 10 years' experience managing multiple large-scale projects. "They'd get the real ugly ones, like the Year 2000 projects," says Kranz.

Small improvements can make a difference, too. Fresh from a recent conference seminar, Jon Hockenberry, a senior project manager, returned to his Houston office at Shell Services Co. with a new idea. He would replace the loose, informal scope project statements his teams had been preparing with carefully crafted, mission statements. The new statements would spell out the business case, list the people involved, and identify the people with the most influence over the project.

"It's broader than what we had been using, and it makes people think about the project early on," says Hockenberry. And it doesn't take long: "We [can] nail the first draft in about two hours. It really sets the stage for the project and what you're trying to accomplish.

Of course, even the most thorough plans are no match for quick corporate decisions. After IMCO meticulously planned and implemented a client/server-based shareholder accounting and reporting system, the company chose to outsource its accounting and simply killed the application.

Source: Deborah Asbrand, "Navigating the Corporate Tempest," *LAN Times,* vol. 13, no. 19 (September 2, 1996), p. 49. Copyright © September 2, 1996 by McGraw–Hill, New York. Reprinted by permission of McGraw–Hill, New York.

BUSINESS CASE STUDY QUESTIONS ···

Activities

1. Complete a top-down model for this case by gleaning facts from the case and placing them in the proper layer of the top-down model. After completing the top-down model, analyze and detail those instances where requirements were clearly passed down from upper layers to lower layers of the model and where solutions to those requirements were passed up from lower layers to upper layers of the model.

2. Detail any questions about the case that may occur to you for which answers are not clearly stated in the article.

Business

1. What are some of the challenges network managers face in administering large network infrastructure projects?

2. Why have project management skills become more critical for network managers?

3. What is the pizza theory of project management?

4. What are some of the responsibilities and duties of a project manager beyond simple task management?

5. What training or certification options in project management are available for information systems professionals?

6. What are the key pieces of information that should be included in a project's mission statement?

Application

1. What are some statistics that indicate the extent and cost of ineffective management of major application development projects?

Network

1. How do network development projects tend to differ from application development projects and how does this difference affect required project management skills?

Technology

1. What types of technology can be employed to assist in project management? Give examples.

2. What are some criteria for choosing the right project management technology?

CHAPTER 13

NETWORK SECURITY

Concepts Reinforced

OSI Model	Internet Suite of Protocols Model
Top-Down Model	Standards and Protocols

Concepts Introduced

Security Policy Development	Virus Protection
Firewalls	Authentication
Encryption	Applied Security Technology

OBJECTIVES

After mastering the material in this chapter, you should

1. Understand the many processes involved with the development of a comprehensive security policy.

2. Understand the importance of a well developed and implemented security policy and associated people processes to effective security technology implementation.

3. Understand the concepts, protocols, standards, and technology related to virus protection.

4. Understand the concepts, protocols, standards, and technology related to firewalls.

5. Understand the concepts, protocols, standards, and technology related to authentication.

6. Understand the concepts, protocols, standards, and technology related to encryption.

■ INTRODUCTION

As interest and activity concerning the Internet have mushroomed, and as telecommuters and remote users are increasingly in need of access to corporate data, network security has become a dominant topic in data communications. As the various processes, concepts, protocols, standards, and technology associated with network security are reviewed in this chapter, it is important to remember the importance of people and their basic honesty and integrity as the underlying foundation for any successful network security implementation. Merely throwing network security technology at a problem without the benefit of a comprehensive, vigorously, enforced network security policy including sound business processes will surely not produce desired results. As the saying goes, such action "Is like putting a steel door on a grass hut."

■ BUSINESS IMPACT

What is the impact on business when network security is violated by on-line thieves? Consider these facts:

- According to federal law enforcement estimates, more than $10 billion worth of data is stolen annually in the United States.

- In a single incident, 60,000 credit and calling card numbers were stolen.

- It is estimated that 50% of computer crimes are committed by a company's current or ex-employees.

- In a survey of 1320 companies in 1996, 78% said they lost money from security breaches, 63% said they suffered losses from viruses, and at least 20 respondents admitted to losing over $1 million.

One of the problems with gauging the true business impact of security breaches is that many companies are understandably reluctant to publicly admit that they have suffered significant losses due to failed network security. Network security is a business problem. It is not merely a network problem nor an information technology problem. The development and implementation of a sound network security policy must start with strategic business assessment followed by strong management support throughout the policy development and implementation stages.

However, this management support for network security policy development and implementation cannot be assumed. For example, 71% of executives surveyed stated that they lacked confidence in the ability of their company's network security to fend off attacks from within or without. This stated lack of confidence has not translated into an infusion of support for network security efforts. From the same survey previously referenced, 73% of responding companies had three or fewer employees dedicated to network security, and 55% of respondents said that less than 5% of their information technology budgets went to network security. In another survey, although 82% of surveyed companies had a security policy in place in 1992, only 54% of respondents had a security policy in place in 1996.

Enterprise network security goals must be set by corporate presidents and/or the board of directors. The real leadership of the corporation must define the vision and allocate sufficient resources to send a clear message that corporate information and network resources are valuable corporate assets that must be properly protected.

■ SECURITY POLICY DEVELOPMENT

The Security Policy Development Life Cycle

One methodology for the development of a comprehensive network security policy is known as the **security policy development life cycle (SPDLC).** As illustrated in Figure 13-1, the SPDLC is aptly depicted as a cycle since evaluation processes validate the effectiveness of original analysis stages. Feedback from evaluation stages cause renewed analysis with possible ripple effects of changes in architecture or implemented technology. The feedback provided by such a cycle is ongoing but will only work with proper training and commitment from the people responsible for the various processes depicted in the SPDLC.

Each of the processes identified in the SPDLC are explained further in Figure 13-2.

A successful network security implementation requires a marriage of technology and process. Roles and responsibilities and corporate standards for business processes and acceptable network-related behavior must be clearly defined, effectively shared, universally understood, and vigorously enforced for implemented network security technology to be effective. Process definition and setting of corporate security standards must precede technology evaluation and implementation.

Security Requirements Assessment

Proper security requirements assessment implies that appropriate security processes and technology have been applied for any given user group's access to/from any potential corporate information resource. The proper development and application of these security processes and technology require a structured approach to ensure that all potential user group/information resource combinations have been considered.

To begin to define security requirements and the potential solutions to those requirements, a network analyst can create a matrix grid mapping all potential user groups against all potential corporate information resources. An example of such a

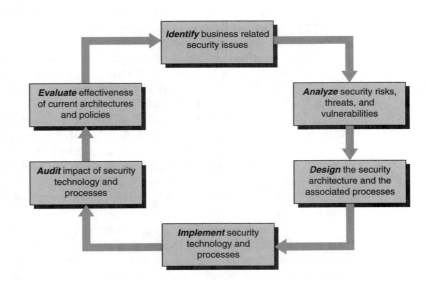

Figure 13-1   The Security Policy Development Life Cycle

SPDLC Process	Explanation/Importance
Identification of business-related security issues	• Security requirements assessment • What do we have to lose? • What do we have worth stealing? • Where are the security holes in our business processes? • How much can we afford to lose? • How much can we afford to spend on network security?
Analysis of security risks, threats, and vulnerabilities	• Information asset evaluation—What do you have that's worth protecting? • Network architecture documentation—What is the current state of your network? • How many unauthorized modems are dialing in? • Identify all assets, threats, and vulnerabilities • Determine risks and create protective measures
Architecture and process design	• Logical design of security architecture and associated processes • What must be the required functionality of the implemented technology? • What business processes implemented and monitored by people must complement this security architecture?
Security technology and process implementation	• Choose security technology based on logical design requirements • Implement all security technology with complementary people processes • Increase the overall awareness of network security and implement training • Design ongoing education process for all employees, including senior management
Audit impact of security technology and processes	• Assure that implemented policy and technology are meeting initial goals • Institute a method to identify exceptions to security policy standards and deal with these exceptions swiftly
Evaluation of effectiveness of current architecture and processes	• Based on results of on-going audits, evaluate effectiveness of current policy and architecture of meeting high-level goals • Adjust policy and architecture as required and renew the cycle

Figure 13-2   Processes of the Security Policy Development Life Cycle

security requirements assessment grid is illustrated in Figure 13-3. While the user groups and corporate information resources form the row and column headings of the grid, the intersections of these rows and columns will be the suggested security processes and policies required for each unique user group/information resource combination. These security processes refer to not just restrictions to information access imposed upon each user group but also the responsibilities of each user group

User Group	Legacy Data Access	Intranet Access	Internet-Inbound Access	Internet-Outbound Access	Global E-Mail Access
Corporate HQ employees					
Executives					
I.S. development staff					
Network management					
Network technicians					
Department management					
End-users					
Remote branch employees					
Telecommuters					
Trading partners					
Customers					
Vendors					
Browsers					
Casual browsers					
Prospective customers					
Consultants and outsourcers					

Figure 13-3   Security Requirements Assessment Grid

for security policy implementation and enforcement. Another category of information for each intersection would be the security technology to be applied to each unique user group/information resource combination to implement the documented security processes.

The security requirements assessment grid is meant to provide only an example of potential user groups and information resource categories. The grid should be modified to provide an accurate reflection of each different corporate security environment. Furthermore, the grid should be used as a dynamic strategic planning tool. It should be reviewed on a periodic basis and should be modified to reflect changes in either user groups or information resources. Only through ongoing auditing, monitoring, evaluation, and analysis can a security requirements assessment plan remain accurate and reflective of a changing corporate network environment.

Scope Definition and Feasibility Studies

In many ways, the software policy development life cycle is similar to the network development life cycle introduced in Chapter 12. Throughout the initial stages of these security policy development efforts, it is essential to remember the critical success factors of the network development life cycle described in Chapter 12. Before proceeding blindly with a security policy development project, it is important to properly define the scope or limitations of the project. In some cases, this scope may be defined in advance due to a management edict to develop a corporate-wide security policy perhaps in response to an incident of breached security. In other cases, feasibility studies may be performed in advance of the decision that determines the scope of the full security policy development effort.

The pilot project or feasibility study provides an opportunity to gain vital information on the difficulty of the security policy development process as well as the assets (human and financial) required to maintain such a process. In addition, vital information concerning corporate culture, especially management attitudes, and its readiness to assist in the development and implementation of corporate network security can be gathered. Only after the feasibility study has been completed can one truly assess the magnitude of the effort and assets required to complete a wider scope policy development effort.

One of the key issues addressed during scope definition or feasibility studies is deciding on the balance between security and productivity. Security measures that are too stringent can be just as damaging to user productivity as can a total lack of enforced security measures. The optimal balance point that is sought is the proper amount of implemented security process and technology that will adequately protect corporate information resources while optimizing user productivity. Figure 13-4 attempts to graphically depict this balance.

Another issue that is commonly dealt with during the scope definition stage is the identification of those key values that a corporation expects an implemented security policy and associated technology to be able to deliver. By defining these key values during scope definition, policy and associated architecture can be developed to assure that each of these values is maintained. These key values represent the ob-

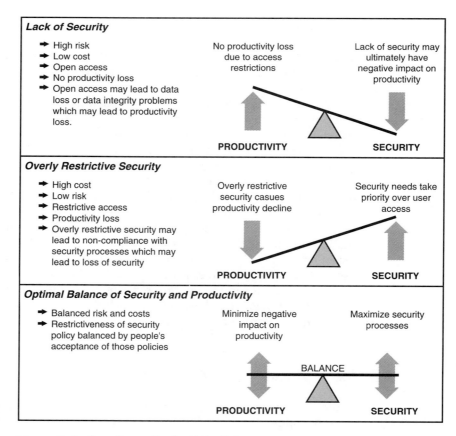

Figure 13-4   Security vs. Productivity Balance

Value of Network Security Policy Development	Explanation/Implication
Identification/authorization	Want to be assured that users can be accurately identified and that only authorized users are allowed access to corporate resources
Access control	Want to be assured that even authorized users are only allowed access to those information and network resources that they are supposed to access
Privacy	Want to be assured that network-based communication is private and not subject to eavesdropping
Data integrity	Want to be assured that data is genuine and cannot be changed without proper controls
Nonrepudiation	Want to be assured that users cannot deny the occurrence of given events or transactions

Figure 13-5 Fundamental Values of Network Security Policy Development

jectives or intended outcomes of the security policy development effort. Figure 13-5 lists and briefly explains the five most typical fundamental values of network security policy development.

Yet another way to organize an approach to security policy and architecture development is to use a model or framework such as **ISO 7498/2,** the **OSI Security Architecture.** This framework maps 14 different security services to specific layers of the OSI seven-layer reference model. The OSI model security architecture can be used as an open framework in which to categorize security technology and protocols, just as the OSI seven-layer model can be used to categorize internetworking technology and protocols. Although more specific and varying slightly in terminology from the five fundamental values listed in Figure 13-5, the OSI security architecture is consistent with and includes all of these fundamental values. As illustrated in Figure 13-6, the ISO 7498-2 security architecture could be used as a grid or checklist to assess whether or not the listed security service has been provided for each associated OSI model layer protocol and by what technologies each service is to be provided. Not all services will necessarily be provided to all suggested layers in all corporate settings. This does not diminish the value of the OSI security architecture as a planning framework however.

Assets, Threats, Vulnerabilities, and Risks

Although Figure 13-4 graphically illustrates the theoretical goal of the security policy development process, balance between productivity and security, how can such a balance actually be delineated within the context of a structured methodology

ISO 7498-2 Security Architecture	Associated OSI Model Layer(s)
Peer entity authentication: Verifies that a peer entity in an association is the one claimed. Verification is provided to the next layer	Application, transport, network
Data origin authentication: Verifies that the source of the data is as claimed. Verification is provided to the next layer	Application, transport, network
Access control service: Protects against unauthorized access of network resources, including by authenticated users	Application, transport, network
Connection confidentiality: Provides for the confidentiality of all data at a given layer for its connection to a peer layer elsewhere, provided primarily by encryption technology	Application, transport, network, data link
Connectionless confidentiality: Same security as above applied to a connectionless communication environment	Application, transport, network, data link
Selective field confidentiality: Provides for the confidentiality of selected fields of application level information on a connection. For example, a customer's PIN (personal ID number) on an automated teller machine transaction	Application, transport, network, data link
Traffic flow confidentiality: Protects against unauthorized traffic analysis such as capture of source and destination addresses	Application, network, physical
Connection integrity with recovery: Provides for data integrity for data on a connection at a given time and detects any modifications with recovery attempted	Application, transport
Connection integrity without recovery: Same as above except no recovery attempted	Application, transport, network
Selective field connection integrity: Provides for the integrity of selected fields transferred over a connection and determines whether the fields have been modified in any manner	Application
Connectionless integrity: Provides integrity assurances to layer above it and may also determine if any modifications have been performed	Application, transport, network
Selective field connectionless integrity: Provides for the integrity of selected fields and may also determine if any modifications have been performed	Application
Nonrepudiation, origin: The recipient of the data is provided with proof of the origin of the data. Provides protection against the sender denying the transmission of the data	Application
Nonrepudiation, delivery: The sender is provided with proof that the data was delivered. Protects against attempts by the recipient to falsify the data or deny receipt of the data	Application

Figure 13-6 OSI 7498-2 Security Architecture

such as the security requirements assessment grid? Most security policy development methodologies boil down to the following five major steps:

1. Identify assets.

2. Identify threats.

3. Identify vulnerabilities.

4. Consider the risks.

5. Take protective measures.

The terms used within these five major steps are related in a process-oriented manner.

Assets are corporate property of some value that require varying degrees of protection. In the case of network security, assets most often include corporate data and the network hardware, software, and media used to transport and store that data.

Threats are processes or people that pose a potential danger to identified assets. A given asset can be potentially threatened by numerous threats. Threats can be intentional or unintentional, natural or man-made. Network-related threats include hackers, line outages, fires, floods, power failures, equipment failures, dishonest employees, or incompetent employees.

Vulnerabilities are the manner or path by which threats are able to attack assets. Vulnerabilities can be thought of as weak links in the overall security architecture and should be identified for every potential threat/asset combination. Vulnerabilities that have been identified can be blocked.

Once vulnerabilities have been identified, how should a network analyst proceed in developing defenses to these vulnerabilities? Which vulnerabilities should be dealt with first? How can a network analyst determine an objective means to prioritize vulnerabilities? By considering the **risk,** or probability of a particular threat successfully attacking a particular asset in a given amount of time via a particular vulnerability, network analysts are able to quantify the relative importance of threats and vulnerabilities. A word of caution however: risk analysis is a specialized field of study, and quantification of risks should not be viewed as an exact science. In identifying the proper prioritization of threats and vulnerabilities to be dealt with, network analysts should combine subjective instincts and judgment with objective risk analysis data.

Once the order in which threats and vulnerabilities will be attacked has been determined, **protective measures** are designed and taken that effectively block the vulnerability to prevent threats from attacking assets. Recalling that multiple vulnerabilities (paths) may exist between a given asset and a given threat, it should be obvious that multiple protective measures may need to be established between given threat/asset combinations. Among the major categories of potential protective measures are

- Virus protection.

- Firewalls.

- Authentication.

- Encryption.

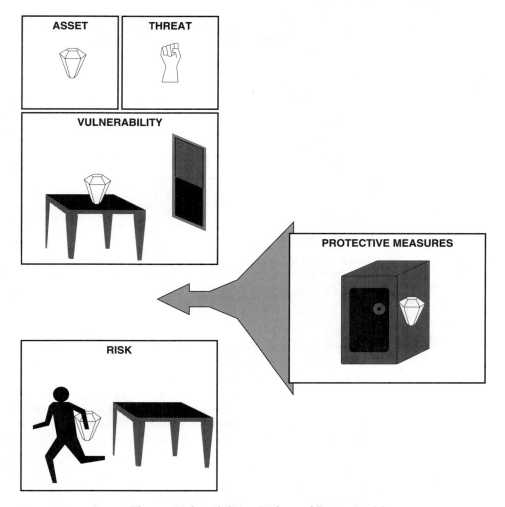

Figure 13-7   Assets, Threats, Vulnerabilities, Risks, and Protective Measures

An explanation of each of these categories of protective measures and relevant examples and applications of each category are supplied in the remainder of this chapter. Figure 13-7 illustrates the relationships between assets, threats, vulnerabilities, risks, and protective measures, whereas Figure 13-8 lists some specific examples of network and information systems vulnerabilities and associated protective measures. Both the vulnerabilities and protective measures listed in Figure 13-8 will be further explained in the remainder of the chapter.

Management Role and Responsibilities

Once the scope of the security policy development effort has been determined and assets, threats, vulnerabilities, risks, and protective measures have been identified, it is time to secure management buy-in for the security policy development process before proceeding any further. Results of the feasibility study will form the basis of the presentation for management.

Network/Information System Vulnerability	Protective Measure
Masquerading	Authentication
Eavesdropping	Encryption
Man-in-the-middle attack	Digital certificates, digital signatures
Address spoofing	Firewalls
Data diddling	Encrypted message digest
Dictionary attack	Strong passwords
Replay attack	Time stamping or sequence numbering
Virus attack	Virus management policy
Trojan horse attack	Firewalls
Denial of service attack	Authentication, service filtering

Figure 13-8   Network/Information System Vulnerabilities and Protective Measures

Be certain that this presentation for management is objective and that any esti-mates of financial losses due to security threats can be substantiated. You will be ask-ing for financial and moral support from management. Your success at securing this support will be a simple matter of management's perception of the cost/benefit analysis of your threat/asset/protective measure scenarios. In other words, have you clearly proven that the costs involved to provide protective measures for corporate assets are outweighed by the benefits of assuring proper protection of those assets?

Now that the existence of security threats and vulnerabilities has been substan-tiated, the next step is to propose your plan of action to develop and implement a solution. It is important not to underestimate the manpower and time requirements necessary to scale up your security analysis from a limited scope feasibility study to a full-fledged enterprise-wide security policy development and implementation process.

But what are the responsibilities of executives and managers beyond merely ap-proving budgets and providing policy enforcement? Figure 13-9 provides a brief listing of key executive responsibilities and Figure 13-10 provides a brief list of man-agement responsibilities. These lists were summarized from publications available from the National Institute of Standards and Technology. NIST publishes a series of Federal Information Processing Standards (FIPS) as well as a series of special publi-cations on a variety of computer and network security related topics.

Policy Development Process

It is important to reiterate that although technology may well be implemented as part of the protective measures to eliminate vulnerabilities and protect assets from their associated threats, it is the processes and policies associated with each of those protective measures that really determine the success or failure of a network secu-rity policy implementation.

Executive's Responsibilities for Protection of Information Resources (excerpted from NIST Special Publication SP 500-169, *Executive Guide to the Protection of Information Resources*)

1. Set the security policy (acceptable-use policy) of the entire organization

2. Allocate sufficient staff, funding, and positive incentives to successfully implement policy

3. State the value of information as a corporate resource to your organization

4. Demonstrate your organization's commitment to the protection of its information resources

5. Make it clear that the protection of the corporate information resources is everyone's responsibility

6. Assign ultimate responsibility for information and network security to specific individuals

7. Require computer and network security and awareness training

8. Hold employees personally responsible for the resources in their care including network access and corporate information

9. Monitor and assess security through external and internal audits (overt and covert)

10. State and follow through on penalties for nonadherence to network security policies

11. Lead by example

Figure 13-9   Executive's Responsibilities for Protection of Information Resources

Management's Responsibilities for Protection of Information Resources
(excerpted from NIST Special Publication SP 500-170, *Management Guide to the Protection of Information Resources*)

1. Assess the consequences of a security breach in the area for which you are responsible. Risks include inability or impairment to perform necessary duties; waste, misuse, or theft of funds or resources; and internal or external loss of credibility

2. Find the optimal balance between security needs and productivity needs

3. Assess vulnerabilities. How long can each information resource be unavailable before business processes become threatened?

4. Assure data integrity within the systems for which you are responsible

5. Maintain required confidentiality and data privacy

6. Assure that nonrepudiation and auditing are present in the systems for which you are responsible

7. Adhere by and enforce corporate acceptable-use policies

Figure 13-10   Management's Responsibilities for the Protection of Information Resources

Again, many of the critical success factors associated with the network development life cycle in Chapter 12 should again be applied to the security policy development process. Be sure that all affected user groups are represented on the policy development task force. Start from a business perspective with a positive philosophy and a universally supportable goal: "The purpose of this policy is to protect our vital corporate resources in order to assure that we can all keep our jobs. This is in our collective best interests." The emphasis should be on corporate-wide awareness and shared values as to the importance of protecting corporate resources such as information and network access. The policy should not be portrayed as administrative edicts to be obeyed under consequence of termination.

Areas that may be considered for development of acceptable-use policies are listed in Figure 13-11.

The list of suggested areas for policy development in Figure 13-11 is not meant to be exhaustive or all-inclusive. Each corporation should amend such a list to include those areas of policy development most appropriate to their corporation. Once policies have been developed for those agreed-upon areas, those policies should be measured against the user group/information resource matrix produced in the security requirements assessment grid (Figure 13-3) to be sure that all potential needs for acceptable-use policies have been met.

Potential Areas for Development of Acceptable-Use Policies

1. Password protection and management (i.e., it is against corporate policy to write your password on a post-it note and paste it to your monitor; it is against corporate policy to allow anyone else to use your user ID or password)

2. Software license policy (policy on using illegal or pirated software on corporate machines, policy on use of shareware on corporate machines, policy regarding who is allowed to install any type of software on corporate machines)

3. Virus protection policy (policy regarding use of diskettes on network-attached PCs, policy on use of corporate computing resources by consultants and outsource personnel, policies related to Internet access)

4. Internet access policy (policies regarding acceptable use of Internet for corporate business)

5. Remote access policy (policies regarding use of single-use passwords, Smart Cards, and secure transfer of corporate data)

6. E-mail policy (policies regarding enrollment in e-mail newsgroups, and personal use of e-mail systems)

7. Policies regarding penalties, warnings, and enforcements for violation of corporate acceptable-use policies

8. Physical access policies (policies regarding access to locked areas, offices, and computer and telecommunications rooms, policy on limited-access areas, visitor policies, policy regarding logging out or locking keyboard when leaving office)

Figure 13-11   Potential Areas for Development of Acceptable-Use Policies

Policy Implementation Process

Once policies have been developed, it is up to everyone to support those policies in their own way. The responsibilities of executives and managers were listed in Figures 13-9 and 13-10, respectively. Having been included in the policy development process, users should also be expected to actively support the implemented acceptable-use policies. Users' responsibilities for the protection of information resources are included in Figure 13-12.

At this point, an effective security policy, including associated technology and processes, should have been developed and be ready for implementation. If user involvement was substantial during the policy development stage and if buy-in was assured at each stage of the policy development, then implementation stands a better chance of succeeding. However, policy implementation will inevitably force changes in people's behaviors, which can cause resistance. Resistance to change is both natural and to be expected. Handled properly, resistance to change can be just

---

User's Responsibilities for Protection of Information Resources (excerpted from NIST Special Publication SP 500-171, *Computer Users' Guide to the Protection of Information Resources*)

1. You are ultimately responsible for protecting the data to which you have access

2. Know which information is especially sensitive or confidential. When in doubt, ask

3. Information is a valuable, shared corporate asset—as valuable as buildings, stock price, sales, or financial reserves

4. The computing resources that the company provides for you are the property of the company and should only be used for purposes which benefit the company directly

5. Familiarize yourself with the acceptable-use policies of your company and abide by them

6. Understand that you will be held accountable for whatever actions you take with corporate computing or networking resources

7. If you ever observe anything or anyone unusual or suspicious, inform your supervisor immediately

8. Never share your password or user ID with anyone

9. If you are allowed to choose a password, choose one that could not be easily guessed

10. Always log off before leaving your computer or terminal

11. Keep sensitive information, whether on diskettes or on paper, under lock and key

12. Don't allow others to look over your shoulder if you are working on something confidential

13. Don't smoke, eat, or drink near computer equipment

14. Know the location of the nearest fire extinguisher

15. Backup your data onto diskettes early and often

Figure 13-12   Users' Responsibilities for the Protection of Information Resources

---

Critical Success Factors for Network Security Policy Implementation

---

1. The policy must have been developed in a team effort with all affected parties feeling that they had input to the process. Policy development must be a bottom-up, grass-roots effort rather than a top-down, administration-imposed effort.

---

2. The security policy must be coordinated with and in compliance with other corporate policies regarding disaster recovery, employee rights, and personnel policies.

---

3. It is important to assure that no part of the security policy is illegal. This is particularly important for corporations that do business in multiple states or countries. For example, in some localities it is illegal to monitor phone conversations of employees.

---

4. Technology must not be promoted as a security solution. Dedicated people, implementing well-designed processes on a consistent basis, combined with the effective use of technology, are the only means to a true security solution.

---

5. The network security policy must not be put on a shelf and forgotten. Security awareness must be a priority and on-going auditing and monitoring should assure that security remains at the forefront of people's thoughts.

---

6. An attitude must be fostered that security threats are indeed real and that they can, and will, happen in your company if people do not follow corporate security procedures.

---

7. Management must be ready to impose prescribed penalties on employees that fail to follow corporate security policy. To do otherwise will quickly send the message that the security policy is a farce.

---

8. Corporate culture may indeed need to change. This is especially true for growing companies that started out as very open, entrepreneurial cultures. Such companies often have difficulty adjusting to structure and controlled access to corporate resources imposed by corporate security policies.

Figure 13-13   Critical Success Factors for Network Security Policy Implementation

a temporary implementation hurdle. Handled improperly, it can spell disaster for an otherwise effective network security policy. Figure 13-13 summarizes some of the key behaviors and attitudes that can help assure a successful network security policy implementation.

Auditing

Manual Audits   To judge whether or not a corporate security policy is successful, it must be audited and monitored on a continual basis. Auditing as it relates to network security policy may be either automated or manual. Manual audits can be done by either internal or external personnel. Manual audits serve to verify the effectiveness of policy development and implementation, especially the extent to which people understand and effectively execute their assigned processes in the overall corporate security policy. Manual audits are also referred to as **policy audits** or off-line audits. Consulting firms that specialize in network security have generated some rather startling results during security audits when they were able to gain entry to a corporate president's office, access his e-mail account, and send e-mail to the chief information officer informing him that he was fired for his lack of effective security policy. As it turns out, the CIO was not really fired. In fact, it was poorly designed and poorly executed people processes that allowed this incident to occur. A receptionist was solely responsible for physical access security to the executive offices and the president left his PC logged in.

Automated Audits Automated audits, otherwise known as **event detection** or **real-time audits,** depend on software that is able to assess the weaknesses of your network security and security standards. Most audit software depends on capturing large amounts of event data and then filtering that data for exceptional or unusual events. Captured events can be telephone calls, login attempts, network server directory access attempts, access to Internet news groups or Web sites, or remote access attempts via dial-up lines. To generate meaningful exception reports, audit software allows users to create filters that will allow only those events deemed exceptional by the users to appear on reports.

Some automated audit tools are able to analyze the network for potential vulnerabilities and make recommendations for corrective action whereas others merely capture events so that you can figure out who did what and when after a security breach has occurred. Other automated tools are able to benchmark or compare events and security-related parameters to a set of government-issued security standards known as C2 or Orange Book standards (officially known as the Trusted Computer System Evaluation Criteria or TCSEC) and issue a report card or "Top 10 Risks" list as to how well a given network measures up. The C2 standards and other security standards will be explained later in the chapter. Some audit tools are able to save previous audit data as baseline information so that network analysts and security specialists can measure improvement in network security including the impact of any security improvements that may have been implemented. Among currently available security auditing tools are the following:

Security Auditing Tool	Vendor
BindView EMS	Bindview Development Corp.
LT Auditor+	Blue Lance, Inc.
AuditTrack	e.g. Software, Inc.
Kane Security Analyst	Intrusion Detection, Inc.

Security Probes Rather than passively gathering network statistics like auditing tools, **security probes** actively test various aspects of enterprise network security and report results and suggest improvements. **Intrusion detection systems** test the perimeter of the enterprise network through dial modems, remote access servers, Web servers, or Internet access. In addition to merely detecting intrusions, such as unsuccessful login attempts over a preset limit, some tools are also able to provide automated responses to these intrusion attempts. Also, some of the more sophisticated intrusion detection systems are dynamic or self-learning and are able to become better at detecting intrusions or to adjust exception parameters as they gain experience in a given enterprise network environment.

Another security probe known as **Security Analyzer Tool for Analyzing Networks (SATAN)** is able to probe networks for security weak spots. The SATAN probe is especially written to analyze UNIX and TCP/IP based systems, and once it has found a way to get inside an enterprise network, it continues to probe all TCP/IP machines within that enterprise network. Once all vulnerabilities have been found, SATAN generates a report that not only details the vulnerabilities found but also suggests methods for eliminating the vulnerabilities. SATAN tries to start TCP/IP sessions with target computers by launching applications such as Telnet, FTP, DNS, NFS, and TFTP. It is able to target specific computers since all TCP/IP-based machines use the same 16-bit address or port number for each of these previously mentioned applications. This application-specific port address plus the 32-bit IP address is known as a socket. Although SATAN was developed as a tool for network managers to detect weaknesses in their own networks, it is widely available on the Internet and can easily be employed by hackers seeking to attack weaknesses in target networks of their choice. Because of the potential for unscrupulous use of SATAN, tools such as Courtney, from the Department of Energy's Computer Incident Advisory Capability, and Gabriel, from Los Altos Technologies, are able to detect the use of SATAN against a network and are able to trigger alarms.

Internet Security Systems has developed a security probe known as RealSecure that looks for 130 known security weaknesses on firewalls, routers, UNIX machines, Windows machines, Windows NT machines, or any other device that uses TCP/IP as its transport protocol stack. RealSecure combines network analyzer, attack signature recognition, and attack response in a single unit. If an attack is detected, RealSecure is able to terminate the connection by spoofing both hosts involved in the communication.

■ VIRUS PROTECTION

Virus protection is often the first area of network security addressed by individuals or corporations. A comprehensive virus protection plan must combine policy, people, processes, and technology to be effective. Too often, virus protection is thought to be a technology-based quick fix. Nothing could be farther from the truth. A survey conducted by the National Computer Security Association in 1996 revealed the following:

- Computer viruses are the most common microcomputer security breach.
- Of the organizations surveyed with 500 or more PCs, 90% experience at least one virus incident per month.
- Complete recovery from a virus infection costs an average of $8100 and 44 hr over a period of 10 working days.
- In June 1996 there were over 6000 known viruses with as many as 200 new viruses appearing per month.

Virus Categories

Although definitions and parameters may vary, the term *computer virus* is generally used to describe any computer program or group of programs that gains access to a computer system or network with the potential to disrupt the normal activity of that system or network. Virus symptoms, methods of infection, and outbreak mechanisms can vary widely but all viruses do share a few common characteristics or behaviors:

- Most viruses work by infecting other legitimate programs and causing them to become destructive or disrupt the system in some other manner.

- Most viruses use some type of replication method to get the virus to spread and infect other programs, systems, or networks.

- Most viruses need some sort of trigger or activation mechanism to set them off. Viruses may remain dormant and undetected for long periods of time.

Viruses that are triggered by the passing of a certain date or time are referred to as **time bombs** whereas viruses that require a certain event to transpire are known as **logic bombs**. Logic bombs in event-driven or visual programs may appear as a button supposedly providing search or some other function. However, when the button is pushed, the virus is executed, causing a wide range of possibilities from capturing passwords to wiping out the disk drive. One of the ways in which viruses are able to infect systems in the first place is by a mechanism known as a **trojan horse.** In such a scenario, the actual virus is hidden inside an otherwise benign program and delivered to the target system or network to be infected. The Microsoft Word Macro (or Concept) virus is an example of a trojan horse virus because the virus itself is innocently embedded within otherwise legitimate Word documents and templates.

Although new types of viruses will continue to appear, Figure 13-14 lists the major virus categories and gives a brief explanation of each.

Antivirus Strategies

An effective antivirus strategy must include policy, procedures, and technology. Policy and procedures must be tied to those vulnerabilities that are specific to virus infection. Viruses can attack systems at the client PC, the server PC, or the network's connection to the Internet. By far, the most common physical transport mechanism for the spread of viruses is the diskette. Effective antivirus policies and procedures must first focus on the use and checking of all diskettes before technology-based solutions are pursued. In fact, 61% of all viral infections are caused by infected diskettes. However, the macro viruses that infect Word documents and Excel spreadsheets are becoming a predominant virus transport mechanism due to the frequency with which such documents are shared between co-workers and across networks as e-mail attachments. Figure 13-15 lists some examples of antivirus strategies although this list should be tailored for each situation and reviewed and updated on a regular basis.

As collaborative applications such as groupware have become more commonplace in corporations, a new method of virus infection and virus reinfection has emerged. Since groupware messages and data are stored in a shared database and since documents can be distributed throughout the network for document conferencing or workflow automation, the virus is spread throughout the network. Moreover, since groupware servers usually replicate their databases to assure that all servers on the network are providing consistent information, the virus will continue to spread. Even if the virus is eliminated from the originating server, responses from still-infected replicated servers will reinfect the original server as the infection/reinfection cycle continues. Virus scanning software specially designed for groupware

Virus Category	Explanation/Implication

File infectors	• Attach themselves to a variety of types of executable files
	• Subcategories of file infectors include the following:
	   • Direct-action file infectors infect a program each time it is executed
	   • Resident infectors use the infected program to become resident in memory from where they attack other programs as they are loaded into memory
	   • Slow infectors infect files as they are changed or created, thus ensuring that the infection is saved
	   • Sparse infectors seek to avoid detection by striking only certain programs on an occasional basis
	   • Companion viruses create new infected programs that are identical to the original uninfected programs
	   • Armored viruses are equipped with defense mechanisms to avoid detection and antivirus technology. **Polymorphic viruses** change their appearance each time an infected program is run to avoid detection

System/boot infectors	• Attack the files of the operating system or boot sector rather than application programs • System/boot sector viruses are memory resident
Multipartite viruses	• Also known as boot-and-file viruses, these viruses attack application files as well as system and boot sectors
Hostile applets	• Although specific to Web technology and Java embedded programs, hostile applets could still be considered viruses. **Attack applets** are intent on serious security breaches, whereas **malicious applets** tend to be annoying rather than destructive. Hostile applets are unknowingly downloaded during Web surfing. Hostile ActiveX components present a similar threat. Some people would argue that such malicious code is not technically a virus. However, there is little doubt as to the potential destructiveness of the code.
Cluster/file system viruses	• Attack the file systems, directories, or file allocation tables so that viruses can be loaded into memory before requested files

Figure 13-14   Virus Categories

databases is available to combat this problem. Figure 13-16 illustrates the collaborative software infection/reinfection cycle.

Managerial Perspective

Antivirus awareness and a mechanism for quickly sharing information regarding new virus outbreaks must accompany the deployment of any antivirus technology. These antivirus awareness and communications mechanisms must be enterprise-wide in scope rather than being confined to a relatively few virus-aware departments. Procedures and policies on how and when antivirus technology is to be employed must be universally understood and implemented.

Antivirus Strategies

1. Identify virus infection vulnerabilities and design protective measures.

2. Install virus scanning software at all points of attack. Assure that network-attached client PCs with detected viruses can be quarantined to prevent the spread of the virus over the network.

3. All diskettes must be scanned at a stand-alone scanning PC before being loaded onto network-attached clients or servers.

4. All consultants and third-party contractors are prohibited from attaching notebook computers to the corporate network until the computer has been scanned in accordance with security policy.

5. All vendors must run demonstrations on their own equipment.

6. Shareware or downloaded software should be prohibited or controlled and scanned.

7. All diagnostic and reference diskettes must be scanned before use.

8. Write protect all diskettes with .EXE and .COM files.

9. Create a master boot record that disables writes to the hard drive when booting from a floppy or disable booting from a floppy, depending on operating system.

Figure 13-15   Antivirus Strategies

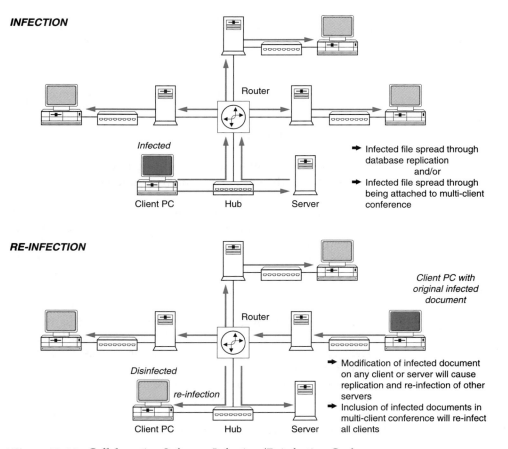

Figure 13-16   Collaborative Software Infection/Reinfection Cycle

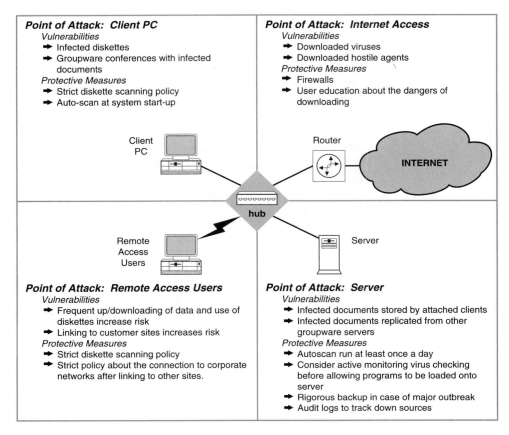

Figure 13-17   Virus Infection Points of Attack and Protective Measures

Antivirus Technology

Since viruses can attack locally or remotely attached client platforms, server platforms, and/or the entrance to the corporate network via the Internet, all four points of attack must be protected. Viruses must be detected and removed at each point of attack. **Virus scanning** is the primary method for successful detection and removal. However, virus scanning software most often works off a library of known viruses, or more specifically the unique digital signatures of these viruses, while new viruses are appearing at the rate of nearly 200 per month. Because of this, it is important to buy virus scanning software whose vendor supplies updates of virus signatures at least once per month. As virus introduction accelerates, it is likely that virus signature updates to virus scanning software will become more frequent as well. Also, some virus scanners can remove a virus from an infected file whereas others merely destroy the infected file as a remedy. Because virus scanners are really scanning for known digital signatures of viruses, they are sometimes referred to as **signature scanners.**

In an effort to be more proactive than reactive, **emulation technology** attempts to detect as yet unknown viruses by running programs with a software emulation program known as a **virtual PC.** In so doing, the executing program can be examined in a safe environment for any unusual behavior or other telltale symptoms of resident viruses. The advantage of such programs is that they identify potentially unknown viruses based on their behavior rather than by relying on identifiable signatures of known viruses. Because of their ability to monitor behavior of programs, this category of antivirus technology is also sometimes known as **activity monitors.** Such programs are also capable of trapping encrypted or polymorphic viruses that are capable of constantly changing their identities or signatures. In addition, some of these programs are self-learning, thereby increasing their knowledge of viruslike activity with experience. Obviously, the key operational advantage is that potentially infected programs are run in the safe, emulated test environment before they are run on actual PCs and corporate networks.

A third category of antivirus technology known as **CRC checkers** or **hashing checkers** creates and saves a unique cyclical redundancy check character or hashing number for each file to be monitored. Each time that file is subsequently saved, the new CRC is checked against the reference CRC. If the CRCs do not match, then the file has been changed. These changes are then evaluated by the program to determine the likelihood that the change was caused by a viral infection. The shortcoming of such technology is that it is only able to detect viruses after infection, which may already be too late.

Figure 13-17 illustrates the typical points of attack for virus infection as well as potential protective measures to combat those attacks.

■ FIREWALLS

When a company links to the Internet, a two-way access point out of as well as *into* that company's confidential information systems is created. To prevent unauthorized access from the Internet into a company's confidential data, specialized software known as a **firewall** is often deployed. Firewall software usually runs on a dedicated server that is connected to, but outside of, the corporate network. All network packets entering the firewall are filtered, or examined, to determine whether or not those users have authority to access requested files or services and whether or not the information contained within the message meets corporate criteria for forwarding over the internal network. Firewalls provide a layer of isolation between the inside network and the outside network. The underlying assumption in such a design scenario is that all of the threats come from the outside network. As evidenced by the statistic cited earlier, this is often not the case. In addition, outside threats may be able to circumvent the firewall entirely if dial-up modem access remains uncontrolled or unmonitored. In addition, incorrectly implemented firewalls can actually exacerbate the situation by creating new, and sometimes undetected, security holes.

Firewall Architectures

Another difficulty with firewalls is that there are no standards for firewall functionality, architectures, or interoperability. As a result users must be especially aware of how firewalls work to evaluate potential firewall technology purchases. Firewall functionality and architectures are explained in the next few sections.

Packet Filtering   Every packet of data on the Internet is uniquely identified by the source address of the computer that issued the message and the destination address of the Internet server to which the message is bound. These addresses are included in a portion of the packet called the header.

A **filter** is a program that examines the source address and destination address of every incoming packet to the firewall server. Network access devices known as routers are also capable of filtering data packets. **Filter tables** are lists of addresses whose data packets and embedded messages are either allowed or prohibited from proceeding through the firewall server and into the corporate network. Filter tables can also limit the access of certain IP addresses to certain directories. This is how anonymous FTP users are restricted to only certain information resources. It obviously takes time for a firewall server to examine the addresses of each packet and compare those addresses to filter table entries. This filtering time introduces **latency** to the overall transmission time. A filtering program that only examines source and destination addresses and determines access based on the entries in a filter table is known as a **port-level filter, network-level filter,** or **packet filter.**

Packet filter gateways can be implemented on routers. This means that an existing piece of technology can be used for dual purposes. However, maintaining filter tables and access rules on multiple routers is not a simple task, and packet filtering does have its limitations in terms of the level of security it is able to provide. Dedicated packet-filtering firewalls are usually easier to configure and require less in-depth knowledge of protocols to be filtered or examined. Packet filters can be breached by hackers in a technique known as **IP spoofing.** Since packet filters make all filtering decisions based on IP source and destination addresses, if a hacker can make a packet appear to come from an authorized or trusted IP address, then it can pass through the firewall.

Application Gateways   **Application-level filters,** otherwise known as **assured pipelines, application gateways,** or **proxies,** go beyond port-level filters in their attempts to prevent unauthorized access to corporate data. Whereas, port-level filters determine the legitimacy of the party asking for information, application-level filters assure the validity of what they are asking for. Application-level filters examine the entire request for data rather than just the source and destination addresses. Secure files can be marked as such and application-level filters will not allow those files to be transferred, even to users authorized by port-level filters.

Certain application-level protocol commands that are typically used for probing or hacking into systems can be identified, trapped, and removed. For example, SMTP (simple mail transfer protocol) is an e-mail interoperability protocol that is a member of the TCP/IP family and used widely over the Internet. It is often used to mask attacks or intrusions. MIME (multipurpose Internet mail extension) is also often used to hide or encapsulate malicious code such as Java applets or ActiveX components. Other application protocols that may require monitoring include World Wide Web protocols such as HTTP, as well as Telnet, FTP, Gopher, and Real Audio. Each of these application protocols requires its own proxy and each application-specific proxy must be intimately familiar with the commands within each application that will need to be trapped and examined. For example an SMTP proxy should be able to filter SMTP packets according to e-mail content, message length, and type of attachments. A given application gateway may not include proxies for all potential application layer protocols.

Application gateways are concerned with what services or applications a message is requesting in addition to who is making that request. Connections between requesting clients and service-providing servers are only created after the application gateway is satisfied as to the legitimacy of the request. Even once the legitimacy of the request has been established, only proxy clients and servers actually communicate with each other. A gateway firewall does not allow actual internal IP addresses or names to be transported to the external nonsecure network. To the external network, the proxy application on the firewall appears to be the actual source or destination as the case may be.

An architectural variation of an application gateway that offers increased security is known as a **dual-homed gateway.** In this scenario, the application gateway is physically connected to the private secure network and the packet-filtering router is connected to the nonsecure network or the Internet. Between the application gateway and the packet-filtering router is an area known as the screened subnet. Also attached to this screened subnet are information servers, WWW servers, or other servers that the company may wish to make available to outside users. However, all outside traffic still goes through the application gateway first, and then to the information servers. TCP/IP forwarding is disabled, and access to the private network is only available through one of the installed proxies. Remote logins are only allowed to the gateway host.

An alternative to the dual-homed gateway that seeks to relieve all the reliance on the application gateway for all communication, both inbound and outbound, is known as a **trusted gateway** or trusted application gateway. In a trusted gateway, certain applications are identified as trusted and are able to bypass the application gateway entirely and establish connections directly rather than be executed by proxy. In this way, outside users can access information servers and WWW servers without tying up the proxy applications on the application gateway. Figure 13-18 differentiates between packet filters, application gateways, proxies, trusted gateways, and dual-homed gateways.

Proxies are also capable of approving or denying connections based on directionality. Users may be allowed to upload files but not download. Some application-level gateways have the ability to encrypt communications over these established connections. The level of difficulty associated with configuring application-level gateways vs. router-based packet filters is debatable. Router-based gateways tend to require a more intimate knowledge of protocol behavior whereas application-level gateways deal with more upper level, application layer, protocols. Proxies introduce increased latency as compared to port-level filtering. The key weakness of an application-level gateway is its inability to detect embedded malicious code such as trojan horse programs or macro viruses.

Internal Firewalls   Not all threats to a corporation's network are perpetrated from the Internet by anonymous hackers and firewalls are not a stand-alone, technology-based quick fix for network security as evidenced by the following facts:

- Sixty percent of network attacks are made by internal users, people inside the firewall.

- Disgruntled employees, former employees, or friends of employees are responsible for 568 out of 600 incidents of network hacking.

- Thirty percent of Internet sites that reported breaches had firewalls in place.

In response to the reality that most episodes of computer crime are inside jobs, a new category of software known as **internal firewalls** has begun to emerge. Internal firewalls include filters that work on the data-link, network, and application layers to examine communications that occur only on a corporation's internal network, inside the reach of traditional firewalls. Internal firewalls also act as access control mechanisms, denying access to any application for which a user does not have

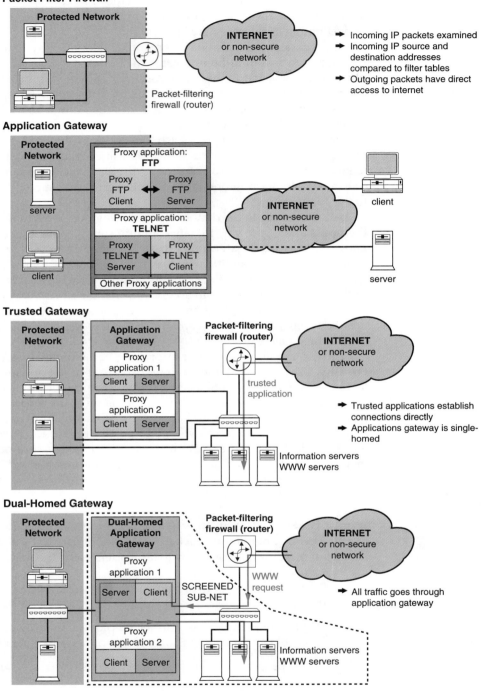

Figure 13-18 Packet Filters, Application Gateways, Proxies, Trusted Gateways, and Dual-Homed Gateways

specific access approval. To assure the security of confidential or private files, encryption may also be used, even during internal communication of such files. Firewall Plus from Network-1 Software and Technology is an example of an internal firewall product.

Firewall Functionality and Technology Analysis

Commercially available firewalls usually employ either packet filtering or proxies as a firewall architecture and add an easy-to-use graphical user interface to ease the configuration and implementation tasks. Some firewalls even use industry-standard Web browsers as their GUIs. Firewall technology is now certified by the **National Computer Security Association.** The NCSA certifies the following:

- That firewalls meet the minimum requirements for reliable protection.

- That firewalls perform as advertised.

- That Internet applications perform as expected through the firewall.

Figure 13-19 summarizes some of the key functional characteristics of firewall technology and Figure 13-20 lists some of the leading firewalls and their vendors.

Firewall Functional Characteristic	Explanation/Importance
Encryption	• Allows secure communication through firewall • Encryption schemes supported: DES RSA, DSA, 3DES, ECC, IDEA, MDS, RSA • Encryption key length supported: 40, 56, 128 bits
Virtual private network support	• Allows secure communication over the Internet in a virtual private network topology • VPN security protocols supported: IPsec
Application proxies supported	• How many different application proxies are supported? Internet application protocols? (HTTP, SMTP, FTP, Telnet, NNTP, WAIS, SNMP, rlogin, ping traceroute)? Real Audio? • How many controls or commands are supported for each application?
Proxy isolation	• In some cases, proxies are executed in their own protected domains to prevent penetration of other proxies or the firewall operating system should a given proxy be breached
Operating systems supported	• UNIX and varieties, Windows NT, UNIXWare
Virus scanning included	• Since many viruses enter through Internet connections, it would stand to reason that the firewall would be a logical place to scan for viruses

Figure 13-19 Functional Characteristics of Firewall Technology

Firewall Functional Characteristic	Explanation/Importance
Web tracking	• To assure compliance with corporate policy regarding use of the World Wide Web, some firewalls provide Web tracking software. The placement of the Web tracking software in the firewall makes sense since all Web access must pass through the firewall. Access to certain URLs can be filtered.
Violation Notification	• How does the firewall react when access violations are detected? Options include SNMP traps, e-mail, pop-up windows, pagers, and reports
Authentication supported	• As a major network access point, the firewall must support popular authentication protocols and technology. Options include SecureID, Cryptocard, Enigma Logic, DES Gold, DES Silver, Safeword, Radius, ASSUREnet, FW-1, Digital Pathways, S/Key, and OS Login
Network interfaces supported	• Which network interfaces and associated data-link layer protocols are supported? Options include Ethernet, Fast Ethernet, FDDI, token ring, high-speed serial for CSU/DSUs, ATM, ISDN, T-1, ,T-3, HDLC, and PPP
System monitoring	• Are graphical systems monitoring utilities available to display such statistics as disk usage or network activity by interface?
Auditing and logging	• Is auditing and logging supporting? • How many different types of events can be logged? • Are user-defined events supported? • Can logged events be sent to SNMP managers?
Attack protection	• Following is just a sample of the types of attacks that a firewall should be able to guard against: TCP denial-of-service-attack, TCP sequence number prediction, source routing and routing information protocol (RIP) attacks, exterior gateway protocol infiltration and Internet control message protocol (ICMP) attacks, authentication server attacks, Finger access, PCMAIL access, domain name server (DNS) access, FTP authentication attacks, anonymous FTP access, SNMP access remote access remote booting from outside networks; IP, media access control (MAC) and address resolution protocol (ARP) spoofing and broadcast storms; trivial FTP and filter to/from the firewall, reserved port attacks, TCP wrappers, Gopher spoofing, and MIME spoofing
Administration interface	• Is the administration interface graphical in nature? Forms-based? • Is a mastery of UNIX required to administer the firewall?

Figure 13-19 Continued

Firewall Technology	Vendor
Firewall-1	Checkpoint Software Technologies
CyberGuard Firewall	CyberGuard Corp.
Borderware Firewall Server	Secure Computing Corp.
Sidewinder Security Server	Secure Computing Corp.
Interceptor	Technologic
Turnstyle Firewall System	Atlantic Systems Group
Alta Vista Firewall	Digital Equipment Corporation
Black Hole	Milky Way Networks Corp.
Eagle Firewall	Raptor Systems
Gauntlet	Trusted Information Systems

Figure 13-20   Firewall Technology (NCSA Certified)

■ AUTHENTICATION AND ACCESS CONTROL

The overall purpose of **authentication** is to assure that users attempting to gain access to networks are really who they claim to be. Password protection was the traditional means to assure authentication. However, password protection by itself is no longer sufficient to assure authentication. As a result, a wide variety of technology has been developed to assure that users really are who they say they are. Authentication products break down into three overall categories:

- *What you know:* Authentication technology that delivers **single sign-on (SSO)** access to multiple network-attached servers and resources via passwords.

- *What you have:* Authentication technology that uses one-time or session passwords or other techniques to authenticate users and validate the authenticity of messages or files. This category of technology requires the user to possess some type of smart card or other token authentication device to generate these single-use passwords.

- *What you are:* Authentication technology that validates users based on some physical characteristic such as fingerprints, hand geometry, or retinal scans.

Token Authentication

Token authentication technology provides one-time-use session passwords that are authenticated by associated server software. This token authentication technology may take multiple forms:

- Hardware-based **smart cards** or smart IDs that are about the size of a credit card with or without a numeric keypad.

- In-line token authentication devices that connect to the serial port of a computer for dial-in authentication through a modem.

- Software tokens that are installed on the client PC and authenticate with the server portion of the token authentication product transparently to the end-user. The user must only enter a personal ID number (PIN) to activate the authentication process.

Token authentication technology is really a system of interacting components that could include any or all of the following:

- A smart card to generate the session password.

- Client software to enter session passwords and communicate with the token authentication server software.

- Server software to validate entries for session passwords and keep track of which smart cards are issued to which users.

- Application development software to integrate the token authentication technology with existing information systems.

There are two overall approaches to the token authentication process.

- **Challenge-response token authentication.**
- **Time-synchronous token authentication.**

Challenge-response token authentication involves the following steps:

1. The user enters an assigned user ID and password at the client workstation.

2. The token authentication server software returns a numeric string known as a challenge.

3. The challenge number and a PIN are entered on the hand-held smart card.

4. The smart card displays a response number on the LCD screen.

5. This response number is entered on the client workstation and transmitted back to the token authentication server.

6. The token authentication server validates the response against the expected response from this particular user and this particular smart card. If the two match, the user is deemed authentic and the login session is enabled.

Time-synchronous token authentication uses slightly more sophisticated technology to simplify the challenge-response procedure somewhat. The result is that in time-synchronous token authentication, there is no server-to-client challenge step.

1. Every 60 sec, the time-synchronous smart card and the server-based software generate a new access code.

2. The user enters a user ID, a PIN, and the access code currently displayed on the smart card.

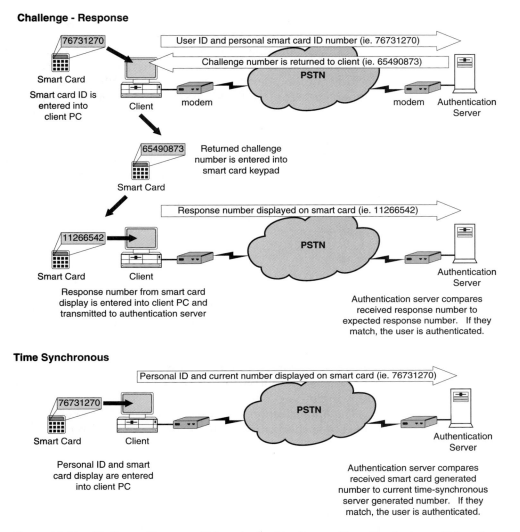

Figure 13-21   Challenge-Response Token Authentication vs. Time-Synchronous Token Authentication

3.   The server receives the access code and authenticates the user by comparing the received access code to the expected access code unique to that smart card that was generated at the server in time-synchronous fashion.

Figure 13-21 differentiates between challenge-response token authentication and time-synchronous token authentication.

Biometric Authentication

If the security offered by token authentication is insufficient, **biometric authentication** can authenticate users based on fingerprints, palm prints, retinal patterns, **voice** recognition, or other physical characteristics. Passwords can be stolen, smart cards can be stolen, but fingerprints and retinal patterns cannot. All biometric authentication devices require that valid users first register by storing copies of their fingerprints, voice, or retinal patterns in a validation database. This gives the biometric device something to reference each time an intended user logs in.

Biometric authentication devices are not yet perfect or foolproof. Most biometric authentication devices must be calibrated for sensitivity. If the biometric device comparison algorithm is set too sensitively, then **false rejects** will occur when valid users are denied access because of slight variations detected between the reference biometric characteristic and the current one. If the biometric device comparison algorithm is not set sensitively enough, then **false accepts** will occur when impostors are allowed access because the comparison was not detailed enough. Users of biometric authentication equipment must calibrate the sensitivity of the equipment to produce acceptable levels of false rejects and false accepts.

Authorization

Sometimes perceived as a subset of authentication, authorization is concerned with assuring that only properly authorized users are able to access particular network resources or corporate information resources. In other words, whereas authentication assures that only legitimate users are able to log into the network, authorization assures that these properly authenticated users only access the network resources for which they are properly authorized. This assurance that users are able to log into a network, rather than each individual server and application, and be only able to access resources for which they are properly authorized is known as **secure single login.**

The authorization security software can be either server-based, also known as **brokered authorization,** or workstation-based, also referred to as **trusted node.**

Kerberos

Perhaps the most well known combination authentication/authorization software is **Kerberos,** developed originally at the Massachusetts Institute of Technology and marketed commercially by a variety of firms. The Kerberos architecture is illustrated in Figure 13-22.

As illustrated in Figure 13-22, a Kerberos architecture consists of three key components:

- Kerberos client software.
- Kerberos authentication server software.
- Kerberos application server software.

To be able to assure that only authorized users are able to access a particular application, Kerberos must be able to communicate directly with that application. As a result, the source code of the application must be "Kerberized" or modified to be compatible with Kerberos. If the source code is not available, perhaps the software vendor sells Kerberized versions of their software. Kerberos is not able to offer authorization protection to applications with which it cannot communicate. Kerberos enforces authentication and authorization through the use of a ticket-based system.

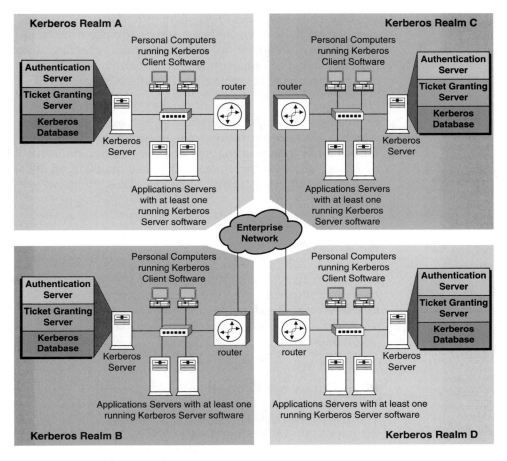

Figure 13-22 Kerberos Architecture

An encrypted **ticket** is issued for each server-to-client session and is valid only for a preset amount of time. The ticket is only valid for connections between a designated client and server, thus precluding users from accessing servers or applications for which they are not properly authorized.

Logically, Kerberos works as follows:

1. Users are first authenticated by the Kerberos authentication server, which consults its database and grants a ticket for the valid user to communicate with the ticket-granting server (TGS). This ticket is known as a **ticket-granting ticket.**

2. Using this ticket, the user sends an encrypted request to the TGS requesting a ticket for access to a particular applications server.

3. If the TGS determines that the request is valid, a ticket is issued that will allow the user to access the requested server. This ticket is known as a **service-granting ticket.**

4. The user presents the validated ticket to the application server, which evaluates the ticket's validity. If the application determines that the ticket is valid, a client/server session is established. This session can optionally be encrypted.

Enterprise networks implementing Kerberos are divided into Kerberos **realms,** each served by its own Kerberos server. If a client wishes to access a server in another realm, it requests an **inter-realm** ticket-granting ticket from its local ticket-granting server to authorize access to the remote ticket-granting server which can authorize access to the remote applications server.

Managerial Perspective

From a network analyst's perspective, concern should be centered on the amount of overhead or network bandwidth consumed by the addition of Kerberos security. Research has indicated that, in fact, the network impact is minimal. However, the additional administrative responsibility of maintaining the Kerberos databases that indicate which users are authorized to access which network resources should not be ignored.

■ ENCRYPTION

Encryption involves the changing of data into an indecipherable form prior to transmission. In this way, even if the transmitted data is somehow intercepted, it cannot be interpreted. The changed, unmeaningful data is known as **ciphertext.** Encryption must be accompanied by decryption, or changing the unreadable text back into its original form.

DES—Private Key Encryption

The decrypting device must use the same algorithm or method to decode or decrypt the data as the encrypting device used to encrypt the data. For this reason **private key encryption** is sometimes also known as symmetric encryption. Although proprietary standards do exist, a standard known as **DES (data encryption standard),** originally approved by the National Institute of Standards and Technology (NIST) in 1977, is often used, allowing encryption devices manufactured by different manufacturers to interoperate successfully. The DES encryption standard actually has two parts, which serve to offer greater overall security. In addition to the standard algorithm or method of encrypting data 64 bits at a time, the DES standard also uses a 64-bit key.

The encryption key customizes the commonly known algorithm to prevent anyone without this private key from possibly decrypting the document. This private key must be known by both the sending and receiving encryption devices and allows so many unique combinations (nearly 2 to the 64th power) that unauthorized decryption is nearly impossible. The safe and reliable distribution of these private keys among numerous encryption devices can be difficult. If this private key is somehow intercepted, the integrity of the encryption system is compromised.

RSA—Public Key Encryption

As an alternative to the DES private key standard, **public key encryption** can be utilized. The current standard for public key encryption is known as **RSA,** named after the three founders of the protocol (Rivest–Shamir–Adelman). Public key encryption could perhaps more accurately be named public/private key encryption as the process actually combines usage of both public and private keys. In public key encryption, the sending encryption device encrypts a document using the intended recipient's public key and the originating party's private key. This public key is readily available in a public directory or is sent by the intended recipient to the message sender. However, to decrypt the document, the receiving encryption/decryption device must be programmed with the intended recipient's own private key and the sending party's public key. In this method, the need for transmission of private keys between sending and receiving parties is eliminated.

Digital Signature Encryption

As an added security measure, **digital signature encryption** provides an electronic means of guaranteeing authenticity of the sending party and assurance that encrypted documents have not been altered during transmission.

With digital signature encryption, a document's digital signature is created by the sender using a private key and the original document. The original document is processed by a hashing program such as Secure Hash Algorithm, Message Digest 2, or Message Digest 5, to produce a mathematical string that is unique to the exact content of the original document. This unique mathematical string is then encrypted using the originator's private key. The encrypted digital signature is then appended to and transmitted with the encrypted original document.

To validate the authenticity of the received document, the recipient uses a public key associated with the apparent sender to regenerate a digital signature from the received encrypted document. The transmitted digital signature is then compared by the recipient to the regenerated digital signature produced by using the public key and the received document. If the two digital signatures match, the document is authentic (really produced by alleged originator) and has not been altered. Figure 13-23 illustrates the differences between private key encryption, public key encryption, and digital signature encryption, and Figure 13-24 summarizes some key facts about currently popular encryption standards.

Key Management Alternatives

Public key dissemination must be managed in such a way that users can be assured that public keys received are actually the public keys of the companies or organizations that they are alleged to be. This added level of assurance is provided by **public key certificates. X.509** is an international standard for public key certificates. Third-party key certification services, or **certificate authorities (CA),** issue the public keys along with a certificate assuring the authenticity of the key. Such certification authorities issue public keys of other organizations, along with certificates of authenticity, assured by their own digital signature. VeriSign is one example of a trusted third-party issuer of X.509 public key certificates. The U.S. Postal Service has also announced plans to begin issuing public key certificates.

Digital certificates or **Digital IDs** issued from CAs such as VeriSign contain an organization's encrypted public key along with a minimal amount of information about the organization such as e-mail address, department, company, state or province, and country. Once a certificate has been issued by a CA, an organization can post their Digital ID on a Web page and be assured that the CA will stand behind the Digital ID's authenticity.

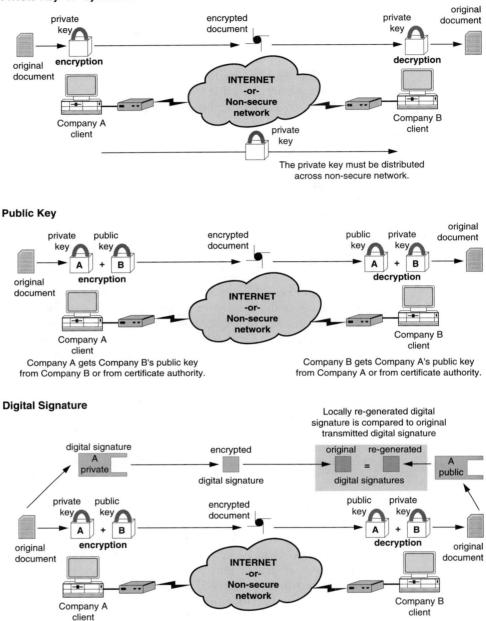

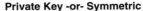

Figure 13-23   Private Key Encryption, Public Key Encryption, and Digital Signature Encryption

Digital IDs may one day replace passwords for Internet-based communications. Recognizing the potential for electronic commerce vendors to quickly gather demographic data about their customers, VeriSign has enhanced their Class 1 Digital ID format to include additional fields in which to store demographic data such as gender, age, address, zip code, or other personal data. Information stored in the encrypted Class 2 Digital ID could allow customized Web pages to be built based on

Standard	Type	Key Size	Explanation
3DES	private	40, 56 bits	Triple DES, uses two or three keys and multiple passes
DES	private	40, 56 bits	Digital encryption standard, widely used for private key encryption
DSA	digital signature	1024 bits	Digital signature algorithm generates appended digital signatures based on original document to assure document has not been altered
ECC	public	160 bits	Elliptical curve cryptography, claims to produce equivalent security of 1024-bit RSA key in only 160 bits
IDEA	private	128 bit	International data encryption algorithm, generates one-time-use session keys, used in PGP (pretty good privacy)
MD5	Digest		Produces 128-bit hash number based on original document. Can then be incorporated into digital signature. Replaced MD4 and MD2
RSA	public	512 to 2048 bits	Rivest–Shamir–Adelman, popular public key encryption standard, minimum key length of 1024 bits recommended
Skipjack	private	80 bits	Used for Clipper and Capstone encryption chips and Defense Messaging System (DMS)

Figure 13-24   Encryption Standards

the information contained therein. The Digital ID service from VeriSign costs $6.00/year for a Class 1 Digital ID and $12.00/year for a Class 2 Digital ID.

■ APPLIED SECURITY SCENARIOS

Integration with Information Systems and Application Development

Authentication products must be integrated with existing information systems and applications development efforts. APIs (application program interfaces) are the means by which authentication products are able to integrate with client/server applications. Beyond APIs are application development environments or software development kits that combine an application development language with the supported APIs. APIs or application development environments must be compatible with the programming language in which applications are to be developed.

AT&T provides a software development kit that includes a library of C language security APIs and software modules for integrating digital signature and other security functionality into Windows NT and Windows 95 applications.

Security Dynamics, who markets SecurID time-synchronous token authentication products, also provides software development kits known as BSAFE 3.0 and Toolkit for Interoperable Privacy Enhanced Messaging.

Microsoft's CryptoAPI allows security services such as authentication, encryption, certificate management services, and digital signatures to be integrated with applications.

An open API, which would allow applications to communicate with a variety of security authorization programs, is known as **GSS-API (generic security service-applications program interface)** and is documented in RFCs 1508 and 1509. Security products companies such as Nortel, producers of the Entrust file signing and encryption package, and Cybersafe Corporation support the GSS-API. GSS-API is described as open because it interfaces between user applications and a variety of security services such as Kerberos, secure FTP, or encryption services. The applications developer does not need to understand the intricacies of these security services and is able to flexibly choose those security services that best meet the needs of the application under development.

Remote Access Security

The biggest challenge facing remote access security is how to manage the activity of all of the remote access users that have logged in via a variety of multivendor equipment and authentication technology. A protocol and associated architecture known as the **remote authentication dial-in user service (RADIUS)** is supported by a wide variety of remote access technology and offers the potential to enable centralized management of remote access users and technology. The RADIUS architecture is illustrated in Figure 13-25. This architecture is referred to as three-

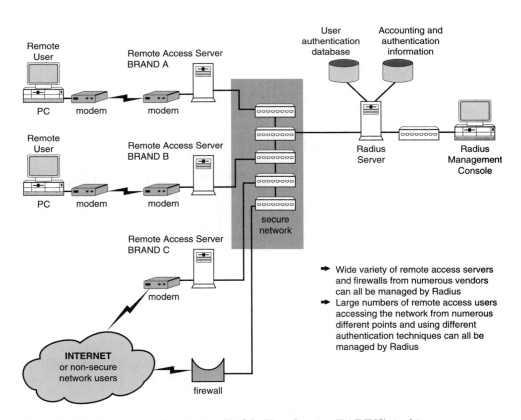

Figure 13-25   Remote Authentication Dial-In User Service (RADIUS) Architecture

tiered because it enables communication between the following three tiers of technology:

- Remote access devices such as remote access servers and token authentication technology from a variety of vendors.

- Enterprise database that contains authentication and access control information.

- RADIUS authentication server.

RADIUS allows network managers to centrally manage remote access users, access methods, and logon restrictions. It allows centralized auditing capabilities such as keeping track of volume of traffic sent and amount of time on-line. RADIUS also enforces remote access limitations such as server access restrictions or on-line time limitations. For authentication, it supports **password authentication protocol (PAP), challenge handshake authentication protocol (CHAP),** and SecurID token authentication. Some RADIUS-based centralized management products may require that a new centralized database of remote access user information be built, whereas others, such as Funk Software's Steel Belted RADIUS, are able to use an existing network operating system's directory services, such as NetWare's NDS, as the management database.

RADIUS is not the only open protocol for communication between centralized remote access management technology and multivendor remote access technology. **Extended terminal access control access system (XTACACS)** is another example of a remote access management protocol that supports three-tiered remote access management architectures.

E-Mail, Web, and Internet/Intranet Security

The two primary standards for encrypting traffic on the World Wide Web are

- **S-HTTP (secure hypertext transport protocol).**
- **SSL (secure sockets layer).**

S-HTTP   Secure HTTP is a secure version of HTTP that requires both client and server S-HTTP versions to be installed for secure end-to-end encrypted transmission. S-HTTP, based on public key encryption, is described as providing security at the document or application level since it works with the actual HTTP applications to secure documents and messages. S-HTTP uses digital signature encryption to assure that the document possesses both authenticity and message integrity.

SSL   SSL is described as wrapping an encrypted envelope around HTTP transmissions. Whereas S-HTTP can only be used to encrypt Web documents, SSL can be wrapped around other Internet service transmissions such as FTP, Telnet, and Gopher as well as HTTP. SSL is a connection-level encryption method providing security to the network link itself. SSL Version 3 (SSL3) added support for more key exchange and encryption algorithms as well as separate keys for authentication and encryption.

SSL and S-HTTP are not competing or conflicting standards although they are sometimes viewed that way. In an analogy to a postal service scenario, SSL provides the locked postal delivery vehicle whereas S-HTTP provides the sealed, tamper-evident envelope that allows only the intended recipient to view the confidential document contained within.

Another Internet security protocol directed specifically toward securing and authenticating commercial financial transactions is known as **Secure Courier** and is offered by Netscape. Secure Courier is based on SSL and allows users to create a secure digital envelope for transmission of financial transactions over the Internet. Secure Courier also provides consumer authentication for the cybermerchants inhabiting the commercial Internet.

PAP/CHAP   Password authentication protocol is the simpler of the two authentication protocols designed for dial-in communication. PAP repeatedly sends the user ID and password to the authenticating system in clear text pairs until it is either acknowledged or the connection is dropped. There is no encryption performed with PAP. Challenge handshake authentication protocol provides a more secure means for establishing dial-in communication. It uses a three-way challenge that includes the user ID, password, and also a key that encrypts the ID and password. The process of sending the pair to the authentication system is the same as with PAP, but the encryption reduces the chance that someone will be able to pick up the ID and password and use it to access a system. The problem with this, and any single-key system for that matter, is that some mechanism must be in place for both the receiver and sender to know and have access to the key. To address this problem, a public key technique may be used to encrypt the single private key for transmission.

PCT   Microsoft's version of SSL is known as **PCT** or **private communications technology**. The key difference between SSL and PCT is that PCT supports secure transmissions across unreliable (UDP rather TCP based) connections by allowing decryption of transmitted records independently from each other, as transmitted in the individual datagrams. PCT is targeted primarily toward on-line commerce and financial transactions, whereas SSL is more flexibly targeted toward Web and Internet applications in general.

PEM   **Privacy enhanced mail (PEM)** was the application standard encryption technique for e-mail use on the Internet used in association with SMTP (simple mail transport protocol). It was designed to use both DES and RSA encryption techniques, but it would work with other encryption algorithms as well. PEM did not receive much support, however, and has been placed in "historical status" by the IETF, meaning that it is no longer being implemented. The reason for this is that PEM did not gain support from either the vendor or user populations. Vendors had their own products they supported and users preferred using other e-mail programs and protocols such as PGP and S/MIME.

PGP   An Internet e-mail-specific encryption standard that also uses digital signature encryption to guarantee the authenticity, security, and message integrity of received e-mail is known as **PGP**, which stands for **pretty good privacy**. PGP overcomes inherent security loopholes with public/private key security schemes by implementing a Web of Trust in which e-mail users electronically sign each other's public keys to create an interconnected group of public key users. Digital signature encryption is provided using a combination of RSA and **MD5** (Message Direct Version 5) encryption techniques. Combined documents and digital signatures are then encrypted using **IDEA (international data encryption algorithm),** which makes use of one-time 128-bit keys known as **session keys**. PGP/MIME overcomes PGP's inability to encrypt multimedia (MIME) objects.

SET **Secure Electronic Transactions (SET)** are a series of standards to assure the confidentiality of electronic commerce transactions. These standards are being largely promoted by credit card giants VISA and MasterCard. SET standards are specifically aimed at bank card transactions over the Internet. However, the assurance of e-commerce confidentiality is not without costs in terms of processing overhead. A single SET-compliant electronic transaction could require as many as six cryptographic functions, taking from one-third to one-half of a second on a high-powered UNIX workstation. The impact of thousands or millions of transactions per second could be enormous.

A large part of assuring the authenticity of e-commerce will be dependent on trusting the e-customers and e-vendors are really who they say they are. An important aspect of the SET standards is the incorporation of digital certificates or Digital IDs, more specifically known as SET Digital IDs that are issued by such companies as VeriSign.

S/MIME **Secure multipurpose Internet mail extension** secures e-mail traffic in e-mail applications that have been **S/MIME** enabled. S/MIME encrypts and authenticates e-mail messages for transmission over SMTP-based e-mail networks. S/MIME will enable different e-mail systems to exchange encrypted messages and is able to encrypt multimedia as well as text-based e-mail.

Virtual Private Network Security

To provide virtual private networking capabilities using the Internet as an enterprise network backbone, specialized **tunneling protocols** needed to be developed that could establish private, secure channels between connected systems. Two rival standards are examples of such tunneling protocols:

* Microsoft's **point-to-point tunneling protocol (PPTP).**
* Cisco's **layer two forwarding (L2F).**

An effort is underway to have the Internet Engineering Task Force (IETF) propose a unification of the two rival standards known as **layer 2 tunneling protocol (L2TP).** One shortcoming of the proposed specification is that it does not deal with security issues such as encryption and authentication. Figure 13-26 illustrates the use of tunneling protocols to build virtual private networks using the Internet as an enterprise network backbone.

Two rival specifications currently exist for establishing security over VPN tunnels.

* **IPsec** is largely supported by the firewall vendor community and is intended to provide interoperability between VPN firewalls from different vendors.
* PPTP is Microsoft's tunneling protocol that is specific to Windows NT Servers and remote access servers. It has the backing of several remote access server vendors.

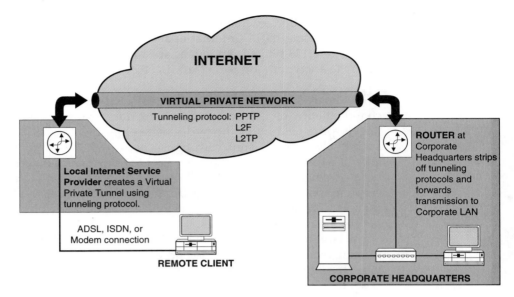

Figure 13-26   Tunneling Protocols Enable Virtual Private Networks

IPsec is a protocol that ensures encrypted communications across the Internet via virtual private networks through the use of manual key exchange. IPsec supports only IP-based communications. IPsec is a standard that, in theory at least, should enable interoperability between firewalls supporting the protocol. Although firewalls of the same brand seem to interoperate sufficiently via IPsec, that does not seem to be the case between different brands of firewall technology.

PPTP is essentially just a tunneling protocol that allows managers to choose whatever encryption or authentication technology they wish to hang off either end of the established tunnel. PPTP supports multiple network protocols including IPX, NetBEUI, and IP. PPTP is primarily concerned with secure remote access in that PPP-enabled clients would be able to dial in to a corporate network via the Internet.

In addition to IPsec, which is specifically targeted at firewall interoperability, the IP network protocol itself is also proposed to be able to support both authentication and encryption. These capabilities are optional for IPv4 and mandatory for IPv6 and are outlined in IETF RFCs 1825 through 1829. To deliver these functions, two new headers are added to the existing IP header:

- The **authentication header** provides data integrity and allows for the authentication of IP packets. It can specify the security association to provide authentication between the source and destination parties and it can also supply data to be used by the agreed-upon particular authentication algorithm to be used.

- The **encapsulating security payload header (ESP)** assures the privacy of the transmission. The ESP header can be used in two different modes depending on the user's privacy needs:
  - **Transport mode ESP** is used to encrypt the data carried by the IP packet. The contents of the data field of an IP (network layer) packet are the upper layer or transport layer protocols TCP (connection-oriented) or UDP (connectionless). These transport layer envelopes encapsulate upper layer data.

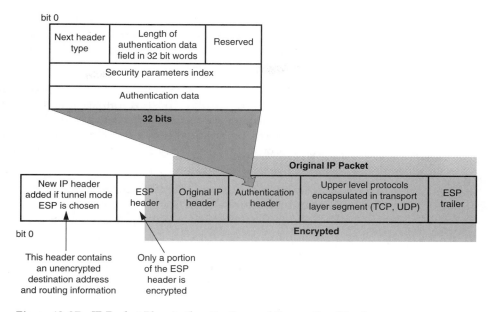

bit 0

Next header type	Length of authentication data field in 32 bit words	Reserved
Security parameters index		
Authentication data		

32 bits

Original IP Packet

New IP header added if tunnel mode ESP is chosen	ESP header	Original IP header	Authentication header	Upper level protocols encapsulated in transport layer segment (TCP, UDP)	ESP trailer

bit 0

Encrypted

This header contains an unencrypted destination address and routing information

Only a portion of the ESP header is encrypted

Figure 13-27   IP Packet Plus Authentication and Encryption Headers

- **Tunnel mode ESP** encrypts the entire IP packet including its own header. This mode is effective at countering network analyzers or sniffers from capturing IP address information. Tunnel mode is most often used in a network topology that includes a firewall that separates a protected network from an external nonsecure network.

It is important to note that the mere inclusion of fields in a protocol does not assure implementation. Applications, authentication products, and trusted security associations would all have to modify hardware and/or software technology to avail themselves of the protocol's new functionality. Figure 13-27 illustrates an IP packet with authentication and encryption headers added.

Enterprise Network Security

To maintain proper security over a widely distributed enterprise network, it is essential to be able to conduct certain security-related processes from a single, centralized, security management location. Among these processes or functions are the following:

- **Single point of registration (SPR)** allows a network security manager to enter a new user (or delete a terminated user) from a single centralized location and assign all associated rights, privileges, and access control to enterprise resources from this single point rather than having to enter this new user's information on multiple resources distributed throughout the enterprise.

- **Single sign-on (SSO),** also sometimes known as secure single sign-on (SSSO), allows users to log into the enterprise network and to be authenticated from their client PC location. It is not necessary for users to remember a variety of different user IDs and passwords to the numerous different enterprise servers from which they may request services. Since this is the single entry point onto the enterprise network for users, auditing software can be used to keep nonrepuditable records of all activities and transactions. Any of the variety of authentication technologies discussed earlier can be used in support of single sign-on.

- **Single access control view** allows the user's access from their client workstation to only display those resources that the user actually has access to. Any differences between server platforms should be shielded from the user. The user should not need to memorize different commands or control interfaces for the variety of enterprise servers that a user may need to access.

- **Security auditing and intrusion detection** is able to track and identify suspicious behaviors from both internal employees and potential intruders. In addition to detecting and reporting these instances, it is essential to be able to respond in an appropriate and automated fashion to these events. Although the intrusions may take place anywhere on the widely distributed network, the detection and response to such events must be controlled from a centralized security management location.

■ GOVERNMENT IMPACT

Government agencies play a major role in the area of network security. The two primary functions of these various government agencies are

- Standards-making organizations that set standards for the design, implementation, and certification of security technology and systems.

- Regulatory agencies that control the export of security technology to a company's international locations.

Standards-Making Organizations

Although many standards-making organizations are involved to varying degrees in the field of network security, the following are some of the most significant ones.

ANSI   The American National Standards Institute (ANSI) is the United States representative to the International Standards Organization (ISO). Any submissions to the ISO from other U.S. standards organizations must first be submitted to ANSI.

NIST   The National Institute of Standards and Technology (NIST) was formed in 1987, but it was formerly known as the National Bureau of Standards. This organization issues publications called the Federal Information Process Standards, or FIPS publications. Category 5 FIPS publications deal with computer security standards and guidelines and include subcategories of access control, cryptography, general computer security, risk analysis and contingency planning, and security labels. NIST also publishes a series of Special Publications related to computer security included in the SP 500 and SP 800 series. NIST also operates a very useful Computer Security Resource Clearinghouse on the World Wide Web at http://csrc.ncsl.nist.gov/

IAB   The Internet Architecture Board is the policy setting and decision review board for the Internet. The Internet Engineering Task Force (IETF) is a subgroup of the IAB that is responsible for setting the technical standards that run the Internet. This is the group responsible for issuing and gathering the responses to RFCs (requests for comment).

ISO   The International Standards Organization is a voluntary organization sanctioned by the United Nations. It is responsible for international standards in a variety of fields, not just data communications. Besides the OSI seven-layer reference model, the ISO is also responsible for the security-related addendum to the OSI model known as ISO 7498/2, the OSI Security Architecture.

NSA   The National Security Agency is a secretive governmental organization that works closely with NIST and is responsible for the design and use of nonmilitary encryption technology. NSA also runs the NCSC, or the National Computer Security Center.

NCSC   The purpose of this organization is to work with members of the computer industry to provide guidelines that are designed to help them develop trusted systems and computer products. This organization is also known for a security certification program called the Trusted Computer System Evaluation Criteria (TCSEC). It is commonly known as the Orange Book because of the color of the jacket. There is also a Red Book from the NCSC, which was developed in 1987 as a supplement to the Orange Book. These "colored book" security guidelines have been criticized for their focus primarily on computer security rather than network security.

Orange Book Certification: The primary focus of the Orange Book is on providing confidential protection of sensitive information based on six fundamental requirements:

- Security policy: An explicit and well-defined security policy must be enforced by the system.

- Marking: Access control labels must be associated with all objects.

- Identification: Individual users must be identified.

- Accountability: Audit information must be kept and protected so that actions affecting security can be traced to the responsible party.

- Assurance: The system must contain hardware and/or software components that can be evaluated independently to provide sufficient assurance that the security policy and accountability criteria can be enforced.

- Continuous protection: The components above that enforce these basic requirements must be continuously protected against tampering and/or unauthorized changes.

It is broken into two primary parts; the first is illustrated in Figure 13-28. It specifies the criteria that must be met to achieve a specific rating. The criteria are defined in hierarchical fashion, with four different ratings possible. The "A" rating is the most secure possible and the "D" rating corresponds to the least secure rating possible.

Division	Protection	Class	Protection	Description
D	Minimal	D	Minimal	Evaluated but does not meet any higher class requirements
C	Discretionary	C1	Discretionary security	Confidence in hardware and software controls Isolates and authenticates users and data
		C2	Controlled access	Encapsulates resources; login and explicit auditing
B	Mandatory	B1	Labeled security	Explicit protection model; execution domains, file labels, system security officer, and documentation required
		B2	Structured	Formal security model, kernelized, covert channel ID, mandatory controls including communication lines required
		B3	Security domains	Central encapsulation, reference monitor, tamper proof, recovery procedures, protected against authentication attacks
A	Verified	A1	Verified design	Extensive security considerations during all developmental phases. Math tools, formal models with explicit math theorems, formal top-level specifications, trusted software distribution required
		Beyond A1		Developmental; source verification

Figure 13-28   Orange Book Certification Criteria

The second portion of the Orange Book contains information about the basic objectives, rationale, and government policy behind the development of each of the criteria. It is also intended to provide guidelines for product developers to aid them in achieving specific criteria.

The Orange Book certification process is both costly and lengthy. Typically, the certification process is projected to take 2 years to complete at a cost of $17 million. To date, both NetWare and NT Server have achieved the **C-2 certification**. An important point to be aware of is the fact that many products may advertise a certification compliance with an Orange Book level; however, compliance and certification are two very different terms. Any vendor can claim compliance, but only vendors that have spent the time and money to pursue the certification process can claim that their products are C-2 certified.

Encryption Export Policy and Key Recovery

Many corporations and organizations depend on the need for private and confidential communication on an international basis. However, in the United States, export of encryption software is tightly controlled. The traditional limit on exportable encryption technology was a 40-bit key. However, 40-bit keys can be cracked in a matter of minutes and do not offer much protection. Businesses conducting operations internationally obviously want to be able to use stronger encryption technology. The government, on the other hand, wishes to gain greater control over international encrypted communication as evidenced by its **Clipper Chip** initiative.

The Clipper Chip initiative proposed that every phone and data communications device in the United States would be equipped with a Clipper Chip to support encryption. The part of the proposal that had businesses and individuals concerned was that the government would hold a spare set of keys that could decrypt any message encrypted by a Clipper Chip device. The notion of trusting the government with a spare set of keys caused quite an uproar and the proposal was subsequently not pursued. However, the initiative clearly showed the government's intention to seek greater control of international encrypted communications.

The current proposal, which some might consider a compromise, is that U.S. companies with international subsidiaries may now export 56-bit key-based encryption technology provided that they establish within 2 years a **key recovery mechanism** that will offer a back door into encrypted data for the government. Once the key recovery mechanism is in place, the companies are allowed to export keys of any length. All banks, whether U.S. based or not, are also allowed to export 56-bit encryption technology. However, even 56-bit keys can be cracked. Experts estimate that 56-bit keys can be cracked in 19 days at a cost of $500,000. The new regulation also moved responsibility for encryption product export from the U.S. State Department to the U.S. Commerce Department, thereby no longer classifying encryption technology as munitions and speeding the export permit approval process.

Key recovery schemes basically assure that a spare set of encryption keys is always available. With key recovery, the actual information used to reconstruct a key travels with the message header. However, someone with the key decryption codes (the spare set of keys) must combine the decryption codes with the key information in the message header to decrypt the message. The big question seems to be, "Who will hold the keys?" **Key escrow agencies,** otherwise known as trusted third parties, are the most commonly proposed solution. Other proposals say that large multinational corporations should be able to act as their own key escrow agents. At the moment there are about 13 different key recovery mechanisms, and no single standard has been proposed although an IBM-led key-recovery alliance with 40 corporate members has been formed. If key recovery were to be extended to a domestic basis, the implications could be phenomenal. Everyone who uses the Internet for communication would need a key and a key escrow agent. This could mean tens of millions of keys unless some type of key sharing was initiated.

SUMMARY

Without question, the overriding theme in this chapter has been that the implementation of security technology in the absence of a comprehensive security policy including senior management support is a waste of time and money. Security policy must be developed as part of an overall increase in security awareness on the part of all users. It must be accompanied by a clear understanding of business processes and personal responsibilities as they relate to security policy implementation. Only in the context of a dynamic, constantly audited security policy can security technology implementation be successful.

The first security process that is generally addressed is virus protection, most often in response to a virus incident. Virus scanning technology is of little use without comprehensive, enforced policies regarding use and handling of diskettes and downloaded files. Activity monitors and signature scanners are two major types of virus scanning software.

The next security process that is generally addressed is authentication, assuring that users attempting to log into network resources are really who they claim to be. Authentication technology includes challenge-response and time-synchronous token authentication systems.

Authorization and access control assure that authenticated users are only able to access those files, directories, and applications to which they are entitled. Kerberos is the best example of a comprehensive authentication/authorization system.

Firewalls are an effective means of shielding private, secure, internal networks from nonsecure external networks. Like other security technology, they must be implemented correctly and in accordance with the overall security policy. Two major categories of firewalls are packet filters, which discriminate between traffic based on source and destination addresses, and application gateways of proxies, which examine individual commands within applications.

Privacy of network communications is assured by encryption. Private key encryption, public key encryption, and digital signature encryption are the major categories of encryption technology. Encryption sessions are customized through the use of keys. The longer the key, in bits, the more secure the transmission.

Encryption technology is regulated as to the key length that can be exported from the United States. Key recovery mechanisms are plans through which the government would be able to decipher encrypted communications. In order for organizations to be able to encrypt communication internationally, they must be willing to submit a key recovery mechanism to the U.S. government.

KEY TERMS

activity monitors, 548
application gateways, 550
application-level filters, 550
assets, 536
assured pipelines, 550
attack applets, 546
authentication, 555
authentication header, 568
biometric authentication, 557
brokered authorization, 558
C-2 certification, 572
CA, 561
certificate authorities, 561
challenge handshake authentication
  protocol, 565
challenge-response token
  authentication, 556
CHAP, 565
ciphertext, 560
Clipper Chip, 573
CRC checkers, 548
data encryption standard, 560

DES, 560
Digital IDs, 561
Digital signature encryption, 561
dual-homed gateway, 551
emulation technology, 548
encapsulating security payload
  header, 568
ESP, 568
event detection, 543
extended terminal access control
  access system, 565
false accepts, 558
false rejects, 558
filter, 550
filter tables, 550
firewall, 548
generic security service-applications
  program interface, 564
GSS-API, 564
hashing checkers, 548
IDEA, 567
inter-realm, 560

internal firewalls, 551
international data encryption
  algorithm, 567
intrusion detection systems, 543
IP spoofing, 550
IPsec, 567
ISO 7498/2, 534
Kerberos, 558
key escrow agencies, 573
key recovery mechanism, 573
L2F, 567
L2TP, 567
latency, 550
layer 2 tunneling protocol, 567
layer two forwarding, 567
logic bombs, 545
malicious applets, 546
MD5, 566
National Computer Security
  Association, 553
network-level filter, 550
OSI Security Architecture, 534

REVIEW QUESTIONS

1. What are some recent changes in the business and networking worlds that have brought network security to the forefront?
2. What is the importance of the cyclical nature of the security policy development life cycle?
3. What is the purpose of the security requirements assessment grid?
4. What is the dilemma involved with the security/productivity balance?
5. How do the critical success factors introduced with the network development life cycle apply to security policy development?
6. What is the purpose of the OSI Security Architecture and how does it relate to the OSI seven-layer reference model?
7. Differentiate between and give an example, in a network security context, of each of the following: asset, threat, vulnerability, risk, protective measures.
8. Are all of the entities listed in the previous question related by one-to-one relationships? Give an example to defend your answer.
9. Briefly summarize the roles of executives, management, and users in the successful development and implementation of security policy.
10. What is the difference between off-line audits and real-time audits?
11. What is the difference between event detection technology and intrusion detection technology?
12. What is the difference between security audit tools and security probes?
13. What is a virus?
14. What is the difference between a logic bomb and a time bomb?
15. What is a trojan horse?
16. What is a polymorphic virus?
17. What are hostile applets and which environment are they particular to?
18. Why are collaborative applications such as groupware an especially friendly environment for viruses?
19. Differentiate between virus scanning and activity monitors as antivirus technology.
20. What is the shortcoming of CRC and hashing checkers as antivirus solutions?
21. What is a firewall?
22. Differentiate between packet-filtering firewalls and application gateway firewalls?
23. Describe the advantages and disadvantages of proxies.

24. What is a dual-homed gateway?
25. What is a trusted gateway?
26. How does a trusted gateway differ from a dual-homed gateway?
27. What is an internal firewall and what is the motivation for such a device?
28. What is authentication?
29. Differentiate between challenge-response authentication and time-synchronous authentication.
30. What is biometric authentication? Give some examples of biometric authentication technology.
31. What is Kerberos?
32. How does Kerberos assure both authentication and authorization?
33. Differentiate between private key encryption, public key encryption, and digital signature encryption.
34. Why are public key certificates and certificate authorities necessary?
35. Why are APIs and application development environments required to integrate security services with information systems? What would be the alternative?
36. What is RADIUS and what added functionality does it offer over an environment without a three-tiered approach?
37. Differentiate between S-HTTP and SSL.
38. Differentiate between PAP and CHAP.
39. What is PGP? What are its advantages and disadvantages?
40. What is SET and what industry is it targeted toward?
41. What is a tunneling protocol and why is it necessary?
42. What is Secure IP (IPv6) and what services can it offer?
43. What is the difference between transport mode ESP and tunnel mode ESP?
44. What is the difference between single sign-on, single point of registration, and single access control view? What do they all have in common?
45. What is Orange Book or C-2 certification?
46. What is the Clipper Chip?
47. What is the purpose of a key recovery mechanism and how does it work?
48. What is the role of a key escrow agency in enabling a key recovery mechanism?
49. What are the potential implications if all Internet users were required to use key recovery mechanisms?

ACTIVITIES

1. Research topics such as network security losses or computer crime and report on your results. What is the trend of the statistics over the past 5 years? How valid are the statistics in terms of being an accurate reflection of the entire extent of the problem?
2. Find an organization or business that will let you prepare a security policy document. Run the entire process as a well-organized project using project management software if possible. Start with a small feasibility and report your results before defining the full project scope. Use the planning tools supplied in the chapter and adapt them to your own situation as needed.
3. Choose any network security related topic of interest and research it using only Internet resources. Two good sites to start with are http://www.ncsa.com and http://csrc.ncsl.nist.gov/.
4. Consider the statement: The implementation of security technology in the absence of a comprehensive security policy is like putting a steel door on a grass hut. Find actual examples of network security implementations to either support or refute the statement.
5. Download a copy of Security Analyzer Tool for Analyzing Networks from ftp://ftp.win.tue.nl/pub/security/index.html. After obtaining proper permissions, run the analysis tool and report on your results.
6. Log into Internet Security Systems web site at www.iss.net and review information regarding their RealSecure network-based attack analyzer. Compare its features with those of SATAN. What would be the most appropriate use for each technology?
7. Create a virus clearinghouse and information center for your school, business, or organization if one does not already exist. Does your organization have a published antivirus strategy? If not, create one. Report on your results.
8. Research the problem of hostile applets and components? What are the potential solutions to the problem? Is this a problem with the development languages?
9. What is Word Macro Concept virus? Find out exactly how it works and figure out how it can be eradicated and kept from spreading. How much of the solution is technology vs. procedures?
10. Design and prepare a budget for a safe remote

access network including remote access server, firewall, authentication technology, and modems. Prepare alternative budget proposals for challenge-response vs. time-synchronous token authentication technology. Was the price difference significant? If so, how could the price difference be justified?

11. Research the field of biometric authentication technology. What are the most stable and dependable products? What are the latest products? Can you find data on false accept and false reject rates of biometric authentication technology?

12. What is the current rate of acceptance and implementation of Kerberos in industry? What are the strengths and limitations of the architecture?

13. Research the issue of privacy in the age of electronic commerce. What impact might Digital IDs and key recovery schemes have on an individual's right to privacy? Consider debating the issue in class. What are the conflicting motivations or goals that are behind the issue?

14. Research virtual private networks. What is the extent of actual implementation of virtual private networks as opposed to the amount of press coverage and technology development? Explain your results.

15. Research and prepare a presentation, time-line, bulletin board on the government's role in encryption technology control, especially in terms of export control. Begin with the Clipper Chip initiative and follow it through the present day.

CASE STUDY

Tackling Internet Security

Network managers moving toward networks based on TCP/IP standards have been told that intranets—because they are all based on the same standards—will become easier to manage. Unfortunately, security may have been left out of the picture.

Security products lag behind other Internet products in terms of interoperability and integration with network software and hardware, say many of those involved with planning security strategies.

"The current piecemeal approach to information security cannot provide adequate security for business," said Michael Miora, president of Miora Systems Consulting Inc. in Playa Del Rey, Calif. "We need an integrated approach and the development of better standards."

Scary Solutions

Miora describes security management as a "nightmare" in which managers string together solutions such as firewalls, encryption, and authentication from a variety of vendors. Among firewalls alone, there are dozens to choose from. Each re-

quires a complicated knowledge of the configuration and architecture, and few offer much integration with other network components.

The proliferation of firewalls—without the full development of other aspects of security—is complicating security-management tasks, said Carl Howe, senior analyst at Forrester Research Inc. in Cambridge, Mass.

"Most people have many firewalls that they have to manage remotely, but it's not safe to do so," said Howe. Additional problems include the lack of cross-platform support, the need for specialized hardware, and the need to learn management interfaces for each firewall product.

Howe said that to deliver true security, firewalls will have to be integrated with other technologies such as encryption and digital certificates, and all of these elements need to be built into existing network products.

Experts argue that firewalls and other specialized security products—such as encryption and authentication directories—will be

easier to manage when they become integrated with other network components such as hardware and applications software.

Sales of standalone firewall products have taken off, but because they are generally loaded on dedicated servers, they are becoming more of a management burden.

"The biggest problem with firewalls is configuration and testing," said Chris Caldwell, chief technical officer at NetDaemons Associates Inc., a security consultancy in Woburn, Mass. "If you have it properly configured, it will work 99 percent of the time, but if the configuration is wrong it gets much worse than that."

Internetworking players such as Cisco Systems Inc. and Bay Networks Inc. have already made security a part of routers and switches by buying firewall components and integrating them into their respective internetworking software.

"I don't think the firewall business, as a separate business, is a viable solution in the long term," said Forrester's Howe. "Security will become more integrated with existing LAN equipment."

It's less likely that managers will want firewalls to be integrated with NOSes because security experts regard this as a breach of basic security principles, in which the NOS server is separated from the firewall.

"I would avoid using technology that's packaged as part of an NOS," said Caldwell.

In addition to requiring the integration with LAN equipment, Forrester's Howe says that encryption and digital certificates need to become standardized in network applications.

"Eventually you will get to a point where you will have your corporate ID, and all security and certificates are managed from a central point."

Confusion Abounds

But for the time being, no such central point exists for network administrators.

"We're hearing from customers that they're very confused and that they're being bombarded by nifty features in security products," said Roger Farnsworth, marketing manager for security products at Cisco in San Jose, Calif. "Security, including point-to-point encryption, authentication, and firewalls, have got to become a service of the network."

Wider standardization of security protocols would help the situation, according to NetDaemon's Caldwell, who believes that technologies such as encryption and digital certificates should be built into IP now that it has become the de facto protocol for networking. "Encryption should be automatic," he said.

In the past year, security vendors have made strides toward standards that will make security more interoperable. Last year, a group of firewall vendors agreed on the IPsec for point-to-point encryption be-

tween firewalls. Also last year, The Firewall Product Developers' consortium, managed by the National Computer Security Association in Carlisle, Pa., was started in an effort to standardize firewall technology.

More recently, Cisco, Cylink Corp., RSA Data Security Inc., Network Systems Corp., FTP Software Inc., TimeStep Corp, and NetManage Inc. announced support for the Internet Security Association Key Management Protocol (ISAKMP) standard, which defines a security architecture for managing the cryptographic keys necessary for electronic commerce and virtual private networks.

Eventually, managers hope to get security that is transparently built into the network.

"Realistically, it should be possible to invent technology that is secure whenever a connection is made," said Caldwell.

Source: R. Scott Raynovich, "Tackling Internet Security," *LAN Times*, vol. 13, no. 23 (October 14, 1996), p. 57. Copyright © October 14, 1996 by McGraw–Hill, New York. Reprinted by permission of McGraw-Hill, New York.

BUSINESS CASE STUDY QUESTIONS ·····

Activities

1. Complete a top-down model for this case by gleaning facts from the case and placing them in the proper layer of the top-down model. After completing the top-down model, analyze and detail those instances where requirements were clearly passed down from upper layers to lower layers of the model and where solutions to those requirements were passed up from lower layers to upper layers of the model.

2. Detail any questions about the case that may occur to you for which answers are not clearly stated in the article.

Business

1. What are some of the problems unique to network security management?
2. What are the sources of these problems?
3. What are some potential solutions to these problems?

4. What is the likely long-term trend for network security technology such as firewalls?
5. How might standardization efforts affect the current dilemma with network security management's lack of integration and interoperability?

Application

1. What is the problem with Internet security products as compared to other Internet applications?

2. List and differentiate between the major categories on Internet security applications.

Data

1. What are the current limitations or weaknesses of digital certificates and data encryption technology?

2. What are some likely solutions to these problems?

Network

1. What are the major categories of network security elements that must become better integrated?

2. What is IPsec?
3. What is ISAKMP?

Technology

1. What are some of the problems associated with deployment of firewalls?

2. What are some potential solutions to the problems associated with the current generation of firewalls?

CHAPTER **14**

NETWORK MANAGEMENT

Concepts Reinforced

OSI Model
Enterprise Network Architectures
Distributed Information Systems

Top-Down Model
Network Development Life Cycle
Protocols and Interoperability

Concepts Introduced

Enterprise Network Management
Server Management
Desktop Management
Distributed Applications Management
Internetwork Device Management
Distributed Network Management

Systems Administration
Help Desk Management
Consolidated Services Desk
LAN Management
Internet/WWW Management
Network Management Technology

After mastering the material in this chapter, you should

1. Understand the business motivations and forces at work in the current systems administration and network management arena.

2. Understand the relationship between network management processes, personnel, and technology in order to produce a successful network management system.

3. Understand the differences between systems administration processes and network management processes.

4. Understand the protocols and technology associated with each area of systems administration and network management.

5. Understand how systems administration and network management technology can be most effectively implemented.

■ BUSINESS ASPECTS OF NETWORK MANAGEMENT

In much the same manner as network security, the successful implementation of a network management strategy requires a combination of policy, process, people, and technology. Merely throwing network management technology in a vacuum at a network management opportunity will not produce the desired results. What these desired results are may be a matter of perspective.

From the top-down, or business-first, perspective, senior management may look to the proper management of network resources to enable a competitive advantage and to be able to deploy new network services quickly and as needed at a reasonable cost. Meanwhile, the desired result of business unit management might be that end-users can successfully execute those applications that have been implemented to enable business processes and achieve business objectives. Successful execution of applications can be quantified in terms such as transactions per second, mean time between failures, average response time to database queries, etc. Such guarantees of proper execution and delivery of end-user applications are sometimes quantified in terms of **quality of service (QOS)** guarantees. Network management personnel tend to take a more infrastructure-centric approach by concentrating on those elements of the network infrastructure that support the enterprise applications. Examples of such infrastructure components could be server performance, network traffic analysis, internetwork device performance, WAN analysis, etc.

How can network managers simultaneously deploy new services, control costs, provide competitive advantage, and provide guaranteed quality of service in an increasingly complicated, multivendor, multiplatform, multiprotocol environment? To a great extent, the answer is to combine the processes embedded in the top-down model and the network development life cycle. The top-down model forces the network manager to constantly evaluate business objectives, the nature of the applications that will meet those business objectives, the nature of the data that will support those applications, the functional requirements of the network that will deliver that data, and finally, the configuration of the technology that will provide the required network functionality. The network development life cycle forces the network manager to engage in an ongoing process of network monitoring, planning, analysis, design, modeling, and implementation based on network performance.

Network infrastructures must be flexible as well as reliable. The ability to have networks change in response to changing business conditions and opportunities is of critical importance to the successful network manager. Some of the details on how network managers are able to deliver reliability, flexibility, and financial accountability in a simultaneous manner are addressed in the following sections as well as in the remainder of this chapter.

Cost Containment

Before a network manager can contain or reduce costs, it is first necessary to have an accurate representation of the source of those costs. Although this may sound like simple common sense, it is easier said than done, and sometimes not done at all. Figure 14-1 lists some practical suggestions for systems administration and network management cost containment.

Cost-Containment Issue	Importance/Explanation
Take inventory	• Gather accurate statistics and information as to every device, including hardware and software configuration information, that is currently requiring support • This initial inventory will produce an overall accounting of how many different platforms and standards must be supported
Determine support costs	• Perform task analysis on network support personnel to determine how costly personnel are spending their time • Are there too many fires? • Are networking personnel being managed effectively? • What is the cost of supporting multiple platforms and standards? • Are networking personnel required at all corporate sites? • Are more networking personnel required as networks become more complex?
Consolidate and centralize	• Consolidate support personnel and deliver one-stop-support for end-users • Centralize purchasing authority • Pool network support personnel to optimize use of costly personnel • Implement centralized license metering and software distribution to help standardize software platforms deployed throughout the enterprise • How can network management functions and technology be centralized to cap or reduce the number of network personnel required to support enterprise networks? • Centralize standardized applications on a server rather than allowing desktops to install a wide variety of applications
Support process redesign	• Once task analysis has been performed on network support personnel, redesign network support processes to optimize end-user support while minimizing support costs • Use consolidated help desk and trouble-ticketing systems to organize user support efforts while minimizing fire-fighting mentality
Standardize	• Standardize on hardware and software platforms, network architectures, network protocols, and network management platforms to simplify management tasks and reduce costs • Standardized desktop platforms will lead to reduced support and maintenance costs • Implement a software version control program so that network support people don't have to deal with multiple versions of multiple software packages

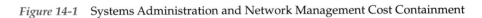

Figure 14-1   Systems Administration and Network Management Cost Containment

Outsourcing

In terms of cost control, one of the key weapons in the arsenal of network managers is **outsourcing,** or the selective hiring of outside contractors to perform specific network management duties. Outsourcing is also becoming increasingly necessary for global corporations to cost-effectively secure required systems and network support personnel throughout the world. There are several keys to outsourcing success:

- The successful identification of those processes that can be most appropriately outsourced is the first key issue. Which processes does the company really need to manage themselves and which could be more cost-effectively managed by a third party? Which skills are worth investing in for the strategic needs of the corporation itself, and which skills are better hired on an as-needed basis? Which tasks can an outsourcer do more cheaply than internal personnel? Which tasks can outsourcers supply new or on-demand expertise for? Which tasks can be outsourced to free corporate personnel for more strategically important issues? Are there tasks that could be more effectively managed by outside experts?

- The successful management of the outsourcing process is required once network management activities have been outsourced as appropriate. It is a good idea to establish communication and evaluation mechanisms as part of the contract negotiation. Issues to be discussed include reporting requirements from the outsourcer to the customer as to performance reports on systems they are responsible for, problem resolution mechanisms, change negotiation mechanisms, performance criteria to be used for outsourcer evaluations, and penalties or bonuses based on outsourcer performance.

- Choosing the right outsourcing provider for the right job is also a key issue. For example, any or all of the following areas may be outsourced although it is unlikely that any one outsourcer could be considered as expert in all areas: application development, application maintenance, client/server systems migration, data center operation, server management, help desk operations, LAN management, end-user support, PC and workstation management, network monitoring, off-site backup and recovery, remote network access, user training and support, and WAN management. The two most common outsourcing areas are application development and data center operation, accounting for 60% of outsourcing in 1996. Among the key evaluation criteria that could be used to narrow the choices of outsourcing vendors are the following: financial stability, networking skill set, geographic coverage, customer references, and pricing structure.

Flexibility

Delivering network flexibility at a reasonable cost to respond quickly to pending business opportunities has become a priority for many network managers. Most network managers that have achieved success in this area cite a few key underlying philosophies:

- Remove dependencies on customized or proprietary hardware and software.

- Move toward adoption of open protocols and off-the-shelf hardware and software technologies. Examples of open protocols include TCP/IP for network transport and SNMP for management information.

- Adopt network management and systems administration packages that support open APIs and can easily accommodate add-in modules.

How can such an acquisition process be managed? Again the top-down model provides the framework to build the technology analysis grid in which technologies to be considered are measured against requirements as dictated by the upper layers of the top-down model.

■ NETWORK MANAGEMENT ARCHITECTURE

To delineate the processes and technology involved with network management, one must first define those components that comprise the network to be managed. This definition of which components are part of the network and which are not is not absolute. Many corporations divide up responsibility for systems administration and enterprise network management in many different ways. There is no single right or wrong way to divide the processes or responsibility for their management. For the purposes of this chapter, the topic of network management is segmented into the following components:

- **Systems administration** focuses on the management of client and server computers and the operating systems and network operating systems that allow the client and server computers to communicate.

- **Enterprise network management** focuses on the hardware, software, media, and network services required to seamlessly link and effectively manage distributed client and server computers across an enterprise.

Both systems administration and enterprise network management consist of several subprocesses as illustrated in Figure 14-2.

As local area networks, internetworks, and wide area networks have combined to form enterprise networks, the management of all of these elements of the enterprise has been a key concern. LANs, internetworks, and WANs have traditionally each had their own set of management tools and protocols. Once integrated into a single enterprise, these disparate tools and protocols do not necessarily meld together into an integrated cohesive system.

Figure 14-3 summarizes the key functional differences between enterprise network management and systems administration and lists some representative technologies of each category as well.

The Network Management Forum associated with the OSI reference model has divided the field of network management into five major categories in a document known as the **ISO Management Framework** (ISO 7498-4). This categorization is somewhat arbitrary as standards and network management technology apply to multiple categories and even the categories themselves are interdependent. However, it is important for the network analyst to be aware of this categorization as it is often referred to when discussing network management architectures and technology. Figure 14-4 lists and explains the five OSI categories of network management.

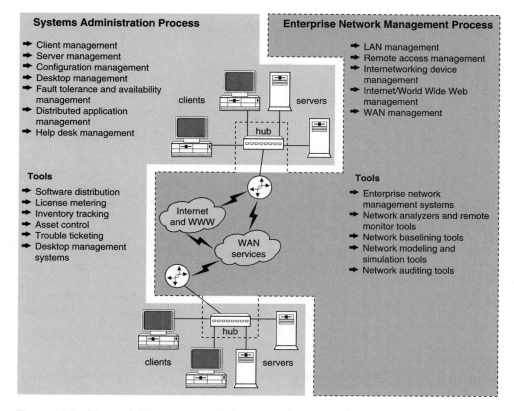

Systems Administration Process

➜ Client management
➜ Server management
➜ Configuration management
➜ Desktop management
➜ Fault tolerance and availability
   management
➜ Distributed application
   management
➜ Help desk management

Tools

➜ Software distribution
➜ License metering
➜ Inventory tracking
➜ Asset control
➜ Trouble ticketing
➜ Desktop management
   systems

Enterprise Network Management Process

➜ LAN management
➜ Remote access management
➜ Internetworking device
   management
➜ Internet/World Wide Web
   management
➜ WAN management

Tools

➜ Enterprise network
   management systems
➜ Network analyzers and remote
   monitor tools
➜ Network baselining tools
➜ Network modeling and
   simulation tools
➜ Network auditing tools

clients   servers
hub
Internet
and WWW
WAN
services
hub
clients   servers

Figure 14-2   Network Management Architecture: Systems Administration and Enterprise Network Management

	Functionality	Technology
Enterprise network management	• Monitor and manage internetwork, technology—switches, routers, bridges, hubs • Monitor and manage WAN links	• HP OpenView • IBM SystemView • Sun Solstice Enterprise Manager
System administration (also known as desktop management)	• Track hardware and software inventory • Perform license metering • Monitor LAN and server activity • Software distribution • Asset management • Server monitoring	• SaberLAN Workstation (McAfee) • Brightworks (McAfee) • LANDesk Suite (Intel) • Norton Administrator for Networks (Symantec) • Frye Utilities for Desktops (Seagate) • System Management Server (Microsoft) • ManageWise (Novell)

Figure 14-3   Systems Administration vs. Enterprise Network Management

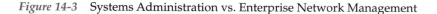

OSI Category of Network Management	Explanation/Importance
Fault management	• Monitoring of the network or system state • Receipt and processing of alarms • Diagnosis of the causes of faults • Determination of the propagation of errors • Initiation and checking of error recovery measures • Introduction of trouble ticket system • Provision of a user help desk
Configuration management	• Compile accurate description of all network components • Control updating of configuration • Control of remote configuration • Support for network version control • Initiation of jobs and tracing of their execution
Performance management	• Determination of quality of service parameters • Monitor network for performance bottlenecks • Measure system and network performance • Process measurement data and produce reports • Capacity planning and proactive performance planning
Security management	• Monitor the system for intrusions • Provide authentication of users • Provide encryption to assure message privacy • Implement associated security policy
Accounting management	• Record system and network usage statistics • Maintain usage accounting system for chargeback purposes • Allocation and monitoring of system or network usage quotas • Maintain and report usage statistics

Figure 14-4   OSI Categories of Network Management

Consolidated Service Desk

Although the division of network management processes into systems administration and enterprise network management is helpful in terms of distinguishing between associated function, protocols, and technology, how are these various processes actually supported or implemented in an enterprise? Reflective of the evolution of information systems in general, network management has undergone an evolution of its own. The current trend in network management is to offer a **consolidated service desk (CSD)** approach to end-user and infrastructure support. Such an approach offers a number of benefits:

- As a single point of contact for all network and application problem resolution, appropriate personnel processes can be matched with associated network management technologies. This match of standardized processes with technology yields more predictable service levels and accountability. CSD software should include features to support problem escalation, trouble ticketing and tracking, and productivity management reporting. Users should be able to easily check on the status of the resolution of reported problems.

- The consolidation of all problem data at a single location allows correlations between problem reports to be made, thereby enabling a more proactive rather than reactive management style. Incorporated remote control software will allow CSD personnel to take over end-user computers and fix problems remotely in a swift manner.

- Resolutions to known user inquiries can be incorporated into intelligent help desk support systems to expedite problem resolution and make the most effective use of support personnel. On-line knowledge bases allow users to solve their own problems in many cases.

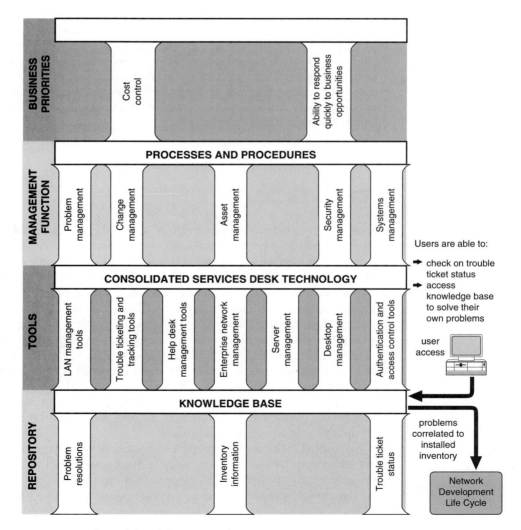

Figure 14-5   Consolidated Service Desk

- The CSD can also handle other processes not directly related to problem resolution such as inventory and asset tracking, asset optimization through the use of such technology as license metering software, and coordination of hardware and/or software upgrades. Software upgrades could be centrally handled by electronic software distribution technology. The management of these systems changes is referred to as change management.

- Network security policies, procedures, and technology can also be consolidated at the CSD.

- Eliminates or reduces "console clutter" in which every monitored system has its own console. In large multinational corporations, this can lead to well over 100 consoles. Recalling that all of these consoles must be monitored by people, console consolidation can obviously lead to cost containment.

Figure 14-5 conceptually illustrates how policy, procedures, personnel, and technology all merge at the CSD. It is important to note the inclusion of policy and procedures in the illustration. The formation of a CSD provides a marvelous opportunity to define or redesign processes to meet specific business and management objectives. Any technology incorporated in the CSD should be chosen based on its ability to support the previously defined corporate policies and procedures in its area of influence. It is important not to first choose a CSD tool and let that tool dictate the corporate processes and procedures in that particular area of management. The actual tools and technology mentioned in Figure 14-5 are discussed in further detail in the remainder of the chapter.

■ SYSTEMS ADMINISTRATION

Server Management

At the heart of systems administration is the administration of the servers that are the workhorses and providers of basic system functionality. As servers are continuing to take on increasingly important roles to the entire enterprise such as electronic messaging servers and enterprise directory servers, it is becoming more important to be able to effectively manage, troubleshoot, and remotely configure these critical elements of the enterprise infrastructure. Server management software seeks to ease systems administrators' chores by effectively monitoring, reporting, troubleshooting, and diagnosing server performance. Some server management software is particular to a certain brand of server, whereas other server management software is able to manage multiple different brands of servers. Ultimately, to be especially useful in meeting overall goals of systems reliability and end-user satisfaction, server management software must provide **server capacity planning** capabilities by monitoring server performance trends and making recommendations for server component upgrades in a proactive manner.

An important point to remember about server management software is that it most often requires a software and/or hardware module to be installed on all servers to be monitored and managed. This module will require varying amounts of system resources (CPU cycles, memory) and will have varying degrees of impact on system performance. Some server management systems perform most of the processing on the managed servers, whereas others perform most of the processing on the server management console or workstation. Likewise, some server management systems require a dedicated management workstation, whereas others will operate on a multifunction management workstation. Figure 14-6 summarizes some of the key potential functional areas of server management software, and Figure 14-7 illustrates the implemented architecture of a server management system.

Server Management System Function	Importance/Explanation
Diagnose server hardware problems	• Can alarm thresholds and status be flexibly defined? • How many alarm levels are possible? • Can RAID drive arrays be monitored and diagnosed? • Is predictive hardware failure analysis offered? • Is a diagnostic hardware module required? • Can server temperature and voltage be monitored? • Can bus configuration and utilization be reported?
Diagnose server software problems	• Does the server management software track version control and correlate with currently available versions? • Can version control indicate potential impacts of version upgrades? • What diagnostics or routines are supplied to diagnose server software problems?
Server capacity planning and performance enhancement	• Are performance enhancement and capacity planning capabilities included? • Are trend identification routines included? • Are inventory, asset management, and optimization modules included?
Share data with other management platforms	• Can data be passed to frameworks and integrated suites such as HP OpenView or IBM SystemView? • Can alerts and alarms trigger pagers, e-mail, and dial-up? • Can data be exported to an ODBC-compliant database?
Remote configuration capability	• Can servers be remotely configured from a single console? • Is out-of-band (dial-up) management supported? • Is remote power cycling supported? • Is screen redirection/remote console supported?
Report generation	• Are alert logs automatically generated? • Can reports be flexibly and easily defined by users?

Figure 14-6   Server Management Software Functionality

Server Management System Function	Importance/Explanation
Protocol issues	• Is TCP/IP required for the transport protocol? • Is IPX supported? • Is SNMP the management protocol? • Are any proprietary protocols required?
Server platforms managed	• Possibilities include Windows NT, NetWare 3.*x*, NetWare 4.*x*, SCO UNIX and other UNIX varieties, OS/2, and Vines
Console requirements	• Is a Web browser interface supported? • Is a dedicated workstation required for the console? • Operating system requirements for console? • Hardware requirements for console?
Statistics tracked and reported	• Logged in users • Applications running • CPU utilization • I/O bus utilization • Memory utilization • Network interface card(s) utilization • Disk(s) performance and utilization • Security management • System usage by application, user
Mapping capabilities	• Can the administrator map or group servers flexibly? • Can statistics be viewed across multiple server groups defined by a variety of characteristics? • How effective is the server topology map? • Can screen displays be easily printed?

Figure 14-6   Continued

Help Desk Management

Although some help desk management technology is aimed at setting up small help desks on a single PC or workstation to provide simple trouble ticketing and tracking, the higher end of help desk technology supports the processes included in the consolidated help desk such as

- Asset management.

- Change management.

- Integration with event management systems.

- Support of business-specific processes and procedures.

The basic objective of this higher end technology is the same as the objective of the consolidated service desk:

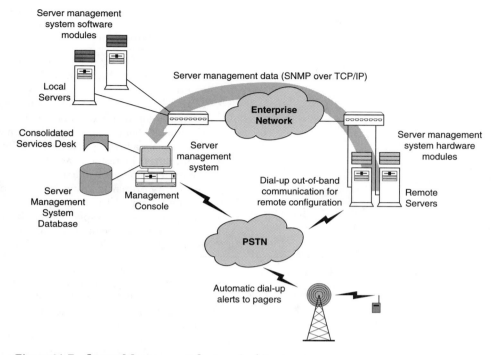

Figure 14-7   Server Management System Architecture

- Rather than merely reacting to system or network problems, proactively manage system and network resources to prevent problems.

Because the consolidated service desk is held accountable for its level of service to end-users, it is essential that help desk management technology be able to gather the statistics necessary to measure the impact of the consolidated service desk. Since a significant amount of the interaction with a consolidated service is via the phone, it is important for help desk management software to be able to interact with call center management technology such as **automatic call distributors (ACD)** and **interactive voice response units (IVRU).** The overall integration of computer-based software and telephony equipment is known as **computer telephony integration (CTI).**

The heart of any help desk management software package is the **knowledge base,** which contains not just the resolutions or answers to problems but the logic structure or decision tree that takes a given problem and leads the help desk staff person through a series of questions to the appropriate solution. Interestingly, the knowledge bases supplied with help desk management software may be supplied by third parties under license to the help desk management software vendor. Obviously, the knowledge base is added to by consolidated service desk personnel with corporate-specific problems and solutions, but the amount of information supplied initially by a given knowledge base can vary. The portion of the software that sifts through the knowledge base to the proper answer is sometimes referred to as the **search engine.**

Figure 14-8 summarizes some of the other key functional areas for help desk management software.

Help Desk Management Software Functionality	Explanation/Importance
Administration, security and utilities	• What types of adds, deletes, and changes can be made with the system up and running and what types require a system shutdown? • Must all help desk personnel be logged out of the system to perform administrative functions? • Can major changes be done on a separate version off-line, followed by a brief system restart with the new version? • Can changes be tested in an off-line environment before committing to live installation? • Is security primarily group level or individual? Can agents belong to more than one group? • Can priorities and response times be flexibly assigned? • Can information be imported and exported in a variety of formats?
Call logging	• How easy is it to log calls? • Can call logging link to existing databases to minimize amount of data that must be entered? • Can number of steps and keystrokes required to add a user or log a call be controlled? • Can multiple calls be logged at once? • Can one call be suspended (put on hold) while another one is logged? • Can special customers or users be flagged as such?
Call tracking and escalation	• How flexible are the call escalation options? • Call escalation options should be able to support internally defined problem resolution and escalation policies and processes • Can the system support both manual and automatic escalation? • Can automatic escalation paths, priorities, and criteria be flexibly defined? • Can calls be timed as part of service-level reporting? • How flexibly can calls be assigned to individual or groups of agents? • Is escalation system tied to work schedule system? • Can subject area or problem experts be identified and used as part of the escalation process?
Customizability	• Customizability is an issue at both the database level and the screen design level • How easy is it to add knowledge and new problems/solutions to the knowledge base? • Does the software offer customizability for multinational companies? • Can entire new screens or views be designed? • Do existing screens contain undefined fields?

Figure 14-8   Help Desk Management Software

Help Desk Management Software Functionality	Explanation/Importance
Integration with other products	• Computer telephony integration with automatic call distributors and interactive voice response units • Which other integrated modules are included: asset management, change management, scheduling, training, workstation auditing • Does the software link to enterprise network management software such as HP OpenView or IBM SystemView?
Performance	• Variables to consider when evaluating performance: number of simultaneous users on-line, number of calls per hour, required platform for database/knowledge base and search engine, required platform for agents • Which SQL-compliant databases are supported? • Can searches be limited to improve performance?
Problem resolution	• Products can differ significantly in how they search knowledge bases. This can have a major impact on performance. Decision trees, case-based retrieval, troubleshooting tools, and embedded expert systems or artificial intelligence are the most intelligent, most complicated, and most expensive options for problem resolution methodologies. • Many products provide more than one search engine or problem resolution method • Some problem resolution products learn about your environment as more problems are entered • Some problem resolution methods can use numerous different knowledge sources or problem databases
Reporting	• How many standard reports are included? • How easily can customized reports be created? • How easily can data (especially agent performance data) be exported to spreadsheet or database programs for further analysis?

Figure 14-8   Continued

Configuration Management

Single Sign-on   Providing single sign-on services for distributed applications deployed across multiple servers is a benefit to users as well as systems administrators. By establishing a distributed security directory housed on a central security server, single sign-on software is able to provide a single login location for multiple, different types of computing platforms. This precludes users from having to remember multiple passwords and allows systems administrators to maintain user accounts and privileges for an entire enterprise from a single location. Single sign-on software is ideally deployed as part of the consolidated service desk. Among multiplatform single sign-on technology and vendors are the following:

Single Sign-on Software	Vendor
OmniGuard/Enterprise SignOn	Axent Technologies
CKS MyNet	CKS North America
AccessManager	ICL, Inc.
Connection	Open Horizon

Configuration Management Tools   Once hardware and software desktop configuration standards have been established and enforced, ongoing maintenance and monitoring of those standards can be assured by configuration management tools such as electronic software distribution tools, license metering tools, and automated inventory tools. To more easily integrate configuration management tools with corporate policy and standards regarding desktop configurations, a new breed of **policy-based management tools** has emerged.

Policy-based management tools in their simplest form are able to automate certain tasks by using job-scheduling utilities to schedule background and after-hours jobs. Another key point about these tools is that they are able to administer multiple different types of client platforms such as DOS, Windows 3.x, Windows 95, Windows NT, OS/2, HP-UX, AIX, SunOS, and Solaris, to name but a few. More advanced tools not only automate administrative tasks but also provide an interface for managing the corporate desktop configuration policies themselves. Administrators are able to set policies for an entire global enterprise, for specified domains, or for individual workstations. For example, some policy-based management software can store policies in a knowledge base that arranges the policies in a hierarchical fashion to identify policy conflicts. However, once again, merely throwing technology at a problem will not provide an adequate solution. First, internal policies must be developed within the corporate environment before they can be entered into the policy-based management system. This policy development may involve a tremendous amount of work before the software can ever be implemented. Examples of the types of policies that might be enforced by policy-based management tools could be any of the following:

- User access rights to files, directories, servers, and executables.
- Desktop start-up applications and background colors or corporate-approved screen savers.
- Deny user access to network if desktop virus checking or metering has been disabled.
- Facilitate changes when applications move or devices are added to the network.
- Prevent users from trying to install and run programs their desktops can't support.

A few examples of policy-based management tools and their vendors are as follows:

Policy-Based Management Tool	Vendor
Saber Tools	McAfee
Norton Desktop Administrator	Symantec
AdminCenter	Hewlett-Packard
Tivoli/Admin	IBM/Tivoli

Desktop Management

Desktop management is primarily concerned with the configuration and support of desktop workstations.

Desktop Management Architecture and Protocols   Desktop management systems rely upon an architecture and associated protocols proposed by the **Desktop Management Task Force (DMTF),** which consists of over 50 companies, including Intel, Microsoft, IBM, Digital, Hewlett-Packard, Apple, Compaq, Dell, and Sun. The overall desktop management architecture is known as the **DMI,** or **desktop management interface,** and is illustrated in Figure 14-9.

Although differing in both strategic intent and governing standards-making organizations, it is still important for desktop management and enterprise management systems to be able to transparently interoperate. Since DMI-compliant desktop management systems store performance and configuration statistics in a **MIF (management information format)** and enterprise management systems employ a MIB, a MIF-to-MIB mapper is required to link desktop and enterprise management systems. The DMI architecture consists of four primary components:

- **DMI services layer** is the DMI application that resides on each desktop device to be managed. The DMI services layer does the actual processing of

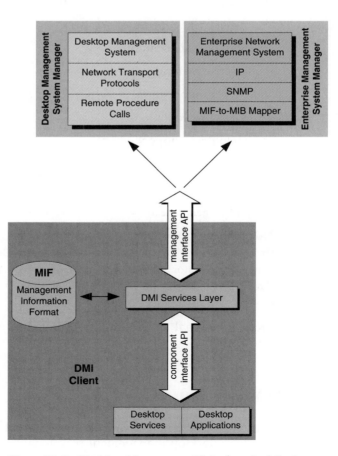

Figure 14-9   Desktop Management Interface Architecture

desktop management information on the client platform and serves as an interface to two APIs.

- The **management interface API** is designed to interface to the desktop system management program that will consolidate the information from this client with all other desktop information.

- The **component interface API** is designed to interface to the individual application programs or desktop components that are to be managed and monitored on the local client.

- Information about the local desktop components is stored locally in a MIF, or management information format.

Desktop Management Technology   Desktop management technology offerings from different vendors are best characterized as suites of associated desktop management applications. Current offerings differ in the variety of management modules included within a given suite as well as the extent of integration between suite modules. Among the modules that some, but not necessarily all, desktop management suites include are the following:

- Hardware and software inventory.
- Asset management.
- Software distribution.
- License metering.
- Server monitoring.
- Virus protection.
- Help desk support.

Examples of desktop management suites and their vendors are as follows:

Desktop Management Suites	Vendor
LANDesk Management Suite	Intel
Saber LAN Workstation	McAfee
Norton Administrator Suite	Symantec
Desktop Management Suite	Seagate

Key functional characteristics of desktop management systems are listed in Figure 14-10.

LAN Management

Desktop management software assumes that a LAN infrastructure will be available over which desktop management functionality can be delivered. As a result, LAN management, once considered a separate functional area from desktop manage-

Functional Category	Importance/Implication
Integration	• Are all desktop management applications tied together through a single interface to a single console? • Do all desktop management applications share information with each other via a single database? • Can software modules be added individually as needed? Suites may be either modular or tightly integrated in design. • Does the system support the DMI architecture? Is output data in management information format?
Network operating system compatibility	• Which network operating system must the desktop management console or server run over? • Which network operating system is the desktop management system able to monitor? Some desktop management systems can only monitor a single NOS. For example, Novell's ManageWise is only able to monitor NetWare networks and Microsoft's System Management Server is only able to manage Microsoft networks, although this may not always be the case. • Examples of supported network operating systems include NetWare, Windows NT, IBM LAN Server, Banyan Vines, Artisoft LANtastic, DEC Pathworks, and AppleTalk
Desktop compatibility	• Since the primary objective of this software category is to manage desktops, it is essential that as many desktop platforms as possible are supported • Examples of supported client platforms include DOS, Macintosh, OS/2, Windows 95, Windows NT Workstation, Windows for Workgroups, and Windows 3.11
Hardware and software inventory (asset management)	• Can the inventory software auto-detect client hardware and software? • Can changes in files or configuration be tracked? • Can versions of software be detected and tracked? • How many applications can be identified? Libraries of 6000 are not uncommon • Can CPU types and speeds be correctly identified? • Is a query utility included to identify workstations with given characteristics?
Server monitoring	• Does the software support the setting of threshold limits for CPU activity, remaining disk space, etc.? • What server attributes can be tracked? CPU activity, memory usage, free disk space, number of concurrent logins or sessions?
Network monitoring	• Can data-link layer traffic be monitored and reported on? • Can network layer protocol traffic activity be monitored and reported on? • Can MAC layer addresses be sensed and monitored? • Can activity thresholds be established for particular data-link or network protocols?
Software distribution	• Can software be distributed to local client drives as well as network servers? • Can updates be automatically installed?

Figure 14-10   Functional Categories of Desktop Management Systems

Functional Category	Importance/Implication
Software distribution	• Can the system track which software needs to be updated through ties with the software inventory system? • Can updates be uninstalled automatically? • Can progress and error reports be produced during and after software distribution?

License metering	• Where can software licenses be tracked?
	    • Clients
	    • Server
	    • Across multiple servers
	• Can license limit thresholds be set?
	• Will the manager be notified before the license limit is reached?
	• Will users be notified if the license limit has been reached?
	• Will users be put into a queue for the next available license after the license limit has been reached?

Virus protection	• Can virus protection be provided for both clients and servers? • Can diskette drives as well as hard drives be protected? • Can viruses embedded within application programs be detected?
Help desk support	• Are trouble-ticketing and call-tracking utilities included? • Are query capabilities included to search for similar problems and solutions? • Are reports available to spot trends and track help desk effectiveness and productivity?
Alarms	• Can managers be notified of changes to files or configuration? • Can violations or preset thresholds be reported? • Can alarms be sent by e-mail, pager, fax, and cellular phone?
Remote control management	• Can managers take over remote client workstations for monitoring or troubleshooting purposes? • Can this be done via modem as well as over the local LAN? • Can files be transferred to/from the remote client? • Can files on the remote client be viewed without taking over complete control of the remote client? • Can remote reboots be initiated?
Reporting capabilities	• How many predefined reports are available? • Can users define their own reports? • Can information be exported to documents, spreadsheets, or databases? • Which export file formats are supported?

Figure 14-10   Continued

ment, has actually become integrated into desktop management suites. The delivery of effective LAN management faces numerous simultaneous challenges:

• Servers are being consolidated into data centers to more effectively manage them from a centralized location.

• Servers are multiplatform in nature, with varying percentages of Windows NT, NetWare, and UNIX servers present.

- Interoperability requirements and distributed client/server applications are increasing the complexity of the LANs to be managed.

- Information systems organizations are continuing to be under intense pressure to deliver cost-effective services that can be measured and/or justified in the face of outsourcing alternatives.

The keys to meeting these challenges have already been identified:

- Establishment of a consolidated service desk.

- Introduction of LAN management technology that is consistent with previously developed and implemented corporate policies and procedures related to LAN management.

Those functional areas of desktop management suites that are particularly focused toward LAN management are as follows:

- Inventory management and optimization.

- Electronic software distribution.

- License metering.

- Remote control support/troubleshooting.

- Server monitoring.

- Network monitoring.

- Web server monitoring.

- Help desk support.

One key manner in which LAN management suites may differ is scalability. Whereas some management suites are focused strictly on workgroup management, others can scale to enterprise proportions and are able to integrate with enterprise management frameworks such as Tivoli Management Environment or HP OpenView. Such integration is enabled through support of enterprise management protocols such as SNMP, RMON, and RMON2. LAN management tools tend to be more focused on problem identification than enterprise-wide consolidated service desk software with characteristics such as problem diagnosis or problem avoidance.

Distributed Application Management

Although distributed applications can be developed for client/server information systems that possess the power equivalent to those deployed on mainframes, client/server-based applications have not yet matched mainframe applications in terms of reliability and manageability. This is primarily due to a lack of effective application management tools and underlying application management protocols that can expose an application's dependencies and measure numerous aspects of performance. This lack of application management tools can make it impossible to diagnose and correct application problems ranging from poor performance to system crashes.

Fortunately, an effort is underway to build self-diagnosing intelligence into applications during the development stage. By having these predefined events and **performance metrics** included within the application, management consoles will be able to detect problems with application performance and take corrective action. These embedded performance metrics are sometimes referred to as **instrumentation.** Two such development environments are Unify VISION and Forte Application Environment. In between the intelligent application, reporting on event conditions and performance metrics, and the management console is an autonomous piece of software known as an **agent** that collects these performance statistics and properly formats them for transmission to the application management console. In turn, these agents are able to communicate with a variety of application management consoles or any SNMP-based administrative program. Examples of agents include AgentWorks from Computer Associates and AppMan from Unify. Eventually, it is hoped that such application management information can be consolidated into enterprise management frameworks such as CA-Unicenter and Tivoli Management Environment.

An alternative to developing your own applications with embedded management intelligence is to purchase a prewritten **event management tool** that has been written to monitor specific commercially available applications such as Lotus Notes, SAP R2/R3, Oracle Financials, or a variety of databases including IBM DB2, Oracle, Informix, and Sybase. PATROL from BMC Software, Inc., is an example of such an event management tool.

One of the key stumbling blocks to widespread deployment and support of distributed application management is the lack of a standard of what application performance information should be gathered and how that information should be reported. One proposal for standardizing how instrumentation should be developed within applications is known as the **applications management specification (AMS).** AMS defines a set of management objects that define distribution, dependencies, relationships, monitoring and management criteria, and performance metrics that can subsequently be processed by agents and forwarded to management consoles. An API that can be used by applications developers is known as **application response measurement (ARM)** and can measure several key application statistics. Another possible standard for distributed application management is a proposed IETF standard known as **Web-based enterprise management (WBEM)** that integrates SNMP, HTTP, and DMI (desktop management interface) into an application management architecture that can use common web browser software as its user interface. An-

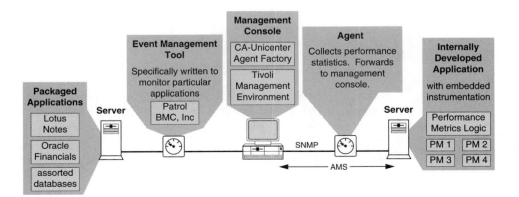

Figure 14-11   Distributed Application Management Architecture

other IETF initiative is developing a two-part applications MIB: the first part, known as the SysAppl MIB, deals with the collection of applications performance data without the use of instrumentation and the second part deals with the collection of performance data that requires instrumentation (performance metrics). As can be seen from the previous paragraph, when it comes to application management, the standards arena is anything but decided. Figure 14-11 illustrates some of the key concepts involved in a distributed application management architecture.

■ ENTERPRISE NETWORK MANAGEMENT

Enterprise Network Management Architecture and Protocols

As illustrated in Figure 14-12, today's enterprise network management architectures consist of a relatively few elements.

Agents are software programs that run on networking devices such as servers, bridges, and routers to monitor and report the status of those devices. Agent software must be compatible with the device that it is reporting management statistics for as well as with the protocols supported by the enterprise network management system to which those statistics are fed. Agents from the numerous individual networking devices forward this network management information to **enterprise network management systems** that compile and report network operation statistics to the end-user, most often in some type of graphical format. Enterprise network management systems are really management application programs running on a management server.

The network management information gathered must be stored in some type of database with an index and standardized field definitions so that network management workstations can easily access this data. A **MIB,** or **management information base,** as these databases are known, can differ in the fields defined for different vendor's networking devices. These fields within the MIBs are known as **objects.** One fairly standard MIB is known as the **RMON MIB,** which stands for remote network monitoring MIB. Finally, a protocol is required to encapsulate the management data for delivery by network and transport layer protocols. Partly due to the dominance of

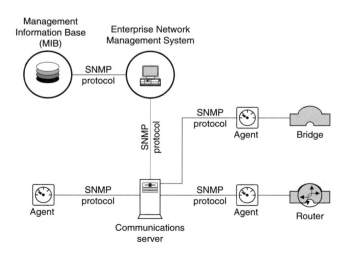

Figure 14-12   Enterprise Network Management Architecture

TCP/IP as the internetworking protocol of choice, **SNMP (simple network management protocol)** is the de facto standard for delivering enterprise management data.

As originally conceived, the enterprise management console would collect the performance data from all of the devices, or elements, comprising an enterprise network in a single, centralized location. However, as networks have grown in both complexity and size and the numbers of devices to be managed have exploded, the amount of management traffic flowing over the enterprise network has begun to reach unacceptable levels. In some cases, management traffic alone can account for 30% of network bandwidth usage, thereby reporting on the problems that it is itself creating.

An alternative to the centralized enterprise management console approach known as the **distributed device manager (DDM)** has begun to emerge. DDM takes more of an end-to-end full network view of the enterprise network as opposed to the centralized enterprise management console architecture that takes more of an individual device or element focus. A DDM architecture relies on **distributed network probes** that are able to gather information from a variety of network devices manufactured by multiple vendors and relay that information to numerous distributed device manager consoles. Probes are strategically placed throughout the enterprise network, especially at junctions of LAN and WAN segments, to isolate the source of network traffic problems. Management traffic is minimized and remains localized rather than monopolizing enterprise network bandwidth supplying the centralized enterprise management console. Figure 14-13 provides a conceptual view of a distributed device manager architecture.

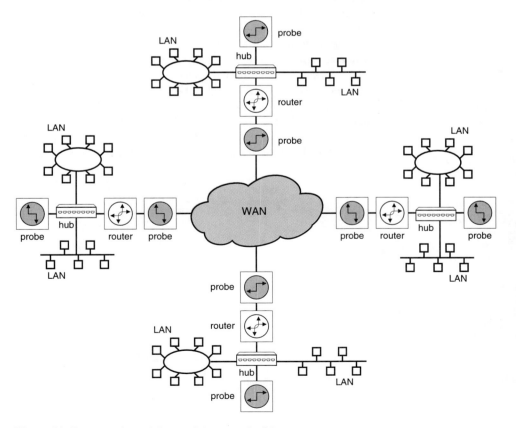

Figure 14-13   Distributed Device Manager Architecture

Another possible evolutionary stage in enterprise network management architectures is web-based enterprise management, first mentioned in the section on distributed application management. The WBEM logical architecture is illustrated in Figure 14-14. The overall intention of the architecture is that the network manager could manage any networked device or application from any location on the network via any **HMMP (hypermedia management protocol)**-compliant browser. Existing network and desktop management protocols such as SNMP and DMI may either interoperate or be replaced by HMMP. Management data from a variety of software agents would be incorporated into the web-based enterprise management architecture via the **HMMS (hypermedia management schema).** All web-based management information is stored and retrieved by the request broker known as **HMOM (hypermedia object manager)**. The WBEM architecture is only a logical design at this point and implemented products and protocols are yet to become reality.

A proposed protocol currently under development by the DMTF (Desktop Management Task Force) that would support HMMS is known as **CIM** or **common information model.** CIM would permit management data gathered from a variety of enterprise and desktop voice and data technology to all be transported, processed, displayed, and stored by a single CIM-compliant web browser. Management data to be used by CIM would be stored in **MOF (modified object format)** as opposed to DMI's MIF or SNMP's MIB format. Figure 14-15 illustrates the interaction of the various types of management data.

Managerial Perspective

Some would argue that CIM is the answer to finally being able to achieve transparency of enterprise management technology. Others would argue that CIM is nothing more than an added layer of complexity on top of an enterprise management system that is already overly complex. An alternative would be to make existing management protocols such as SNMP, DMI, and CMIP more interoperable without the need for additional layers of protocols. However, due to political issues and turf wars, achieving such interoperability is easier said than done, thereby creating opportunities for new all-encompassing protocols such as CIM.

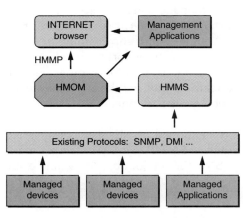

Figure 14-14 Web-Based Enterprise Management Logical Architecture

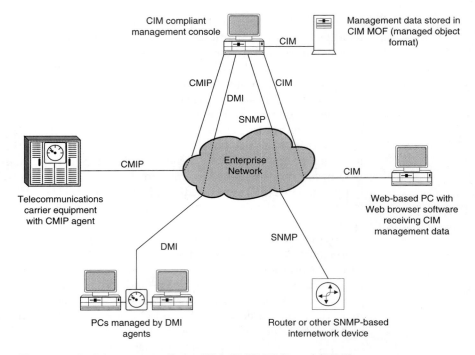

Figure 14-15   Management Data: CIM, CMIP, DMI, and SNMP

Which SNMP Is the Real SNMP?   The original SNMP required internetworking device-specific agents to be polled for SNMP-encapsulated management data. Alarm conditions or exceptions to preset thresholds could not be directly reported on an as-needed basis from the agents to the enterprise network management software. The lack of ability of agents to initiate communications with enterprise network management systems causes constant polling of agents to transpire. As a result of the constant polling, considerable network bandwidth is consumed.

Also, the original SNMP did not provide for any means of manager-to-manager communication. As a result, only one enterprise network manager could be installed on a given network, forcing all internetworked devices to report directly to the single enterprise network manager. Hierarchical arrangements in which regional managers are able to filter raw management data and pass only exceptional information to enterprise managers are not possible with the original SNMP.

Another major shortcoming of the original SNMP is that it was limited to using TCP/IP as its transport protocol. It was therefore unusable on NetWare (IPX/SPX), Macintosh (AppleTalk), or other networks. Finally, SNMP does not offer any security features that would authenticate valid polling managers or encrypt traffic between agents and managers.

The need to reduce network traffic caused by SNMP as well as to deal with other aforementioned SNMP shortcomings led to a proposal for a new version of SNMP known as **SNMP2**, or **SMP (simple management protocol).**

SNMP2's major objectives can be summarized as follows:

• Reduce network traffic.

• Segment large networks.

• Support multiple transport protocols.

- Increase security.

- Allow multiple agents per device.

Through a new SNMP2 procedure known as **bulk retrieval mechanism,** managers can retrieve several pieces of network information at a time from a given agent. This precludes the need for a constant request and reply mechanism for each and every piece of network management information desired. Agents have also been given increased intelligence that enables them to send error or exception conditions to managers when requests for information cannot be met. With SNMP, agents simply sent empty datagrams back to managers when requests could not be fulfilled. The receipt of the empty packet merely caused the manager to repeat the request for information, thus increasing network traffic.

SNMP2 allows the establishment of multiple manager entities within a single network. As a result, large networks that were managed by a single manager under SNMP can now be managed by multiple managers in a hierarchical arrangement in SNMP2. Overall network traffic is reduced as network management information is confined to the management domains of the individual network segment managers. Information is only passed from the segment managers to the centralized network management system via manager-to-manager communication upon request of the central manager or if certain predefined error conditions occur on a subnet. Figure 14-16 illustrates the impact of SNMP2 manager-to-manager communications.

SNMP was initially part of the Internet suite of protocols and therefore was only deployed on those networks equipped with the TCP/IP protocols. SNMP2 works transparently with AppleTalk, IPX, and OSI transport protocols.

Increased security in SNMP2 allows not just monitoring and management of remote network devices but actual **remote configuration** of those devices as well. Furthermore, SNMP2 or a variation of SNMP known as **secure SNMP** will allow users to access carriers' network management information and incorporate it into the wide area component of an enterprise network management system. This ability to actually access data from within the carrier's central office has powerful implications for users and enables many advanced user services such as SDN, or software-defined network.

Perhaps the most significant SNMP2 development in terms of implication for distributed client/server management is the ability to deploy multiple agents per device. As a practical example, on a distributed server, one agent could monitor the processing activity, a second agent could monitor the database activity, and a third could monitor the networking activity, with each reporting back to its own manager. In this way, rather than having merely distributed enterprise network management, the entire distributed information system could be managed, with each major element of the client/server architecture managed by its own management infrastructure.

Unfortunately, considerable debate over portions of the SNMP2 protocol have delayed its deployment for years. Some people feel that features of SNMP2, especially the security aspects, are too difficult to implement and use whereas others blame the delay on concerns over marketing position and competitive advantage from technology vendors. In the interim, alternative upgrades to SNMP have been proposed by both officially sanctioned organizations such as the IETF and ad hoc forums. Figure 14-17 summarizes key points of the various SNMP2 alternatives.

MIBs   Management information bases serve as repositories for enterprise network performance information to be displayed in meaningful format by enterprise network management systems. The original RMON MIB standard that was developed

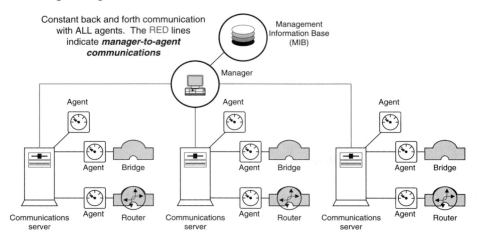

Before: *Manager-to-Agent Communications*

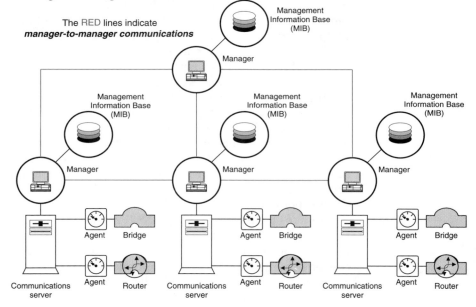

After: *Manager-to-Manager communications*

Figure 14-16 SNMP2 Supports Manager-to-Manager Communications

in 1991 has been updated as **RMON2.** Whereas the original RMON MIB only re-quired compatible technology to be able to collect and analyze statistics on the physical and data-link layers, RMON2 requires collection and analysis of network layer protocols as well. In addition, RMON2 requires compatible technology to be able to identify from which applications a given packet was generated. RMON2 compatible agent software that resides within internetworking devices and reports performance statistics to enterprise network management systems is referred to as an **RMON probe.** Overall, RMON2 should enable network analysts to more effec-tively pinpoint the exact sources and percentages of the traffic that flows through

SNMP Standard	Also Known As	Advantages	Disadvantages
SNMP		• Part of TCP/IP suite • Open standard • Works with defined MIBs	• Excessive polling • No manager-to-manager communication • Only supports TCP/IP • No security
SNMP2	• SMP • Secure SNMP	• Supports bulk retrieval • Supports manager-to-manager communication • Supports multiple protocols • Provides security • Remote configuration	• Never implemented due to squabbling among standards bodies
Updated SNMP2	• SNMP2t • SNMP2c • SNMP1.5	• Supposedly easier to implement due to removal of security features	• No security features • No manager-to-manager communication • No remote configuration
SNMP3	• SNMP2	• Adds security features back into SNMP2	• Lack of support from official standards-making organization • Vendor-specific solutions are being offered as alternatives

Figure 14-17 Alternative SNMP2 Proposals

their enterprise networks. Figure 14-18 summarizes some of the key functional areas of the RMON2 specification.

Although the RMON2 specification may be able to track traffic generated by a particular application, it does not provide the functionality to determine whether or not the application is performing appropriately. To effectively manage distributed information systems, distributed applications must be able to be managed in a manner similar to enterprise network components. Proposals for such an **application MIB** identify three key groups of variables for proper application tracking and management:

- **Definition variables** would store background information concerning applications such as application name, manufacturer, version, release, installation date, license number, number of consecutive users, etc.

- **State variables** would report on the current status of a given application. Three possible states are: up, down, or degraded.

- **Relationship variables** would define all other network-attached resources on which a given distributed application depends. This would include databases, associated client applications, or other network resources.

One of the major difficulties with developing and implementing an application MIB is the vast difference that exists among distributed applications.

Distributed database management is also important to overall enterprise information system management. Although most distributed data management platforms

RMON2 Function	Explanation/Importance
Protocol distribution	• Tracks and reports data-link layer protocols by percentage • Tracks and reports network layer protocols by percentage • Tracks and reports application source by percentage
Address mapping	• Maps network layer addresses to MAC layer addresses • Maps MAC layer addresses to hub or switch port
Network layer host table	• Tracks and stores in table format network layer protocols and associated traffic statistics according to source host
Network layer matrix table	• Tracks and stores in a matrix table format network layer protocols and associated traffic statistics according to sessions established between two given hosts
Application host table	• Tracks and stores in table format application-specific traffic statistics according to source host
Application matrix table	• Tracks and stores in a matrix table format application-specific traffic statistics according to sessions established between two given hosts
Probe configuration	• Defines standards for remotely configuring probes that are responsible for gathering and reporting network activity statistics
History	• Tracks and stores historical traffic information according to parameters determined by the user

Figure 14-18   RMON2 Specifications

provide their own management system for reporting performance statistics, there is currently no way to consolidate these separate management systems into a single enterprise-wide view. The IETF has been working on a **database MIB** specification that would allow any enterprise data management system to report performance statistics back to any SNMP-compliant enterprise network management system.

Enterprise Network Management Technology

Technology Architectures   All of the systems administration and network management processes reviewed in this chapter can be enabled by associated technology. In most cases, network management products offer functionality across more than one category of network or systems management. One way to distinguish between network management technology is to focus on the architecture of that technology. In general, network management technology can be categorized into one of three possible architectures:

- **Point products**, also known as **element managers**, are specifically written to address a particular systems administration or network management issue. The advantage of point products is that they are narrow in scope, provide the sought after solution, and are usually relatively easy to install and understand. The disadvantage to point solutions is that they do not necessarily integrate with other systems administration and network management tools.

Any necessary correlation between point products must be done by network management personnel. Backup and restoral tools, license optimization tools, or management tools specifically written for a particular vendor's equipment are examples of point solutions.

- **Frameworks** offer an overall systems administration or network management platform with integration between modules and a shared database into which all alerts, messages, alarms, and warnings can be stored and correlated. Perhaps more importantly, most frameworks also offer open APIs or an entire application development environment so that third-party application developers can create additional systems administration or network management modules that will be able to plug in to the existing framework and share management information with other modules. The advantages of a well-integrated framework is that it can offer the network administrator a single, correlated view of all systems and network resources. The disadvantage of frameworks is the development or integration of modules within the framework can be difficult and time-consuming. In addition, not all management modules may be compatible with a given framework. Examples of open frameworks include NM-Expert from Alcatel, Command Post from Boole & Babbage, and Net Expert from Objective Systems Integrators.

- **Integrated Suites** could perhaps be looked upon as a subset of frameworks. The difference between integrated suites and frameworks is that integrated suites are filled with their own network management and systems administration applications rather than offering the user an open framework into which to place a variety of chosen applications. The advantage of integrated suites is that the applications are more tightly integrated and linked by a set of common services that tend to offer the user a more consolidated view of network resources. The disadvantage of integrated suites is that they do not offer the open pick-and-choose architecture of the framework. Examples of integrated suites include Computer Associates' Unicenter, IBM System View, Tivoli's TME, and HP OpenView. Some products in this category offer an integrated suite of applications but also support open APIs to accommodate third-party systems administration and network management applications.

Desired Functionality   Beyond the choices of architecture, systems administration and network management technology also differs in the level of functionality offered. For example, although most network management software can report on network activity, detect abnormal activities, and report alarms, fewer packages are able to diagnose or fix problems. Among the commonly listed functions that network administrators would like to see delivered by systems administration and network management technology were the following:

- The ability to track the operational status of distributed applications.

- The ability to automate reporting of system status information.

- The ability to automate repetitive system management tasks.

- The ability to integrate application management and systems administration information with network management information.

- The ability to improve application performance by properly responding to system status messages.

Currently Available Technology Enterprise network management systems must be able to gather information from a variety of sources throughout the enterprise network and display that information in a clear and meaningful format. Furthermore, enterprise network management systems are being called on to monitor and manage additional distributed resources such as

- Workstations and servers.
- Distributed applications.
- Distributed data management systems.

One of the current difficulties with actually implementing enterprise network management systems is a lack of interoperability between different enterprise network management systems and third-party or vendor-specific network management systems. Popular enterprise network management systems include

- HP Openview.
- IBM SystemView.
- Sun Soft Solstice Enterprise Manager.
- Computer Associates' CA-Unicenter TNG (The Next Generation).
- TME 10—IBM/Tivoli Systems (includes IBM SystemView).
- Platinum Technology Systems Management Solution.

Examples of third-party or vendor-specific network management systems, sometimes known as element managers, include

- Seagate NerveCenter.
- Cisco CiscoWorks.
- Bay Networks Optivity.
- UB Networks UB Network Director.
- Xyplex ControlPoint.
- American Power Conversion PowerNet.

Among the manifestations of the lack of interoperability between third-party applications and enterprise network management systems are

- Separate databases maintained by each third-party application and enterprise network management system.
- Redundant polling of agent software to gather performance statistics.
- Multiple agents installed and executed on networked devices to report to multiple management platforms.

The lack of interoperability between different enterprise network management systems makes it difficult if not impossible to

- Exchange network topology information and maps.
- Exchange threshold performance parameter and alarm information.

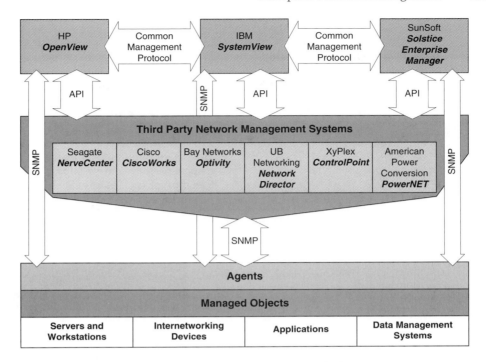

Figure 14-19   Enterprise Network Management System Architecture

The major cause of all of this lack of interoperability is the lack of common APIs both between different enterprise network management systems and between a given enterprise network management system and a variety of third-party network management systems. Figure 14-19 illustrates an architectural view of how enterprise network management systems interface to other enterprise network components. Interoperability APIs included in Figure 14-19 are either proposed or under development.

In addition to interoperability issues previously discussed, key functional areas of enterprise network management software are listed in Figure 14-20.

Analysis—Network Analyzers

The only real effective way to diagnose problems with network performance is to be able to unobtrusively peer into the network transmission media and actually see the characteristics of the packets of data that are causing performance problems. LAN and WAN **network analyzers** are able to capture network traffic in real time without interrupting normal network transmission. In addition to capturing packets of data from the network, most network analyzers are able to decode those packets, monitor packet traffic statistics, and simulate network traffic through traffic generators. Filtering provided by network analyzers can isolate certain types of protocols or traffic from only particular workstations or servers. Given the multitude of protocols and the tidal wave of packets on a given network, effective filtering capabilities are enormously important to network analyzer usefulness.

Some network analyzers are software based (you supply the PC), hardware based (come fully installed in their own dedicated PC), or hybrid, in which an add-

Functional Category	Importance/Implication
Operating system compatibility	• Which operating systems does the enterprise network management system run over? 　• HP UX 　• Sun OS 　• Solaris SPARC 　• IBM AIX 　• Windows NT • How many simultaneous operators of the enterprise network management system are supported? • Can multiple operators be distributed across the enterprise network?
Database compatibility	• Which databases can the enterprise network management system interoperate with? 　• Oracle 　• Ingres 　• SyBase 　• Informix 　• Proprietary 　• DB2 　• Flat file
Network size and architecture	• Is there a limit to the number of nodes supported? • Can the software map all network architectures? Ethernet, token-ring, FDDI, switched LANs, WANs, ATM? • Can mainframes be integrated into the enterprise network management system? • Can IPX as well as IP devices be managed?
Third-party application support	• How many third-party applications are guaranteed to interoperate with this enterprise network management system?
MIB and management protocol support	• How many different MIBs are supported? MIBs can be IETF sanctioned or vendor specific. Enterprise network management systems can easily support over 200 different MIBs. • Are management protocols other than SNMP supported? CMIP (common management information protocol), proprietary, SNMP2
Self-configuration	• To what extent is the enterprise network management software able to self-configure or auto-discover the enterprise network topology? • Can the self-configuration process be customized or controlled?
Cascading or effect alarms	• Is the system able to identify and report alarms triggered by other alarms to more easily pinpoint the cause of problems? This capability may be known as event correlation.

Figure 14-20   Functional Categories of Enterprise Network Management Systems

on hardware device with installed software is linked to your notebook PC via the parallel port. Still other analyzers, such as the Network General Sniffer, are shipped with a PCMCIA (PC Card) Ethernet adapter and software for installation on a limited number of supported notebook computers. Sniffers are also available preconfigured. Network analyzers can also differ in the number of LAN and WAN protocols that can be analyzed, the number of nodes from which traffic can be captured, and the ease of use, understanding, and flexibility of the user interface. Some network analyzers include expert systems that are able to predict oncoming problems based on observed traffic trends.

Network analyzer capabilities are most easily compared and categorized according to the seven-layer OSI model as outlined in Figure 14-21. In some cases, devices are specific to particular layers. For example, layer 1 testers are more commonly known as **cable scanners** or cable testers, whereas devices that test layers 2–7 are often called **protocol analyzers.** Other devices combine both functionalities into a single device. The following gives names of some popular network analyzers and their vendors:

Network Analyzer	Vendor
Sniffer Internetwork Analyzer	Network General
Fluke LANMeter	Fluke
Internet Advisor	Hewlett-Packard
DominoWAN Internetwork Analyzer	Wandel & Goltermann
WAN 900	Digitech Industries

OSI Model Layer	Network Analyzer Functionality
Layer 7—application	• Some analyzers are able to display actual text and numbers being transmitted across a medium. Since passwords and credit card numbers can be displayed by such a device, it is understandable why network analyzers are sometimes considered a security threat. Displaying protocols from layers 4–7 is referred to as embedded protocol decodes.
Layer 6—presentation	• Embedded protocol decodes
Layer 5—session	• Embedded protocol decodes
Layer 4—transport	• Embedded protocol decodes
Layer 3—network	• Network layer protocols: X.25, ISND Q.931, IP, IPX, AppleTalk
Layer 2—data link	• Hardware interface modules (LAN): Ethernet, token ring, switched Ethernet, Fast Ethernet, FDDI • Hardware interface modules (WAN): ISDN BRI, DDS, ATM • Data-link WAN protocols: BiSync, HDLC, SDLC, PPP, LAPB, LAPD, SLIP, frame relay, SNA
Layer 1—physical **(also known as cable scanners or cable testers)**	• Cable scanners are able to pinpoint cable problems including locations of breaks, short circuits, miswiring, and polarity problems • Although a variety of different media types might be tested, the two most popular are Category 5 unshielded twisted pair and fiber optic cable • Layer 1 protocols: V.35, RS-232, RS-449, 423, 422, 530, T-1 (variety of interfaces)

Figure 14-21 Network Analyzer Functional Capabilities by OSI Model Layer

OSI Model Layer	Network Analyzer Functionality

Layer i—physical	• Among the key features and measurements of cable testers are the following:
	   • Ambient noise: level of external noise (from fluorescent lights, motors) where a cable is installed
	   • Attenuation: loss of signal strength over the distance traveled through media
	   • Attenuation-to-cross talk: extent to which a medium resists cross talk
	   • BERT (bit error rate tester): able to determine percent of bits received in error
	   • capacitance: capacity of the medium to store an electrical charge
	   • continuity: an uninterrupted electrical path along the medium
	   • impedance: opposition to flow of a signal within a medium, measured in ohms; the lower the impedance, the better the conductor
	   • loopback device: cable tester function that sends a transmitted signal out through the medium and back into the device for test and measurement
	   • loop resistance: resistance encountered in completing a full electrical circuit
	   • injector device: part of cable tester that creates signal, verifies transmission, and manages testing
	   • NExT (near-end cross talk): signals being transmitted on one end overcoming and interfering with the weaker signals being received on the same end
	   • NVP (nominal velocity of propagation): the speed of the data transmission through the tested media compared to speed of light transmission through a vacuum
	   • OTDR (optical time division reflectometer): device that measures the time it takes for light to be reflected through a medium in order to detect breaks, crimps, etc.
	   • SNR (signal to noise ratio): comparison of signal strength to background noise; measured in (dB)
	   • split pair: when a wire of one pair gets spliced to the wire of an adjacent pair
	   • TDR (time domain reflectometer): able to measure cable lengths, distance to breaks, etc. by reflected electrical signals through a medium
	   • Two-way NExT: measures near-end cross talk as well as far-end cross talk, which is cross talk in same direction as signal
	   • Wire map: verifies pin-to-pin continuity and checks for polarity reversal, short circuits, and open circuits; displayed graphically

Figure 14-21   Continued

Monitoring — Network Baselining Tools

By combining the ability to monitor and capture SNMP and RMON data with the abilities to analyze the captured data and report on trends and exceptions, **network baselining tools** are able to track network performance over extended periods of time and report on anomalies or deviations from the accumulated baseline data. Such tools usually need several weeks of data to establish realistic baseline network performance averages. Network baselining tools may possess auto-discovery capabilities that allow them to build graphical representations of networks by monitoring network management traffic. Such tools also exhibit characteristics such as flexible polling and event correlation that allow them to proactively seek information from network-attached devices and assimilate that information with previously collected data in order to form conclusions and make recommendations. Most network baselining tools share the results of their efforts through a wide variety of predefined and user-defined reports.

Typical reports would offer statistics such as

- Current network volume by day, week, and month as compared to historical averages.

- Network traffic volume leaders by node, actual vs. expected.

- Nodes that are in violation of a variety of user-defined thresholds.

- Predicted number of days before a node will cross a user threshold.

- Nodes whose performance is degrading.

The following gives some examples of network baselining tools and vendors:

Network Baselining Tool	Vendor
Network Health	Concord Communications
Monitoring System	Kaspia Systems
Network PM	3DV Technology

Simulation — Network Modeling and Simulation Tools

Simulation software tools are also sometimes known as **performance engineering** software tools. All simulation systems share a similar trait in that the overall network performance that they are able to model is a result of the net effect of a series of mathematical formulas. These mathematical formulas represent and are derived from the actual performance of the circuits and networking equipment that comprise the final network design.

The value of a simulation system is in its ability to predict the performance of various networking scenarios otherwise known as **what-if analysis.** Simulation software uses the current network configuration as a starting point and applies what-if scenarios. The benefits of a good network simulation package include the following:

- Ability to spot network bottlenecks such as overworked servers, network failures, or disk capacity problems.

- Ability to test new applications and network configurations before actual deployment. New applications may run well in a controlled test environment but may perform quite differently on the shared enterprise network.

- Ability to re-create circumstances in order to reproduce intermittent or occasional network problems.

- Ability to replicate traffic volume as well as traffic transaction type and protocol mix.

The key characteristics that distinguish simulation software are listed in Figure 14-22.

Among network simulation packages and vendors are the following:

Network Simulation Package	Vendor
ComNet Predictor	CACI Products
ComNet III	CACI Products
CANE-RAD	ImageNet
CANE	ImageNet
NetMaker XA	Make Systems, Inc.
BONES	Systems & Networks
AutoNet	Network Design & Analysis Group

Auditing—Network Auditing Tools

Network auditing tools have not enjoyed the popularity to date of other previously described network management technology. This trend is slowly changing as network managers realize the value that network auditing tools can provide in such areas as consolidated services desks, inventory management, network management, and security. What network auditing tools all seem to have in common is the ability to provide records of which network files have been accessed by which users. The value provided by network auditing tools is sometimes provided at a performance cost. Auditing software must be installed and constantly executed on every client and server PC to be audited. The audit statistics gathered can consume significant amounts of disk space and may or may not warn of impending disk storage problems. Among the other capabilities that some, but not necessarily all, network auditing tools offer are the following:

- Ability to keep time logs of file accesses.

- Ability to determine which users are deleting files that just seem to disappear.

- Ability to audit when users copy files to diskettes.

- Ability to audit which software programs (authorized and unauthorized) are installed and/or running on any computer.

- Ability to audit only specified files and/or specified users.

- Ability to integrate with security, systems management, or help desk products.

- Ability to produce text-based, graphical reports and ability to export to spreadsheet, word processing, or database products.

- Ability to track and report on configuration changes.

- Ability to track logins and logouts.

Network Simulation Software Characteristic	Importance/Explanation
Network types	• Which different types of networks can be simulated? Circuit-switched, packet-switched, store-and-forward, packet radio, VSAT, microwave?
Network scope	• How many of the following can the simulation software model either individually or in combination with one another? Modems and multiplexers, LANs, NetWare only, internetworks, WANs, MANs?
Network services	• How many of the following advanced services can be modeled? Frame relay, ISDN (BRI and PRI), SMDS, X.25, ATM?
Network devices	• Some simulation systems have developed performance profiles of individual networking devices to the point where they can model particular networking devices (bridges, routers, MUXs) made by particular manufacturers
Network protocols	• In addition to the network transport protocols listed in the analysis and design section, different router-to-router or WAN protocols can have a dramatic impact on network performance. Examples: RIP, OSPF
Different data traffic attributes	• As studied in previous chapters, all data traffic does not have identical transmission needs or characteristics. Can the software simulate data with different traits? For example: bursty LAN data, streaming digitized voice or video, real-time transaction-oriented data, batch-oriented file transfer data
Traffic data entry	• Any simulation needs traffic statistics to run. How these traffic statistics may be entered can make a major difference in the ease of use of the simulation system. Possibilities include manual entry by users of traffic data collected elsewhere, traffic data entered "live" through a direct interface to a protocol analyzer, a traffic generator, which generates simulated traffic according to the user's parameters, or auto-discovery from SNMP and RMON data generated by enterprise network management systems
User interface	• Many simulation software tools now offer easy-to-use graphical user interfaces with point-and-click network design capability for flexible what-if analysis. Some, but not all, produce graphical maps that can be output to printers or plotters. Others require users to learn a procedure-oriented programming language.
Simulation presentation	• Some simulation tools have the ability to animate the performance of the simulated network in real time whereas others perform all mathematical calculations and then playback the simulation when those calculations are complete.

Figure 14-22   Network Simulation Software Functionality

Among network auditing packages and vendors are the following:

Network Auditing Package	Vendor
Site Inventory (part of DP Umbrella Suite)	McAfee Associates
LT Auditor+	Blue Lance, Inc.
AuditTrack	E. G. Software, Inc.
LANAuditor	Horizons Technology, Inc.
CentaMeter	Tally Systems Corp.

SUMMARY

Network management, like other network-related technology-based solutions, can only be effectively implemented when combined with the proper processes, people, and procedures. As information technology departments have had to become more business-oriented, network management has become more focused on cost containment. Outsourcing is one way in which costs may be contained. However, outsourcing opportunities must be properly analyzed and managed to assure the delivery of quality network management.

The overall field of network management can be logically segmented into systems administration, which is most concerned with the management of clients, servers, and their installed network operating systems, and enterprise network management, which is more concerned with the elements of the enterprise network that connect these distributed systems. One solution to providing comprehensive systems administration and enterprise management services is known as the consolidated service desk.

Server management, help desk management, configuration management, desktop management, LAN management, and distributed application management are all segments of systems administration. Although each of these segments may contain unique functionality and require unique technology, there is a great deal of integration of functionality and overlap of technology.

Enterprise network management architectures and protocols can vary from one installation to the next. New architectures and protocols are under development in order to bring some order to the multiplatform, multivendor, multiprotocol mix of today's enterprise networks.

A variety of enterprise network management technology is available to allow network managers to be proactive rather than reactive. Besides a wide variety of enterprise network management integrated suites and element managers, other enterprise network management tools include network analyzers, network baselining tools, network modeling and simulation tools, and network auditing tools.

KEY TERMS

ACD, 591
agent, 600
AMS, 600
application MIB, 607
application response measurement, 600

applications management specification, 600
ARM, 600
automatic call distributors, 591
bulk retrieval mechanism, 605
cable scanners, 613

CIM, 603
common information model, 603
component interface API, 596
computer telephony integration, 591
consolidated service desk, 586

REVIEW QUESTIONS

1. Describe some of the business-oriented pressures faced by network managers as well as some of the responses to those pressures.
2. What are some of the advantages and disadvantages to outsourcing?
3. Differentiate between systems administration and enterprise network management.
4. Differentiate between the various layers of management defined by the OSI Management Framework.
5. What is a consolidated service desk and what unique functionality or advantages does it offer? How does it differ from previous network management technologies?
6. What are some of the important advantages and disadvantages of server management software?
7. Why is it important for help desk software to be able to integrate with call center technology?
8. What is the difference between a knowledge base and a search engine and why is each important?
9. What are the unique features of policy-based management tools and what is the significance of such features?
10. What is the purpose and structure of the DMI?
11. How does desktop management software

functionality differ from enterprise network management software functionality?
12. What are the key limitations of distributed application management and how are these limitations overcome?
13. What is the difference between distributed device management and centralized enterprise network management?
14. What disadvantage of centralized network management does distributed network management attempt to overcome?
15. Differentiate between the following terms: agent, MIB, RMON, object, SNMP.
16. What is a distributed network probe and how does it differ from an SNMP agent or an RMON probe?
17. What is CIM and what interoperability issues does it hope to overcome?
18. Describe the relationship between the various components of WBEM.
19. What are some of the shortcomings of SNMP and how are they overcome in SNMP2?
20. Why has SNMP2 not been widely accepted and implemented?
21. Differentiate between RMON and RMON2.

22. Differentiate between point products, frameworks, and integrated suites as alternate enterprise network management technology architectures.
23. What are some of the most important functional characteristics of enterprise network management systems?
24. What are some of the important functional characteristics of network analyzers?
25. What is the difference between a cable scanner and a protocol analyzer?
26. What is the overall purpose or value of a network baselining tool?
27. What is the overall purpose or value of a network modeling and simulation tool?
28. What are some of the ways in which current network configuration information can be loaded into a network modeling and simulation package?
29. What is the overall purpose of network auditing tools?
30. Why are network auditing tools becoming more popular than they once were?

ACTIVITIES

1. Investigate the current status of SNMP2. Is the IETF still working on the standard? What are businesses doing in the meantime? What are the key issues that are the cause of debate?
2. Survey businesses or organizations that have implemented enterprise network management systems. Which enterprise network management system was chosen? Why? Which third-party network management systems (if any) does the enterprise system interface with? What functionality of the enterprise network management system has actually been implemented? What do the organizations feel has been the benefit of these systems? What has been the investment in terms of effort to implement and support these systems?
3. Investigate the current state of the desktop management systems market. What percentage of products support the DMI architecture? What percentage of products interface directly to enterprise network management systems? Does one product have a dominant market share? Analyze and report on your results.
4. Research the outsourcing phenomenon. Is outsourcing still increasing in popularity? What has been learned about the advantages and disadvantages of outsourcing? Which types of activities are most often outsourced? Find an organization that has hired an outsourcer and interview them. Find a company that provides outsourcing services and interview them. Do you think outsourcing is a passing phenomenon?
5. Review currently available help desk technology and report on your findings. Find a corporation using help desk software and determine how well the software fits the corporation's business processes and policies. Investigate the technology selection process to determine whether or not evaluation criteria were established before the purchase.
6. Review currently available policy-based management technology and report on your findings. Find a corporation using policy-based management software and determine how well the software fits the corporation's business processes and policies. Investigate the technology selection process to determine whether or not evaluation criteria were established before the purchase.
7. Investigate the field of distributed application management. Has the percentage of applications managed via embedded instrumentation increased? Are application developers including more embedded instrumentation within their applications? Survey corporations in your area to determine how many are using or planning to use distributed application management?
8. Investigate the current status and availability of products supporting the WBEM architecture.
9. Investigate the extent to which network simulation, network baselining, and network auditing tools are being used by corporations in your area. What common characteristics do the corporations using these tools share?

CASE STUDY

Pepsi's Net Expansion

When members of Pepsi-Cola Co.'s network-management team heard they would soon be responsible for supporting an additional 6,000 nodes in the company's restaurant divisions, among the group's first thoughts were to "run for the border."

Although Pepsi's restaurant chains—Taco Bell, Kentucky Fried Chicken, and Pizza Hut—are currently networked to Pepsi's environment, they have kept their own management systems. Integrating them into Pepsi's main management structure would provide the divisions with a centralized-management design to ensure no changes to the network can be made that would affect other divisions. Additionally, Pepsi believes that bringing in management responsibility for the chains will save on resources by sharing equipment and expertise.

In conjunction with upping its responsibilities by 6,000 nodes to about 30,000 nodes, Pepsi's management group is also in the process of upgrading to Hewlett-Packard Co.'s Tornado management platform, HP OpenView 4.1.

The company plans to use the distributed capabilities of HP OpenView 4.1 to partition the management system so that not all of the monitoring information or traps are sent to a single location, according to Ray Shemer, director of technology services for Pepsi-Cola Information Technology. So instead of receiving all the management information at its Somers, N.Y., headquarters, the company will spread the information among three data centers located in Somers, Dallas, and Winston-Salem, N.C.

Where It Stands

Pepsi's main management console monitors about 24,000 nodes and runs on HP OpenView 3.31. It resides in Somers where it receives alerts from 172 sites across the country. In addition, a help desk in Winston-Salem receives notification of events from another 135 offices. These alarms are also passed on to Somers.

According to Tony Travaglini, project manager for network management at Pepsi, the Somers management station receives approximately 1,000 events a day.

To filter through these alerts, Pepsi has implemented Seagate Technology Inc.'s NerveCenter. NerveCenter determines which alarms are repeats from the same device and does not pass on the duplicates. This reduces the number of problems the event log lists and lets network managers view only critical alerts, according to Travaglini.

Other management tools used include Bay Networks Inc.'s Optivity, Cisco Systems Inc.'s Cisco-Works, and Concord Communications Inc.'s Network Health Trakker. Pepsi also uses Remedy Corp.'s Action Request System to automatically generate trouble tickets, which are sent to administrators via E-mail by pagers.

Currently, the management teams are divided into three levels and are assigned events on the basis of the severity of the problem. In addition, 50 LAN technical-support analysts are located at various remote sites to provide immediate help with new implementations, training, and network problems, according to Shemer.

With the addition of the restaurant divisions, the number of remote sites managed will grow to

nearly 360. Initially, the management team will be responsible for monitoring the restaurants' Cisco routers, DSU/CSU (data service unit/channel service unit) connections, and WAN links, which range in speed from 56Kbps to 1.544Mbps.

A second phase of integration with the restaurants may extend management down to the server level—potentially increasing the responsibility of Travaglini's team by 500 to 600 file servers.

Choice of Pepsi's New Generation

To distribute management duties, Pepsi is working to implement HP OpenView 4.1. According to Travaglini, this latest HP OpenView platform will let the company divide network information among the data centers, thereby placing less of a burden on the database in Somers and providing remote administrators with the management information they need.

As of now, the database resides on an HP G70 midrange server that houses 24,000 objects. With HP OpenView's distributed capabilities, "the OpenView database will be smaller, so it will be faster to query information," said Travaglini.

As HP OpenView is implemented at the data centers, Travaglini said Pepsi will bring in new machines to house the management information. The HP G70, currently in Somers, will be moved to Winston-Salem, and Somers will gain a newer HP server, the K220 with 1GB of RAM and 3.8GB of storage. Information in Dallas will reside on an HP D350—an entry-level server.

One of the benefits of moving to HP OpenView 4.1's distributed approach is to lessen the bandwidth used when polling the network. "Status polling will take its toll when you have a 30,000-node network," said Travaglini. "If you can envision the network right now, you see all the traffic is brought back to Somers across the country" via the WAN. By keeping some of the alerts local, Pepsi expects to cut bandwidth use by two-thirds.

Distributing the information has another benefit. Managers at Somers and remote network analysts will see better performance when accessing network information. Each time a remote network manager logged in via an X-terminal application, it would kick off another HP OpenView session and slow down the CPU on the server for all users, noted Travaglini. "Our box couldn't handle it. We were going to have to either limit the number of users coming in or buy a bigger box," he said.

Travaglini admits that "the Tornado installation is going to take an extreme amount of work." But he is optimistic that his team of eight will meet the Labor Day deadline.

Although Shemer and Travaglini do not expect the installation to be completely smooth—"there's always something that's unforeseen, and with the size of our network, we always find it," said Travaglini—they said the fact that they can manage their network proactively rather than reactively will provide a lot of help.

Travaglini credits the preplanned implementation of standards and procedures with enabling this comfort. One of Pepsi's standards is using uniform hardware across the network. For example, all routers are from Cisco and all hubs from Bay Networks. "If you do your planning on day one, it makes day two that much easier," said Travaglini.

With all of the planning and with the expected benefits of the new management platform, Pepsi may be saying to itself: "You've got the right one, baby."

Source: Monica Snell, "Pepsi's Net Expansion," *LAN Times*, vol. 13, no. 14 (June 24, 1996), p. 43. Copyright © June 24, 1996 by McGraw-Hill New York. Reprinted by permission of McGraw-Hill, New York.

BUSINESS CASE STUDY QUESTIONS

Activities

1. Complete a top-down model for this case by gleaning facts from the case and placing them in the proper layer of the top-down model. After completing the top-down model, analyze and detail those instances where requirements were clearly passed down from upper layers to lower layers of the model and where solutions to those requirements were passed up from lower layers to upper layers of the model.

2. Detail any questions about the case that may occur to you for which answers are not clearly stated in the article.

Business

1. In what business was the corporation described in the case primarily involved?
2. What business event triggered a major change in network management responsibilities?
3. What business-level benefits or objectives were expected from integrating the network management systems of Pepsi's restaurant chains with its corporate headquarters network management system?
4. What steps had Pepsi taken in terms of business processes and procedures to assure that the implementation of the new network management system went as smoothly as possible?

Application

1. Which network management application is used at Pepsi headquarters?
2. How many sites are managed by Pepsi headquarters in Somers, NY?
3. How many sites are managed by Winston-Salem?
4. How many sites will be managed after the net expansion?
5. Is this management data shared? How?

Data

1. How will the network management data be distributed?
2. Would you describe the network management system as centralized or distributed? Defend your answer.
3. How many alarms per day are received?

4. How are these alarms filtered?
5. What is the benefit of filtering alarms?
6. Where does the database with all of the network management data currently reside?

7. What is the plan for the future location(s) of this data?

Network

1. What was the objective of combining the network management systems of all of Pepsi's restaurant chains with the corporate network management systems?
2. How many nodes were on Pepsi's network after the expansion?
3. What network components are the management team currently responsible for?

4. How might the types of components for which the management team is responsible change?
5. What is the potential bandwidth impact of gathering management data from a 30,000-node network?
6. How can this polling be minimized? By how much?

Technology

1. What network management technology is employed by Pepsi? Describe the function of each

component technology or network management application.

APPENDIX A

Law 1: You will never know all there is to know in Data Communications.

Law 2: Be honest with yourself concerning what you don't know.

Law 3: There are no Data Communications police.

Law 4: If the network doesn't make good business sense, it probably makes no sense.

Law 5: Technical details are important, technical details are important, technical details are important.

Law 6: There is no such thing as a data communications failure, only networking solutions as yet unfound.

Law 7: Beware of self-proclaimed data communications experts.

Law 8: It is more important to be able to ask data communications questions than it is to be able to supply data communications answers.

Law 9: If you're not moving forward, then you're losing ground to someone who is.

Law 10: In data communications, nearly anything is possible. The real question is whether the proposed solution is affordable.

APPENDIX B

■ **TOP 10 REASONS TO BE IN DATA COMMUNICATIONS**

1. It's a great way to meet Star Trek fans.

2. You will understand Dilbert comic strips.

3. You get to carry a beeper, walkie-talkie, cell phone, mobile fax, laptop computer, and a bunch of other really cool gadgets.

4. You always have an excuse to miss important family events due to "networking emergencies."

5. You get to work long hours doing interesting things for decent money. (You probably won't get rich.)

6. You get fascinating calls in the middle of the night.

7. You get to work on weekends and holidays so you don't interfere with *normal* working people.

8. You can speak entire sentences in acronyms and not use a single English word.

9. Bloodshot eyes from late-night troubleshooting are so attractive.

10. Having a predictable workday is no fun at all!

GLOSSARY

10/100 NICs Most of the 100BaseT NICs are called 10/100 NICs which means that they are able to support either 10BaseT or 100BaseT, but not simultaneously

100BaseFX physical layer standard for 100Mbps transmission over Fiber optic cable.

100BaseT4 physical layer standard for 100Mbps transmission over 4 pair of Category 3, 4, or 5 UTP.

100BaseTX this is the most common of the three 100BaseX standards and the one for which the most technology is available. It specifies 100Mbps performance over 2 pair of Category 5 UTP (Unshielded Twisted Pair) or 2 pair of Type 1 STP (Shielded Twisted Pair).

100VG-AnyLAN 100VG-AnyLAN is a 100Mbps alternative to 100BaseT which replaces the CSMA/CD access methodology with Demand Priority Access or DPA, otherwise known as Demand Priority Protocol or DPP

10Base2 A 10Mbps Ethernet standard for thin coaxial cable media

10Base5 A 10Mbps Ethernet standard for thick coaxial cable media

10BaseFL A 10Mbps Ethernet standard for fiber optic cable media

10BaseT A 10Mbps Ethernet standard for unshielded twisted pair media

16-bit sub-system A shared memory address space, sometimes referred to as a 16-bit sub-system, allows 16bit applications to execute in a 32 bit operating environment

16QAM 16 point quadrature amplitude modulation—a modulation scheme with sixteen different potential detectable events, would allow 4 bits/baud or quadbits to be produced or detected per signaling event. In this case the transmission rate in bps would be 4 times the baud rate

1Base5 A 1Mbps Ethernet standard for unshielded twisted pair

23B+D 23 bearer channels (64Kbps ea.) plus one 64K D channel. Configuration of PRI ISDN

2B+D 2 64Kbps B channels plus one 16K D channel. Configuration of BRI ISDN

30B+D 30 64Kbps bearer channels plus one 64K D channel. European PRI which maps to an E-1.

3270 protocol conversion card 3270 Protocol Conversion card is inserted into an open expansion slot of a PC. Additional protocol conversion software, which may or may not be included with the protocol conversion card, must be loaded onto the PC in order to make the PC keyboard behave like a 3270 terminal keyboard

7 Hop limit One very important limitation of source routing bridges as applied to large internetworks is known as the 7 Hop Limit. Because of the limited space in the RIF (Router Information Field) of the explorer packet, only 7 hop locations can be included in the path to any remote destination

AAL ATM adaptation layer protocols convert user input payloads into ATM cells

ABR Available bit rate, ATM bandwidth management scheme that takes a fixed minimum amount of bandwidth plus whatever VBR (variable bit rate) is not using

absolute path names In Unix, Absolute path names start at the root directory in the listing of the path to the destination directory while relative path names start at the current directory

access charges RBOCs were allowed to charge access charges for co-location of the alternate carrier's equipment in their COs

access control list See ACL

access line Local loop from customer premises to network service entry point

access methodologies Since the LAN media is to be shared by numerous PC users, then there must be some way to control access by multiple users to that media. These media sharing methods are properly known as access methodologies.

ACD Incoming calls are routed directly to certain extensions without going through a central switchboard. Calls can be routed according to the incoming trunk or phone number. Often used in customer service organizations in which calls may be distributed to the first available agent.

ACE Adverse Channel Enhancements, a collection of 4 MNP 10 protocols designed to work with circuits subject to impairment such as cellular

ACK/NAK Acknowledgment/negative acknowledgement, used with ARQ error correction to indicate whether or not retransmission is required

acknowledgment & polling traffic The first characteristic of SNA which can cause trouble on a LAN is the great amount of acknowledgment and polling traffic between SNA processors and SNA end-user devices. This constant chatter could quickly monopolize the better part of the LAN bandwidth.

acknowlegement Postive acknowledgment indicating data block was received without error

ACL NT's security reference monitor compares the requested object's security description as documented in access control lists (ACL), with the requesting user's security information as documented on their security access token.

active monitor In a token passing access methodology, the token is generated in the first place by a designated PC known as the active monitor and passed among PCs until one PC would like to access the network.

Adaptive Differential Pulse Code Modulation See ADPCM

adaptive protocols Protocols that are able to change transmission characteristics as circuit quality varies

Adaptive Size Packet Assembly A MNP 4 protocol that changes the amount of data transmitted in each block dependent on circuit quality

address bit order reversal In the case of IEEE 802.3, the least significant bit is the right-most bit of the byte and in the case of IEEE 802.5, the least significant bit is the left-most bit of the byte. This bit order reversal is especially troublesome for translating bridges which must translate between token ring and Ethernet frames

address caching In order to avoid constantly flooding the network with explorer packets seeking destinations, source routing bridges may employ some type of address caching or RIF caching, so that previously determined routes to known destinations are saved and re-used.

ADPCM By transmitting only the approximate difference or change in amplitude of consecutive amplitude samples, rather than the absolute amplitude, only 32Kbps of bandwidth in required for each conversation digitized via ADPCM as opposed to PCM.

ADSL Asymmetric digital subscriber line. Local loop data service able to offer 6Mbps download and 640Kbps upload over existing copper pairs without interfering with existing POTS service

advanced intelligent network See AIN

Advanced Parallel Technology See APT

Advanced Peer to Peer Networking See APPN

Adverse Channel Enhancements See ACE

AIN Signaling System 7 and the intelligent services that it enables are often described as part of an all-encompassing interface between users and the PSTN (Public Switched Telephone Network) known as AIN or Advanced Intelligent Network

American Standard Code for Information Interchange See ASCII

Amplifier Device used on analog circuits to strengthen and retransmit signals

amplitude carrier wave charateristic which is manipulated to represent 1s and 0s (wave height)

amplitude modulation a modulation scheme in which amplitude is manipulated in order to represent discrete detectable events which are then interpreted into 1s and 0s

analog transmission method characterized by continuously varying tones within a given bandwidth or range of frequencies

analog simultaneous voice/data See ASVD

ANI Automatic number identification, also known as caller ID

API Application program interface, series of commands supported by both application programs and operating systems that insures compatibility between the two

Application program interface See API

application services It is the server network operating system which is responsible for application services which includes not only executing the back-end engine portion of the application, but also supplying the messaging and communications services to enable interoperability between distributed clients and servers.

applications layer The application layer, layer 7 of the OSI Model is also open to mis-interpretation. Application layer protocols do not include end-user application programs. Rather, they include utilities which support end-user application programs. Some people include network operating systems in this category. Strictly speaking, the best examples of application layer protocols are the OSI protocols X.400 and X.500

applications software Applications software on a LAN is divided into client front-ends and server back-ends or engines and is concerned with accomplishment of a specific type of task or transaction. LAN applications software can be divided into two major sub-categories: LAN productivity software & LAN resource management software

APPN APPN-Advanced Peer to Peer Network is IBM's answer to multiprotocol networking on a peer to peer basis using the SNA architecture, rather than a LAN-based network architecture

APT Microcom protocol that allows modems to connect to PCs via parallel port in order to avoid serial port bottlenecks

ARQ Automatic retransmission request, error correction protocol that requires retransmission of data blocks received in error

ASCII standardized method for encoding humanly readable characters. ASCII uses a series of 7 bits to represent 128 ($2^7 = 128$) different characters

ASVD Analog simultaneous voice/data does not transmit voice and data in a truly simultaneous manner. Instead, it switches quickly between voice and data transmission. Voice transmission always takes priority, so data transfers are paused during data transmissions. ASVD has been formalized as ITU standard V.61

Asymmetric digital subscriber line See ADSL

asynchronous frames In FDDI, while synchronous frames are being transmitted, any unused network capacity can still be used by other workstations transmitting asynchronous frames.

asynchronous transfer mode See ATM

asynchronous transmission synchronization is reestablished with the transmission of each character in asynchronous transmission via the use of start and stop bits

AT&T 5ESS Switch One of the switches that supports ISDN

ATM Asynchronous Transfer Mode is a switch-based WAN service using fixed length frames, more properly referred to as cells. Fixed length cells assure fixed length processing time by ATM switches, thereby enabling predictable, rather than variable, delay and delivery time

ATM access switches Interface between ATM switches and legacy LANs

ATM adaptation layer See AAL

ATM gateway switches See ATM access switches

ATM LAN emulation ATM service that allows ethernet or token ring traffic to travel across higher speed ATM networks without requring changes to LAN workstations

Attachment Units See AU

attenuation Loss of signal strength during transmission due to resistance of the media

AU Iso-Ethernet hubs are known as Attachment Units (AU) and cost between $400–$500 per port

Audiotex These systems deliver audio information to callers based on responses on the touch-tone keypad to pre-recorded questions. Primarily used for information hot-lines.

auditing system In NetWare 4.1, an extensive auditing system monitors and reports on what valid users are doing. The auditor acts independently of the supervisor and separately monitors activity on both the file system and the NetWare Directory Services database

authentication Authentication in NetWare 4.1 uses a combination of private encryption keys and passwords, while the VLM requester security agent on the client workstation and NDS file server combine to assure that users are properly authenticated before being logged in

auto restoral Ability of dial back up units to restore communications to leased lines from dial-up backup lines once the leased lines have been repaired

auto-detection & configuration Auto-detection & configuration of installed controllers, interface cards and peripherals by network operating systems is dependent on the network operating system possessing a compatible driver for that device

automated attendant Allows callers to direct calls to a desired individual at a given business without necessarily knowing their extension number

automatic call distribution See ACD

automatic failover Automatic failover implies that a clustered server will automatically and transparently take over for another failed server in the same cluster

automatic number identification Service available via either ISDN or in-band signalling

Automatic retransmission request See ARQ

available bit rate See ABR

B channel In Isochronous Ethernet, The 6.144 Mbps C channel is in fact further sub-divided into 96 64Kbps ISDN B channels which carry the actual multimedia traffic. Applications are able to aggregate these B channels as needed up to the 6.144Mbps limit.

backbone network In a hierarchial enterprise network design, the high speed inter-LAN portion of the network is often referred to as the backbone network

backward compatibility A very important aspect of any migration plan to a new client network operating system is the extent of support for backward compatibility is terms of application support, also known as legacy application support. In other words, will current applications run without modification on the new network operating system?

backward explicit congestion notification See BECN

bandwidth range of frequencies

bandwidth on demand interoperability group See BONDING

baseband transmission baseband transmission means that the entire bandwidth of the media is devoted to one data channel

Basic input output system See BIOS

basic rate interface See BRI

baud   timed opportunities to identify ones and zeroes by sampling the carrier wave are known as signaling events. The proper name for one signaling event is a baud

baud rate   the number of baud, or signalling events, per second

bearer channels   ISDN channels that actually bear, or carry, data and voice.

BECN   backward explicit congestion notification, a frame relay flow control mechanism

Bell 103   Bell system modem standard for 300bps modem using FSK modulation

Bell 212A   Bell system modem standard for 1200bps modem using 4PSK

benchmarking   One way to demonstrate the impact of implemented technology by tying networking costs to business value is through a process known as benchmarking

BER   bit error rate, measurement of errors on a given transmission line

bindery   Network operating systems have always depended on some sort of naming service or directory in which to store information about users as well as systems resources such as disks, servers, and printers. NetWare 3.x servers stored this type of information in a bindery

BIOS   Basic input output system, interface between operating system and PC hardware components

B-ISDN   Broadband ISDN. ATM switching plus SONET transmission

bit   a binary digit, a 1 or 0

bit error rate   See BER

Block Sequence Number   Used in ARQ error control to identify which data blocks were received in error

BONDING   bandwidth on demand interoperability group Inverse multiplexing standard

boundary router   In the case of boundary or branch office routers, all routing information is kept at the central site router. This allows the boundary router to require less technical configuration and to be available for a lower cost than central site routers

bps   bits per second

breakout boxes   a device used to monitor and manipulate transmission signals

BRI   Basic rate interface. 2B+D ISDN

bridge   A bridge uses MAC layer addressing to logically segment traffic between attached LANs

Broadband ISDN   See B-ISDN

broadband transmission   In general, any transmission service at the T-1 level or greater are considered broadband

broadcast   In a broadcast logical topology, a data message is sent simultaneously to all nodes on the network. Each node decides individually if the data message was directed toward it. If not, the message is simply ignored

broadcast filtering   Instead of allowing explorer packets onto the internetwork, routers can filter these broadcast packets out of the traffic, read the destination address to which the PC is seeking a route, and supply the PC directly with that information after consulting its own routing tables.

broadcast storm   In the case of improperly addressed frames or frames destined for non-existent addresses, frames can be infinitely perpetuated or flooded onto all bridged LANs in a condition known as a broadcast storm

brouters   At one time, specialized devices which could either bridge or route were referred to as brouters, however, today most advanced routers include bridging functionality

Buffer Memory   Memory included in modems to hold transmitted blocks of data in order to implement sliding window or continuous ARQ

bus   The bus topology is a linear arrangement with terminators on either end and devices connected to the "bus" via connectors and/or transceivers.

bus and tag   A standard for high speed data channels between FEPs and IBM mainframes, Bus and Tag has a transmission rate of 4.5 Mbps and has been available since 1967.

business process re-engineering   When businesses delineate business layer objectives as part of a top down analysis, they critically re-examine their business processes in an analysis methodology known as business process reengineering (BPR).

byte   a collection of 8 bits which represents a character

C channel   In Isochronous Ethernet, A 6.144 Mbps ISDN C channel is reserved for streaming time sensitive traffic such as multimedia applications.

CAI   PBX-integrated wireless phones support the CT2 (Cordless Telephony Generation 2) Common Air Interface (CAI) global standard for low-power wireless transmission

call accounting system   Call Accounting Systems can pay for themselves in a short amount of time by spotting and curtailing abuse as well as by allocating phone usage charges on a departmental basis.

call control   Using computer-based applications users are more easily able to use all of the features of their phone system or PBX, especially the more complicated but seldom used features. Includes use of features like on-line phone books, auto-dialing, click-and-point conference calls, on-line display and processing of voice mail messages

Call pickup Allows a user to pickup or answer another user's phone without the need to actually forward calls.

call set-up packets used to establish virtual circuits in frame relay networks

callback security Modem security feature that verifies users and dials them back at pre-determined numbers

CAP CAP is a defacto standard, deployed in many trial ADSL units, and was developed by AT&T Paradyne.

CAP Companies which seek to offer local access service in competition with RBOCs are known as Competitive Access Providers or CAPs

Carrier Sense Multiple Access with Collision Detection See CSMA/CD

carrier wave a reference wave which is manipulated by modems to represent 1s and 0s

carrierless amplitude & phase See CAP

carriers A carrier, or phone company, offers phone services to the general public in a given geographic area

CBR Constant bit rate. An ATM bandwidth management scheme that provides a guaranteed amount of bandwidth to a given virtual path, thereby producing the equivalent of leased T-1 or T-3 line

CBS Commited Burst Size defines the extent to which a user can exceed their CIR over a period of time in a frame relay network

CCIS A more official name for out-of-band signaling is Common Channel Interoffice Signaling

CDDI Copper Distributed Data Interface employs FDDI over twisted pair media. The official ANSI standard for CDDI is known as TP-PMD (Twisted Pair-Physical Media Dependent).

cell relay fast packet switching technology employing fixed length cells

cells ATM (Asynchronous Transfer Mode) is a switch-based WAN service using fixed length frames, more properly referred to as cells.

central clock A central clock or timing device in the TDM gives each input device its allotted time to empty its buffer into an area of the TDM where the combined data from all of the polled input devices is conglomerated into a single message frame for transmission over the composite circuit.

Central Directory Server In APPN, The Central Directory Server can save time as well as network traffic for the Network Nodes. Instead of each Network Node on an internetwork doing their own information gathering and internetwork exploration and inquiry, they can simply consult the Central Directory Server.

central office See CO

central site router Central site routers, otherwise known as enterprise or backbone routers are employed at large corporate sites, while boundary or branch office routers are employed at remote corporate locations with less routing requirements and fewer technical support personnel

channel bank When a bank of codecs are arranged in a modular chassis to not only digitize analog voice conversations but also load them onto a shared high capacity (T-1:1.544Mbps) circuit, the hybrid device is referred to as a channel bank

Channel Service Unit/Data Service Unit See CSU/DSU

channel-attached gateways As an alternative to LAN-based gateways, channel-attached gateways are able to interface directly to the mainframe's high speed data channel, thereby bypassing the FEP entirely. Physically, the channel attached gateways are often modules which are added to enterprise routers

character encoding process required to render humanly readable characters into machine language through representation of characters as a series of 1s and 0s

checksums Error check character calculated using decimal face values of characters in transmitted data blocks

CIR Committed Information Rate refers to the minimum bandwidth guaranteed to users for "normal" transmission in a frame relay network

circuit switched network A network based on circuit switched services in which users are able to use the entire bandwidth of physical circuits created solely for their transmissions

circuit switching A switching process in which physical circuits are created, maintained and terminated for individual point-to-point or multi-point connections

Class 1 regional center Highest capacity switching office in PSTN network hierarchy

Class 2 sectional center 2nd highest capacity switching office in PSTN network hierarchy

Class 3 primary center 3rd highest capacity switching office in PSTN network hierarchy

Class 4 toll center 4th highest capacity switching office in PSTN network hierarchy

Class 5 office   Local switching office

clear request packet   In frame relay networks, the special packet which terminates virtual circuits

client   A client PC is a computer which a user logs into in order to access LAN-attached resources and services

Client front-ends   portion of distributed client/server application program that runs on the client PC

client network operating systems   Client network operating systems integrate traditional operating system functionality with advanced network operating system features to enable communication with a variety of different types of network operating system servers

Client/server CTI   In this CTI architecture, a CTI server computer interfaces to the PBX or ACD to provide overall system management while individual client-based CTI applications execute on multiple client PCs.

client/server network operating systems   Client/Server network operating systems offer the ability to support hundreds of users, and the ability to interact with other network operating systems via gateways. These client/server network operating systems are both considerably more expensive and considerably more complicated to install and administer than peer-to-peer network operating systems.

cluster controller   A cluster controller is a device which allows connection of both 3270 terminals as well as LANs with possible wide area links to packet switched networks (X.25) or high speed leased lines. A cluster controller concentrates the transmissions of its numerous input devices and directs this concentrated data stream to the FEP either locally or remotely

CO   A central office is a facility belonging to the local phone company in which calls are switched to their proper destination

codec   coder/decoder used to digitize analog voice signals

co-location   Through a mandated process known as co-location, RBOCs had to allow alternate local loop carriers, to install their equipment in the RBOC's central office

committed burst size   See CBS

committed information rate   See CIR

Common Air Interface   See CAI

common channel interoffice signalling   See CCIS

Common Control Area   software programs that reside in and are executed on specialized computers within the PBX in an area sometimes referred to as the PBX CPU, Stored Program Control or Common Control Area.

Common Transport Semantics   In the New SNA architecture, Common Transport Semantics layer offers independence between the applications and the transport protocols which deliver those applications across the internetwork

communications server   LAN-based server dedicated to modem control for incoming and outgoing calls

competitive access providers   See CAP

composite message frame   The frame that is built by combining the contents of individual channel buffers in a multiplexer

Computer telephony integration   See CTI

configuration bridge protocol data unit   Spanning Tree Algoritm bridges accomplish path management by communicating with each other via configuration bridge protocol data units (Configuration BPDU)

connectionless   A packet switched service that supports globally addressed unreliable datagram service

connection-oriented   A packet switched service that supports virtual circuits

constant bit rate   See CBR

constellation points   a plotted point on a quadrant which represents a particular phase shift and amplitude of a modulation scheme

Continuous ARQ   Also known as sliding window ARQ, continues to transmit data while waiting for ACK/NAK. Slides back to NAK'd block and begins retransmission from there.

convolutional encoding   Encoding methodology used with trellis coded modulation, a forward error correction protocol

Copper Distributed Data Interface   See CDDI

Cordless Telephony Generation 2   See CT2

CPE   Customer premises equipment, generic name for customer owned PBX

CRC   A 32 bit cyclical redundancy check (CRC) is generated over the address, type, and data fields as a frame check sequence in Ethernet networks

CRC-16   16 bit cyclic redundancy check, traps multiple bit errors up to 15 bits 100% of the time

CRC-32   32 bit cyclic redundancy check, traps multiple bit errors up to 31 bits 100% of the time

CSMA/CD   Carrier Sense Multiple Access with Collision Detection or CSMA/CD is the access methodology used by Ethernet media sharing LANs

CSU/DSU   Channel service unit/data service unit used to interface to carriers' digital transmission services

CT2   PBX-integrated wireless phones support the CT2 (Cordless Telephony Generation 2) Common Air Interface (CAI) global standard for low-power wireless transmission

CTI   Computer telephony integration

CTI application development tool   generates application code in a language such as Visual Basic and incorporates TAPI or TSAPI system commands into the program

CTI voice card   key functions of a CTI voice card are as follows: Record and playback digitized video, Create and recognize DTMF tones (Dual Tone Multiple Frequency), Answer and place phone calls,Recognize and process incoming Caller ID (Automatic Number Identification) information

customer premises equipment   See CPE

cyclic redundancy check   See CRC

d channel   delta channel, in ISDN used for transport of management & control information

D channel   In Isochronous Ethernet, 1 64Kbps ISDN D channel is used for management tasks such as call control and signaling.

D-4   A type of T-1 framing in which 24 8bit time slots are combined with a framing bit to form 193 bit frames

DARPA   TCP/IP was developed during the 1970's and widely deployed during the 1980's under the auspices of DARPA or Defense Advanced Research Projects Agency

DAS   Dual Attachment Station devices attach to both of FDDI's rings

data circuit terminating equipment   See DCE

data communications   the encoded transmission of data via electrical or optical means

Data Compression   Procedure is which redundant data is removed from the data stream and repesented by shorter codes thereby increasing overall throughput for a given transmisssion rate

data display channel   See DDC

Data Link Switching   See DLSw

data migration   Data migration utilities manage the migration of data among different types of storage devices as part of a comprehensive hierarchical storage management (HSM) program

data over voice   Data over voice unit. a type of frequency division multiplexer

data terminal equipment   See DTE

datagrams   globally addressed message packets found in connectionless frame relay networks

data-link layer   The data-link layer (layer 2 of the OSI model) is responsible for providing protocols which deliver reliability to upper layers for the point-to-point connections established by the physical layer protocols. The data-link layer is of particular interest to the study of local area networks as this is the layer in which network architecture standards are defined

DB-25   A 25 pin physical connector associated with both serial and parallel transmission protocols

DB-9   A 9 pin physical connector associated with a variety of serial protocols

DCE   Data circuit terminating equipment; a generic designation to indicate directionality in a serial transmission. Modems are DCE

DDC   PnP compliant monitors will be controlled and configured according to the PnP DDC or Data Display Channel standard.

DDS   Digital data service; a digital carrier transmission service offering speeds up to 56Kbps

DE   discard eligibility. flag in frame relay frame indicating those frames that can be discarded in the event of network congestion

de-encapsulation   In de-encapsulation, each successive layer of the OSI model removes headers and/or trailers and processes the data which was passed to it from the corresponding layer protocol on the source client.

delta file synchronization   Delta file synchronization is perhaps the most significant file synchronization option in terms of its potential impact on reducing required bandwidth and file transfer time to accomplish the synchronization. Rather than sending entire files across the dial-up or LAN link, delta file synchronization only transfers the changes to those files.

Demand Priority Access   See DPP

Demand Priority Protocol   See DPP

demodulation   conversion of an analog signal to equivalent digital data

deregulation   As a result of deregulation, both AT&T and the RBOCs were allowed to enter into other non-regulated industries by forming additional subsidiaries

desktop CTI   In this CTI architecture, individual PCs are equipped with telephony boards and associated call control software. Each Desktop CTI-equipped PC controls only the phone to which it is directly attached.

destination address   Rather than merely transferring all data between LANs or LAN segments, a bridge reads the destination address (MAC layer address of destination NIC) of each data frame on a LAN, decides whether the destination is local or remote (on the other side of the bridge), and only allows those data frames with non-local destination addresses to cross the bridge to the remote LAN.

dial backup Ability of leased line modems to restore transmission via dial-up circuits in the event of a leased line failure

dial-up line circuit switched connection or local loop used to access PSTN

dial-up router In those cases where the amount of inter-LAN traffic from a remote site does not justify the cost of a leased line, dial-up routers may be the appropriate choice of internetworking equipment

dial-up server See remote node server

dibit two bits

DID Direct inward dialing Allows calls to bypass the central switchboard and go directly to a particular user's phone.

digital a transmission method characterized by discrete voltage levels used to represent logical 1s and 0s

digital data services See DDS

digital service hierarchy Series of standards defining high speed digital services (DS-1 = 1.544Mbps)

digital signal processors take the digitized PCM code and further manipulate and compress it.

digital signal processors See DSP

digital simultaneous voice/data See DSVD

direct inward dial See DID

directory services Network operating systems have always depended on some sort of directory or naming service in which to store information about users as well as systems resources such as disks, servers, and printers.

directory synchronization software See file synchronization

discard eligibility See DE

Discrete ARQ Also known as stop and wait ARQ. Transmitting modem waits for an ACK or NAK for each transmitted block before transmitting the next block

discrete multitone See DMT

distance vector RIP uses a distance vector algorithm which only measures the number of hops to a distant router, to a maximum of 16

distinct layer 2 switching & layer 3 routing An internetwork evolutionary design scenario in which separate Layer 2 switches and Layer 3 routers cooperatively contribute what each does best in order to deliver internetwork traffic as efficiently as possible.

distributed parallel processing See DPP

distributed queue dual bus See DQDB

distributed routing An internetwork evolutionary design scenario in which layer 2 switching and layer 3 routing functionality are combined into a single device sometimes referred to as a multi-layer switch.

divestiture Divestiture broke up the network services of AT&T into separate long-distance and local service companies

DLSw IBM's version of TCP/IP encapsulation is known as Data Link Switching or DLSw and has been proposed as a standard to the IETF (Internet Engineering Task Force) as RFC (Request for Comment) 1434. DLSw does not propose anything radically new but incorporates many vendor-specific TCP/IP encapsulation features into a single standard which will hopefully be widely supported

DLUR/S The specific APPN protocol which deals with SNA/LAN integration is known as DLUR/S (Dependent Logical Unit Requester/Server).

DMT discrete multitone DMT has been approved as an ADSL standard (ANSI Standard T1.413) by the ANSI T1E1.4 working group.

domain directory services Network operating systems have always depended on some sort of naming service or directory in which to store information about users as well as systems resources such as disks, servers, and printers. Windows NT uses a domain directory service.

domains Domain directory services see the network as a series of linked sub-divisions known as domains.

DPA See DPP

DPP Future versions of NetWare will support clustering through a systems architecture which Novell refers to as distributed parallel processing (DPP).

DPP Demand Priority Protocol (Demand Priority Access) is the access methodology of 100VG-AnyLAN. Ports can be designated as high priority, thereby giving priority delivery status to time-sensitive types of traffic such as video or voice which require guaranteed delivery times for smooth presentation. This makes 100VG-AnyLAN especially well suited for multimedia traffic.

DQDB distributed queue dual bus, SMDS network architecture

DS Digital service, see digital service hierarchy

DS-0 a 64Kbps digital carrier transmission service

DS-1 1.544Mbps

DSE Data Switching Exchanges, otherwise known as packet switched networks

DSP digital signal processor; specialized computer chip able to process digital signals quickly, used in echo cancellation

DSVD digitizes all voice transmissions and combines the digitized voice and data over the single analog transmission line (ITU V.70)

DTE data terminal equipment; a generic designation to indicate directionality in a serial transmission. PCs are DTE in a point to point, PC to modem transmission

DTMF Touch tone dialing is technically known as DTMF, or Dual Tone Multi-Frequency, because the tone associated with each number dialed is really a combination of two tones selected from a matrix of multiple possible frequencies

Dual Attachment Station See DAS

dual homing In FDDI, a given server may be connected to more than one FDDI concentrator to provide redundant connections and increased fault tolerance. Dual connecting servers in this manner is known as dual homing.

dual ring of trees Multiple concentrators attaching multiple devices to the FDDI rings as illustrated in Figure 7-13 is known as a dual ring of trees.

dual tone multi frequency See DTMF

dynamic reconfiguration PnP standards also include support for dynamic reconfiguration which will enable such things as: PCMCIA cards being inserted into and removed from computers without a need to reboot, Hot docking (powered up) of laptop computers into docking bays or stations., Dynamic reconfiguration-aware applications software which could automatically respond to changes in system configuration

dynamic scalability clustering can also imply using the CPU power of multiple CPUs located in separate computing platforms to produce a single, more powerful, virtual computer in a process known as dynamic scalability

Dynamic Speed Shifts MNP 10 protocol that allows modems to automatically raise or lower transmission speeds in response to variable circuit conditions

E-1 European stamdard for high speed digital transmission 2.048Mbps

early token release mechanism 16Mbps Token Ring network architectures use a modified form of token passing access methodology known as early token release mechanism in which the token is set to free and released as soon as the transmission of the data frame is completed rather than waiting for the transmitted data frame to return to the source workstation.

EBCDIC Extended binary coded decimal interchange code; 8 bit encoding scheme, 256 characters

echo cancellation sophisticated technique which allows some modems to offer full duplex transmission over two wire circuits

edge switches Edge switches deployed within the LANs will be programmed with minimal routing information. Edge switches will consult distributed route servers for "directory assistance" when they encounter routing situations which they are not equipped to handle

EMI Electro Magnetic Interference

encapsulating bridges The encapsulating bridge merely takes the entire Ethernet data link layer frame and stuffs it in an "envelope" (data frame) which conforms to the FDDI data link layer protocol.

encapsulation a data message emerges from a client front end program and proceeds down the protocol stack of the network operating system installed in the client PC in a process known as encapsulation. Each successive layer of the OSI model adds a header according to the syntax of the protocol which occupies that layer

End nodes In APPN, end Nodes are end user processing nodes, either clients or servers without any information on the overall network, available internetwork links, or routing tables

end-to-end network links The network layer protocols are responsible for the establishment, maintenance, and termination of end-to-end network links. Network layer protocols are required when computers which are not physically connected to the same LAN must communicate

engine See server back-end

enterprise network The enterprise network is the transportation system of the client-server architecture. Together with middleware, it is responsible for the transparent cooperation of distributed processors and databases

enterprise network management system Systems which are able to manage multi-vendor, multi-platform enterprise networks. Examples include HP OpenView, IBM SystemView and Sun SunNet Manager

equal access Equal access means that any other long distance carrier must be treated equally by the local BOCs in terms of access to the local carrier switching equipment, and ultimately to their customers.

Error Correction Process of re-transmitting data blocks received in error

Error Detection Process of identifying data blocks received in error via techniques such as parity, LRC, checksum, or CRC

Error Prevention Process of trying to prevent data errors by either reducing interference on circuits or by employing adapative protocols that are able to adjust to impairments of varying circuit quality

ESCON   A standard for high speed data channels between FEPs and IBM mainframes, ESCON II (Enterprise System CONnection) has a maximum transmission rate of 70Mbps, has been available since 1990, and is able to transmit up to 30 miles over fiber optic cable.

ESF   24 D-4 frames

Ethernet   Although strictly speaking , Ethernet and IEEE 802.3 are conflicting standards, the term Ethernet is commonly used to refer to any IEEE 802.3 compliant network

Ethernet II   The first Ethernet standard was developed by Digital, Intel and Xerox corporation in 1981 and was known as DIX 1.0, sometimes referred to as Ethernet I. This standard was superseded in 1982 by DIX 2.0, the current Ethernet standard, also known as Ethernet II.

explorer packet   In an internetwork connected via source routing bridges, the PC sends out a special explorer packet which determines the best path to the intended destination of its data message. The explorer packets are continually propagated through all source routing bridges until the destination workstation is finally reached.

extended binary coded decimal interchange code   See EBCDIC

extended superframe   See ESF

EZ-ISDN   In order to try to further simplify the ISDN ordering process, an alternative ordering code scheme known as **EZ-ISDN** has been proposed by the National ISDN Users Forum.

fallback   When an analog circuit, dial-up or leased, degrades or has some kind of transmission impairment, many modems use fallback or lower speeds automatically and continue with data transmissions.

Fax-on-demand   By combining computer-based faxing with interactive voice response, users can dial in and request that specific information be faxed to their fax machine.

FCS   frame check sequence, error detection technique

FDDI   Fiber Distributed Data Interface (FDDI) is a 100Mbps network architecture which was first specified in 1984 by the ANSI (American National Standards Institute) subcommittee entitled X3T9.5.

FDM   frequency division multiplexing, each channel gets a portion of the bandwidth for 100% of the time

FECN   forward explicit congestion notification, a flow control mechanism in frame relay networks

FEP   A front end processor is a computer which offloads the communications processing from the mainframe, allowing the mainframe to be dedicated to processing activities. A high speed data channel connects the FEP to the mainframe locally although FEPs can be deployed remotely as well.

Fiber Distributed Data Interface   See FDDI

file synchronization software   File synchronization software is able to synchronize versions of files on laptops and desktop workstations and is now often included as a standard or optional feature in client network operating systems. Also known as version control software or directory synchronization software

filtering   Filtering is when a bridge reads the destination address on an Ethernet frame or Token Ring packet and decides whether or not that packet should be allowed access to the internetwork through the bridge

filtering rate   Measured in Packets/sec or Frames/sec, a measure of the filtering performance of a given bridge

first-party call control   Also known as desktop CTI

fixed callback   Callback mechanism that is only able to call remote uses back at pre-determined phone numbers entered in a directory

Flow Control   Mechanism that stops and starts data transmission in order to avoid overflow of buffer memory

format converter   A special type of bridge which includes a format converter can bridge between Ethernet and Token Ring. These special bridges may also be called multi-protocol bridges or translating bridges.

Forward Error Correction   Error correction protocols that seek to avoid the need for retransmission by sending redundant data along with actual data in order to assist the receiving modem in correctly interpreting received signals

forward explicit congestion notification   See FECN

forward if not local   Since only frames with destination addresses not found in the known local nodes table are forwarded across the bridge, bridges are sometimes known as a "Forward-if-not-local" devices.

forward if proven remote   Once the router is satisfied with both the viability of the destination address as well as with the quality of the intended path, it will release the carefully packaged data packet via processing known as forward-if-proven-remote logic.

forwarding   Forwarding is the bridge process necessary to load the packet onto the internetwork media whether local or remote.

forwarding rate   Measured in Packets/sec or Frames/

sec, a measure of the forwarding performance of a given bridge

four-wire circuit   A four-wire circuit is comprised of two wires capable of simultaneously carrying a data signal each with its own dedicated ground wire. Typically, four wire circuits are reserved for leased lines

fractional T-1   See FT-1

Fractional T-1 multiplexers   A T-1 multiplexer that is able use less than a full T-1 as its composite output channel

FRAD   The access device to the frame relay network, known as a frame relay access device or FRAD must be able to respond to requests from the frame relay network to "throttle back" or slow down the input to the network or risk losing transmitted packets due to network overload.

frame check sequence   See FCS

Frame Relay   A WAN packet switched network service known as Frame Relay has become a popular alternative SNA/LAN integration WAN service. The key positive attribute of Frame Relay is that charges are based on actual amounts of traffic transmitted rather than fixed monthly rates

frame relay access device   See FRAD

frame relay switch   Network switch capable of switching frame relay frames

frame status flags   In a token passing access methodology, Successful delivery of the data frame is confirmed by the destination workstation setting frame status flags to indicate successful receipt of the frame and continuing to forward the original frame around the ring to the sending PC

frames   The data-link layer provides the required reliability to the physical layer transmission by organizing the bit stream into structured frames which add addressing and error checking information.

framing   In T-1 framing, Differentiating between channels is accomplished through a technique known as framing which is really an adaptation of the TDM

framing bit   The 193rd bit added to the 24 8 bit time slots to indicate the end of one D-4 frame

frequency   a wave characteristic which can be manipulated in order represent 1s and 0s

frequency division multiplexing   See FDM

frequency modulation   process of manipulating carrier wave frequency in order to represent 1s and 0s

frequency shift keying   See FSK

front end processor   See FEP

FSK   frequency shift keying; shifting carrier wave frequency on analog circuits in order to represent digital 1s and 0s

FT-1   Fractional T-1, broadband service that allows customer to access less than the full 24 DS-0s in a T-1

full-duplex   simultaneous transmission in both directions on a given circuit

gateway   A LAN server-based, shared protocol converted access to a mainframe is known as a gateway

global address   Address attached to a datagram in a frame relay network that allows it to be properly delivered

global directory services   See NDS

granularity   How finely access can be controlled (by disk, directory, or file level) is sometimes referred to as the granularity of the access control scheme.

GSM   Global system for mobile communications, a voice compression technique

guardbands   Portions of the 4000Hz voice bandwidth, reserved to protect against interference

half-duplex   transmission in both directions, only one direction at a time on a given circuit

handshaking   modem initialization which takes place in order to allow modems to agree on carrier wave frequency, modulation scheme, error correction protocols, etc.

hardware flow control   Flow control mechanism that uses RS-232 pins CTS/RTS, clear-to-send/request to send

Hayes AT Command Set   Series of commands understood by both communications software and modems that allows the communications software to control and respond to modem activity

Hayes compatible   Term that indicates that a modem is able to understand and respond to commands in the Hayes AT command set

Hayes ESP communications accelerator   Serial port replacement hardware that is able to support transmissions up to 921.6Kbps, thereby eliminating the traditional serial port bottleneck

HDLC   high level data link control. Data link layer protocol for X.25

header   Additional information added to the front of data is called a header

hierarchical networking   An internetworking design strategy known as hierarchical networking isolates local LAN traffic on a local network architecture such as Ethernet or Token Ring while transmitting internetwork traffic over a higher speed network architecture such as FDDI or Fast Ethernet. Servers are often directly connected to the backbone network while individual workstations access the backbone network only as needed through routers.

high level data link control   See HDLC

horizontal software compatibility Horizontal software compatibility is concerned with transparency between *similar* software layers *between* different clients and servers

HPR/AnyNET Recent enhancements to APPN known as HPR (High Performance Routing) /AnyNET now allow multiple transport protocols such as IP and IPX to travel over the APPN network simultaneously with SNA traffic. In such an implementation, APPN rather than TCP/IP serves as the single backbone protocol able to transport multiple LAN protocols as well as SNA traffic simultaneously.

hub The hub provides a connecting point through which all attached devices are able to converse with one another. Hubs must be compatible with both the attached media and the NICs which are installed in client PCs

Huffman encoding Encoding mechanism that replaces ASCII code with variable length codes, shorter codes (4 bits) for most frequently used characters, longer (11bit) codes for least frequently used characters

hunting Hunt groups are established to allow incoming calls to get through on alternate trunks when a primary trunk is busy

IBM3270 In micro-mainframe connectivity, the micro (Standalone or LAN-attached PC) pretends to be or "emulates" a mainframe terminal such as an IBM 3270 attached and logged into the mainframe

ICP Intelligent Call Processing (ICP) service, customers are able to re-route incoming 800 calls among multiple customer service centers in a matter of seconds.

IEEE 802 Local area network architecture standards are defined, debated and established by the IEEE (Institute of Electrical and Electronic Engineers) 802 committee

IEEE 802.1 See Spanning Tree Algorithm

IEEE 802.12 Details of the 100VG-AnyLAN network architecture are contained in the proposed IEEE 802.12 standard

IEEE 802.14 The access methodologies for sharing cable bandwidth via cable modems are being standardized as IEEE 802.14 cable network specifications.

IEEE 802.2 The upper sub-layer of the data-link layer which interfaces to the network layer is known as the logical link control or LLC sub-layer and is represented by a single IEEE 802 protocol (IEEE 802.2)

IEEE 802.3 Although strictly speaking , Ethernet and IEEE 802.3 are conflicting standards, the term Ethernet is commonly used to refer to any IEEE 802.3 compliant network

IEEE 802.3u The details of the operation of 100BaseT are in the IEEE 802.3u proposed standard.

IEEE 802.3z Proposed standard for gigo bit ethernet

IEEE 802.5 IBM has been the driving force behind the standardization and adoption of Token Ring with a prototype in IBM's lab in Zurich, Switzerland serving as a model for the eventual IEEE 802.5 standard.

IEEE 802.6 IEEE specification for DQDB, the SMDS network architecture

IEEE 802.9a Details of the Iso-Ethernet network architecture are contained in the IEEE 802.9a standard which is officially known as Isochronous Ethernet Integrated Services

in-band signalling when signal bandwidth is robbed to transport managerial or control information

Institute of Electrical and Electronic Engineers 802 Committee See IEEE 802

Int14 Interrupt 14 is the redirection interface that PC-based communications software must redirect modem output to on Microsoft networks

integrated client/server management system In addition to managing a multi-vendor enterprise network, an integrated client-server management systems must also be able to supply the following management capabilities: Enterprise Database Management, Enterprise Desktop Management, Enterprise Transaction Processing Management, Enterprise Distributed Processing Management

Integrated Services Digital Network See ISDN

Integrated Services Terminal Equipment See ISTE

integration Integration refers to that transitionary period of time in the migration process when both network operating systems must be running simultaneously and interacting to some degree

intelligent call processing See ICP

interactive voice response See IVR

Interdomain Trust In the case of a domain directory service such as Windows NT 3.51, the remote or foreign server receives the user authentication from the user's primary domain controller (local server) in a process known as Interdomain Trust (IT).

inter-exchange carriers See IXC

interface The logical gap between two communicating hardware or software components is commonly referred to as an interface.

interface specification bit by bit layout of frames that user data must be transformed into before entering network switches

Internet protocol See IP

Internet Suite of Protocols TCP/IP (Transmission

Control Protocol/Internet Protocol) is the term generally used to refer to an entire suite of protocols used to provide communication on a variety of layers between widely distributed different types of computers. Strictly speaking, TCP and IP are just two of the protocols contained within the family of protocols more properly known as the Internet Suite of Protocols.

internet suite of protocols model a four-layered communications architecture in which upper layers use the functionality offered by the protocols of the lower layers

internetworking Linking multiple LANs together in such as way as to deliver information more efficiently from cost, business, and performance perspectives.

Interrupt 14 See Int14

intersymbol interference Interference between constellation points in a given modulation scheme which can cause misinterpretation is known as intersymbol interference

intranets Internet type services available for use by in-house, authorized employees

inverse multiplexing process of conglomerating multiple high speed WAN links to support a single high bandwidth demand application

IOC Depending on what combinations of voice, video or data traffic a user wishes to transmit over ISDN, up to 20 or more ISDN Ordering Codes (IOC) are possible

IP Internet protocol, network layer protocol of the internet suite of protocols

IP Switching By implementing IP routing software directly on ATM switching hardware, IP switching combines switching and routing capabilities into a single device and discriminates between which traffic should be switched and which should be routed

IP-based voice transmissions Voice transmission over any IP-based network such as LANs, modem to modem, or the internet

I-P-O model The I-P-O model provides a framework in which to focus on the difference between the data that came into a particular networked device (I) and the data that came out of that same device(O). By defining this difference, the processing (P) performed by the device is documented.

ISDN Integrated Services Digital Network is a circuit-switched digital WAN service which is the support network transport service for Isochronous Ethernet

ISDN data/voice modem Not truly a modem, but a ISDN terminal adpater that supports analog phones as well as data transmission

ISDN ordering codes See IOC

ISDN switch Switch that supports circuit switching for ISDN services

ISDN terminal adapters Allows analog devices (phones, fax machines) to hook to ISDN services

ISO 10646 More commonly known as Unicode, this encoding scheme used 16bit characters to represent most known languages and symbols (over 65,000 possible characters)

isochronous The term isochronous refers to any signaling system in which all connections or circuits are synchronized using a single common clocking reference. This common clocking mechanism allows such systems to offer guaranteed delivery times which are very important to streaming or time-sensitive traffic such as voice and video.

Isochronous Ethernet See Iso-Ethernet

Iso-Ethernet Isochronous Ethernet, also known as Iso-Ethernet offers a combination of services by dividing the overall 16.144 Mbps bandwidth delivered to each workstation into several service-specific channels.

ISTE A workstation with an Iso-Ethernet NIC installed is properly referred to as Integrated Services Terminal Equipment

IT See Interdomain Trust

ITU H.323 The ITU H.323 standard for interoperability among client software for low bandwidth audio (voice) and video conferencing

IVR Interactive voice response systems support on-line transaction processing rather than just information hot-line applications.

IXC Any phone traffic destined for locations outside of the local LATA must be handed off to the Long Distance or Inter-Exchange carrier (IXC) of the customer's choice

Kermit Kermit is a popular file transfer protocol best known for being available on nearly any computing platform of any type

known local nodes Data-Link protocols such as Ethernet contain source addresses as well as the destination addresses within the pre-defined Ethernet Frame layout. A bridge checks the source address of each frame it receives and adds that source address to a table of known local nodes

LAN A Local Area Network (LAN) is a combination of hardware and software technology which allows computers to share a variety of resources such as: printers and other peripheral devices, data, application programs, storage devices

LAN productivity software   LAN productivity software is application software which contributes directly to the productivity of its users. In other words, this is the software which people use to not only get their work done, but more importantly, to get their work done more quickly, effectively, accurately, or at a lower cost than if they did not have the benefit of this software

LAN resource management software   LAN resource management software is concerned with providing access to shared network resources and services. Examples of such shared network-attached resources include printers, fax machines, CD-ROMs, modems and a variety of other devices and services.

LAN software architecture   In order to organize and illustrate the inter-relationships between the various categories of LAN software, a LAN Software Architecture can be constructed divided into two major categories: Network operating systems and applicaitons software. Also included are security software and management software

LAP-B   Link access procedure-balanced, data link layer protocol for X.25

LAP-D   the frame definition for frame relay networks. This frame definition is said to be a subset of the LAP-D protocol. LAP-D stands for Link Access Procedure—D Channel, where the D channel refers to the 16Kbps Delta Channel in BRI (Basic Rate Interface) ISDN (Integrated Services Digital Network).

LAP-M   Link Access Protocol for Modems, V.42 error control protocol that implements selective ARQ

LATA   All local phone traffic within a local access transport area is handled by the local phone company, more formally known as a local exchange carrier or LEC, most often one of the RBOCs.

LCR   Using routing and pricing information supplied by the user, the PBX chooses the most economical path for any given call

leased line   a dedicated phone circuit which bypasses central office switching equipment, no dialtone

Least cost routing   See LCR

least significant bit   Both Ethernet and token ring believe that bit 0 on byte 0, referred to as the least significant bit, should be transmitted first

LEC   Local exchange carriers, or local phone company which handles all local phone traffic within a LATA

legacy applications   See backward compatibility

line cards   PBX cards that attach to users phones

Line conditioning   Value added service available from carriers in order to reduce interference on analog leased lines

link access procedure-D channel   See LAP-D

link access procedure-balanced   See LAP-B

Link access protocol for modems   See LAP-M

link state   OSPF protocol uses a more comprehensive link state algorithm which can decide between multiple paths to a given router based upon variables other than number of hops such as delay, and capacity, throughput, and reliability of the circuits connecting the routers

link state packets   See LSP

links   Links are a unique aspect of the Unix file system which allow a given file to be known by, and accessed by more than one name. A link is nothing more than an entry in a directory which points to a file stored in another directory, or another whole directory

LLC   In order for an IEEE 802.3 compliant network interface card to be able to determine the type of protocols embedded within the data field of an IEEE 802.3 frame, it refers to the header of the IEEE 802.2 Logical Link Control (LLC) data unit.

LLC sub-layer   The upper sub-layer of the data-link layer which interfaces to the network layer is known as the logical link control or LLC sub-layer and is represented by a single IEEE 802 protocol (IEEE 802.2)

load balancing   The effective use of a network's redundant paths allows routers to perform load balancing of total network traffic across two or more links between two given locations

load balancing   In SMP, all CPUs are kept equally busy in a process known as load balancing

local access transport area   See LATA

local area network   See LAN

local exchange carrier   See LEC

local loop transmission   Narrowband Tramsnission services from customer premises to CO

local loops   The circuits between a residence or business and the local Central Office or CO are known as local loops

local security authority   In Windows NT, the platform-specific login process interacts with the local security authority which actually provides the user authentication services

logical channel   virtual circuit in frame relay network

logical channel number   identifier assigned to virtual circuit in frame relay network

logical link control   See LLC

logical network design   Network performance criteria could be referred to as *what* the implemented network must do in order to meet the business objectives outlined at the outset of this top-down analysis. These requirements are also sometimes referred to as the logical network design.

Logical Ring Physical Star IBM's Token Ring network architecture, adhering to the IEEE 802.5 standard, utilizes a star configuration, sequential message delivery, and a token passing access methodology scheme. Since the sequential logical topology is equivalent to passing messages from neighbor to neighbor around a ring, the token ring network architecture is sometimes referred to as: Logical Ring, Physical Star.

logical topology The particular message passing methodology , or how a message will be passed from workstation to workstation until the message ultimately reaches its intended destination workstation. is more properly known as a network architecture's logical topology

logon process The Logon process is responsible for the interaction with the user on whatever computer platform they may wish to log in on

longitudinal redundancy checks See LRC

LRC Longitudinal redundancy checks, two dimensional parity that overcomes simple parity's inability to detect multiple bit errors

M block connector physical connector most often associated with V. 35 serial transmission standard

MAC sub-layer The media access control or MAC sub-layer is a sub-layer of the data-link layer that interfaces with the physical layer and is represented by protocols which define how the shared local area network media is to be accessed by the many connected computers

management information base See MIB

management software management software must be incorporated in order to provide a single, consolidated view of all networked resources, both hardware and software

media access control See MAC

media sharing LANs Local area networks which use access methodologies to control the access of multiple users to a shared media are known as media sharing LANs.

message Transport layer protocols also provide mechanisms for sequentially organizing multiple network layer packets into a coherent message.

MIB Performance statistics are often gathered and stored in databases known as MIBs (Management Information Base)

Microcom Networking Protocols See MNP

micro-mainframe connectivity In micro-mainframe connectivity, the micro (Standalone or LAN-attached PC) pretends to be or "emulates" a mainframe terminal such as an IBM 3270 attached and logged into the mainframe

micro-segmentation When segmentation is taken to the extreme of limiting each LAN segment to only a single workstation, the internetworking design strategy is known as micro-segmentation. A micro-segmented internetwork requires a LAN switch which is compatible with the NICs installed in the attached workstations

middleware Middleware resides in the middle of the distributed processing system, serving as a transparent insulator surrounding the enterprise network over which the client-server communication actually travels.

migration Migration features are aimed at easing the transition from NetWare 3.12 to either NetWare 4.1 or Windows NT.

mini-PBX offer multiple workers the ability to share a small number of phone lines with integrated advanced features

mirrored server link In NetWare 4.1 SFT III, the synchronization of the servers is accomplished through a dedicated link known as the Mirrored Server Link (MSL)

MNP A series of 10 classes of error control and data compression protocols that have become defacto standards for modem transmission

MNP Class 5 MNP protocol that offers data compression at up to a 2:1 ratio

modem data communications device which modulates/demodulates analog/digital conversion

modem cable cable which attaches a modem to a PC. Pinned straight through

modem setup string Initialization string of Hayes AT commands that establishes communication between a modem and the local PC's communication software

modulation process of converting discrete digital signals into continuously varying analog signals

MPTN A layer of the New SNA architecture, the Multiprotocol Transport Networking Layer supports numerous transport protocols including SNA/APPN

multi-function telephony boards See mini-PBX

multi-layer switch A single device in which layer 2 switching and layer 3 routing functionality are combined

multiplexing process that combines outputs of several channels into a single composite output

multi-protocol bridges See translating bridge

multiprotocol routers Multiprotocol routers have the capability to interpret, process and forward data packets of multiple routable and non-routable protocols

multiprotocol routing Multiprotocol routing provides the functionality necessary to actually process and understand multiple network protocols as well as translate between them. Without multiprotocol routing software, clients speaking multiple different network protocols cannot be supported.

Multiprotocol Transport Networking Layer See MPTN

multirate ISDN Multirate ISDN uses a technique known as inverse multiplexing in which a collection of 64Kbps B channels are dialed up and combined together into a single logical channel of sufficient bandwidth to meet application needs such as videoconferencing.

narrowband digital services digital carrier services offering bandwidth of less than 1.544 Mbps

Narrowband ISDN Narrowband ISDN , is a switched digital network service offering both voice and non-voice connectivity to other ISDN end users.

NASI NetWare Asynchronous Service Interface, is the redirection interface that PC-based communications software must redirect modem output to on NetWare networks

National ISDN-1 See NISDN-1

NDS Network operating systems have always depended on some sort of naming service or directory in which to store information about users as well as systems resources such as disks, servers, and printers. . NetWare 4.1 employs a global directory service known as NDS or NetWare Directory Services.

negative acknowledgement NAK, control character sent to the transmitting modem from the receiving modem when a data block is received in error

NetWare 4.1 SFT III NetWare 4.1 SFT III offers an automatic failover version known as server duplexing

NetWare 4.1 SMP SMP version of NetWare that loads a second operating system kernel, known as the SMP kernel, which works cooperatively with the first or native operating system kernel.

NetWare Asynchronous Service Interface See NASI

NetWare Connect NetWare remote access server software

NetWare Directory Services See NDS

network architecture switching architecture + transmission architecture = network architecture

Network File System See NFS

network hierarchy A hierarchy of switching offices from class 5 to class 1. Higher levels on the network hierarchy imply greater switching and transmission capacity as well as greater expense

network interface card The data-link layer frames are built within the network interface card installed in a computer according to the pre-determined frame layout particular to the network architecture of the installed network interface card. Network interface cards are given a unique address in a format determined by their network architecture

network layer The network layer protocols are responsible for the establishment, maintenance, and termination of end-to-end network links. Network layer protocols are required when computers which are not physically connected to the same LAN must communicate

Network nodes In APPN, Network Nodes are processing nodes with routing capabilities. They have the ability to locate network resources, maintain tables of information regarding internetwork links, and establish a session between the requesting end-node and the internetwork service requested.

network objects In some cases, directory services may view all users and network resources as network objects with information concerning them stored in a single database, arranged by object type. Object attributes can be modified and new network objects can be defined

network operating systems network operating systems are concerned with providing an interface between LAN hardware, such as network interface cards, and the application software installed on a particular client or server. The network operating system's job is to provide transparent interoperability between client and server portions of a given application program.

network service network services are offered to customers by carriers dependent upon the capabilities of their network architecture

network termination unit-1 See NTU-1

network-to-network interface See NNI

New SNA The New SNA architecture would allow customers to integrate multi-vendor, multi-platform, multi-protocol information systems without being locked into one vendor's proprietary network architecture.

NFS NFS or Network File System was originally developed by Sun Microsystems as part of their Open Network Computing (ONC) environment. NFS allows multiple, different computing platforms to share files

night mode Many companies close their switchboard at night but still have employees working who must be able to receive and make phone calls.

NISDN-1   NISDN-1 (National ISDN-1) defines a national standard for ISDN switches as well as inter-switch communication.

NNI   Standards that govern inter-switch communication

non-routable   Protocols processed by some routers are actually data link layer protocols without network layer addressing schemes. These protocols are considered non-routable.

non-routable protocol   Non-routable protocols can be processed by routers by either having the routers act as bridges or by encapsulating the non-routable data link layer frame's upper layer protocols in a routable network layer protocol such as IP

Northern Telecom DMS100 Switch   One of the switches that is able to support ISDN services

NT-1   See NTU-1

NTU-1   A Network Termination Unit-1 (NTU-1) or (NT-1) is required to physically connect the ISDN line to a user's ISDN CPE. Most integrated ISDN equipment includes built-in NT-1s, although stand-alone models are available.

object oriented user interfaces   Object Oriented User Interfaces present the user with a graphical desktop on which objects such as files, directories, folders, disk drives, programs, or devices can be arranged according to the user's whim

OC   optical carrier, standards for optical transmission

OC-1   optical transmission standard, 51.84 Mbps

octet   An octet is a unit of data 8 bits long. The term byte is often used to refer to an 8 bit character or number. Since today's networks are likely to carry digitized voice, video, and images as well as data, the term octet is more often used to refer to these 8 bit packets of digital network traffic

open shortest path first   See OSPF

optical carrier   See OC

OSI Model   The OSI Model consists of a hierarchy of 7 layers which loosely group the functional requirements for communication between two computing devices. The power of the OSI Model lies in its openness and flexibility. It can be used to organize and define protocols involved in communicating between two computing devices in the same room as effectively as two devices across the world from each other.

OSPF   OSPF or Open Shortest Path First (RFC 1247) is an example of a link state protocol which was developed to overcome some of RIP's shortcomings such as the 15 hop limit and full routing table broadcasts every thirty seconds. OSPF uses IP for connectionless transport

out of band signalling   management & controlling signalling using a separate channel other than that used for data or voice transmission

outsourcing   the purchase of services from outside vendors rather than supporting internal staffs

P channel   In Isochronous Ethernet, A 10Mbps ISDN P channel is reserved for Ethernet traffic and is completely compatible with 10BaseT Ethernet

packet assembler/disassembler   See PAD

packet layer protocol   See PLP

packet signing   In NetWare 4.1, every packet transmitted from a particular client workstation can have a unique, encrypted digital signature attached to it which can only be authenticated by the server in a process known as packet signing. However, a performance price of 5-7% is paid for the increased security as valuable CPU cycles are spent encrypting and decrypting digital signatures.

packet switched network   As opposed to circuit switched networks, physical circuits are shared by numerous users transmitting their own packets of data between switches

packet switches   Used to route user's data from source to destination

packet switching   As opposed to circuit switching, user's data shares physical circuits with data from numerous other users

packetizing   process of adding overhead or management data to raw user data in order to assure proper delivery

packets   Network layer protocols are responsible for providing network layer (end-to-end) addressing schemes and for enabling inter-network routing of network layer data packets. The term packets is usually associated with network layer protocols while the term frames is usually associated with data link layer protocols

PAD   device which transforms raw data into properly formatted packets

paging   Ability to use paging speakers in a building. May be limited to specific paging zone

PAM   Pulse amplitude modulation, a voice digitization technique

parallel networks model   A network design in which separate networks for SNA and LAN traffic had to be established between the same corporate locations.

parallel transmission   transmission method in which all bits in a given character travel simultaneously through a computer bus or parallel transmission cable

parity   Simple error checking mechanism that adds a single bit per character

password protection   Modem security mechanism that requires passwords for access to dial-up network resources

path names   Path names are used in Unix to identify the specific path through the hierarchical file structure to a particular destination file

payload   generic term referring to data, voice, or video that may be transmitted over WANs

PBX   Private branch exchange, a customer owned telephone switch

PBX CPU   Software program execution area in a PBX

pbx-to-host interfaces   Interface between PBXs and host computers for sharing information in order to enable CTI

PCM   Pulse code modulation. voice digitization technique that digitizes voice into 64Kbps by assigning voice levels to one of 256 eight bit codes

PDC   Domain directory services associate network users and resources with a primary server known as a PDC or Primary Domain Controller

PDM   Pulse duration modulation, a voice digitization technique

PDN   public data network, another name for packet switched network

peer-to-peer internetworking   With full peer to peer internetworking, the PC can exchange data with any mainframe or any other PC on a host-to-host level rather than acting like a "dumb" terminal as in the case of micro-mainframe connectivity

peer-to-peer network operating systems   Peer-to-peer network operating systems, also known as DOS-based LANs or Low-cost LANs offered easy to install and use file and print services for workgroup and departmental networking needs.

performance monitoring   Performance monitoring software should offer the ability to set thresholds for multiple system performance parameters. If these thresholds are exceeded, alerts or alarms should notify network management personnel of the problem, and offer advice as to possible diagnoses or solutions. Event logging and audit trails are often included as part of the performance monitoring package.

periodic framing   Framing used in T-1 services to combine 24 DS-0s into a D-4 frame

Perl language   The Perl language (Practical Extraction & Reporting Language) adds the following functionality to that offered by the Korn and Bourne shells: list processing, associative arrays, modern subroutines & functions, more control statements, better I/O, full function library

permanent virtual circuit   See PVC

phase   one characteristic, (analogous to the wave's pattern) of a wave which can be manipulated in phase modulation schemes in order to represent logical 1s and 0s.

phase modulation   manipulation of a carrier wave's phase via phase shifting in order to represent logical 1s and 0s on an analog transmission circuit

phase shift keying   See PSK

physical layer   The physical layer, also known as layer 1of the OSI model, is responsible for the establishment, maintenance and termination of physical connections between communicating devices. These connections are sometimes referred to as point-to-point data links

physical network design   The delineation of required technology determining *how* various hardware and software components will be combined to build a functional network which will meet pre-determined business objectives. is often referred to as the physical network design.

physical topology   Clients and servers must be physically connected to each other according to some configuration and be linked by the shared media of choice. The physical layout of this configuration can have a significant impact on LAN performance and reliability and is known as a network architecture's physical topology.

piggyback updates   A dial-up router update mechanism in which updates are performed only when the dial-up link has already been established for the purposes of exchanging user data.

Plain Old Telephone Service   See POTS

PLP   Network layer protocol for X.25

Plug-n-play   See PnP

PnP   The goal of plug-n-play is to free users from having to understand and worry about such things as IRQs (Interrupt Requests) , DMA (Direct Memory Access) channels, memory addresses, COM ports, and editing CONFIG.SYS whenever they want to add a device to their computer.

PnP BIOS   A PnP BIOS (Basic Input Output System) is required to interface directly to both PnP and non-PnP compliant hardware.

point of presence   See POP

point-to-point data links   The physical layer, also known as layer 1of the OSI model, is responsible for the establishment, maintenance and termination of physical connections between communicating devices. These connections are sometimes referred to as point-to-point data links

poll spoofing Poll Spoofing is the ability of an internetworking device, such as an SDLC converter or router, to respond directly to, or acknowledge, the FEP's constant polling messages to the remote cluster controller. By answering these status check messages locally, the inquiry and its answer never enter the wide area link portion of the internetwork

polling In TDM multiplexing, the process of emptying each channels buffer in order to build the composite frame

POP Competing long distance carriers wishing to do business in a given LATA maintain a switching office in that LATA known as a POP or Point of Presence

port cards also known as line cards or station cards. PBX cards through which user phones are attached

POTS Dial-up, circuit-switched, analog phone service

PPM Pulse position modulation, a voice digitization technique

predictive dialing also known as outbound dialing, uses a database of phone numbers, automatically dials those numbers, recognizes when calls are answered by people, and quickly passes those calls to available agents.

presentation layer The presentation layer protocols provide an interface between user applications and various presentation-related services required by those applications. For example, data encryption/decryption protocols are considered presentation layer protocols as are protocols which translate between encoding schemes such as ASCII to EBCDIC

primary domain controller See PDC

Principle of Shifting Bottlenecks Principle that states that as one network bottleneck is overcome, the network bottleneck merely shifts to a different network location. (From the modem to the serial port)

prioritization gives priority access to available trunks to certain users

private branch exchange See PBX

productivity paradox The fact that little if any documented increase in productivity results from massive investments in technology

promiscuous listen Promiscuous listen means that transparent bridges receive all data packets transmitted on the LANs to which they are connected.

propagation Forwarding messages by bridges to all workstations on all intermittent LANs is known as propagation.

propagation delay propagation delay is the time it takes a signal from a source PC to reach a destination PC. Because of this propagation delay, it is possible for a workstation to sense that there is no signal on the shared media, when in fact another distant workstation has transmitted a signal which has not yet reached the carrier sensing PC.

protected memory mode Client network operating systems may execute 32 bit applications in their own address space, otherwise known as protected memory mode

protocol A protocol is a set of rules which govern communication between hardware and/or software components.

protocol conversion Converting between two or more protocols in order to enable communication between two or more networked computing devices

protocol discriminator In order to differentiate which particular non-compliant protocol is embedded, any packet with AA in the DSAP and SSAP fields also has a 5 octet SNAP header known as a protocol discriminator following the Control field

protocol stack The sum of all of the protocols employed in a particular computer is sometimes referred to as that computer's protocol stack.

protocols Protocols are nothing more than rules for how communicating hardware and software components bridge interfaces or talk to one another.

proxy polling Proxy polling emulates the FEP's polling messages on the remote side of the network, thereby assuring the remote cluster controller that it is still in touch with an FEP.

PSE Packet switched exchange, another name for packet switched network

PSK A type of phase modulation in which different phase shifts represent different combinations of 1s and 0s

PSN The Public Switched Network or dial-up phone system through which local access to phone services is gained.

PSTN Public switched telephone network, the analog voice network

public data network See PDN

public switched network See PSN

Public Switched Telephone Network See PSTN

pulse older style of dialing with rotary phone that produces pulses of electricity to represent numbers

Pulse Amplitude Modulation See PAM

Pulse Code Modulation See PCM

Pulse Duration Modulation See PDM

Pulse Position Modulation   See PPM

Pulse Width Modulation   See PWM

PVC   Packet switched equivalent of a leased line

PWM   Pulse width modulation, a voice digitization technique

Q.931   an ISDN Standard known as Q.931 which allows PBX features to interoperate with Public Switched Network Features.

Q.sig   Q.Sig standardizes features among different PBX manufacturers and delivers those standardized features within the limitations of the feature set offered by ISDN

QAM   quadrature amplitude modulation; modulation scheme in which both phase and amplitude are manipulated

QPSK   Phase shift modulation with four different phases is more properly referred to as quadrature phase shift keying or QPSK.

quadrature amplitude modulation   See QAM

quadrature phase shift keying   See QPSK

RADSL   Rate adaptive digital subscriber line is able to adapt its data rate to the level of noise and interference on a given line. Currently, it is not able to support this adaptive rate on a dynamic basis, however.

RAS   Windows NT's remote access server software

rate adaptive DSL   See RADSL

RBOC   Regional Bell Operating Company Divestiture caused the former Local Bell Operating Companies to be grouped into new Regional Bell Operating Companies (RBOCs) to offer local telecommunications service

real-mode device drivers   Programs or sub-routines which write directly to computer hardware are sometimes referred to as employing real-mode device drivers.

receiver   earpiece on a phone handset

regulatory agencies   State, local, and federal authorities charged with overseeing the operation of companies in the telecommunications industry.

relative path names   In Unix, Absolute path names start at the root directory in the listing of the path to the destination directory while relative path names start at the current directory

reliable   refers to connection-oriented packet switched services which offer guaranteed delivery

remote access server   Dedicated LAN-based server that controls remote access via modems to LAN based resources

remote node server   An alternative to server-based remote access software is a standalone device alternatively known as a dial-up server or remote node server. Such a self-contained unit includes modems, communications software, and NOS-specific remote access server software in a turnkey system.

repeater   A repeater's job is to: Repeat the digital signal by regenerating and retiming the incoming signal, Pass all signals between all attached segments, Do not read destination addresses of data packets, Allow for the connection of and translation between different types of media, Effectively extend overall LAN distance by repeating signals between

Repeater   Device used by carriers on digital transmission lines to regenerate digital signals over long distances

Rexx   The Rexx scripting language offers an easier to learn and use alternative to Perl which supports structured programming techniques such as modularity while still offering access to shell commands

RFI   Radio Frequency Interference

RIF   One very important limitation of source routing bridges as applied to large internetworks is known as the 7 Hop Limit. Because of the limited space in the RIF (Router Information Field) of the explorer packet, only 7 hop locations can be included in the path to any remote destination

ring logical topology   See sequential

ring physical topology   In a ring physical topology, each PC is actually an active part of the ring, passing data packets in a sequential pattern around the ring. If one of the PCs dies, or a network adapter card malfunctions, the "sequence" is broken, the token is lost, and the network is down.

RIP   RIP is a router-to-router protocol associated with TCP/IP. RIP uses UDP as a transport protocol and broadcasts its routing tables to all directly connected routers every thirty seconds

RJ48c   Jack in which T-1 services are typically terminated

round robin polling scheme   In 100VG-AnyLAN, the Demand Priority Protocol access methodology uses a round robin polling scheme in which the hubs scan each port in sequence to see if the attached workstations have any traffic to transmit. The round robin polling scheme is distributed through a hierarchical arrangement of cascaded hubs.

router servers   An internetwork evolutionary design scenario in which Route Servers will provide a centralized repository of routing information while edge switches deployed within the LANs will be programmed with minimal routing information.

Routing Information Field   See RIF

routing information protocol   See RIP

routing tables   Routers consult routing tables in order to determine the best path on which to forward a particular data packet.

RPC   RPC (Remote Procedure Call) is a session layer protocol responsible for establishing, maintaining, and terminating communications sessions between distributed applications in an NFS environment

RS-232-C   An EIA serial transmission standard officially limited to 20Kbps over 50 ft distance

RSVP   (Resource Reservation Protocol) enables routing software to reserve a portion of network bandwidth known as a virtual circuit

RT24   A voice compression algorithm

run length encoding   Encoding mechanism that looks for repeating characters and replacements multiple repeating characters with a repetition count code

S/N   signal to noise ratio; expressed in decibels, measures power of data signal as compared to power of circuit interference or noise

SAS   Single Attachment Stations attach to only one of FDDI's two rings

SBA   In FDDI, frames transmitted in a continuous stream are known as synchronous frames and are prioritized according to a methodology known as synchronous bandwidth allocation or SBA which assigns fixed amounts of bandwidth to given stations.

SCAM   PnP compliant SCSI controllers will be configured according to a PnP standard known as SCAM or SCSI Configured Automatically.

SCSI configured automatically   See SCAM

SDLC   IBM SNA's data link layer protocol. SLDC frames do not contain anything equivalent to the OSI network layer addressing information for use by routers which makes SDLC a non-routable protocol

SDLC conversion   SDLC frames are converted to Token Ring Frames by a specialized internetworking device known as a SDLC Converter.

SDLC converter   See SDLC conversion

SDN   software defined network implies that the user has some control over the flexible configuration of their wide area telecommunications service and network

SDSL   Symmetric digital subscriber line differs from ADSL in that it offers upstream and downstream channels of equal bandwidth

security   As important corporate data is transferred over network links, precautions must be taken to prevent unauthorized access to transmitted data, as well as to corporate networks and computer systems.

Security Account manager   In Windows NT, all of the user and user group ID and permission level information is stored in and maintained by the security account manager which interacts with the local security authority to verify user Ids and permission levels

security ID   See SID

security reference monitor   See SRM

segmentation   Segmentation is usually the first internetworking approach employed to reduce shared media congestion. By having fewer workstations per segment, there is less contention for the shared bandwidth

selective ARQ   ARQ error control mechanism that is able to retransmit only those particular data blocks received in error

sequential   In a sequential logical topology, also known as a ring logical topology, data is passed from one PC (or node) to another. Each node examines the destination address of the data packet to determine if this particular packet is meant for it. If the data was not meant to be delivered at this node, the data is passed along to the next node in the logical ring.

serial transmission   transmission method in which all bits of a given character are transmitted in linear fashion, one after the other

server back-end   portion of a distributed client/server application that runs on the server PC

server duplexing   In such a case, not only are the contents of the disks synchronized, but the contents of the servers' memory and CPUs are also synchronized. In case of the failure of the primary server, the duplexed server takes over transparently.

server isolation   Instead of assigning all workstations to their own LAN segment as in micro-segmentation, only selected high-performance devices such as servers can be assigned to their own segment in an internetworking design strategy known as server isolation. By isolating servers on their own segments, guaranteed access to network bandwidth is assured

server network operating systems   Server network operating systems are able to be chosen and installed based on their performance characteristics for a given required functionality. For example, NetWare servers are often employed as file and print servers whereas Windows NT, OS/2, or UNIX servers are more likely to be employed as application servers

servers   Servers such as application servers and print servers are usually dedicated computers accessed only through LAN connections. Whereas a client could be considered a service requester, servers are characterized as service providers

Service Profile Identifier Numbers   See SPID

session layer   The session layer protocols are responsible for establishing, maintaining, and terminating sessions between user application programs. Sessions are interactive dialogues between networked computers and are of particular importance to distributed computing applications in a client/server environment

shared media LANs   The various connected computers and peripheral devices will all share some type of media to converse with each other. As a result, LANs are sometimes more specifically referred to as shared media LANs or media-sharing LANs.

shell   In Unix, the command interpreter which is the user's interface to the system is a specialized user process known as a shell.

SID   In Windows NT, the local security authority generates a security access token for authorized users which contains security Ids (SID) for this user and all of the user groups to which this user belongs.

signal to noise ratio   See S/N

signalling system 7   See SS7

simple network management protocol   See SNMP

Single Attachment Station   See SAS

single point of failure   Any network attached device or piece of technology whose failure would cause the failure of the entire network

sinks   packet destinations

Sliding Window Protocols   Continuous ARQ, for example, continues to transmit and slides back to NAK'd data blocks when a NAK is received

slot time   In Ethernet networks, The time required for a given workstation to detect a collision is known slot time and is measured in bits.

slow convergence   The delay which occurs while all of the routers are propagating their routing tables using RIP, known as slow convergence, could allow certain routers to think that failed links to certain networks are still viable

small business network operating systems   Small business network operating systems have had to differentiate themselves from client network operating systems and peer-to-peer network operating systems by offering more advanced features such as: dedicated 32-bit server software, bundled workgroup software, and an easy migration path to server-based network operating systems

Small Office Home Office   See SOHO

SMDR   station message detail recording; an individual detail record is generated for each call for call accounting systems

SMDS   Switched multimegabit data service, a connectionless high speed data service

SMP   Symmetrical multiprocessing is a system architecture in which multiple CPU's are controlled by the SMP operating system and individual threads of application processes are assigned to particular CPUs on a first-available basis.

SMP kernel   In the SMP version of NetWare , a second operating system kernel, known as the SMP kernel, is loaded which works cooperatively with the first or native operating system kernel.

SMP scalability   SMP scalability refers to the percentage of increased performance achieved for each additional CPU

SNA   Systems Network Architecture, IBM's proprietary network architecture, was originally designed to link mainframes

SNAP   In order to ease the transition to IEEE 802 compliance, an alternative method of identifying the embedded upper layer protocols was developed, known as SNAP or Sub-Network Access Protocol. Any protocol can use SNAP with IEEE 802.2 and appear to be an IEEE 802 compliant protocol.

SNMP   Performance management information can be communicated to Enterprise Management Systems such as HP OpenView or IBM SystemView in the proper SNMP (Simple Network Management Protocol) format

software defined network   See SDN

software flow control   Used control characters XON, XOFF to control data transmission into and out of buffer memory

SOHO   New market for mini-PBXs and desktop CTI

SONET   synchronous optical network, dual ring, high speed fiber based transmission architecture

SONET superframe   Rather than fitting 24 channels per frame delineated by a single framing bit, a single SONET frame or row is delineated by 3 octets of overhead for control information followed by 87 octets of payload. Nine of these 90 octet rows are grouped together to form a SONET Superframe

source address   Data-Link protocols such as Ethernet contain source addresses as well as the destination addresses within the pre-defined Ethernet Frame layout. A bridge checks the source address of each frame it receives and adds that source address to a table of known local nodes

source routing bridge   A source routing bridge is used to connect two source-routing enabled Token Ring LANs. Data messages arrive at a source routing bridge with a detailed map of how they plan to reach their destination

source routing transparent bridge   Bridges which can support links between source routing Token Ring

LANs or transparent LANs, are known as Source Routing Transparent (SRT) bridges

Spanning Tree Algorithm The Spanning Tree Algorithm (STA) has been standardized as IEEE 802.1 for the purposes of controlling redundant paths in bridged networks and thereby reducing the possibility of broadcast storms.

SPE The 87 octets of payload per row in each of the time rows or the Superframe is known as the Synchronous Payload Envelope or SPE.

SPID In order to properly interface an end-user's ISDN equipment to a carrier's ISDN services, desired ISDN features must be specified. In some cases, end user equipment such as remote access servers must be programmed with Service Profile Identifier Numbers (SPID) in order to properly identify the carrier's equipment with which the user equipment must interface.

spoofing Spoofing is a method of filtering chatty or unwanted protocols from the WAN link while assuring that remote programs which require on-going communication from these filtered protocols are still re-assured via emulation of these protocols by the local dial-up router.

SRM The security reference monitor is primarily concerned with authorization or authentication for processes that wish to access objects and users that wish to access the system via the logon process. It is the only kernel mode portion of the NT security system.

SS7 signalling system 7, a common inter-switch signallig protocol for call managment and control

standards An agreed upon protocol as determined by officially sanctioned standards making organizations, market share, or user group concensus

star The star physical topology employs some type of central management device. Depending on the network architecture and sophistication of the device, it may be called a hub, a wiring center, a concentrator, a MAU (Multiple Access Unit), a repeater or a switching hub

station cards PBX cards that attach to users phones

station message detail recording See SMDR

statistical time division multiplexing See STDM

STDM Advanced form of TDM multiplexing that seeks to overcome TDM inefficiencies by dynamically adapting polling of channels

store-and-forward Message passing process employed by X.25 in which messages are kept by packet switched until ACK is received from destination switch

Stored Program Control location in PBX where software is executed

streaming protocol File transfer protocol that continues to transmit until it encounters an end of file indicator. Relies on modems to provide error control

STS-1 The electrical equivalent of the OC-1 , the optical SONET Superframe standard is known as the STS-1 or Synchronous Transport Signal

sub-network access protocol See SNAP

superframe 12 D-4 frames

SVC Switched virtual circuit, packet switched equivalent of a circuit switched dial up line

switched line as opposed to a leased line, a switched line is connected to a CO switch, provides dial-tone, and reaches different destinations by dialing different phone numbers

switched multimegabit data service See SMDS

switched virtual circuit See SVC

switching Process by which messages are routed from switch to switch en route to their final destination

switching architecture major component of network architecture along with transmission architecture

switching matrix location in CPU where circuits are switched to complete calls

symmetric DSL See SDSL

symmetric multiprocessing See SMP

synchronous bandwidth allocation See SBA

Synchronous Data Link Control See SDLC

synchronous frames In FDDI, frames transmitted in a continuous stream are known as synchronous frames and are prioritized according to a methodology known as synchronous bandwidth allocation or SBA which assigns fixed amounts of bandwidth to given stations.

synchronous optical network See SONET

synchronous payload envelope See SPE

synchronous TDM In a technique used in T-1 transmission service known as periodic framing or synchronous TDM, twenty-four channels of eight bits each (192 bits total) are arranged in a frame

synchronous transmission transmission method in which timing is provided by a clocking signal supplied by either modems or the carrier

Systems Network Architecture See SNA

T.120 standard for multipoint audioconferences

T-1 1.544 Mbps digital WAN service adhering to the DS-1 standard

T-1 channel bank   Device which can take a variety of voice and data inputs, digitize them, and multiplex them onto a T-1 circuit

T-1 CSU/DSU   Device which interfaces between a T-1 circuit and another device such as a mux, bridge or router

T-1 IMUX   Inverse multiplexer that can combine four or more T-1s for bandwidth on demand applications

T-1 inverse multiplexer   See T-1 IMUX

T-1 multiplexers   Multiplexers that combine several digitized voice or data inputs into a T-1 output

T-1 switches   Switches that are able to re-direct T-1s or the DS-0s contained therein

T-3   a leased line digital broadband service of 44.736Mbps

tandem office   establishes the intra-LATA circuit and also handles billing procedures for the long distance call.

TAPI   CTI API promoted by Microsoft & Intel

TCM   Trellis coded modulation, a forward error correction technique that transmits redundant data in hopes of avoiding retransmission

TCP/IP   TCP/IP (Transmission Control Protocol/Internet Protocol) is the term generally used to refer to an entire suite of protocols used to provide communication on a variety of layers between widely distributed different types of computers. Strictly speaking, TCP and IP are just two of the protocols contained within the family of protocols more properly known as the Internet Suite of Protocols.

TCP/IP encapsulation   Each non-routable SNA SDLC frame is "stuffed" into an IP "envelope" for transport across the network and processing by routers supporting TCP/IP internetworking protocol

TCP/IP Model   Although not identical to the OSI 7 layer model, the 4 layer TCP/IP Model is no less effective at organizing protocols required to establish and maintain communications between different computers.

TDM   time division multiplexing With TDM, from a connected terminal's point of view, 100% of the bandwidth is available for a portion of the time.

telecommunications   Usually used to indicate a broader market than data communications, including voice, video, and image services

Telecommunications Act of 1996   The Telecommunications Act of 1996 seeks to encourage competition in all aspects and markets of telecommunications services including switched and dedicated local and inter-LATA traffic as well as cable TV companies and wireless services such as paging, cellular, and satellite services

telephony API   See TAPI

telephony services API   See TSAPI

throughput   PC to PC data rate, transmission rate x data compression ratio

time division multiplexing   See TDM

time slot   8 bits of digitized information collected in one sample and assigned to one of 24 channels in a T-1 D-4 frame

timed updates   A dial-up router update mechanism in which updates are performed at regular pre-determined intervals

timing limitation   The second SNA characteristic which can cause problems when run over a shared LAN backbone is that SNA has timing limitations for transmission duration between SNA hosts and end-user devices. Thus on wide area, internetworked LANs over shared network media, SNA sessions can "time-out", effectively terminating the session.

token   In a token passing access methodology, a specific packet (24 bits) of data is known as a token

token passing   Token Passing is an access methodology that assures that each PC User has 100% of the network channel available for their data requests and transfers by insisting that no PC accesses the network without first possessing a specific packet (24 bits) of data known as a token

toll quality   The ITU standard for 32Kbps ADPCM is known as G.721 and is generally used as a reference point for the quality of voice transmission known as toll quality

tone   common name for DTMF dialing

top down model   Insisting that a top-down approach to network analysis and design is undertaken, through the use of the top down model, should assure that the network design implemented will meet the business needs and objectives which motivated the design in the first place.

TP-PMD   The official ANSI standard for CDDI is known as TP-PMD (Twisted Pair-Physical Media Dependent).

trailer   Information added to the back of data is called a trailer

translating bridges   A special type of bridge which includes a format converter can bridge between Ethernet and Token Ring. These special bridges may also be called multi-protocol bridges or translating bridges.

transmission architecture   key component of network architecture along with switching architecture

Transmission Control Protocol/Internet Protocol   See TCP/IP

transmission rate rate of actual bits transmitted end-to-end measured in bps, equal to bits/baud × baud rate

transmitter mouthpiece on telephone handset

transparent Bridges are passive or transparent devices, receiving every frame broadcast on a given LAN. Bridges are known as transparent due to their ability to only process data link layer addresses while transparently forwarding any variety of upper layer protocols safely embedded within the data field of the datalink layer frame

transparent bridge Bridges that connect LANs of similar data link format are known as transparent bridges

transport layer the transport layer protocols are responsible for providing reliability for the end-to-end network layer connections. Transport layer protocols provide end-to-end error recovery and flow control and also provide mechanisms for sequentially organizing multiple network layer packets into a coherent message.

Trellis Coded Modulation See TCM

triggered updates A dial-up router update mechanism in which updates are performed whenever a certain programmable event, such as a change in available services, occurs

trunk cards cards in PBX that attach to local loops

TSAPI CTI API promoted by Novell and AT&T

turnaround time time it takes two half-duplex modems to change from transmit to receive mode by manipulating RTS and CTS signals

two-wire circuits common local loop circuit in which one of these two wires serves as a ground wire for the circuit, thereby leaving only one wire between the two ends of the circuit for data signaling

UART (Universal Asynchronous Receiver Transmitter) acts as the interface between the parallel transmission of the computer bus and the serial transmission of the serial port.

UDP User datagram protocol, transport protocol that is part of the internet suite of protocols, used in IP voice transmission

UNI user network interface, In ATM, cell format that carries information between the user and the ATM network

Unicode 16 bit character encoding scheme identical to ISO 10646

unified messaging also known as the Universal In-Box will allow voice mail, e-mail, faxes, and pager messages to all be displayed on a single graphical screen. Messages can then be forwarded, deleted, or replied to easily in point and click fashion.

universal asynchronous receiver transmitter See UART

universal client A client workstation's ability to interoperate transparently with a number of different network operating system servers without the need for additional products or configurations is described as a universal client capability.

universal in-box see unified messaging

Unix system kernel The Unix system kernel fulfills requests for services from Unix systems programs by interacting with the hardware layer and returning requested functionality to the systems programs and utilities.

Unix systems programs Unix systems programs and utilities deliver requested functionality to users by issuing system calls to the Unix system kernel

unreliable connectionless networks with globally addressed datagrams cannot guarantee delivery and are referred to as unreliable

user accounts database In Windows NT, the user accounts database is physically stored on the primary domain controller except in those cases when an individual workstation may have a need to verify specific User Ids for remote access to that workstation

user datagram protocol See UDP

user demands the top layer of the wide area network architecture

user network interface See UNI

V.32 ITU standard for modem transmitting at 9600bps, 4 QAM & TCM modulation

V.32bis ITU standard for modem transmitting at 14.4Kbps, 6QAM & TCM modulation

V.32ter Proprietary standard for modem transmitting at 19.2Kbps, 8 QAM & TCM modulation

V.34 ITU standard for modem transmitting at 28.8Kbps, 9QAM & TCM

V.42 ITU standard for error control, supports MNP 4 and LAP-M

V.42bis ITU standard for data compression, compression ratios up to 4:1

V.Fast Proprietary standard for 28.8Kbps modems prior to ratification of V.34

V.Fast Class Proprietary standard for 28.8Kbps modems prior to ratification of V.34

V.FC Proprietary standard for 28.8Kbps modems prior to ratification of V.34

variable bit rate See VBR

variable callback Callback security mechanism for modems that supports callback to phone numbers entered at dial-in time after password verification

VBR   Variable Bit Rate provides a guaranteed minimum threshold amount of constant bandwidth below which the available bandwidth will not drop. However, as bursty traffic requires more bandwidth than this constant minimum, that required bandwidth will be provided.

VDSL   Very High Speed DSL—provides 52Mbps downstream and between 1.6–2.3Mbps upstream over distances of up to only 1,000 ft. It is being explored primarily as a means to bring video on demand services to the home

version control software   See file synchronization

vertical redundancy check   See VRC

vertical software compatibility   Vertical software compatibility is concerned with making sure that all necessary compatible protocols are in place in order for all of the software and hardware within a single client or server to operate harmoniously and transparently

very high speed DSL   See VDSL

virtual circuit   dedicated path for voice over frame relay that minimizes or eliminated delay usually associated with frame relay

virtual circuit table   The details that relate the LCN to a physical circuit consisting of an actual series of specific packet switches within the packet switched network are stored in a virtual circuit table.

virtual device drivers   See VxDs

virtual machines   Some client network operating systems, such as Windows NT, have the ability to support multiple APIs and multiple different operating system sub-systems, sometimes known as virtual machines

virtual parallel machines   See VPM

virtual tributary   See VT

voice digitization   technique by which analog voice is converted into digital signals

voice over the Internet   also known as IP-based voice

voice/data multiplexers   device that interfaces to T-l leased lines to carry voice and data

voice-grade leased line   analog leased line with 3100Hz of bandwidth

VPM   Clusters are also sometimes referred to as Virtual Parallel Machines (VPM)

VRC   Simple parity checking, adds one parity bit per character

VT   flexibly defined channels within the SONET payload area are known as virtual tributaries or VTs.

VT1.5   SONET virtual tributary equivalent to a mapped T-1

VxDs   More secure 32 bit operating systems control access to hardware and certain system services via virtual device drivers. otherwise known as VxDs

wavelength   The distance between the same spots on two subsequent waves is called the wavelength. The longer the wavelength, the lower the frequency and the shorter the wavelength, the greater the frequency

Wavelength Division Multiplexing   See WDM

WDM   Wavelength Division Multiplexing—technique in fiber optic transmission in which multiple bits of data can be transmitted simultaneously over a single fiber by being represented by different light wavelengths.

wireless bridge   Wireless bridges use spread spectrum radio transmission between LAN sites (up to 3 miles) and are primarily limited to Ethernet networks at this time.

X.25   Packet switching standard that defines interface specification for packet switched networks

X.500   As enterprise networks become more heterogeneous comprised of network operating systems from a variety of different vendors, the need will arise for different network operating systems to share each other's directory services information. A directory services specification known as X.500 offers the potential for this directory services interoperability

XDR   XDR (External Data Representation) is a presentation layer protocol responsible for formatting data in a consistent manner so that all NFS clients and servers can process it, regardless of the computing platform or operating system on which the NFS suite may be executing

XMODEM   Public domain File transfer protocol, widely used, 128 bytes/block, checksum error control

XON/XOFF   Control characters used in software flow control. XOFF stops data transmission, XON restarts it.

YMODEM   File transfer protocol, 1KB data blocks, CRC-16 error control, batch execution

ZMODEM   File transfer protocol, dynamically adjusts data packet size, automatic recovery from aborted file transfers

Index